The World Wide Web Complete Reference

KÖNEMANN

www.koenemann.com

Editor: Ágnes Lakos
Responsible co-editors: András Kemenes, Tamás Zászkaliczky
Technical editor: Dezső Varga
Engraved by Kottamester Bt., Budapest

ISBN 978-3-7419-1500-0

Printed in China by Reliance Printing

K 131

The World Wide Web Complete Reference

Rick Stout

Osborne **McGraw-Hill**
Berkeley New York St. Louis San Francisco
Auckland Bogotá Hamburg London Madrid
Mexico City Milan Montreal New Delhi Panama City
Paris São Paulo Singapore Sydney
Tokyo Toronto

Osborne **McGraw-Hill**
2600 Tenth Street
Berkeley, California 94710
U.S.A.

For information on translations or book distributors outside the U.S.A., or to arrange bulk purchase discounts for sales promotions, premiums, or fundraisers, please contact Osborne McGraw-Hill at the above address.

The World Wide Web Complete Reference

1234567890 DOC 99876

ISBN 0-07-882142-8

Publisher
Lawrence Levitsky

Acquisitions Editor
Scott Rogers

Technical Editor
Gordon Miller

Project Editor
Linda Comer

Copy Editor
Heidi Steele

Proofreader
Cynthia Douglas

Computer Designer
Roberta Steele

Illustrator
Rhys Elliott

Series Design
Roberta Steele

Quality Control Specialists
Joe Scuderi
Kristie Reilly

Cover Design
Compass Marketing

To the person who has had the largest influence in my life,
my father, Ron Stout of Arizona.
Thanks for everything, Dad.

About the Author

Rick Stout is the coauthor of Osborne's acclaimed *The Internet Complete Reference, The Internet Yellow Pages* and *Internet Yellow Pages: Science, Research and Technology*. Stout is a Certified Public Accountant and holds degrees in business administration and accounting. Formerly a consulting manager at the accounting firm Ernst & Young, Stout is a specialist in business computer and accounting systems. He is the author of several books, including *The Peter Norton Introduction to Computers*, and numerous articles for computer magazines. Stout lives in the San Diego area, where he works on literary projects, develops software, and consults. He can be reached at rick@cts.com.

Contents at a Glance

Contents

Acknowledgments

I couldn't have written this book without a great deal of help from many people. First and foremost, I want to thank the greatest acquisitions editor in the business—Scott Rogers of Osborne McGraw-Hill. Without Scott's unending patience, guidance, and prodding, I would never have written this book. And congratulations to Scott on his promotion to Executive Editor. I would also like to thank Larry Levitsky, the publisher at Osborne, for the opportunity to do this book.

Also at Osborne, I'd like to thank the entire team involved with the book: Daniela Dell'Orco, Scott's excellent Editorial Assistant; Project Editor Linda Comer; and Kelly Barr, for help with some of the more arcane features of Microsoft Word. And not with Osborne, but equally important, was copy editor Heidi Steele, who did an excellent job with the book. Thanks to Brad Shimmin for filling Scott's big shoes on occasion, and to Rhys Elliott for the outstanding artwork in the book.

I also thank Gordon Miller of G3 Systems, Inc., in Blacksburg, Virginia, for his technical review of my manuscript. Thanks, too, to Kenn Nesbitt for reviewing several of the chapters, and to Ronda Stout for her fast and furious editing of the catalog copy.

The excellent directory of businesses on the Web at the back of this book is the result of many hours of hard work on the part of a world-class team of researchers. My deepest appreciation goes to each of them. They are:

Catherine Bagley, Williams College
Lindsay Gordon, Princeton University

Jim Hall, San Diego, California
Lee Jenkins, Vanderbilt University
Frances Marshall, Northwestern University
Ben Plouganou, Sinaloa, Mexico
Julie Zures, Vanderbilt University

Next, I extend my sincerest thanks to Bill Blue and the folks at CTS Network Services in San Diego for being the finest Internet service providers in Southern California. Without their expert know-how and prompt service, it would have been much harder to do this book. Specifically, I want to thank Morgan Davis and Jay Curtis for their wizardry with hardware and software systems, as well as with ISDN, and for working into the wee hours of the morning with me when it was necessary.

A special thanks is also in order to Joe Salame of AmeriNet and ATMNET in San Diego. Joe's knowledge about and enthusiasm for ISDN had a significant impact on this book. Thanks also to Joe for his help sorting out his awesome array of ISDN products, for his expert help in implementing my ISDN connection, and for going the extra mile for a client.

I would like to express my gratitude and appreciation to Tom Lettington of ATMNET in San Diego for providing my ISDN connection. Tom's professionalism and the skill and knowledge of the crew at ATMNET are a credit to Internet service providers.

Finally, I'd like to thank each of the following people and organizations that contributed to this work through direct participation, by lending hardware or software to the project, or by granting me permission to reference their works:

Mark Burgeous, Data Transfer Group (San Diego, California)
Dennis Clark, SIMS Internet Matrix Southeast (Charleston, South Carolina)
Bob Crowe, Internet Products Inc. (San Diego, California)
Ellen Elias, O'Reilly & Associates
David Gulbransen, Indiana University
Hal Lenox, Pacific Bell (San Diego, California)
Desirree Madison-Biggs, Netcom Online Communications
Ruffin Prevost, Author
Jim Sims, SIMS Internet Matrix Southeast (Charleston, South Carolina)
Farley Stewart, Internet Products Inc. (San Diego, California)

Introduction

Whether you're an old pro with the Internet or just getting started, this book has a great deal to offer you. If you're new to the Internet and the World Wide Web, we'll take you by the hand and start at the very beginning. If you've been exploring the Web for a while and want to learn more about it, or even create your own Web site, this book will show you each step of the process.

There are many other good books about the Web. However, many of them focus narrowly on specific tools you can use with the Web (such as Mosaic or HTML), or they discuss the Internet in general and don't give the World Wide Web the attention it deserves.

Indeed, for a whole new generation of Internet users, the term "Internet" is synonymous with the Web. These users are coming to the Web in large numbers from online services such as America Online, CompuServe, and Prodigy. Some come aboard by buying software packages or operating systems that promise to put them on the "information superhighway." Others get their access the old-fashioned way—by finding out how it all works, buying an account, collecting the software, and setting everything up themselves.

Regardless of the method you choose to get onto the Internet and into the Web, this book has the answers you need. Whether you're just starting out and want to learn it all or you're an experienced Web user and want to know how to create clickable imagemaps or complex interactive forms, this book is your one-stop reference for the World Wide Web.

New Internet and Web Users

The good news for brand-new Web users is that, unlike the Internet in general, the Web is conceptually quite simple. With your Macintosh or your PC running Windows, you can quickly learn to browse the Web like a pro. In fact, once your system is set up, all you really need are basic mousing skills and a desire to travel the Web and see what it has to offer.

To get to that point, though, you have a hurdle to jump: finding an Internet service provider and setting up your system. Part 1 of this book is your guide through this territory. Once you've emerged on the other side with a system that's ready to go, you'll be free to explore on your own, and this book provides pointers to hundreds of interesting places to start your investigations.

Part 1 begins with an explanation of what the Internet is, where it came from, and what you need to get connected. It then describes how to establish your own connection to the Internet. You'll learn about operating systems and software packages that offer turnkey connections, and you'll find out about the Internet and Web access provided by the major online information services. Part I ends with a discussion of Web browsers—the programs you use to access the World Wide Web. You'll see what to look for in a browser and how to use one, and you'll get a closer look at two of the most popular browsers.

Experienced Users

Because the Web is so simple, you might wonder what more there is to learn once you know how to browse it. After you've begun your journey on the Web, it won't be long before you're thinking about creating your own Web pages and making them available to the world at large. Tens of thousands of people and organizations have set up their own Web servers (programs that send Web pages to readers over the Internet), and *Business Week* magazine estimates that the number of Web servers doubles every 53 days. A research computer scientist at Carnegie-Mellon University estimates that Web sites currently contain five million Web pages and that this number is doubling every six months to a year.

You may also wonder what you could offer that would interest anyone else. After you've netsurfed around the world a few times, your imagination, creativity, and desire to participate in this phenomenon will come together and inspire you to create your own information-age version of the welcome mat.

One of the most practical examples of what you might put on your Web pages is information about your business. If you sell products or services, you can announce them to the world in a way that would have been impossible before the World Wide Web.

Part 2 focuses on how to create Web pages. The first chapter of Part 2 addresses the theories and philosophies that will guide you in designing a good Web page. Then you'll learn the basic mechanics of structuring a Web page or a collection of Web pages. Finally, you'll delve into the nitty-gritty details of putting those pages together—how to create Web pages, format your text, create links to other documents and multimedia objects, and create tables and gateway programs.

Part 3 concentrates on a number of topics that are especially important if you're considering establishing your own presence on the Web. You'll learn what you need to know about leasing computer space and Internet bandwidth, then explore the issues involved in putting your own computers or networks onto the Internet. Among the topics in Part 3 are designing a network from the ground up for integration into the Internet, choosing the right type of high-speed connection, sorting out the dizzying array of Web server software, analyzing Web server statistics, and creating imagemaps. Part 3 closes with a chapter of tips and advice on doing business on the Internet. We'll let you in on some good ideas and try to steer you around the pitfalls wherever possible.

Catalog of Commercial Services and the Appendices

In the catalog at the back of this book, you'll find pointers to the Web pages of hundreds of companies that have established their own presence on the Web. The companies in the catalog range from some of the largest corporations in the world right down to home entrepreneurs, such as the one selling exotic hot sauces out of his garage.

The appendices bring together information that should be at the fingertips of every Web author. In Appendix A, we've compiled a reference of the HTML markup codes and special characters you'll use when creating HTML documents. This is something we have found missing in most every other book about the World Wide Web, even those that focus exclusively on creating Web pages.

In Appendix B, we present a reference for finding Web software on the Internet. For all the commercial products available today, some of the best Internet and Web software is free and available to anyone. Finding it, though, can be a challenge. In this appendix, we list public-domain and shareware software packages that you can use to put your computer onto the Internet, including Web browsers and Web servers for practically every type of computer, graphics tools, video utilities, HTML editing tools, imagemapping tools, server log analysis tools, and much more. The list even contains freeware and shareware email programs you can use to send electronic mail anywhere in the world.

Contacting the Author

If you have a question or a gripe, or just want to send me a comment, I welcome your feedback. You can always reach me through Osborne McGraw-Hill (the address is at the front of the book), but why not just email me instead? My email address is rick@cts.com.

I look forward to hearing from you!

Part 1

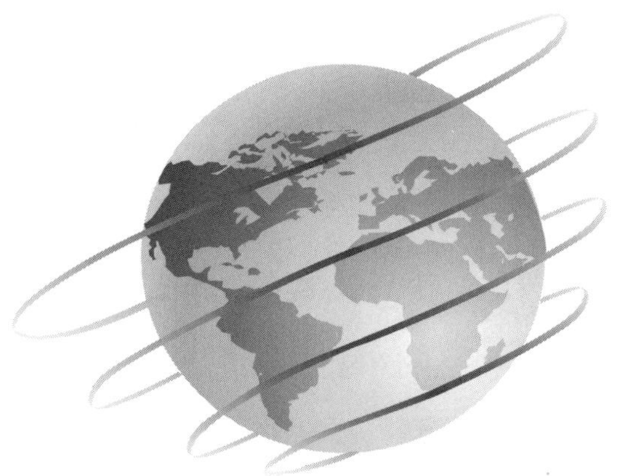

Getting Started with the Web

Chapter 1

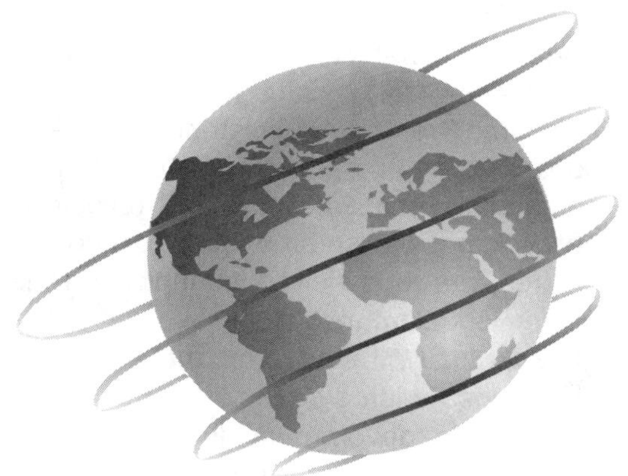

An Introduction to the Web

Discussion of the Internet and the World Wide Web is everywhere. Nearly every major news magazine and newspaper has featured articles about the Web, and everyone from your local florist to the TV news networks is proudly displaying a Web address.

But what exactly are the Internet and World Wide Web? Who owns them? Who runs them? How do they work?

This chapter introduces you to the Internet and the World Wide Web and answers some of the fundamental questions people ask when they begin to take an interest in these new tools.

The Internet

The Internet was created nearly 25 years ago as a project of the U.S. Department of Defense. Technically, the group that created it was the Defense Advanced Research Projects Administration, or DARPA. Its goal was to create a way for widely separated computers to transfer information and data and to make these data communications as robust and reliable as possible. DARPA wanted to make a network that was smart enough to recover on its own from problems such as power failures, interruptions in communication lines—even a nuclear attack. DARPA called its network *Darpanet*.

Eventually, the government dropped the idea that its network was only useful for defense-related projects, and the network became known as *Arpanet*. Around this time, the government also began connecting many of the country's universities to the network. By now, generations of students have studied, used, and improved what is today the Internet.

Only five years ago, the Internet was still relatively unknown outside of scientific and technical communities. That would soon change, however. After two decades of development and improvements, the Internet was ready to explode into the mainstream.

Many people were initially attracted to the Internet because it connected them to the world at large. They could exchange electronic mail, participate in discussions (via *Usenet newsgroups*), and easily exchange programs and data with others around the world using the Internet's file-transfer facilities.

Technically, the Internet isn't a network of computers—it's a network of networks. Local networks throughout the world are tied together by wires, telephone lines, fiber-optic cables, microwave transmissions, and satellites in orbit. But the details of how data gets from one computer on the Internet to another are invisible to the user.

NOTE *The Internet is dramatically different from online services such as CompuServe and America Online. These companies sell access to their computers; think of them as gigantic bulletin board systems owned and operated by a company. What you see and what you can do with them are limited to what they allow you to see and do. To avoid losing their entire memberships to the Internet, these services have found it necessary to offer access to the Internet and the World Wide Web. They determine which parts of the Internet you can access, however, and some of them charge extra for Internet access (even for sending email to an Internet address).*

Until recently, using the Internet generally meant using programs and tools on Unix computers. Long after the personal computer craze was in full swing, the Internet was still an arcane concept to many PC and Mac users—even to many people who considered themselves experts with personal computers, software, and networking.

All of this began to change, though, with the development of high-speed modems and a software hack called *Serial Line Internet Protocol* (SLIP). When 14.4 Kbps modems entered the market, it suddenly became practical to connect PCs and Macintosh computers to the Internet, and SLIP software made it possible to extend the Internet from centrally located networks to the PC user at home or in the office.

High-speed modems and SLIP have resulted in a blizzard of new products—both hardware and software—that make it easy to connect a home or office computer to the Internet. As a result, excitement about the Internet has been snowballing for nearly two years.

Although the Internet began as a government research project and was funded by tax dollars for years, the government is not involved in it anymore. It might still be one of the largest single users of the Internet, but it no longer funds new development or supports any of the costs associated with maintaining the network. The Internet is completely self-sufficient.

So who does own it, and who pays for it? No single person or company owns the Internet. After all, the only things to own are the wires and communications paths that carry bits and bytes from one network to another. Somebody does own these lines; it just it isn't a single company or individual, but many.

The huge high-speed trunk lines that run between countries and major cities are usually owned and maintained by big telecommunications companies. For example, AT&T and Sprint own and maintain some good-sized chunks of the trunk lines that snake around the country and the world. For the most part, it's not terribly important to these companies that their lines are being used for Internet traffic; that's just what a telecommunications company does. When there is demand for data communications, the companies try to meet that demand with service. When the demand is high enough, they lay another fiber trunk or launch another satellite.

The ones asking these large telecommunications companies for more or faster communications lines are often smaller communications companies such as the regional Bells (PacBell, Mountain Bell, Bell Atlantic, and so on). These smaller companies are also just trying to meet the demand for more and faster access from their customers—local phone companies and Internet service providers.

An Internet service provider, or ISP, is a company that buys a relatively high-speed line from a telecommunications company, then splits up and resells its available bandwidth to local businesses and individuals.

Now take the case of small businesses on the Internet. Small businesses usually pay their ISP for the amount of bandwidth they need or can afford. If a company is very small and only has a few computers on its local network, it may be able to get away with just a modem connection. A nondedicated (not full-time) modem connection costs less than $30 a month. If a company wants a permanent connection at modem speeds, it will pay around $300 a month.

Large businesses (and even some smaller ones) normally want a faster connection to their ISPs than they can get with a modem connection. Some of the faster services used by large businesses are direct leased lines to their service providers, frame relay, and ISDN. (These terms are explained in Chapter 17.) Many ISPs themselves have direct leased lines, which cost about $3,000 per month.

As you can see, the companies and individuals in the chain each own and pay for their own piece of the Internet. Those that want to can resell their access to try to cover their costs or make a profit—and then there's a new piece of the Internet owned and paid for by another user.

What is the World Wide Web?

For all its technological wonder, the Internet has suffered for years from a reputation of being difficult to learn, hard to use, and downright homely compared to the sexy interfaces of bulletin board systems, online services, and most of the software people use on personal computers.

The World Wide Web has changed all this. The Web has quickly become the graphical user interface to the Internet, and it stands unrivaled by any online service in terms of both aesthetics and flexibility.

To access the Web, you use a program called a *Web browser*. A Web browser is just a program on your own computer that knows how to retrieve "pages" of text and graphics from other computers on the Internet. Embedded in these pages are symbols (called *links*) telling your Web browser where to find other related pages on the Internet. A browser displays links differently from the surrounding text. (For example, it may display links in blue, as underlined text, or as 3-D buttons.) When

you click on a link, it loads another page of text and graphics. This is called *following a link*, and the concept of following links to related pages of information is called *hypertext*.

Part of the reason for the Web's huge and rapid success is that it's easy to use: It's as simple as clicking a mouse button. And although you need to understand some of the details, creating your own Web pages is easy and downright fun.

Another key to the Web's magic is its simplicity. Web "pages" are simply files lying around on the hundreds of thousands of computers connected to the Internet. To "serve" the pages when they're requested by a browser, all a computer needs is another simple program called a *Web server*. The Web server just waits and listens for requests from Web browsers. When a request comes in, it finds the requested file and sends it back to the browser.

Of course, it's not quite as random as it might sound at this point. A company or organization that wants to welcome visitors to its Web site sets up a special page called a *home page*. The home page is an organization's (or a person's) electronic welcome mat. It tells visitors who the organization is and what it does, and it may offer links to other related pages. For example, a business's home page might display the name and logo of the company and offer links to other pages on its computer with information about the company's products, employees, customers, and so on. Because businesses want to put their best foot forward, they carefully craft their pages to be attractive and offer useful information to potential customers and to the public in general.

The Web isn't only for business. As you'll see in Chapter 6, many pages on the Web are just for fun, and many are completely frivolous. But that's okay. Who's to say that people can't use their own disk space and bandwidth to publish anything they want? By and large, though, businesses and organizations take their Web pages (and their Web site as a whole) very seriously. Most people will never set foot in the lobbies of IBM, Microsoft, Boeing, Chase Manhattan, or the myriad of smaller companies with which they do business. If they have Web access, however, they are quite likely to pull up a business's home page, which gives people every bit as much of a first impression.

Most technology companies (especially computer hardware and software companies) have recognized this for some time, and most have already established a presence on the Web. These companies realized the benefits of using the Internet (and the Web) early on, and they now provide valuable and serious services through their Web sites.

For example, many computer software and hardware companies offer technical support through their Web pages. A couple of years ago, everyone thought that bulletin boards and faxback technology would be the next rage. (With faxback, you dial a voice phone number and navigate an automated menu of selections to have a computer fax a document back to you that explains how to do something.) Faxback is still around, but the Web is much better; it's much easier to browse through the visual interface of a Web site than to respond to a computer-generated voice.

Also, many technology companies put their entire product catalogs online. By following menus of hypertext links, you can zero in on products that interest you, and in many cases even order them online. Potential customers can get specifications, find out about prerequisite products, and even see what a company's products look like before buying them. For customers who have already purchased products, many companies offer free software updates and new utilities and drivers online.

Today, even companies that have nothing at all to do with computer technology are racing to get online. Florists, automotive shops, graphic artists, consultants, locksmiths, agricultural businesses, banks, finance companies—they're all on the Web. Some have established their presence to better serve their existing customers. Some are on the Web to promote their business and sell their products. Still others simply offer information and resources to the public at large. Whatever their reasons (and there are plenty), more are arriving every day and staking their claims.

What Type of Computer Do You Need?

Virtually every type of computer can connect to the Internet, but this book focuses on PCs running Windows (Windows 3.1, Windows 95, or Windows NT); PCs running Unix systems, such as SCO Unix and the various BSD-based systems (such as BSDI, Linux, FreeBSD, and NetBSD); and Macintosh computers.

From time to time, we will discuss Unix computers, Unix commands, and setting up and using programs for Unix. In fact, in the discussion in Chapter 16 about how to set up a local area network for connecting a small business to the Web, we even suggest that our ideal small business network would include a Unix computer. If you don't know Unix but you're inclined to tinker with computers and software, you might want to explore it; Unix systems are powerful and robust, and they integrate very nicely into the Internet and the Web.

Despite the occasional mention of Unix, however, you needn't worry about learning it—or even using it, for that matter. As a user of the Web, you can do everything you need to from the comfort of Windows or your Mac. You can even get a permanent connection to the Internet and provide a variety of Internet services—including serving Web pages, mail, and files—from a Windows computer or a Mac.

What Extra Equipment or Software Do You Need?

Beyond your computer, the only hardware you need to browse the Web is a modem. You can use a 14.4 Kbps modem, but we recommend 28.8 Kbps modems to anyone who hasn't bought one yet; the small difference in price justifies the doubled speed.

If you plan to set up your own permanent Web site on the Internet with a faster connection than a modem can provide, you may need some additional network hardware. We'll look at faster connections and the hardware you need for them in Chapter 17.

As far as software is concerned, you may already have everything you need if you use Microsoft's Windows 95 or Windows NT or IBM's OS/2 Internet Connection. These operating systems include everything you need to get connected to the Internet. With Windows 95, making your first connection to the Internet can be as easy as clicking an icon on your desktop. And once you're connected, you can go find more and better programs to use with the Internet and even investigate the rates and services of other local Internet service providers. We'll take a closer look at these operating systems and their Internet connectivity in Chapter 3.

If you're still using Windows 3.1 or you use a Mac, everything you need is freely available on the Internet. Of course, this presents a chicken-or-the-egg problem for people who aren't connected yet: How can you download the software from the Internet if you're not connected? The next chapter explores some ways around this problem. Briefly, one solution is to get the necessities from your ISP when you sign up. Once you're connected, you can find the best of the free software yourself on the Web.

Alternatively, you can buy an Internet access package at your local software store that includes the utilities and programs you need. Some of these even include an Internet account with a service provider. All you have to do is load the software and make a call to start up your account. We'll also look at these turnkey packages in Chapter 3.

Finally, the major online information services such as CompuServe, America Online, and Prodigy are beginning to offer access to the Internet. (These are discussed in Chapter 4.) While the access they offer isn't as complete as what you get with an ISP, and they often charge for the access they do offer, using them can be a convenient way to get connected quickly and begin exploring the Internet.

Chapter 2

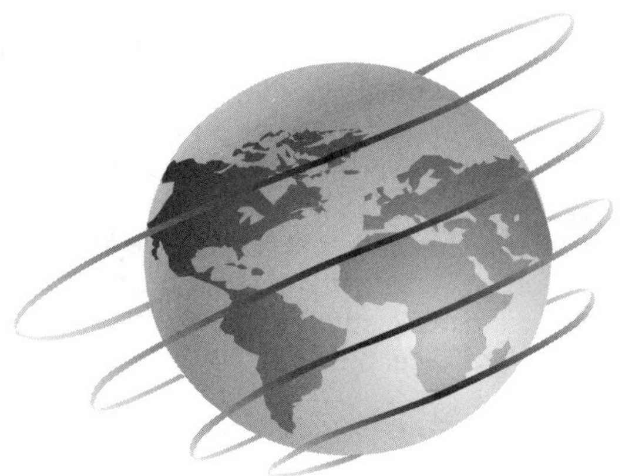

Getting Connected

Without a doubt, the hardest part about using the Web is getting your connection to the Internet and setting up your computer to use it. There are so many variables to take into account, and so many options for different types of computer systems, that it can all be very confusing.

In this chapter, we will cut through the confusion and show you how to get your system connected. We won't go into each and every intricate detail and option you might want to consider in the future, but we will give an overview of the many possibilities and help you find the provider and type of connection that's best for you.

Types of Connections

If you have access to the Internet through a Unix computer and a shell account, you may already know that you can use nongraphical programs to browse the Web. But accessing the Web without the graphics is like eating a sundae without the fudge, whipped cream, and cherry. Figure 2-1 shows a Web page as it appears when you view it with a Web browser called Lynx, which runs under command-line Unix. Figure 2-2 shows the same Web page as it looks when you view it with Netscape, a graphical browser that is available for most of the popular graphical user interfaces, including Microsoft Windows, the Mac, and X Window on Unix computers. Clearly, browsing the Web with a graphical browser is more exciting and rewarding than with a nongraphical browser.

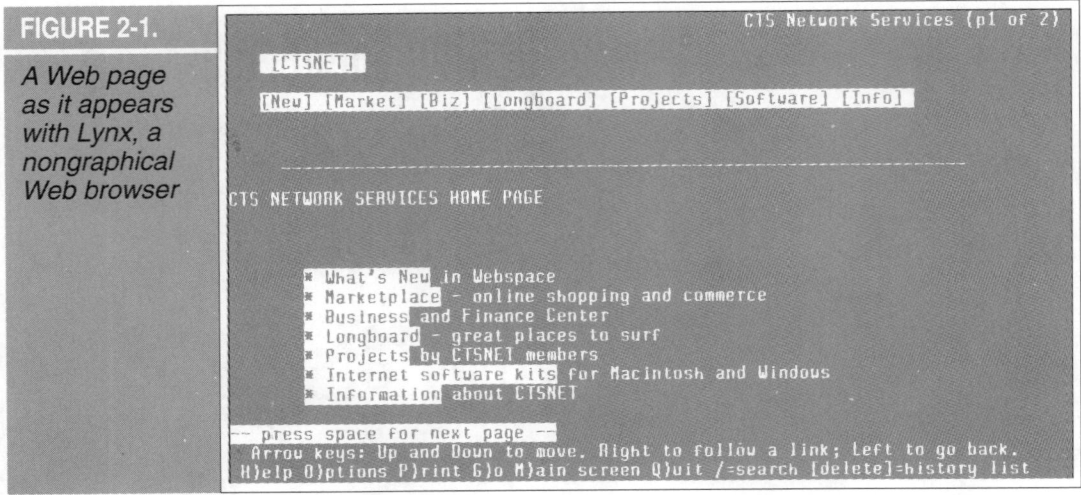

FIGURE 2-1. *A Web page as it appears with Lynx, a nongraphical Web browser*

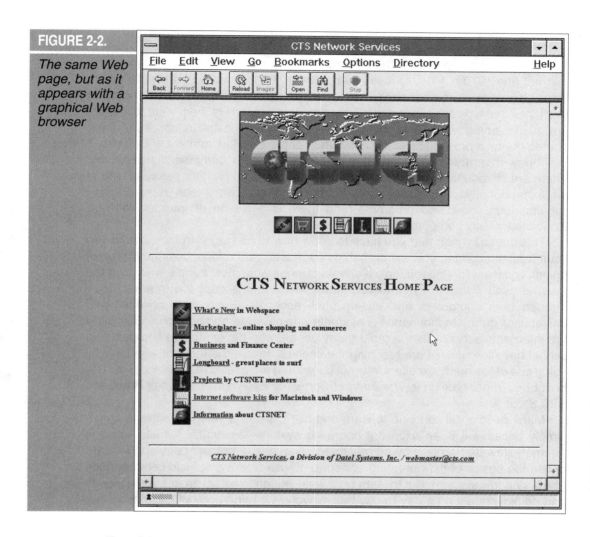

FIGURE 2-2. *The same Web page, but as it appears with a graphical Web browser*

For all intents and purposes, the World Wide Web has become the graphical user interface for the Internet. So why would new users want to learn Unix and use nongraphical Web browsers when they can use graphical browsers on their own computers and peruse the Web in all its illustrated glory? Given this choice, most people will choose to use Windows, OS/2, or Macintosh programs to browse the Web, so that they can enjoy all its fantastic multimedia capabilities.

In the next sections, we will give you an overview of why the Unix operating system is still important, but then we will explain how you can connect to the Internet without having to worry about arcane things like Unix.

Shell Accounts and the Dreaded "U" Word

The Internet grew up around the Unix operating system. In the early years of the Internet (the 1970s), virtually every computer on the Internet was a Unix. In those days, Unix computers were almost always very large, very expensive, and complex machines that typically supported hundreds of users. Many of them were located at universities and government installations—often military bases. In fact, the Internet started out as a project to link the computers of the U.S. Department of Defense.

Today, most Internet service providers still use Unix computers themselves. There are several technical reasons for this. For the most part, it's because Unix is an exceptionally robust and mature operating system; it can handle many simultaneous users and programs, and there is a wealth of Internet software available for Unix computers.

This doesn't mean that *you* have to know how to use Unix. In fact, unless you want a shell account, you will probably never even see a Unix command prompt unless you want to. (Indeed, only a couple of years ago, most people who used the Internet used it this way.) However, many people still access the Internet today through Unix computers and dial-up shell accounts. Each year, colleges and universities graduate thousands of students who have learned how to use Unix and the Internet in school. Also, a great many people who never studied computers in school have learned, or are teaching themselves, to use the Internet with Unix by using one of the many excellent Internet books that are available in bookstores. The best book in our opinion is *The Internet Complete Reference* by Harley Hahn and Rick Stout.

Many people will continue to learn and use Unix for a very long time to come, simply because it is an excellent operating system—especially for use with the Internet. However, Unix is by no means for everyone. It doesn't take long to learn to use the basics of the operating system or to use Unix's graphical user interface (the X Window system). But to learn Unix well enough to set up an Internet gateway and administrate it on a day-to-day basis involves a huge body of knowledge that most people would find overwhelming.

The Graphical Connection—SLIP and PPP Accounts

Like most people, you probably want to use the Internet with graphical programs. This means that you will have to get a particular type of account from an Internet service provider. When you buy a shell account on an Internet service provider's computer, you are buying an account for *you* (the person) to log into. To be able to use graphical programs with the Internet, you have to buy a special account for *your*

computer (rather than for you) to log into. These accounts are called *SLIP* or *PPP* accounts. (We will explain what these terms mean in a minute.)

The fundamental difference between an account for *you* and an account for *your computer* is this: When you use a communications program such as ProComm or ZTerm to call a Unix computer, you in effect transport yourself to that remote computer. This is no different from dialing into any local bulletin board system, except that the remote computer is on the Internet and your own computer is not. In contrast, when you get a SLIP or PPP account for your computer, you actually extend the Internet to your own computer—your computer is really on the Internet. These concepts are illustrated in Figure 2-3.

FIGURE 2-3.

Conceptual differences between dial-up shell accounts and SLIP/PPP accounts

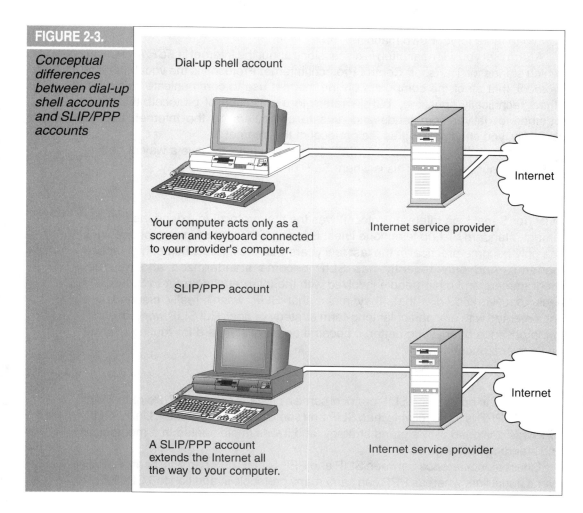

Dial-up shell account

Internet

Your computer acts only as a screen and keyboard connected to your provider's computer.

Internet service provider

SLIP/PPP account

Internet

A SLIP/PPP account extends the Internet all the way to your computer.

Internet service provider

The graphical programs that you use with your Internet connection (email programs, Web browsers, file-transfer programs, Usenet newsreaders, and so on) are written to use the Internet directly. This means that your computer has to be on the Internet.

Besides being able to use the Web graphically, there are many advantages to having your own computer on the Internet instead of using a remote computer that is on the Internet. For example, your email messages will all be stored on your own machine, and this gives you physical control over their security and privacy. Also, when you retrieve files from FTP (File Transfer Protocol) servers, the files come directly to your own machine. This is much more convenient than when you use a remote computer with a shell account. With a shell account, you have to first use FTP to bring files to the remote computer, then use a communications program to download them to your own machine.

A term that you will hear often in discussions about the Internet is *TCP/IP*. TCP/IP (which stands for Transport Control Protocol/Internet Protocol) is the vocabulary, or *protocol*, that all of the computers on the Internet use to communicate with each other. Technically speaking, TCP/IP refers to a collection of protocols that work together to deliver commands and data to computers on the Internet, but for simplicity, you can think of it as the protocol of the Internet.

To put your own computer onto the Internet, you have to have a way of getting TCP/IP to your computer. This is where SLIP or PPP comes into play.

SLIP

SLIP (for Serial Line Internet Protocol) was the first protocol to extend the Internet through standard dial-up telephone lines. Bringing TCP/IP through telephone lines has only become practical in the last few years with the introduction of high-speed modems. And only recently has SLIP become standardized and reliable. Programmers and other people involved with the Internet often refer to SLIP as "a hack that worked." By that, they mean that SLIP wasn't really planned and implemented with any particular long-term strategy or goal. But SLIP worked—and, in the absence of anything better, it became an early standard for routing Internet traffic over a phone line.

PPP

Virtually on the heels of the SLIP protocol came a protocol called *PPP* (Point-to-Point Protocol). PPP is more reliable than SLIP and sometimes slightly faster. Unlike SLIP, PPP was designed with a grand strategy, and it was implemented in a methodical and standardized way.

One major difference between SLIP and PPP is that SLIP can only carry TCP/IP over a serial line, whereas PPP can carry many protocols in addition to TCP/IP over

a variety of connections. For example, a PPP link can carry Novell network or Macintosh network protocols at the same time that it carries TCP/IP for an Internet connection. And PPP can work both over a local area network and on computers connected by serial cables. You probably won't ever need to be concerned with the details of these examples, but you can see that PPP is the more robust and flexible protocol.

Turnkey Packages

One way to get connected to the Internet is to go down to your software store and buy one of the many Internet access packages that are offered by software companies and book publishers. Some of these packages offer all the software you need to get started, including the low-level drivers for SLIP or PPP and an assortment of Internet client programs (native Windows or Mac programs that use the Internet, such as an email program, a Web browser, or a file-transfer utility).

Sometimes these packages also include an Internet access agreement with a large Internet service provider. For the most part, these bundled access agreements include a standard SLIP or PPP account that you could also arrange for yourself. If you do decide to establish an account yourself, it might be a little harder to get and configure the software you need. However, the advantage of setting up the system on your own is that you will learn quite a bit about the Internet in the process.

In Chapter 3, we will look in detail at several of the most popular Internet packages that you can buy off the shelf.

Information Services

In Chapter 4, we will look at what America Online, CompuServe, and Prodigy are doing to allow their users access to the World Wide Web. Companies like these are called *information services*. Typically they have one very large computer with many local telephone numbers across the country that their users can dial into with a modem. Among other things, they often provide news, articles, discussion forums, and shopping services—and usually charge fees for accessing most of the best resources they offer. These information services are quickly jumping onto the Internet bandwagon. If they don't, they will probably lose their members to the Internet!

Most of the large information services offer email access to the Internet. Some also offer access to Internet Usenet newsgroups and file transfers, and most of those that don't already offer access to the World Wide Web are planning to do so in the near future. Unfortunately, most of the information services charge by the hour or even by the minute for access to the Internet. Some even still charge to deliver email to or from the Internet.

If you are interested in a turnkey package or an information service, you may want to read the sections "Choosing the Right Modem" and "Getting the Software and Making the Connection" later in this chapter. If you are not an experienced modem user (or if you don't even have a modem yet), you may find these sections helpful.

Finding an Internet Service Provider

If you have already tried to find an Internet service provider, you may have found that it's not as easy as looking up "Internet" in your phone company's yellow pages—at least not yet! Finding a provider can be a real paradox, too. If you already have access to the Internet, it is very easy to find providers and get information about their services. But if you don't already have access (which is probably why you are reading this section), finding a provider can be a real mystery at first. While we can't give you any absolute answers, like a telephone number to call, we will give you some good pointers and places to begin your search. There are a couple of approaches you can take to finding an Internet service provider.

Large Internet Service Providers

One way to find a service provider is to contact some of the Internet providers that service very large portions of the country. Several companies have emerged as leaders in this market and are committed to establishing a presence in every major city. When an Internet service provider puts a connection point into service, it's called a *point of presence*, or sometimes a *POP*. (POP is also an acronym for Post Office Protocol—something completely different that we will talk about later.)

If you are in or near any sizable city, it is likely that one or more of the large Internet service providers can help you. Most of them are listed in the catalog at the back of the book in the section "Internet Service Providers."

Local Internet Service Providers

Even though large Internet providers are easier to find and use, you shouldn't quickly dismiss smaller local providers. Often, local providers can provide better service at market prices and offer all the features of their larger competitors. They can, however, be harder to find.

Many medium-sized and larger cities have local weekly computer magazines. You can usually find them at computer stores, bookstores that carry computer books, and newsstands. Sometimes you can find advertisements in these magazines for local companies that sell access to the Internet.

If you can't find any advertisements for local Internet service providers, try the section virtually all of these magazines have that lists local bulletin board systems. Many BBSs are on the Internet, and more BBS operators are putting their systems on the Internet all the time. You won't get full access to the Internet through a BBS (you won't get access to the Web), but you can often get access to Usenet newsgroups. If you can find a BBS with access to Usenet newsgroups, read the newsgroups alt.internet.service and alt.internet.access.wanted. If you don't get any immediate leads, try posting an article to alt.internet.access.wanted explaining that you are looking for a local Internet provider. If there are any, chances are someone will know of one or more of them and reply to your article.

Finally, it can never hurt to check the yellow pages. Many Internet providers are not even listed in the yellow pages yet, but some are. Check under "Data Communications," "Computer - Bulletin Boards," and "Computer - Networking."

If you do all of this and still can't find a local provider, you might consider getting an account with one of the large providers. Some of them offer a trial period during which you can use their services. That will give you a chance to evaluate their system while you investigate other possibilities.

Comparing Services and Prices

It is hard to enjoy browsing the Web if you have to keep reminding yourself that the meter is running. In most major cities, you should be able to find a provider that will give you a local access number. If you can't, or if you are in a rural area, you can use one of the larger Internet providers that offers 800 number access. However, they will charge you by the minute or by the hour for that service.

Some providers still charge by the minute or by the hour for your online time (in addition to any 800 number charges), but many of them are moving to flat monthly fees or combination fees. With combination fees, you get a low monthly fee and a relatively low hourly charge for a certain number of hours. After the specified number of hours, the hourly rate goes up.

Of course, you should first try to find a provider that offers a local number and charges a flat monthly fee with no additional connect-time charges. The simplest and least expensive type of account is a shell account. A reasonable flat-fee rate for a shell account is between $17 and $20 per month. The rate for a SLIP or PPP account can range between $20 and $30 per month.

Some of the larger providers offer several different service plans (just in case all this is too simple). IBM, for example, has two plans: the basic plan, which includes six hours per month of access time for around $13, with additional hours billed at

$4 per hour; and the comprehensive plan, which includes 30 hours of access time for $30, with additional hours billed at $3 per hour. Clearly, IBM's comprehensive plan is a better buy than its basic plan. With the comprehensive plan, if you spend an hour a day browsing the Web, your monthly bill will be around $30.

Of course, if IBM doesn't have a POP near you, you will have to pay a higher phone bill to your long-distance utility or pay IBM an additional amount for using its 800 number service. IBM charges an additional $6 per hour for 800 number access. If you have to use its 800 number for the same 30 hours, your monthly bill will be $210 ($30 plus $180)!

As a guideline, try to find a provider that will sell you a SLIP or PPP account for around $30 per month and not limit you to less than 30 hours per month. Also, be sure to ask about other charges—some providers charge for each email message you send out or find other ways to get more of your money. Try to avoid providers that impose ancillary charges if you can.

Paying for Your Account

With most every Internet service provider, you can arrange to pay your monthly bill automatically with a credit card. In fact, some of the major providers require you to provide a credit card for billing. If you can't or don't want to pay by credit card, some providers will bill you the old-fashioned way—by sending you a monthly statement.

A word of caution about paying by credit card: Don't put your credit card information (card name, number, or expiration) in any electronic correspondence. Electronic mail is not secure. In all likelihood, nobody will ever care to read your mail, but don't count on its security. It just isn't worth the risk. Only give out sensitive information like this over the telephone to the appropriate billing personnel, through postal mail, or in person.

Email on the Infobahn

Even though this book is primarily about the World Wide Web, we need to take a few minutes to note the other kinds of things you can do on the Internet for those of you who have just begun this journey. You can access most of these resources through a Web browser, and the important ones are discussed in the context of the World Wide Web in later chapters. Electronic mail is the exception to this, since it is the one Internet resource that you may not be able to access through your Web browser (although a few do have facilities for sending email built in). Nonetheless,

you need to know how your email will work. After everything you might go through to gain access to the Web, you wouldn't want to have to buy another book to learn how to set up your email, so we will give you an email primer here.

As mentioned earlier, this book departs from the tradition of the many Internet books available in that its focus is almost exclusively on the World Wide Web. There is a good reason for this: Of all the things you can do with the Internet (and there are many), regular Internet users are most interested in only about a dozen of them:

- Anonymous FTP—FTP is a program you can use to retrieve files from computers on the Internet.
- Archie—Archie servers are computers on the Internet with databases of the names of many of the files stored on FTP servers on the Internet. You can use an Archie client program to find the locations of files (the names of the FTP servers) when you know the name, or part of the name, of a file you want.
- Electronic Mail—You will probably find email to be one of the best parts of being connected to the Internet. You will be able to exchange messages with people all over the world in a matter of seconds.
- Finger—The Finger program will give you information about other people with accounts on Unix computers on the Internet. For example, Finger will tell you when users last logged onto their computer, if they are logged on currently, and the last time they read their mail.
- Gopher—The Gopher system is a worldwide menu system. It is similar in concept to the World Wide Web, but Gopher "pages" have only menu choices on them and no graphics at all.
- Internet Relay Chat—IRC is a worldwide real-time chat program. By tuning in a particular IRC channel, you can converse with others with similar interests in a sort of typist's CB radio environment.
- Mailing Lists—Mailing lists are the Internet's answer to the postal mailing lists you find in the real world. You can join mailing lists for many hundreds of subjects. Subscribing and unsubscribing are usually completely automated, and the "distributions" are delivered to your regular email address.
- Telnet—A telnet program allows you to connect to and log into other computers on the Internet. Of course, to log into another computer, you have to have a user name and a password on that computer.

- Usenet Newsgroups—The Usenet newsgroups form a sort of global bulletin board system; you can join discussion groups for a myriad of topics, both general and esoteric. Globally, there are well over 10,000 newsgroups (topics).
- WAIS—WAIS (for Wide Area Information Service) is a collection of databases you can search for information about any topic on the Internet.
- World Wide Web—Of course, the Web is the worldwide system of interlinked and interwoven hypertext documents.

Of these 11 main resources on the Internet, by far the most important to casual (and often very serious) users are

- Anonymous FTP
- Electronic mail
- Gopher
- Mailing lists
- Usenet newsgroups
- The World Wide Web

Most of the newer Web browsers we will look at in Chapter 5 serve not only as front-ends to the World Wide Web, but also as front-ends to Anonymous FTP archives and Gopher servers. Through various Web sites, you have access to all the Usenet newsgroups. A couple of the browsers (Netscape and the latest versions of Mosaic) even have built-in support for reading Usenet newsgroups. This leaves only one of the important resources of the Internet that can't generally be accessed directly through a Web browser or the Web itself: electronic mail. This is why we will briefly cover email programs, and what you need to get your email working, in this section.

Electronic Mail with a Shell Account

As we explained earlier in this chapter, when you use a communications program such as ProComm or ZTerm to call a computer on the Internet and log in, you are actually using the remote computer. In this scenario, your own computer is not actually on the Internet—you are just dialing into, and using, the remote computer as you might dial into any bulletin board system.

When you have a shell account on a Unix computer on the Internet, you already have an email address. Your email address consists of your login name followed by the "@" character, then the name of the computer or network your account is on.

For example, let's say you have a shell account with one of the largest Internet service providers—Netcom. Netcom has many individual computers on its network, but the name of the whole network (as it is known on the Internet) is *netcom.com*. Let's also say that your name is Woody Boyd and that you've chosen for your login name "woodyb". In this case, your email address would be "woodyb@netcom.com".

When you (Woody) log into your account on Netcom, the computer you log into will check your mail and tell you if you have any messages waiting. You can use any one of the many mail programs on most Unix computers to read and respond to your email.

Electronic Mail with a SLIP or PPP Account

If you ask your Internet provider to set up a SLIP or PPP account for you, chances are it will also set up a mail account, but you should ask just to be sure. A mail account that comes with a SLIP or PPP account is very similar to a shell account, but you won't need to log into it.

Unlike with a shell account, the login name you get for a SLIP or PPP account will not be part of your email address. This is because with SLIP or PPP, the login name is really for your computer, not for you. In fact, once you get your software configured, you probably won't ever need to think about the login name or password for your computer's SLIP or PPP account again—unless, of course, you want to change your password.

Think about a mail account as a shell account that you will never log into. In fact, you might not even have a password. However, the Internet service provider's computer will queue incoming mail for you just as though you had a regular shell account.

So how do you get your mail to your own computer so you can read it? You will use an email program that uses a protocol called *POP* (for Post Office Protocol—this is where POP does not mean point of presence) to log into the computer your mail account is on and download your mail. When you configure your mail program, you will specify how often it checks for mail. While you are online, you can have your mail program check for new mail. For example, you could configure your mail program to check for new mail every 10 or 15 minutes. When new mail arrives, your mail program will download your mail. Some of them notify you by playing a tune and possibly raising a flag on a mailbox icon.

Eudora is a popular commercial mail program with versions for both the Macintosh and Microsoft Windows. Eudora was developed by a company named Qualcomm, which makes slightly out-of-date versions of Eudora freely available on the Internet. Qualcomm's FTP site is ftp.qualcomm.com.

Choosing the Right Modem

A modem is the only actual piece of hardware that you must have to use the World Wide Web (aside, of course, from an adequate computer). Your modem is the device that allows your computer to "talk" to your Internet service provider's computer. Or, more accurately, your modem talks to your provider's modem, which in turn talks to the provider's computer. Before we talk about the specifications and capabilities of modems, you should understand that they come in two basic flavors—internal and external.

Internal vs. External Modems

An *internal* modem is a circuit board (or *card*) that you slip into a slot on the inside of your computer. You connect it to the phone company by unplugging the wire from your telephone and plugging it into the end of the card, which is accessible from the back of your computer. Typically, modems have two phone plugs. If you get another phone wire, you can run it between your telephone and the modem. That way, you don't have to fumble with telephone wires whenever you want to use the Internet, and your phone will work normally when you are not using the line. Of course, if you will be cruising the Web a lot, you may want to consider getting a second telephone line so you don't tie up your telephone while you're on the Web.

An *external* modem is also a circuit board, but the board is enclosed in a small box that can sit on your desktop or by your computer. External modems have three connectors on the back—two for the phone wires and another that you use to run a cable to one of your computer's serial ports. For PCs this is usually a 25-pin (DB-25) connector. For Macs, the connector is a smaller one, but the proper cable for your computer will usually come with your modem.

Whether you use an internal or external modem is really a matter of personal preference. Each has its benefits. The decision usually comes down to four questions:

- Does your computer have an available serial port (needed for an external modem)?

- Does your computer have an available slot inside (needed for an internal modem)?
- Do you want to see the flashing lights on the front of an external modem that show you what is going on with the modem?
- Do you mind paying slightly more for an external modem?

Internal and external modems function in the same way. In our opinion, however, it is nice to be able to see what is going on with your modem by viewing the lights on the front, and it's also helpful to be able to turn the modem off separately from your computer.

Modem Standards

In the old days (all of two or three years ago), using a modem and communications software could be a real ordeal. If you didn't know what you were doing, you could easily drown in the alphabet soup. You had to learn about terms like parity, stop bits, and data bits and about standards like MNP (for Microcom Network Protocol), compression, and error correction. Thankfully, this is all pretty much standardized now.

There are really only two types of modems you should consider for your Internet connection:

- A fast modem
- A slower, but cheaper, modem

The fastest modems widely available today transfer data at 28,800 bits per second. You don't need to worry about what a bit is—just understand that this is a rate (like miles per hour or gallons per minute). All modem speeds are measured against this same rate, so you can be sure that when you compare them, you are dealing with similar numbers. Most modem manufacturers abbreviate modem speeds by expressing them in thousands of bits per second, or Kbps. Thus, a modem that can transfer data at 28,800 bits per second is a 28.8 Kbps modem (you call these "twenty-eight eight" modems).

Before 28.8 Kbps modems came onto the market, the fastest modems generally available were 14.4 Kbps (these are called "fourteen four" modems). Since 28.8 Kbps modems are the rage now, you can find some good bargains on 14.4 Kbps modems. Both of these modems can actually transfer data at rates that are higher than their base ratings. This is because modems can compress the data you send through them, sometimes very effectively. By using built-in compression techniques, these modems can sometimes quadruple their throughput. Thus a 28.8 Kbps modem has a theoretical maximum throughput of 115,200 bits per second, and a 14.4 Kbps modem has a theoretical maximum throughput of 57,600 bits per second.

Happily, you don't have to remember all these numbers. All the capabilities of these two types of modems are defined in two international specifications. Modems with a base speed of 28.8 Kbps are defined by a standard called *V.34* (pronounced "vee dot thirty-four" or sometimes just "vee thirty-four"). Modems with a base speed of 14.4 Kbps are defined by the standard called *V.32bis* ("vee dot thirty-two bis" or "vee thirty-two bis"; "bis" rhymes with the word "bliss").

Getting the Software and Making the Connection

In the first sections of this chapter, we looked at the different ways you can connect to the Internet; we also discussed communication protocols, Internet resources, electronic mail, and modems. In this section, we will give you some pointers on the software you will need to put on your computer to make your SLIP or PPP connection to the Internet and how you go about installing it. We provide the most help for Microsoft Windows 3.1 users because this operating environment is so widely used and because it is probably the most difficult type of system to configure for a SLIP or PPP account.

If you have bought, or intend to buy, a bundled access package, you probably don't need to worry about this section. (You can read Chapter 3 for more information about these programs.) Also, we won't go into detail about getting connected with Windows 95 or OS/2 Warp here. These systems already have the software you need and, to some extent, are preconfigured for Internet connections. We will also go into more detail about using both of these operating systems on the Internet in Chapter 3.

The Basics

Getting the software you need for the Internet can sometimes seem like a "chicken or the egg" proposition. This is because you can get the software so easily from the Internet, but you have to have access to the Internet first. If Internet providers have an office in your city, the easiest way to get the software is to walk in their front door and ask for a diskette with the software you need. It's more likely, though, that they won't have an office in your city, so you will have to set up your account over the telephone and get the software another way.

Table 2-1 summarizes the software you need to get started with a PPP or SLIP account. This table doesn't include any of the client software you will use after you get your system connected (such as Web browsers, email programs, or FTP clients); it just lists the low-level tools for getting TCP/IP running on your system and making the connection to your provider. We cover Web browsers in Chapter 5.

TABLE 2-1. *Software You Will Need for SLIP or PPP Accounts*

OPERATING SYSTEM	SOFTWARE YOU NEED
Windows 3.1 and Windows for Workgroups	Trumpet Winsock (shareware), Chameleon (commercial), other SLIP/PPP packages
Macintosh	MacTCP (commercial) and a SLIP/PPP package such as TCP/Connect II (commercial)
Windows 95	(nothing needed—it is all included)
Windows NT	(nothing needed—it is all included)
OS/2 Warp	(nothing needed—it is all included)

For establishing a SLIP/PPP connection with any operating system, you need two software components—a TCP/IP driver and the SLIP/PPP software itself, which takes control of your modem and makes the connection to your Internet service provider. For Windows 3.1, the TCP/IP driver is largely a single file (named *WINSOCK.DLL*) that just has to exist on your system. Because this file is included with most SLIP/PPP packages (such as Trumpet Winsock and Chameleon), it is easy to slip into the notion that all you need is the SLIP/PPP package, but you will be better off if you understand the distinction between the TCP/IP component and the SLIP/PPP component.

Regardless of which operating system you use, the procedure you follow to establish your connection will be about the same. Generally, here's how it all works:

First, arrange for your PPP or SLIP account with your Internet provider. Remember that a PPP or SLIP account is really an account for your *computer* (rather than you). Your provider will give you a login name and password for your computer to use when it logs in, the phone number for your computer to call, an *IP number,* and perhaps several other bits of information such as a number called a *netmask*, a number for a *domain name server*, and information for your email account (see Table 2-2 for an explanation of these terms).

Your computer's IP number is its unique address on the Internet. IP addresses are usually made up of four groups of numbers, separated by periods. For example, 199.100.81.100 is a valid IP address. Some providers will assign you a permanent number; others will have their computer assign a number to your computer each time it connects to their computer. If your provider assigns a permanent number to your computer, you may also have to choose a unique name for your computer to

TABLE 2-2. *Some Terms You Need to Understand to Set Up Your SLIP/PPP Connection*

TERM	WHAT IT MEANS
domain	The domain is the Internet name of your Internet provider's network—the network that your computer will be part of. For example, if your provider is PSI, your domain will probably be *psi.com*.
domain name server	One of the computers on your provider's network is set up to translate computer names into their corresponding IP numbers for all the computers on your provider's network (including yours). For example, let's say you want to look at Pacific Bell's home page, so you type **http://www.pacbell.com** into your Web browser. Before your browser can load that Web page, it has to check with your domain name server to get the IP number for the computer "www.pacbell.com". The domain name server will inform your system that the computer's IP number is 192.150.170.2.
IP number	An IP number is a sequence of four numbers separated by periods that uniquely identifies every computer on the Internet. Some Internet providers assign IP numbers permanently so that your computer's IP number will never change. Other providers set up their systems to assign IP numbers dynamically, which means that each time you establish your connection, you may have a different IP number.
mail server	Some Internet providers dedicate a computer to serving mail for all the other computers on their network. If this is the case for your network, your provider will give you the machine name or IP number so you can enter it into the setup screen for your mail program.
netmask	Your provider may give you an additional number for your network called a *netmask*. If so, just enter it into the setup screen for your SLIP/PPP system.
news server	Many providers dedicate a computer to storing Usenet news articles and serving them to the users on their networks. If this is the case with your provider, you will have to enter the name or IP number of your news server into the configuration screen for the program you will use to read the news.

TABLE 2-2. *Some Terms You Need to Understand to Set Up Your SLIP/PPP Connection* (continued)

TERM	WHAT IT MEANS
router *or* gateway	This is the computer your computer will dial into to establish your connection to the Internet.
router login	This is the name your computer will use to log into the router computer. A convention that some (but not all) providers follow is to begin PPP account names with a "p" (like "pdhayes" for someone whose name is Don Hayes) and to begin SLIP accounts with an "s" (like "sjwarren" for someone whose name is Jennifer Warren). Most often, this login name will not correspond to your email address—it's just an identifier for your computer.
router password	Just as when a person logs into a computer, when your computer logs into the router, it has to supply both a login name and a password. This string of characters is the password your computer will need to complete the login sequence.

be associated with its IP number. Table 2-2 summarizes and defines the terms associated with the information you'll get from your service provider.

Your provider will create the account for your computer on its computer while you set up your own system. On your system, you will open a Setup dialog box (it may also be called an Options or Configuration dialog box) in your SLIP or PPP software (such as Trumpet Winsock or MacTCP) and enter the information your provider gave you in the appropriate edit boxes. You also need to tell your software which communications port your modem is on. Figure 2-4 shows the Network Configuration dialog box for Trumpet Winsock.

Once you have entered the information, you can choose Login or Dial from a menu in your SLIP or PPP software and your computer will initiate the connection. Unlike a shell account where a person logs in and the provider's computer runs a shell, when your computer logs in, the provider's computer initiates the SLIP or PPP protocol on the line and makes a TCP/IP connection with your computer. At this point, your computer will be on the Internet.

We have given you a general overview of what you need to do to get connected, independent of any operating-system-specific terms. In the next section, we will look more specifically at what you need to do if you use Microsoft Windows, then briefly

FIGURE 2-4. *Trumpet Winsock's Network Configuration dialog box*

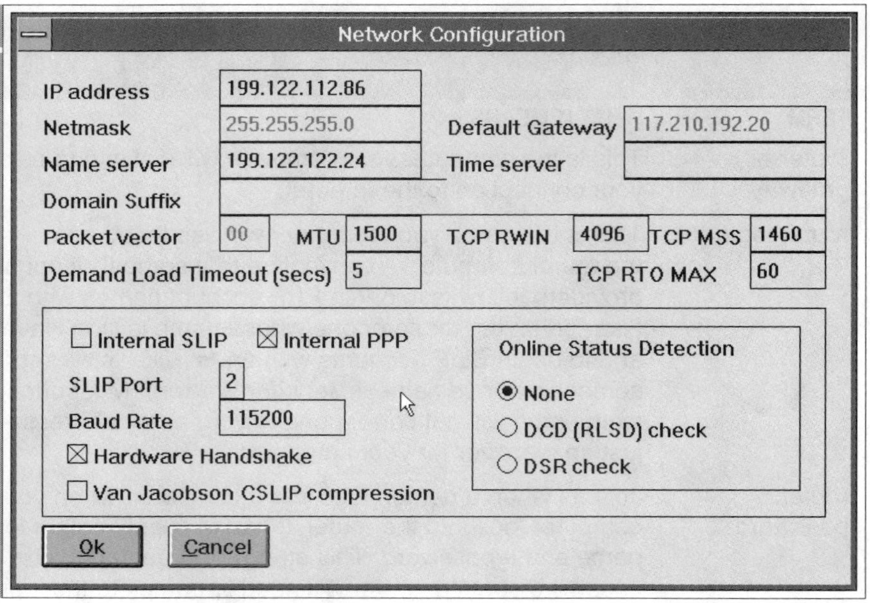

give you some suggestions for connecting to the Internet with Windows 95, OS/2 Warp, or a Macintosh.

Windows 3.1 and Windows for Workgroups

There are a handful of SLIP/PPP packages that you can use with Microsoft Windows. Some of the best of them are shareware, but there are also fully commercial packages. One good one (that is also shareware) is Trumpet Winsock from Trumpet International. Trumpet Winsock is widely used for SLIP and PPP accounts because it is reliable and easy to use. Trumpet Winsock also lets you take control of your modem and dial out to your Internet provider, so it's everything you need in one program.

If you already have access to the Internet, you can get the latest version of Trumpet Winsock from Trumpet International's FTP server at ftp.trumpet.com.au, from any number of software archive sites on the Internet, or from local bulletin board systems.

One popular commercial SLIP/PPP package is Chameleon. Chameleon, or a scaled-down version of it, comes with some of the turnkey packages. In the rest of this section, we talk about Trumpet Winsock only, but the procedures and concepts are similar for all the packages.

Trumpet Winsock comes as a ZIP file. Files archived in the ZIP format need to be "unzipped" using the shareware program PKUNZIP. Some of the desktop managers for Windows (such as Norton Desktop for Windows) have built-in support for ZIP files, so you can easily extract them. If you don't have such a utility, you can get PKUNZIP from practically any local bulletin board system.

To install Trumpet Winsock, follow these steps:

1. Create a directory for Trumpet Winsock. For example, issue the DOS command **MKDIR C:\TRUMPET**.
2. Extract the files in the ZIP file to that directory with PKUNZIP or another unarchiving utility.
3. Add the directory *C:\TRUMPET* to your PATH statement by editing the PATH line in your *AUTOEXEC.BAT* file, and reboot your computer to allow the new PATH statement to take effect.
4. Run the TCPMAN program that is included in the Trumpet package by opening the File|Run dialog box and typing **TCPMAN** into the command-line edit box.
5. When you run TCPMAN for the first time, the Network Configuration dialog box appears (shown in Figure 2-4). Enter the information supplied by your Internet service provider into the edit boxes in the dialog box. The boxes you should be most concerned with are those for the IP address, the name server, either Internal SLIP or Internal PPP, the SLIP port number, and the baud rate. You may or may not need the other boxes; your provider will tell you if you do. If you can't match up the descriptions for the information your provider gave you and the edit boxes, ask your provider to clarify them for you. Finally, you close the dialog box.
6. From the Dialer menu, choose *setup.cmd*. This is a script file that will prompt you for the phone number of your Internet service provider's modem, your SLIP or PPP login name, and the password.

Finally, you can establish your connection to the Internet by choosing Login from the Dialer menu. That's all there is to it. Once Trumpet establishes the connection, you can minimize the TCPMAN program to an icon and leave it on your desktop while you explore the Internet.

To disconnect from your provider's computer, just open TCPMAN and choose Bye from the Dialer menu.

Windows 95 and OS/2 Warp

If you run Windows 95 or Warp, you already have all the software you need to get started. Both systems come with a TCP/IP and a PPP software program, as well as a few rudimentary client programs, including a telnet program, an FTP client, and a Web browser.

In Chapter 3 we will take a closer look at configuring Windows 95 and Warp for your Internet connection.

Macintosh

The Macintosh community benefits from a wealth of quality Internet software. The other benefit to using a Mac with the Internet is that getting SLIP or PPP to run is generally easier than it is for a PC running Windows 3.1. You will, however, still need to enter the information your Internet provider gives you into a setup screen. To get your Mac onto the Internet, you will first have to collect some software (refer back to Table 2-1).

MacTCP

For the Mac, the TCP/IP driver is the package called *MacTCP*, which you must have on your system. In addition to MacTCP, you have to have a SLIP/PPP package. As with the SLIP/PPP packages for Windows 3.1 systems, this can be a little confusing because some packages will include MacTCP and others won't. You don't have to worry about MacTCP if your Mac runs System 7.5 or later because MacTCP is included with the operating system.

If you use a version of the Macintosh operating system prior to System 7.5, the best way to get MacTCP may simply be to upgrade your system to System 7.5 or the latest version. You may also be able to get MacTCP directly from Apple Computer without upgrading to System 7.5 if, for some reason, you don't want to upgrade your computer.

Another way to get MacTCP is bundled with other products. If you will also need a SLIP/PPP package (which we'll look at in the next section), some of them will include MacTCP. Also, Eudora, a popular email program from Qualcomm, includes MacTCP. When you install Eudora, the installation program will take care of installing MacTCP if it isn't already on your system. Qualcomm is listed in Appendix B.

If you can't get MacTCP from any of these sources, you can get it from the excellent book *The Internet Starter Kit for Macintosh* by Adam Engst (Hayden Books). This book includes all the software you need on a diskette. In addition to some good Internet client software, you will get both MacTCP and a SLIP/PPP package.

PPP/SLIP and Dialers

Some Anonymous FTP sites on the Internet offer a shareware PPP package called MacPPP. If you can find it, MacPPP will get you started. A commercial product that is highly recommended by some Mac users is TCP/Connect II from InterCon Systems Corporation. InterCon is also listed in Appendix B.

Clearly, we have focused on explaining what Microsoft Windows 3.1 and Windows for Workgroups users need to do to get connected. This is because these folks need the most help! Indeed, installing software on a Mac can be very simple (e.g., "Insert the diskette and drag the icon onto your desktop..."). Windows users have more options, which complicates things even more. We've found that for Mac users, the best tactic is to explain the concepts behind what they need to do, rather than focusing on the specifics of how to do them. For Windows 95 and OS/2 Warp users, getting connected isn't quite as simple as it is for Mac users, but it is still fairly straightforward. We will jump into the details about Warp and Windows 95 in the next chapter.

Chapter 3

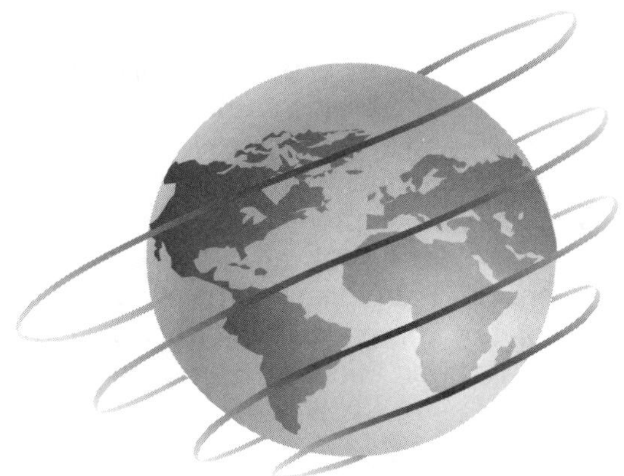

Turnkey Solutions for Connecting to the Internet

Not long ago, connecting a PC running Windows or OS/2 to the Internet was a trying experience—even for users who were experienced with both PCs and the Internet. Pulling together applications, dialer programs, and utilities with arcane names like WINSOCK.DLL could quickly have you pulling out your hair. And once you had all the software, getting it all in the right place and configured properly was a hit-or-miss proposition.

The Unix operating system has had Internet connectivity almost since its creation. With built-in TCP/IP and other protocols—such as electronic mail, network file systems, and, more recently, HTTP (the protocol of the Web)—Unix systems are virtually ready to play on the Internet when they come out of the box.

Toward the end of Windows 3.1's life cycle, a number of software bundles from various publishers eased the pain of configuring a Windows system to connect to the Internet. But with Windows NT, Windows 95, and OS/2 Warp Connect, the operating system developers finally delivered; these operating systems now include the drivers and protocols for connecting to the Internet. And configuring them is as easy as filling in your network address and clicking an OK button.

In this chapter, we'll look at these turnkey solutions (packages and operating systems), which promise to include everything you need to get onto the Internet in one box. We'll look at two operating systems—Windows 95 and OS/2 Warp Connect—that promise to have you surfing the Net in no time. We'll finish up this chapter by taking a quick look at a couple of software bundles that make connecting to the Net with Windows 3.1 nearly as easy as it is for Windows 95 and OS/2.

Windows 95

Windows 95 is a truly amazing new generation of Microsoft Windows. Not only is it easier to install and configure than previous versions of Windows, but it's a pleasure to use. Windows 95 includes many new features, tools, and enhancements over Windows 3.1. Gone are the days when it took an entire afternoon to configure a Windows system with a reasonable desktop manager, system scheduling and monitoring software, utility software, network drivers, protocols, and dialers. The Windows 95 CD has everything you need for a robust and very well-connected desktop operating system.

Sorting Out the Options

Before we explore the details of connecting a Windows 95 system to the Internet, you should understand what you get with Windows and what you don't.

First, the basic operating system includes tools for connecting to a new Microsoft online service called *The Microsoft Network*. MSN is an information service—like a

large computer bulletin board system—along the same lines as CompuServe and America Online. And, like the other information services, your computer accesses MSN by using its modem to place a call to a local telephone number. Through MSN, you can read news, join discussion groups, even purchase products and services online. You can also access the Internet through MSN. However, we won't cover MSN in this chapter; since it's essentially an online service competing directly with other online services, it's discussed in Chapter 4 along with the others.

Second, Microsoft sells a companion product to Windows 95 called *Plus!*. The Plus! package offers some utility programs, a few applications, and custom configurations for your desktop. One of the Plus! pack's best features is a wealth of custom desktop schemes for your Windows 95 system, including background patterns and images, cursor customization, and interesting sound schemes. The Plus! package also includes a few additional Internet utilities, such as a Web browser, that don't come with the basic operating system. While the Plus! package is nice, it contains nothing that you must have for connecting to and using the Internet.

Finally, the basic Windows 95 operating system includes all the underlying protocols and utilities you need to connect to the Internet. It even includes a few TCP/IP applications—such as a telnet program, FTP, and ping—but not a Web browser. If you want Microsoft's version of Mosaic, you'll have to get the Plus! package.

Networking with Windows 95

When you install the Windows 95 operating system, it goes through an exhaustive examination of your computer's hardware, identifying each adapter card and peripheral attached to your system. Among the adapters and peripherals it will find are network interface cards and modems. Once installation is complete, Windows 95 will know about your modem and network hardware and will load drivers for them automatically during the boot-up process.

Windows 95 also includes more than a dozen common network protocols. Among these protocols are:

- Banyan VINES
- DEC Pathworks
- IBM DLC
- IPX/SPX
- NetBEUI
- TCP/IP
- Novell IPX
- SunSoft's PC-NFS

The beauty of networking with Windows 95 is the simplicity of its approach. The operating system recognizes all the hardware you might want to use for networking (modems and network interface cards) and includes most of the protocols you would want to use. All that's left for you to do is create associations between the networking hardware and those protocols. In fact, during the installation process, Windows 95 automatically creates some of these associations.

For example, let's say you have an Ethernet network interface card in your PC and that it's attached to an Ethernet network. The Windows 95 installation process will detect your Ethernet card and automatically associate the two most common protocols with it: IPX/SPX and NetBEUI. If you also want to run the TCP/IP protocol on your network because you plan to connect your entire network to the Internet, you'll have to create an additional association between your Ethernet card and the TCP/IP protocol. (We'll show you how to do this in a moment.)

Here's another example: You have a single computer, not a network, and you want to use a dialup PPP account with an Internet service provider (ISP). In this case, you'll also need to use the TCP/IP protocol, but it will have to be associated with your dialup connection (your modem) rather than a network card.

The process of creating associations between a network protocol and a network device is called *binding*. Before we show you how to bind a protocol to a device, we should briefly explain the three protocols you're most likely to need.

The protocol of Novell networks is called *IPX*. It's been around as long as Novell, and if you plan on connecting your Windows 95 machine to a Novell network, you'll need it. Microsoft calls its version of this protocol *IPX/SPX*, but Novell's own version is also included with the operating system. If you had a network card in your PC when you installed Windows 95, the installation program probably created a binding for IPX/SPX to the card automatically. If you don't connect to a Novell network, you can safely delete that binding. You can easily re-create the binding at any time in the future if you need it. (This stuff is pretty easy to figure out, but you should probably at least wait until you're done with this section before you start deleting protocol bindings.)

The protocol of Microsoft networks (and LanManager networks) is *NetBEUI*. In the old days, this protocol was called NetBIOS. Again, if there was a network card in your system during your Windows 95 installation, a binding for NetBEUI was probably

created automatically. If there are other Windows machines (Windows 95, Windows NT, or Windows for Workgroups) on your network, you'll probably want to keep NetBEUI. This protocol lets you easily share resources such as printers, CD-ROM drives, disk folders, and even entire hard disks with other Windows computers.

As you learned in the last chapter, TCP/IP is the protocol of the Internet. The Windows 95 installation doesn't automatically create a binding for TCP/IP, but it's easy enough to add yourself. However, you might not even need to add it manually, depending on how you intend to access the Internet; if you plan to use MSN or some of the tools in the Plus! package, Windows will handle the setup for you.

You can access the Internet with Windows 95 in three ways:

- A dialup connection to the MSN online service
- A dialup PPP connection to an ISP
- A TCP/IP network connected to the Internet through a router or gateway

If you plan to use MSN, you don't have to worry about any of this; just skip ahead to Chapter 4.

Setting Up a PPP Connection with an ISP

If you have, or plan to get, a dialup PPP account with an ISP, you also don't have much to worry about; a Wizard will walk you through the process of setting it up under Windows. (*Wizard* is what Microsoft calls the small programs Windows provides to automate tasks and help you through complicated procedures.)

To use this Wizard, open the My Computer icon on your desktop, double-click the Dial-Up Networking icon, and then double-click the Make New Connection icon. The Wizard creates an icon that represents the PPP connection to an ISP that you're defining. The first page of this Wizard (see Figure 3-1) prompts you for a name for your connection (and the icon) and confirms the modem to use. The second page prompts you for the phone number for the connection (see Figure 3-2), and the final screen just confirms that the connection was created and saves it under the name you assigned to it.

To check or change the connection settings, right-click on the connection's icon in the Dial-Up Networking folder and select Properties. This will display the following dialog:

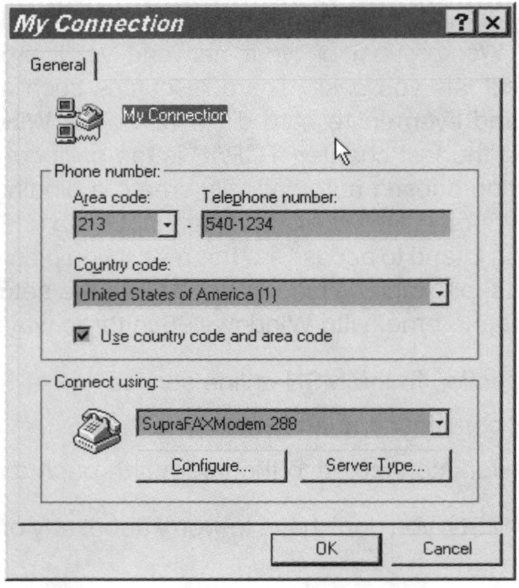

This dialog shows only the phone number and modem; to see the actual connection settings, click the Server Type button in the Connect Using box. This will display the following dialog, which includes a field for the server type, options, and checkboxes with a check mark for each protocol associated with the connection.

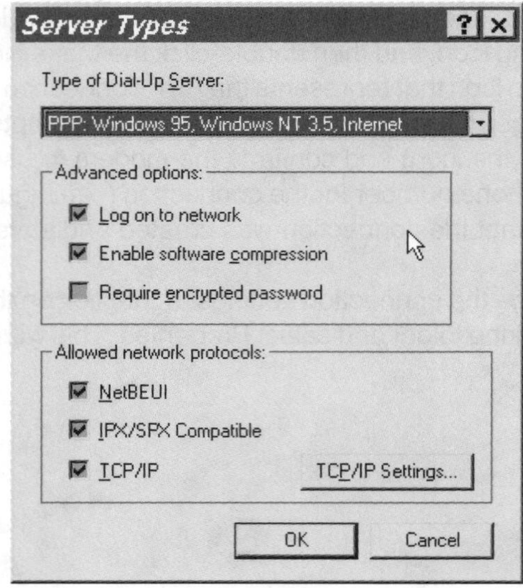

FIGURE 3-1.
Page 1 of the Dial-Up Networking Wizard

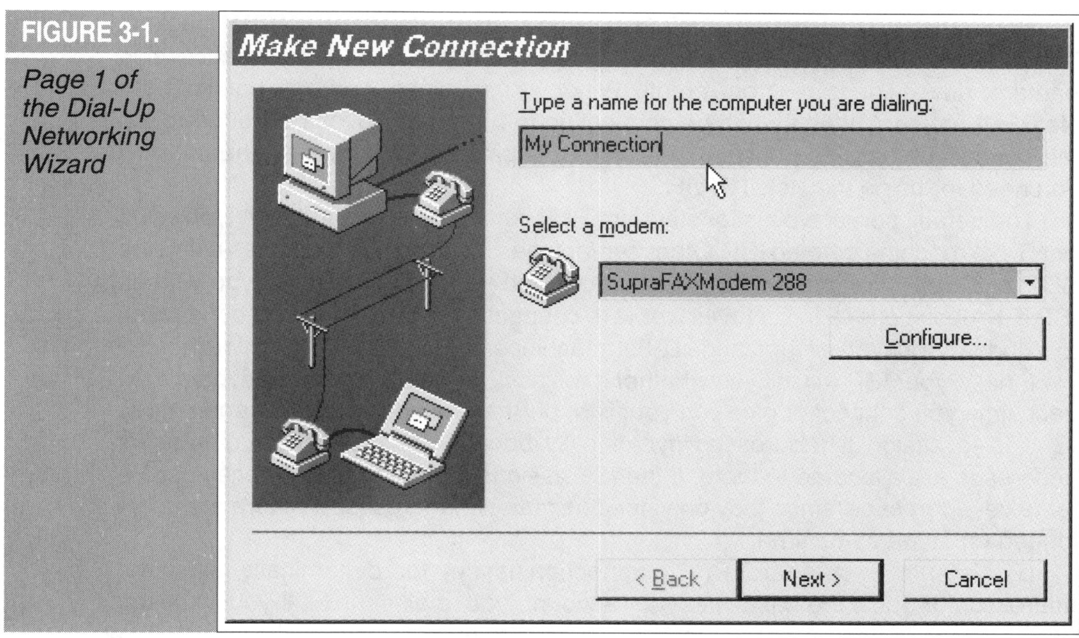

FIGURE 3-2.
Page 2 of the Dial-Up Networking Wizard

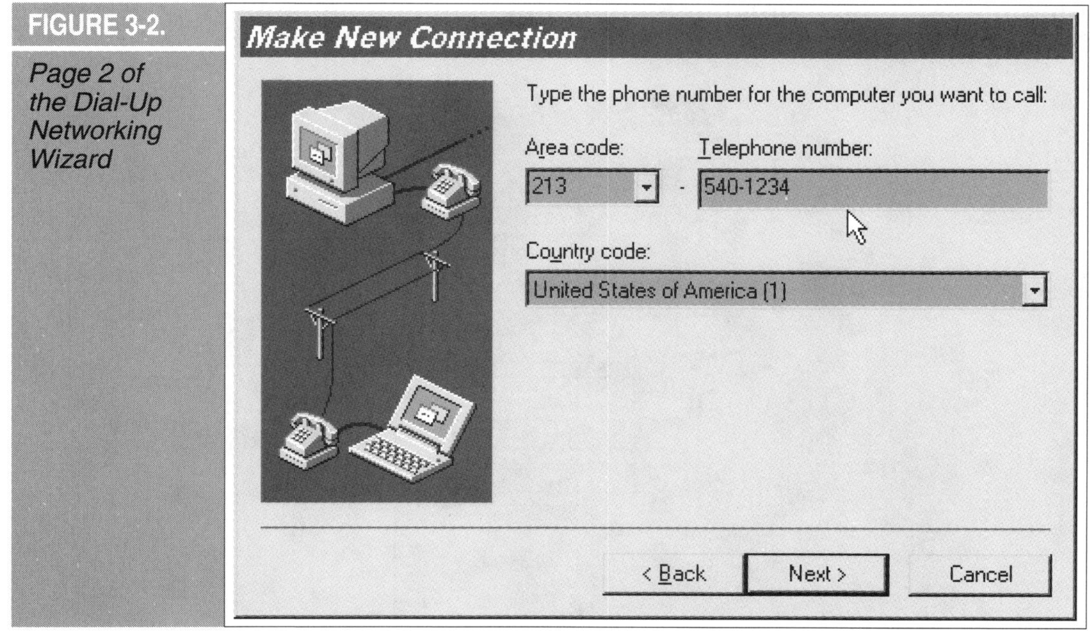

Notice that all three protocols in the Allowed Network Protocols box are checked. This is the default for a PPP Internet connection. If you don't plan on accessing printers, drives, or folders on remote Windows machines, you can uncheck the NetBEUI protocol. If you won't be connecting to a remote Novell network through the connection, you can uncheck the IPX/SPX protocol. That leaves the protocol you need for using the Net: TCP/IP.

The default server type is for standard PPP connections to another Windows 95 or NT 3.5 machine or to an ISP. Other server types include Unix machines using the SLIP or CSLIP (compressed SLIP) protocol (you might also use this type with an ISP if it doesn't offer PPP), Novell Netware connections, and servers for connecting to Windows for Workgroups and NT 3.1 machines.

Finally, your ISP will tell you whether it will assign you IP addresses dynamically each time you connect or give you your own permanent address. The trend among ISPs is to assign IP addresses dynamically because only a certain number of addresses are allocated to them. If the ISP assigns them dynamically, they use up far fewer addresses, since they only need as many IP addresses as there are users logged on at the same time.

By default, a standard PPP connection is set for dynamically allocated addresses. If that's the case with your account, you're all set. But if your provider does give you a permanent address, you'll have to record it along with some other information. Do this by clicking the TCP/IP Settings button in the Server Types dialog to display the following panel:

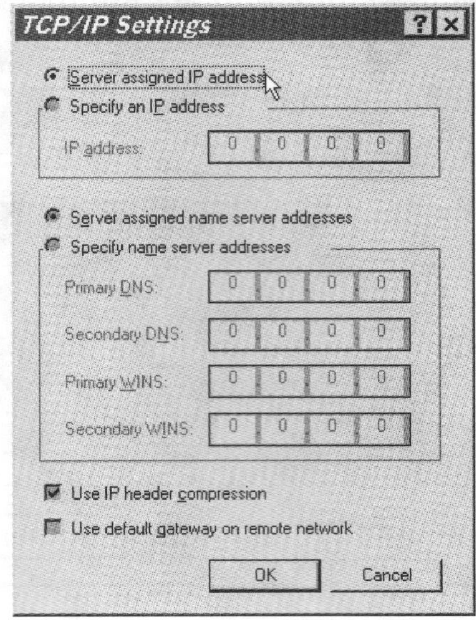

To record your IP address, click the Specify an IP Address radio button and enter the address in the IP Address field. Your ISP may also give you IP addresses for DNS and WINS servers. If it does, you'll need to specify those as well.

That's all there is to setting up a PPP connection to an ISP with Windows 95. To use your new connection profile, just pull up the Dial-Up Networking folder and double-click the icon for your connection. (You can also drag the icon out onto your desktop so it's easier to access.) When you double-click the icon, Windows will dial out to the ISP and establish the network connection.

Setting Up a Connection Through a TCP/IP Network

The third way to connect to the Internet with Windows 95 is through a local area network that's connected to the Internet through a router or gateway. In Chapters 16 and 17, you'll learn how to make such a connection between a network and an ISP. In this section, you'll see how to configure Windows 95 to use that network connection.

There isn't a Wizard for configuring a network connection to the Internet, but the process is simple enough that it really doesn't matter. All you have to do is bind the TCP/IP protocol to the network adapter, then enter your TCP/IP options. Here's how to do it:

Open the Network applet in the Control Panel. The Network dialog will be displayed:

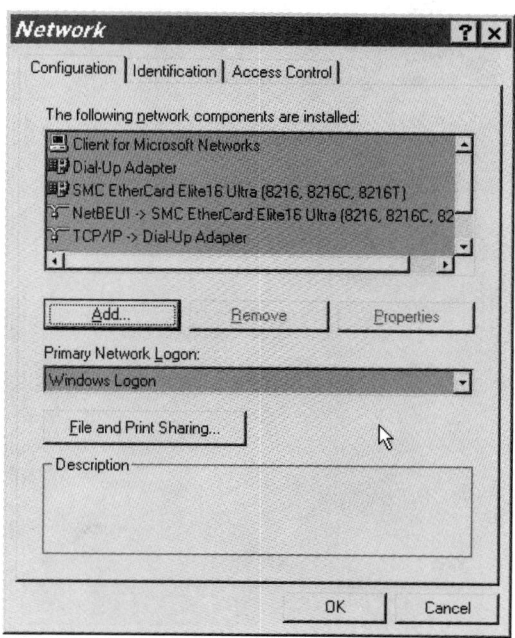

First, look through the entries in the scroll box to make sure the TCP/IP protocol isn't already configured and bound to your network card. (It's OK if TCP/IP is bound to a dialup adapter; you just won't be using that with your network connection.)

Once you've confirmed that TCP/IP isn't already bound to the network card, click the Add button to add the TCP/IP protocol. The Select Network Component Type dialog shown in Figure 3-3 is displayed. Choose Protocol and then click Add. This brings up the Select Network Protocol dialog (see Figure 3-4). Click Microsoft in the box on the left side of the dialog, then click TCP/IP in the box on the right side. Finally, click OK until you're back to the Network dialog.

Now there should be a new line in the scroll box that looks like this:

```
TCP/IP -> SMC EtherCard Elite16 Ultra
```

except that instead of *SMC EtherCard Elite16 Ultra*, you should see a description of the network interface card in your system. Select this line in the scroll box by clicking it with your mouse, then click the Properties button. (Alternatively, you can just double-click on the line.) This displays the TCP/IP Properties dialog, which has tabs at the top for each subject relating to your TCP/IP protocol:

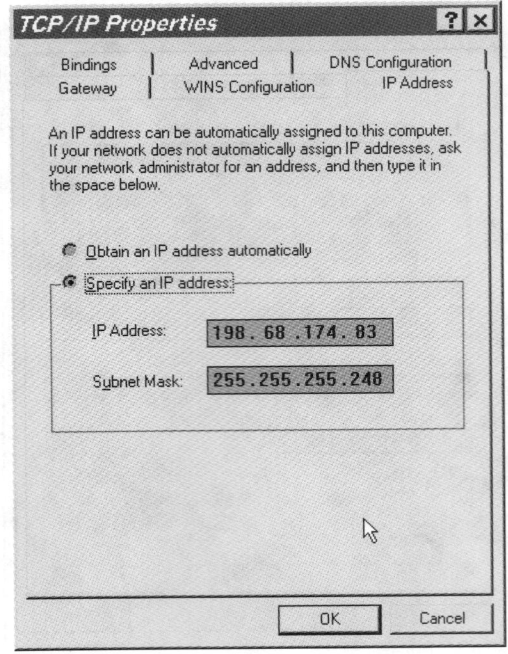

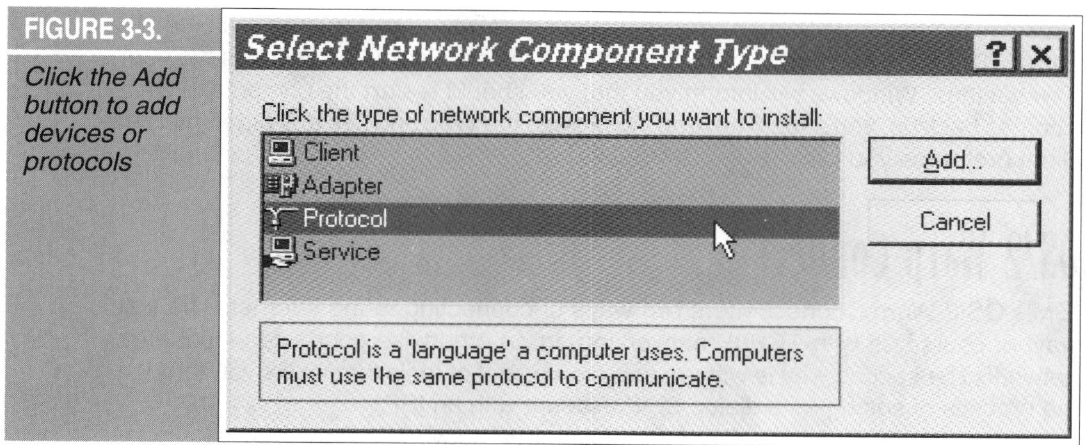

FIGURE 3-3. *Click the Add button to add devices or protocols*

First, click on the IP Address tab and enter your IP address and subnet mask. (Your ISP or system administrator will give you both of these numbers.) Next, go to the DNS Configuration tab and fill in the name of your machine on your network, your domain name, and the IP addresses for your DNS servers. Finally, go to the

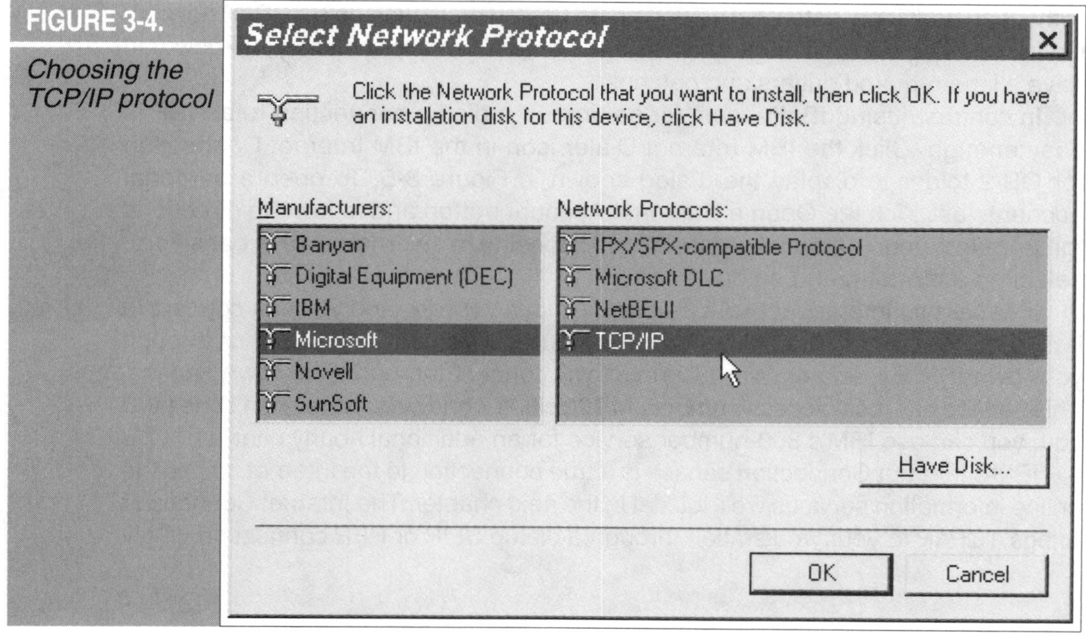

FIGURE 3-4. *Choosing the TCP/IP protocol*

Gateway tab and enter the IP address of your gateway or router, then click the OK button. This will bring you back to the Network dialog. Click OK again to save your new settings. Windows will inform you that you should restart the computer. When it comes back up, you should be ready to browse the Web and use any other Internet client programs you like.

OS/2 Warp Connect

IBM's OS/2 Warp Connect offers two ways of connecting to the Internet. The first way, of course, is with TCP/IP networking on an otherwise connected local area network. The second way is with an easy-to-use set of tools that walks you through the process of setting up a dialup SLIP account with an ISP.

Unfortunately, setting up OS/2 for a local area network isn't as easy as it is for Windows 95. It can be straightforward enough if your system happens to have hardware—such as network interface cards—for which OS/2 includes drivers. Out of the box, however, OS/2 lacks support for some common hardware, and getting drivers isn't always an easy proposition. Also, IBM has a tendency to surprise you by informing you only after you're deep into an installation that you need to get patches or additional software. We tested one of the first versions of OS/2 Warp Connect and found at the last minute that OS/2 can't do domain-name service without an additional patch. So setting up an OS/2 workstation on a TCP/IP network isn't something you should plan on doing in an hour or two, unless you know you have all the required drivers and patches.

In contrast, using IBM's tools for setting up a dialup connection to an ISP is easy enough. Click the IBM Internet Dialer icon in the IBM Internet Connection for OS/2 folder to display the dialog shown in Figure 3-5. To open a personal account, just click the Open a Personal Account button and follow the directions for entering your personal information, choosing a username and password, selecting a modem, and so on.

IBM calls its Internet network *The IBM Global Network*, and you can connect to it through IBM's own Internet access service (the *Internet Connection*) or through your own ISP. By default, Warp Connect will connect through IBM's own service. This service has local access numbers in 700 cities worldwide; if there isn't one near you, you can use IBM's 800-number service for an additional hourly charge.

IBM's Internet Connection service is a true connection to the Internet, unlike the online information services we'll look at in the next chapter. The Internet Connection brings TCP/IP to your workstation through a dialup SLIP or PPP connection. (Only

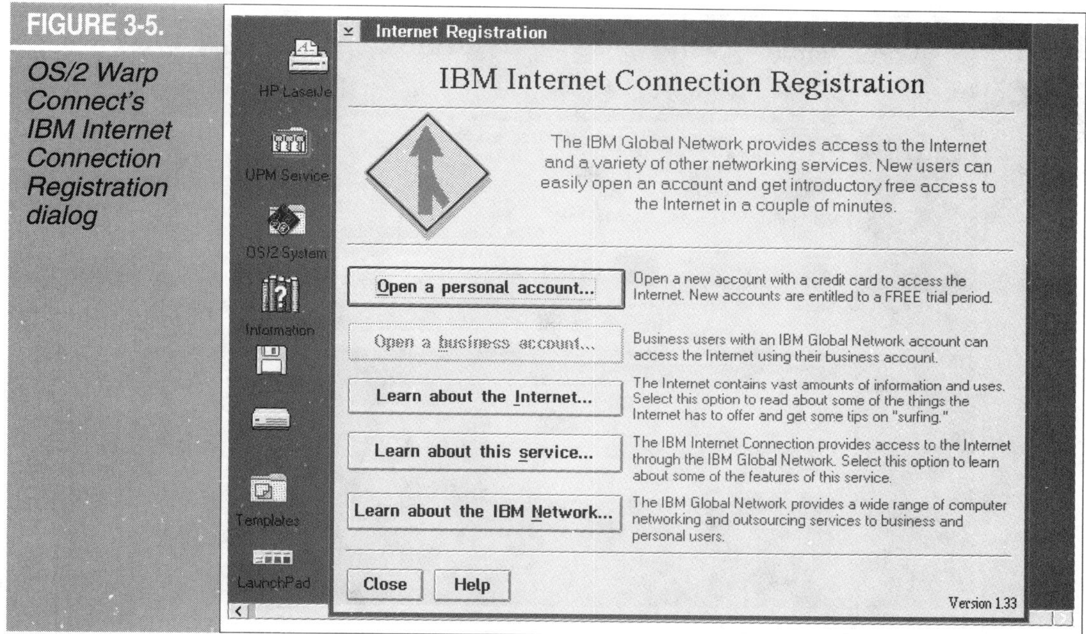

FIGURE 3-5. *OS/2 Warp Connect's IBM Internet Connection Registration dialog*

SLIP is included with the package; for PPP you may have to get another package.) But once you're connected, you can use IBM's included Internet client programs or any other Internet clients that run under OS/2 or Microsoft Windows.

Figure 3-6 shows the contents of the Internet Connection and Internet Utilities folders. Tools built into the basic operating system include a Web browser called *WebExplorer*, a Gopher client, email programs, a telnet program, and an FTP client for file transfers.

WebExplorer (IBM's Web browser) is adequate for reading most of the pages on the Internet, but it falls short when it encounters new features such as custom backgrounds, inline figures, background and foreground colors, and tables. Figure 3-7 shows WebExplorer displaying the Internet Connection home page.

Because all current Web browsers should work with the Internet's Gopher menu system, it's somewhat redundant to include a separate Gopher client program. However, IBM's Gopher client is fast, efficient, and cute (see Figure 3-8).

There is no doubt that IBM's latest generation of OS/2 Warp is a powerful and robust operating system. Once it's configured, it's stable and solid. Unfortunately, it's seldom easy to get it to that point.

FIGURE 3-6. *Internet Connection and Internet Utilities folders*

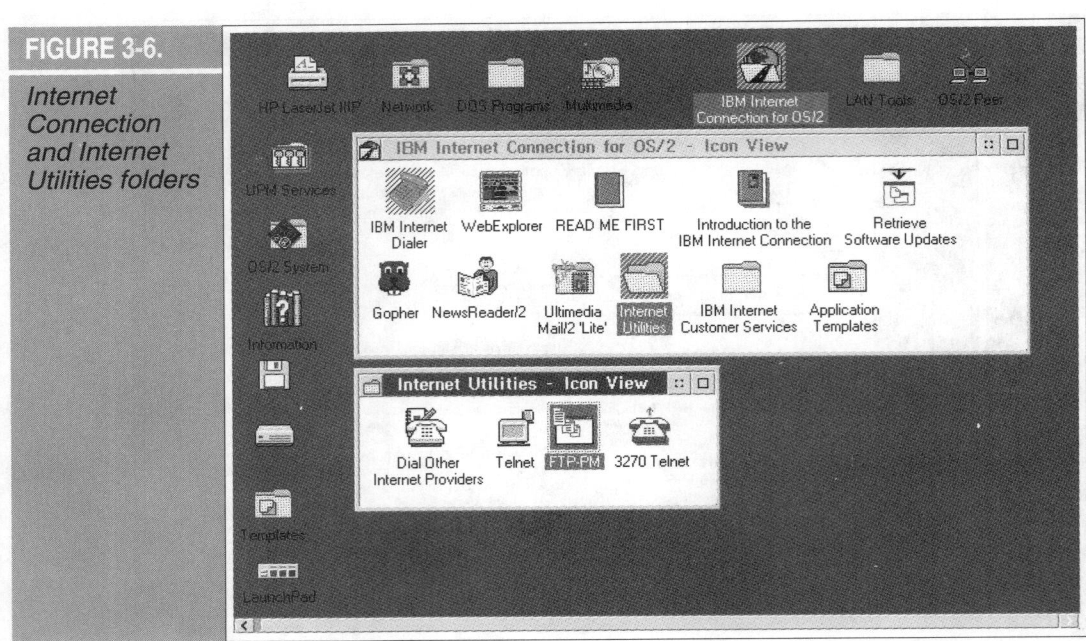

FIGURE 3-7. *IBM's WebExplorer*

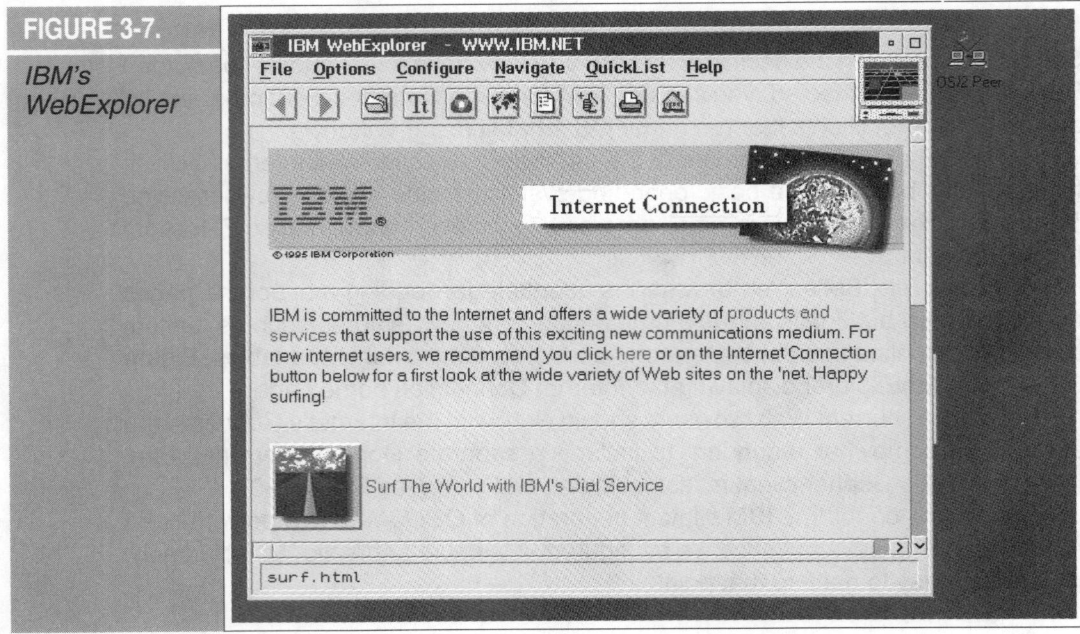

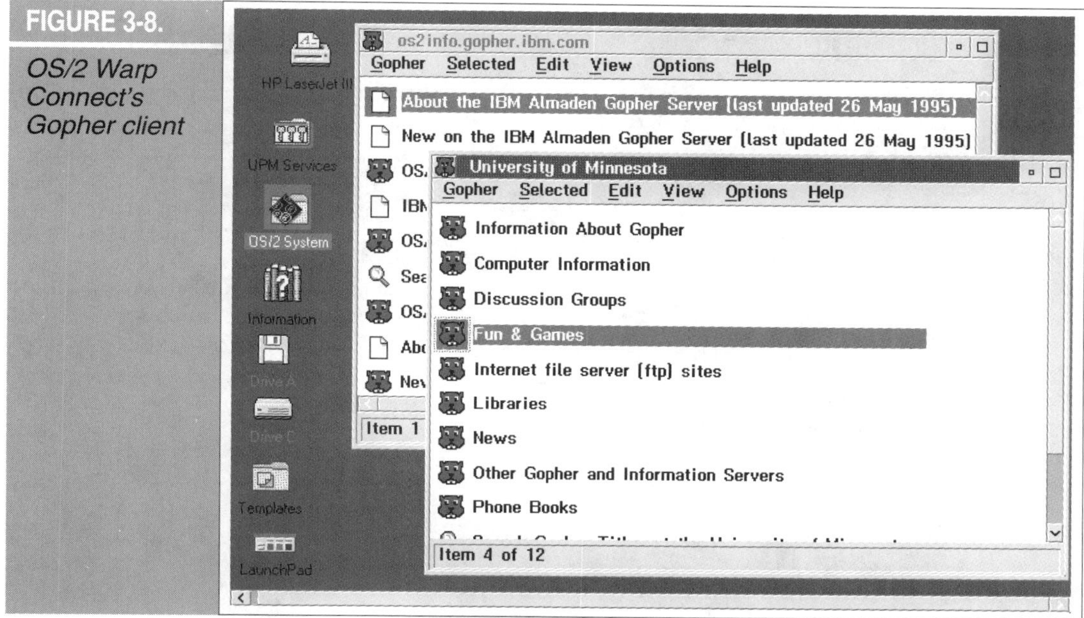

FIGURE 3-8.

OS/2 Warp Connect's Gopher client

Netcom's NetCruiser

Netcom On-Line Communications is certainly one of the largest ISPs in the U.S. With points of presence in nearly every major American city, Netcom may well be the largest ISP in the world.

Netcom offers all the traditional services of an ISP, including dialup shell accounts on Unix computers, SLIP and PPP accounts, and high-speed network connections. Netcom also offers its own software package, which integrates nearly everything you might want to do with the Internet and the World Wide Web into a single program. Netcom calls this program *NetCruiser*.

Figure 3-9 shows the main program window of NetCruiser. The interface is simple, and it provides toolbar buttons to let you read and send electronic mail, browse the World Wide Web and Gophers, read and post to Usenet newsgroups, transfer files using the Internet's FTP protocol, and use telnet, Finger, and IRC (an interface to the Internet's chat facility).

Bringing all these services together into one program can greatly simplify using the Internet for new users, but it does have some drawbacks.

For one, you have to wait for the developers at Netcom to issue new versions of the NetCruiser package. This means you'll seldom have the latest features of any

FIGURE 3-9. *The NetCruiser main program window*

of the tools. For example, the Web browser in the current version (shown in Figure 3-10) doesn't yet support background images, custom colors, or tables—features already supported by nearly every major browser.

Another drawback of NetCruiser is that, due to its popularity, it may be difficult to connect to Netcom's point of presence in your area. Since many people like to surf the Web at the same time, the phone banks can fill up quickly. And since Netcom is so large, it can't always respond to complaints of endless busy signals as quickly as the smaller providers can.

However, NetCruiser does have its strengths. It makes the process of connecting to the Internet simple, especially for people with Windows 3.1 systems. It comes on a single floppy disk, and the setup program is straightforward and easy to use. Once the software installation is complete, the setup program asks if you'd like to go ahead

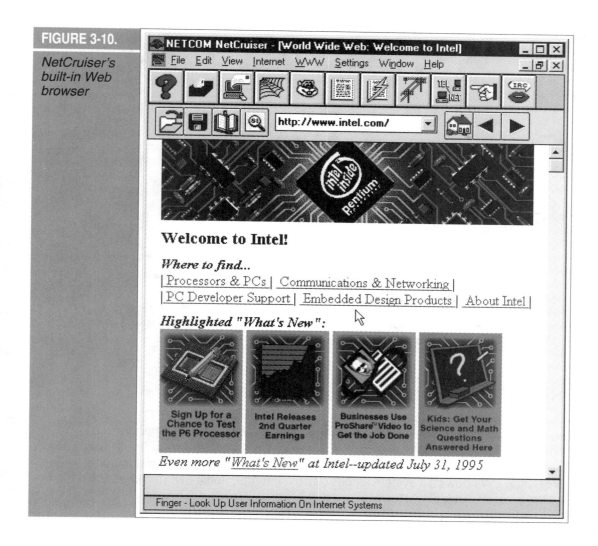

FIGURE 3-10. *NetCruiser's built-in Web browser*

and register the software. Figure 3-11 shows the main registration form. You just fill in your name, address, username, and password, then click the Continue button.

Next, NetCruiser asks you how you would like to be billed for the service. With the billing details out of the way, NetCruiser displays a list of phone numbers you can use to connect to Netcom (Figure 3-12). Pick the number nearest you, and you're all set. When you double-click on the NetCruiser icon, NetCruiser connects to the service and you see the main program window.

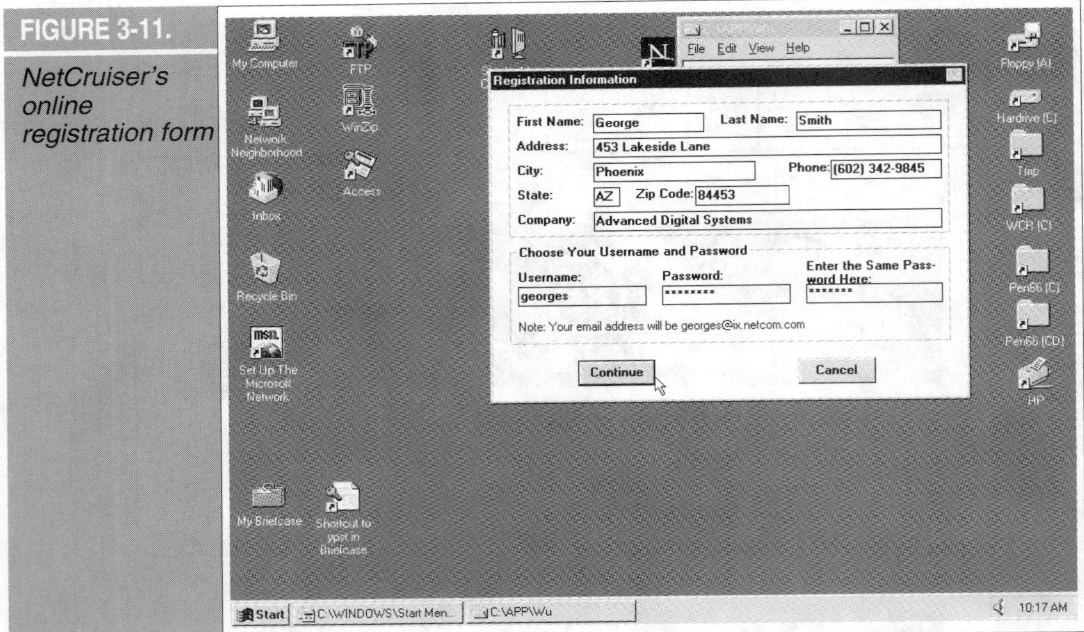

FIGURE 3-11. *NetCruiser's online registration form*

Windows 3.1 TCP/IP Connectivity Packages

As you saw in the last section, NetCruiser is a product of a large ISP. Other ISPs have also begun to bundle software with their access services, and other types of companies are getting into this market as well. Book publishers and software developers are filling the shelves of software stores with packages to automate configuring a Windows 3.1 system for use with the Internet. Some even include SLIP or PPP accounts with an ISP.

A few of the most popular of these packages are:

- Netmanage's Chameleon
- SPRY's Internet in a Box
- SPRY's Mosaic in a Box
- BookLink Technology's InternetWorks

There are many others; just take a tour of your local software store to see what's available.

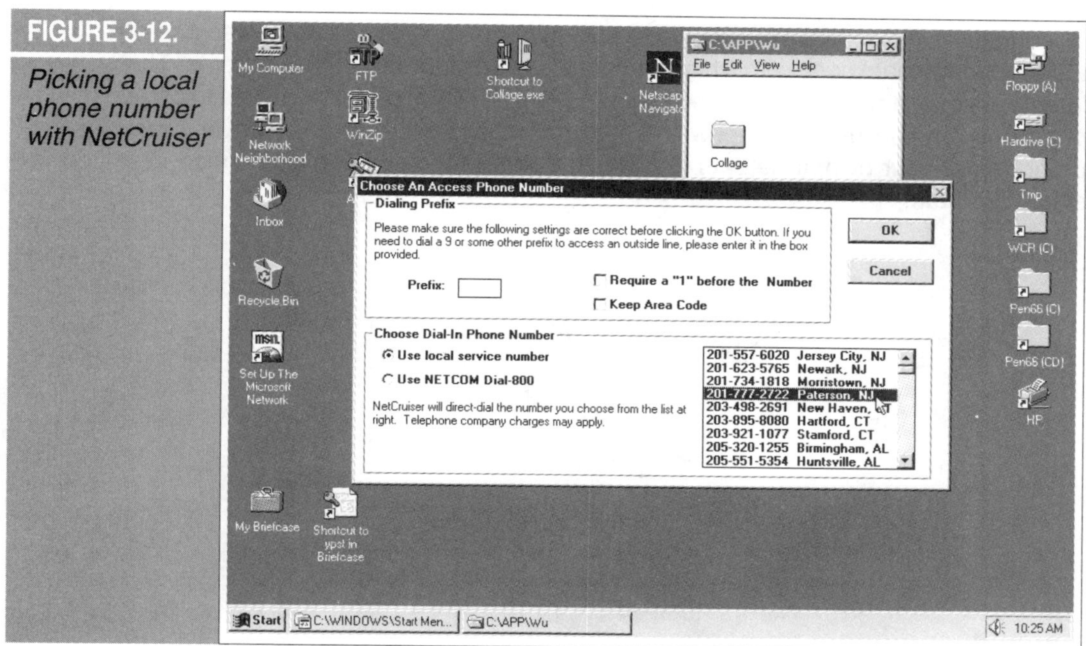

FIGURE 3-12. *Picking a local phone number with NetCruiser*

The most important thing to understand about these packages is that there are two types: those that install the TCP/IP protocol into your Windows 3.1 machine and those that use their own proprietary protocol for communications between the program interface and a remote host.

The programs that install TCP/IP on your system might explicitly use the term *TCP/IP*, but they might also use the term *Winsock* or *TCP/IP stack*. These packages are preferable to the ones that use proprietary protocols because you can use your own TCP/IP applications with them. For example, if you use a package that installs TCP/IP on your system, you can use the Netscape Web browser and other Internet clients available for free on the Internet, such as FTP clients, chat clients, and email programs.

The packages that install TCP/IP on your system typically also come with their own suite of reasonable Internet client programs. For example, Chameleon's product comes with the company's own versions of a Web browser, an FTP client, ping, chat, email, and a Gopher client. The leading programs in each category (email, FTP, Web browsers, and so on) tend to be the nicest to use, and these programs don't usually come with software bundles. Even if you like the bundled programs, you'll probably need to upgrade them to the latest versions anyway.

Originally, Netcom's NetCruiser (discussed in the previous section) was one of the proprietary packages with which you couldn't use your own Internet clients. The latest versions, however, make NetCruiser's internal TCP/IP stack available to other programs running under Windows. While that means you can use newer client programs of your own, it defeats the purpose of having everything you need in a single program.

Chapter 4

Web Access Through Online Services

Over the past few years, a silent revolution has been redefining new users' options for connecting to the Internet. In this whirlwind of change, major hardware and software companies are forging alliances with telecommunications companies and Internet service providers (ISPs) to offer their own online services. Moreover, they are building Internet connectivity and even Internet applications into their software packages.

The most celebrated (and criticized) example of this trend is Microsoft's decision to include in Windows 95 the programs necessary to set up and use its new online service, *The Microsoft Network* (MSN). This venture into a completely new market for Microsoft pits the software giant against a whole new field of competitors—the other online services, including America Online, CompuServe, and Prodigy.

Many online services now offer Internet connectivity to their member bases. The demand for Internet connectivity arises largely out of the overwhelming popularity of the World Wide Web, which, coincidentally, represents the biggest threat to online services.

In this chapter, we'll look at the Web access provided by America Online, CompuServe, MSN, and Prodigy. However, before we look at the individual services, we'll discuss the more general question of whether or not to use an online service for Internet (and Web) access in the first place.

Internet Access Through Online Services

It's tough for Internet old-timers to take online services seriously. To them, using an online service for Internet access is like picking one store where you'll do all your shopping. You could probably find a single store that has everything you need, from diapers and green beans to tires and novels—but why would you want to? On the other hand, if getting to malls and other stores is a problem, and the store right across the street has everything you need, shopping there might seem like a good idea.

Whatever reasons people have for using them, online services play an important role in the online society because they're easy to set up and easy to use. That role was even more important in the past, when using the Internet meant learning to use a command-line Unix computer with a 2400-baud dialup connection. However, online services still fill at least a few important needs.

As the online services have implemented their own Internet connectivity, they've introduced many of their members to the Internet in a gentle and gradual way. Online services are also very helpful for people who are completely new to the world of computers. They keep the learning curve gradual, yet offer enough interesting services and resources to keep the users' curiosity piqued. As these people learn more about using computers and software, they can venture out into the vast Internet

whenever they like, while staying shielded from most of the harsh technology they would otherwise encounter.

The online services do a better job with some services than does the Internet. Even today, the Internet is largely a nonsecure world where hackers can spy on all kinds of Internet traffic, including confidential conversations and even financial transactions. By using direct phone connections and controlling the software running on the computers at both ends of those phone lines, online services are more (although never completely) secure from intruders.

For individuals joining up to see the online world, security isn't much of an issue—except when your credit-card numbers are involved. But for businesses, the security issue can be compelling. For example, many computer hardware and software companies have beta-testing programs for their products and want to offer online assistance and support, but confidentiality can be a big problem on the Internet. Online services can provide discussion forums where attendance is restricted to authorized participants.

Also, companies offering certain types of services find it easier to control access to their services and bill for them with online services. For example, the large information search and retrieval services, such as Iquest and Knowledge Index, can automatically bill an online service for database searches performed by members, and the online service then bills the member. These types of businesses are beginning to come to the Internet and the World Wide Web as well, but they are arriving slowly because of concerns related to keeping their databases and user billing information secure.

Finally, online services can make navigating the online world a more organized experience for people than it would be if they jumped directly into the Internet. By offering resources people like to use and organizing them in a clever way, online services do indeed provide a valuable service.

On the other hand, if it's the Internet, and especially the World Wide Web, that you're interested in, you can often do a lot better if you "go solo" than if you join an online service. With most online services, you're limited to using the company's own software for navigating not only their own system, but the Internet and the Web as well. Proprietary software for accessing the Internet and cruising the Web is almost always at least a generation behind other shareware and public-domain packages freely available on the Internet and are only useful if you have a real SLIP or PPP connection to the Internet.

Another disadvantage of online services is that your choices for connecting to them are often severely restricted. With several of the top online services, a 14.4 Kbps connection is the fastest they support. Most are in the process of upgrading to 28.8 modem speeds, but ISDN and other high-speed connections are still out of the question.

Another drawback is that establishing a Web presence for yourself or your company with an online service is difficult and expensive at best. This is because online services aren't really set up to host Web pages on the Internet. While they do it on occasion, it's almost always through a high-level agreement and not a normal business transaction for them.

While most of the major online services now offer access to the Internet, they don't provide full access. People with computers that are actually on the Internet have a wealth of tools and programs at their fingertips. Most of the online services offer only a very small subset of these—electronic mail, Usenet newsgroups, FTP, telnet, and a Web browser. You won't get Archie, Finger, Veronica, Jughead, the Wide Area Information Service (WAIS), and many other useful tools.

Finally, problems frequently occur with the connections between users and online services and between online services and the Internet. Busy phone numbers and stuck modems are a common occurrence with online services. ISPs' phone lines are also busy on occasion, but in general ISPs are better equipped to monitor phone usage closely and respond quickly to increased demand for phone lines. And once you're connected to an online service, you may discover that some Internet sites that should be accessible just aren't.

America Online

America Online (AOL) is a relative newcomer in the online service industry, but it has quickly become a very popular service with several million members. AOL offers email connections to other online services and to the Internet as well as "departments" you can visit for current news, entertainment, travel information, sports— there's even a kids-only department. Figure 4-1 shows AOL's main menu.

AOL's Internet menu (see Figure 4-2) offers easy access to the most popular Internet facilities, including Usenet newsgroups, the World Wide Web, and FTP (for file transfers). In addition to buttons you can click to access these services directly, the Internet menu also provides a scroll window with a collection of interesting and useful resources on the Internet.

AOL's software interface is freely available from many sources; it's included in several computer-related magazines and books and is available separately at most computer and software stores. AOL doesn't charge for its software, but it does charge for access to AOL and the Internet. During the sign-up process, you enter your full name and address and give a credit-card number for billing.

The AOL software is all you need to access AOL (and the Internet through AOL); there are no protocols, dialers, or other utility programs to worry about. The first time you sign on, however, you may have to update your version of the AOL software to

FIGURE 4-1.

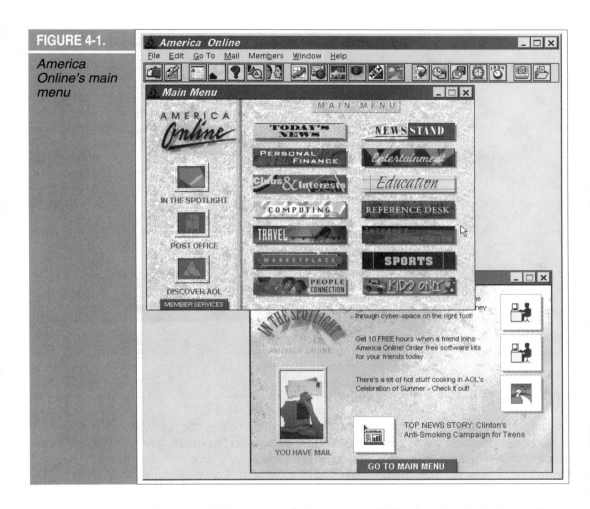

America Online's main menu

access the Internet. AOL has made this process fairly easy by displaying a dialog box notifying you that you need to update your software. When you click the OK button, AOL takes care of the details of downloading the new version.

AOL's Web browser (shown in Figure 4-3) is adequate, but it falls short of taking advantage of the newest and best of the Web (as do all the browsers that come with online services). The browsers that AOL and most of the other services offer are necessarily behind the premier Web browsers because of the time it takes to integrate new features into them.

AOL charges around $10 per month for its service, and this includes five hours of usage each month. Additional hours are billed at just under $3 an hour.

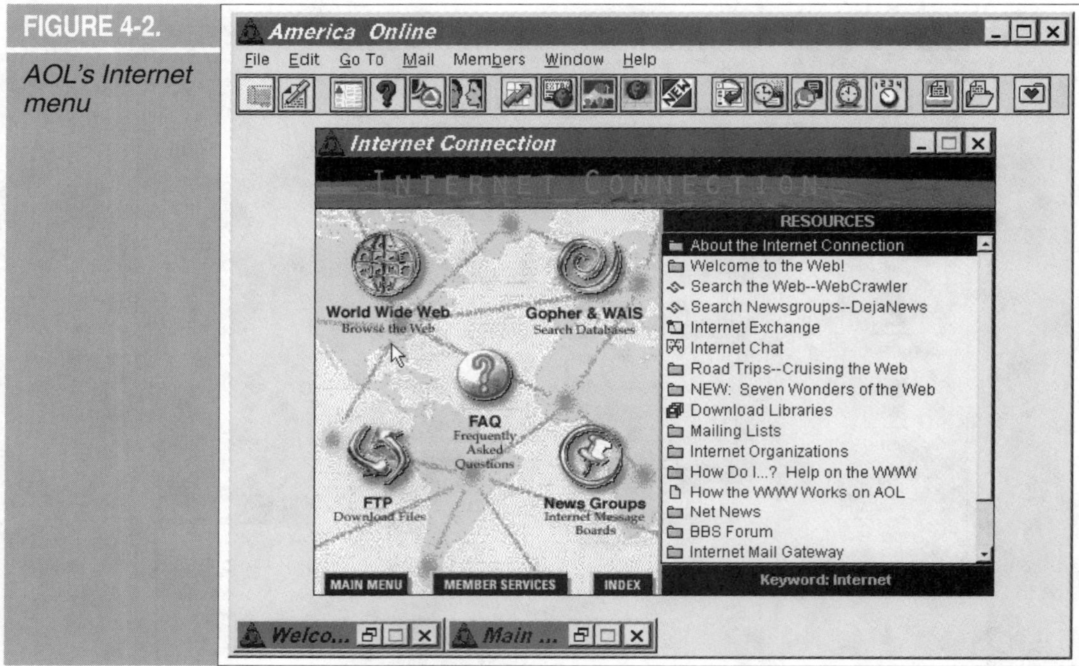

FIGURE 4-2. *AOL's Internet menu*

CompuServe

CompuServe is one of the oldest and largest online services and offers a wide variety of services, including news, online magazines, discussion forums on many topics, research reference services, shopping, and—most recently—access to the Internet. Figure 4-4 shows the introductory screen as it looks with CompuServe's interface software for Microsoft Windows, called *WinCIM*.

CompuServe's Internet access is fairly limited, but it does offer email exchange with the Internet and other online services. It also offers access to Usenet newsgroups, the Internet's FTP file-transfer service, and a telnet program that you can use to log into computers on the Internet on which you have accounts. CompuServe also provides access to the World Wide Web, but it implements Web connectivity in a completely different way from the other online services. (We'll talk about this in a minute.)

Like AOL and the other online services, CompuServe's front-end programs (such as WinCIM, shown in Figure 4-4) establish a direct connection between your

FIGURE 4-3.

AOL's Web browser

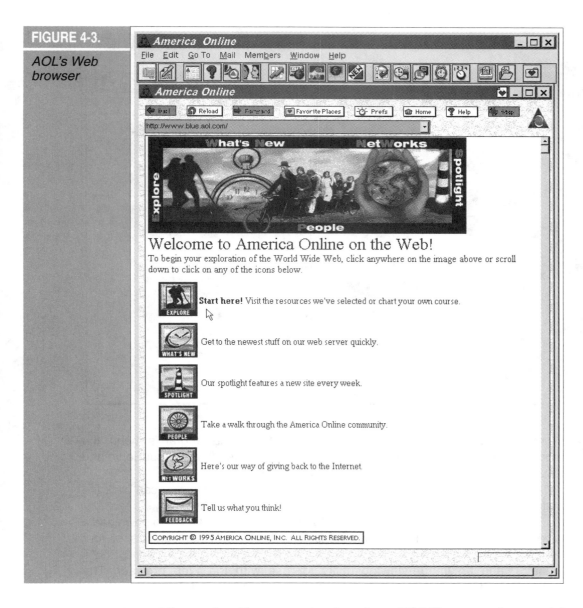

computer and the service. Your computer doesn't run TCP/IP or any other special protocol besides those the front-end program itself uses (this is invisible to the user). These interface programs handle all interaction between the user and CompuServe.

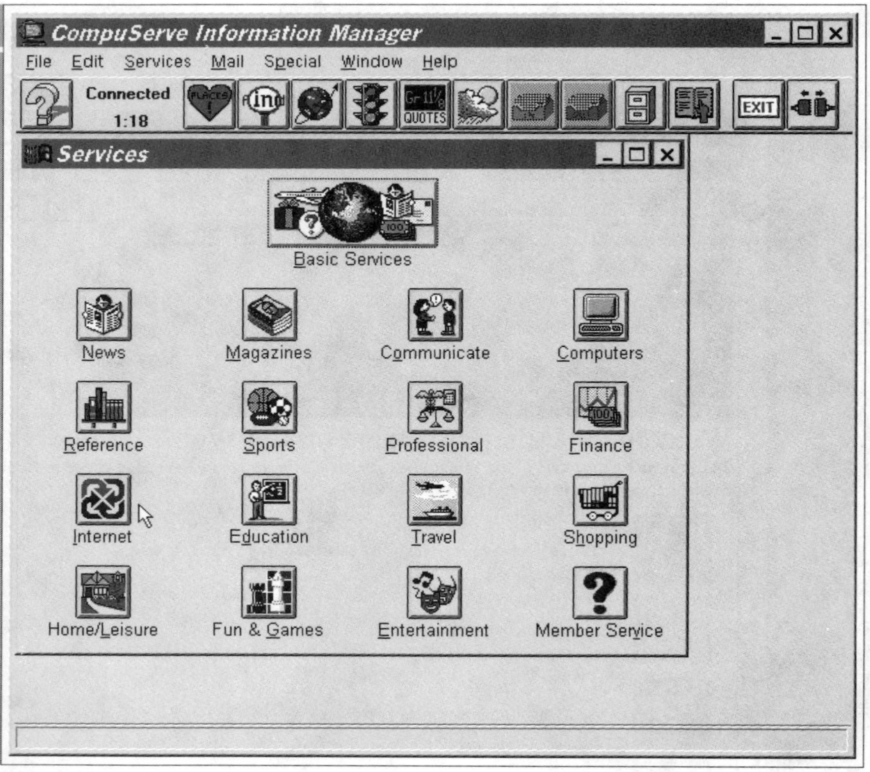

FIGURE 4-4. *CompuServe's WinCIM program*

When you click on a button or make a selection from the program's menu, the program retrieves the information or service you requested from CompuServe and displays it in a window or offers you more selections.

Figure 4-5 shows CompuServe's Internet Services section. You can click the buttons for Usenet, FTP, and telnet to launch each of these services.

To access the World Wide Web with CompuServe, you first have to download a program called NetLauncher from CompuServe. NetLauncher consists of four programs: an installation and setup program, a PPP dialer, a Web browser (SPRY's Mosaic), and an image-viewing utility for use with the Web browser. The CompuServe version of the SPRY browser is shown in Figure 4-6.

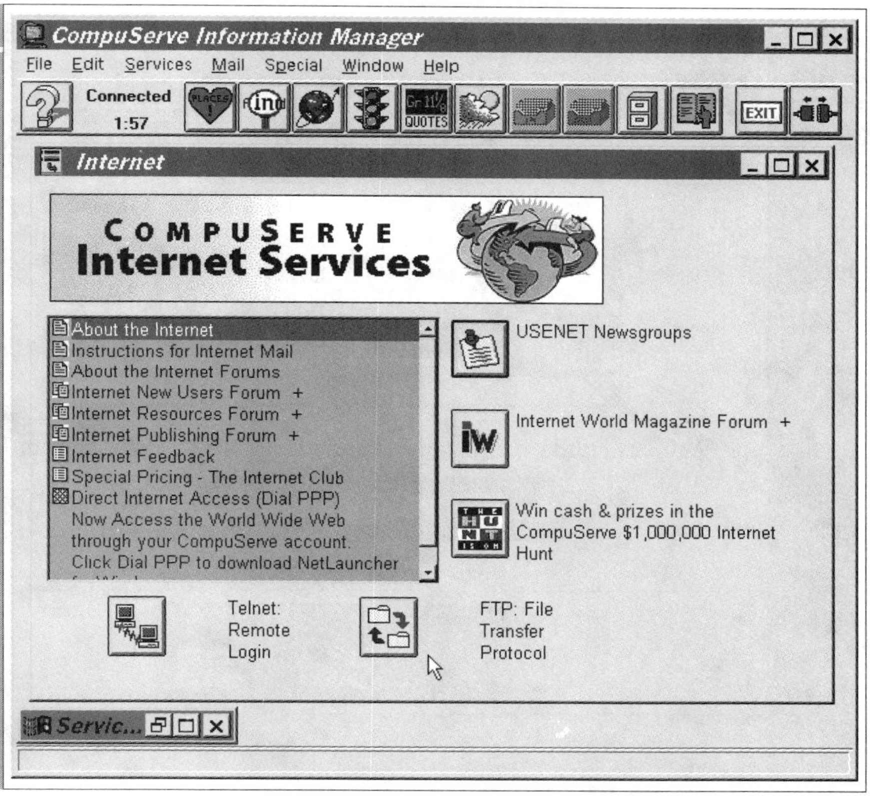

FIGURE 4-5. *CompuServe's Internet Services folder*

Interestingly, NetLauncher works just like other turnkey Internet access packages (discussed in the previous chapter) by installing the TCP/IP protocol on your computer. The dialer program is preconfigured for establishing a PPP connection to CompuServe. Once that connection is established, your system is on the Internet just as if you had used Internet in a Box or installed Trumpet Winsock yourself. And, since your system is really connected to the Internet with TCP/IP, you can use any Internet software you'd like to read news, browse the Web, and transfer files. After you install NetLauncher, CompuServe becomes your ISP (at least for Web access).

FIGURE 4-6. *CompuServe's SPRY Mosaic Web browser*

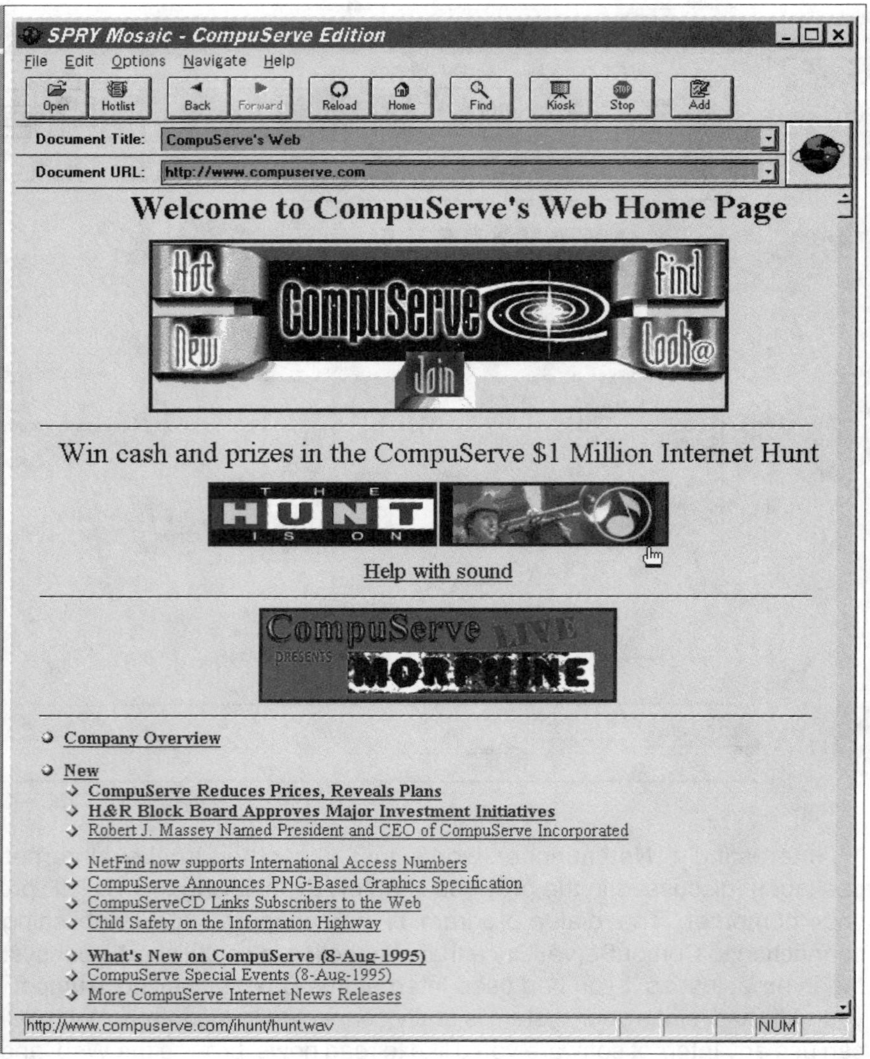

CompuServe charges just under $10 per month for unlimited access to its basic services, which include three hours per month of Internet access. Each additional hour is billed at $2.95.

The Microsoft Network

In the last chapter, we discussed the three ways you can connect to the Internet with Microsoft's newest operating system, Windows 95. We looked at how to connect a Windows 95 system using its built-in dialup networking software and how to connect through a local area network. We saved the discussion of MSN for this chapter because it competes directly with the other online services. (In fact, MSN competes *so* directly with the other services that the U.S. Department of Justice nearly blocked Microsoft from including MSN with Windows 95).

Signing up for MSN is as easy as double-clicking an icon on your desktop. Provided your system has a modem, Windows 95 dials out to MSN and begins the process of setting up your account. You simply enter your personal information (Figure 4-7), choose whether you want a personal or business account, and enter your payment options, and you'll be up on MSN in no time.

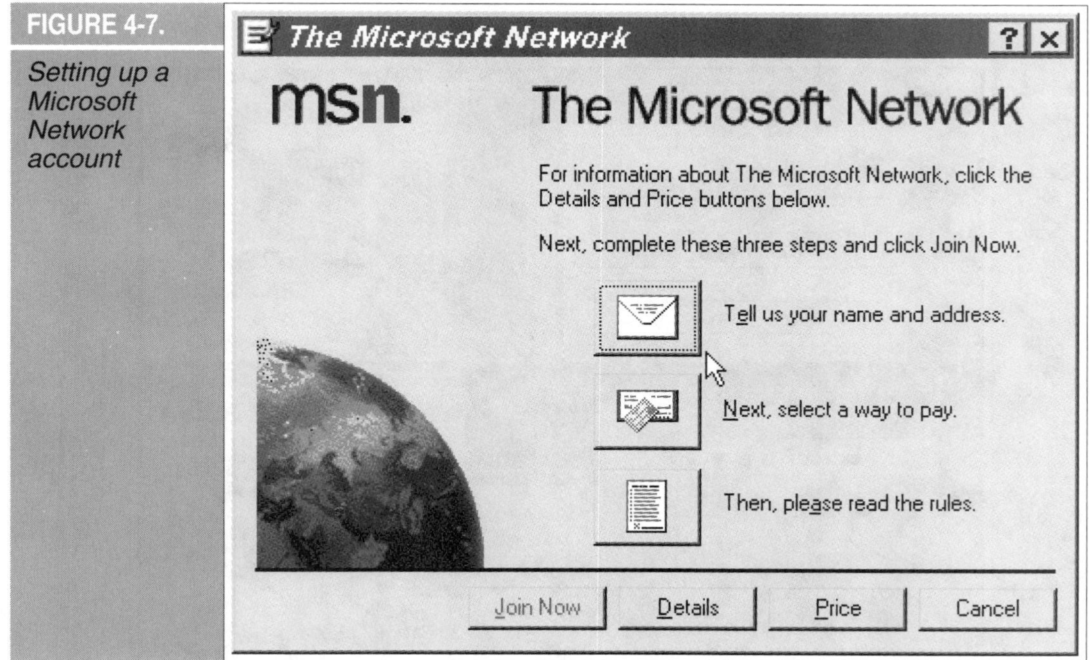

FIGURE 4-7. *Setting up a Microsoft Network account*

The first thing to realize about MSN is that it is fundamentally different from the other online services in a subtle but important way: Both AOL and CompuServe provide programs that act as front-ends, or interfaces, to their online services. Anything you do with these services takes place inside that single program interface. Within the front-end's program window, you can open multiple windows to follow menu links, read your email, and so forth at the same time, but it all happens inside the program window.

MSN is different in that it is integrated tightly with the Windows 95 operating system. When you follow a menu choice or navigate to other services in MSN, you get a new window that isn't constrained by the boundaries of a program window. And each new window has all the same controls and options as other windows in Windows 95; they look just like the windows that allow you to navigate the computer's disk drives and folders, the Briefcase, and so on.

Figure 4-8 shows Windows 95 running with an open connection to MSN. Notice that each service and menu is in its own window, which can be placed anywhere on the desktop or minimized to the Windows 95 task bar. The ability to use MSN in the

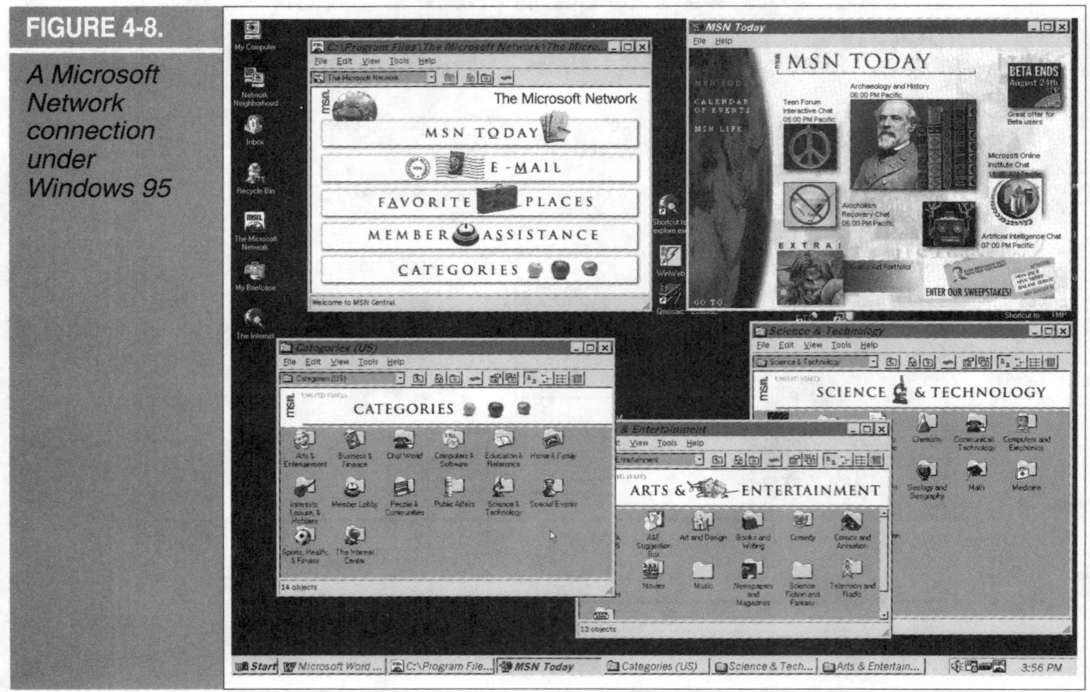

FIGURE 4-8. *A Microsoft Network connection under Windows 95*

native Windows environment is an appealing feature; don't be surprised if the other online services offer it in the future.

Like the other online services, MSN offers a rich variety of interesting resources, including forums for arts and entertainment, business and finance, education and reference, home and family, leisure pursuits and hobbies, public affairs, sports and fitness, health, and much more.

MSN's Internet Center offers access to Usenet newsgroups, some Internet-specific file libraries, and chat rooms (these function as an interface to the Internet's Internet Relay Chat service). Presumably, Microsoft assumes that if you want to browse the Web or access FTP file archives, you'll use the other tools available in Windows 95 and its companion product, the Plus! pack.

Microsoft offers two pricing plans for members of MSN. The standard plan is just under $5 per month, and it includes three hours of usage per month. Additional hours are billed at $2.50 an hour. The frequent-user plan is just under $20 per month; it includes 20 hours of usage per month, with additional hours billed at $2 an hour.

Prodigy

Prodigy is one of the oldest online services. Early on, it won a large share of the home online service users. In recent years, Prodigy's popularity has waned, but it has struggled back into one of the top spots among online service providers.

Prodigy offers a respectable collection of services, including areas for business and finance, computing, entertainment, news and weather, travel, and Internet access, with separate areas for kids and teens.

In the past, one of Prodigy's worst features was a dreadful interface reminiscent of a DOS screen, even in the Windows versions. However, in the past year Prodigy has made headway toward making better use of the Windows environment; it now uses more drop-down menus and more attractive fonts and controls. If you connect to Prodigy by using one of the free disks (they seem to be everywhere), you'll probably want to update Prodigy's front-end software right away.

Upgrading the Prodigy software is easy, and with some of the upgrades you won't even have to exit the program; just click Update when it asks if you want to update the software, and Prodigy takes care of the details. After you download and reconfigure the system, your interface will be updated to the latest version automatically. Figure 4-9 shows Prodigy's introductory screen.

Another complaint in the past was that Prodigy displayed intrusive advertisements and sent junk mail to its members. In the newer versions of the software and the service, Prodigy has made great strides toward toning down its advertisements.

FIGURE 4-9. *Prodigy's Highlights page*

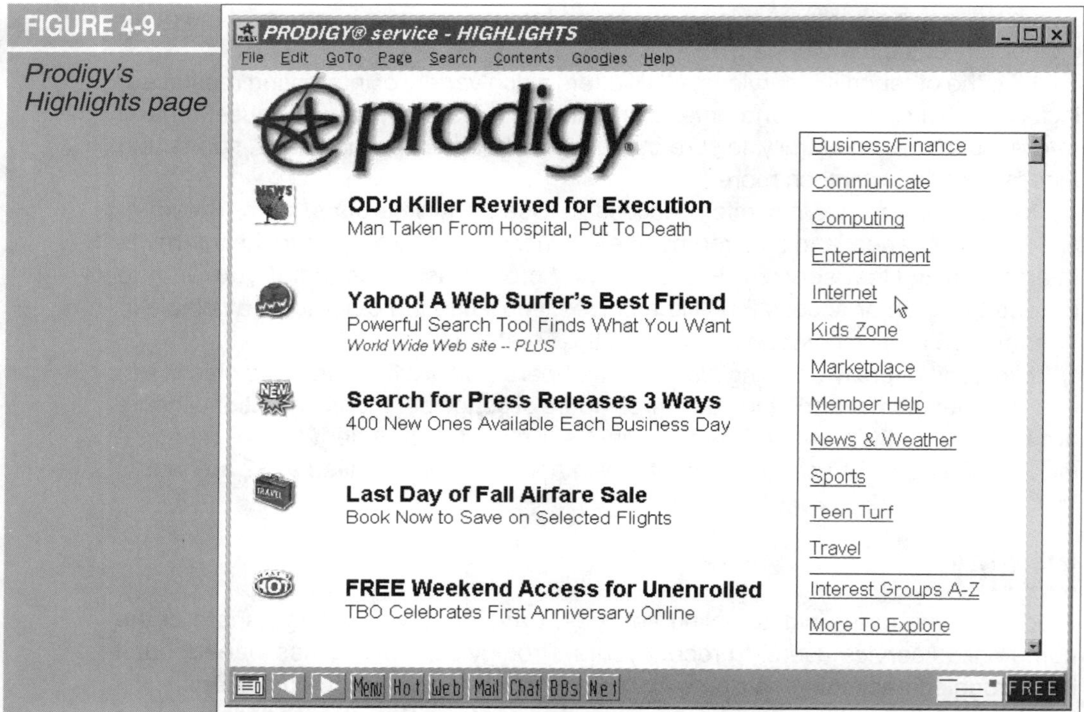

Prodigy's Web access is surprisingly good. Although you wouldn't expect it given the mundane feel of most of Prodigy's menus and screens, a nice Web browser is included (Figure 4-10).

Prodigy has menu options for FTP and Gopher, but when you choose them, a note informs you that you can use the Web browser to access these Internet services (a reasonable reminder that the other online services should provide as well).

Unfortunately, Prodigy currently only offers access at 14.4 Kbps. This is a little slow for browsing the Web, but by the time you read this, Prodigy will probably have begun upgrading to 28.8 Kbps modems.

Prodigy offers a basic plan and a frequent-user plan, which it calls the *30/30* plan. The basic plan is just under $10 per month and includes five hours of access. The 30/30 plan is around $30 per month and includes 30 hours of use. With both plans, each additional hour is billed at $2.95.

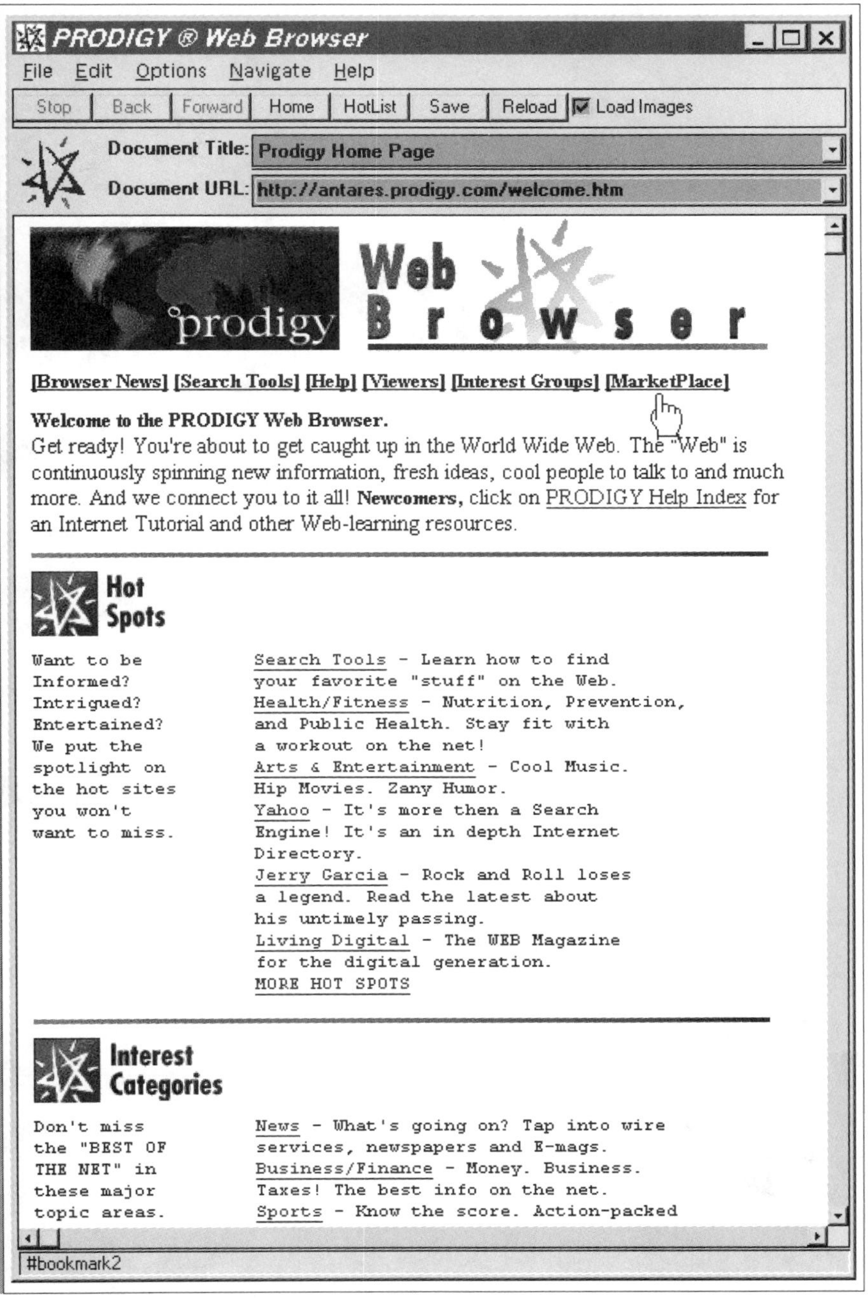

FIGURE 4-10.

Prodigy's Web browser

PRODIGY ® Web Browser

File Edit Options Navigate Help

Stop | Back | Forward | Home | HotList | Save | Reload | Load Images

Document Title: Prodigy Home Page

Document URL: http://antares.prodigy.com/welcome.htm

prodigy Web Browser

[Browser News] [Search Tools] [Help] [Viewers] [Interest Groups] [MarketPlace]

Welcome to the PRODIGY Web Browser.
Get ready! You're about to get caught up in the World Wide Web. The "Web" is continuously spinning new information, fresh ideas, cool people to talk to and much more. And we connect you to it all! **Newcomers,** click on PRODIGY Help Index for an Internet Tutorial and other Web-learning resources.

Hot Spots

Want to be Informed? Intrigued? Entertained? We put the spotlight on the hot sites you won't want to miss.

Search Tools - Learn how to find your favorite "stuff" on the Web.
Health/Fitness - Nutrition, Prevention, and Public Health. Stay fit with a workout on the net!
Arts & Entertainment - Cool Music. Hip Movies. Zany Humor.
Yahoo - It's more then a Search Engine! It's an in depth Internet Directory.
Jerry Garcia - Rock and Roll loses a legend. Read the latest about his untimely passing.
Living Digital - The WEB Magazine for the digital generation.
MORE HOT SPOTS

Interest Categories

Don't miss the "BEST OF THE NET" in these major topic areas.

News - What's going on? Tap into wire services, newspapers and E-mags.
Business/Finance - Money. Business. Taxes! The best info on the net.
Sports - Know the score. Action-packed

#bookmark2

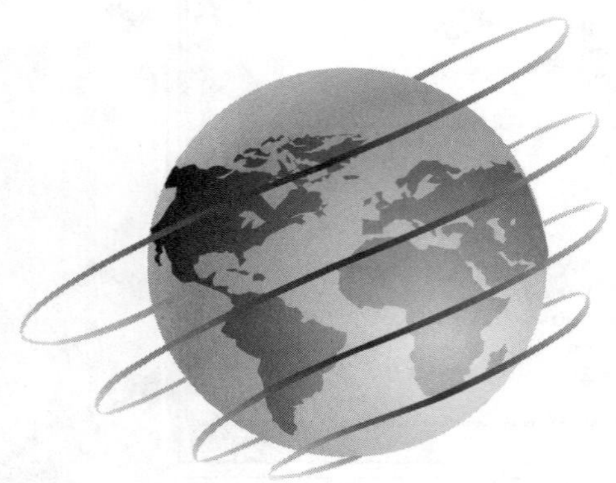

Chapter 5

Using Web Browsers

Few programs you'll ever use regularly on your computer are as conceptually simple as a Web browser. In fact, once you've learned to use one of them, you'll essentially know how to use them all. One reason for a Web browser's simplicity is that it attempts to be a transparent application; it's simply there to display pages and serve as a window onto the World Wide Web. In a way, you look *through* the browser rather than at it. It follows that the mechanics of using the browser have more to do with the documents it displays than with the browser itself.

Your biggest task will be deciding on the right browser. To speak of the collection of available Web browsers as a *market* would be a little misleading. Few are actually commercial products yet. They eventually will be, however, and choosing a browser will involve the same sorts of personal preferences that come into play when choosing a word processor or any other software application.

This chapter covers the basics of Web browsers. You'll learn how to use a browser, gain some techniques for better surfing, and find out what types of settings and options should be available in a browser. Finally, you'll be introduced to some of the many browsers that are available.

What Is a Browser?

Your Web browser is your window onto the World Wide Web. In fact, since most browsers now support other Internet protocols, many people find they can use their Web browser as a graphical user interface to the Internet.

Using your Web browser, you can view Web documents containing integrated or linked graphics, or even video and audio clips. You can also use your browser to navigate FTP sites and retrieve software and data files, read Usenet newsgroups, and send email messages.

As you saw in Chapter 1, Web documents are hypertext documents; they contain links to other documents, which may in turn contain links to yet more documents. It's easy to identify the links on a Web page because the browser displays link text differently from normal text; it's usually shaded in a different foreground color and is often underlined.

When you move the mouse pointer over normal text in a Web page, the pointer looks like an arrow. When you move the pointer over link text, however, your browser probably changes the pointer shape from an arrow to a hand, with the index finger pointing to the link text. Although you can't see the color cue, Figure 5-1 shows a page with some link text.

To select a link, click on it with the left mouse button. Your browser will clear the window and retrieve the document to which the link refers. Figure 5-2 shows how

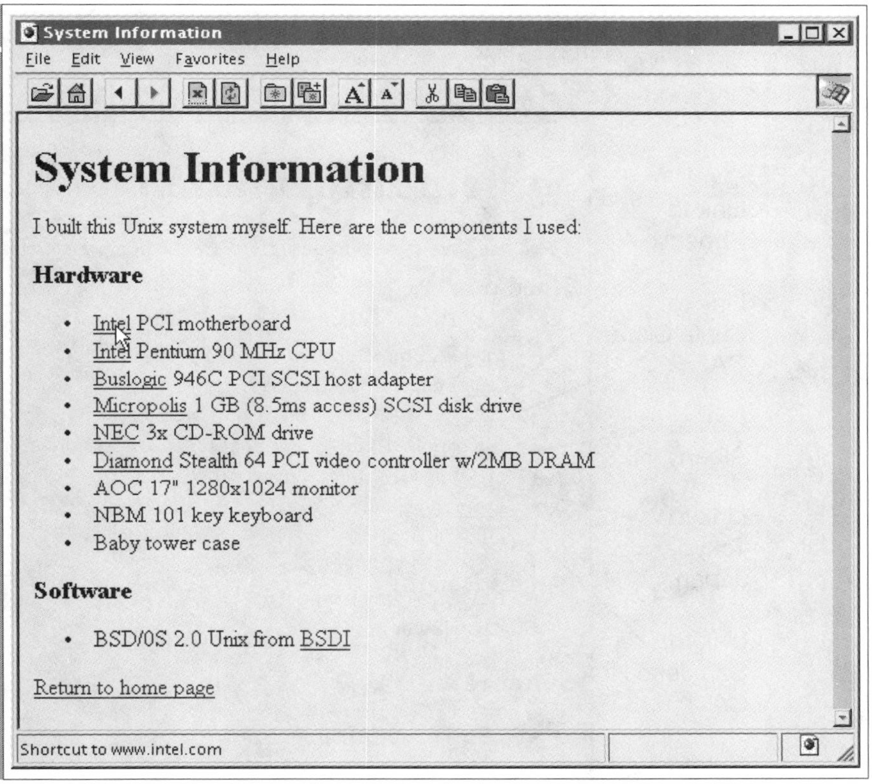

FIGURE 5-1.

Link text is shaded in a different color and is often underlined

System Information

File Edit View Favorites Help

System Information

I built this Unix system myself. Here are the components I used:

Hardware

- Intel PCI motherboard
- Intel Pentium 90 MHz CPU
- Buslogic 946C PCI SCSI host adapter
- Micropolis 1 GB (8.5ms access) SCSI disk drive
- NEC 3x CD-ROM drive
- Diamond Stealth 64 PCI video controller w/2MB DRAM
- AOC 17" 1280x1024 monitor
- NBM 101 key keyboard
- Baby tower case

Software

- BSD/0S 2.0 Unix from BSDI

Return to home page

Shortcut to www.intel.com

this process works. The links in a Web page create invisible ties between your own computer and remote computers, which may be physically located in the next room or on another continent.

Figure 5-3 shows a very popular Web browser called *NCSA Mosaic* running under Windows 95. *NCSA* stands for the National Center for Supercomputing Applications, an organization sponsored by the University of Illinois at Urbana-Champaign. NCSA has been actively involved in developing the Internet, and it offers to the Internet community a wealth of software and technological studies and information. NCSA's World Wide Web address is http://www.ncsa.uiuc.edu/.

NCSA Mosaic is so popular mostly because it was one of the first browsers for the World Wide Web. Even though competing browsers have since appeared on the scene, NCSA has done a tremendous job of keeping up with the trends and even leading new development in some areas. One such area is Web security.

FIGURE 5-2. *Hypertext links can connect you to the computer in the next room or one around the globe*

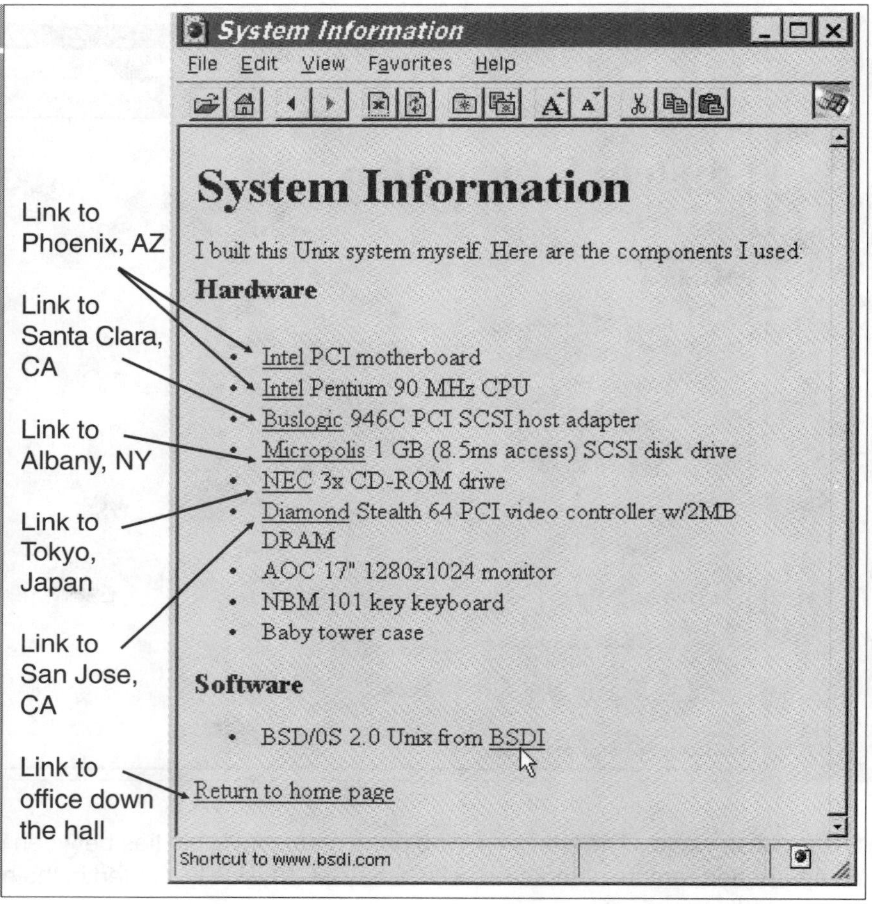

Link to Phoenix, AZ

Link to Santa Clara, CA

Link to Albany, NY

Link to Tokyo, Japan

Link to San Jose, CA

Link to office down the hall

System Information

File Edit View Favorites Help

System Information

I built this Unix system myself. Here are the components I used:

Hardware

- Intel PCI motherboard
- Intel Pentium 90 MHz CPU
- Buslogic 946C PCI SCSI host adapter
- Micropolis 1 GB (8.5ms access) SCSI disk drive
- NEC 3x CD-ROM drive
- Diamond Stealth 64 PCI video controller w/2MB DRAM
- AOC 17" 1280x1024 monitor
- NBM 101 key keyboard
- Baby tower case

Software

- BSD/0S 2.0 Unix from BSDI

Return to home page

Shortcut to www.bsdi.com

NCSA Mosaic was the first, and is still one of the few, to use some of the security features that come with firewalls and proxy servers. (These terms are discussed in Chapter 16.)

Another reason for NCSA Mosaic's popularity is that it set the early standards for ease of use, providing an interface that included a toolbar and other elements to assist the user. Figure 5-3 shows the Mosaic program window. Although the version of Mosaic shown here is a recent one, the toolbar and the globe icon in the upper right-hand corner of the window have been a part of Mosaic from the beginning.

FIGURE 5-3.

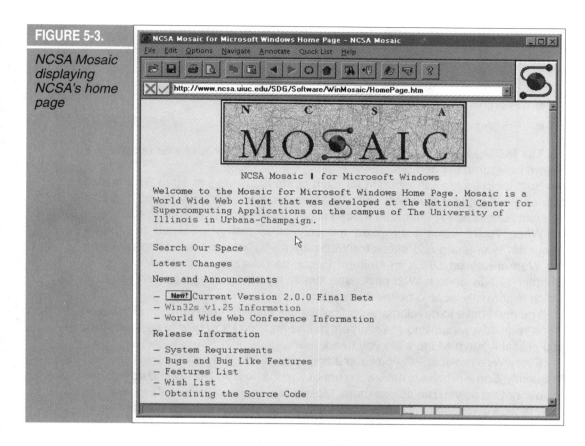

NCSA Mosaic displaying NCSA's home page

When you surf the World Wide Web, most of your time will be spent interacting with Web documents displayed in the browser window—reading text, looking at pictures, and clicking on link text to display other pages. Besides interacting with the Web pages themselves, you will do only a few other things with any frequency:

- Use the browser window's scroll bar to pan your window up or down
- Click a button on the toolbar to go back to a previous page
- Click another button on the toolbar to return to the home page

In a normal browsing session, you'll perform these functions virtually every minute you're on the Web.

Some other actions you might perform fairly frequently include:

- Clicking a button on the toolbar to follow a link forward
- Reloading a page currently being displayed by the browser
- Searching for a word or phrase in a page
- Printing a page

The NCSA Mosaic and Netscape toolbars, along with some of their options, are shown in Figures 5-4 and 5-5.

Both toolbars provide a button for each of the functions just listed. This is also true of other popular browsers' toolbars. Web browsers are easy to use because you can access all the important functions by clicking toolbar buttons.

When you're using a browser, the only other task you'll need to perform frequently is entering addresses for Web pages you want to view. (Addresses on the Web are called *URLs,* or Uniform Resource Locators, and are discussed in Chapter 11.) To go to a Web page, you simply type the address into an edit box, which is normally located below the toolbar.

You don't have to develop any particular skills to use a Web browser effectively. If you've used a windowing environment before and you know how to use a mouse, you probably have all the skills you need.

Every Web browser lets you keep a *bookmark* list, a "hot list" of pages you visit frequently. Some browsers have a toolbar button that lets you easily add new pages to your hot list as you run across them. Mosaic has such a button on its toolbar, but in Netscape you have to click the Add Bookmark command in the Bookmark menu (see Figure 5-6). After you bring up the bookmark list, you can go to one of the pages you've stored in the list simply by clicking its name in the list.

FIGURE 5-4. *NCSA Mosaic's toolbar*

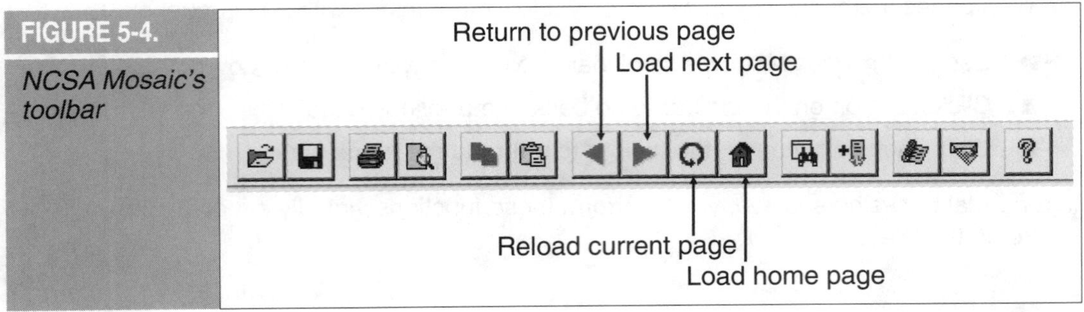

FIGURE 5-5.

Netscape's toolbar

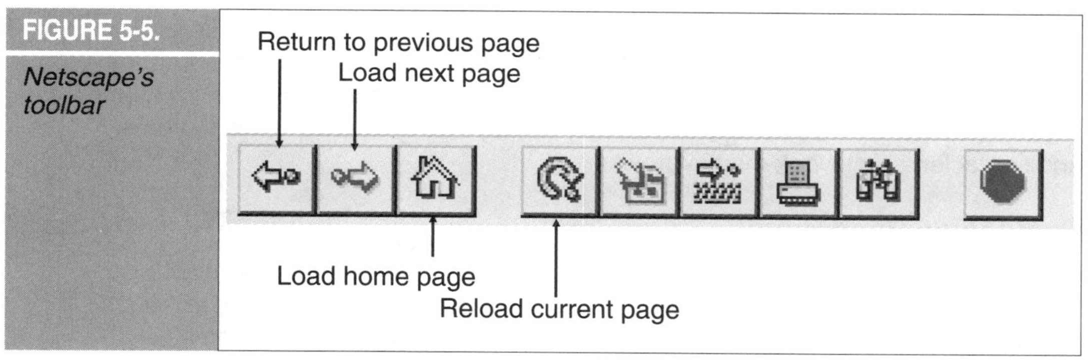

FIGURE 5-6.

Adding a bookmark with Netscape

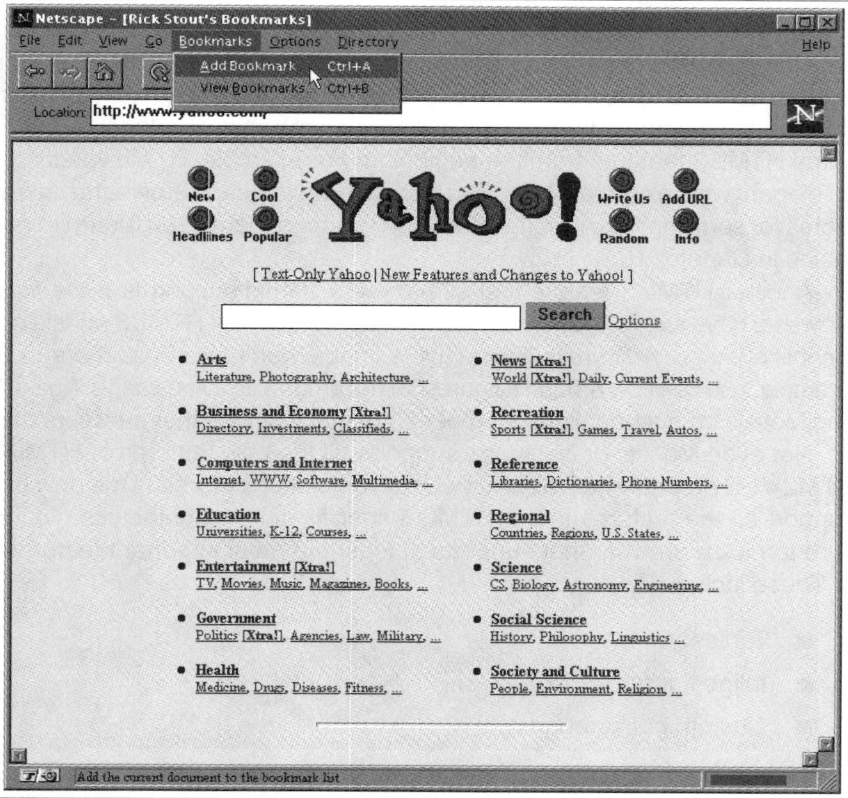

Netscape - [Rick Stout's Bookmarks]

File Edit View Go Bookmarks Options Directory Help

Add Bookmark Ctrl+A

View Bookmarks... Ctrl+B

Location: http://www.yahoo.com/

New Cool Headlines Popular Yahoo! Write Us Add URL Random Info

[Text-Only Yahoo | New Features and Changes to Yahoo!]

Search Options

- **Arts**
  Literature, Photography, Architecture, ...
- **Business and Economy** [Xtra!]
  Directory, Investments, Classifieds, ...
- **Computers and Internet**
  Internet, WWW, Software, Multimedia, ...
- **Education**
  Universities, K-12, Courses, ...
- **Entertainment** [Xtra!]
  TV, Movies, Music, Magazines, Books, ...
- **Government**
  Politics [Xtra!], Agencies, Law, Military, ...
- **Health**
  Medicine, Drugs, Diseases, Fitness, ...
- **News** [Xtra!]
  World [Xtra!], Daily, Current Events, ...
- **Recreation**
  Sports [Xtra!], Games, Travel, Autos, ...
- **Reference**
  Libraries, Dictionaries, Phone Numbers, ...
- **Regional**
  Countries, Regions, U.S. States, ...
- **Science**
  CS, Biology, Astronomy, Engineering, ...
- **Social Science**
  History, Philosophy, Linguistics ...
- **Society and Culture**
  People, Environment, Religion, ...

Add the current document to the bookmark list

What to Look for in a Browser

With all these options, you may be wondering how to choose a browser. In this section, we'll point you in the right direction by identifying the most important features and characteristics to look for in a browser.

Compatible Rendering

When you're deciding on a browser, the single most important thing to check is whether or not the browser renders documents adequately. You may be surprised to learn that not all Web browsers render (or display) documents in the same way, but it's true. Web browser developers try to make their products render documents the way the others do, but the planners and programmers don't always interpret features of the markup language (HTML) in the same way, especially those features that are new to the HTML specification.

An even more common problem is that some developers simply can't include new features and capabilities as quickly as others. The specification for the latest version of HTML (version 3) is expected to be finalized this year. It's been in development for more than a year, and several browser developers have supported some HTML 3 features from the beginning. For example, HTML version 3 provides an elegant way to create tables. The Mosaic and Netscape browsers have supported tables for some time, while others still don't support them. (You'll learn about creating tables in Chapter 10.)

Another HTML 3 feature that all browsers should support is *inline figures*. Most browsers have supported inline images for some time, but HTML 3 adds a new twist to the inline image. A *figure* is like an inline image, but it gives you more flexibility. For example, text can flow around a figure, but not around an inline image. Again, Netscape and Mosaic both render figures properly, but many of the other browsers don't.

Not even Mosaic or Netscape supports all the new features of HTML 3. In fact, HTML 4 will probably be well on its way to completion before the majority of browsers support all the features in the HTML 3 specification. Nonetheless, you should be sure to pick a browser that supports at least the most important features of HTML 3. These include:

- Tables
- Inline figures
- Custom backgrounds

Using Internet Services

As you know, you can use a Web browser to access Internet resources other than the World Wide Web. Sometimes it isn't obvious when you're connecting to a non-WWW resource because you connect to it simply by following a link in a Web page. For example, someone might include a link to a Usenet newsgroup in a page. When you click on that link text, your browser will display a list of subject lines of articles posted to that newsgroup. Each displayed subject line will also be link text that you can click to read the individual articles and follow-ups.

In addition to accessing Internet resources through Web pages, you can also access them directly with your browser—or at least you should be able to. In the last year or so, browser developers have begun to build in support for other Internet services, such as newsgroups and email. As a result, many people who publish pages on the Web have begun to include links to access Usenet newsgroups and to send electronic messages. So if a browser you're considering doesn't support mail and Usenet, you should probably choose another one.

It only takes a moment to determine whether a browser can support these services. All you do is type a special URL into the edit box where you enter URLs for normal Web pages. As a test, type

```
news:rec.aviation
```

into the edit box. If a page of article subjects comes up, your browser supports Usenet. Figure 5-7 shows how it should look. (We'll look more at URLs for Usenet newsgroups in Chapter 11.)

To find out if a browser supports mail, type

```
mailto:maryk@cosmetics.com
```

into the edit box. Of course, you can substitute any email address you like, but it doesn't really matter because you'll get either an error message (if your browser doesn't support mail) or a dialog, such as the one shown in Figure 5-8, in which you can type the text of a message. You can click the Cancel button to close the dialog.

Nearly every browser today supports FTP, but try it out just to be sure. Type

```
ftp://ftp.ncsa.uiuc.edu/Web/Mosaic/Windows
```

FIGURE 5-7. *Mosaic displaying a page of Usenet article subjects*

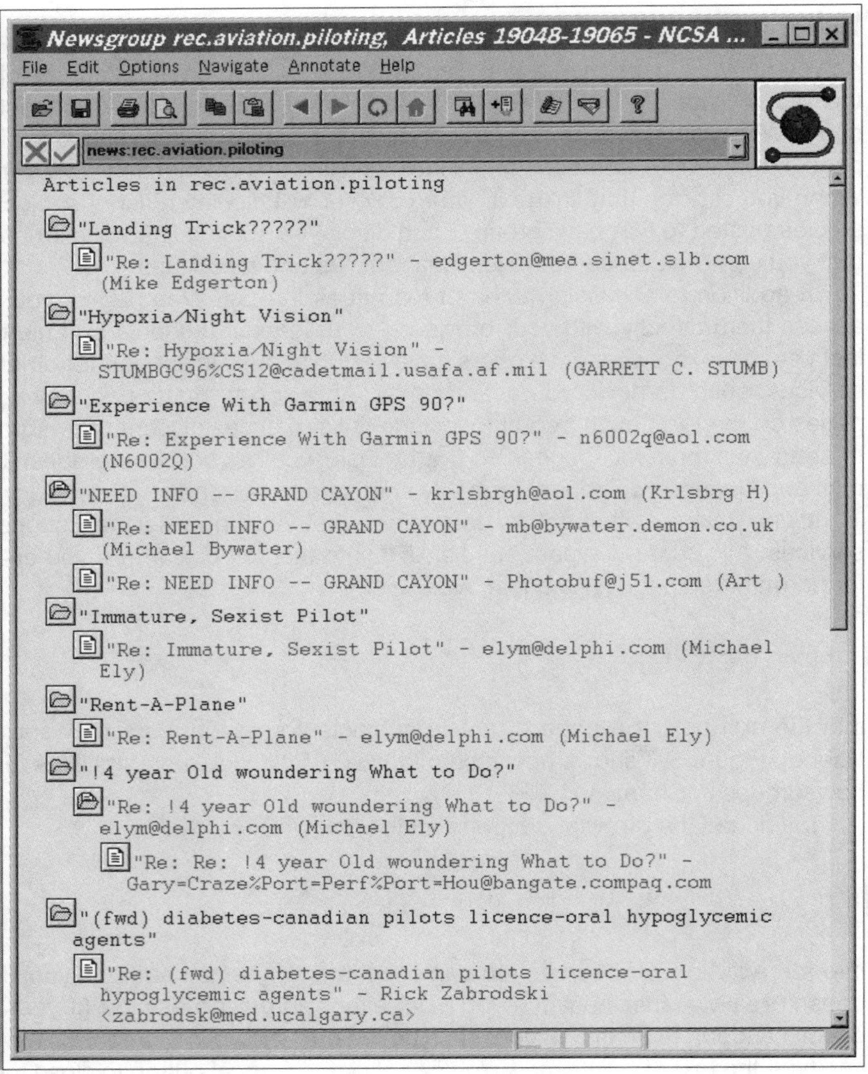

Newsgroup rec.aviation.piloting, Articles 19048-19065 - NCSA ...

File Edit Options Navigate Annotate Help

news:rec.aviation.piloting

```
Articles in rec.aviation.piloting
"Landing Trick?????"
  "Re: Landing Trick?????" - edgerton@mea.sinet.slb.com
  (Mike Edgerton)
"Hypoxia/Night Vision"
  "Re: Hypoxia/Night Vision" -
  STUMBGC96%CS12@cadetmail.usafa.af.mil (GARRETT C. STUMB)
"Experience With Garmin GPS 90?"
  "Re: Experience With Garmin GPS 90?" - n6002q@aol.com
  (N6002Q)
"NEED INFO -- GRAND CAYON" - krlsbrgh@aol.com (Krlsbrg H)
  "Re: NEED INFO -- GRAND CAYON" - mb@bywater.demon.co.uk
  (Michael Bywater)
  "Re: NEED INFO -- GRAND CAYON" - Photobuf@j51.com (Art )
"Immature, Sexist Pilot"
  "Re: Immature, Sexist Pilot" - elym@delphi.com (Michael
  Ely)
"Rent-A-Plane"
  "Re: Rent-A-Plane" - elym@delphi.com (Michael Ely)
"!4 year Old woundering What to Do?"
  "Re: !4 year Old woundering What to Do?" -
  elym@delphi.com (Michael Ely)
    "Re: Re: !4 year Old woundering What to Do?" -
    Gary=Craze%Port=Perf%Port=Hou@bangate.compaq.com
"(fwd) diabetes-canadian pilots licence-oral hypoglycemic
agents"
  "Re: (fwd) diabetes-canadian pilots licence-oral
  hypoglycemic agents" - Rick Zabrodski
  <zabrodsk@med.ucalgary.ca>
```

This should bring up an index of the files in the */Web/Mosaic/Windows* subdirectory at NCSA's FTP site (see Figure 5-9). This is also where you can get Mosaic, if you don't already have it.

FIGURE 5-8. *Netscape's mail dialog box*

Send Mail / Post News

From: Jean Randall <Jean@rls.com>

Mail To: jpeters@rls.com

Post Newsgroup:

Subject: Conference call tomorrow

Attachment: Attach...

```
Joe,

Let's make the call tomorrow at 11:00.  It will be 2:00 PM
there and they should be back from lunch by then.

-Jean
-------------------------------------------------------------
-Jean Randall
(jean@rls.com)
```

Send | Quote Document | Cancel

Caching

Another important feature to insist on in your browser is *caching*. A browser that caches keeps copies of the pages you visit so that it doesn't have to download them again if you want to return to them. Reloading a page from the cache is much quicker than downloading it again from the original source.

There are actually two types of caches: *disk cache* and *memory cache*. Browsers may have one or both types. As you might have guessed, with disk cache the browser stores the page locally on your own hard disk and gives it a special name that allows the browser to match it up with the URL for the original page. When you request a page in the cache, the browser encodes the URL into a file name, then looks to see if the page is in the cache directory. If it is, it loads the page from the disk rather than downloading it again.

Memory cache is similar to disk cache, but instead of storing pages on your hard disk, a memory cache holds the whole document in your computer's memory. This provides for even faster access than reloading the document from disk.

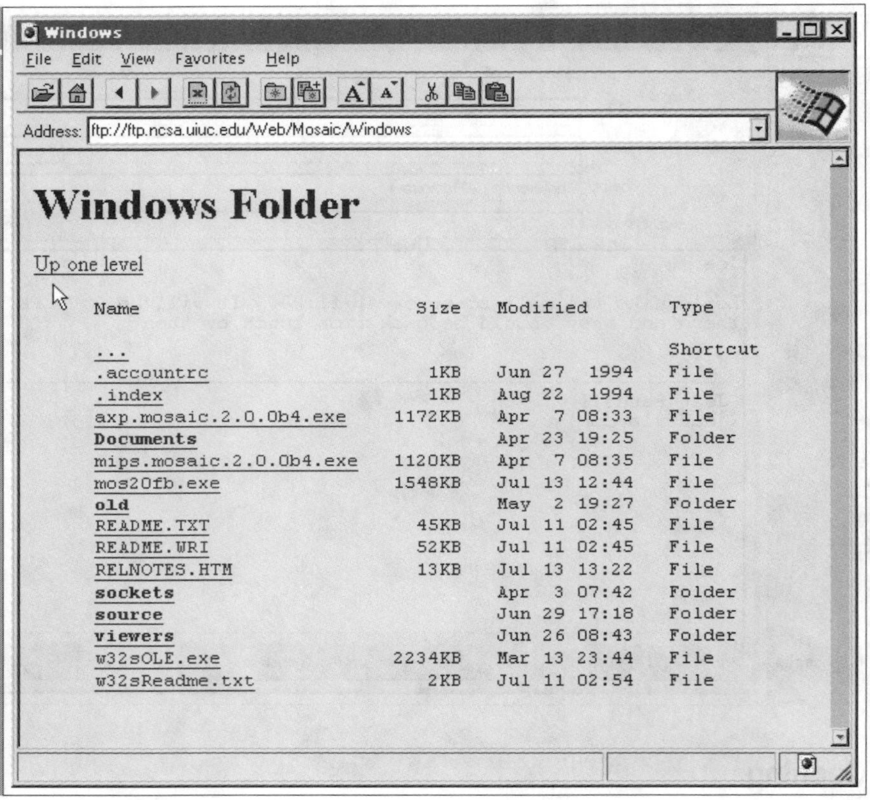

FIGURE 5-9. *Microsoft's Internet Explorer displaying a directory at an FTP site*

For more on configuring your browser for caching, see the section "Caching" later in the chapter.

Ease of Use

While all Web browsers are fundamentally simple to use, the one you settle on should be very easy to work with; it should function as a transparent window onto the Web.

Of course, your personal tastes and preferences will play the biggest part in deciding on a browser, and you won't know how it feels to work with each one until you try it out. However, we can suggest a few basic features. For one, you'll probably want your browser to provide a toolbar with buttons for the functions you perform most frequently. Most popular browsers do contain toolbars, but a number of them don't.

Another feature to look for is a visible edit box for Web page URLs, and it's best if the browser allows you to cut and paste to the edit box. This allows you to copy a URL from a Web page, or another document, into the edit box instead of having to type it in. You may also want to get a browser that lets you open multiple windows to view different pages at the same time, or at least lets you run multiple instances of the browser at the same time.

Finally, with some browsers you have to configure the typefaces and fonts for every HTML element—each heading level, normal text, emphasized text, and so on—before the browser can display pages adequately. The ability to change the typeface and font for each element is a nice feature, even though it comes close to violating the very premise of HTML (that documents should look the way the author intended, not the way the reader may like).

Security Features

If you will be browsing the Web from within a secured network, you may have to configure your browser to work through a special computer on your network called a *proxy server*. Most popular browsers let you configure them to work with a proxy server, but some don't, so find out if you'll be working through a proxy before deciding on your browser. If you are, your Internet service provider or system administrator will tell you if you need to do anything special to use your browser. See Chapter 16 for more on proxy servers and firewalls.

Installing and Configuring a Browser

If you purchase your Web browser at a software store or get it as part of an Internet access package, more than likely it will come on a diskette with an installation program. If this is the case, just follow the included directions to install it.

If you download a browser from the Internet, it may also come with an installation program. Before you can use the program, however, you'll have to extract the setup program and other files from an archive file. These days, most archive files are self-extracting .EXE programs—you run the .EXE program directly under DOS or Windows to create the files you need to install the browser. The archive file may also be a ZIP file, in which case you'll need to open it using WinZip (or the shareware program PKUNZIP if you're using DOS).

It's a good idea to extract the archive file into a temporary subdirectory. That way, when the installation is complete, you can easily clean up the leftover installation files and the original archive file by deleting them or by deleting the whole subdirectory.

After you extract the installation files, you'll usually find files named README.TXT and SETUP.EXE in the subdirectory. Use an editor or a text viewer to read the README.TXT file in its entirety. README files usually contain installation instructions and important information about using the browser with different operating systems. Of course, by the time you can access the README file, you've already completed much of the installation procedure. However, README files may give you important tips about locating the browser's program files, using the setup program, or averting problems that may arise from incompatibility with your hardware or other programs.

When you've read the README file and are satisfied that you're ready to proceed, just double-click on the SETUP.EXE program. This program will ask you where you want to locate the browser's program and data files and may ask you about other configuration options, such as caching and helper applications. A setup program normally creates a program group window for the various programs and utilities that come with the browser or, in the case of Windows 95, creates a group for your Start/Programs menu.

The installation guidelines given here are primarily for Windows users. If you use a Mac, the procedure will likely be even easier. As soon as you download the Mac archive file, you can just double-click on its icon to install your new browser.

Basic Options

One of the first things you should do after installing a new browser is set some of the basic options in its configuration dialog box. Figure 5-10 shows the General tab in the options dialog for NCSA Mosaic, and Figure 5-11 shows the Services tab.

Browsers are usually preconfigured with a home page address that points to the company that developed the browser. For example, Netscape is preconfigured to point to Netscape's own web, making it your starting point. While a developer's web usually isn't a bad choice for a starting point, you may find yourself wanting to start elsewhere. You can change the default home page to your own if you have one, to your service provider's, or to a Web directory such as Yahoo. To change the home page, simply type its URL into the home page edit box. In the case of Mosaic, this edit box is under the General options tab (see Figure 5-10). In Netscape, you set the home page in the Options/Preferences/Styles panel (see Figure 5-12).

While you may want to change your home page immediately, several other configuration options are even more important. These include telling your browser:

- Your name
- Your email address
- The location of your signature file

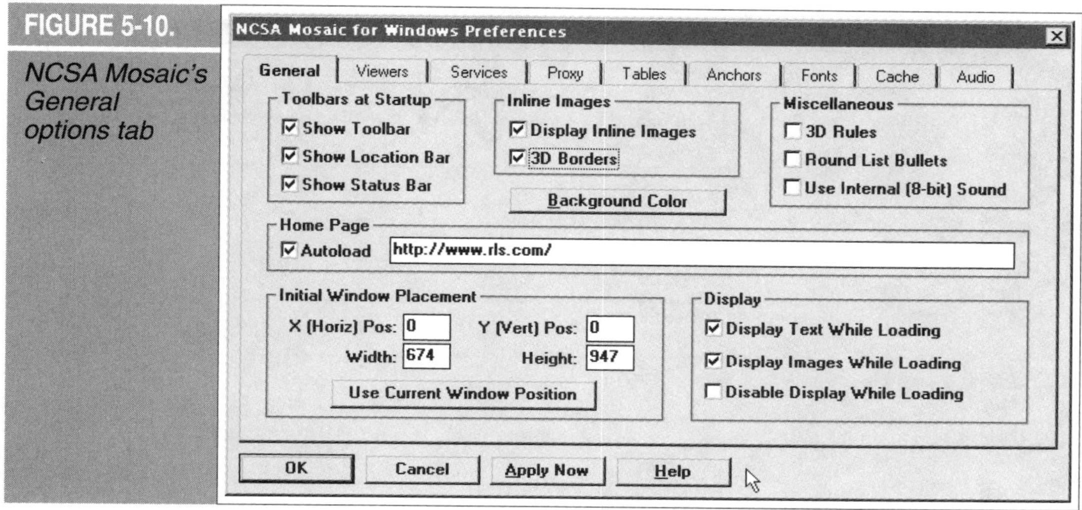

FIGURE 5-10. *NCSA Mosaic's General options tab*

- The name of the news server it should use
- The name of the mail server it should use

Your Internet provider or system administrator should be able to tell you the names of the servers your browser will use to deliver mail and provide access to

FIGURE 5-11. *NCSA Mosaic's Services options tab*

NCSA Mosaic for Windows Preferences
General | Viewers | Services | Proxy | Tables | Anchors | Fonts | Cache | Audio
Mail:
Name: Rick Stout
E-mail Address: rick@rls.com
SMTP Server: smtp.rls.com
FTP:
Use Extended FTP
Display FTP Messages
News
Display Options:
Thread View
Group View
Tree View
Number of articles to load: 30
Number of articles to display: 20
NNTP Server: news2.rls.com
.sig file:
Subscriptions
Telnet
C:\PCTCP\TN.EXE
Browse
Host:port
Host port
OK | Cancel | Apply Now | Help

FIGURE 5-12. *Netscape's Options/ Preferences/ Styles dialog*

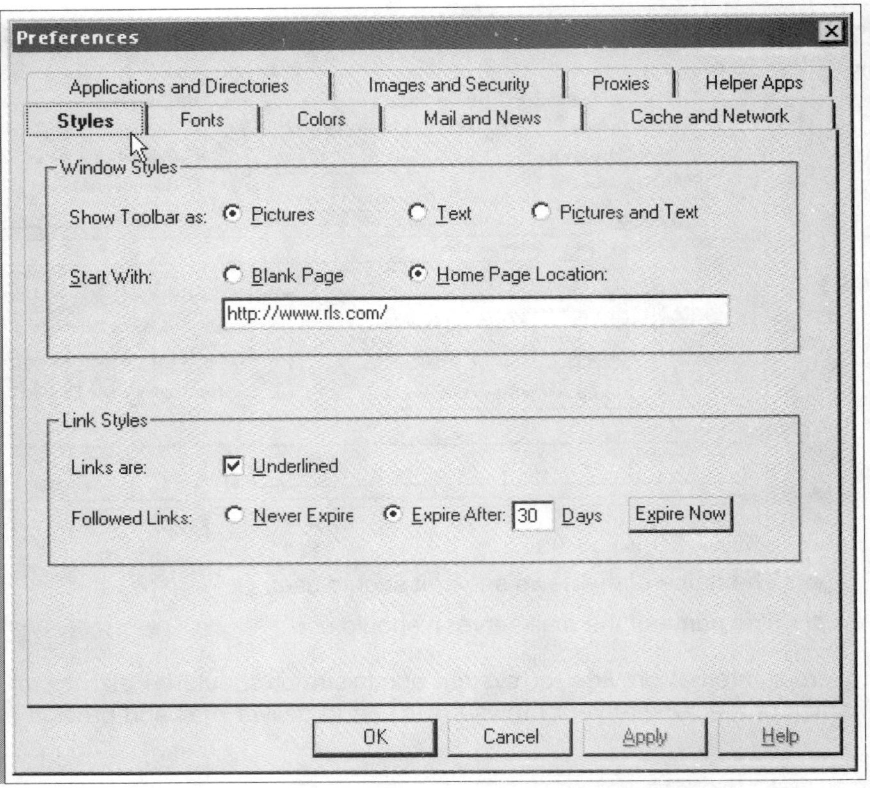

Preferences
Applications and Directories | Images and Security | Proxies | Helper Apps
Styles | Fonts | Colors | Mail and News | Cache and Network
Window Styles
Show Toolbar as: Pictures Text Pictures and Text
Start With: Blank Page Home Page Location:
http://www.rls.com/
Link Styles
Links are: Underlined
Followed Links: Never Expire Expire After: 30 Days Expire Now
OK Cancel Apply Help

Usenet newsgroups (see Figure 5-11). The server names are generally those of machines on your service provider's network (or your own network), and they usually follow a convention for machine names. For example, computers that serve news are usually named *news*, and computers that provide mail services are usually named *mail* or *smtp*. Some browsers even come preconfigured for these standard server names, and for most people they won't need to be changed. Unless you need to use a computer that's not on your provider's network or your own network for these services, you won't need to enter the full domain name (such as *news.netcom.com*).

Beyond these necessities, there are several other options you may want to change. Most browsers give you the option of displaying or hiding some components of the browser. For example, you can choose to display or hide the toolbar, the edit box for addresses, and other items such as buttons that take you directly to the developer's web or to directories.

You may also be able to change the way the browser displays Web documents. Some browsers allow you to specify a custom background color (most browsers use gray or tan by default). In addition, you might be able to customize the appearance of link text. Most browsers can display link text in at least three ways. A link you've recently followed that is still in a memory cache is called an *active link*. A link you've followed in the past (but not as recently) will probably be in the disk cache. This type of link is called a *followed link*. Finally, a link you've never visited or haven't followed in a long time is called an *inactive link*. Alternatively, some browsers (including NCSA Mosaic) use the terms *cached anchor*, *visited anchor*, and *unvisited anchor* to refer to these types of links.

By default, Mosaic uses blue for unvisited anchors, green for cached anchors, and red for visited anchors. Netscape uses blue for inactive links and purple for followed links, but it always underlines link text regardless of its cache status.

Although you can change the default appearance of elements such as link text and backgrounds, you should understand that these settings can be overridden by Web pages that specify their own properties. When you come across such a page, don't think your browser is broken; the author has just customized the page to have a specific appearance.

Once you've got your browser running, take a few minutes to explore the options panels. Most of the options will be self-explanatory, but some browsers do offer online help or even pages on the developer's web to explain the options in detail.

Caching

With some browsers, such as NCSA Mosaic and Netscape, you can specify the amount of data the browser maintains in the memory and disk caches. First you have to decide whether or not you want the browser to maintain a cache at all. You should always let the browser cache data, unless you really don't have enough free disk space. The disk space it costs you to have an adequate cache is well worth it for the performance boost you'll get loading documents locally rather than from their original sources.

Assuming you do want the browser to maintain a cache, you have a couple of options for determining the amount of data it should keep in the cache. Usually, you set a maximum number of kilobytes for the disk cache and either a number of kilobytes or a number of documents for the memory cache. Figure 5-13 shows Mosaic's Cache options panel, configured to maintain four documents in the memory cache and one megabyte of disk cache.

Netscape gives you three options for determining how frequently it verifies cached documents: Once per Session, Every Time, and Never. If you set this option to Every Time, Netscape will verify that the source document (the Web page) still

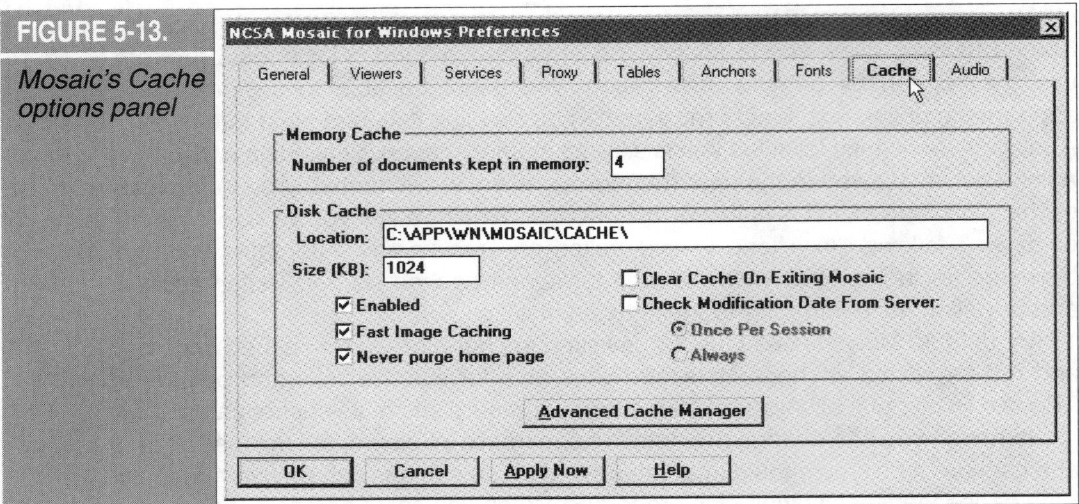

FIGURE 5-13. *Mosaic's Cache options panel*

exists and hasn't changed from the cached copy. If it still exists and hasn't changed, Netscape will use the cached copy. If the option is set to Once per Session, Netscape will perform this verification once for each document retrieved during the Netscape session (from the time you start the Netscape program until you exit it). With the option set to Never, Netscape will always use the cached document without verifying it against the original at all.

Styles and Fonts

We mentioned earlier that some browsers allow you to override the default typeface and font for each HTML element. NCSA Mosaic is an example of this type of browser. A more common approach, one that many other browsers use, is to let you set a base font from which the browser derives the sizes of all the other elements.

For example, if you run your computer's display at a high resolution, you may want to increase the base font size so you can read pages more easily. If the default font size for normal text is 8 points and you increase it to 12 points, each of the other HTML elements is adjusted to a larger point size, resulting in a 50% increase in size for every element.

The ability to adjust font size is important, especially to people who use high-resolution monitors and to those who already have sight impairments. Changing the typeface style is somewhat less important but nevertheless something you may want to do, depending on your taste and which font the browser uses as its default. For example, Mosaic uses the Courier font as its default. Courier is reminiscent of the

old typewriter fonts, and it's understandably a default setting that many users will want to change immediately.

Helper Applications

Every Web browser should be able to display still images (regular GIF or JPEG pictures) in the browser window. This capability is built right into the browser—you don't need any special programs or utilities. There are, however, many types of files that neither your browser nor your computer will be able to recognize or use without a little help from you.

If you use a Mac, chances are your system already has built-in support for playing sounds and displaying images and video clips. The chances are also good that any browser you buy or download will be preconfigured to work with your Mac's operating system and will be able to play sounds and display images and video automatically (as long as the image, sound, and video files are in formats that Macs recognize).

If you use a PC, though, you may have to do a little work to get things set up. Still images aren't a problem; any browser will be able to display images in the common GIF and JPEG formats. It's the sound and video that can present a problem. These might not be a problem for you if you have a newer PC with multimedia capabilities, but older PCs didn't come with the ability to play sounds and display video clips.

For a PC to play sounds (beyond the rudimentary ones the built-in PC speaker can play), it has to be equipped with an adapter card called a *sound card* and external speakers. Sound cards are very common add-ons, and most computer stores have them stacked to the ceiling. For around $100, you should be able to find a sound card that will play 16-bit sounds and music; it may even come with a connector for a CD-ROM drive and a joystick. Sound cards also come with the software they need to let Microsoft Windows know you have a sound card and how to use it.

To play video sequences, you need a graphics-capable monitor and a video card. If you already run Windows, you probably have the hardware you need, but you also need some software. The video format native to Windows is Microsoft's own *AVI* (for Audio/Video Interleave) format. The drivers for playing AVI video clips come with a number Microsoft's multimedia products, but you can also get them separately in Microsoft's Video for Windows package. If you're running Windows 95, you already have all the software you need—it's built into the operating system.

So Mac computers can already play sounds and video in the Mac's native formats, and with a little help Windows computers can play sounds and video in Windows' own formats. But, as you may have guessed, there's still a problem: When you run across a link to a sound or video clip on the Web, how will you know if it's in a format your computer can play?

The answer is that you may not be able to play every sound or video file you find, but you can increase your odds dramatically. Web page publishers usually try to provide audio sequences and video clips in at least two formats. To increase the likelihood that you'll be able to play the sounds and video you find on the Web, you can install additional programs to play other sound and video formats and then configure your browser to work with these "helper applications."

In Chapter 12 ("Working with Multimedia Objects"), we'll look at the details of image, audio, and video file formats. You'll learn where to get the helper applications to display and play them and how to set up your browser to work with these helper applications.

Browsers for Every System and Taste

Without question, the most popular browsers today are Netscape's browsers, NCSA Mosaic, and a handful of commercial variants of Mosaic. Netscape's browsers are commercial products, but so far Netscape has had a very flexible beta program that you can almost always use to get the latest and greatest version free. If you decide to take advantage of Netscape's beta program, be sure to read the licensing agreement and hold up your end of the deal.

NCSA Mosaic is copyrighted and owned by the University of Illinois, but the university licenses the program freely for academic, research, and internal business purposes.

Besides the fact that the Netscape and NCSA Mosaic browsers are powerful, flexible, and easy to use, one of their biggest draws is that they are available for the most important platforms, including all the variants of Microsoft Windows, Macintosh computers, and Unix computers running the X Window system. So whatever type of computer you use, there's a good chance you can use a Netscape or NCSA Mosaic browser.

If, for some reason, you just can't live with a Netscape or NCSA Mosaic browser and you want to try out others, there are plenty available. Table B-1 in Appendix B shows where you can find Netscape and Mosaic; it also lists many additional browsers, the platforms they run on, and where you can find them (or at least get more information about them).

For an updated list of available browsers, check the current World Wide Web FAQ at http://sunsite.unc.edu/boutell/faq/www_faq.html and the Yahoo directory's listing at http://www.yahoo.com/Computers/World_Wide_Web/Browsers/. These sites list many more browsers as well, both commercial and freeware. You can get more information on them and even download many of them directly.

Part 2

Creating Web Pages

Chapter 6

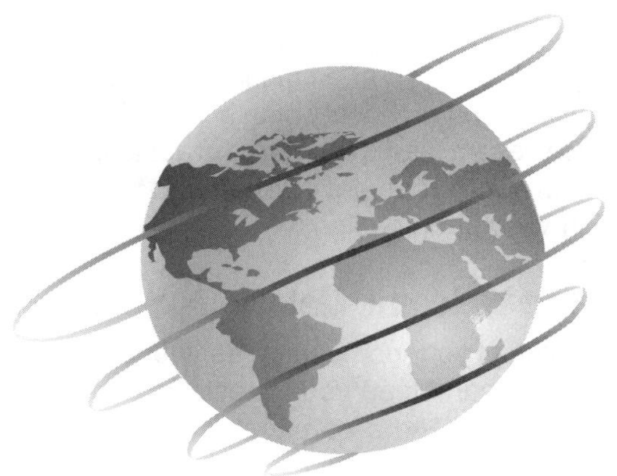

Weaving a Better Web

The Phenomenon of the Home Page

It isn't often that a new idea takes off like a wildfire in a dry wheat field. But that's exactly what has happened with the Web. The wind driving this force of nature is our need to communicate with others, combined with our desires to show off, help people, and help ourselves. For the first time, we've found a way to put out a welcome mat and attract hundreds—perhaps even thousands—of visitors.

With our new visibility, though, come some significant challenges and responsibilities. The biggest challenge is to be interesting enough for people to want to spend some time and even visit again. The biggest responsibilities are to offer something of value or of interest to the Internet community and to be thoughtful of users who don't have high-speed direct connections to the Internet.

Before we go into the details of creating Web pages in the rest of Part II, we're going to take some time in this chapter to look at some general considerations. We will show you how to plan a web of pages, and we'll give you some pointers on how to present information, use graphics, and use color in your pages. We'll also discuss some nice features you can add to your Web pages that have become conventions in Web page design.

The Welcome Mat

Think of your home page as your electronic welcome mat—but one that does much more than clean your guests' shoes. A home page serves as a welcome mat, an entryway, and a personal greeting all rolled into one. You offer your visitors both information about yourself and gifts and opportunities. If you want to attract people's attention, you have to be attractive, courteous, and interesting. Everyone has a story to tell, and you might be surprised at how often you will find yourself absorbed by the intellect and wit of people you will probably never meet.

People use the term *home page* in a couple of ways that have slightly different meanings. For businesses, a home page usually refers to an introductory page with a logo and a short blurb about the company. From that page, you can navigate to other related pages for background information and product- or service-related information. Each of these related pages usually has links back to the home page. In the context of a business, the term *home page* means the first, or beginning, page of a web of pages.

For individuals, a home page is also an introductory page that often features a picture of the page owner and any other personal information that the page owner may want to publish. But most individuals don't go to the trouble of creating an intricate web of interconnected pages. More often, an individual's home page is a

single page, and it's more a destination than a beginning. For example, many small companies include a page in their web about the staff of their company. From such a page, you can sometimes follow links to individual pages about each employee of the company. And often, these home pages are at the bottom of a company's web hierarchy. That is, there often aren't more links to follow logically beneath an employee's home page.

Here's another example: Many people who use the Web aren't employed by companies that have an Internet presence, so they create their pages themselves and make them available on another organization's computer. In either case, individuals' home pages are more often a starting point.

Of course, the nature of a home page will usually reflect the context of the pages around it. For example, an individual's home page on a company's web will be professional and will include a personal resume or biography, and possibly a picture. Figure 6-1 shows such a page for an employee of a small business.

On the other hand, many people create their own home pages outside of any endeavor that requires them to conform to social etiquette. They can advertise their political or social orientations, offer links to their favorite Internet resources, such as a band fan page, and otherwise let their hair down. Figure 6-2 shows an example of a personal home page.

The Corporate Entryway

Businesses are flocking to the Web in droves. Although businesses were slow to get involved in the Internet initially, many are here now, and more are coming aboard every day. Businesses and entrepreneurs bring both the best and the worst of their community, but for the most part their participation is a great boon for Internet and Web users. The allure of the marketplace is extending the Internet into the homes and offices of anyone willing to open the door. As a consequence, the infrastructure of the Internet is being strengthened, the quality of the content is improving, and availability of products and services is soaring.

One reason the Web is such a great marketplace is that the playing field is inherently level. A large corporation might have the resources to create and maintain a huge web of interconnected pages that provide product information, customer support services, and so on, but everyone has a single front door: a home page that fits nicely in a Web browser's window. This puts the person selling gourmet sauces out of her home on the same footing as a multinational corporation and allows a wide array of products to flourish, from flowers to financial services.

FIGURE 6-1. *An employee home page*

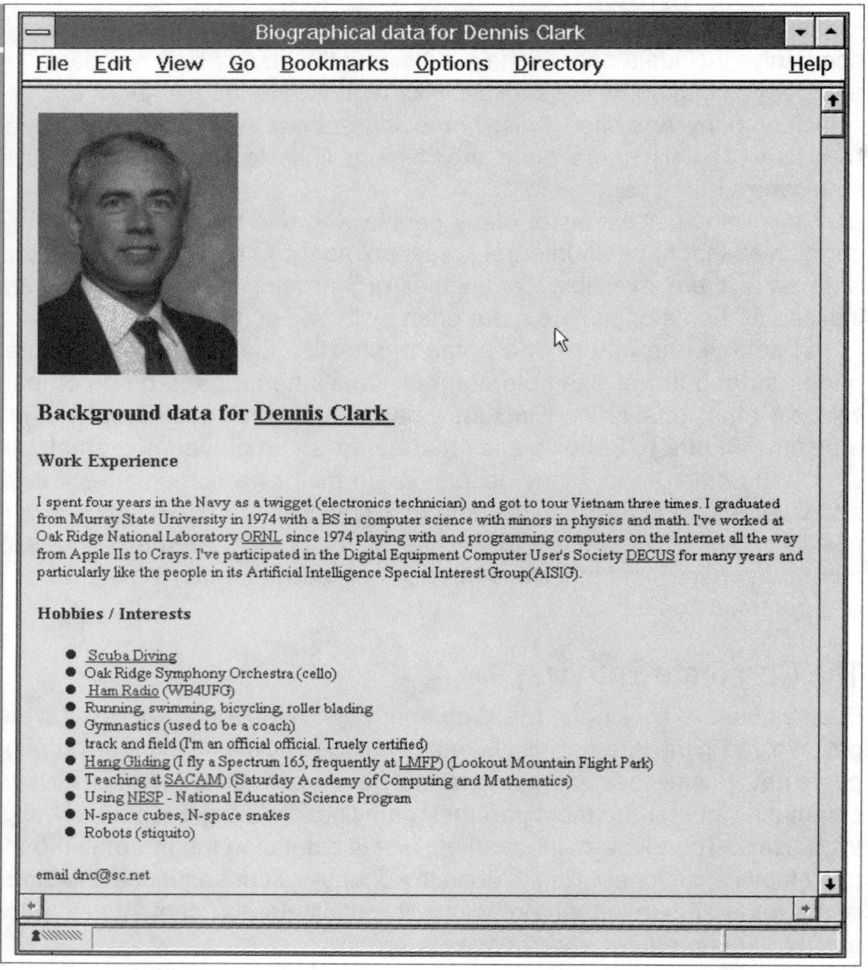

Biographical data for Dennis Clark

File Edit View Go Bookmarks Options Directory Help

Background data for Dennis Clark

Work Experience

I spent four years in the Navy as a twigget (electronics technician) and got to tour Vietnam three times. I graduated from Murray State University in 1974 with a BS in computer science with minors in physics and math. I've worked at Oak Ridge National Laboratory ORNL since 1974 playing with and programming computers on the Internet all the way from Apple IIs to Crays. I've participated in the Digital Equipment Computer User's Society DECUS for many years and particularly like the people in its Artificial Intelligence Special Interest Group(AISIG).

Hobbies / Interests

- Scuba Diving
- Oak Ridge Symphony Orchestra (cello)
- Ham Radio (WB4UFG)
- Running, swimming, bicycling, roller blading
- Gymnastics (used to be a coach)
- track and field (I'm an official official. Truely certified)
- Hang Gliding (I fly a Spectrum 165, frequently at LMFP) (Lookout Mountain Flight Park)
- Teaching at SACAM) (Saturday Academy of Computing and Mathematics)
- Using NESP - National Education Science Program
- N-space cubes, N-space snakes
- Robots (stiquito)

email dnc@sc.net

What Makes a Good Web

There really aren't any secrets to building a web that users will like. Make it simple, make it interesting, and make it useful. Of course, nothing in real life is ever quite that easy. In this section, we will arm you with a few important guidelines for designing pages that will attract, and hopefully hold, your readers' attention.

FIGURE 6-2.

A personal home page

Brian Hefferan's Living Room

File Edit View Go Bookmarks Options Directory Help

Welcome to Brian Hefferan's Living Room...

As you walk in my front door, you see to your right a fancy old upright piano. A few selections from my collection of old sheet music are on the ledge above its keyboard. There's a ukulele hanging on the wall and a banjo leaning against an overstuffed chair. Across the room are dozens of stacked crates filled with lp's and 78rpm records. If you look around more closely, you'll learn more about my musical interests.

It's hard not to notice the prototype the **Heftone String Bass** I'm developing. It looks like nothing you've seen before...

On the coffee table are some mail order music catalogs from my employer, Elderly Instruments.

My computer and modem are to your left, and there's a good chance they are on line right now. To see some of my favorite net hangouts, check out my hotlist

brianhef@heftone.com

I like to play banjo (bluegrass, old-time, tenor, & others) ukulele, fiddle, saxophone, guitar, Heftone string bass, lap steel, and probably a few more. I like to sing popular songs from the 1920's, which I learn mostly from the old sheet music and 78rpm records I collect. Vocally, my main influences are Cliff Edwards (Ukulele Ike), Johnny Marvin, Nick Lucas, Frank Crumit, and Gene Austin.

I have a modest collection of old 78's. I'm especially interested in popular singers from the 1920s, ukulele players, early 5-string banjoists (Ossman, Bacon, VanEps, ect), Hawaiian music, western swing, bluegrass, old-timey, early country, black gospel, & jump R&B.

brianhef@heftone.com

E-mail your comments to me.

back to the living room...

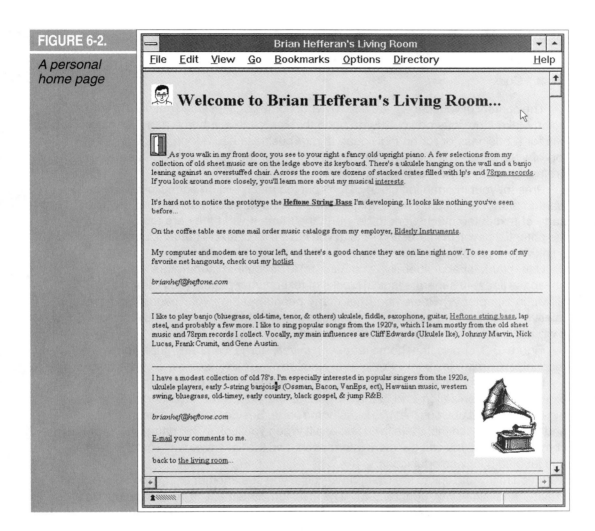

How to Hook the Casual Browser

People say that the first impression is the most important. Try to put your best foot forward on your home page and entice readers to explore the rest of your Web pages. One of the best general guidelines to use as you design your Web pages is to follow the three "C"s:

- Content
- Clarity
- Color

The content of your pages—especially your home page—should get right to your point. Make it obvious on your home page that the page *is* a home page, whether it is for a business or for an individual. If your business has a logo, place it at the top of your page. This gets your logo out in front of the public and adds an air of professionalism to your whole presentation.

Present your information clearly. Don't put too much text on pages to which you want to attract attention. People might make a snap decision that reading a whole page of text is too much work to be worth their time if what they are looking for is the potential payoff of interesting links. If you have a lot of text to present, put it under a link where people can choose to read it if they are interested.

Use blank space liberally, and use HTML's built-in separators (graphical horizontal lines) to separate logical blocks of text on your pages. (You'll learn about HTML in Chapter 7.) Remember that many people reading your pages will have relatively small computer screens; if you use plenty of blank space and separators, it will make it easier for them to read your text.

Figure 6-3 shows the home page of a very large company that you may recognize. Companies from virtually every industry you can imagine are on the Web!

Figure 6-4 shows a home page of a small company. This page is an excellent example of organization and clarity. It gets to the point—the logo and welcome message make it obvious that this is the home page. Besides the welcome message and the links, notice that there is no text at all! When you look at this page, you know immediately that you can get more information, and the links are neatly categorized and labeled by six colorful icons.

If you follow the link to the Company Profile, you see another example of clarity, brevity, and simplicity (Figure 6-5). The mission statement is to the point, it's separated nicely into paragraphs, and the text of the page is bracketed by horizontal lines. Notice that this page has only two links on it. Of course, there is nothing wrong with having several links on a page—especially in lists. But keep in mind that your pages should be simple and not crowded with unnecessary links.

Pictures and Sound

One way to grab a person's attention is with pretty pictures. Figure 6-6 shows a real attention-getter. This page starts off with an engaging graphic that depicts a group

FIGURE 6-3.

The home page of a familiar large company

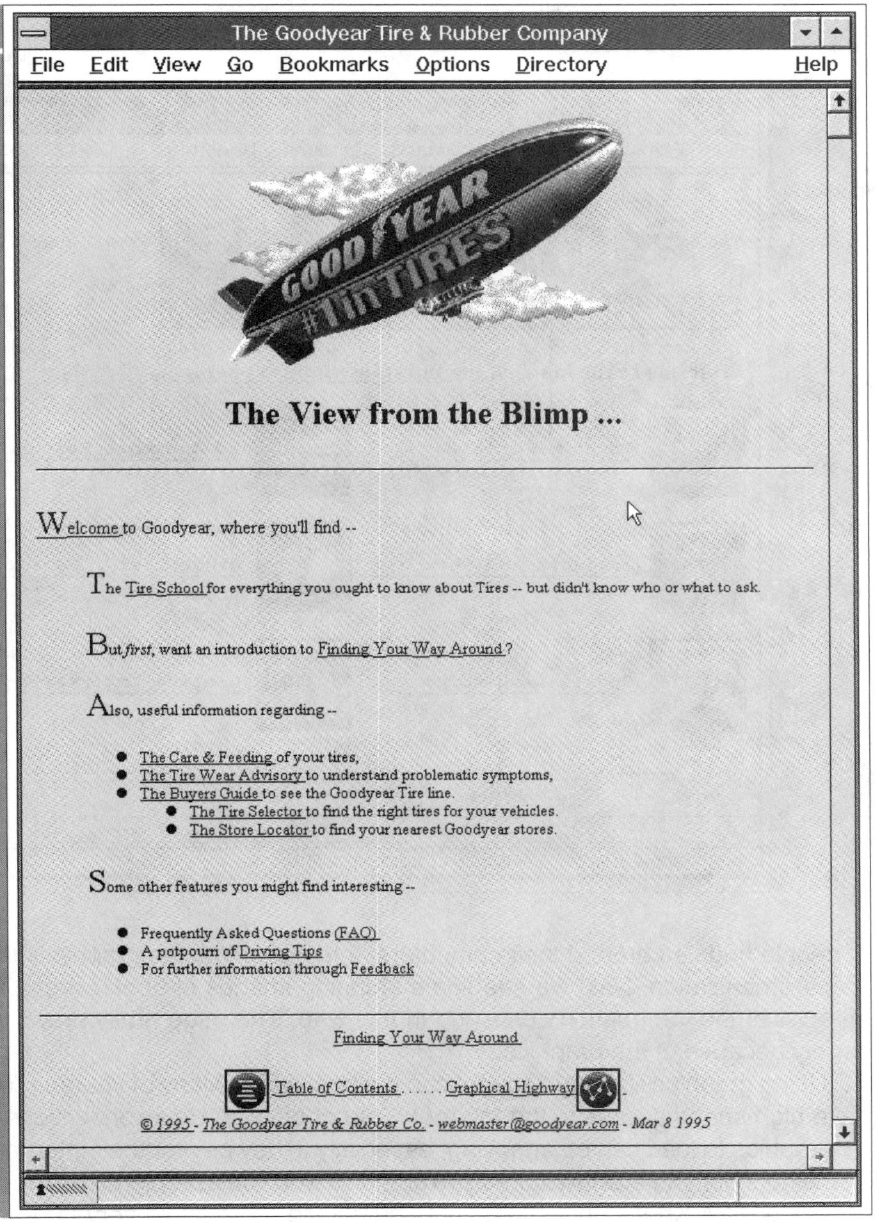

The Goodyear Tire & Rubber Company

File Edit View Go Bookmarks Options Directory Help

GOODYEAR #1 in TIRES

The View from the Blimp ...

Welcome to Goodyear, where you'll find --

The Tire School for everything you ought to know about Tires -- but didn't know who or what to ask.

But *first*, want an introduction to Finding Your Way Around?

Also, useful information regarding --

- The Care & Feeding of your tires,
- The Tire Wear Advisory to understand problematic symptoms,
- The Buyers Guide to see the Goodyear Tire line.
  - The Tire Selector to find the right tires for your vehicles.
  - The Store Locator to find your nearest Goodyear stores.

Some other features you might find interesting --

- Frequently Asked Questions (FAQ)
- A potpourri of Driving Tips
- For further information through Feedback

Finding Your Way Around

Table of Contents ...... Graphical Highway

© 1995 - The Goodyear Tire & Rubber Co. - webmaster@goodyear.com - Mar 8 1995

FIGURE 6-4. *The home page of a small Internet business*

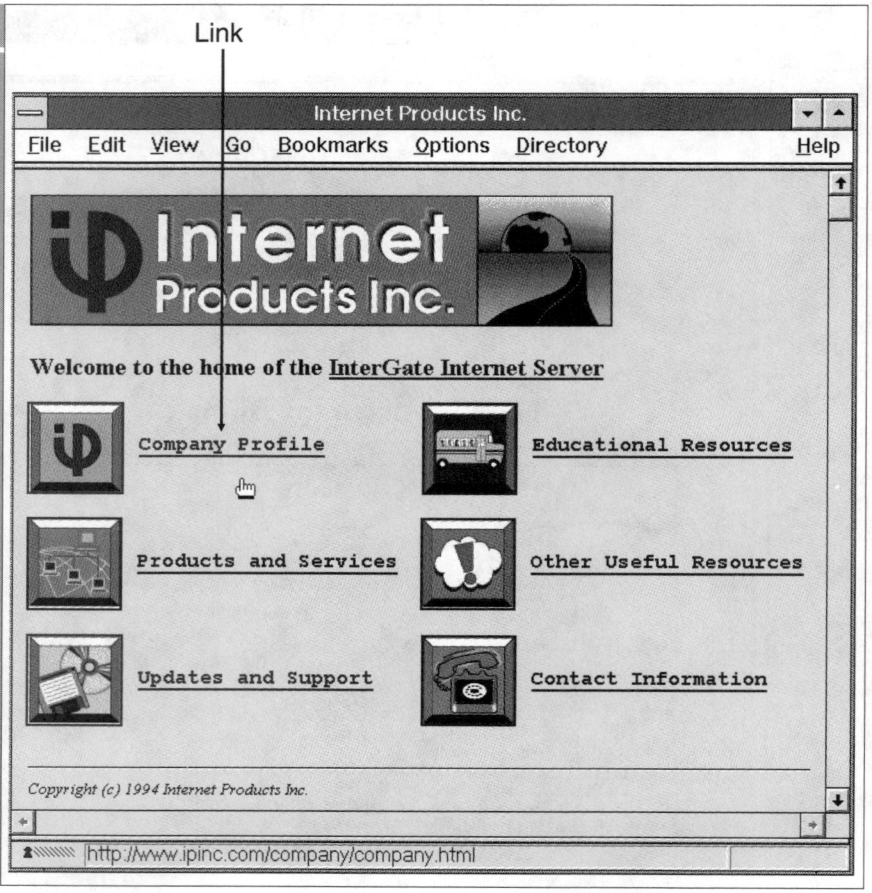

of people huddled around their computers. Integrated into the graphic is the name of the organization. Next we see some stunning images of book covers, followed by a list of the information contained in this web. The page really draws you in—largely because of the graphics.

Using graphics liberally, though, can cut both ways. Many of your readers won't have high-speed access to the Internet. For people with slow connections, waiting for graphics to load can be annoying, especially if they pay for their Internet access by the hour or minute. A few icon-sized graphics won't be a problem, even for readers with slow 14.4 Kbps connections, but you should try to avoid very large graphics wherever possible.

FIGURE 6-5.

The Company Profile page

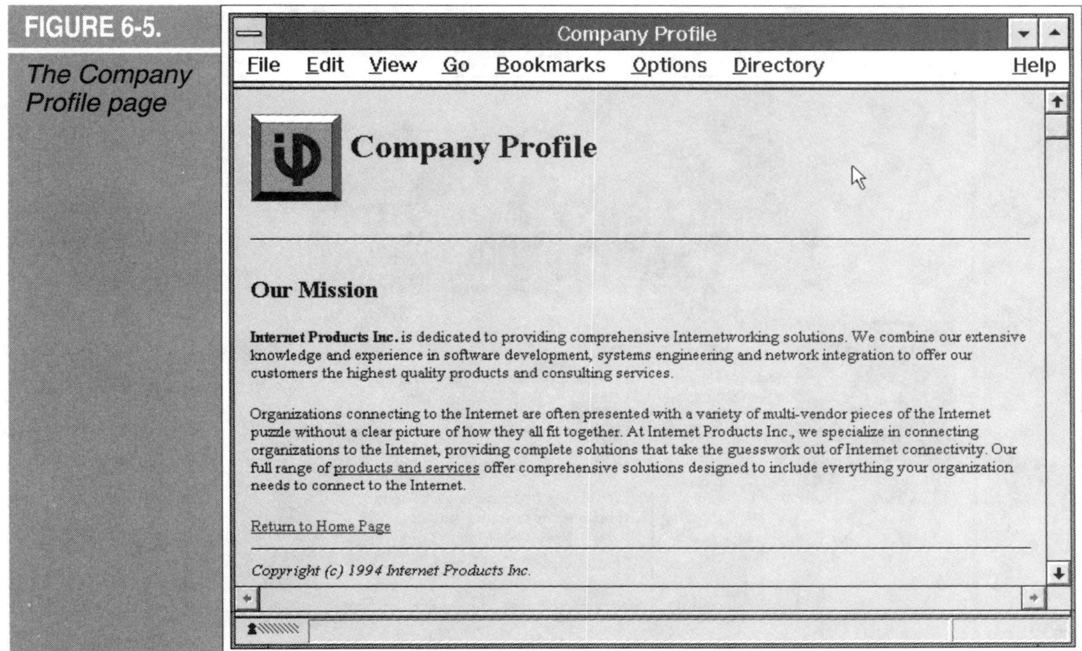

Many people like to put a picture of themselves on their home page. A polite way to do this is to put your picture behind a link entitled something like "A picture of me." Another way is to have two versions of your picture—the full-sized one and a small one that will load quickly. Instead of putting the full-sized version on your home page, put the small picture there and make it a link to the full-sized version. You can put a label next to the small version to tell readers that they can click on it to view your mug at full size.

Another interesting link you can put on your page is a verbal welcome message that you record in your own voice. Audio messages are a great personal touch, but if you decide to use audio clips, you should *only* put them behind links on your pages. Even short audio segments can take a long time for your readers to load, and some of the people reading your page may not be interested, or may not have the capability to hear them anyway.

The Magic of Color

If you use color well, it can do wonders for your Web pages. Although you can't usually control things like the color of the window background on which people will

FIGURE 6-6. *A highly graphical and attractive page*

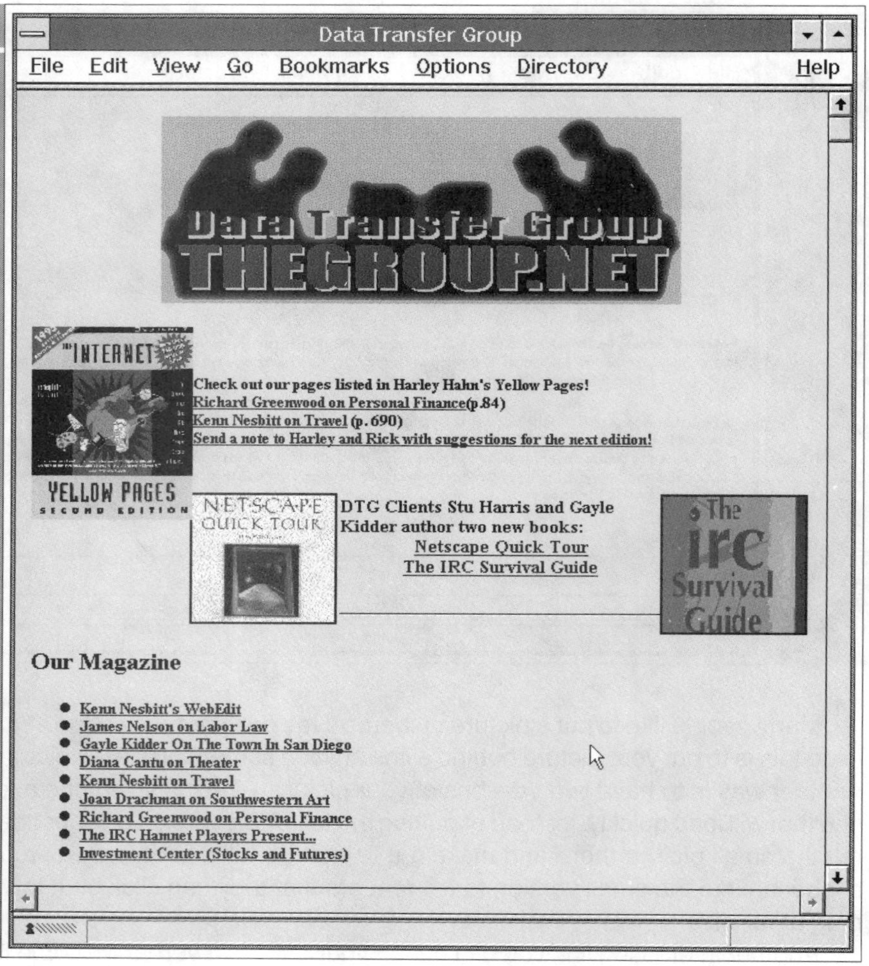

view your page or the colors in which links are displayed, you can control the color of your graphic images and icons. There is a body of science surrounding colors and their effects (both conscious and subconscious) on the mind. Whether our responses to colors are learned or intuitive is up for grabs. Nonetheless, we do seem to react to various colors in fairly predictable ways.

While we won't delve deeply into this science (or art form, depending on your point of view), we can give you a few guidelines. Some of these suggestions may

seem obvious, but if you can work them into your overall design, you (and your readers) might really enjoy the results.

Yellow is the color of information. It doesn't signify that the information is good, bad, urgent, or nonurgent; it just tells you that there is information for you. This may be one reason informative street signs are often yellow. It's also why the original Post-it notes and the telephone yellow pages are yellow. Yellow is a great color to use if you want to reach out and grab someone's attention, then deliver an informative message.

Red, of course, means "danger" or "warning." If you combine a red background with a familiar shape, such as a stop sign, you can convey a powerful message at a deeper level than that of the text.

Some color combinations work better than others. Blue, gold, and wine red are often called *royal colors*. Apparently, many of us have a positive reaction to the combination of these colors, perhaps because they do blend nicely. While you can certainly use any combinations of colors you like, you should try to stay with colors that combine well without clashing. Try to avoid combining dark colors, such as blue, with either green, red, or black. Also, green and red don't combine well (except at Christmas!).

The following shows two excellent examples of graphic panels that were thoughtfully designed with color and imagery in mind:

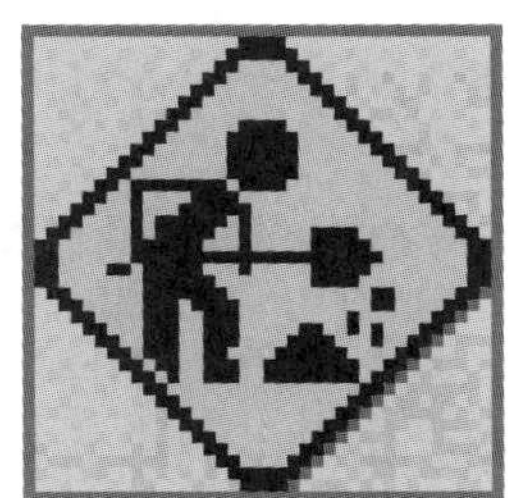

Many people and organizations use these "CAUTION—UNDER CONSTRUCTION" icons to signify that Web pages are under development and might not always work perfectly. Since you can't tell from the black-and-white versions here, in the image on the left the "Danger" sign has white letters on a red background. The face is brown, the hard hat is red, and the border is yellow. In the image on the right, the stick figure is black on a yellow background (this is the more common, but less artistic, of the two icons).

Creating a Web of Pages

You will design a better web if you take the time to do a little planning in advance. The last thing you want to do is bore people—or, worse, get them lost—in a convoluted collection of pages that jump around like the Internal Revenue Code.

Designing from the Top Down

First decide what information you want to convey to your readers, then design the paths you would like your readers to follow as they browse through your web. This is sometimes called *storyboarding* your web. Of course, many of your pages will have more than a single link to another page, so you can't strictly control the paths that your readers will follow. However, you can do a lot to help them along their journey. Let's work through a simple example.

Let's say you own a surf shop and you want to put information about your business and products on the Web. First, make a list that describes in general terms what you offer. On your list you have:

- A home page with general information about your surf shop.
- A link to a page with a list of the company's products.
- Links from each item in the product list to a page with more detailed information, including specifications, prices, and a picture of the product.
- Links from each product-information page to a page where people can place an order.
- A page with information about the company's employees that includes a list of the employees; each employee's name in the list points to a page with more information about that person.
- A page with links to information about the local weather and surf conditions, and even to a current picture of the prized local surf spot.
- A page with links to other interesting surf-related resources on the Web.

Next, take a piece of paper and draw a picture of how you would like your readers to be able to navigate through your pages. Always start with your home page and draw your links to each subsequent page. You don't have to worry about the specific content of each page at this point; this exercise will simply help you understand and plan how your web will ultimately work. Figure 6-7 shows what the storyboard for your web might look like when you're done.

In addition to the arrows shown in Figure 6-7, there are some links that are assumed; you don't want to clutter your storyboard with too many arrows. Every

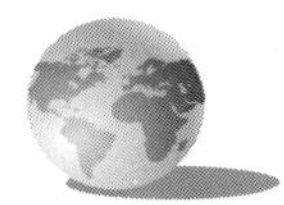

FIGURE 6-7.

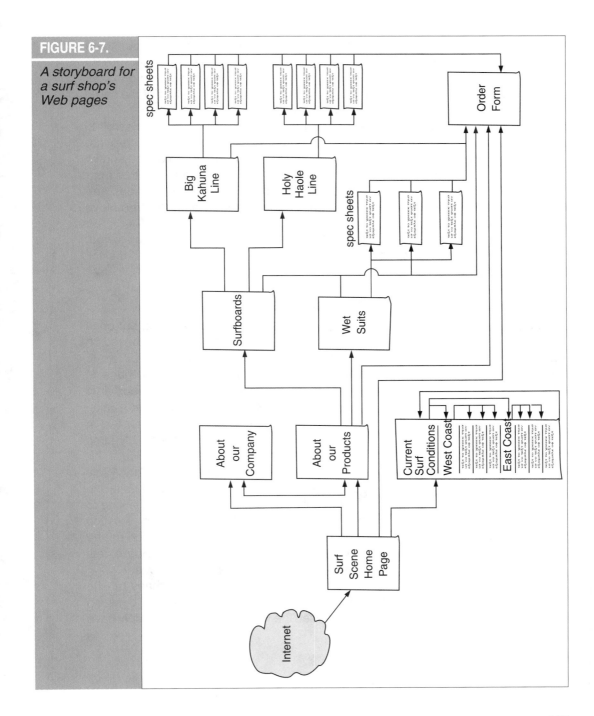

A storyboard for a surf shop's Web pages

page in your web should provide a link the reader can use to get back to your home page. (You can see such a link near the bottom of the page shown in Figure 6-5.) This is a common convention, and it's a courtesy you should always extend to your readers. Most Web designers put these buttons at, or near, the bottom of the page, so users have come to expect them to be there.

Finally, if you like to create long pages that your readers will need to scroll to read, there are two more conventions you should be aware of. One is to provide a short list of links at the top of a long page to allow readers to go directly down to the place on the page that interests them. The other is to provide a button near the bottom of the page to return quickly to the top of the page. As you can see in Figure 6-8, the "Current Surf Conditions" page is a long page that employs both of these suggestions.

Whether or not you employ buttons for navigating on a single page is up to you. These conveniences are a courtesy, but not as important or as expected as the link back to the home page.

Make the Most of the Medium: Hypertext

It's easy to think of the World Wide Web only in terms of linked pages, but don't make this mistake. Keep in mind that the medium you are working with is based on hypertext. *Hypertext* is the concept of linking key terms and words *in your text* to *other related text*. This is a conceptual level lower than links from one page to another page. An excellent example of hypertext is the help system built into Microsoft Windows applications. In hypertext (and, of course, with the Web), links, or *keywords*, are highlighted or displayed in a different color from the other text in the document. By clicking on a highlighted word or phrase, you immediately jump to the related information.

But Web documents are not merely hypertext. You might say that the World Wide Web is the mother of all hypertext systems. This is because you aren't limited to providing links to text that you create yourself. You aren't even limited to linking to documents on your own computer. You have at your disposal every existing document on the World Wide Web. So use them! Not only will you spruce up the appearance and functionality of your Web pages, but you'll also provide a real service to your readers if you offer them links to other interesting resources.

Of course, you have to temper your desire and ability to create many off-site links with the goals of clarity and simplicity. You will have to find the balance between simplicity and functionality. If you have browsed the Web already, you probably have a good idea of how much is too much.

FIGURE 6-8.

On long pages, it's nice to provide links at the top of the page for readers to jump immediately to the section that interests them

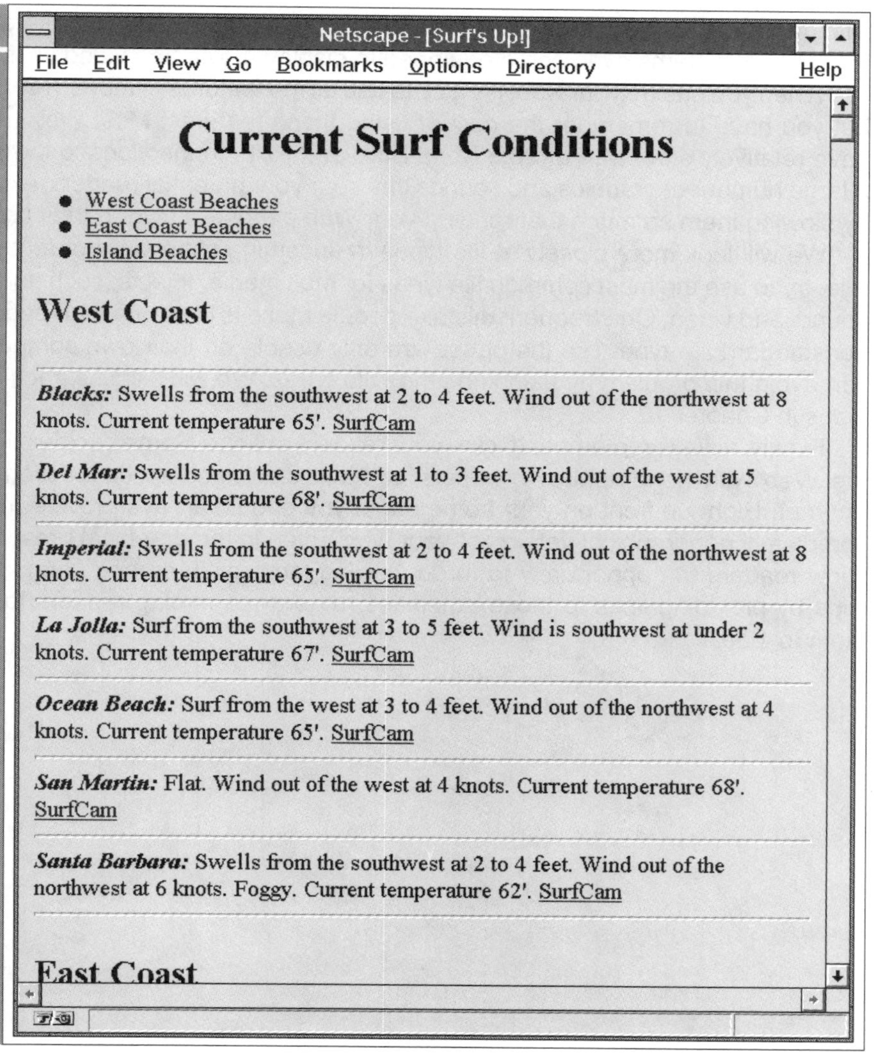

Netscape - [Surf's Up!]

File Edit View Go Bookmarks Options Directory Help

Current Surf Conditions

- West Coast Beaches
- East Coast Beaches
- Island Beaches

West Coast

Blacks: Swells from the southwest at 2 to 4 feet. Wind out of the northwest at 8 knots. Current temperature 65'. SurfCam

---

Del Mar: Swells from the southwest at 1 to 3 feet. Wind out of the west at 5 knots. Current temperature 68'. SurfCam

---

Imperial: Swells from the southwest at 2 to 4 feet. Wind out of the northwest at 8 knots. Current temperature 65'. SurfCam

---

La Jolla: Surf from the southwest at 3 to 5 feet. Wind is southwest at under 2 knots. Current temperature 67'. SurfCam

---

Ocean Beach: Surf from the west at 3 to 4 feet. Wind out of the northwest at 4 knots. Current temperature 65'. SurfCam

---

San Martin: Flat. Wind out of the west at 4 knots. Current temperature 68'. SurfCam

---

Santa Barbara: Swells from the southwest at 2 to 4 feet. Wind out of the northwest at 6 knots. Foggy. Current temperature 62'. SurfCam

---

East Coast

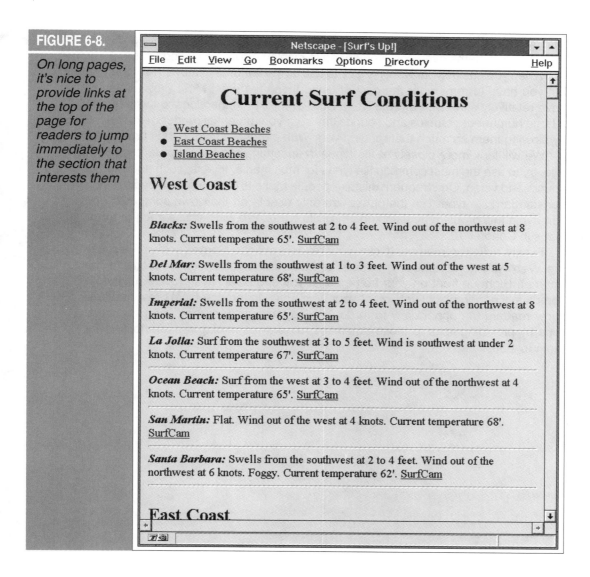

Design for Multimedia

The world of computers has changed dramatically in the last few years. Today, most every computer system that finds its way out of a computer store is equipped for multimedia. This means that the computer can display graphics and play sounds with far more quality and clarity than the old standard PC speakers. Some multimedia systems even come equipped to display movie and video clips.

When you design your web, it's nice to use all the features of modern computers, but you have to remember the cost of using these features. Most Web users still have relatively slow 14.4 or 28.8 Kbps SLIP and PPP connections to the Internet. A large number of graphics and sounds can sour your potential readers' experience by slowing them so much that reading your Web pages isn't worth their time.

We will look more closely at file types in upcoming chapters, but as a general rule, try to use the most common file types for multimedia objects, such as pictures, sound, and video. One frequent mistake people make is to create their pages using nonstandard file types, so the pages are only usable on their own computer. You can avoid this problem by using common file types. We will discuss each of these types in Chapter 12.

Finally, always remember to give your readers options. Some people still access the Web with nongraphical browsers or have slow modem connections to the Internet. Right up front on your home page, you should always provide a link to a completely nongraphical version of your web. Even in the graphical presentations, allow readers the opportunity to forgo viewing large pictures and sound or video clips by providing links to those amenities rather than forcing readers to wait for them to load.

Chapter 7

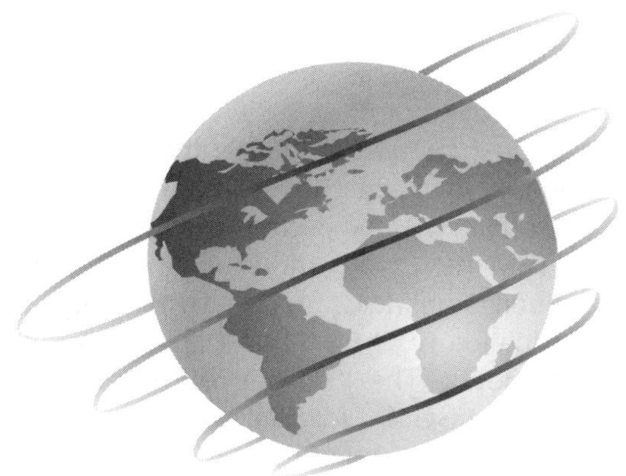

The Language of the Web—HTML

What Is HTML?

Back in the early '80s, when IBM still set most of the standards in the world of computers and information systems, IBM had a pretty good idea that was a little ahead of its time. That idea was based on the recognition that documents have a great deal in common. Documents have titles, addresses, headings, body text, and other elements that are all very similar from one document to the next. Furthermore, from document to document, these elements often share similar attributes such as font sizes and typefaces.

IBM toyed with the idea of creating a document system that would identify each of the elements of a document within the document itself with a kind of tag. This way, displaying or printing documents could be more or less independent of the specific hardware, although such a system would require some software to display or print documents for each different type of computer system the documents would be displayed or printed by. The avenue that IBM explored was to develop a sort of pseudo-computer language that combines plain text and formatting instructions. Such a language is called a *markup language*, and IBM called its version *Generalized Markup Language*, or *GML*.

IBM never did much with GML, but in 1986 the International Standards Organization (ISO) decided that IBM had a good concept, and it produced a publication (ISO 8879) that defined a markup language for creating standardized documents. The ISO derived its language from IBM's GML but called the new language SGML, for *Standard Generalized Markup Language*. (Perhaps the ISO was getting weary of IBM setting so many of the standards in those days.)

NOTE *The title of ISO 8879:1986 is* Information Processing—Text and Office Systems—Standard Generalized Markup Language (SGML). *It's interesting to note that at the time, the ISO believed SGML would be most useful in information processing departments for text and office systems. Contrary to ISO's expectations, SGML—and its more important offspring, HTML—became most important to the millions of individuals who use their PCs and workstations to browse the World Wide Web, whether or not they even know what it is.*

SGML defines many different types of documents, but the type that we are interested in is the hypertext document. HTML, which stands for *Hypertext Markup Language*, is the subset of SGML that defines hypertext documents. People use the term HTML to refer to both the hypertext document itself (which is a specific type of SGML document) and the markup language that you use to create a hypertext document.

You can consider an HTML document from two different points of view. You can regard HTML as plain text that contains some formatting instructions (in the form of

HTML markup codes, or *tags*) that tell Web browsers how to display and print documents, or you can look at HTML as a document-formatting language that also contains the text of documents. The way you choose to look at any particular HTML document will probably depend mostly on the volume of formatting tags as compared to the volume of plain text. For example, here is the HTML code for a simple Web page that presents a paragraph of text:

```
<head>
<title>A Page with a Paragraph of Text</title>
</head>
<body>
A graph can rapidly become more complex as you add new data series
to it. The table has three rows of data. A single line, or a single
series of bars, cannot represent more than a single row of data.
This is one reason why there are many different types of graphs.
</body>
```

The HTML tags are the words and symbols enclosed in the less-than ("<") and greater-than (">") symbols. Don't worry about learning these tags at this point; you'll see them all at length in the next few chapters.

Aside from the tags defining the document title, the only other tags in the code are the two that mark the beginning and end of the body section of the document. Although this document only contains one paragraph, it could just as easily contain many pages of text, and it would still not require any additional HTML tags except a <P> tag to separate each paragraph. Figure 7-1 shows what this code looks like when it is rendered by a browser. Note that in the HTML code, the lines in the paragraph break in different places from when they are rendered by the browser. This is because the Web browser decides where to break lines, depending on the width of the browser window.

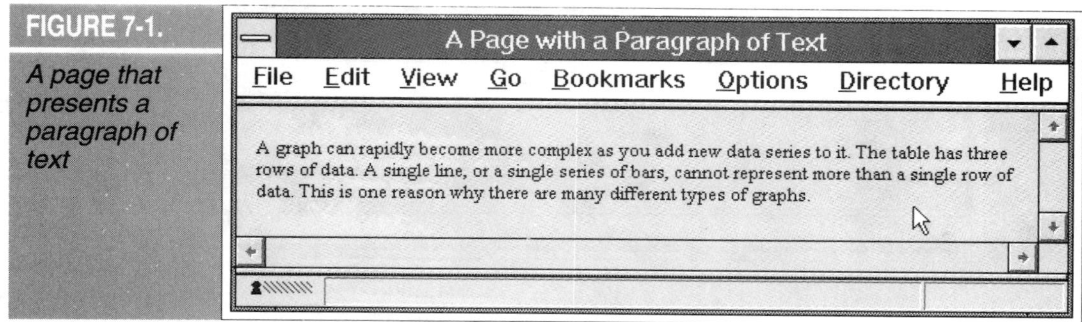

FIGURE 7-1. *A page that presents a paragraph of text*

Here is the source code for another page that displays a short list of items:

```
<head>
<title>A Page with a List of Items</title>
</head>
<body>
<ul>
<li>Line item 1
<li>Line item 2
<li>Line item 3
<li>Line item 4
<li>Line item 5
</ul>
</body>
```

Notice that with this document, the text content of the document is overshadowed by the larger number of HTML tags defining the formatting of the list. Figure 7-2 shows what this code looks like when it is rendered by a browser. As you can see, it takes more markup code to produce a list than it does a simple paragraph. When you add more lists, nested lists, and other elements such as headings, pictures, captions, and tables, a document can begin to look like the markup codes make up the overwhelming majority of the document.

Although you can look at a document as textual content with markup codes, or as a presentation language with embedded content, it's best to try to keep in mind that your textual content is the most important part of your document. This will help you stay focused on your content.

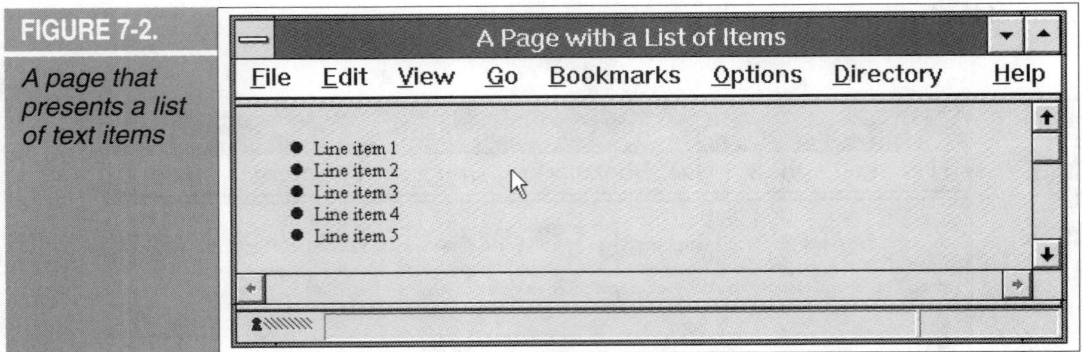

FIGURE 7-2. *A page that presents a list of text items*

As the World Wide Web continues to grow, HTML is quickly eclipsing SGML in importance and scope. One interesting paradox involving the roles of SGML and HTML is that developers are moving toward incorporating style sheets into HTML to allow authors more flexibility in formatting. In a sense, SGML was designed to act as a container for numerous types of documents, and each document type was to have a specific set of styles (typefaces and font sizes) for the various elements in the document, such as head levels, titles, addresses, and so on.

Originally, HTML documents were defined as one of these document types, so the style for each head level, title, caption, and so on was fairly strictly defined. But now, Web authors designing HTML documents are finding that they want more control over formatting. As a result, proposals are in the works now for versions of HTML that will include style sheets with an assortment of predefined styles. The author will be able to pick and choose which styles to use in each HTML document he or she creates. This is just one example of how HTML is becoming more robust than its "parent," SGML. In fact, HTML is driving the technology of markup languages today.

Versions of HTML

Today, HTML is in its fourth generation. Each version of HTML is a superset of earlier versions. This means that each new version of HTML adds new capabilities and functionality but generally doesn't change the way tags worked in previous versions. (With each new version, however, the HTML developers have cleaned up minor problems and have removed a few unnecessary features.)

Before we explain the differences between the versions of HTML, we should take a minute to make sure that you understand the importance of HTML *versions* (or *levels*) and the relationship between the version of HTML and the browsers you use. Remember that Web pages on the Internet are simply text files (HTML documents) that lie around on computers on the Internet waiting for someone to read them with a Web browser. When you point your browser at a particular Web page, it goes to the computer where that file resides and retrieves the file in its entirety. Your browser loads the HTML file into your own computer's memory and interprets each of the tags to display the page the way the author intended.

If the author of a Web page used only the basic tags that have been part of HTML since the first version, you would probably never have a problem displaying the page with any common browser. If, on the other hand, the author used some of the additional capabilities of the newer versions of HTML, your browser might not be able to interpret those tags. When this happens, your browser might give you an error message, or it might simply ignore or display the tags that it can't interpret as text. The latest version of HTML (Level 3) calls for documents to include version information, so that eventually browsers will be able to identify the HTML level of a page.

HTML Levels 0 and 1

HTML Level 0 is the common denominator of all Web browsers. To work at all with the Web, a browser has to support all the HTML Level 0 tags. This will seldom be a problem because all the common browsers do support at least Level 0.

HTML Level 0 embodies the original adaptation of SGML for the hypertext document type. Even after three new generations, most of the HTML tag types are still HTML Level 0 tags. Take a quick look at Appendix A to get an idea of the total number of tag types and note that most of them originated in HTML Level 0.

HTML Level 1 includes all the Level 0 features, but it adds a few new tags for highlighting text and for displaying images as an integral part of a Web page. Images that are embedded in a Web page are called *inline images*. The drawback to Level 1 images is that there is no way to make text flow around an image. This is resolved in Level 3 with the introduction of *figures*. These are essentially the same as images, but text can flow around them.

HTML Level 2

HTML Level 2 includes all the features of Level 1, plus support for forms. You can use forms in Web pages when you want to get input from the reader. Forms can include edit boxes, into which the reader can type; list boxes, from which the reader can pick a value; and buttons, which the reader can click to perform actions. Figure 7-3 shows such a page with a form for entering criteria to search a database.

With HTML Level 2 and its support for forms, the World Wide Web has become an interactive medium—where information can flow in both directions—rather than a passive, read-only text-retrieval system. Most of the browsers available today support HTML Level 2.

HTML Level 3

HTML Level 3 (which used to be called *HTML+*) is fully backward-compatible with HTML Level 2 but adds many new features. Most notably, Level 3 adds tags for rendering tables on a page. Prior to Level 3, if you wanted to put a table on a page, you had to use the old SGML table tools, which were complicated and clumsy, or you had to include them as a block of preformatted text. Level 3 makes using tables easy. Figure 7-4 shows a Web page with such a table.

Level 3 also adds a new tag type for *inline figures.* Inline figures are an improvement over inline images because text can flow around a figure. Figures also

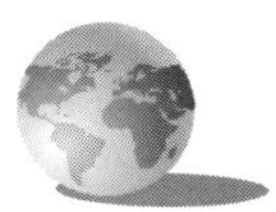

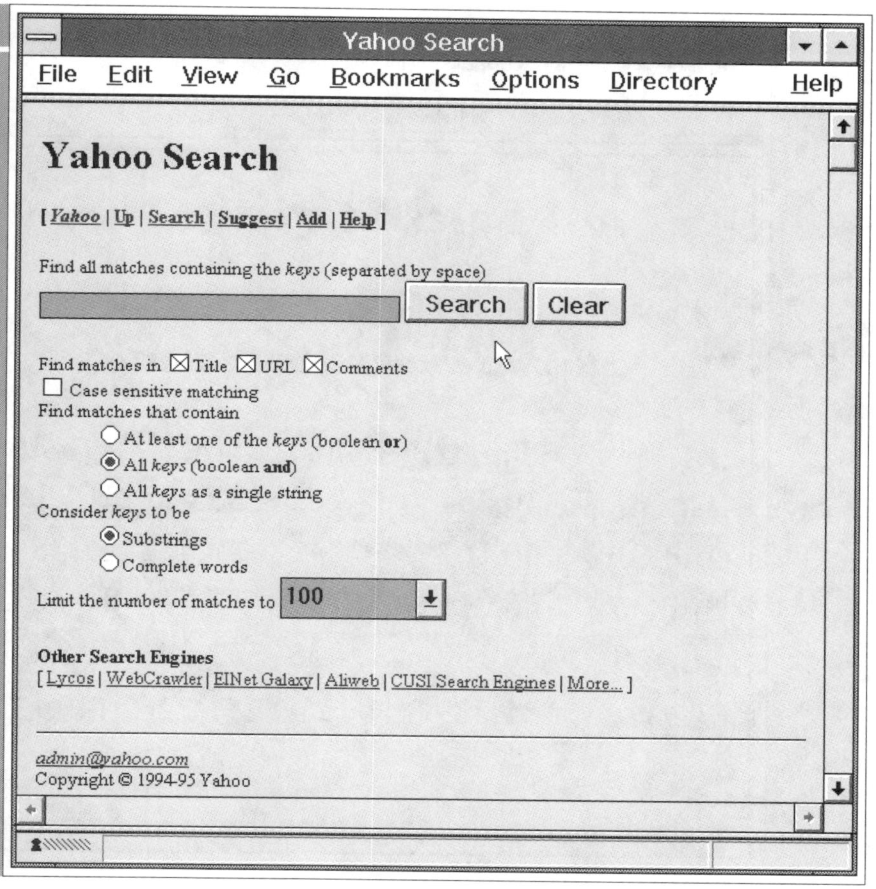

FIGURE 7-3.

A form for entering search criteria into a database

Yahoo Search

File Edit View Go Bookmarks Options Directory Help

Yahoo Search

[*Yahoo* | Up | Search | Suggest | Add | Help]

Find all matches containing the *keys* (separated by space)

Search Clear

Find matches in ☒ Title ☒ URL ☒ Comments

☐ Case sensitive matching

Find matches that contain

○ At least one of the *keys* (boolean **or**)

◉ All *keys* (boolean **and**)

○ All *keys* as a single string

Consider *keys* to be

◉ Substrings

○ Complete words

Limit the number of matches to 100

Other Search Engines

[Lycos | WebCrawler | EINet Galaxy | Aliweb | CUSI Search Engines | More...]

admin@yahoo.com

Copyright © 1994-95 Yahoo

allow for faster browsing because images can be rendered in a new way (if the browser supports it). When a Web page contains several similar figures (such as icons with minor differences) or when several nearby pages have similar graphics (such as slightly different logos), Level 3 browsers can render the additional images by overlaying the differences between the original base figure and the new images onto the original image, which is still in the browser's disk cache. This is much faster than simply downloading each image separately.

Other enhancements in Level 3 include support for math equations and formulas, better character-positioning control, a banner area on pages for static displays of logos or disclaimer information, and the ability to dynamically customize a browser's menus or toolbars from within an HTML document.

FIGURE 7-4. *HTML Level 3 makes formatting tables easy*

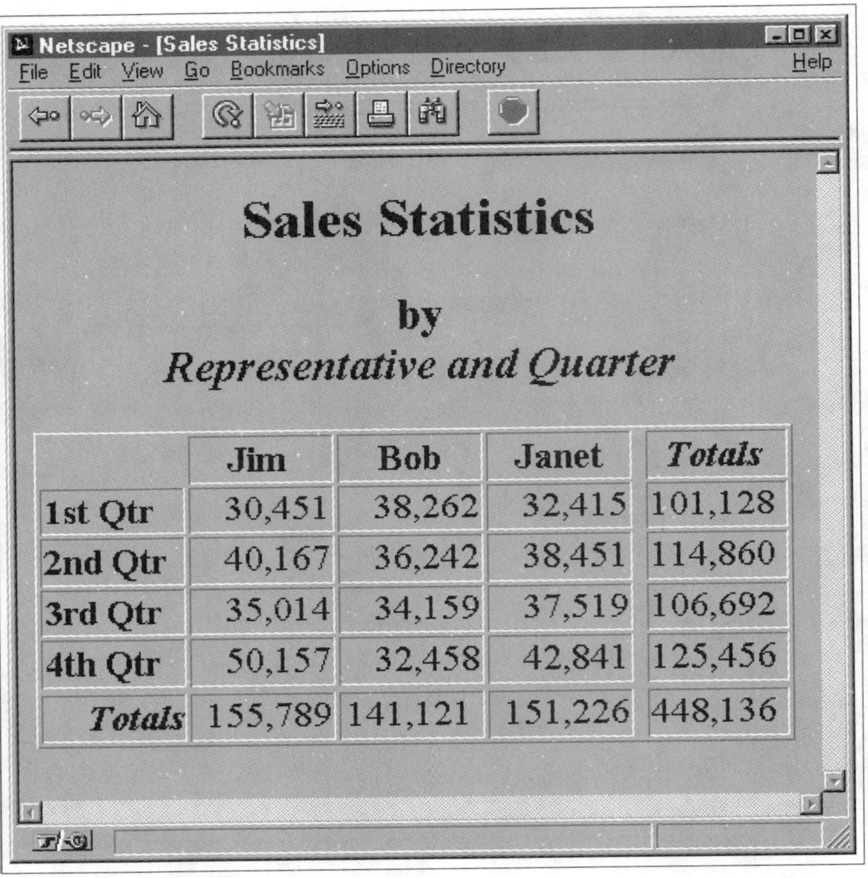

Netscape - [Sales Statistics]

File Edit View Go Bookmarks Options Directory Help

Sales Statistics

by
Representative and Quarter

	Jim	Bob	Janet	*Totals*
1st Qtr	30,451	38,262	32,415	101,128
2nd Qtr	40,167	36,242	38,451	114,860
3rd Qtr	35,014	34,159	37,519	106,692
4th Qtr	50,157	32,458	42,841	125,456
Totals	155,789	141,121	151,226	448,136

Without a doubt, the HTML Level 3 specification represents the most radical enhancements to the HTML language in its short life. Unfortunately, most browsers available today don't fully support HTML Level 3. In fact, it could be as much as another year before most browsers do provide full support for Level 3 enhancements.

Nonstandard Extensions

Some companies that create Web browsers add their own enhancements to HTML. The most notable company that does this is Netscape. An example of such an enhancement is Netscape's <BLINK> tag, which causes text following this tag to blink if it is viewed with one of Netscape's browsers. Currently, there is no such tag in any HTML level specification, nor in any proposals.

Purists will say that these kinds of initiatives hinder the HTML development process and will keep HTML from becoming a robust and open standard. Others, however, believe that there is no harm done by creative initiatives such as these. Moreover, most Web browsers are designed to be forgiving of tags they don't recognize. For the most part, browsers ignore unsupported tags, so it really doesn't hurt to add minor enhancements to the language. Besides, developers do tend to come up with good ideas from time to time. And in all likelihood, ideas like a <BLINK> tag will probably find their way into the standard, eventually.

Directions for the Future

The development of HTML is an ongoing process that is spearheaded by the World Wide Web consortium (or W3 consortium) at the Laboratory for Computer Science at the Massachusetts Institute of Technology (MIT).

TIP *For a wealth of information on every level of HTML as well as on outstanding proposals and ideas under development, visit the W3 organization at* http://www.w3.org/ *and MIT's Laboratory for Computer Science pages at* http://www.lcs.mit.edu.

The W3 consortium regularly publishes its draft HTML version specifications and requests for comments. You can read all about the plans for new and improved features in upcoming versions of HTML. W3 also offers plenty of information on Usenet newsgroups you can read and mailing lists you can join if you are interested.

Indeed, upcoming versions of HTML have some real gee-whiz features. Some of the most exciting things include virtual-reality document types and audio input fields into which you can record vocal messages. Unfortunately, however, the gap between new specifications and the time it takes software developers to deliver browsers that incorporate all the new features is widening. Nevertheless, the World Wide Web's future—and its position as the graphical user interface to the Internet—seems assured, and Web pages are destined to become ever more capable and feature-rich.

Chapter 8

Defining an HTML Page

Web pages can run the gamut from exceedingly simple to very complex. In this chapter, we will start at the very beginning of the process of creating a Web page. We'll look at the parts of a Web page, then for the rest of this chapter focus mainly on the first of those parts—the head section. In the following chapters, we'll look at the body section.

HTML documents have two main sections—a *head* section and a *body* section. The head section of a document is always short; there are usually only a couple of things you need to do there. The body section is where you define the content of your page. The items that you define in each of these sections are called *elements*; thus, things you define in the head sections are *head elements*, and things you define in the body section are *body elements*. The diagram in Figure 8-1 shows the relationship of these two sections in a typical HTML document.

In this chapter, and in the following several chapters, we will jump into the details of writing HTML documents. Here, we will look at prologues and the elements you use in the head section of documents to define documentwide characteristics. In the chapters following this one, we will focus on the elements you use in the body sections to mark up the bulk of the content of your HTML documents.

File Formats and Editing Tools

An HTML document is a plain text file. By that, we mean a file that contains only the characters you can enter directly from your computer's keyboard. These include all

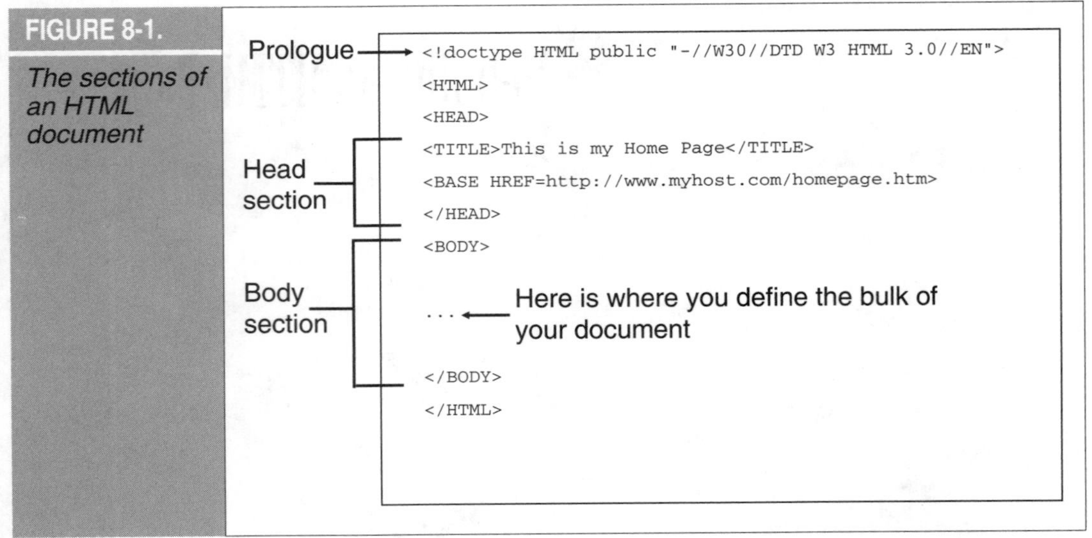
Prologue
<!doctype HTML public "-//W30//DTD W3 HTML 3.0//EN">
<HTML>
<HEAD>
<TITLE>This is my Home Page</TITLE>
<BASE HREF=http://www.myhost.com/homepage.htm>
</HEAD>
<BODY>
...
Here is where you define the bulk of your document
</BODY>
</HTML>
Head section
Body section

FIGURE 8-1. *The sections of an HTML document*

the alphabetic and numeric characters, punctuation, and other symbols that you can type directly into a file. This means you can use a simple text editor to create Web pages—you don't need any specialized program, or even a word processor, to create your pages.

Text editors are easy to find and are built into most computer operating systems. If you use Windows, you can use the Notepad applet that comes with Windows in the Accessories group. If you use DOS, you can use the Edit program. With Unix, you can use vi, emacs, or pico. These are just a few of the common text editors. There are many more, including commercial packages you can buy at the software store.

A text editor is not the same as a word processor. A word processor saves its documents in a format that is native only to that particular word processor. For example, a WordPerfect document file is in a format that WordPerfect recognizes with embedded codes for fonts, typefaces, page breaks, and so on. You can use a word processor to create HTML documents, but you have to be sure to save them as plain ASCII text files or they will be in the word processor's native format.

There are also specialized programs, templates, and macros you can use with word processors to create HTML documents. We'll look at some of these in Chapter 14, but it is probably best if you start out writing HTML with a plain ASCII text editor. This way, you won't be shielded from the actual HTML code. As with learning anything new, it's best to start at the beginning and use new tools to automate your tasks only after you have a solid understanding of those tasks.

The Prologue

In addition to head elements and body elements, an HTML document has an additional element that you may not find in many documents yet: the prologue. A *prologue* is a line of text at the beginning of an HTML document that will tell future browsers which HTML version the document conforms to. The reason you won't find many Web pages with prologues is that they aren't required, and not many browsers know what to do with them yet, so they just ignore them. But beginning with HTML 3, prologues may become more important.

The official definitions for each version of HTML (and SGML) are called DTDs (for *Document Type Definitions*). The DTD for HTML 3 actually contains two definitions: a strict definition that conforms more tightly to SGML, and a relaxed definition that uses more HTML conventions. For example, the stricter definition requires that you use the SGML convention of marking the beginning of a paragraph with a <P> tag and the end of a paragraph with the </P> tag. The more relaxed definition, on the other hand, recognizes that marking both the beginning and end of a paragraph is somewhat redundant and has dropped this requirement. Instead of marking both ends, you *separate* paragraphs with a single <P> tag.

The HTML prologue identifies the DTD to which an HTML document conforms. Right now, prologues aren't used for much except allowing authors to use some SGML authoring tools that expect to find them. But as HTML 3 browsers become available, and as new document types such as 3-D Web pages and video pages become more common, prologues may become more important.

If you want to publish Web pages for the Internet as it is today, you probably don't need to worry about prologues. And if you're writing HTML 3 documents, you can also forget about prologues because the default DTD for HTML 3 documents is the relaxed, HTML-style DTD. Also, the HTML version of a Web page is implied for Web browsers because it is encoded into the MIME content type served by HTTP servers (if you don't know what that means, don't worry about it). But if you want to write strict, SGML-compliant documents in HTML 3, your document should begin with the prologue

```
<!doctype HTML public "-//W30//DTD W3 HTML 3.0//EN">
```

There is one other reason you might want to consider using prologues from the outset of your Web publishing. Most of the popular browsers available today are a hodgepodge of capabilities. While most of them support all the HTML 0 and HTML 1 tags, many don't support all the HTML 2 tags, and only a few support some HTML 3 tags. To complicate this, most browsers have no way of identifying which version of HTML was used to write a document. They simply understand the tags, or they ignore them. This passive interpretation was good for HTML and the Web in the past, when HTML was simple. But with all the new capabilities coming down the pipeline, browsers need at least to be able to display a warning message when they are about to try to render a document that may have tags they won't be able to interpret. If you include a prologue that contains a version number, future browsers may be able to use it to identify the HTML version of a document and supply such a warning if necessary.

One other tag doesn't relate to either the head or body section of a document. This is the <HTML> tag and its terminator, </HTML>. The <HTML> tag simply confirms for your browser that the text following the tag is marked up with HTML. Either the <HTML> tag is the first line of an HTML document, or it immediately follows the prologue. The terminating </HTML> tag is usually the last line of an HTML document. Like the prologue, these tags are optional. Some authors don't use them, but generally it is good form to put them in.

The Head Section

The head section is where you define attributes that apply to your HTML document as a whole. Perhaps the most important of these (and the one people use most often) is the title of the Web page, but there are other useful tags you can use in this section as well.

We will introduce you to most of the common head elements in this section, but not all of them. For an exhaustive list and the most up-to-date information, you should check the current HTML specifications. You can find links to the current specifications for each HTML version in the W3 web at MIT at

```
http://www.w3.org/hypertext/WWW/MarkUp/
```

Every document should have a head section, if only to define a title for the page. You identify the beginning of your head section with the <HEAD> tag and terminate it with the </HEAD> tag.

Titles

Browsers display the title of an HTML document in the title bar of the window your browser is in. Whether you use a Mac, X Window, or one of the versions of Microsoft Windows, all graphical programs display a title in the bar at the top of the program window (see Figures 8-2 and 8-3). Also, when you minimize, or *iconize*, a running browser program, the title of the open Web page will be displayed under the icon your operating system uses to represent your browser.

Setting the title of a page is straightforward. In the head section, just sandwich your page title between the <TITLE> and </TITLE> tags, like this:

```
<HEAD>
<TITLE>The Home of Pete's Online Rare Lizard Emporium</TITLE>
</HEAD>
```

Some references claim that a title is a required element of HTML. In real life, though, if a document doesn't have a title, a browser will usually just display the file name or URL in place of the title, or it will simply display the word "Untitled." However, defining a title is easy, and it gives an identity to your page. It is almost always worth the effort.

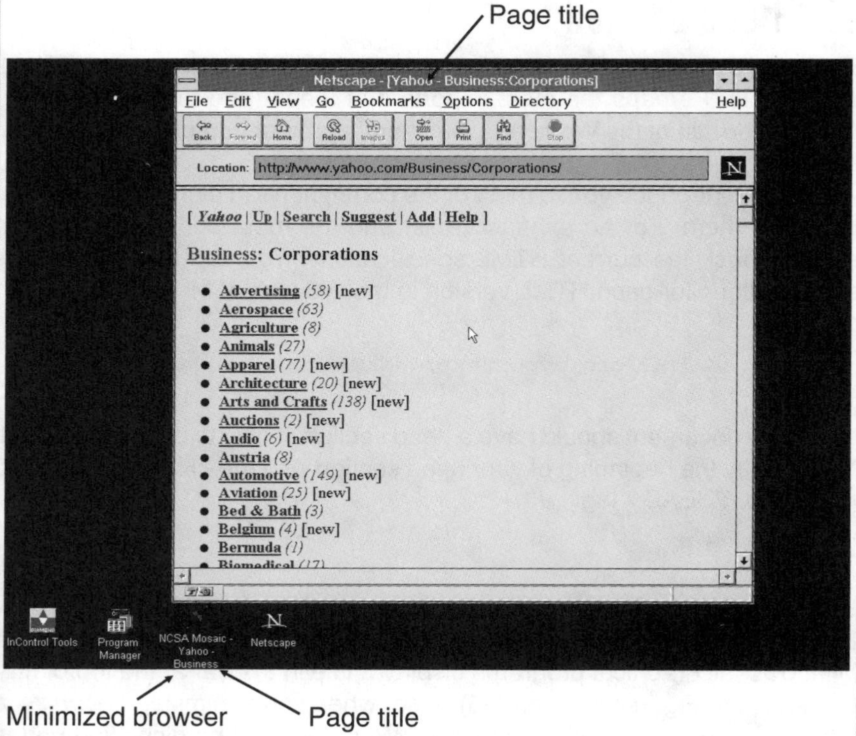

FIGURE 8-2. *Netscape running under Windows 3.1. Mosaic is minimized*

Page title

Minimized browser

Page title

A Little about Anchors

Anchors put the hypertext into HTML. They're the tools you use to reference other HTML documents, other locations in the same document, and other external files, such as image files and audio/video clips. We will leave most of the discussion about anchors and links to Chapter 11, because they are actually body elements—not head elements. But you need to know just a little about anchors for the discussion here about head elements.

An anchor tag is similar in some respects to the tags you've learned about so far. The <HTML>, <HEAD>, and <TITLE> tags all refer to text that follows them, and each is terminated with a terminating tag (such as </TITLE> or </HEAD>). An anchor element also begins with the tag itself, refers to the text that immediately follows it, and ends with a terminator. However, since an anchor element defines a hypertext hot-spot, it needs an additional piece of information besides the text that

FIGURE 8-3.

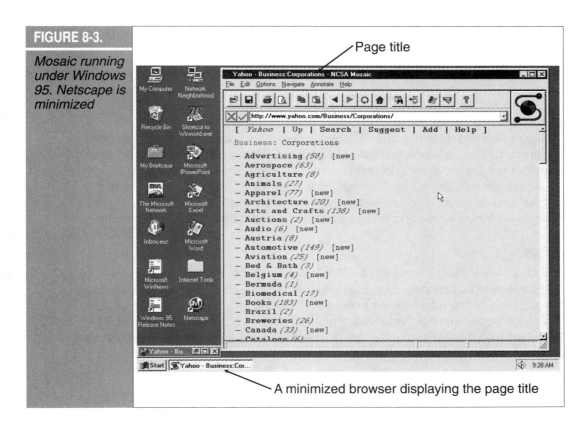

Mosaic running under Windows 95. Netscape is minimized

Page title

A minimized browser displaying the page title

will form the hot-spot—you have to supply the address of the document to which the anchor refers.

You place the reference inside the anchor tag itself. For example, the format of an anchor tag looks like this:

```
<A (address of the linked document)>The text that browsers will
display</A>
```

Anchors have several uses, one of which is to reference other documents. And for each of these uses, the anchor tag may need a different kind of information where we have included a page address here for a hypertext link. The information you insert in an anchor tag (the text enclosed in parentheses in the example above) is called the anchor *attribute*. An anchor that references another document is called an *HREF anchor* because the attribute for a hypertext link anchor starts off with the characters HREF (for *Hypertext REFerence*). For example, an anchor tag that creates a link to another Web page looks like this:

```
<A HREF="http://www.myhost.com/homepage.html">My Home Page</A>
```

This anchor will display the text "My Home Page" on a Web browser as a hot-spot. (Some browsers display hot-spots as colored text; others display them as underlined text or even 3-D elevated text that looks like a button.) When a reader clicks this hot-spot, the browser will retrieve the document referred to by the HREF attribute.

Again, anchors are not head elements (they are body elements), but we wanted to give you a basic introduction to them here so that you would have some background for understanding the Link and Base elements, which we will look at next.

Links

The Link element has been part of HTML since the beginning, but with HTML 3, it has some new functionality. The original purpose of the Link element was to allow the author to define relationships between HTML documents, such as to associate other Web pages with the "Next" and "Previous" buttons on Web browsers. In HTML 3, you will also be able to use the Link element to define a page banner that will be fixed in position even as readers scroll through the content of the page. Such a banner might be used for company logos or legal disclaimers. The other major new function of the Link element is to attach a style sheet to a document. In this section, we will look at using the Link element for both banners and style sheets. Our look at these types of links will be brief because, as of yet, no browsers support banners, and the method that will ultimately be used to implement style sheets (beyond assigning them with the Link element) is still uncertain.

The tag for a Link element is <LINK>, and the Link element is called an *empty* element because it doesn't sandwich any text between an opening tag and a terminator. A Link element doesn't have a terminator because it doesn't need to create any hot-spot text on the face of a Web page. Links generally apply to an entire document, which is why they are head elements.

Document Relationships

The attribute for defining relationships is *REL*, and you can define several types of relationships with it. As we mentioned above, you can define other Web pages to be the "Next" and "Previous" pages for a browser's toolbar, which a reader can use for a guided tour of some subject matter. There are other relationships as well, including pages to go to when a reader clicks on a "Home" or "Help" button. When

the Link element is fully supported, you will also be able to create document-specific toolbars. For example, each individual page you publish can have its own custom toolbar at the top. The toolbar could contain buttons for going directly to the next or previous document as well as to custom help screens, a home page, a table of contents, an index, and other places. Most people who publish large webs of pages build these links into the body of their documents with conventional HREF anchors. Unfortunately, the ability to create a custom toolbar with buttons that stay put instead of hypertext links that scroll with the text of the page is a great facility that few browsers implement. Hopefully, software developers who write Web browsers will wake up to this feature of HTML.

Although few browsers support HTML 3 links at this point, here's what a typical head section that defines some relationships might look like:

```
<HEAD>
<TITLE>Product Information Page</TITLE>
<LINK REL=Previous HREF="CompanyInfo.html">
<LINK REL=Next HREF="OrderForm.html">
<LINK REL=Home HREF="Homepage.html">
</HEAD>
```

The Link elements in this sample head section define documents for the "Next," "Previous," and "Home" buttons on a toolbar.

Banners

With HTML 3, you can also use a Link element to define a *banner* for your document. A banner is a fixed part of the page that will stay on the screen even when you scroll down through the text of the page. The HTML 3 specification suggests that this will be used for company logos and disclaimers, but we're betting that creative people will think of many more uses for banners. In fact, banners may negate, to some extent, the motivation for software developers to implement custom toolbars with the Link REL attribute.

NOTE *Another body element (the <BANNER> tag) can implement a banner from the body of a page. However, we don't think placing a banner in the body section is very intuitive because a banner is a component of a whole page; it is not associated with the textual content of the body section. Moreover, if you define a banner with the <LINK> tag in the head section, you define it by referencing another HTML document. This means you can share a single common banner among many different documents.*

To define a banner in the head section, use the <LINK> tag like this:

```
<LINK REL=Banner HREF=banner.html>
```

This tag defines a banner for a page. The banner itself is defined in a separate file named *banner.html.*

Style Sheets

Today, some Web browsers will allow you to customize the appearance of the pages you read with the browser by changing the associations between body elements (such as heading levels and addresses) and the native display fonts on your computer. The trouble with this is that your changes only affect your own system, and the authors of the pages you read have no control over what you see. For example, say a company puts a copyright notice or an admonishment on a banner in the pages they publish and, for some legal reason, that this message should always be displayed in a particular font. If you've changed the font on your own system for the admonishment element, you will see that message in a different font from the one the author intended.

One of the most celebrated enhancements of HTML 3 is the introduction of style sheets. Although the specification for style sheets isn't settled at the time of this writing, it probably will be soon. You will use the Link element to implement style sheets with HTML 3. The definitions of style sheets reside in files that are external to your HTML document. The format for style-sheet specifications isn't settled yet either, but they will most likely use a format called DSSSL (*Document Style Semantics and Specification Language*), or a scaled-down version of DSSSL called *DSSSL-Lite*.

You will be able to declare a style sheet in two ways. One way will be to use an attribute of the Link element. Here's what a style-sheet declaration with a Link element will look like:

```
<LINK REL=StyleSheet HREF="inhouse.dsssl">
```

The other way will be to use another head element called a Style element. Here's what a Style element declaration will look like:

```
<STYLE NOTATION="inhouse.dsssl">
```

Declaring a style sheet this way will require a terminating tag:

```
</STYLE>
```

When you point your HTML 3 browser at a Web page that includes a style-sheet declaration, it will first load the referenced style sheet so that it can render the page the way the author intended. Style-sheet declarations will override any local font changes you have made in your browser's setup or options screen.

Like the other Link elements we've looked at here, style-sheet declarations are head elements, but they can also be *cascaded*, or temporarily changed, at any point in a document simply by putting another style-sheet declaration in the body section of your document at the point where you want the style to change.

When browsers that support HTML 3 style sheets arrive, you can be sure the event will be accompanied by much fanfare.

Base

With the Base element, you can define a starting point for all the HREF tags that will follow. This will be useful if someone someday reads your page out of its original context. For example, say that you incorporate into your HTML document some graphics and links to other pages, and these graphics and pages physically reside in the same directory as the page itself. If you should ever move the document, or if people download it to read it locally on their own computer, the references to the graphics and other pages won't be valid anymore because the referenced pages and graphics are on your computer—not theirs.

By setting the Base element, you eliminate that problem. The Base element points to the final resting spot of your HTML document, so relative addresses remain intact. For example, say your document has a link that points to an image file named *BLUEDOT.GIF*. That file resides in a subdirectory named *IMAGES*, which is below the directory the document is in. The relative address of the image is

```
IMAGES/BLUEDOT.GIF
```

If people download this document and read it locally on their own machines, it's unlikely that they will have an image file named *BLUEDOT.GIF* sitting in a directory named *IMAGES* directly under the directory they put your HTML document into. When the browser renders the page, it won't be able to find and display the image.

You can solve this problem by defining a Base element for your page. The Base element is, in effect, simply an absolute reference to your HTML document. After you define the Base element, references to other files, such as pages and images, can be in relative format and will work properly even if they are read out of context. To continue the previous example, if someone reads your document out of context, with a Base element pointing at the original location of the document, their browser will know to go back to that original location to find the subdirectory *IMAGES* with the file *BLUEDOT.GIF*. The <BASE HREF> tag in the following code segment shows how you define a Base element:

```
<HTML>
<HEAD>
<TITLE>The Home of Pete's Online Rare Lizard Emporium</TITLE>
<BASE HREF="http://www.myhost.com/homepage.html" >
</HEAD>
```

This Base element tells browsers that any future relative addresses in the document are relative to the original location of this file—namely the root Web directory on the computer "www.myhost.com." So a reference such as

```
<IMG SRC="IMAGES/BLUEDOT.GIF">
```

will resolve to

```
<IMG SRC="http://www.myhost.com/IMAGES/BLUEDOT.GIF">
```

Isindex

The Isindex element tells Web browsers that a page is a *searchable index document*. A searchable index document is an interactive page that allows readers to enter some criteria and search a database. Of course, this only works if the Web server you use has a search engine. (We'll look more at Web servers in Chapter 16.) If your server does have a search engine, you can make your pages interactive by getting keywords from readers, searching a database, and presenting your readers with the results of their searches. The syntax for the <ISINDEX> tag works like this:

```
<ISINDEX HREF="reptiles.db" PROMPT="What kind of reptile are
you interested in?">
```

The parameter to the HREF attribute describes the database to search, and the PROMPT attribute is the text, or prompt, that the reader will see next to an edit box.

This Isindex element will create an edit box on your page, like the one shown in Figure 8-4 (if you view the document with Netscape) or Figure 8-5 (if you view it with Mosaic). Your readers can use the search engine by typing keywords into the edit box and pressing the ENTER key. Their Web browser will submit a query to a database named (in this case) reptiles.db.

FIGURE 8-4.

Netscape's Isindex element edit box

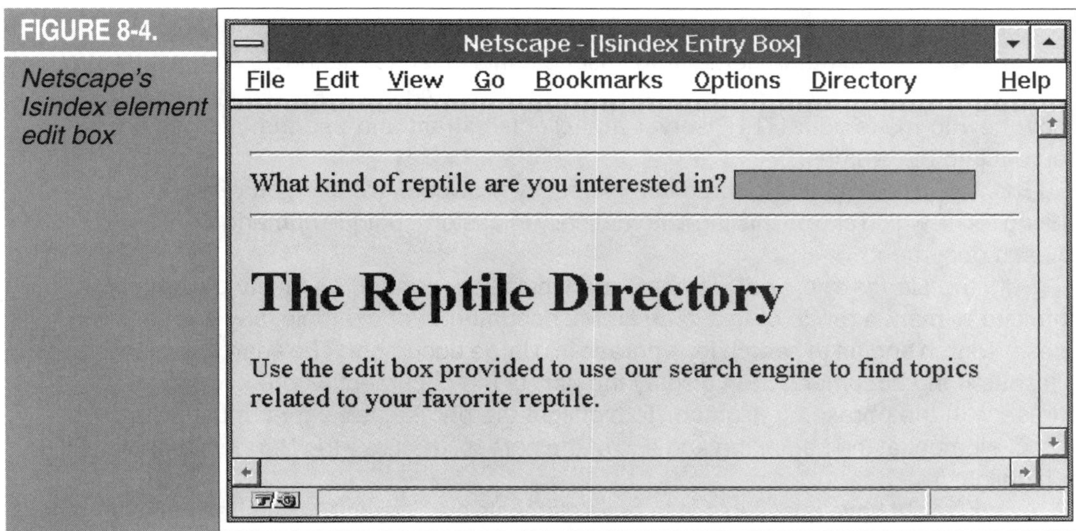

Most of the time, Isindex is actually in HTML code that is generated on the fly by a Web server. Ordinarily, you won't create an HTML document by hand where you would manually enter an <ISINDEX> tag. We'll take a closer look at Web servers and search engines in Part III.

Other Head Elements

Of the head elements we've introduced you to here, by far the most important are the Title and Base elements. However, there are a few other head elements that you might run into on occasion. These are the Meta, NextID, Range, and Spot elements.

FIGURE 8-5.

Mosaic's Isindex element edit box

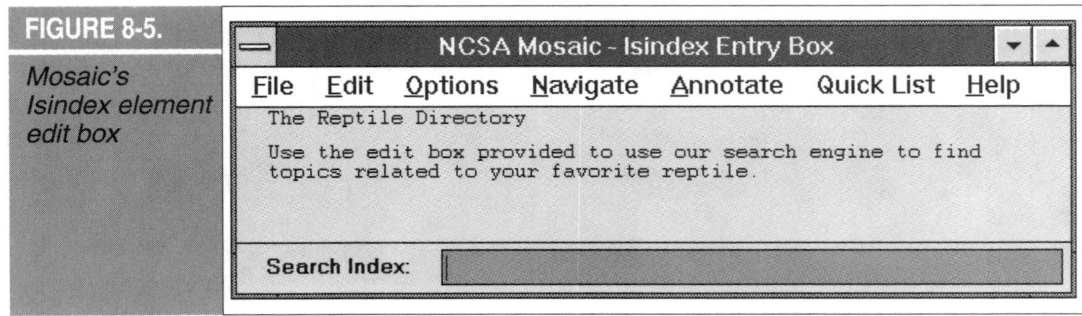

The *Meta* element allows you to embed information into your HTML document for which there is no other element. In essence, this is a user-definable element. If you use the Meta element to define some piece of information, presumably you will know how to make your HTTP server and clients extract and use the information you put into the element.

The *NextID* element is ignored completely by browsers. It's used only by HTML editing tools, which create this tag automatically to assign a unique numeric identifier to each document.

Both the *Range* and *Spot* elements are typically generated on the fly by server software to mark a range of text in an HTML document. For example, say a reader uses a search engine to search for a phrase in a large document. The search engine will search the document, then display the part of the document where it found the phrase with the phrase highlighted. To highlight the phrase, the server must insert a Spot element at the beginning and end of the phrase, then use the Range element to highlight it.

As you might have guessed, these head elements aren't exactly mainstream tools that you will need to use right away. In fact, you may never need them at all. If you ever do, check the current HTML specification for the latest information on them.

Chapter 9

Formatting Text and Displaying Special Characters

In this chapter, we will learn about the HTML elements that you can use in your documents to define the way browsers will render your text. You will also learn how to apply special attributes to your text, such as bold and italics, and how to represent special characters in your documents.

Formatting Text

If you've read the preceding chapters, you may already understand the dichotomy in the concept of formatting text in HTML. It's important to understand this contradiction because it is the reason HTML authors don't have complete control over the way Web browsers will display their documents. HTML is one of the markup languages defined by the *Standard Generalized Markup Language*, or *SGML*. SGML is the ISO standard for describing how different types of documents look with respect to things like typefaces and fonts.

From the viewpoint of SGML, an HTML document is simply one particular document type (a hypertext document) among many other *Document Type Definitions* (or *DTDs*). Therefore, the typefaces and fonts for each component of an HTML document are already defined. How Web browsers render a document depends on the capabilities of the browser itself and the particular computer it runs on. This device independence was one of the primary goals of SGML.

But due to the explosion and popularity of the first real-world application of SGML—the World Wide Web—publishers find that they want more control over the way their documents are rendered. To some extent with style sheets in HTML 3, and probably to a larger extent in future HTML versions, publishers are getting that greater level of control. But since most of the browsers don't yet support style sheets, we have to work with what we have.

What we have now is a system that isn't very elegant, but for the most part, you can use the building blocks of HTML to produce pages that most browsers will render in a way that is close to what you want.

We're going to look at these building blocks in this chapter. Both the good and bad news is that you really don't have very many choices. This is good because it's easy to learn and remember your options. Of course, it's not so great because you don't have much flexibility in how you format the content of your pages.

Headings

A heading is a word or phrase that is highlighted in some way to indicate the title of a section of text. The term *heading* is pretty standard throughout the publishing world. For example, the heading for this section of text is "Headings."

HTML provides for six heading levels. The theory is that first-order heads are the most prominent, and each successive head is slightly less prominent in some way. Here's how the DTD for HTML 2 suggests browsers render headings:

- Level 1 Heads: Bold, very large font, centered. One or two blank lines above and below.
- Level 2 Heads: Bold, large font, flush left. One or two blank lines above and below.
- Level 3 Heads: Italic, large font, slightly indented from the left margin. One or two blank lines above and below.
- Level 4 Heads: Bold, normal font, indented more than a 3 head. One blank line above and below.
- Level 5 Heads: Italic, normal font, indented as a 4 head. One blank line above.
- Level 6 Heads: Bold, indented same as normal text, more than a 5 head. One blank line above.

In practice, though, browsers almost universally render headings flush left. And most of them don't implement the italic typefaces suggested for level 3 and level 5 heads.

NOTE *The programmers who write the browsers that we use to read Web pages tend to interpret HTML specifications differently. That's the case not only with headings, but with every element of HTML. This is why the same page won't always look the same in every browser you use to view it and why, when you develop Web pages, you should always check your work with several different browsers to make sure you get the result you want.*

You specify a heading in your text with the <H*x*> tag, where *x* is the head level, and you terminate the heading tag in the usual way. For example, to make browsers display the text "The Dinosaur Detour" as a level 1 head, you would do this:

```
<H1>The Dinosaur Detour</H1>
```

Figures 9-1, 9-2, and 9-3 show what each heading looks like with three different browsers running under Microsoft Windows. The browsers are Netscape, the W3 organization's testbed browser Arena, and WinWeb, respectively.

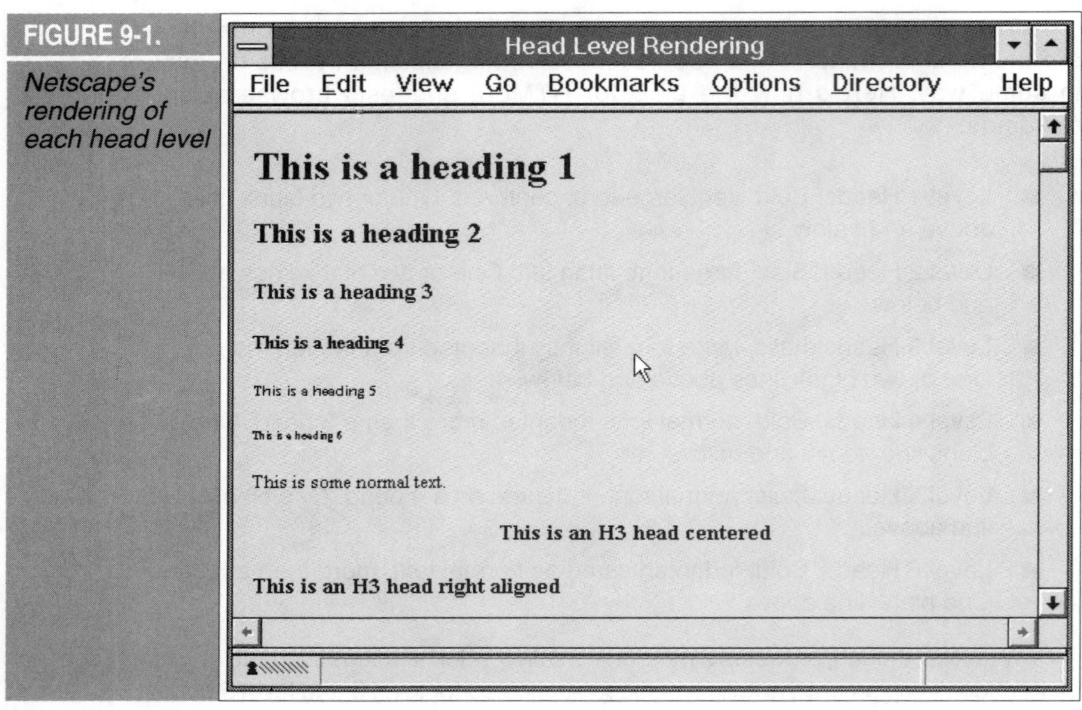

FIGURE 9-1. *Netscape's rendering of each head level*

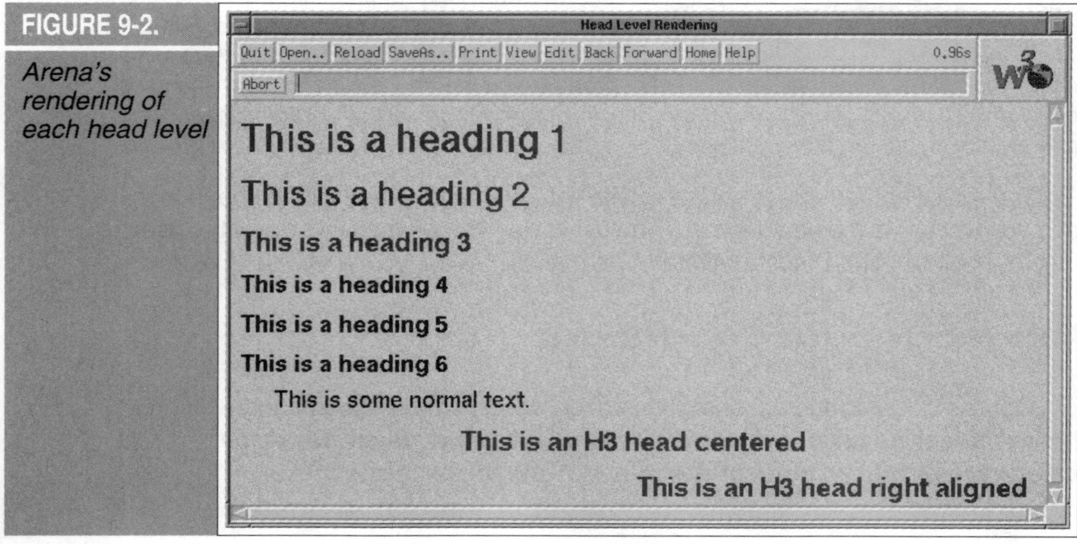

Head Level Rendering
Quit Open.. Reload SaveAs.. Print View Edit Back Forward Home Help 0.96s
Abort
This is a heading 1
This is a heading 2
This is a heading 3
This is a heading 4
This is a heading 5
This is a heading 6
This is some normal text.
This is an H3 head centered
This is an H3 head right aligned

FIGURE 9-2. *Arena's rendering of each head level*

FIGURE 9-3.

WinWeb's rendering of each head level

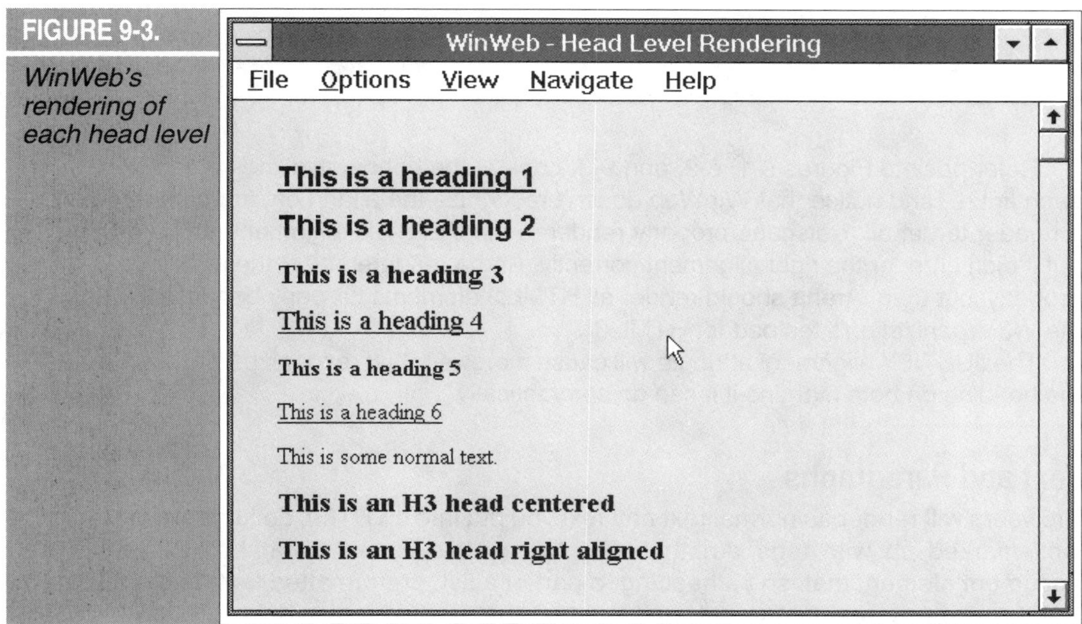

Notice that none of these browsers implement the HTML specification's suggestions for rendering heads exactly. Netscape relies most heavily on different font sizes to distinguish between heads. WinWeb renders 1, 4, and 6 heads underlined. Notice that, by default, NCSA Mosaic doesn't distinguish between head levels at all. This is because Mosaic leaves determination of the typefaces and fonts for every document element up to the users—they must go into a preferences screen and assign the characteristics they want for each element.

With HTML 3, you can use the ALIGN attribute to specify the horizontal alignment of headings. Valid alignments are:

- Left
- Center
- Right
- Justify

Include the ALIGN attribute with the opening header:

```
<H3 ALIGN=right>This is right aligned</H3>
```

or

```
<H3 ALIGN=center>This is a centered heading</H3>
```

Refer back to Figures 9-1, 9-2, and 9-3. Look at the bottom two lines of text in each figure, and notice that WinWeb doesn't recognize the alignment attribute for a header tag at all. Netscape properly rendered the CENTER alignment attribute, but it didn't render the right alignment correctly. Arena rendered all of the headings properly, but then, Arena should render all HTML 3 elements properly because it's the W3 organization's testbed for HTML 3.

The JUSTIFY alignment attribute will cause a browser that recognizes it to align the heading on both margins if it can do so practically.

Text and Paragraphs

Browsers will render as normal text any text you put into an HTML document that isn't marked up with tags. Another way to say this is that normal text is a document element that isn't a heading, a part of a list, preformatted text, and so on. As with any real document, units of text that should logically be grouped together are called *paragraphs*.

Most browsers render normal text flush left and wrap the text to the next line at a white-space character (a space or a tab) where necessary to fit each line in the window in which they are displaying the text. A few browsers indent the first line of paragraphs, but most render paragraphs as blocks of text that are aligned on the left margin.

The Paragraph Element

The original concept of the paragraph in HTML was that paragraphs should be enclosed by beginning and terminating tags—the beginning tag is <P>, and the terminator is </P>. However, in practice this proved to be redundant and unnecessary. For example, here is the HTML code for a sequence of four paragraphs:

```
<P>This is the beginning of a paragraph of normal text. This paragraph
will be terminated with a tag to mark the end of the paragraph.</P>
<P>This is a second paragraph of text.</P> <P>And this is a third
paragraph.</P>
<P>And finally, this is the fourth paragraph.</P>
```

Here's what this text looks like when it's displayed with a browser:

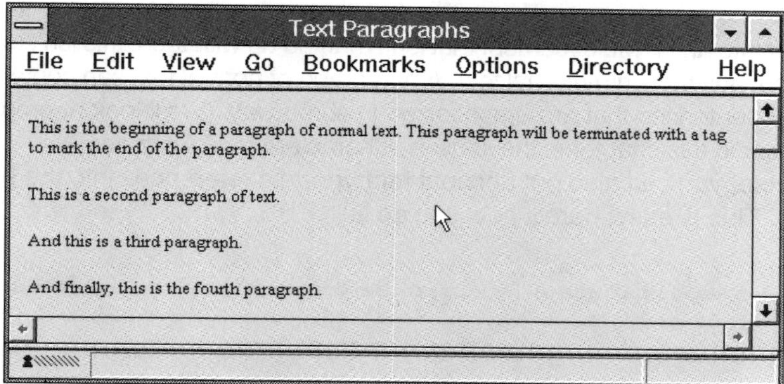

Notice that the tags separating each paragraph are always both the terminating </P> tag and the <P> tag that marks the beginning of the next paragraph. Instead of doing this, it's easier to visualize and more productive if you use a single paragraph tag (the <P>) to separate paragraphs. Virtually every browser looks at the <P> tag as a signal to insert a blank line and begin a new paragraph, and ignores the </P> altogether.

There is something else to take note of in this example. First, notice that the third paragraph starts on the same line that the second ends on. As you can see, it doesn't matter to the browser where in a line you begin a paragraph—the <P> tag always marks the beginning of the new paragraph. However, it's much easier to read and maintain your HTML code if you put a blank line between your paragraphs. Thus, you can rewrite these paragraphs to look like this:

```
<P>This is the beginning of a paragraph of normal text. This paragraph
will not be terminated with a tag to mark the end of the paragraph.

<P>This is a second paragraph of text.

<P>And this is a third paragraph.

<P>And finally, this is the fourth paragraph.
```

Your browser will render this page identically to the example you just saw, and it's easier to read the HTML when you separate your paragraphs with a blank line.

Including Elements Within Normal Text

Although we began this section by saying that browsers will render as normal text any text you put into an HTML document that isn't marked up with tags, this isn't to say that you can't put any tags into normal text. A paragraph of normal text can contain words, phrases, or sentences that are emphasized in some way. (We'll look at emphasizing your text later in this chapter in the section "Character-Level Attributes.")

Of course, you can also put anchors for hypertext references into the body of a paragraph. This is easy; here's how you do it:

```
<P>You can easily place a hypertext reference anywhere in the middle
of a block of text. To do so, just <A HREF="page2.htm">sandwich</A> the
text of your hot-spot between the beginning and ending tags.
```

Here's how a browser will display this paragraph:

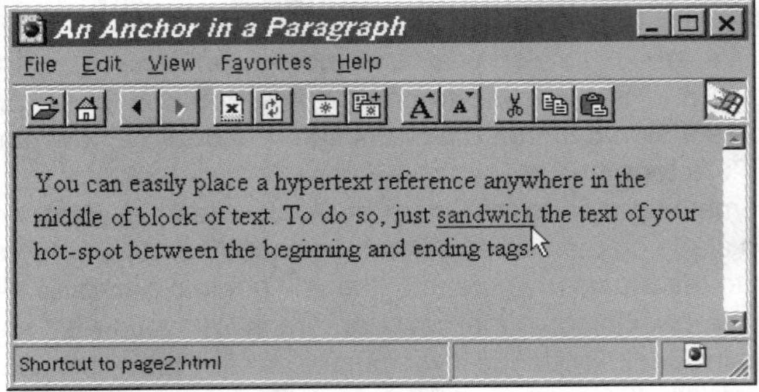

This particular browser highlights the hot-spot by displaying it in blue and underlining it.

Line Breaks and Nonbreaking Spaces

Sometimes you need a little more control over your text than you have with paragraphs alone. Since browsers decide where to break lines of normal text based on the size of the window, this leaves you with a lack of control in two ways: sometimes you want to break a line before a browser would break it regardless of window size, and once in a while you may want to make sure a line isn't broken at all. The line-break element and nonbreaking-space character solve these problems.

Breaking Lines

You can insert a line break at any point in your text with the line-break (<BR>) tag. The difference between a line break and a paragraph tag is that the line-break tag

wraps the following text down to the next line, while a paragraph tag leaves more space (a blank line) between the tag and the following text. For instance:

```
Tickets are available at Dodger Stadium at:<P>
Dodger Stadium<BR>
1000 Elysian Park Avenue<BR>
Los Angeles, CA<P>
```

The first line of this code is followed by a paragraph tag. The next two lines (the first two lines of the address) are followed by <BR> tags. When a browser renders this code, it looks like this:

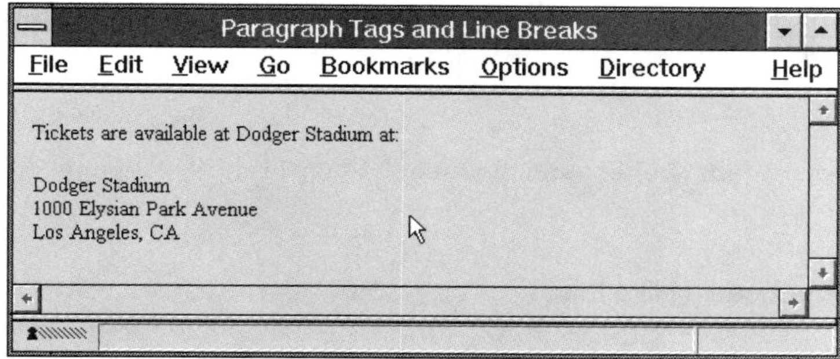

Notice that the paragraph mark at the end of the first line causes the browser to skip an entire line, but the line breaks at the end of the first two lines of the address cause the browser to wrap to the left margin without leaving any blank lines. You can use the line-break tag within any HTML element, including headings and special elements such as the address element.

Netscape has added an additional tag that you can use to suggest where to break a line if it needs to be broken. The tag is <WBR>. This tag isn't in the HTML specifications, but it could be in the future. Right now, it only works with Netscape browsers.

Preventing Line Breaks

Occasionally, you may want to make sure a browser doesn't break a line where it normally would. For example, say you want the main heading of your page to display the name of your company without breaking it, even if the reader's browser is displaying a very narrow page. To do this, rather than using the regular space character between the words of the heading, you use a special nonbreaking-space character. The nonbreaking space isn't really a single character in the HTML code, although it looks like a normal space when it's rendered. And a nonbreaking space isn't a typical tag, either.

You signify a nonbreaking space with a type of markup code you haven't seen yet, called an *entity*. Entities represent special characters that are otherwise difficult to represent in HTML codes, either because they aren't normal ASCII characters or because they need special interpretation by browsers. This is the case with the nonbreaking space—it tells browsers to display a normal space character, but that they can't break the line there.

Entities have the format *"&xxxx;"* where "*xxxx*" is a string of characters to identify the particular entity. The code for a nonbreaking space is *" "*.

Let's say the name of your company is "North American Washer and Household Appliance Company" and that for some reason (perhaps the name is part of a legal trademark that must be displayed just so) you don't want browsers to wrap the name. So instead of

```
<H1>
North American Washer and Household Appliance Company
</H1>
```

you code your heading like this:

```
<H1>
North American Washer and Household 
Appliance 
Company</H1>
```

Be careful if you want to use the nonbreaking-space entity. Even though this entity has been around awhile, some of the most popular browsers still don't support it. Hopefully this will change in future releases.

Netscape has also added an element to prevent line breaks. Rather than specifying nonbreaking-space characters with a special entity, you can mark the beginning of a section of text that shouldn't be broken with the <NOBR> tag and terminate it with the </NOBR> tag. Like the <WBR> tag, these tags aren't part of the HTML specification, but they do work with Netscape browsers.

Horizontal Tabs

If you put tab characters (ASCII 9) directly into an HTML document, browsers will simply ignore them. Tabs are new with Level 3, so be aware that if you use

them, not every browser will be able to display them. You can use tabs in a document in two ways; both are equally acceptable.

The first way you can use tabs is to define them and give them names. You define a tab relative to some other text in your document above the place where you want to use that tab. For example, say that you want to set a tab in about an inch from the left margin. First you find a line of text (or a heading, or whatever) in your document that extends beyond the point where you want to set the tab. Then you pick a character in that line where you want your tab to be, move your cursor to that character, and insert the defining tab tag.

Assume that you have the following line of text in a document:

```
<P>Here's a list of my favorite spots on the Web:<P>
```

and you have looked at your document in a browser and decided that the tab you want to use should be at the same place as the character "s" in the word "list." To define and name that tag, you insert the <tab> tag into that line:

```
<P>Here's a li<tab id=tab1>st of my favorite spots on the Web:<P>
```

It's ugly, but it works. This defines a tab named "tab1" at the beginning point for the letter "s" in the word "list." Keep in mind that the tab will be where a browser renders that letter, not where it is in the related HTML code. A browser will start the word "Here's" at the left margin, but in the HTML code the characters are actually farther to the right because of the <P> tag at the beginning of the line. Also, proportionally spaced fonts might cause letters to be somewhere other than where you expect them.

To use *tab1*, you use the <tab> tag again, but with a different attribute:

```
<tab to=tab1>The Internet Shopping Network
```

This tag will cause the text "The Internet Shopping Network" to begin at the same point as the "s" in the word "list" where you defined *tab1*.

The other way to define a tab is to use the INDENT attribute to the <tab> element. The INDENT attribute takes a number that represents a number of *en units*. An en unit is a typographical unit equal to one-half of the current point size, or about one-half of the width of the letter "M" in any given font. For example:

```
<tab id=tab1 indent=8>
```

Rule Lines

A rule is a single horizontal line that you can use to separate logical sections of your documents. Figure 9-4 shows a page that uses rules liberally to make the text of the page easier to read. The tag for a rule line is <HR>, for *Horizontal Rule*. The rule-line tag has no terminator, and browsers will render rules at the point in a document where they encounter them. Browsers render a rule from the left margin to the right margin.

With HTML 3, you will eventually be able to specify an alternative image file for browsers to use instead of the default image, which is simply a horizontal line. For example, you will be able to design a stylized image and reference it in the rule tag with the SRC (source) attribute:

```
<HR SRC="fancyline.gif">
```

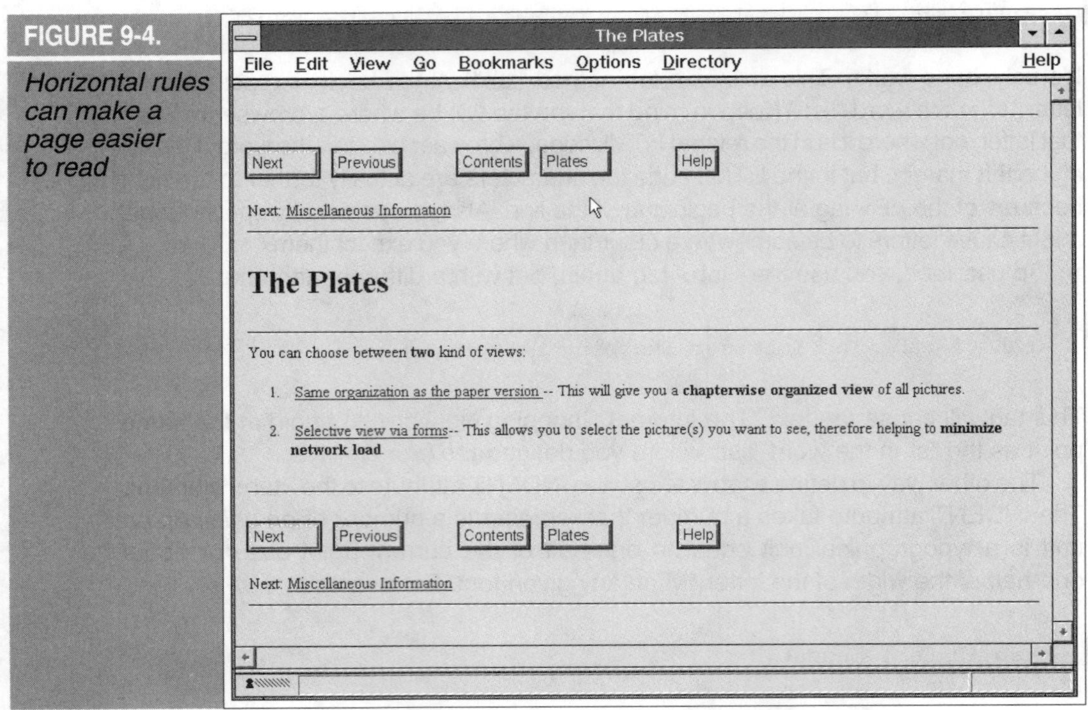

FIGURE 9-4. *Horizontal rules can make a page easier to read*

Referencing an alternative image file this way doesn't work yet with most browsers, but this feature is not far off.

Netscape has also introduced of couple of enhancements to horizontal rules. Newer versions of Netscape can display rules with different thicknesses and lengths. The SIZE attribute controls the thickness of the rule, and a WIDTH attribute controls the length of the rule. Figure 9-5 shows several examples.

A SIZE of 1 results in a solid black line, and larger values result in a 3-D effect. The width of a rule is specified as a percentage, with 100% being the default—from margin to margin.

NOTE *The 3-D effect of wide rules doesn't work particularly well on pages with custom backgrounds or a custom background color. For wide rules on these pages, you will probably want to use a custom image for the rule as well.*

Both of these enhancements are useful and will probably find their way into a future HTML specification.

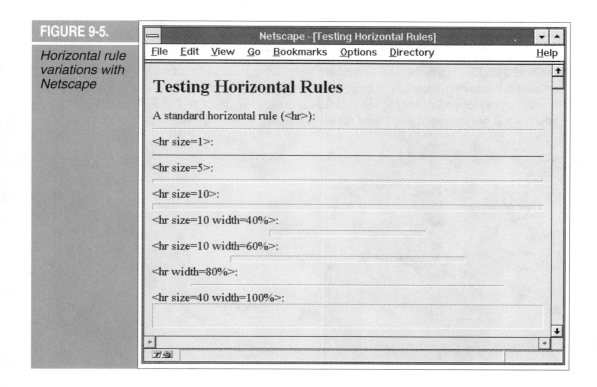

FIGURE 9-5. *Horizontal rule variations with Netscape*

Netscape - [Testing Horizontal Rules]

File Edit View Go Bookmarks Options Directory Help

Testing Horizontal Rules

A standard horizontal rule (<hr>):

<hr size=1>:

<hr size=5>:

<hr size=10>:

<hr size=10 width=40%>:

<hr size=10 width=60%>:

<hr width=80%>:

<hr size=40 width=100%>:

Lists

HTML defines three categories of list elements, with several variations and options for each:

- Unordered lists
- Ordered lists
- Definition lists

Before we go into the details of each of these list types, let's go over some of the basic properties of a list element. A list element has a start tag, where you might define some special options with an attribute; the line items in the list; and a terminating tag. Generically, the HTML code looks like this:

```
<start tag ATTRIBUTES>
<list line items>
<...>
<terminating tag>
```

You can also nest lists inside other lists.

UNORDERED LISTS Think of unordered lists as bulleted lists. Most browsers render them with a bullet mark, usually a heavy dot, on the left side of the list's line items. The opening tag for an unordered list is <UL>, and the terminator is </UL>. The <LI> tag marks the beginning of line items for all list types.

```
<H3>Agricultural Crops of Southern Arizona</H3>
<UL>
<LH>Field crops</LH>
<LI>Apples
<LI>Corn
<LI>Cotton
<LI>Wheat
</UL>
```

When a browser renders this list, here's what you get:

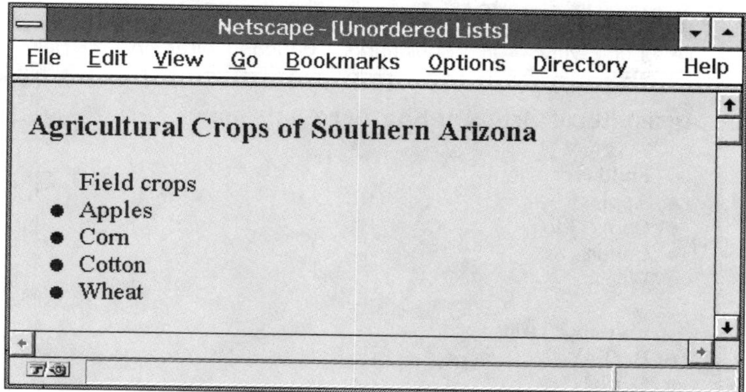

You can also include other elements in a list. The following list is separated into two sections—field crops and livestock crops. The sections are separated physically by the paragraph tag <P>, and each section has a list header element denoted by the <LH> tag and terminated with the </LH> tag.

```
<H3>Agricultural Crops of Southern Arizona</H3>
<UL>
<LH>Field crops</LH>
<LI>Apples
<LI>Corn
<LI>Cotton
<LI>Wheat
<P><LH>Livestock crops</LH>
<LI>Beef
<LI>Ostrich
<LI>Pork
</UL>
```

This code will produce this output:

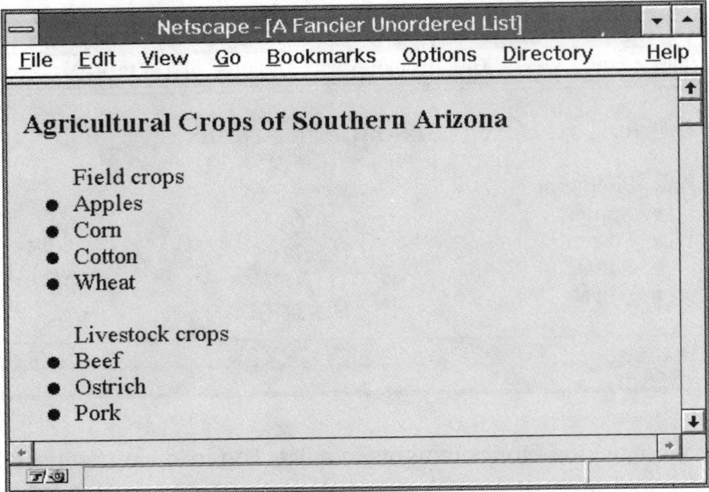

Of course, you can also split this list into two separate lists and get the same effect. This example just points out some of the flexibility you have with lists.

You can also change the bullet image that displays next to each line item in an unordered list. The default bullet is a heavy dot, but you can use the TYPE attribute with the <UL> tag to choose among a disc, a circle, and a square. For example:

```
<UL type=square>
```

Menu Lists

The menu list and the directory list (which we will look at next) have both been superseded in HTML 3 by variations on the standard unordered list. A menu list is for relatively short line items, and browsers display it indented slightly more than a normal unordered list. Most browsers display menu lists without any bullets. The old-style tag format for a menu list is:

```
<MENU>
<LI>Microsoft: Word for Windows
<LI>Novell: WordPerfect for Windows
<LI>Lotus Development: Word Pro
</MENU>
```

In HTML 3, there is no menu list. Instead, you use an unordered list, and you use the PLAIN attribute to remove the bullets. Thus, the HTML 3 code for the same list looks like this:

```
<UL PLAIN>
<LI>Microsoft: Word for Windows
<LI>Novell: WordPerfect for Windows
<LI>Lotus Development: Word Pro
</UL>
```

Directory Lists

Directory lists are for lists of items that each have 20 or fewer characters. The intent of the directory list is to display the list items in columns the way the Unix command **ls -c** or the MS-DOS command **dir/w** lists the contents of a disk directory in columns. However, few browsers ever supported the directory list element. They just treat a directory list as a normal unordered list. For the sake of completeness, here's an example of the old-style (and seldom supported) HTML code for a directory list:

```
<DIR>
<LI>files
<LI>mail
<LI>programs
</DIR>
```

Although the directory list is obsolete, HTML 3 does provide a way to display a list of short line items in a columnar format. As with the menu list, you use a special attribute to the standard unordered list. Actually, you give it two attributes. The first is the same PLAIN attribute that you use with the menu list. The second is WRAP=HORIZ. Thus, the Level 3 version of the list will look like this:

```
<UL PLAIN WRAP=HORIZ>
<LI>files
<LI>mail
<LI>programs
</UL>
```

It remains to be seen how many browsers will ultimately implement the directory list. Use it cautiously, and remember that browsers that don't render the directory list correctly will treat it as a normal, vertical unordered list.

ORDERED LISTS An *ordered list* is one where the line items are numbered. An ordered list has the characteristics of an unordered list in virtually every respect except that instead of bullets, it displays numbers for each line item. The tag for an ordered list is <OL>. Here's an example:

```
<OL>
<LH>Follow this procedure to install the software.
<LI>Insert the diskette into the floppy drive and close the door.
<LI>Choose <I>File¦Run</I> from the main menu.
<LI>Type &quot;a:setup&quot; in the edit box.
<LI>Press return or click the <B>OK</B> button.
</OL>
```

Here's what it looks like when a browser renders it:

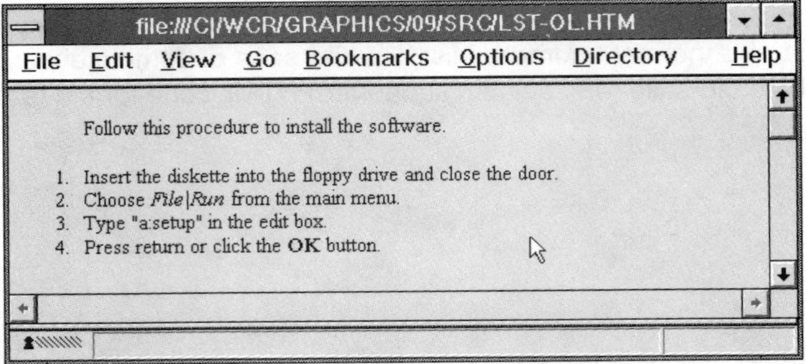

With HTML 3, you can begin the numbering sequence of an ordered list at any number you like. Of course, numbering begins with 1 by default; if you want to start your list at another number, just use the SEQNUM attribute to the <OL> tag. For example:

```
<OL SEQNUM=11>
```

As with other new HTML 3 features, this may not work with some browsers yet.

DEFINITION LISTS A *definition list* (sometimes called a *glossary list*) is a special list for defining terms. Definition-list line items have two parts:

- The word or term to be defined
- The definition of the word or term

You begin a definition list with a <DL> tag and terminate it in the usual way, with a </DL> tag.

Since the line items in a definition list have two components, you need to identify them separately. Definition lists use two tags, where the other lists use the single <LI> tag: You identify the word or term to be defined with a <DT> tag (for *definition term*) and the definition with a <DD> tag.

Most browsers render the terms to be defined on a line by themselves, then drop down and indent the definition. For example:

```
<DL>
<DT>Modem <DD>A device for converting a digital data stream into audio
signals that can be transmitted over a telephone line.
<DT>Monitor <DD>A computer's display device. The main output device for
most computers.<DT>Mosaic<DD>A computer program written by students at the
University of Illinois for reading HTML documents on the World Wide Web.
</DL>
```

Most browsers will render this code in a way that looks like a typical book glossary:

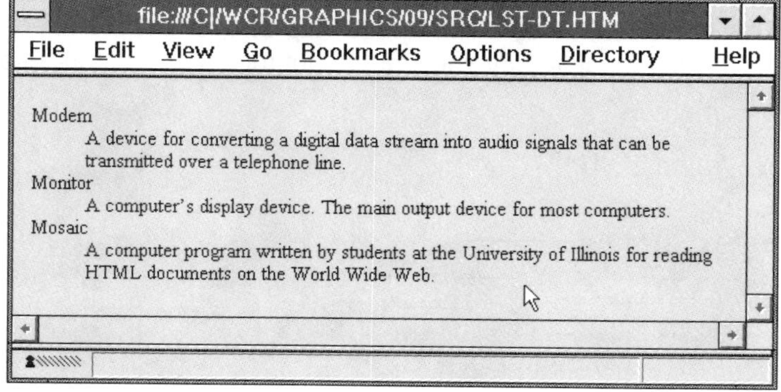

Notice that it doesn't matter where you begin a term or a definition. The browser will properly format the output as it encounters each tag. Of course, you can clean up your code considerably to make it easier to read and maintain. Browsers won't complain if you indent with tabs or spaces. Clearly, this is easier to read:

```
<DL>
<DT>Modem
    <DD>   A device for converting a digital data stream into audio
           signals that can be transmitted over a telephone line.
<DT>Monitor
    <DD>   A computer's display device. The main output device for
           most computers.
<DT>Mosaic
    <DD>   A computer program written by students at the University of
           Illinois for reading HTML documents on the World Wide Web.
</DL>
```

Preformatted Text

Sometimes you want to make sure that browsers render some text exactly the way it appears in your HTML code, preventing any line breaks or use of special fonts. Text that this might apply to includes ASCII art, poems for which you want each stanza to be intact, tables of numbers, or any document for which you want to preserve the existing formatting.

For this job, you use the <PRE> tag and its corresponding terminator </PRE>. Browsers render the text following a <PRE> tag exactly as it appears in your HTML document. This means that they also have to display this text in a fixed-space font such as Courier. For example, say you want to put this ASCII picture of an airplane onto a page:

```
           _____
  ¦        ¦ ___\          /~~~¦
 _:________¦/'(..)`\______/  ¦ ¦
<_¦ ``````  \__~~__/ USAF ___¦_¦
  :\_____(=========,(*),-\__¦_/
  ¦       \       /--'
           ¦ (*) /  Mustangs
           ¦____/   Forever
```

Without the <PRE> and </PRE> tags, browsers would destroy this picture because they treat the space character and tabs symbolically rather than literally.

The <PRE> element tells them to treat white-space characters literally and preserve all existing characters and lines exactly.

To use the <PRE> tags, just put the opening tag before your preformatted text and the terminator immediately after it.

```
<PRE>

             _____
   ¦        ¦ ____\          /~~~¦
  _:________¦/'(..)'\________/  ¦ ¦
 <_¦'''''''  \__~~__/  USAF ____ ¦_¦
   :\______(=========,(*),-\__¦_/
   ¦       \       /---'
            ¦ (*) /  Mustangs
            ¦____/   Forever
</PRE>
```

Here's how it will look in browsers:

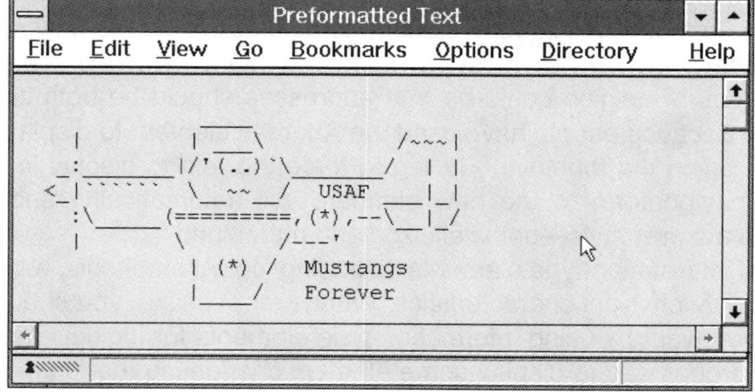

Character-Level Attributes

So far in this chapter we have looked at HTML elements that describe the general formatting of text. HTML also has facilities for you to add character-level attributes to any text in your document, including headings, paragraphs, anchors, and text in lists. By *character-level attributes*, we mean any special formatting you might want to apply to a sentence, phrase, word, or even a single character.

Generally, there are two categories of character formatting elements: *font-style elements* and *information-type elements*. These are also called *physical formatting elements* and *logical formatting elements*, respectively.

A font-style element is an attribute you might want to assign to any type of text regardless of its basic element type. For example, you might want to make a particular word or phrase in a paragraph show up in italics or bold. A few of the font-style elements are:

- Boldface
- Italics
- Underlined

An information-type element is different in that, while it might look like normal text that has an attribute assigned (italics, for example), it is actually an elemental type of text on its own. For example, the Address element looks just like normal text with italics applied to it, but it is actually an element. One reason for using information-type elements is that if you define these elements separately, future HTML specifications and browsers can change the way browsers render these elements without affecting other text.

For example, as the Address element is defined today, the only special thing about it is that it displays on most browsers in an italic font. Two years from now, the consensus of opinion could be that addresses should be both italicized and underlined. Because people have used the Address element to display addresses rather than using the font-style <I> tag to force the text to display in italics, new browsers that conform to the new standard will automatically render Address elements in the new style—both italicized and underlined.

Think of information-type elements as adding logical emphasis, while font-style elements apply physical characteristics. Whenever possible, you should try to get the effect you want by using information-type elements for logical emphasis. This way, if the proper way to display some element changes in the future, you'll have nothing to fix. New browsers that incorporate the change will simply display those elements in a different way. But when you simply want to make a word italic or bold, and the word doesn't correspond to any information-type element, you can always use the font-style elements.

Figure 9-6 shows the font-style elements rendered in Arena. Figure 9-7 shows a few of the information-type elements; others are listed in Table 9-1.

As you are well aware by now, some characters have special meanings in HTML and to Web browsers. These characters include the less-than (<) and greater-than (>) symbols that you use for HTML tags, quotation marks ("), and the ampersand symbol (&) that you learned about with the nonbreaking-space character.

In the section where you learned about the nonbreaking-space character ( ), we explained that this type of symbol is called an *entity* and that other

FIGURE 9-6.

Font-style elements

Font-style elements

Tags	Description
<B>...</B>	***This is bold text***
<I>...</I>	*This is italic text*
<U>...</U>	This is underlined text
<S>...</S>	~~This is struck through text~~
<TT>...</TT>	`This is teletype text`
<BIG>...</BIG>	This is big text
<SMALL>...</SMALL>	This is small text
_{...}	This is $_{\text{subscript}}$ text
^{...}	This is ^{superscript} text

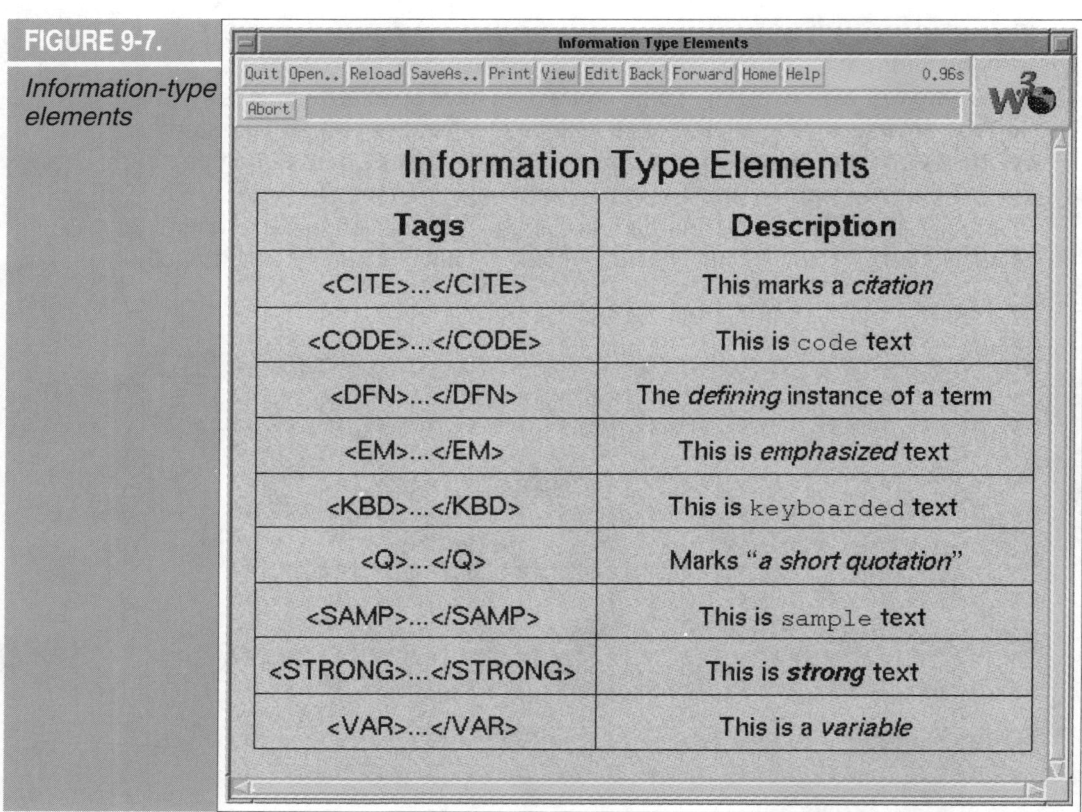

Information Type Elements

Quit Open.. Reload SaveAs.. Print View Edit Back Forward Home Help 0.96s

Abort

Information Type Elements

Tags	Description
<CITE>...</CITE>	This marks a *citation*
<CODE>...</CODE>	This is `code` text
<DFN>...</DFN>	The *defining* instance of a term
<EM>...</EM>	This is *emphasized* text
<KBD>...</KBD>	This is `keyboarded` text
<Q>...</Q>	Marks "*a short quotation*"
<SAMP>...</SAMP>	This is `sample` text
<STRONG>...</STRONG>	This is ***strong*** text
<VAR>...</VAR>	This is a *variable*

FIGURE 9-7. *Information-type elements*

entities have other uses. You learned that entities have the format "*&xxxx;*", where *xxxx* is a string of characters that identify the particular entity, and that you put entities into a document to signify some special single character. In the case of the nonbreaking-space entity, it notifies Web browsers reading the document that they should display a regular space character on the screen but that the space character does not qualify as white space, so that browsers will not choose to break the line at that character.

Similarly, other entities represent characters that have special meaning in HTML, preventing you from typing them directly into your document, or that you have no

TABLE 9-1. *Additional Information-type Elements*

START TAG	DESCRIPTION	TERMINATOR
<ABBREV>	Marks abbreviated text	</ABBREV>
<ACRONYM>	Marks acronyms	</ACRONYM>
<AU>	Identifies the author of a document	</AU>
<INS>	Marks inserted text	</INS>
<DEL>	Marks deleted text	</DEL>
<LANG>	Changes the language context of the document	</LANG>
<PERSON>	Identifies a person's name	</PERSON>
<ADDRESS>	Displays addresses in an italic font	</ADDRESS>
<BLOCKQUOTE>	Marks large blocks of quoted text	</BLOCKQUOTE>
<ADMONISHMENTS>	Marks warnings and caution statements	</ADMONISHMENTS>
<FN>	Identifies footnotes	</FN>
<NOTE>	Used for a variety of note classes	</NOTE>

easy way of typing on the typical computer keyboard. Figure 9-8 shows samples of some of these entities in a browser window. Table 9-2 summarizes the most common entities you will need or run into in other HTML documents.

Unfortunately, not all browsers recognize every entity yet. Some of them even recognize an entity when they shouldn't—a few look only for the "&" followed by a string of recognizable characters and ignore the semicolon. If that is the case with your browser, don't leave off the semicolons; the HTML specification clearly calls

FIGURE 9-8. *Some of the common entities*

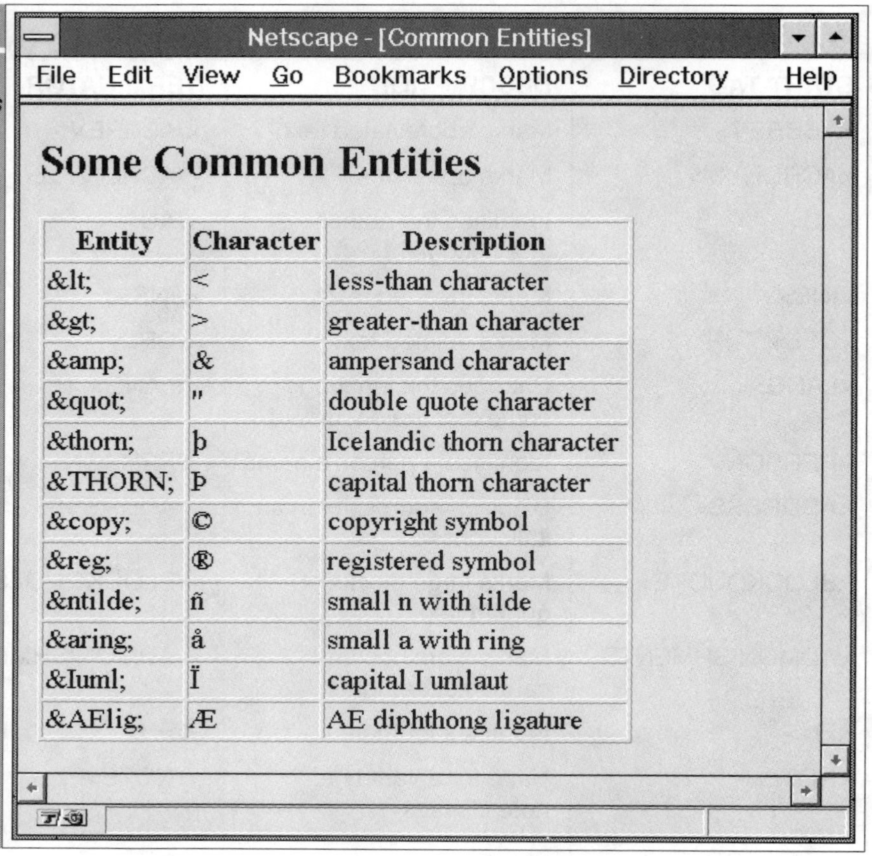

Netscape - [Common Entities]

File Edit View Go Bookmarks Options Directory Help

Some Common Entities

Entity	Character	Description
<	<	less-than character
>	>	greater-than character
&	&	ampersand character
"	"	double quote character
þ	þ	Icelandic thorn character
Þ	Þ	capital thorn character
©	©	copyright symbol
®	®	registered symbol
ñ	ñ	small n with tilde
å	å	small a with ring
Ï	Ï	capital I umlaut
Æ	Æ	AE diphthong ligature

for it, and some browsers do look for the semicolon. If they don't find it, they will render the entity literally and display it on the screen.

There are actually a great deal more entities than the ones in Table 9-2. Most of them are for displaying Latin and Greek characters in your documents. We won't go into those here. If you are interested in learning more about how to display these characters, check out these Web pages:

- http://www.ncsa.uiuc.edu/demoweb/html-primer.html
- http://www.hpl.hp.co.uk/people/dsr/html/latin1.html
- http://www.w3.org/hypertext/WWW/MarkUp/ISOlat1.html

TABLE 9-2. *A Few Additional Entities*

ENTITY	DESCRIPTION
	A nonbreaking space
&endash;	A hyphen (a line about one-half the width of the letter "M")
	A blank space about one-half the width of the letter "M"
&emdash;	A dash about the width of the letter "M"
	A space about the width of the letter "M"
	A soft hyphen
"	A double quote mark
©	The copyright symbol
™	The trademark symbol

Other new entities with HTML 3 deal with math and expressing equations. We will look at some of these in Chapter 10.

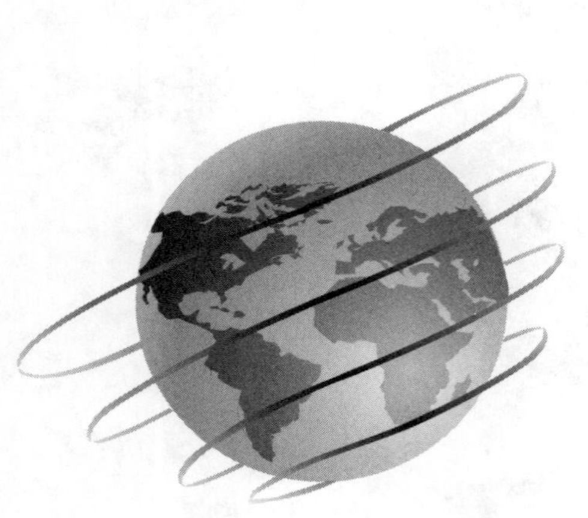

Chapter 10

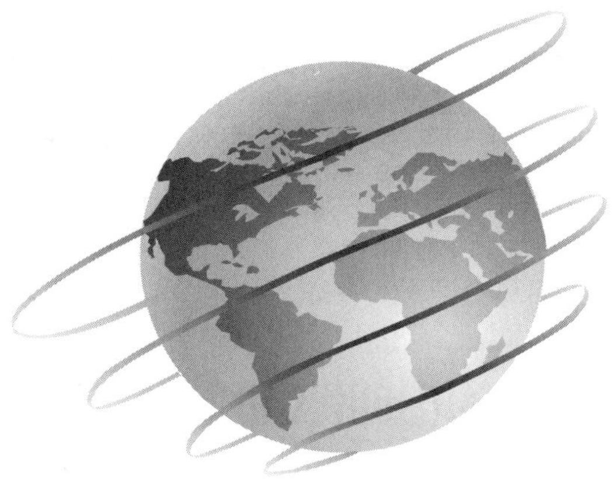

What's New with HTML 3

Up to this point in the book, we've mentioned some of the new features and changes that HTML 3 brings to the Web. In this chapter, we will look more closely at the changes and enhancements HTML 3 brings to existing HTML tags, and at some of the new features of HTML 3, including tables, math, and style sheets.

We should mention again at this point that, while the specification for HTML 3 is likely to be finalized by the time you read this, most browsers still don't support all of the new features in HTML 3. Browser developers don't tend to release a whole new version of their browsers when a new HTML version comes out. Instead, they implement new features one at a time, and a great deal of time can pass before they make the transition from full support of one HTML version to the next. Some browser developers actually lead the HTML specification and implement new tags and attributes that aren't even discussed in the specification, while other developers choose never to implement some features of the specification.

This isn't to imply that the new features aren't finding their way into the browsers you will use today. The major ones, such as Netscape and Mosaic, already support HTML 3 tables and many of the new attributes to old elements. The rule that you should write your Web pages to be as compatible as possible with the old standards will probably always stand. Luckily, browsers just ignore tags and attributes that they don't understand.

New Attributes to Old Tags

Most of the head and body elements we discussed in the previous two chapters have existed in HTML since HTML 0. And through HTML 2, they worked the same way. But the HTML 3 specification brings some new functionality to each of them. We discussed some of this new functionality when we introduced you to the individual tags, but we saved some of the new stuff for this chapter because these new features are common to many HTML elements and tags.

With HTML 3, nearly every element of HTML has gotten a facelift. In fact, every body element in the language, with the exception of font-style elements such as bold and italic, takes a new attribute—the ID attribute. And nearly all of these body elements take two additional attributes—the LANG and CLASS attributes. Some other new attributes are also common to several elements, while other new attributes are specific to one particular element.

In the first part of this section, we will look at ID, CLASS, and LANG, the three new attributes that you can use with virtually every element. In the next section, we

will look at the new attributes that are common to several elements. And in the final section, we will look at more new attributes, but we will focus on the specific elements that take them, rather than on the attributes themselves.

The Common New Attributes

With HTML 3, nearly every element in the language will accept the three attributes we look at here. The only exceptions are horizontal tabs (which take only the ID attribute), horizontal rules (which take ID and CLASS, but not LANG), and font-style elements (which take no attributes).

ID

Prior to HTML 3, you could define a target for hypertext links anywhere in your document by using the anchor (<A>) tag with the NAME attribute. For example, simply putting the anchor

```
<A NAME="Bibliography"></A>
```

into your document defines a target (named *Bibliography*) for a hypertext link that you define with another anchor tag such as

```
<A HREF="#Bibliography">Jump to the Bibliography</A>
```

For backward compatibility, this still works with HTML 3, but with the new specification you have much more capability.

In HTML 3, you can define a hypertext target in any element type with the exception of font-style elements. Horizontal rules, lists, headings, paragraphs, tables, and all of the rest of the elements—even line breaks—can all serve as targets for HREF references so you can create anchors to jump to virtually any spot in a document.

Instead of using the NAME attribute, though, you use the new ID attribute. Here's how you define a regular line break:

```
<BR>
```

By including the ID attribute, you can use that line break as an HREF target:

```
<BR ID="Bibliography">
```

You can also use any other element (again, with the exception of font-style elements) to define the HREF target. For example:

```
<DIV ID="Bibliography" CLASS=Normal>
<HR ID="Bibliography">
<IMG ID="Bibliography" SRC="liveoak.gif">
<OL ID="Bibliography">
<VAR ID="Bibliography">
```

LANG

The format for identifying a particular language combines two ISO standard codes—the first code represents the language itself (as specified by ISO 639), and the second code represents a dialect or variation of the language (as specified by ISO 3166). Each of these codes is typically two characters. For example, English as it's spoken in the United States is *en.us,* and English as it's spoken in Britain is *en.uk.* Here's how you might use it:

```
<BODY LANG="en.us">
```

Whether you'll ever need to use this attribute—or ever actually see a browser that knows what to do with it—is up for grabs.

CLASS

Eventually, when the HTML 3 specification is solidified, when browsers fully support it, and when the implementation of style sheets is well defined and in use, the CLASS attribute will be an important means to override default properties of document elements. Virtually every element in HTML 3 can accept the CLASS attribute, giving the author a great deal of flexibility. To use the CLASS attribute, you will include it in the tag for the element you want to modify.

For example, say that you want to modify one instance of a Heading 3 element so that browsers will render this heading in capital letters regardless of whether the text between the <H3> tag and the </H3> tag is upper- or lowercase. In the opening tag for that heading element, you would use the CLASS attribute as follows:

```
<H3 CLASS=allcaps>This heading will be in capital letters!</H3>
```

The list of possible parameters to the CLASS attribute will be different depending on the element you use it with, and a definitive list of possible parameters will depend upon the stylesheet in use.

So the CLASS attribute will be important—some day—but you won't have to worry about it for a while.

Other New Attributes

Of the three new attributes we just looked at, by far the most important and useful is the ID attribute. In this section, we will look at some more new attributes, but these are less prevalent than the previous three. These attributes each work with two or more elements. Most of them apply to four, five, or six of the elements.

CLEAR

When you create a block-like element such as a table or a graphic and the text flows around the element (see the note on the <FIG> tag), you sometimes need to halt the free flow of text to force the next element to appear below the table or graphic. You can do this with the CLEAR attribute. Specify the CLEAR attribute in the next element to follow the free-flowing text. For example, consider this markup code:

```
<FIG SRC="manatee.gif">
The manatee is a large mammal that lives in the shallow waters
of the ocean. They come to the surface to breathe every three to
five minutes. They are vegetarians, are docile, and harmless to
humans. Adult manatees can range in weight from 500 to 2000 lbs.
```

NOTE *The <FIG> tag is new with HTML 3. It works like the <IMG> tag, but rather than starting subsequent elements next to the lower-right corner, or even beneath the image or figure, the <FIG> tag starts the element right next to the image (next to the upper-right corner of the image). In the case of text, the text flows around the image.*

Now look ahead to Figure 10-1 to see how this text is rendered to the right of the graphic, and consider how you would begin a new paragraph to start at the left margin below the image. Any number of paragraph tags (<P>) would only leave one blank line below the bottom line of text next to the graphic, and the next element

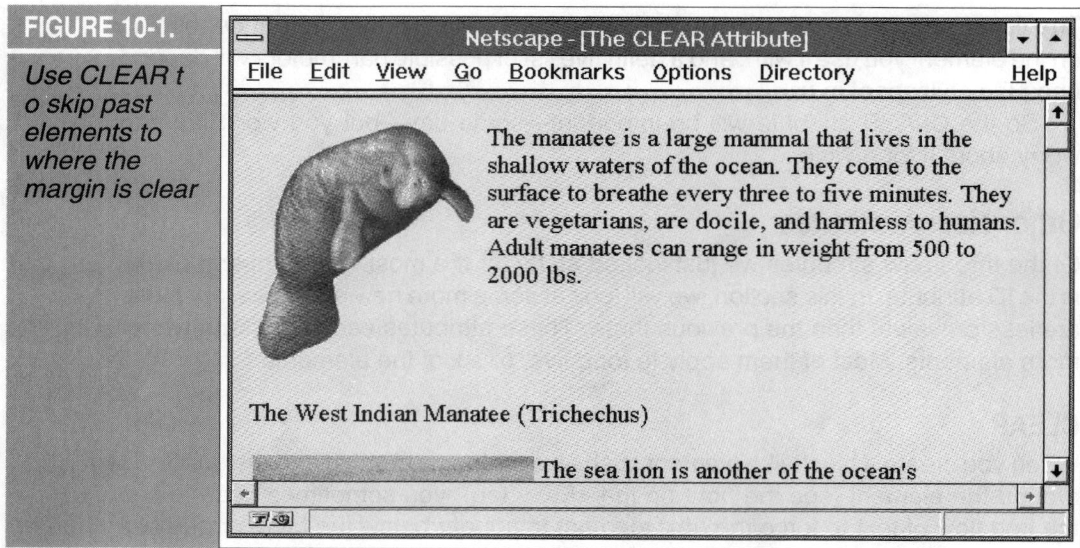

FIGURE 10-1. *Use CLEAR t o skip past elements to where the margin is clear*

would still be to the right of the image. One solution might be to add as many linebreak (<BR>) tags as you need to force the next element below the image. In this example, though, that would require six or eight linebreak tags. Clearly, this isn't an elegant solution.

A better solution is to use the CLEAR attribute in the opening tag of the next element.

```
<FIG SRC="manatee.gif">
The manatee is a large mammal that lives in the shallow waters
of the ocean. They come to the surface to breathe every three to
five minutes. They are vegetarians, are docile, and harmless to
humans. Adult manatees can range in weight from 500 to 2000 lbs.
<P CLEAR=left>The West Indian Manatee (Trichechus)

<FIG SRC="manatee.gif">
The sea lion is another of the ocean's mammals.
```

The *left* parameter to the CLEAR attribute indicates that browsers should drop down as far as they need to in order to get to the left margin. In other words, they should stop flowing elements around any graphics or objects and go to the next location on the page where the left margin is clear.

The CLEAR attribute can take five parameters:

- CLEAR=left
- CLEAR=right
- CLEAR=all
- CLEAR="20 en"
- CLEAR="80 pixels"

The *right* parameter works like the left one, but it causes browsers to drop down until the right margin is clear. The *all* parameter causes browsers to skip down to the first place that both margins are clear. Alternatively, you can specify a number of en units or pixels of horizontal space on a line that must be clear. This causes browsers to skip down to the first line on which there are the specified number of en units or pixels free of any text or objects. (Of course, you specify the number of en units or pixels—we just provided 20 and 80 here as an example.)

Fourteen of the body elements in HTML 3 accept the CLEAR attribute. (See the table in Appendix A to see which attributes each element can use.)

ALIGN

Use the ALIGN attribute to specify an alignment for an element within the margins of the browser window, or within other elements such as a cell in a table. Elements that can include the ALIGN attribute include:

- Divisions
- Headings
- Paragraphs
- Horizontal tabs
- Figures
- Tables

Several of these elements were able to use the ALIGN attribute prior to HTML 3. There are four basic parameters you can use with the ALIGN attribute, and a few extra you can use in some circumstances. The basic parameters are:

- ALIGN=left
- ALIGN=center
- ALIGN=right

- ALIGN=justify

The *left* and *right* parameters align your element along the left and right text margins, respectively. The *center* parameter centers an element between the text margins, and the *justify* parameter attempts to size the element such that its right and left edges are both aligned along the text margins.

There are two additional parameters you can use with figures (the <FIG> tag) and tables (the <TABLE> tag). These are:

- ALIGN=bleedleft
- ALIGN=bleedright

These parameters cause browsers to align figures not with the text margins, but with the window border of your browser (even further to the left than the left text margin, and further right than the right text margin).

One of the elements you can use the ALIGN attribute with is horizontal tabs (the <TAB> tag). However, horizontal tabs don't use the *justify* parameter, and they do use one additional parameter:

- ALIGN=decimal

Use this parameter when you want to line up a column of numbers on a decimal point rather than along the left or right edge of the numbers.

MD

Use the MD attribute to embed a checksum for any link that supports the standard HREF-type link. For example, if you want to make sure that a graphic image referenced in a page is the one you intended, you can generate a checksum of the image and build it right into the element you use to reference the image:

```
<FIG SRC="dingbat.jpg" MD="md5:sa&T>wa/pR+gajadjK21ba7">
```

When browsers open the graphic file, they will run their own checksum on the image. If the checksums match, the browser will display the image. If not, the browser shouldn't display it.

It is somewhat doubtful that the MD attribute (which stands for Message Digest) will ever be an important feature of HTML. Only time will tell.

SRC

The SRC attribute is a familiar one. It's used to indicate the source of an image for the <IMG> tag. But it has other uses too. It works exactly the same way in HTML 3 with the <FIG> tag as it does with the <IMG> tag (both in previous versions and in HTML 3). But four other elements can also use the SRC attribute in HTML 3. These are:

- Headings
- Admonishments
- Unordered lists
- Horizontal rules

For headings and admonishments, the SRC attribute specifies an image to appear before the heading or the note of an admonishment. For example, an admonishment might be a note that cautions users that a page is under construction and might not always work properly. You can use the SRC attribute with the NOTE element to display a caution sign:

```
<NOTE CLASS=warning SRC="caution.gif">This page is under
construction!</NOTE>
```

For unordered lists, you can use the SRC attribute to specify an image to use in place of the usual bullet. The SRC attribute doesn't work with ordered lists because they have numbers instead of bullets.

For horizontal rules, use the SRC attribute to specify an image other than the default flat line:

```
<HR SRC="wavyline.gif">
```

WIDTH

There are several elements that can use the WIDTH attribute. Among these are:

- Figures
- Images
- Preformatted text

- Horizontal rules
- Tables

Generally, the WIDTH attribute instructs Web browsers to try to adjust the width of the associated object if it is possible. With figures and images, the WIDTH attribute amounts to a suggestion to browsers rendering the objects. The browsers will determine if it is even possible to scale images to the suggested width. If they can, they will scale the image. If they can't, they will ideally do their best to approximate the suggested width. When you use the WIDTH attribute with figures and tables, you have to use it along with an associated UNITS attribute to specify the units of your dimensions. The two possibilities for units are en units and pixels. Here are two examples:

```
<IMG SRC="clown.gif" WIDTH=60 UNITS=pixels>
<FIG SRC="clown.gif" WIDTH=16 UNITS=en>
```

You will seldom see the WIDTH attribute used with preformatted text (text formatted with the <PRE> tag), but it is supposed to tell browsers the width, in characters, at which they should display a block of preformatted text. Valid widths are 40, 80, and 132—not coincidentally the widths that printers print fixed-space text in expanded, normal, and compressed modes. Here's what it looks like:

```
<PRE WIDTH=80>
```

It's not likely that many browsers will support the WIDTH attribute for preformatted text.

At the time of this writing, the HTML 3 specification says nothing about horizontal rules (the <HR> tag) supporting the WIDTH attribute. Nevertheless, at least two of the prominent browsers already do.

For horizontal rules, the parameter you give to the WIDTH attribute is a percentage of the distance from the left text margin to the right text margin. For example:

```
<HR SIZE=15 WIDTH=60%>
```

will create a horizontal rule line that spans 60% of the distance from the left margin to the right. It will be centered in the window, but it will only be slightly longer than half of the width of the window.

The specification doesn't say anything about the SIZE attribute to the horizontal rule either, but it works with more than one browser. The size refers to the vertical thickness of the line.

HEIGHT

Like the WIDTH attribute, the HEIGHT attribute is a suggested height for browsers to display an image (either a figure or an image). If you supply both a suggested width and a height, browsers will do their best to scale the image to those dimensions, but if the suggested dimensions aren't possible, they may have to decide for themselves how to adjust them.

Also, as with the WIDTH attribute, browsers will look for a UNITS attribute to determine whether the height you provide is in pixels or en units.

A Closer Look at a Few Elements

In the last section, we looked at some of the new HTML 3 attributes that are common to several HTML elements. For example, we looked at the ALIGN attribute, which you can use with six of the body elements. In this section, we are going to look at some more new attributes, but we're going to do it by focusing on the elements with which they work, rather than on the attributes themselves. We're taking this approach because these attributes are unique to a single element or appear in only one or two elements.

Body

In Chapter 9, we looked at body elements, but we didn't actually focus on the <BODY> tag itself. This was because until HTML 3, the <BODY> tag didn't take any attributes. In the previous sections of this chapter, you saw that the <BODY> tag can now take the ID, LANG, and CLASS attributes, but there is another new attribute that this tag can take in HTML 3. It is an exciting new feature.

CUSTOM BACKGROUNDS With the BACKGROUND attribute, you can specify an image file that browsers will replicate to create a custom background for a Web page. Eventually you will also be able to do this with style sheets (see the last section of this chapter), but the BACKGROUND attribute provides a direct and quick way to change the look of your pages. And it works today with most new browsers. Here's an example:

```
<BODY BACKGROUND="arcade.gif">
```

This tag produces a window that looks like the one shown in Figure 10-2.

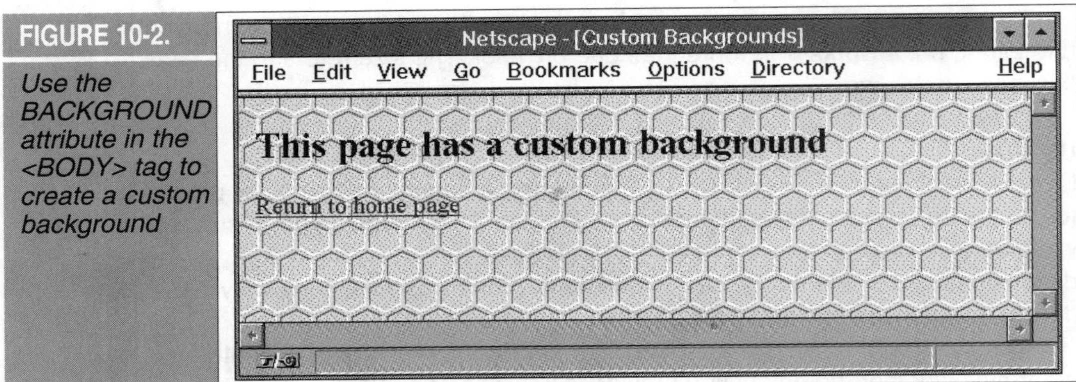

FIGURE 10-2. *Use the BACKGROUND attribute in the <BODY> tag to create a custom background*

ADDING COLOR TO YOUR PAGES Netscape provides a couple of extensions to the <BODY> tag that you may find useful. Netscape's browser recognizes attributes that allow you to change the text color and window background color. This isn't part of the HTML 3 specification, but it would certainly be a nice addition—and it probably won't be long before it is incorporated into the spec.

The attributes are BGCOLOR for setting the background color and TEXT for setting the text color. For the parameters to these attributes, you supply a string of characters that represent three hexadecimal numbers, but that's not as hard as it sounds.

The decimal number system (the one we use all the time in real life) is called the decimal number system because it uses 10 symbols to represent numbers. Of course, these symbols are the numbers 0 through 9. With computers, it's often more convenient to use the hexadecimal number system (or hex). The symbols available in hex are 0, 1, 2, 3, 4, 5, 6, 7, 8, 9, A, B, C, D, E, and F.

The string parameter that you use with both the BGCOLOR and TEXT attributes represents three hexadecimal numbers that specify an intensity for the colors red, green, and blue, respectively. For example, the lowest intensity of a color is 00, and the highest intensity is FF. Thus, pure red would be represented by the string FF0000—the maximum intensity for red, and the minimum intensities of green and blue. Pure green would be 00FF00, and pure blue is 0000FF. These strings are sometimes referred to as *color triads*, or *hex color triads*. Black (which is no color at all) is represented by the number 000000, and white is represented by FFFFFF. You'll soon get the hang of mixing the primary colors to get the shade you want. See Figure 10-3 for more examples of mixtures of the primary colors and some other interesting shades.

FIGURE 10-3.

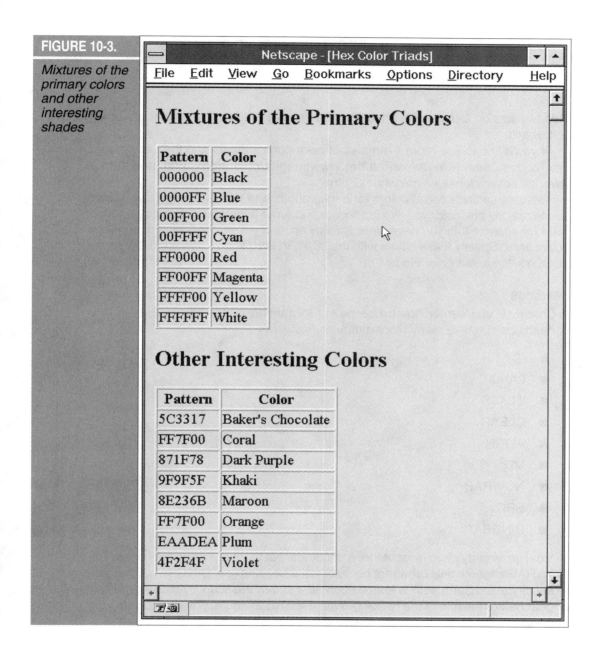

Mixtures of the primary colors and other interesting shades

Netscape - [Hex Color Triads]

File Edit View Go Bookmarks Options Directory Help

Mixtures of the Primary Colors

Pattern	Color
000000	Black
0000FF	Blue
00FF00	Green
00FFFF	Cyan
FF0000	Red
FF00FF	Magenta
FFFF00	Yellow
FFFFFF	White

Other Interesting Colors

Pattern	Color
5C3317	Baker's Chocolate
FF7F00	Coral
871F78	Dark Purple
9F9F5F	Khaki
8E236B	Maroon
FF7F00	Orange
EAADEA	Plum
4F2F4F	Violet

Here's the syntax for using the BGCOLOR and TEXT attributes:

```
<BODY BGCOLOR="#5C3317" TEXT="#FFFF00">
```

This tag sets up a page with a background color of Baker's Chocolate with bright yellow text.

If you'd like to see more examples of color combinations and their associated hex codes, see http://www.infi.net/wwwimages/colorindex.html and http://www.infi.net/wwwimages/colorindex2.html.

Besides setting special colors for backgrounds and text, Netscape also allows you to specify any color you like for anchor text (your hypertext hot-spots), another color for anchors that you have already followed, and yet another color for currently active links. Specify these colors with the LINK, VLINK, and ALINK attributes to the <BODY> tag and a color triad.

Headings

In Chapter 9, you learned how to use the ALIGN attribute with headings. But in HTML 3, headings can take many more attributes, including:

- ID
- LANG
- CLASS
- CLEAR
- ALIGN
- MD
- NOWRAP
- SRC
- DINGBAT

You've already seen most of these attributes, but there are a few new ones. The NOWRAP attribute tells browsers not to break a heading line. DINGBAT allows you to specify a standard, built-in image such as a folder, trashcan, or mouse, that will appear before the text of the heading. With the SRC attribute, you can specify your own custom image file to appear before the text of a heading.

Horizontal Tabs

In Chapter 9, you learned how to use horizontal tabs, both with <tab id= and <tab to=, and with the INDENT attribute.

In HTML 3, tabs will also take an attribute called DP that allows you to specify the decimal point character if you are using the ALIGN=decimal attribute. The default decimal point is a period (for lining up columns of numbers), but you can substitute any other character you wish. For example, to render something like this:

Name:	John Smith
Email address:	jsmith@netcom.com
Status:	current

you can specify the DP character to be the colon (:).

Tables

One of the most exciting new features of HTML 3 is the ability to include text, data, pictures, graphics, anchors, and anything else that the language recognizes in a table. It is now possible to define tables logically and elegantly. With previous versions of HTML, creating tables was such a cumbersome procedure that people often simply created text files and included them in documents as preformatted text with the <PRE> tag. Now, you can create tables with the <TABLE> tag. This process is easy, and it provides much more flexibility.

Elements of a Table

Before we get into the details of how to mark up a table, let's look at the parts of a table to build a foundation for our discussion in this section. Figure 10-4 shows a simple table of three rows and two columns.

The text "Simple Table" above the table is a table element called a *caption*. This term is slightly counterintuitive because other elements, such as images, put captions underneath the object. The table caption actually looks more like a title or a heading, but most browsers render table captions this way—centered above the table.

The grid that you see separating the columns and rows is called the *border*. Some browsers render borders in 3-D style like the one shown here. Others render borders as lines. You can easily choose whether or not to have a border. Tables don't have borders by default, and to specify one, you just include the attribute BORDER in the opening <TABLE> tag. (You'll see how this works soon.)

The table shown in Figure 10-4 has two columns and three rows. The area where a column and row intersect is called a *cell*—just like a spreadsheet. The two cells

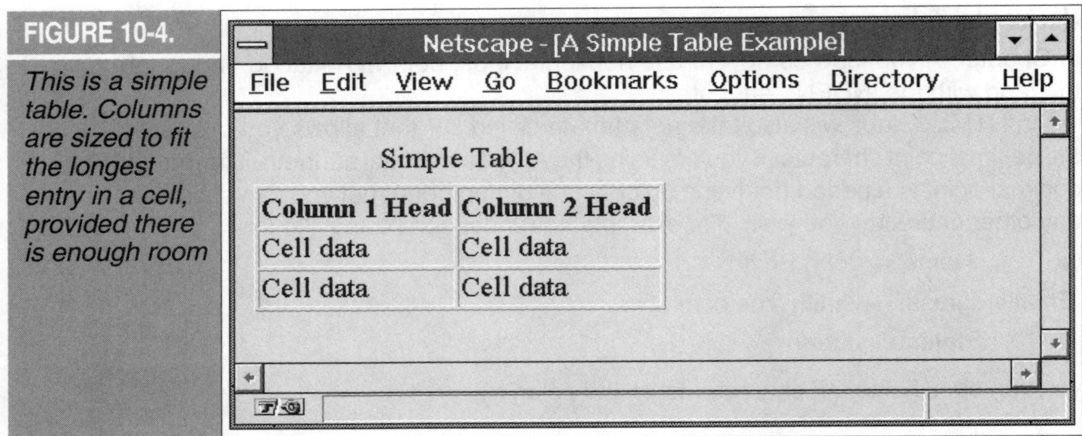

FIGURE 10-4. *This is a simple table. Columns are sized to fit the longest entry in a cell, provided there is enough room*

in the top row of this table contain column headings. There isn't anything particularly special about column headings except that by default, the text of a column head is bold and centered in the cell. The tag to mark a column head is <TH> (for Table Header cell).

The markup tag for cell data is the <TD> tag (for Table Data). By default, cell data looks just like normal text and is left-aligned in the cell.

Basically, that's all there is to tables. Of course, we're going to complicate this a little bit by showing you how to define rows that span multiple columns, how to define columns that span multiple rows, and how to strictly define column specifications. We'll also show you some tricks for working with alignment, images, and widths. But keep in mind that everything you do with a table is just a variation on a simple table like the one we've looked at here.

Defining a Table

If you've looked at the markup code for a particularly fancy or intricate table, you may have had a sinking feeling in your stomach. The HTML code for a table isn't pretty, and it's not easy to follow. The good news, though, is that it's easier to create the code yourself than it is to follow someone else's table markup code. When you see a table that has cells that span several rows or several columns, you might think to yourself that this is going to be complicated—but it really isn't.

Just remember that you define a table one row at a time—from top to bottom. And within your definition of a row, you define that row one cell at a time from left to right.

Here's the HTML code to define the "Simple Table" we looked at in the previous section:

```
<table border>
<caption>Simple Table</caption>
<tr><th>Column 1 Head<th>Column 2 Head
<tr><td>Cell data<td>Cell data
<tr><td>Cell data<td>Cell data
</table>
```

First, notice that the table definition starts with the <TABLE> tag and is terminated with the </TABLE> tag. In this case, the opening <TABLE> tag has the BORDER attribute. Without the BORDER attribute, the table would still be there when you read it with a browser, but you wouldn't see the border. It's a good idea to always turn on the border by including this attribute with the <TABLE> tag, even if you don't intend your finished product to have a border. Doing so will allow you to see more easily what you are doing as you define your table. You can turn off the border later by deleting the BORDER attribute.

The second line of this code segment defines the table caption. As you saw in Figure 10-4, this causes browsers to render the words "Simple Table" centered above the table. Of course, table captions are optional. And if you want your table caption to appear some other way, you can easily do so by using other HTML elements above or below the table. In fact, you could even use the <CAPTION> element outside of the table. This will cause the caption to be displayed like a normal caption element—left-aligned. However, keeping the caption definition inside the table definition associates the caption with the table.

The remaining three rows of our simple table definition define the three rows of the table. Row definitions begin with the <TR> tag and don't require a closing tag. Browsers will properly assume that a new <TR> tag ends the previous row (if there was one) as well as beginning a new row.

After the <TR> tag, you define the contents of the cells in that row. There are only two markup codes you can use for cells: <TH> for header cells, and <TD> for data cells. Both of these codes mark the beginning of your cell content, and neither requires a closing tag. Again, browsers will correctly assume that a new <TH> or <TD> tag ends the previous cell and begins a new one, and a <TR> tag ends a row and begins a new one.

More Control over Tables

Now that you know the basics of defining a table, let's look at some of the tools at your disposal for customizing your tables. We'll start out by learning how to exercise control over column widths. Then you will learn how to create cells that span multiple rows and columns, and how to make the content of your cells line up the way you want.

Controlling Width

In our "Simple Table" example in the previous sections, we didn't discuss how browsers determine column width. Here's the general rule that browsers follow: Columns should be wide enough to display the data in the cells as long as the browser can still display all of the columns that are defined. In the "Simple Table," none of the cell entries are very long, so the browser rendered the columns wide enough to display the longest entry—in this case, the column headings. And since the column headings are about the same size, the column widths are about the same.

Figure 10-5 shows what the "Simple Table" looks like with a longer entry in the lower left-hand cell.

Notice that the browser rendered the first column wider than the second in order to accommodate the longer text in a cell in the first column. So what happens if the text in a cell is *really* long? The browser will choose a point at which to wrap the text in the cell down to another line—not to the next row, but to another line within the cell. Figure 10-6 shows how it looks.

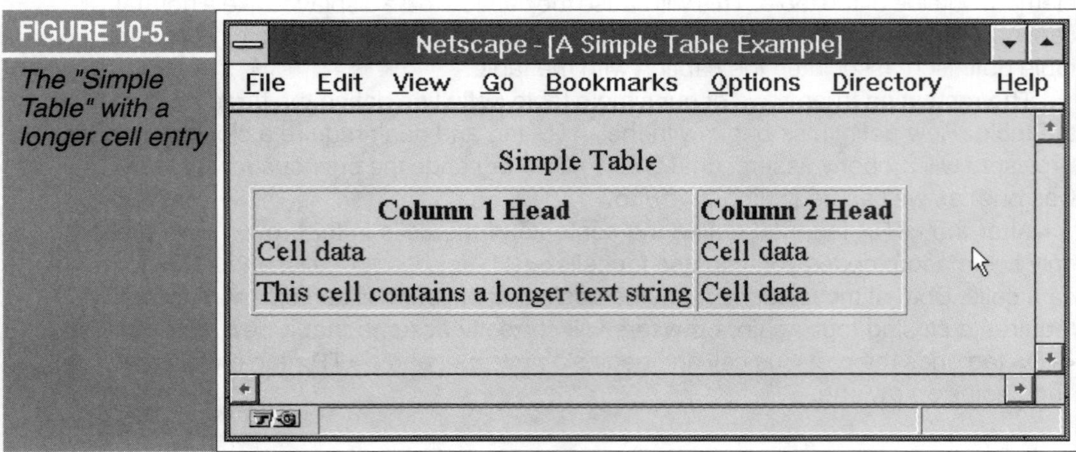

FIGURE 10-5. *The "Simple Table" with a longer cell entry*

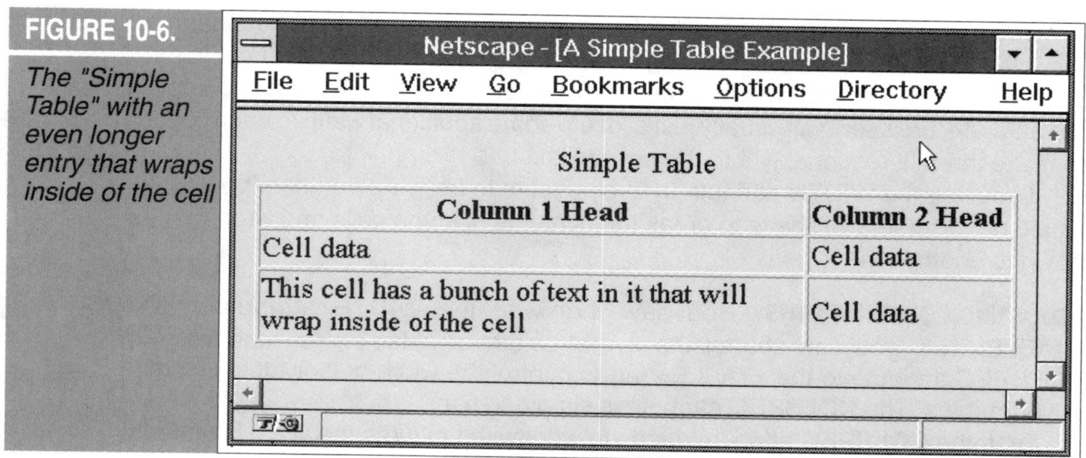

FIGURE 10-6. *The "Simple Table" with an even longer entry that wraps inside of the cell*

Notice that the browser expanded the overall width of the table to extend it from the left margin all the way to the right margin. Then it sized the right-hand column to be as wide as it needed to be, and used the rest of the space for the width of the left-hand column and wrapped the text in the left column where it needed to based on that width. This is how browsers will determine column widths if you don't include any other directions for sizing your columns.

ADJUSTING TABLE WIDTHS You can specify an overall fixed width for a table by using the WIDTH attribute to the <TABLE> tag. Use the WIDTH attribute in conjunction with the UNITS attribute. For example:

```
<TABLE BORDER UNITS=pixels WIDTH=800>
```

This defines a table that will be 800 pixels in overall width. Note that if your computer is running in standard VGA mode (640 x 480 pixels), you don't even have 800 horizontal pixels in which a browser can render such a wide table. The browser will still load the table, though, and display the table at that size. You will just have to use the browser's horizontal scroll bar to pan the table left and right.

The other choices you have for units are:

- en—Specify the width in en units
- pixels—Specify the width in pixels
- relative—Specify the width as a percentage of the width of the window

Of course, specifying an overall table width with the WIDTH attribute changes the rules a little bit for browsers trying to determine how wide to render columns. If you use the WIDTH attribute to force a table to be wider than it would be without the attribute, browsers will usually just allocate some additional width to each column to make them fit reasonably into the new width.

If you use the WIDTH attribute to force a table to be narrower than it otherwise would be, browsers will have to break the contents of some cells and wrap the text down to another line.

ADJUSTING COLUMN WIDTHS You saw that with the WIDTH attribute to the <TABLE> tag, you can control the overall width of a table. You can use the COLSPEC attribute to the <TABLE> tag to control the width of individual columns in your tables. The COLSPEC attribute is simple to use.

First, the COLSPEC attribute needs to work with units (as the WIDTH attribute does), so it uses the same UNITS attribute that the WIDTH attribute uses. And the choices are the same: en units, pixels, or a relative percentage. Here's how it works:

You pass a string parameter to the COLSPEC attribute that describes the justification and width of each column. For example:

```
<TABLE BORDER UNITS=pixels COLSPEC="L80 C55 R68 D50">
```

This COLSPEC parameter defines the alignment and width of the first four columns of the table. The letter in each of the four groups describes the alignment (Left, Center, Right, or Decimal), and the number describes the width of each column (in pixels in this case, since the UNITS attribute is defined as pixels). Similarly,

```
<TABLE BORDER UNITS=en COLSPEC="L25 L20 D32">
```

defines the alignment and width (in en units) for three columns of a table. The first two columns here are left-aligned, and the third is decimal-aligned. (Decimal alignment is useful for aligning a column of numbers on a decimal point.)

Although it's not part of the HTML 3 specification, you can also use a WIDTH attribute in a cell definition to set the width of a column. (At least, this works with some browsers.) Just pass the WIDTH attribute to any cell definition tag (<TD>), like this:

```
<TD WIDTH=60>
```

The default units are pixels. Perhaps you've realized that there is something potentially contradictory about setting a column's width in a cell definition. Which cell in a column do you use—the top cell? The answer is, it doesn't matter. You can use this technique to set a column's width in any cell in the column. Web browsers will just take the largest value and set the width of the whole column to that size.

Clearly, the COLSPEC attribute is the better solution to specifying column widths. Eventually, most browsers will probably support the COLSPEC attribute. But at the time we are writing this, none do that we can find. It won't be difficult for developers to implement, though, and it will give Web authors a simple way to control column width.

Netscape Communications has suggested some new features for tables. One of these suggestions is that the BORDER attribute to the <TABLE> tag take a numeric parameter to specify the thickness of table borders. Netscape has also added two new attributes to the <TABLE> tag for finely controlling cell spacing. These are CELLSPACING and CELLPADDING. You can use CELLSPACING to adjust the amount of space that Netscape browsers put between cells. Effectively, this is the thickness of the border separating cells. The CELLPADDING attribute allows you to adjust the amount of space between a cell border and its contents. Netscape has implemented these features into its browsers, and they may eventually show up in the HTML specification.

Making Cells Span Rows and Columns

The only thing even slightly tricky about tables is making cells span rows and columns. Doing this can create some interesting effects. Figure 10-7 shows a more complicated example of a table than the ones we've worked with so far. The first row of this table is a single cell that contains a label ("Assets"), and it spans all five columns of the table. Directly below the word "Assets" is another cell that also contains a label ("Current") that looks like it spans the next four rows of the table.

You perform this magic with the COLSPAN and ROWSPAN attributes to the <TD> (cell data) tag. The parameters to these attributes are the number of columns or rows that the cell should span. A cell can span multiple columns, multiple rows, or both multiple columns and multiple rows.

So that you don't get confused, here's where you need to keep in mind that you define a table one row at a time. The upper-left cell in this table contains the word "Assets." In the definition of that cell, we used the attribute COLSPAN=5 to make the cell span all five columns of the table. That's all there is to the first row of the table.

In the definition of the first cell in the second row of the table (which contains the word "Current"), we just added the attribute ROWSPAN=4. Thus, the contents of

Netscape - [Balance Sheet]

File Edit View Go Bookmarks Options Directory Help

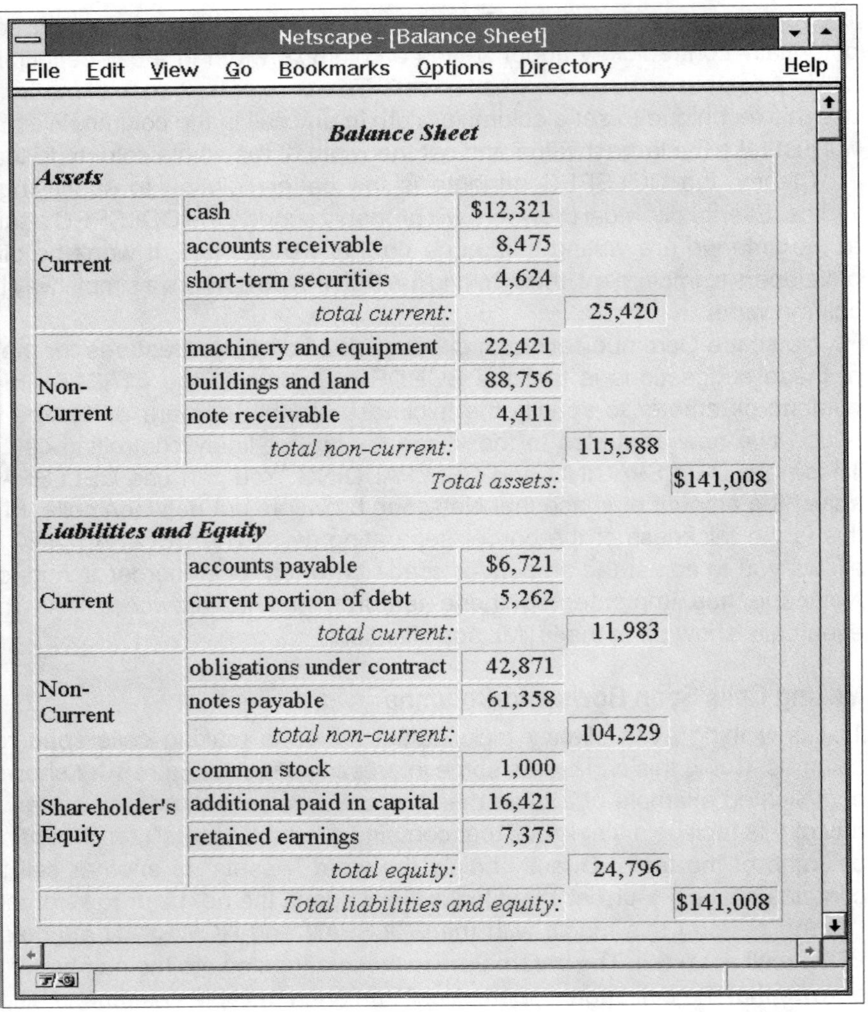

Balance Sheet

Assets				
Current	cash	$12,321		
	accounts receivable	8,475		
	short-term securities	4,624		
	total current:		25,420	
Non-Current	machinery and equipment	22,421		
	buildings and land	88,756		
	note receivable	4,411		
	total non-current:		115,588	
			Total assets:	$141,008
Liabilities and Equity				
Current	accounts payable	$6,721		
	current portion of debt	5,262		
	total current:		11,983	
Non-Current	obligations under contract	42,871		
	notes payable	61,358		
	total non-current:		104,229	
Shareholder's Equity	common stock	1,000		
	additional paid in capital	16,421		
	retained earnings	7,375		
	total equity:		24,796	
			Total liabilities and equity:	$141,008

FIGURE 10-7. *Using a table to present a financial statement*

the cells in the second row are the word "Current," the word "cash," and the amount $12,321; the last two cells in this row are empty (no data or <TD> tags are defined for them).

Since the first cell in the second row spans the three rows beneath that row, this effectively removes the first cell from play when you go to define the third row. In the definition of the third row, keep in mind that the first cell for which you define some data will appear in the second column of the table. So for the third row (through

the fifth), instead of having five columns with which to work, you have only four. The content of the third row is the term "accounts receivable," the value 8,475, and two blank (undefined) cells, for a total of four cells.

Finally, in the fifth row, you also have only four cells in which you can define data. The content of the cells in this row is the term "total current," an empty cell, the value 25,420, and another empty cell. Here's all the HTML code for this table:

```
<table border units=pixels>
<caption><b><i>Balance Sheet<i></b></caption>
<tr><td colspan=5><em><b>Assets</b></em>
<tr><td rowspan=4 width=70>Current<td width=215>cash<td
width=80 align=right>$12,321
<tr><td>accounts receivable<td align=right>8,475
<tr><td>short-term securities<td align=right>4,624
<tr><td align=right><i>total current:</i><td><td width=80
align=right>25,420

<tr><td rowspan=4 width=70>Non-<br>Current<td>machinery and
equipment<td align=right>22,421
<tr><td>buildings and land<td align=right>88,756
<tr><td>note receivable<td align=right>4,411
<tr><td align=right><i>total non-current:</i><td><td width=80
align=right>115,588
<tr><td colspan=3 align=right><i>Total
assets:</i><td><td>$141,008

<tr><td colspan=5>
<tr><td colspan=5>
<tr><td colspan=5><em><b>Liabilities and Equity</b></em>

<tr><td rowspan=3 width=70>Current<td width=215>accounts
payable<td width=80 align=right>$6,721
<tr><td>current portion of debt<td align=right>5,262
<tr><td align=right><i>total current:</i><td><td width=80
align=right>11,983

<tr><td rowspan=3 width=70>Non-<br>Current<td>obligations under
contract<td align=right>42,871
<tr><td>notes payable<td align=right>61,358
<tr><td align=right><i>total non-current:</i><td><td width=80
align=right>104,229
```

```
tr><td rowspan=4>Shareholder's <br>Equity<td>common stock<td
align=right>1,000
<tr><td>additional paid in capital<td align=right>16,421
<tr><td>retained earnings<td align=right>7,375
<tr><td align=right><i>total equity:</i><td><td width=80
align=right>24,796

<tr><td colspan=3 align=right><i>Total liabilities and
equity:</i><td><td>$141,008
</table>
```

Notice that you can use all the font-style elements and alignment attributes you like in the content of your tables. You can even use line breaks (the <BR> tag) and the nonbreaking-space entity (* *).

There is an additional alignment attribute that you can use with table cells. The VALIGN attribute allows you to specify the vertical alignment of a cell's contents. For example, say that you have a cell that vertically spans three or four rows and you want to center a small graphic image in that cell. The default vertical alignment is *top*, so the image will be at the top of the cell, leaving a lot blank space beneath it. Just use the VALIGN attribute in the cell's <TD> tag:

```
<TD valign=middle>
```

Other values you can use with VALIGN are *bottom*, *baseline*, and of course *top*.

Use Your Imagination!

The table we presented in Figure 10-7 is a fairly straightforward example of a table in HTML 3. We used this table to demonstrate the basics of alignment attributes, font-style elements, empty cells, and spanning rows and columns with cells. But you don't have to be limited to such ordinary tables. You can experiment with graphics, forms, lists, and even nesting other tables into the cells of your tables.

Figure 10-8 shows another example. This four-column table has a graphic image in the left-hand column that spans all five rows of the table, a column of labels, and two columns of input form fields. Figure 10-9 shows another variation of this. This table has only a single row that contains a graphic image in one cell, a set of labels separated by line breaks (
 tags) in the next cell, and a collection of form fields in the last cell.

FIGURE 10-8.

Table data can include images and input forms

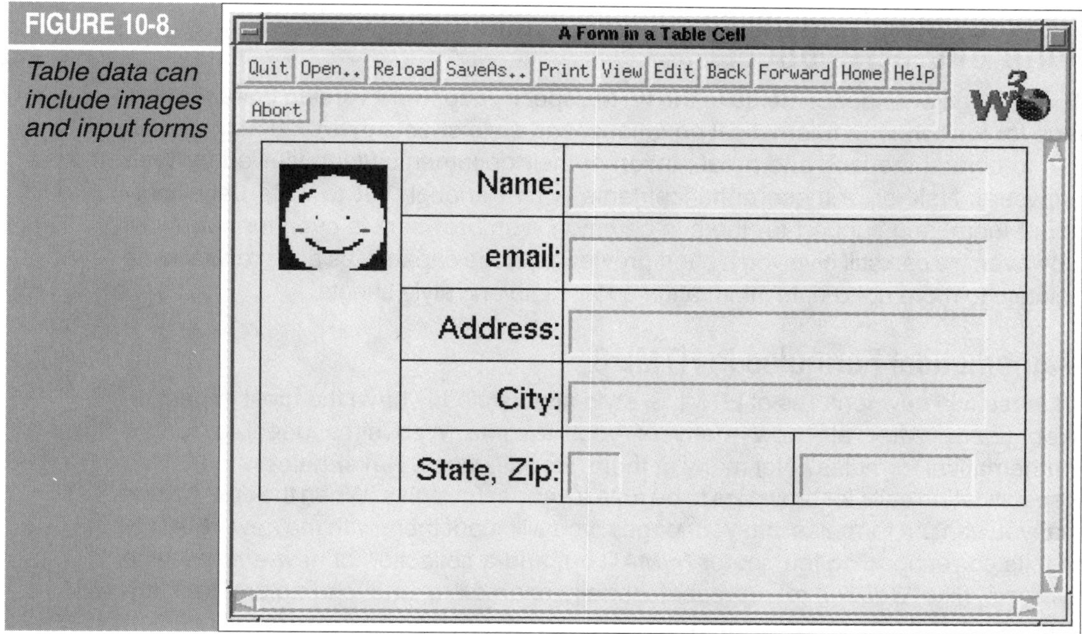

FIGURE 10-9.

A single table cell can contain an entire form

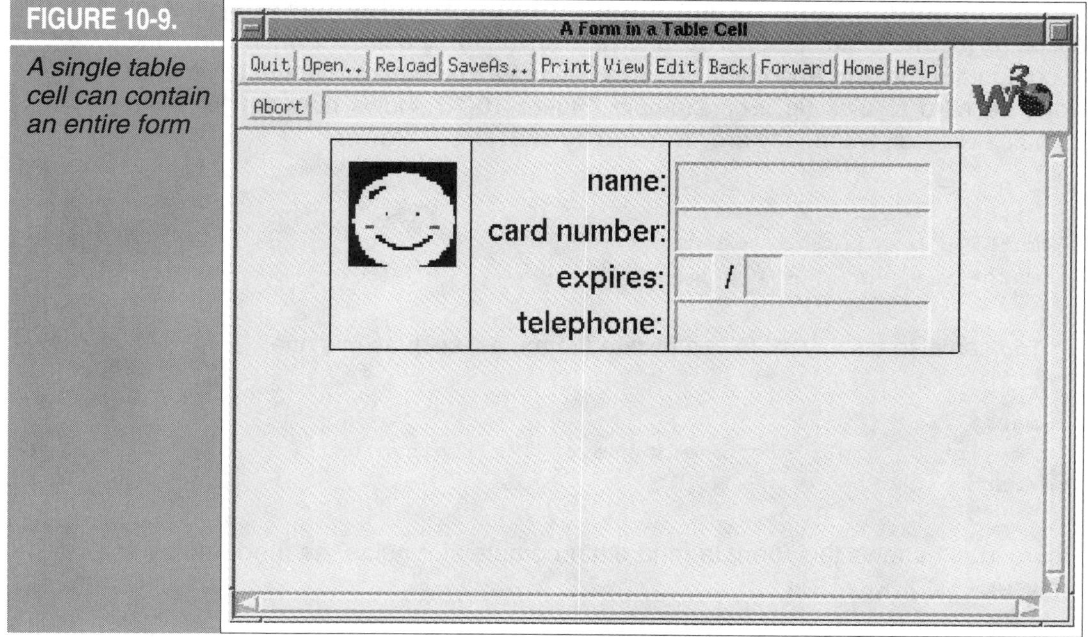

Math and Style Sheets

The final major enhancements to the HTML specification with version 3 are markup tags for rendering mathematical equations, and style sheets that Web authors can use to control the look and presentation of their documents when viewed by Web browsers. Neither of these enhancements is firm enough yet to write definitively about them, and support for them in common Web browsers is even further away. However, we can still give you a short preview of these capabilities and provide some pointers to more up-to-date information about math and style sheets.

Mathematical Formulas in HTML 3

Of these two new features of HTML 3, style sheets clearly have the most impact on Web users. After all, how many of your favorite Web sites need to render mathematical formulas? Not many of them, we will guess. Nevertheless, the HTML 3 specification calls for browsers to be able to render formulas. When the time comes that you can put formulas into your pages, you will mark them with the new $tag, its corresponding terminator ($), and a collection of new *entities*—the symbols (like *"*) to represent certain characters and characters that are impossible to enter with a keyboard.

For the most part, the complex task of rendering a formula graphically will be handled by browsers. The document author can use relatively familiar syntax for encoding them—syntax that will be familiar to anyone who has ever written any kind of computer program. And if you've never written a computer program, the format won't be hard to pick up. For example, Figure 10-10 shows how the following formulas will look when they are rendered by an HTML 3 browser:

```
<math> y = a x + b </math>
<math> a = &pi; r^2^ </math>
<math> y = a x^y^ + b cos x</math>
```

You can also display more complicated formulas, such as this one:

```
<math>
y = {int_0_^&inf;^<left>{sin x<over>1+x} dx}
</math>
```

Figure 10-11 shows this formula (and other complex formulas) as rendered by a browser.

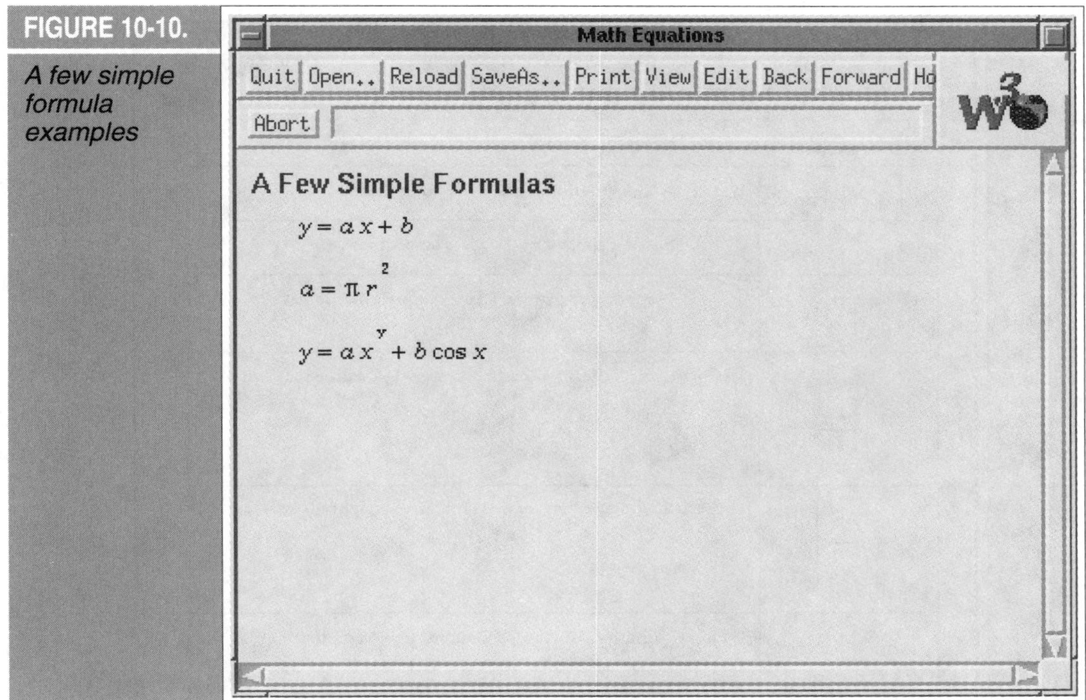

FIGURE 10-10. *A few simple formula examples*

This formula uses two entities you haven't seen yet. The *&inf;* entity represents the infinity symbol (the sideways 8), and the * * entity represents a narrow space (a thin space). In addition to these entities, the HTML 3.0 specification will likely support the entire Greek alphabet with characters like *α*, *β*, *γ*, and so on. Review the current HTML specification to get the most up-to-date information on math in HTML 3, including a complete set of entities.

Style Sheets

We looked briefly at style sheets in Chapter 8 when we discussed the head section of HTML documents. To review briefly, some of the new Web browsers allow users to specify a typeface and font for many of the HTML elements the browser encounters. For example, if readers want to change the look of a 1 heading (the <H1> tag), they can go into an "Options" or "Preference" screen in their browser and choose any typeface and font size available on their computer for that element. The same goes for many other elements, including plain text.

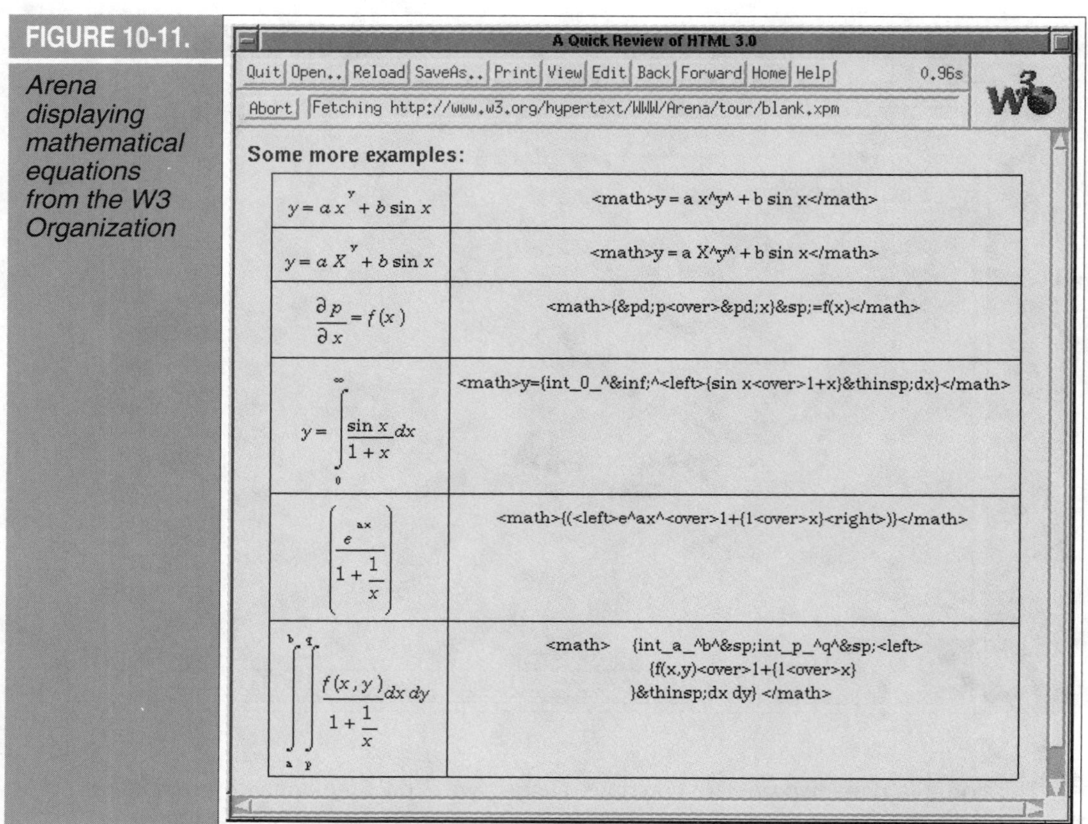

FIGURE 10-11. *Arena displaying mathematical equations from the W3 Organization*

In some respects, this flexibility is good, but the drawback is that Web page authors lose some control over the way their pages will look. There may be legal or artistic reasons that authors need to be able to override any local changes that users will make. But perhaps the most compelling reason is that authors have a sense of ownership and pride in the pages they develop, and they simply *want* them to look a particular way. Style sheets will solve this problem.

However, the ultimate disposition of style sheets in HTML 3 is even less certain and may initially be supported by even fewer browsers than the math element. In fact, at the time we are writing this, the very method for implementing style sheets is still up in the air. The ultimate method could be a subset of the ISO standard for the Document Style Semantics Specification Language (or DSSSL). The subset is called DSSSL Lite and is being promoted by the SGML Open Consortium, although

there are a number of other proposals being submitted and supported by different parties.

If there is a front-runner for the style-sheet implementation plan, it is the one being included in the current draft specification; the plan is called *Cascading Style Sheets: a draft specification* (see http://www.w3.org/hypertext/WWW/Style/css/draft.html).

Regardless of which proposal gets adopted, the way you use styles as a Web page author will probably be the way they are described in the current draft specification (and how we described them in Chapter 8). The current draft is called Cascading Style Sheets because of how they work. Consider this sample head section:

```
<HEAD>
  <TITLE>Implementing Cascading Styles</TITLE>
  <LINK REL=stylesheet HREF="formal.style">
  <STYLE NOTATION=public>
    h1: font.family = roman
    hr: back.color = #F00
    h4, p: font.family = helvetica
  </STYLE>
</HEAD>
```

You can use the <LINK> tag to specify a base, or standard, style sheet for all the documents at your site (your company or organization). In this example, we referenced a style sheet in a file called *formal.style*. Of course, your pages can reference any valid style sheet file that you have on your system or network.

You can override the styles for some elements in the style sheet referenced by the <LINK> tag by including a <STYLE> tag and specifying a particular notation. Here we specified the notation "public," but you can use any keyword that you have set up.

Finally, as the author of the page, you can include suggestions to further override the style sheet and notation for individual elements. You do this inside the <STYLE> element. In the example above, we suggested that browsers override the font for the <H1>, <H4>, and <P> elements. (The paragraph tag, <P>, refers to plain text.)

The term *cascading* refers to this method of starting with a standard style sheet, then overriding parts of it with a style notation, and finally overriding specific elements.

With style sheets, you will be able to explicitly specify the characteristics of virtually every element in HTML. This will include typefaces and fonts, the

characteristics of rule lines, en and em dashes, margins, indentation, foreground and background colors for every element, widths, heights, leading, and many other properties. However, the current consensus seems to be that the readers of your pages should have the ultimate say over how elements are rendered, hence the overrides are called *suggestions*. The reason for this is that Web authors can never predict the capabilities of the equipment and the person reading their pages. For example, a sight-impaired person might need to override all style suggestions to make text very large in order to read the page at all.

Chapter 11

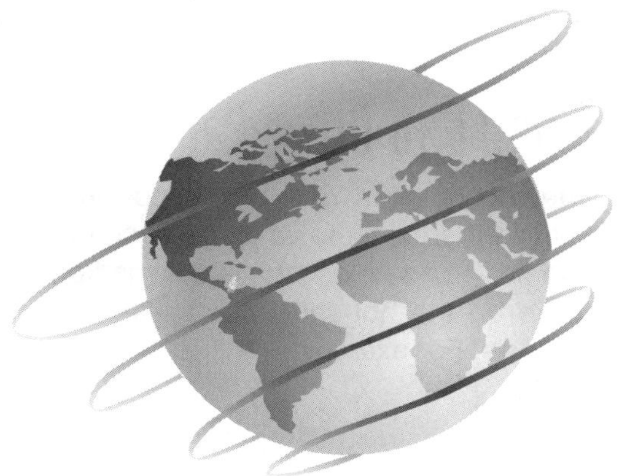

Anchors: The Hypertext Cross-Reference

Whether or not you knew what an anchor was before beginning this book, you probably have some understanding of them now because we've referred to them several times in the chapters leading up to this one.

Anchors are conceptually simple: They're the ingredient in the HTML soup that makes it a hypertext medium. Anchors are the cross-references that define the hypertext links in HTML documents. Using anchors, you can link a hot-spot in a Web page to other pages, to other parts of the same page, and to files and even other Internet services such as FTP servers and the Internet mail system. Up to this point, we've used anchors in a number of examples of Web pages that point to other pages.

In this chapter, we will review what you may already know about anchors, and we will show you how to use anchors to create links to other pages, to certain spots in pages, and to the other Internet services. Think of this chapter as a guide that you can refer back to whenever you're creating hypertext links.

Linking to Other Pages

The anchor tag is <A>, and its most important attribute is the HREF attribute, which defines the object to which the anchor is linked. Any text between the anchor tag and its terminating </A> tag is marked as the *hot-spot* for that anchor. The user clicks on the hot-spot to activate the link to the object defined with the HREF attribute. For example:

```
Combinet has a Web page you can check to
<A HREF="http://www.combinet.com/deploy.html">
see if ISDN service is available</A>in your area.
```

This tag causes a browser to display the the phrase "see if ISDN service is available" in a special way in the browser window — probably underlined and in blue.

When you use your mouse to click on an anchor's hot-spot, your browser will retrieve that Web page and load it into your browser window.

The Uniform Resource Locator

Let's take a closer look at the parameter to the HREF attribute in the anchor above.

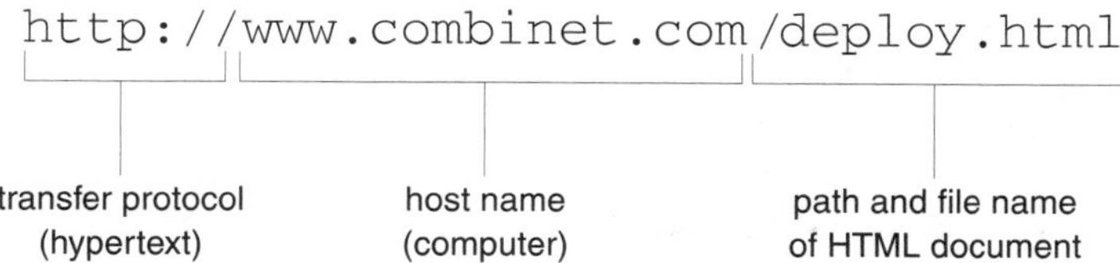

This string of characters is called a *Universal Resource Locator* (or URL). It's called universal because it describes everything about a particular resource that a Web browser needs to know to request and display it. The URL describes the protocol a browser should use to retrieve the resource, the name of the computer it is on, and the path and file name of the resource.

Transfer Protocols

The "http://" is the part of the URL that describes the protocol. The letters *http* stand for *HyperText Transfer Protocol*, the set of rules that a browser will follow to request a document and that the remote server will follow to supply the document. HTML documents almost always use the HTTP protocol, but there are other important ones that Web browsers can use. We'll talk about all of these eventually, but here are a few of the others:

- FTP (for File Transfer Protocol)
- Gopher (for accessing gopher servers)
- Mailto (for access to an SMTP mail server)
- NNTP (for Net News Transfer Protocol)
- Telnet (for remote terminal sessions)

Host Names

The next part of the URL is the name of the remote host. In this example, the host is "www.combinet.com". This host name refers to a computer named "www" that is on the "combinet" network, which has a ".com" extension because it is a commercial domain.

It's become something of a convention for organizations that provide Web servers to put their main public Web server on a machine named "www". Organizations that have a high volume of Web traffic may put a computer on their network dedicated exclusively to serving Web pages. They almost always give that computer the name "www". You'll occasionally run into computers named "www2" or even "www3" at sites that have an especially high volume of traffic.

However, the convention of naming the computer that serves Web pages "www" isn't followed only by large organizations with many computers; even small sites with a single computer frequently use this convention. They simply register the name "www" on their network (or their service provider's network) as an alias for their single machine. We'll show you how to do this in Chapter 16 of this book.

Directories and Paths

The final part of the URL is the path and file name of the HTML document on the remote host. Most system administrators for Web servers organize their collection of Web pages by creating a tree of disk subdirectories to contain the files. The top, or root, of this directory tree is seldom the root directory of the hard disk drive. For example, the top directory for a Web server running on a Unix system might be */var/www/docs*. On a Windows NT or Windows 95 system, it might be *C:\WWW\DOCS*; any subdirectories you reference in a URL are relative to this top directory.

In our example, there are no subdirectories specified in the URL. This URL refers to an HTML document file named *deploy.html* that is physically stored in the top directory of the Web document tree, wherever that is. There is no way to tell (and no reason why you need to know) which actual subdirectory on the remote host serves as the root directory for its Web documents.

Here's another example of a URL:

```
http://www.abc.com/browse/som/dtp.html
```

This URL refers to a Web page file called *dtp.html* in the subdirectory *browse/som/* on the host *www.cts.com*. The subdirectory *browse* is on the root of the Web document tree, and within that subdirectory is another subdirectory called *som* which holds the file *dtp.html*.

Port Numbers

One other part of a URL isn't used in either of the two examples we've looked at: the port number. You won't run into port numbers very often, but we should look at them briefly.

Clients for the different Internet services—FTP, the Gopher system, the Web, and so on—use a default port number when they connect to a remote computer. The servers don't actually have different *physical* ports (it only takes one wire to connect a computer to the Internet), but servers do have different *logical* ports that the connections coming into the system from the Internet attach to. This way, the

server software knows what to expect when a remote computer connects to a certain port and knows what program to run to handle the connections.

By default, Telnet programs use port 23, Gopher programs use port 70, and Web clients connect to port 80. Once in a while you may need to explicitly specify a port number other than the default in a URL. To do that, just follow the host name with a colon and the number of the port.

For example, if you need to create an anchor to a Gopher system that is on port 71 of a remote host (instead of the default 70), you might use a URL like this:

```
gopher://umn.edu:71
```

If you need to retrieve a Web page through a nonstandard port, the URL you use might look like this:

```
http://www.ucsd.edu:81/mammals/bovine.html
```

Default Pages and Directories

If you've browsed through the catalog at the back of the book and looked at the URLs for these companies, you may have noticed that many of them don't include a path or file name. This is because Web servers automatically provide a default file to a browser if you omit a specific file name from a URL. There's nothing special about that default file except its name. On most systems, the default Web page name is *index.html*, but this may vary from system to system. A few servers use *default.html* or *homepage.html*.

The mere existence of a file named *index.html* in any subdirectory in a Web tree makes it the default Web page for that subdirectory. The advantages of this may not be immediately apparent, but it is really a great feature. Since *index.html* is the default name, organizations almost always name their home pages *index.html* and put them in the root of their Web page directory tree. This way, you don't have to know a path and file name to find the home page of many businesses—you can just guess at their host name, and it will often work. For example, the following URLs take you directly to the home pages of each of these companies.

- http://www.ibm.com/
- http://www.microsoft.com/
- http://www.goodyear.com/
- http://www.att.com/

When you specify a subdirectory name in a URL but don't include a file name, the remote server looks for a default file named *index.html* in that subdirectory. If it finds one, it will serve that file. But if there is no default file, the remote server creates a page to show a list of the files in that subdirectory. Let's say, for example, that you provide the anchor

```
<A HREF="http://www.tectron.com/aviation/">
```

where *aviation* is the name of a subdirectory on the root of the Web tree at that host. If there is no file named *index.html* in the *aviation* directory, the server at the host will provide a listing of the files in the directory. The remote server creates the HTML code on the fly to serve this list to the Web browser. Figure 11-1 shows what it looks like.

An easy way to think of this behavior is that the server first looks in a directory for a file named *index.html*. If it finds one, it serves that file. If it doesn't, it creates an "index" of the files in the directory and serves that instead.

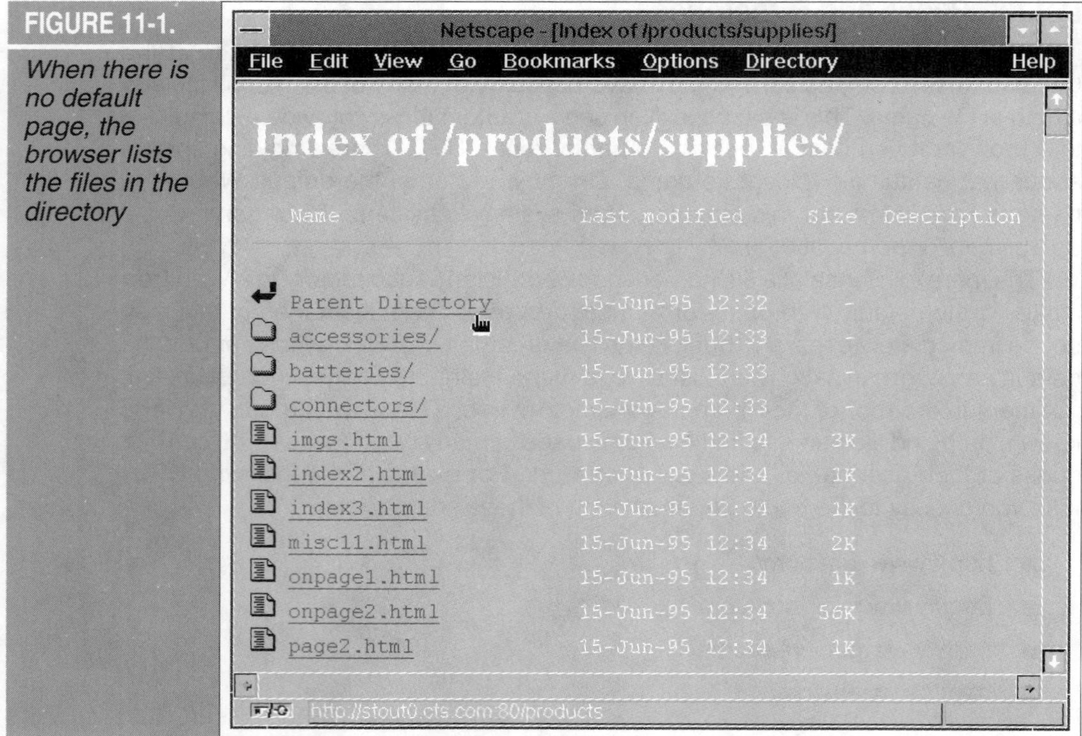

FIGURE 11-1. *When there is no default page, the browser lists the files in the directory*

When you create a web of pages, you can put this feature to work for you. At one extreme, you could make an entire web of pages where every page is named *index.html* and resides in its own subdirectory. This could make for large and cumbersome subdirectory trees. At the other extreme, you could give all the pages of your web unique names and place them in the same subdirectory. This too can become cumbersome if your web has a great many pages. The most logical way to lay out a web is to use a combination of subdirectories with default pages that also contain related page files.

A good practice to follow to find a reasonable medium is to think of the anchors in your Web pages as menu choices (which isn't hard since that's essentially what they are), then create a hierarchy of subdirectories that corresponds to those menu choices. Think of the final page of any sequence of menu choices that a user might take as a *terminal page*—a page that simply presents some piece of information. A terminal page may well have links to other pages in your web or even to remote hosts, but terminal pages don't provide any further categorization of menu choices.

For example, say you are creating a web for a small business that sells electronic equipment and supplies. And let's say the name of the computer your Web server is on is named, or aliased to, *www.tronics.com*. You can create a home page for the company in the root Web directory and name that home page *index.html*. That way, other Web authors can create links to your company's home page by creating the anchor

```
<A HREF="http://www.tronics.com">Tronics, Inc.</A>
```

and people using a browser can find your company simply by typing the URL

```
http://www.tronics.com
```

into their Web browser.

Let's also say that you put a number of anchors in this home page that relate to different subjects, including general company and product information. Among the products your company sells on the Web are batteries; for users to get to the battery information, they have to navigate through several pages in this order:

1. Home page
2. Product information
3. Supplies

4. Batteries
5. Information about a specific battery type

A good way (but by no means the only way) to set up your pages and anchors is to make them correspond to a directory tree.

If a user is interested in size AA batteries, the second to last page they will see in the sequence will present them with a choice of batteries (AA, C, D, 9-volt, and so on). When they click on the link labeled "AA Batteries," they will get a *terminal page* with detailed information about the company's AA batteries. This final page with information about the AA batteries might include links back to the company's home page or to an order form, but it is the last page in a logical sequence of pages.

Now, it doesn't make a lot of sense to create a separate directory for every type of battery because each directory would probably have only one page in it. A better way would be to name the second to the last page (the one that lists the types of batteries) *index.html* and place it in the */products/supplies/batteries* subdirectory along with the pages that describe each of the batteries.

Let's follow the anchors from the beginning. The company home page is named *index.html* and resides in the root Web directory on the server. When a reader clicks on the anchor for "Product Information," the server sends her the default file (named *index.html*) in the directory */products*. When she clicks on "Supplies," the server sends her the file */products/supplies/index.html*. When she clicks on "Batteries," the server sends the file */products/supplies/batteries/index.html*. Finally, when she clicks on "AA Batteries," the server sends the file */products/supplies/batteries/ AA.html*.

Linking to Local Pages

In the discussion of URLs in the previous section, each example of a URL in an anchor tag that we presented included a full host name. But when you are making links to HTML documents on your own system, you don't have to include the host name in every anchor. In fact, it will be faster for people reading your pages from their own machines if you don't include a host name for local files; if you do, their computers will have to re-resolve that host name each time they load a new page.

When you create links to local pages, you can omit the host name completely. To continue the example we began in the previous section, the anchor in Tronics' home page to link to the "Product Information" page can simply look like this:

```
<A HREF="products">Product Information</A>
```

Remember that Tronics' home page is in the root Web directory and that "products" is the name of a subdirectory in that root directory. This reference is relative to the

location of the home page (the directory *products* exists in the same directory as the home page). Follow along with this sequence of events by referring to Figures 11-2 and 11-3.

When users click on the link "Product Information" in the home page, your server sends them the file *index.html* in the directory */products*. So now your reader is looking at a page with a link labeled "Supplies" on it. This link connects to the default page in the *supplies* subdirectory, which also contains another subdirectory named *batteries*. The link for "Supplies" looks like this:

```
<A HREF="supplies">Supplies</A>
```

When your user clicks on the link "Supplies", the server sends him the file *supplies/index.html*. Notice that the way we expressed this path here (*supplies/index.html*) is relative to the location of the page he is looking at. The actual location of this file is */products/supplies/index.html*.

FIGURE 11-2. *Disk directory tree of tronics.com*

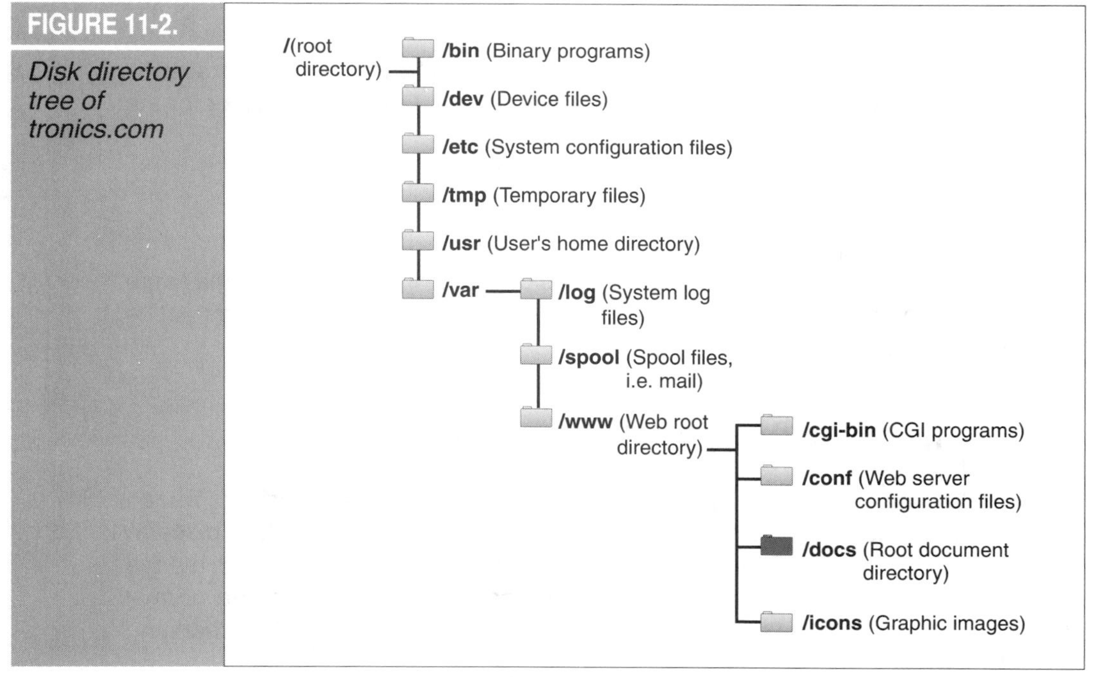

FIGURE 11-3. *Subdirectory tree below the root Web document directory*

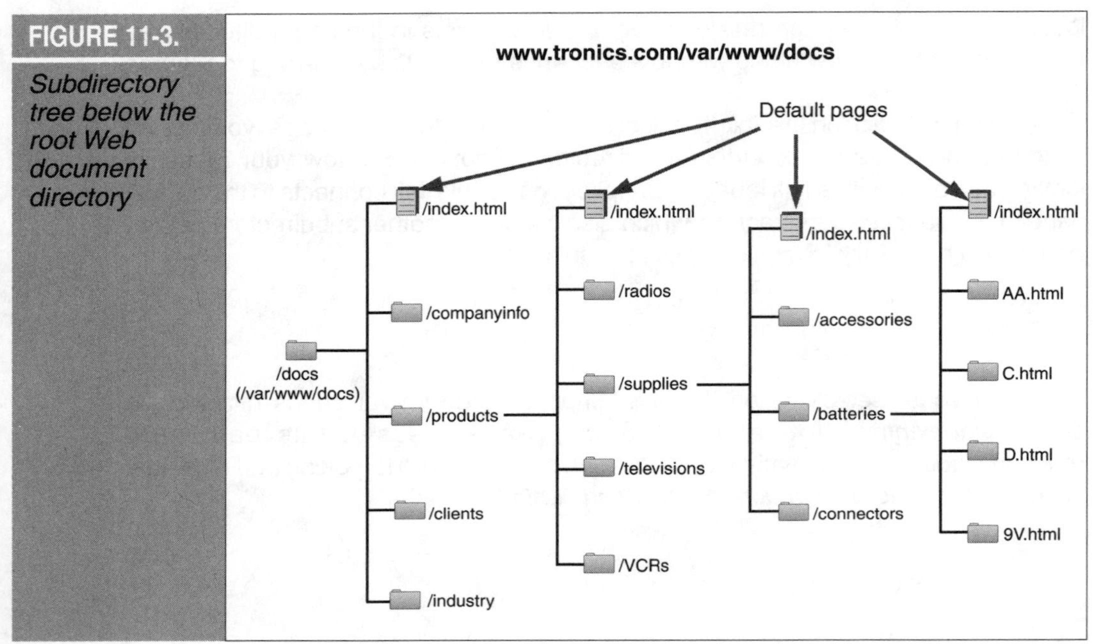

After the reader clicks on the link "Supplies" and then "Batteries," he will see the file *batteries/index.html* (relative to the "Supplies" page). Finally, the anchor for the link to the "AA Batteries" page is

```
<A HREF="AA.html">AA Batteries</A>
```

Like the links to the directories leading up to this page, the file *AA.html* is in the same directory as the page the reader is looking at, so the anchor can specify a relative URL to the page.

Linking to Other Parts of the Same Page

You can also use an anchor to jump to another spot in the same document. You do this by defining not only the hypertext hot-spot, but also the target (the place to which you want to jump). Defining an anchor to jump to a particular spot on a page is simple. It just involves a slight variation on the HREF parameter to a normal anchor tag. However, the way you define the targets of these anchors is changing with HTML 3.

You create a hypertext target inside a document by assigning a unique name to an element. It's this process of assigning names to elements that is changing with HTML 3, but the concept remains the same. Defining a name is like creating a label in a programming language—it's just some code that says "I'm naming this spot in the document, and its name will be Fred." Of course, you would probably use a more descriptive name than Fred—something like "Section2" or "Part_3" or "Bibliography". Names can be anything you want, as long as they haven't already been used in the document.

Let's look for a moment at the anchors you use to jump to a named element, then go back and look at the specifics of creating the targets—the named elements.

To create an anchor that will jump a reader to a named element, just include a pound sign (the # character) after the page's file name in the URL. Follow that with the name you assigned to the element you want the reader to jump to. For example, let's say that in the document at http://www.tectron.com/info/products.html you have created a named element that you called "Radios". And let's say you want to create anchors at the top of the document to allow readers to jump down to the various sections of the document. Such anchors would use relative URLs, as discussed in the previous section. The anchor to jump directly to the "Radios" label would look like this:

```
<A HREF="#Radios">Jump directly to the Radios</A>
```

You can also provide an *absolute* URL that would allow browsers to jump directly to this section of this document from anywhere in the world. The same link with an absolute URL would look like this:

```
<A HREF="http://www.tectron.com/info/products.html#Radios">Jump
from anywhere</A>
```

Prior to HTML 3, the only way to create a hypertext target within a document (a named element) was with an anchor tag. To use this method, you use the NAME attribute to the anchor. (It doesn't matter whether the anchor has an HREF parameter or not; it's perfectly legitimate to use an anchor element only for defining a hypertext target.)

```
<A NAME="Radios">Radio Products</A>
```

This anchor has no HREF attribute. The only thing it does is associate the name "Radios" with this spot in the document, thus making it a potential hypertext target.

With HTML 3, you can still use an anchor as a hypertext target (by adding the NAME attribute to the anchor), but you can also use virtually every other element as a hypertext target as well. The only exceptions are the font-style elements such as Bold and Italic. It's as easy to assign a name to a horizontal rule or a heading (in order to use it as a target) as it is to name an anchor.

Naming these elements works pretty much the same way as it always has for anchors. However, the attribute isn't NAME—it's ID. For example, to assign the name "products" to a heading that displays the text "Product Information," you use the ID attribute with the heading tag directly:

```
<H2 ID="products">Product Information</H2>
```

This displays the label "Product Information" in the header 2 format just the way you would expect, but now the label is also a hypertext hot-spot. The anchor you need to jump to this hot-spot is the same as it's always been:

```
<A HREF="#products">Product Information</A>
```

When readers click on this anchor text, their browser will skip down to the label and position the page in their screen so that the heading is at the top of their browser's window.

Not all browsers support the ID attribute to the elements yet. However, most browser developers are working on it. Some of the developers plan to support the ID attribute in only some elements initially, like the heading elements.

Using Graphic Images as Hypertext Hot-spots

Occasionally you might want to make a graphic image a hypertext hot-spot. For example, you might want the links on your page to look like graphic icons or buttons, as shown in Figure 11-4. You already know all the concepts and tags you need to do this, but to help you put the pieces together, we'll go over the procedure here.

To make an image a hypertext hot-spot, you simply sandwich the tag for your image into an anchor tag. You can even optionally include a text label in the anchor tag to make both the image and the label part of your hot-spot (see Figure 11-5). For example, let's say that your icon image file is called *icon1.gif* and that you want this image to be a hot-spot that leads browsers to the page *page2.html*. Here's how your anchor should look:

```
<a href="page2.html"><img src="icon1.gif">Page 2</a>
```

FIGURE 11-4.

An image can be a hypertext hot-spot

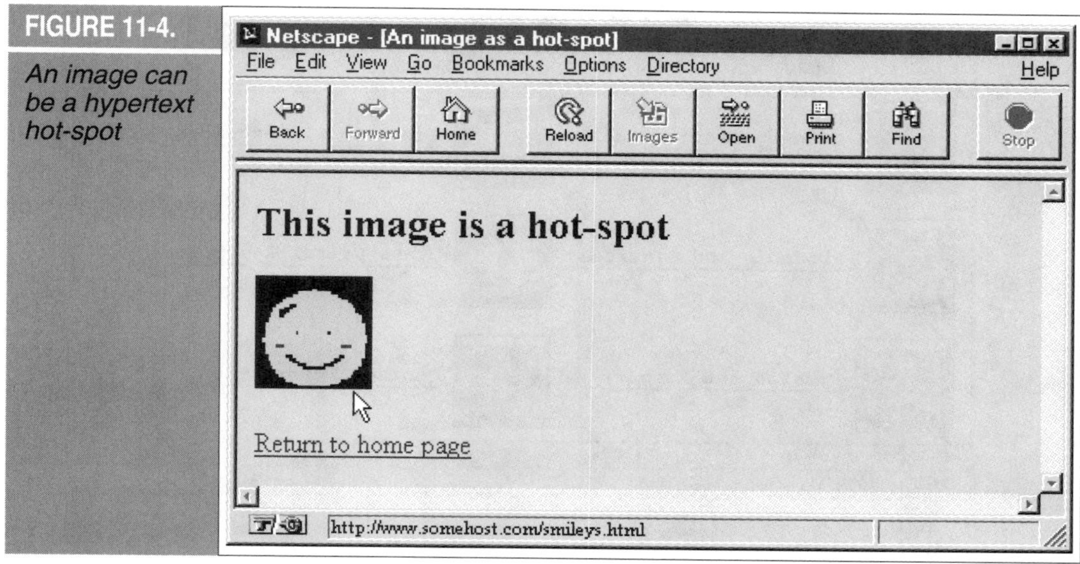

The HREF attribute to the anchor tag points to *page2.html*, just as it would if you were not including an image in the hot-spot. Sandwiched between the opening and terminating tags of the anchor, though, are both an image tag and the text "Page 2".

You can also use multiple images side by side for an interesting effect. Figure 11-6 shows an example.

FIGURE 11-5.

A single image with a label as a hypertext hot-spot

FIGURE 11-6. *Multiple images as hypertext hot-spots*

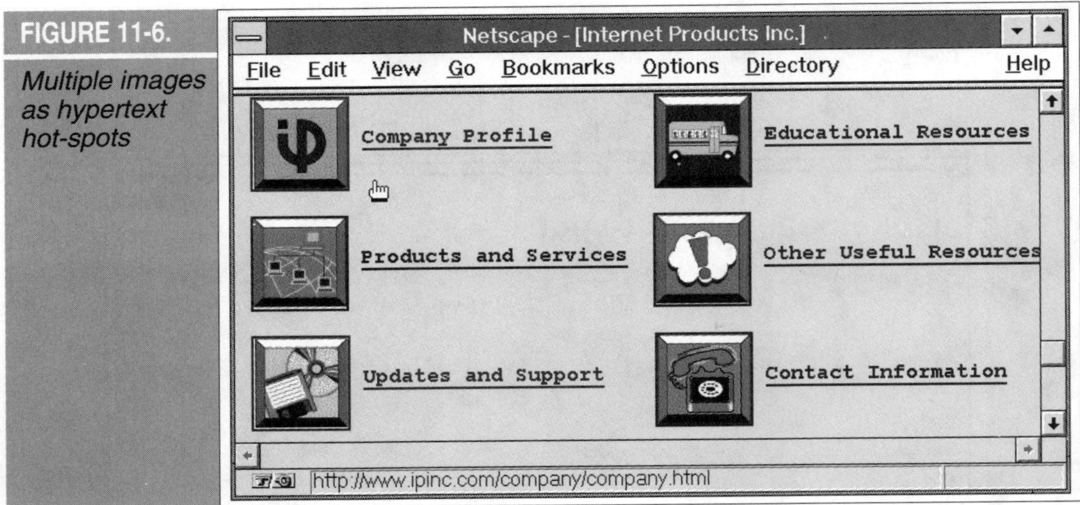

Linking to FTP Servers

The *File Transfer Protocol*, or FTP, is the tool users have relied on for years to send files to and retrieve files from other computers on the Internet. While the FTP command-line interface isn't difficult to use, it gives people the impression that the Internet is arcane and that you have to be some kind of techno-geek to be able to use it. The World Wide Web has changed all that.

While you can't use a Web browser to put a file on a remote computer, you can use one to browse and retrieve files (which is mostly what you would want to use FTP for anyway). As you can see in Figure 11-7, a directory of files on an FTP server as seen through a Web browser is just a list of files that you can click to download.

Before we get into the URL and anchors for FTP resources, you should understand that there are two types of FTP: Anonymous FTP and Non-anonymous FTP.

Anonymous FTP

Anonymous FTP allows you to log into any computer on the Internet that provides an FTP server, whether or not you have an account and password on that computer. In command-line Unix, you would use a program called "ftp" to make such a

FIGURE 11-7.

An FTP directory as shown in a Web browser's window

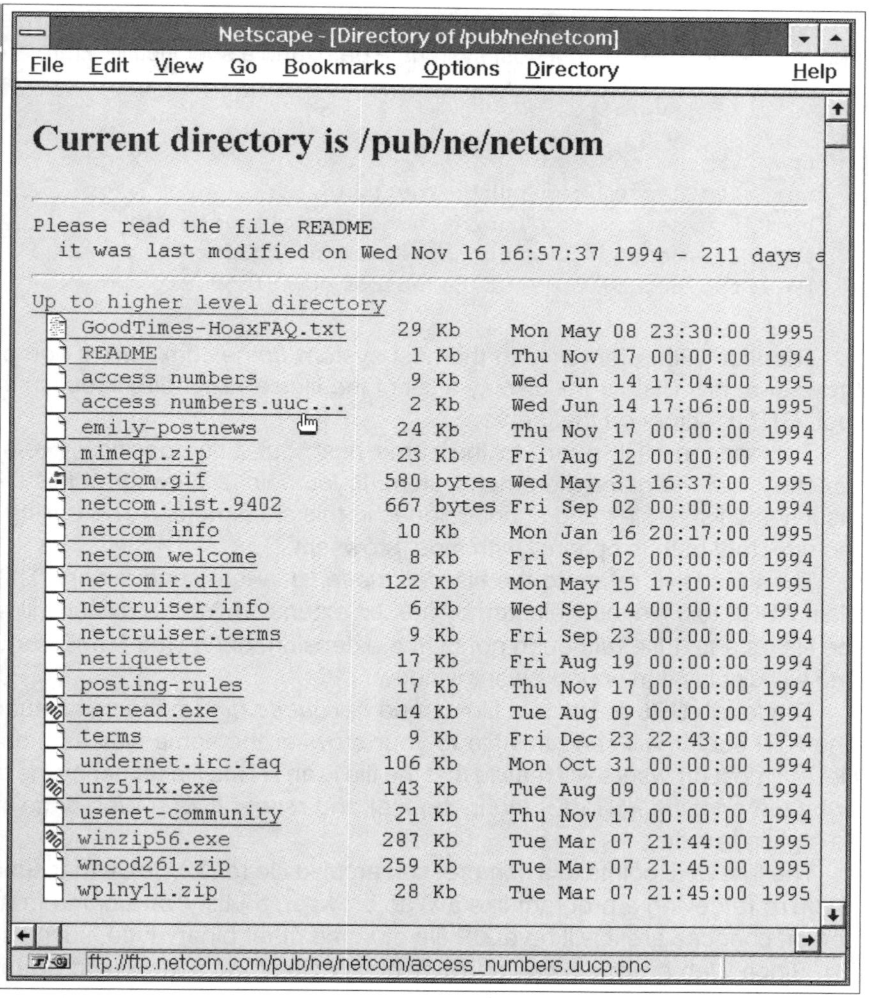

Netscape - [Directory of /pub/ne/netcom]

File Edit View Go Bookmarks Options Directory Help

Current directory is /pub/ne/netcom

Please read the file README
it was last modified on Wed Nov 16 16:57:37 1994 - 211 days a

Up to higher level directory

GoodTimes-HoaxFAQ.txt	29 Kb	Mon May 08 23:30:00 1995
README	1 Kb	Thu Nov 17 00:00:00 1994
access numbers	9 Kb	Wed Jun 14 17:04:00 1995
access numbers.uuc...	2 Kb	Wed Jun 14 17:06:00 1995
emily-postnews	24 Kb	Thu Nov 17 00:00:00 1994
mimeqp.zip	23 Kb	Fri Aug 12 00:00:00 1994
netcom.gif	580 bytes	Wed May 31 16:37:00 1995
netcom.list.9402	667 bytes	Fri Sep 02 00:00:00 1994
netcom info	10 Kb	Mon Jan 16 20:17:00 1995
netcom welcome	8 Kb	Fri Sep 02 00:00:00 1994
netcomir.dll	122 Kb	Mon May 15 17:00:00 1995
netcruiser.info	6 Kb	Wed Sep 14 00:00:00 1994
netcruiser.terms	9 Kb	Fri Sep 23 00:00:00 1994
netiquette	17 Kb	Fri Aug 19 00:00:00 1994
posting-rules	17 Kb	Thu Nov 17 00:00:00 1994
tarread.exe	14 Kb	Tue Aug 09 00:00:00 1994
terms	9 Kb	Fri Dec 23 22:43:00 1994
undernet.irc.faq	106 Kb	Mon Oct 31 00:00:00 1994
unz511x.exe	143 Kb	Tue Aug 09 00:00:00 1994
usenet-community	21 Kb	Thu Nov 17 00:00:00 1994
winzip56.exe	287 Kb	Tue Mar 07 21:44:00 1995
wncod261.zip	259 Kb	Tue Mar 07 21:45:00 1995
wplny11.zip	28 Kb	Tue Mar 07 21:45:00 1995

ftp://ftp.netcom.com/pub/ne/netcom/access_numbers.uucp.pnc

connection, and by convention you could log into the remote computer with the username "anonymous" or "ftp". When the remote computer prompts for a password, you type in your own Internet email address.

When you use Anonymous FTP with a Web browser, the browser takes care of the details of making the connection and logging in. All you have to do is point the browser at the FTP server you want to browse.

As with Web URLs, FTP URLs can refer to a host system only, to a host system and a directory path, or to a host system, a path, and a specific file. Here are several variations on FTP URLs:

```
ftp://ftp.netcom.com
ftp://ftp.netcom.com/pub/ne/netcom/
ftp://ftp.netcom.com/pub/ne/netcom/netiquette.txt
ftp://ftp.netcom.com/pub/ne/netcom/netiquette.html
ftp://ftp.netcom.com/pub/ne/netcom/winzip56.zip
```

The first URL refers only to the host system *ftp.netcom.com.* If you point your browser at this URL, it will display a list of the files and subdirectories in the top, or root, FTP directory on that server.

The second URL refers to the same host, but also specifically refers to the directory */pub/ne/netcom* on that system. If you point a browser at this URL, it will display the list of files and subdirectories in this subdirectory. The trailing slash on the directory path is optional with most browsers.

The third URL refers to the file *netiquette.txt* in that subdirectory. This file is a plain ASCII text file, as indicated by the .txt extension. Your browser will recognize the file as a text file (although not by the extension, but by the MIME content type) and will display it in your browser window.

The fourth URL points to a file named *netiquette.html* in the same subdirectory. The FTP server will send this file to your browser the same way as it does a text file, but most browsers will realize that the file is an HTML file (either by the extension or by the opening <HTML> tag in the file) and render it as a Web page instead of as a plain text file.

The last URL points to a compressed archive file (a ZIP file) in that subdirectory. If you're retrieving a program like a Web browser, a utility, or a game from an FTP server, chances are it will be a ZIP file or some other binary type, such as an .EXE file. Since Web browsers can't display binary files (and you wouldn't want them to if they could), most will pop up a dialog box and ask you if you want to save the file to disk. Retrieving files from an FTP server is as simple as that.

Now that you know how to use FTP URLs with a browser, let's look at how you make anchor elements that you can put into a page for these URLs. There are no tricks here; just put those URLs into an anchor tag along with some anchor text to create a hot-spot.

```
<a href="ftp://ftp.netcom.com">Netcom's Public FTP Server</a>

<a href="ftp://ftp.netcom.com/pub/ne/netcom/">Netcom's FTP
Archive</a>

<a href="ftp://ftp.netcom.com/pub/ne/netcom/netiquette.txt">
Netiquette in text format</a>

<a href="ftp://ftp.netcom.com/pub/ne/netcom/netiquette.html">
The Netiquette Web Page</a>

<a href="ftp://ftp.netcom.com/pub/ne/netcom/winzip56.zip">
A Windows Zip Utility</a>
```

Non-Anonymous FTP

Non-anonymous FTP is different from Anonymous FTP in that you use it to log into a remote computer when you do have your own user account and password on that machine. For example, let's say that you have both a shell account and a PPP account with your Internet provider. And let's say you mostly use only your PPP account because, of course, you spend most of your time browsing the Web. But once in while you do log into your shell account to use some program or facility that you can only access from a command-line shell account. As a result, you've accumulated some files in your home directory on your service provider's machine that you would like to bring home.

In all likelihood, Anonymous FTP couldn't help you in this situation because you wouldn't have access to the files in your home directory. Generally, users' home directories and the FTP directory tree are completely separate. But you know your username and password, so you can use Non-anonymous FTP to get your files.

The URL for a Non-anonymous FTP connection is a little different from those for Anonymous FTP because you have to encode your username and password into the URL. Here's what it looks like:

```
ftp://rickst:GrafX@netcom.com/u3/rickst
```

In this example, "rickst" is the username and "GrafX" is the password. Follow the host name with the full path to your home directory. When you point your browser at a URL like this, it will show you a list of the files in your home directory in the same way that Anonymous FTP displays directories. And also like Anonymous FTP, you can point to a specific file or subdirectory in your home directory.

Here's the same URL in anchor form:

```
<a href="ftp://rickst:GrafX@netcom.com/u3/rickst">My home
directory on Netcom</a>
```

WARNING *If you create links to Non-anonymous FTP accounts and make these links available to the world, you are giving away your username and password to anyone who cares to look at it. Be very careful about keeping your passwords off pages that are publicly available.*

File URLs

Most browsers support a *file* URL. That is, you can display a text file that is on your own computer in a Web browser by simply pointing your browser at it. This isn't a feature that you will use often, because many other programs can serve as better viewers than a Web browser. But you may, on occasion, want to pull up a local text document in your browser. The syntax for a file URL is a little different from other URLs. For example, let's say you have a directory \TMP on your C: drive, and in that directory is an HTML file you are working on named *ORDRFORM.HTM*. You can test this page with your browser by pointing the browser at the URL:

```
file:///C:/TMP/FTPDIR.HTM
```

or, on a Unix system:

```
file:////usr/home/rick/mypage.html
```

Notice that these URLs begin with the file type "file:" and that there are three slashes (four on a Unix system) instead of the usual two. After that, all you need is the drive, path, and file name to your local file.

Although you can use a file URL to load a file on a remote system, there's little point because your browser will simply use FTP to get it anyway.

Also, be careful when building file URLs for a local file into anchors on a Web page. When a browser runs into a file URL, it will expect the file to be on the same system that the browser is running on. So while it may work on your system (because the referenced file is on your system), other people who browse your page and click on that link will get an error because the referenced file is not on their system.

Linking to Gopher Servers

A couple of years ago, the Gopher system held great promise as the new resource that would make the Internet easy to use for the masses. It didn't hold that lofty perch long, though. With the popularity of the Web today, the Gopher system has for the most part become a relic. In fact, many new Web users have never even heard of Gopher. Gopher is a worldwide, Internet-based menu system—a program that displays lists of menu options (see Figure 11-8). The Gopher program allows users to make a selection from the available options, then it transports them to a new set of menu options or displays a document. As with anchors in HTML, a menu choice might take the reader to a new menu, to a document on a machine across the room, or to the other side of the world.

FIGURE 11-8.

Viewing a Gopher menu with a Web browser

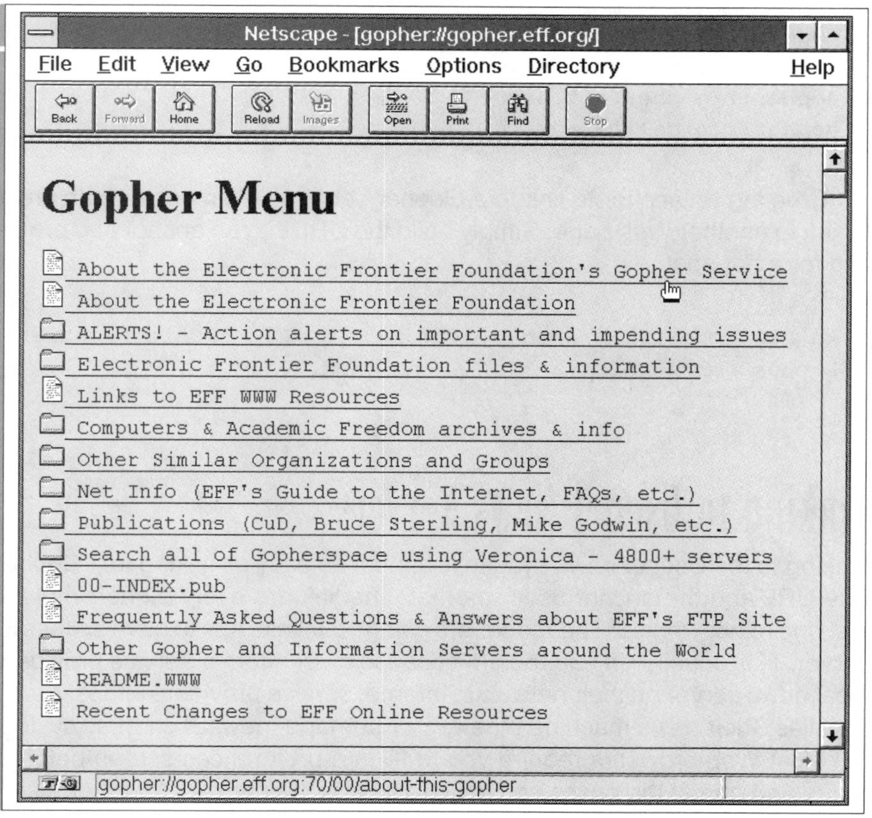

Netscape - [gopher://gopher.eff.org/]
File Edit View Go Bookmarks Options Directory Help
Back Forward Home Reload Images Open Print Find Stop

Gopher Menu

About the Electronic Frontier Foundation's Gopher Service
About the Electronic Frontier Foundation
ALERTS! - Action alerts on important and impending issues
Electronic Frontier Foundation files & information
Links to EFF WWW Resources
Computers & Academic Freedom archives & info
Other Similar Organizations and Groups
Net Info (EFF's Guide to the Internet, FAQs, etc.)
Publications (CuD, Bruce Sterling, Mike Godwin, etc.)
Search all of Gopherspace using Veronica - 4800+ servers
00-INDEX.pub
Frequently Asked Questions & Answers about EFF's FTP Site
Other Gopher and Information Servers around the World
README.WWW
Recent Changes to EFF Online Resources

gopher://gopher.eff.org:70/00/about-this-gopher

Compared to the Web, the Gopher system is exceedingly simple. For one thing, it's completely nongraphical, so there are none of the complexities of images, headings, fonts, and so on. Furthermore, there is no free-form text on Gopher menus—just menu choices—so every menu is like a list of anchors. Of course, this system's simplicity and lack of capability is why the Web is so popular today. However, there are still many popular Gopher servers on the Internet with a wealth of information and resources. And the simplicity of the Gopher system has made it easy for Web browser developers to build Gopher compatibility into their browsers. Gopher menus look better in a Web browser than they ever did on a character-based terminal screen.

Like Web servers and FTP servers, Gopher servers run on many computers around the world (although the majority of them are at universities), and you identify them by their host names and domain. Here are a few typical Gopher URLs:

```
gopher://hawking.u.washington.edu
gopher://riceinfo.rice.edu
gopher://gopher.eff.org
gopher://pipeline.com
```

Creating an anchor to link to a Gopher server is even easier than creating one to link to another Web page: Simply build the URL into an anchor and provide some text for a hot-spot.

```
<a href="gopher://gopher.eff.org">The Electronic Frontier
Foundation Gopher</a>
```

Linking to Usenet News Servers

Linking to the Usenet news system is almost as easy as linking to a Gopher server. The URL and the anchor used to create the link are every bit as simple. There is just one minor wrinkle: The reader browsing your links has to have access to a news server. This usually isn't a problem because most Internet service providers have a local news server on their networks. Internet service providers almost always name (or alias) their news machines "news", or perhaps "news2" on busy systems.

Most Web browsers require you to fill in a preferences screen before you use them, and one of the boxes you have to fill in is the name of your news server. The default name "news" may even be in the box already. Of course, when you're

designing a Web page that provides links to a particular newsgroup, you have no control over whether or not your readers have filled in this information properly. You'll have to assume they have, and if they haven't, they'll get an error message when they try your link to a newsgroup.

There are two types of URLs for news: those that refer to whole subject groups and those that refer to a particular message. Before you make links to specific messages, bear in mind that Usenet messages don't stay around for long. Most Internet service providers make news articles expire in a matter of days.

To create an anchor to a Usenet newsgroup, use the protocol type "news" followed by a colon, then just type in the name of the newsgroup:

```
<a href="news:rec.aviation">Usenet's rec.aviation newsgroup</a>
```

Every message that is posted to the Usenet system gets a unique identifying number called the *message id*. When you read a message, you can see the message id. If you find a particular message to which you want to create a link, you should know its message id. To create a link to a single message, just replace the name of the newsgroup with the unique message id:

```
<a href="news:543521145">A very interesting message</a>
```

Linking to the Internet Mail System

Two of the pieces of information that users should provide to their browsers during setup are their Internet mail address and the name of the computer that serves mail on their network. Given this information, a Web browser can send a piece of email anywhere in the world. You'll often see "mailto" links at the bottom of Web pages for contacting the author or webmaster in case you have questions or problems with their pages.

The mailto URL type causes a browser to pop up a dialog box in which the reader types the text of a message. When the reader is ready to send the message, she clicks an OK or Send button. Nearly all of the most important browsers today support the mailto URL. Here's what a mailto anchor looks like:

```
<a href="mailto:rstout@netcom.com">Send a note to Rick</a>
```

When a browser encounters this URL, it will pop open a dialog box with a message preaddressed to you. In the example shown in Figure 11-9, it is preaddressed to "rstout@netcom.com". The dialog box will probably even include your return address and your signature file, if you have one. The reader can click in the large edit box to edit the body of the message, then click the Send button; the browser will fire off the message to the mail server.

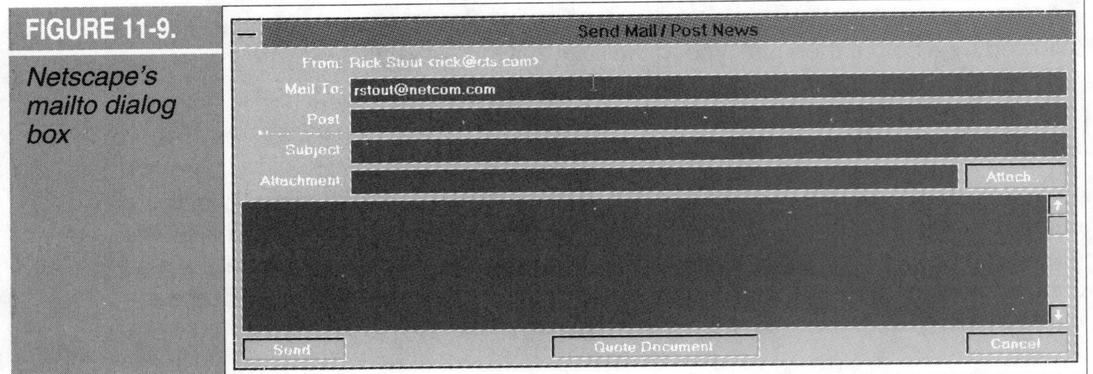

FIGURE 11-9. *Netscape's mailto dialog box*

Chapter 12

Working with Multimedia Objects

Up to this point in Part II, you've learned about creating Web pages with HTML. You've learned what HTML is, how to use it to create pages, and how to create links to a variety of Internet tools and services. In this chapter, we'll take a small detour and explore some areas that don't, strictly speaking, have anything to do with HTML. For starters, you'll learn how to use two variations on the familiar GIF image format that you've seen in most of the examples of inline images up to this point. Next, you'll learn how and why you might use external images.

In the second part of this chapter, we'll look at multimedia objects such as video and sound. You'll learn about the different formats for audio and video clips and how to integrate them into your Web pages.

Advanced Image Topics

By now you're comfortable with displaying inline images on a Web page with the standard image tags in HTML—<IMG> and <FIG> (the latter in HTML 3). In this section, we'll look at some techniques you can use to change the appearance of your inline images. All the tools you'll need are freely available on the Internet, and they're not hard to use.

Transparent Images

All the image formats that display graphics on computers (including the popular GIF and JPEG formats) define rectangular areas on a computer's display. Even the round dots you see so often used as bullets are actually square images. To make a nonsquare image, such as a round dot, appear as a round dot rather than a round dot on a square background, you need to make the background disappear.

Figure 12-1 shows an image we first saw in Chapter 10. The top half should be familiar; the lower shows the original image before it was converted to a transparent GIF. We made this image transparent by using a program that identifies the background pixels and converts them to a transparent color. (As you'll see in a moment, this is easy to do when the background of the image is a solid color.) When a browser displays a transparent image like this one, it looks like it's displaying just the subject of the image.

Figure 12-2 shows how the image background really becomes transparent. A custom background has been set; notice that the page background is visible through the background of the image. A transparent GIF image conforms to a slightly different standard from a normal GIF image. This standard is called *GIF89a,* and it allows you to mark a single color in the image as transparent. Some image viewers don't recognize GIF89a images as being any different from a standard GIF (a GIF87a

FIGURE 12-1. *Transparent and nontransparent images*

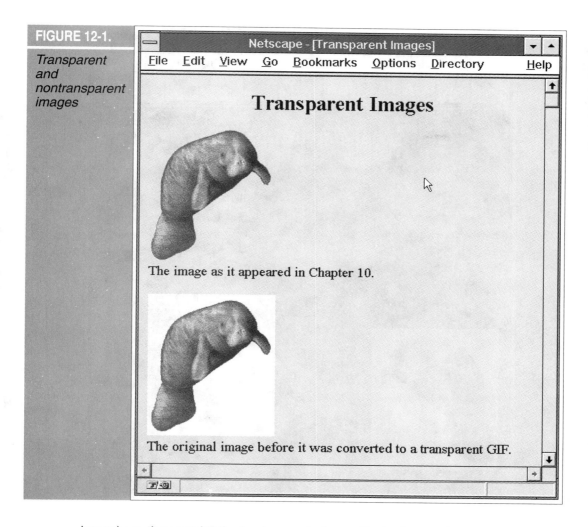

image), so they render the background along with the image. Fortunately, most of the newer viewers and Web browsers do understand GIF89a images.

Several tools can convert a standard GIF87a image to a transparent GIF89a image. Before you try to convert an image, though, take a close look at it to make sure it's a good candidate for conversion.

The process of converting a GIF to a transparent image is simple: You just pick a single color in the image to earmark as transparent. Every pixel of that color in your image will become transparent, so be careful. The conversion programs have

FIGURE 12-2. *The manatee on a custom background*

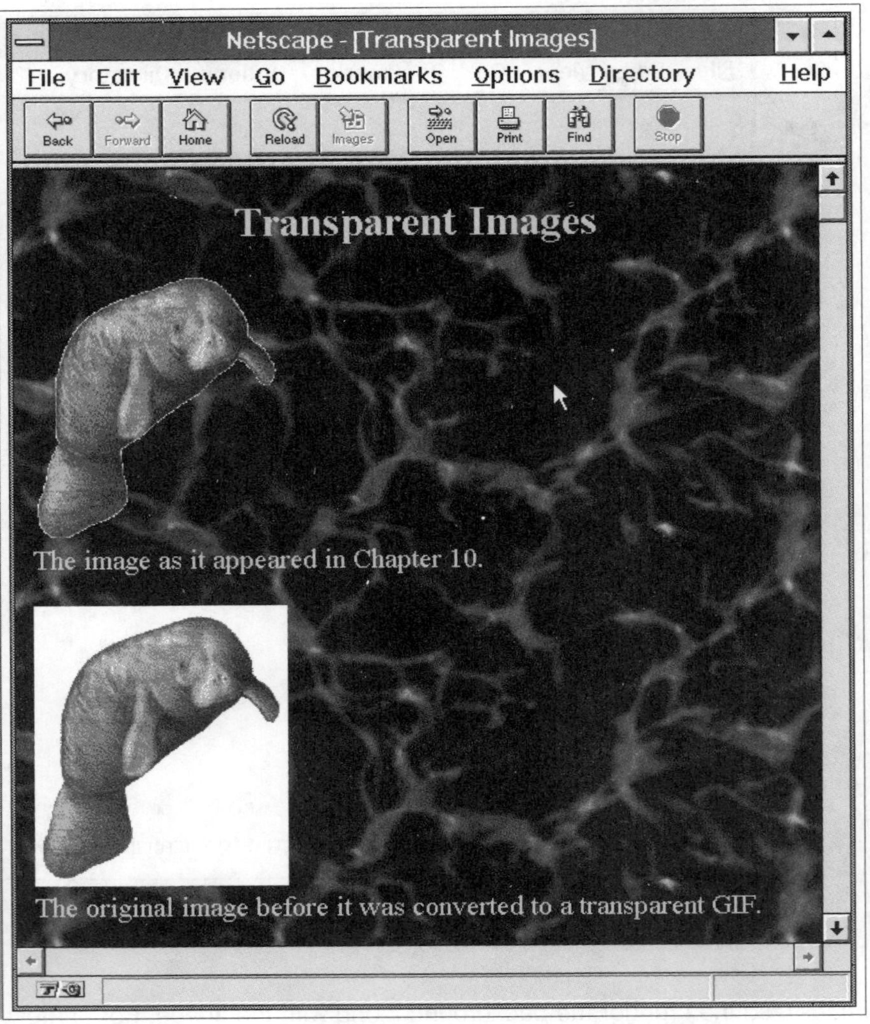

no concept of the geography of your image—they can't differentiate which part is the subject and which part is the background. They simply redefine one of the colors in the colormap to be transparent.

To be on the safe side, you can first load the image into a paint program to make sure the background pixels are a color that's unique to the whole image. An easy way to do this is to use the *floodfill* feature of many drawing programs. Once you're sure all the pixels of the background are the same color (like white, gray, or light

blue) and don't exist anywhere inside the subject of the image, you can use a utility program to convert the image to a GIF89a and make the background transparent.

Several popular programs are available for converting GIF87a images into GIF89a images. Two such programs are GIFTool and GifTrans. Both of these command-line programs are shareware, and they're available for both Unix and DOS. Mac users can use a program called Transparency. Try looking for these utilities at the following locations:

- For GIFTool, see http://www.homepages.com/tools.
- For GifTrans, see ftp://melmac.corp.harris.com/files/giftrans.exe.
- For Transparency, see http://www.yahoo.com/Computers_and_Internet/Software/Graphics.

The first step in converting a GIF to a transparent GIF is figuring out how to identify your background color in the GIF colormap, if it isn't obvious. This is one reason it's nice to use white for a background if you're creating the image yourself and white doesn't appear anywhere inside the subject of your image. If you use GIFTool or GifTrans to convert your images, you make the color transparent by specifying its index in the image colormap, by specifying the combination of red, green, and blue in hexadecimal form, or (with GIFTool) by specifying the name of the color.

For example, let's say you create a logo like the one in Figure 12-3 with a program like Microsoft Draw or CorelDraw and save it as a GIF image. Let's also say that the foreground color of the logo is black and that, when it appears in Web browsers, you want the background to be transparent for a nice effect.

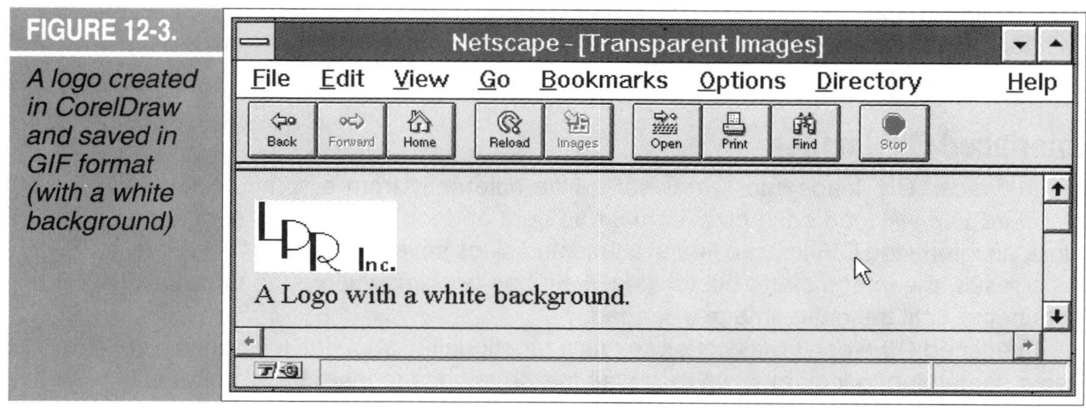

FIGURE 12-3. *A logo created in CorelDraw and saved in GIF format (with a white background)*

The next step is to run this GIF through GIFTool or GifTrans to make the white background transparent. With this image, the process is easy because even before you begin you know you want to make all the white pixels transparent. With GIFTool, the command line is

```
giftool -rgb white -o tlprlogo.gif lprlogo.gif
```

This command takes the file *lprlogo.gif*, makes the white pixels transparent, and saves it with the name *tlprlogo.gif*. The parameter *-rgb white* tells GIFTool to mark white pixels as transparent, and the parameter *-o tlprlogo.gif* tells GIFTool not to overwrite the original file but to make a new file named *TLPRLOGO.GIF*.

With GifTrans, you can't use the word *white* to describe the color you want to make transparent. Instead, you have to either specify the RGB values in hex or find the index in the GIF's colormap for white and use the index. These RGB hex values work exactly the same way as they do for defining background and text colors in Netscape's HTML extensions. (You might want to refer back to Chapter 10, which shows the RGB hex values for the eight primary colors.) Since we know from Figure 10-3 that white is a full "FF" value for each of the three colors red, green, and blue, the RGB hex code for white is "FFFFFF":

```
giftrans -t #ffffff -o tlprlogo2.gif lprlogo.gif
```

The parameter *-t#ffffff* tells GifTrans that the color to mark as transparent is white. The *-o* option specifies the output file name.

We're not going to delve any deeper into using GIFTool and GifTrans to make transparent images; we just wanted to give you an overview of how the programs work. Both GIFTool and GifTrans provide syntax and usage help if you invoke them with an *-h* parameter, and you can learn a lot about the programs by simply experimenting and playing with them.

Interlaced GIF Images

An *interlaced* GIF loads into a browser a little differently from a standard GIF. A standard GIF will load each pixel from left to right and top to bottom in sequence, while an interlaced GIF loads a line at a time and skips several lines after each one. As a result, the image starts out looking like it has poor resolution, then gradually gets better until the entire image is loaded.

Interlaced GIFs don't really offer any new functionality; about all they do is give users something to look at while they wait for the images to load. It's nice if a GIF is interlaced, but it's not an essential feature.

GIFTool converts a standard GIF to an interlaced one in a single command. For example,

```
giftool -B -i tlprlog.gif
```

converts the transparent logo image to an interlaced one. In this command, the *-B* option tells GIFTool to operate in batch mode, reading and writing to the same file. The *-i* option tells it to convert the image to an interlaced GIF. Of course, the benefit of seeing the image quickly is moot with a small image. With larger images, however—especially very detailed ones—the effect is nice.

Building Multimedia into Your Pages

From here to the end of this chapter, we're going to look at three types of external media—external images, sound, and video. The first thing to understand about integrating these media into your Web pages is that none of them have anything to do with HTML. In fact, they really don't even have much to do with the Web; their only connection with the Web is that your readers will use Web browsers to download the external media to their computers.

The fact that these media have nothing to do with HTML has an upside and a downside. The advantage is that integrating them into your pages is exceedingly easy; all you do is create an anchor that points to an image file, an audio file, or a video file. The disadvantage is that browsers can't interpret and render these files. Consequently, your readers have to configure their own systems to work with these files, and there isn't a lot you can do to help them.

In this section, we'll explain how to configure Web browsers to use external media. Then we'll discuss what you can do in your own Web pages to offer the most functionality to your readers, regardless of which computer and browser they have.

Configuring Browsers for External Media

External images are images that are displayed outside a browser window. To display an image outside the browser window, the browser has to run a separate program and pass the image description to it. Audio and video clips also have to be played and displayed by separate programs, and browsers have to know about those programs as well. These separate programs are commonly known as *viewers* or *helper applications*, because they help the Web browser do its work.

To play sounds, a computer has to have the requisite hardware. Macs, of course, have sound built into them. Most of the multimedia PCs on the market today are also equipped for sound right out of the box. Older PCs will need a sound card and speakers.

In Microsoft Windows, the native sound file format is .WAV. One of the applets that come with Windows (in the Accessories group) is a program called Media Player. Media Player can recognize and play a variety of multimedia files, including .WAV, .AVI, and MIDI. When a Web browser follows a link to a .WAV file, it recognizes it as a Microsoft audio file and sends it to Media Player, which then plays the file.

Strictly speaking, browsers don't use file extensions to decide what type of files they're getting. Rather, they identify file types by the MIME content type that the remote server builds into the HTTP header when it sends them. More often than not, however, the Web server at the other end of the wire looks up the file extension in a table and, based on that extension, decides which MIME content type to build into the HTTP header. So the file extension does matter, albeit indirectly.

A computer doesn't need any equipment other than a graphic monitor to display video clips. Of course, Macs have always had graphic monitors, and today virtually all PCs have at least VGA monitors. The software is usually built in, too. The same Media Player applet that plays audio files under Windows can also play video files in Microsoft's .AVI video format.

The key to making audio, video, and external images work with a Web browser is having the browser configured for each type of file (based on the MIME content type) you want the browser to use. Most browsers have a Setup, Configuration, or Preferences screen where you can associate each MIME content type with an application. Figure 12-4 shows Netscape's Preferences dialog, which you use to associate MIME content types with helper applications. The left column in the large window shows the MIME file types. The middle column describes the action the browser should take when it encounters a file of each content type, and the right-hand column lists the common file extensions generally associated with each content type.

Browsers can take several kinds of actions. One action is to display images themselves. They can also run programs—for example, in Figure 12-4, you can see that Netscape will launch the MPLAYER program (Media Player) for a content type of *video/x-msvideo*. Browsers can also prompt the user for an action to take. When browsers prompt you for an action, they usually ask if you want to save the file to disk or configure a viewer for the file.

Figure 12-5 shows the corresponding Preferences panel in NCSA Mosaic. This dialog box works a little differently, but the idea is the same: You associate a program or action with a MIME content type.

The audio and video examples mentioned here (the .WAV audio file and the .AVI video file) both happen to be media formats that are native to Windows. If everyone who might read your Web pages used Microsoft Windows, you wouldn't need to

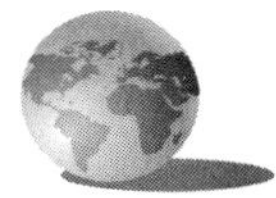

FIGURE 12-4.

Netscape's Options/ Preferences/ Helper Applications dialog

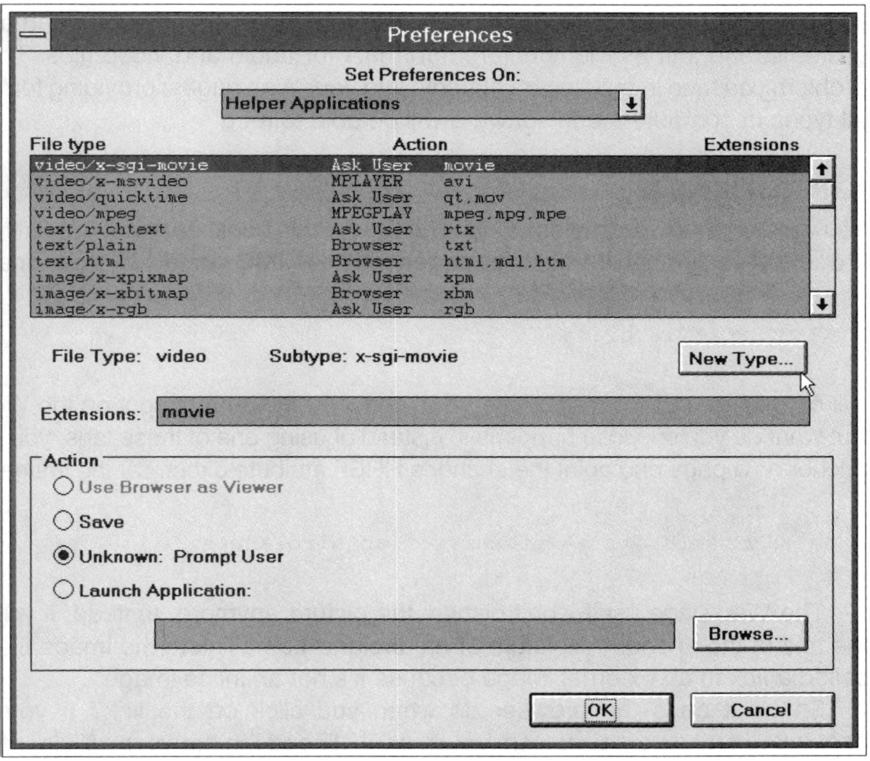

Preferences
Set Preferences On:
Helper Applications
File type
Action
Extensions
video/x-sgi-movie Ask User movie
video/x-msvideo MPLAYER avi
video/quicktime Ask User qt,mov
video/mpeg MPEGPLAY mpeg,mpg,mpe
text/richtext Ask User rtx
text/plain Browser txt
text/html Browser html,mdl,htm
image/x-xpixmap Ask User xpm
image/x-xbitmap Browser xbm
image/x-rgb Ask User rgb
File Type: video
Subtype: x-sgi-movie
New Type...
Extensions:
movie
Action
Use Browser as Viewer
Save
Unknown: Prompt User
Launch Application:
Browse...
OK
Cancel

FIGURE 12-5.

NCSA Mosaic's Options/ Preferences/ Viewers panel

NCSA Mosaic for Windows Preferences
General
Viewers
Services
Proxy
Tables
Anchors
Fonts
Cache
Audio
Associate Mime Type of:
video/x-msvideo
Description of Mime Type (Optional):
Microsoft Video AVI (audio/video interleave)
With this/these extensions:
.avi
To This Application:
C:\WINDOWS\MPLAYER.EXE
Browse...
Add
Remove
OK
Cancel
Apply Now
Help

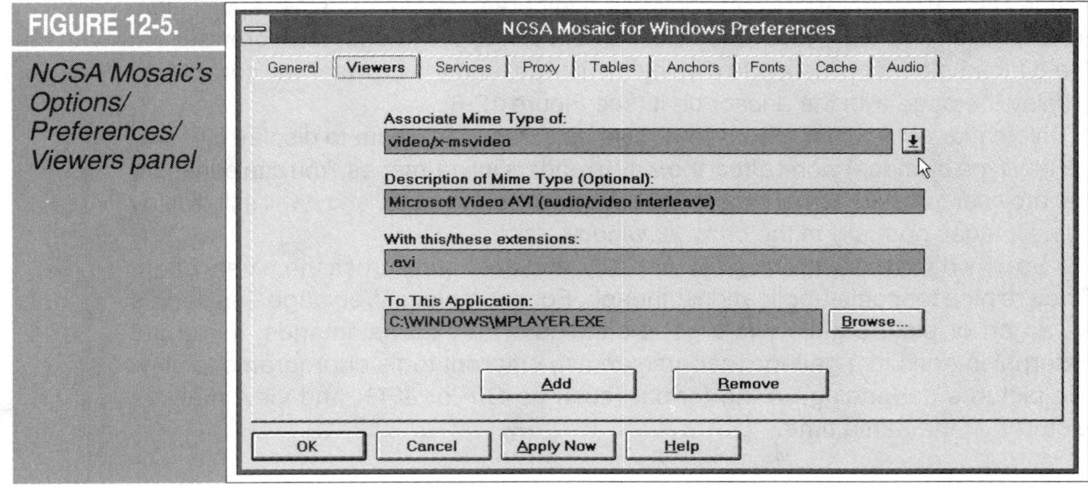

know any other systems. But there are different types of computers and operating systems, and just as many different formats for audio and video files. This is the problem you face in building multimedia into your Web pages: providing formats that all types of computers and software will be able to read.

External Images

You've seen many examples of inline images in this book. To review, an inline image is one that you embed in your Web pages with the <IMG> or <FIG> tag. For example,

```
<IMG SRC="f18.gif">
```

will cause browsers to display the inline image at the current spot on the Web page. But what do you suppose happens if, instead of using one of these tags, you make an anchor on a page and point the anchor's HREF attribute directly at the image file?

```
<A HREF="f18.gif">A picture of an airplane<A>
```

The Web page itself won't display the picture anymore. Instead, it will display the text of the anchor ("A picture of an airplane") as a link to the image file. This is called a *link* to an external image because it's not an inline image.

So what does the browser do when you click on the link? If you haven't configured any external viewers yet, in all likelihood the browser will clear the page and just display the image in the browser window. However, the key to external images is that your readers can configure a separate viewer, or helper application, for GIF files. This way, when they click on the link to the image, their browser will fire off the helper application to display the image, and the browser will continue to display the page with the anchor on it (see Figure 12-6).

Note that configuring a browser to use an external program to display GIF files (or any type of image) won't affect the way it renders inline images. You can configure the browser to use external programs for every type of image, and it will still display inline images normally in the browser window.

So why have external images? Actually, you don't run across them very often. They're nice for some applications, though. For example, a Web page that serves as an art or picture gallery is a good candidate for external images. If you put external images in a gallery, readers can use different tools or programs to view the pictures depending on the format (such as GIF or JPG) and view multiple pictures at the same time.

FIGURE 12-6.

A GIF viewer displaying an external image (browser visible beneath)

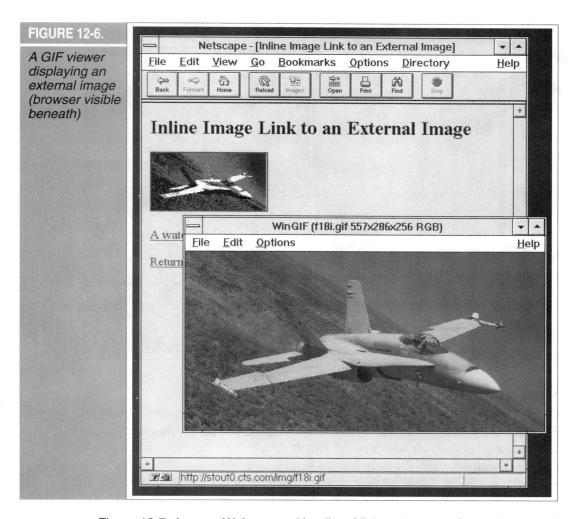

Figure 12-7 shows a Web page with a list of links to images. Several copies of a helper application are also running, each displaying a different picture. The viewer displaying GIF images is a program called WinGIF; the JPG images are being displayed by WinECJ. Both of these programs are shareware and are freely available on the Internet. Check your Archie server for a location near you. For Mac viewers, check http://www.qub.ac.uk/sigweb/mac-comms-utils.html. A popular viewer for the Macintosh is JPEGview, which displays GIFs and other formats along with JPEG files.

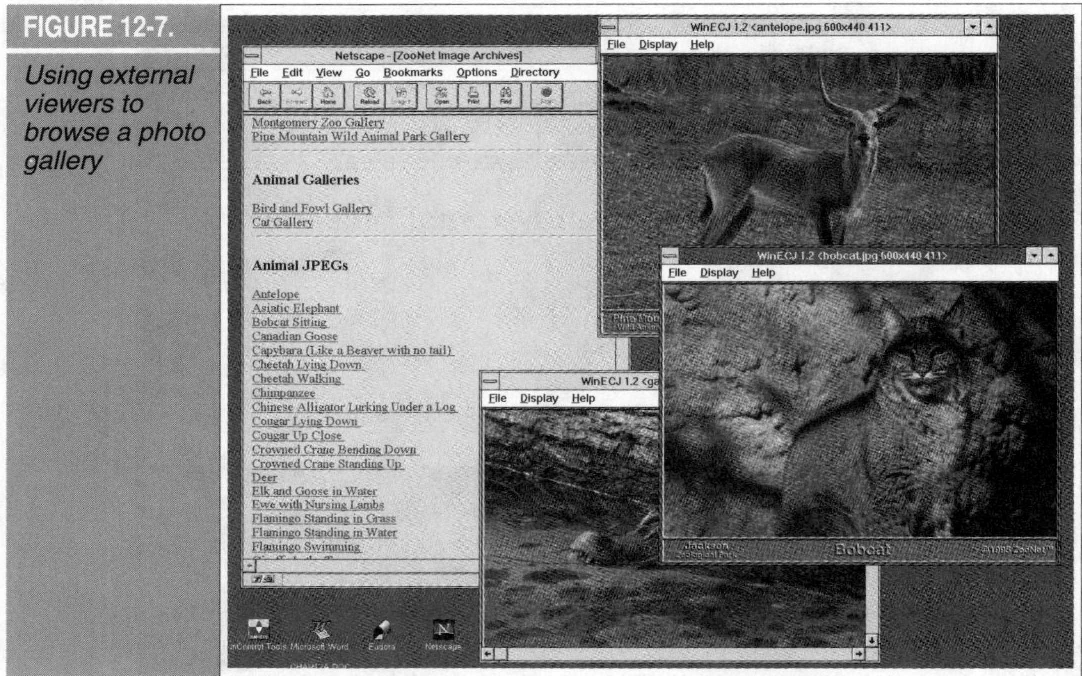

FIGURE 12-7. *Using external viewers to browse a photo gallery*

Working with Sound

Web browsers and HTML don't yet have a facility for inline sound. Thus, browsers have to use helper applications to handle every sound you put on your Web pages. As mentioned earlier, the native sound format for Microsoft Windows computers is .WAV. *Native* means that the software you need to play .WAV files (the Media Player program) is part of Windows itself—you don't need any additional software. Of course, you do need a sound card and speakers. Media Player is also part of Windows 95.

To configure a browser to play sounds automatically when it runs across them, simply configure MPLAYER (the file name of the Media Player program) as the application to launch for .WAV files.

Unfortunately, most of the audio files you find on the World Wide Web are not .WAV files. Sun Microsystems' Unix workstations had audio capabilities years before Windows did, so they use their own audio file format. And Macintosh computers use an altogether different audio file format.

Perhaps hardware and software developers will soon agree on a common format for audio and video files. When that day comes, you can bet the new standard will

draw on the best qualities of each of the existing formats, and the minor confusion we have to endure today won't have been for nothing.

In the meantime, we can do two things to enhance interoperability for sound and video media. First, we can encourage people to seek and use the most capable media players—that is, the ones that can handle the widest variety of sound and video formats—as the helper applications they use with their Web browsers. More importantly, when we offer audio and video links on our Web pages, we have to provide them in at least two—if not three—formats. The most popular sound file formats and their extensions are:

- Sun Microsystems: .au
- Microsoft Windows: .WAV
- Macintosh: .SND and .AIFF

The Sun .au format is the oldest and least capable. These files are extremely common on the Internet due to the huge number of Sun workstations connected to it. Most of the .au files are eight-bit sound samples, however, so they don't take advantage of the capabilities of today's (mostly 16-bit) sound equipment and software.

With the growing number of Microsoft Windows users on the Internet, it's likely that we'll begin to see more and more .WAV files on Web pages. Macs can use both the .SND and .AIFF formats, and Mac users are also a growing presence on the Internet.

For Windows users, a good solution for playing sounds on your system is a shareware program called *WPLANY*. It can play all the most important sound formats, including .WAV, .SND, .au, and even Creative Labs' .VOC and the Amiga .IFF format. WPLANY is freely available on the Internet; use an Archie server to find a site near you.

Converting Sound Formats

A number of utilities freely available on the Internet convert sound files from one format to another. This is important because any sound clip you want to include on a Web page, whether you find it or record it yourself, will be in one of the formats just listed. Since you need to provide your sound clip in at least two, and probably three, formats, you'll have to do the conversion yourself.

If you use Microsoft Windows, you'll most likely record a message in the .WAV format using either the built-in Sound Recorder applet or one of the more capable programs that come with most popular sound cards. If you use a Mac, you'll probably record your message in the .AIFF format.

The two most important sound format options to provide on your pages are .WAV files for Windows users and .AIFF files for Mac users. If you want to provide .au files for Unix users, you'll have yet another conversion to do. Table 12-1 lists a few

TABLE 12-1. Audio File Conversion Programs			
PROGRAM	**PLATFORM**	**CONVERSION**	**LOCATION**
Brian's Sound Tool	Mac	.WAV to Mac	ftp://src.doc.ic.ac.uk/computing/systems/mac/info-mac/snd/util/brians-sound-tool-13.hqx
Snd Converter Pro	Mac	.SND to .AIFF	ftp://src.doc.ic.ac.uk/computing/systems/mac/info-mac/snd/util/snd-converter-pro-20.hqx
WAVany	Windows	all to all	ftp://ftp.netcom.com/pub/ne/neisius/wvany10.zip

conversion programs, the conversions they do, and where you can find them on the Internet. We won't go into the details of using these programs; see the documentation for additional information.

Linking to Sound

To create a link to a sound file, you insert an anchor that references the sound file the same way you create a link to an external image file:

```
<A HREF="bluejay.wav">The call of the bluejay<A>
```

But since you're providing links to three formats, your HTML will look more like this:

```
<A HREF="bluejay.wav">The call of the bluejay (Windows .WAV
format)<A>

<A HREF="bluejay.aiff">The call of the bluejay (Mac .AIFF
format)<A>

<A HREF="bluejay.au">The call of the bluejay (Sun .au format)<A>
```

It's also nice to provide a descriptive icon with sound links and an approximation of the size of the audio file (see Figure 12-8). This way, people know at a glance that they're following a link to an audio clip that may take some time to transfer. An icon also informs readers who may not have a full command of your language that the link leads to a sound clip.

FIGURE 12-8.

Links to three audio formats (with audio icons)

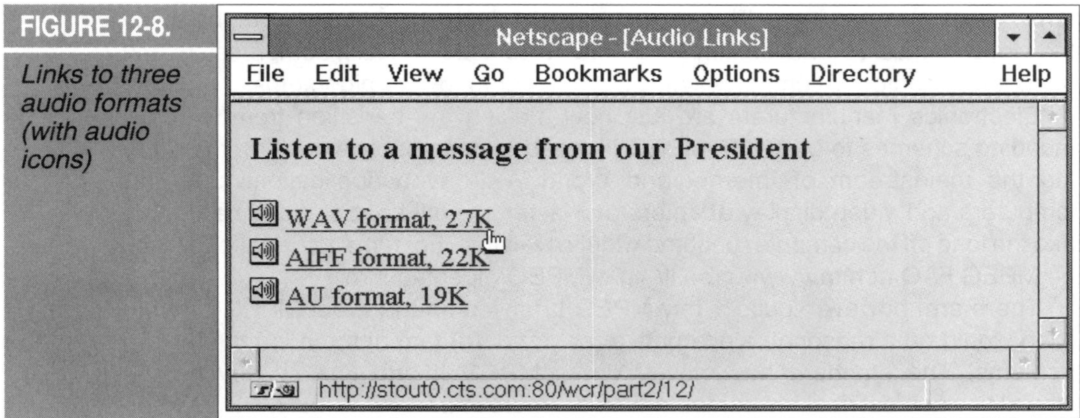

Working with Video

The challenges you face in integrating video clips into your Web pages are much the same as those you face with sound. The problems don't involve HTML, but if you want to provide video clips to people with all kinds of computers and software, you have to convert the clips into the popular formats.

As with audio formats, there are several formats for video images. Of these formats, three are sufficiently popular that you need to offer links to them:

- Microsoft Video for Windows
- QuickTime
- MPEG

The QuickTime format is native to the Macintosh and includes both video and sound.

The third important video format is MPEG, for Motion Picture Expert Group, an organization that was established to create a standard cross-platform format for digitized video. The original MPEG video format didn't include sound. The newer MPEG II standard does include sound, but MPEG compression is so high that decompressing both MPEG audio and MPEG video at the same time puts a severe load on all but the fastest desktop computers available today. To use MPEG II effectively, you really need to equip your computer with an adapter card that will decode the MPEG II files with hardware rather than software.

MPEG is different from AVI and QuickTime in that it's a professional standard for encoding (and decoding) a bitstream of digital audio and video for consumer electronics products. For example, the new satellite TV services use MPEG II encoding for their digital satellite transmissions and build the decoding right into the hardware of their receivers. This allows very fast decompression of both the audio and video signals. High-definition TV (HDTV) also uses MPEG II compression, and in the future cable TV companies may switch over to MPEG algorithms.

Electronics manufacturers are just now making the transition from MPEG I encoding schemes to MPEG II. MPEG II capabilities probably won't find their way into the mainstream of Internet and World Wide Web applications until our computers and video display adapters are faster or until special video cards that take the load off the computer become widely available. For more information, check the MPEG FAQ at http://www.crs4.it/~luigi/MPEG/mpegfaq.html.

There are, however, quite a few MPEG I movies on the Web. MPEG I format video would be a reasonable alternative (or standard) format for video but for two problems: The standard has moved on to MPEG II and is now beyond the capabilities of most desktop computers, and—more importantly—the MPEG I video format does not include sound.

Compared to MPEG II, the AVI and QuickTime formats are simplistic. However, they're superior to MPEG I because they do include sound. Table 12-2 lists some popular software for playing video files and shows the platforms they run on, the formats they play, and some ideas on where to find them.

If you intend to offer an original video clip on a Web page, you'll first have to record it and digitize it. We won't go into the details of how to do that, but we will mention that one strategy is simply to buy a video capture board for your computer

TABLE 12-2. *Popular Video Software*

PROGRAM	PLATFORM	PLAYS	LOCATION
Sparkle	Mac	MPEG QuickTime	ftp://ftp.cc.utexas.edu/microlib/mac/multimedia/
Qtime	Windows	QuickTime	ftp://src.doc.ic.ac.uk/computing/systems/ibmpc/windows3/
MPEGPlay	Windows	MPEG	http://www.geom.umn.edu/docs/mpeg_play/mpeg_play.html
QuickTime for Windows	Windows	QuickTime	http://quicktime.apple.com/
Video for Windows	Windows	AVI	http://www.microsoft.com/

TABLE 12-3. *Video Conversion Programs*

PROGRAM	PLATFORM	CONVERSION	LOCATION
Sparkle	Mac	MPEG↔QuickTime	ftp://ftp.cc.utexas.edu/microlib/mac/multimedia/
AVI→Quick	Mac	AVI→Quick	ftp://hyperarchive.lcs.mit.edu/info-mac/gst/mov/avi_to_qt_converter.hqx
SmartVid	Windows	AVI↔QuickTime	ftp://ftp.intel.com/pub/IAL/multimedia/smartv.exe
XingCD	Windows	AV →MPEG	http://www.xingtech.com/

and plug a camcorder into it. Video capture boards come with the software you need to use them, but they often capture video files to a proprietary format. Your first task, therefore, is to use the software provided by the maker of your video capture device to convert the video clip into one of the standard formats—AVI, QuickTime, or MPEG. Before you buy a video capture board, make sure the software provides a way to do this.

Once you have your clip in a standard format, you'll have to find a conversion program to translate it into the other formats. Table 12-3 lists a few programs you can use to do this.

One additional complication is that the QuickTime format for the Macintosh is different from the QuickTime format for other platforms. If you intend to offer a link to a QuickTime version of a video clip, you'll have to specify whether or not it's for a Mac. QuickTime videos created on Mac platforms have to be *flattened* for other platforms. Two utilities for flattening QuickTime clips are listed in Table 12-4.

TABLE 12-4. *Mac QuickTime Flatteners*

PROGRAM	PLATFORM	LOCATION
Fast Action	Mac	ftp://hyperarchive.lcs.mit.edu/info-mac/gst/mov/fast-action-10.hqx
Qflat	Windows	ftp://venice.tcp.com/pub/anime-manga/software/viewers/qtflat.zip

If you're interested in pulling down some video clips in a variety of formats so that you can experiment with them, check out the archives listed in Table 12-5. For more sites, check the *Internet Yellow Pages* (Osborne McGraw-Hill) in the section "Computers: Multimedia."

Finally, if you're interested in learning more about integrating movies into your web or about making videos in general, take a look at the following sites:

- http://www.el.dorado.ca.us/~homeport/white_paper_toc.html
- http://www.io.org/~mbelli

TABLE 12-5. *A Few Richly Stocked Video Archives*

FORMAT	LOCATION
QuickTime	http://mambo.ucsc.edu/psl/thant/thant.html
MPEG	http://cuiwww.unige.ch/w3catalog/
MPEG	http://w3.eeb.ele.tue.nl/mpeg/
MPEG	http://www.cs.ucl.ac.uk/movies/

Chapter 13

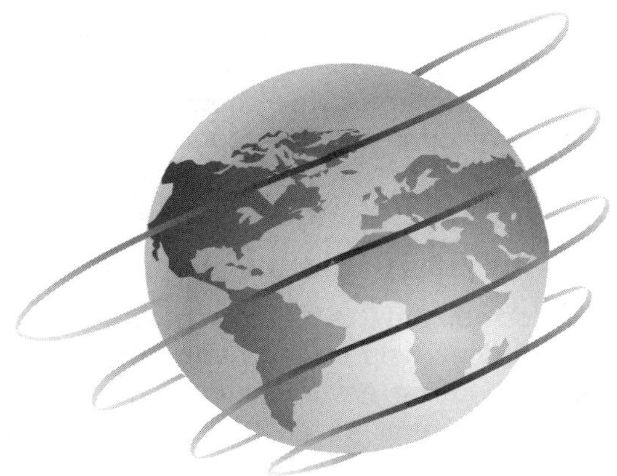

Gateway Interfaces and Forms

The two facilities that make the Web an interactive medium are forms and gateway interfaces. If you haven't run into forms out on the Web yourself, you have at least seen a few examples in the chapters leading up to this one. Since forms and gateway interfaces are closely related, we're going to cover them together in this chapter.

Forms let the readers of your pages send information back to you—or, rather, to a program you've set up to handle that information. This is what allows two-way communications and interactivity.

But the forms that readers type their information into are only half the puzzle. To do anything with the information your readers submit to you, you have to create a computer program that will receive the information from their browsers and do something with it. These programs are called *common gateway interfaces*, *CGI scripts*, or *CGI programs*. To install CGI programs on your system, you have to have access to your Web server or have an agreeable system administrator.

In this chapter, we'll show you the building blocks of interactivity. You'll see how to marry forms and CGI programs to get the functionality you want in your web.

Gateway Interfaces

So, do you have to be a computer programmer to write a CGI program? Not at all. But it does help to have some knowledge of how computer programs work in a command-line environment such as MS-DOS or Unix. You don't need a lot of knowledge that you can't pick up quickly if you've ever written a DOS batch file or edited your AUTOEXEC.BAT. If you have written programs before, you'll be even better off.

Generally, you can use any programming language you like to write a CGI program. The only requirement is that your code be translatable into an executable, stand-alone program (one that doesn't need an interpreter or special environment to run).

Two Types of Interfaces

A person using a browser can send information back to a Web server in two ways. The first method uses the <ISINDEX> tag you learned about in Chapter 8. In that chapter, you learned about the tag itself and saw a figure showing the edit box it puts on a Web page, but we didn't give you all the information you need to use the tag.

The <ISINDEX> tag makes a browser display a single edit box that you can type text into on a Web page. This type of interaction is called a *document-based query*. It's called a *query* because it's used primarily to get a single word, or a few key words, back to some sort of database engine to perform a search. It's called

document-based because the HTML code that defines the searchable index and specifies what to do with the text entered into it is all part of the document itself (we'll explain this in a minute).

The second way to get input from a reader is with a real form (as opposed to the single edit box of a searchable index). A form is a collection of input boxes on a Web page that can accept text and numbers or allow the user to choose between certain options or values. The form in Figure 13-1 prompts readers to fill in name and address information, using checkboxes and radio buttons to let readers make selections and choose between options. When the readers are finished filling in the

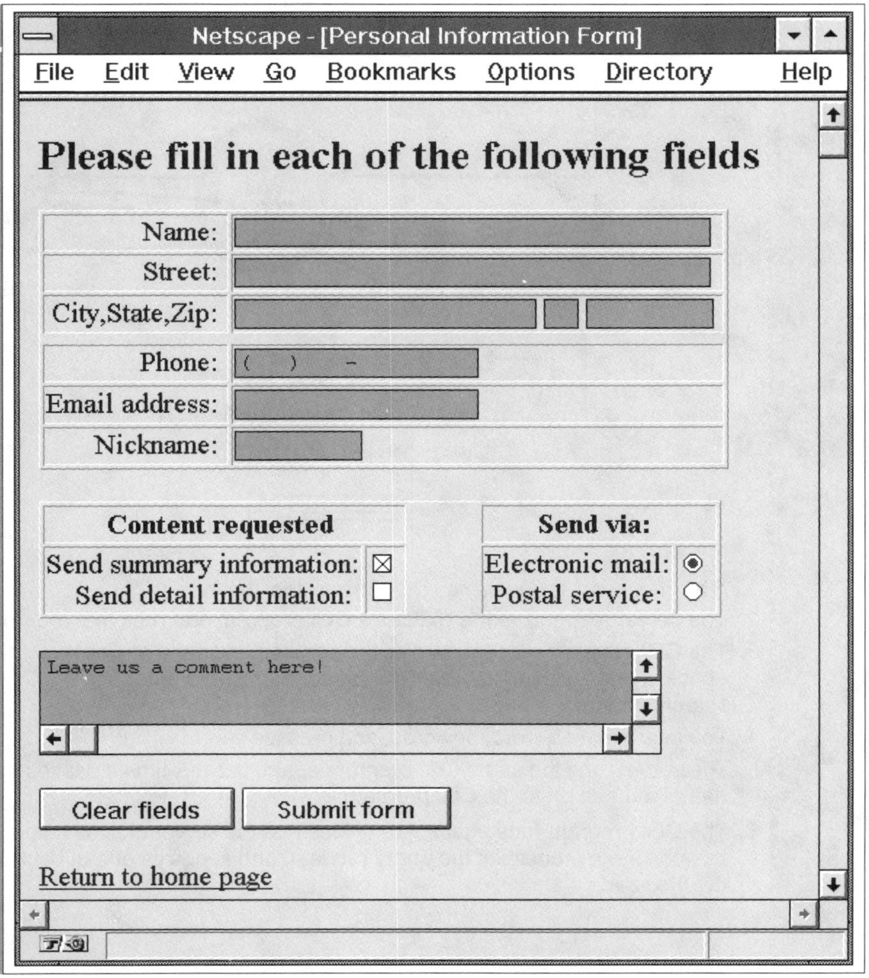

FIGURE 13-1.

A form-based query prompting for a name and addresss

Netscape - [Personal Information Form]

File Edit View Go Bookmarks Options Directory Help

Please fill in each of the following fields

Name:	
Street:	
City,State,Zip:	
Phone:	( ) -
Email address:	
Nickname:	

Content requested		Send via:	
Send summary information:	☒	Electronic mail:	◉
Send detail information:	☐	Postal service:	○

Leave us a comment here!

Clear fields | Submit form

Return to home page

information, they can click on a button to send the information they entered back to the Web server. This type of interaction is called a *form-based query*, although such a form may have nothing at all to do with querying a database; it may just perform an operation like sending mail back to the reader.

As we said in the introduction to this chapter, forms (whether they are document-based or form-based) work closely with gateway programs. Actually, document-based queries *are* gateway programs themselves. That is, the HTML code goes to a browser and displays the edit box and a prompt is generated by the gateway program. Figure 13-2 shows how this works.

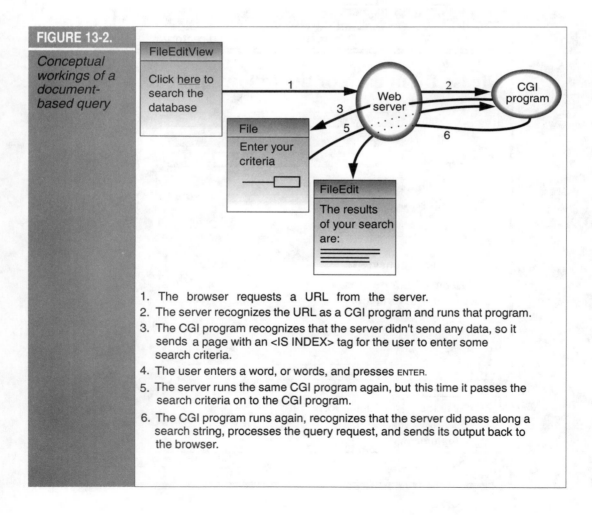

FIGURE 13-2. *Conceptual workings of a document-based query*

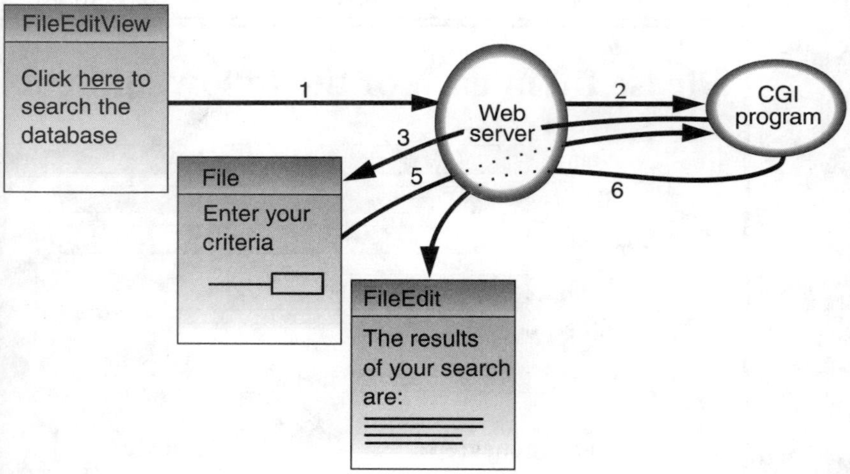

FileEditView
Click here to search the database
1
Web server
2
CGI program
3
File
Enter your criteria
5
6
FileEdit
The results of your search are:

1. The browser requests a URL from the server.
2. The server recognizes the URL as a CGI program and runs that program.
3. The CGI program recognizes that the server didn't send any data, so it sends a page with an <IS INDEX> tag for the user to enter some search criteria.
4. The user enters a word, or words, and presses ENTER.
5. The server runs the same CGI program again, but this time it passes the search criteria on to the CGI program.
6. The CGI program runs again, recognizes that the server did pass along a search string, processes the query request, and sends its output back to the browser.

In some ways, form-based queries are a little more complicated than document-based queries, but in other ways they're more straightforward. With a form-based query, a Web page with a form is actually an HTML file sitting on the server. When you follow a link to a page with a form, the server notices nothing special about the page you load. Your browser takes care of rendering the form, and nothing special takes place until you click the submit button on the form. At that point, your browser sends the name of a CGI program for the Web server to run (the name is built into the HTML of the page) along with the data you entered into the form. The server then recognizes that you want to run a gateway program and passes the data from your form on to that program. This concept is illustrated in Figure 13-3.

FIGURE 13-3.

Conceptual workings of a form-based query

1. The browser requests an HTML document from the server.
2. The server sends the document, which includes a form-based form.
3. The reader enters the requested information into the form.
4. When the reader clicks the submit button, the browser sends the data in the form fields as well as the name of a CGI program to run.
5. The server runs the CGI program passing it the form data.
6. The CGI program processes the data and sends it back to the server, which passes it back to the browser.

So why would you choose one type of query over the other? This question will only come up when a single edit box is sufficient for your input. Since document-based queries only put a single edit box on the browser screen, they just won't do for multifield forms. If you do want a single edit box, it's generally easier to use a document-based query—as long as you can live with the default edit box that the <ISINDEX> tag creates. Netscape sticks the edit box at the top of the page, and Mosaic puts it at the bottom. With form-based queries, you have total control over where your edit boxes and other controls are rendered because you define them with your HTML code.

A Word About the Examples

In this chapter, we'll work through five examples of interactive Web pages. The first four are functionally identical, but we'll use two different programming languages to create both document-based and form-based queries. Here's the scenario:

A number of people have helped us collect the entries for the catalog of business Web sites at the back of this book. To prevent people from sending in entries for URLs we already have in our database, we devised a method that allows them to check and see if we have a particular URL. By loading a Web page into their browsers, they can type or paste their new URL into an edit box, then press the ENTER key or click the submit button. The server then runs a CGI program that checks a text version of our database for the new URL. If it already has the URL, the CGI program says so and displays the name of the company to which the URL belongs. If the new URL isn't in the database, the CGI program says "Sorry, I couldn't find that URL" (which is actually good news for our researchers).

The fifth example is a more complex multifield form that we process with a C program. Since this is a multifield form, it necessarily uses the form-based query method.

The two languages we used for these CGI programs are the Unix Bourne shell scripting language and C. The reason we chose these languages is that both are available on just about every Unix computer in the world, and most of the Web servers on the Internet are Unix computers. (Many people like to use another very popular scripting language for Unix systems, Perl; we chose not to use Perl only because it doesn't exist on every Unix system.)

There is nothing easy about programming in either the Bourne shell or C, but neither is it terribly difficult. So relax; it won't be hard to follow along with the examples. Programming in the Unix Bourne shell is similar to writing a batch file in DOS. And a benefit of writing CGI programs in a shell script language is that you can use other programs that are available on Unix computers, such as *sed*, *cut*, and *tr*, to format text and translate characters. We've used these programs in the Bourne shell examples here.

With C, you can also use external tools to make writing CGI programs easier. In our examples, however, we won't use any of these tools; that way you'll get the clearest picture of what goes on in a CGI program. And this way, when we tell you about some of the external tools you can use, you'll know exactly what they do.

Web servers for other computers and operating systems are also starting to become available. Several are available now for Macintosh computers and for PCs running OS/2, Windows 95, and Windows NT. If you plan to put up a Web server on one of these platforms, this chapter is still important—all the concepts and procedures still apply, even though the syntax of your CGI language may change (if you use C, the syntax won't change at all; C compilers are available for every operating system).

A Simple, Noninteractive CGI Program

Before we jump into interactive queries, let's look at a noninteractive CGI script that simply generates some output at the server and returns the output to a browser. We'll start with a simple Web page that provides a link we can follow with a browser. However, rather than referencing another Web page, this anchor will reference a simple CGI script. Let's begin by writing a Bourne shell script that prints out the local date and time. On Unix computers, the *date* program displays the current date and time; you can run the program simply by typing **date** at the command line. To make a shell script that calls this program, just use a text editor to create a file that contains that command. For example,

```
#!/bin/sh
# A shell script that displays the current local date and time
date
```

tells the Unix operating system what program to use to interpret the commands that follow in the file. This shell script will use a program named *sh* that resides in the directory */bin* on all Unix systems. This program is the Bourne shell interpreter, so this is a Bourne shell script. You can program several other shells with shell scripts, but the Bourne is the oldest and most widely supported program.

Let's save the file under the name *datescript* and see if it works. Before you can run it, though, you have to let Unix know that it's an executable script file. In Unix, you do this with the *chmod* command (for change mode) to flag it as executable. At the command line, just type the command

```
chmod +x datescript
```

Now you can test the shell script by typing its name and pressing ENTER. But unlike DOS, Unix doesn't automatically include your current directory in your PATH statement. If typing **datescript** doesn't work, you may have to preface the file name with ./ to let the operating system know where your script file is located. Here's what it should look like:

```
$ ./datescript
Mon Oct 9 21:58:24 PDT 1995
$
```

The dollar sign is the Unix command prompt (like the C:\> prompt in DOS). When you type the name of your script and press ENTER, the operating system fires off a Bourne shell, which interprets the commands in your script. In this case, the only command is the date command, which displays its output. When the script is finished, the operating system returns control to you by giving you another command prompt.

A couple of details need to be taken care of before your script is finished. The reason the script works now is that the Bourne shell that interprets the commands in the script inherits the PATH statement of your interactive shell (the one that displays the $ prompt when you log in). When the Web server runs your script at the request of a browser somewhere out on the Internet, you can't be guaranteed that your server will know where to look for the *date* program. So it's best to include full path names to any external programs you use in your CGI scripts. For that matter, it's better yet to test and make sure your script can find any external programs before it tries to run them. On most Unix systems, the *date* program resides in the */bin* directory.

The best approach of all is to set a variable at the beginning of your script that defines all the external programs the script uses. Thereafter, you can just reference the variable names in the body of your script. If you ever need to change any of the programs, you only have to make the change at the top of the script rather than searching through a long script to find every occurrence of a program name. It's unlikely that you would ever move or need to change a program that just reports the date. It is common to make your scripts available to others, however, and their *date* program might be in */usr/bin* instead of */bin*.

Every CGI program, whether it's a shell script or a compiled program, has to print out a MIME content type before any other output it may produce. The Web server builds this information into the HTTP header so that browsers receiving the text will know what to do with it. For HTML documents, this will always be the same line of text. The text that defines the MIME content type for an HTML document is

```
Content-type: text/html
```

Sometimes (especially when you're debugging your scripts) you'll want to send your script output to a browser as plain text, in which case the text that defines the MIME content type should be

```
Content-type: text/plain
```

The content type is always followed by two consecutive new-line characters. If you prefer, you can think of this as the line describing the content type followed by a blank line.

Here's a slightly more wholesome version of the *datescript* program that's ready for use as a CGI script:'

```
#!/bin/sh
# A CGI shell script that displays the current local date and
# time
DATE=/bin/date
echo Content-type: text/html
echo
if [ -x $DATE ]; then
   $DATE
else
   echo Where is the date program on this system?
fi
```

The first line after the comment (the fourth line) creates a variable called DATE and assigns it the value "/bin/date", since this is where the *date* program is on most systems. The next two lines print out the MIME content type and follow it with a blank line (the extra ECHO statement creates the second new-line character). Next is an *if* statement to determine if the *date* program is really where we think it will be. If the shell finds the *date* program, it runs it. Otherwise, it prints an error message.

The final hurdle in finishing this CGI script is to put it where the Web server will find it. You can't just leave it in your own home directory and expect the Web server to be able to access it. This is where you need access to the server directories or a good relationship with your system administrator.

A Web server is just another program. Usually, Web servers have names like *httpd* (for HTTP Daemon) and exist in a directory that contains system programs such as */usr/bin* or */usr/contrib/bin.* In a properly configured Unix system, the Web server starts up automatically when the system starts up. And when the server first runs, it reads some configuration files that tell it where to find its files and directories. In Chapter 11, we talked about the root Web directory and about how a file named *index.html* in the root Web directory would be the default Web page for a server. The root Web directory usually contains a subdirectory named *cgi-bin* that houses the CGI programs the server needs to access.

For example, if the root Web directory is */var/www*, the directory for CGI programs would be */var/www/cgi-bin*. Of course, this isn't set in stone; in fact, it's just another configuration option that the system administrator specifies in the server's startup files. But it has become something of a convention that CGI programs go in a subdirectory named *cgi-bin* in the root Web directory.

If you manage your own Unix system, you probably already know where your Web server looks for CGI programs. If so, put your CGI script into that directory. If you don't manage your own Unix system (a little more likely), chances are you won't be able to copy your CGI script into that directory; Unix enforces strict rules about permissions to write files into directories that you don't own. Ask your system administrator to help you with this. Some administrators won't want to put copies of your pages into their Web server's directory tree, but they may give you your own CGI script that you can modify to load all your own pages.

You're almost done! All that remains is to create a simple Web page from which you can call your CGI program. You point an anchor at your CGI program just as you would to reference an HTML document. Here's a sample page to do this:

```
<HTML>
<HEAD>
<TITLE>Call a CGI Program</TITLE>
</HEAD>
<BODY>
<A href="/cgi-bin/datescript">Check the date!</A>
</BODY>
</HTML>
```

When you load this page into your browser, you'll see the single anchor that points to your CGI program. Click on it, and you'll see the current date and time. That's all there is to it!

Interactive forms are a little more complicated, but the principles are pretty much the same. Form-based queries work almost exactly like this simple script except that you pass some information to your CGI program, and you have to write a program to handle it. But before we go into form-based queries, let's look at document-based queries.

Document-Based Queries

Since document-based queries are designed to accept criteria and search a database, they automatically provide a single edit box for the search criteria. Here's how this typically works: When you use a browser to follow a link to a document-based query, you're presented with an edit box for your search criteria and perhaps some text describing what you should do (see Figure 13-4). After you type a search string into the edit box and press the ENTER key, the CGI program receives your search string, processes it, and displays some output on the screen. The output screen may or may not provide another edit box for an additional search.

The tricky part about document-based queries is that they don't originate from an HTML document file sitting on the server. The HTML code that generates both screens (the one with the search index and the output screen) is generated on the fly by the CGI program. That is, the CGI program itself outputs the HTML markup tags and text that define a Web page. If you run your CGI program from the command line, you'll see that the output is HTML.

There are two basic ways to pass information into a computer program when you run it: with *parameters,* or through something called the *standard input stream.* If you've ever used a command-line operating system, you are familiar with passing parameters (which are also sometimes called *arguments*) to a program. For example, the Unix command

```
cal 1 1996
```

FIGURE 13-4. *Document-based queries have only a single input box*

Netscape - [Enter Search Criteria]

File Edit View Go Bookmarks Options Directory Help

Back Forward Home Reload Images Open Print Find Stop

Search Index Page

Enter your search criteria:

Next search

Exit

will display a calendar for the month of January 1996. The name of the program is *cal*, and the numbers *1* and *1996* are parameters you pass into the *cal* program.

When a Web server runs a document-based CGI program, it does the equivalent of typing the program name at a command line and passing the information from your single edit box to the CGI program as a parameter. If you type multiple words into the edit box separated by spaces, these words arrive inside the CGI program as multiple parameters. For example, let's say you're using a document-based query to search a database for documents that contain the words *congress* and *amendments*. You can type both words into the edit box, separated by a space. Let's also say that the name of the CGI program is *wordsearch*. The server will send the whole string of characters to the CGI program as if it typed them at a command line like this:

```
wordsearch congress amendments
```

However, the first time you click on a link that runs a document-based CGI program, your browser won't pass it any parameters at all because you haven't even seen the edit box yet, let alone typed something into it. This is how the CGI program knows whether to display the edit box for you to type in some search criteria or to try to process some criteria: by the number of parameters it receives. Let's go through the process step by step.

The first time you run this document-based CGI program, you just follow an anchor link to the program itself. The server recognizes that you requested a CGI program and runs that program for you. The program first looks at the number of arguments that it was called with. If there were none, it sends a page to your browser that includes the <ISINDEX> tag; the edit box will then be displayed, and you can type your search criteria into it along with any instructions. On the other hand, if it does receive some arguments, the program knows it has already displayed the edit box for you and that you typed some words into it. So, depending upon whether or not it received any arguments, the CGI program decides to either display the edit box and instructions or query the database and display the results of the query. Now let's jump into our first real example.

We keep the information about all the entries in the catalog at the back of this book in a PC database system—Microsoft Access, to be specific. Our researchers submit entries for this database on a text form that they email to us in batches. Whenever we receive a new batch of entries, we process the text file and import the data into the database. Then we run a program that we wrote to dump a smaller ASCII version of the database to a text file. This text file has a line for each entry; on each line is a Web URL followed by a comma, then the name of the company to which that URL belongs. To cut down on space and work, we decided to assume that URLs are prefaced with the required "http://". Here's what a few lines from this file look like:

```
www.abekas.com,Abekas
www.access.digex.net/~dcarson/Lrc.html,Lunar Resources Company
www.adcg.com/,Honeywell, Inc.
www.alden.com/,Alden Electronics
www.amd.com,Advanced Micro Devices (AMD)
```

To use our CGI program, the researchers follow the link to the program and get an edit box and a prompt to enter the URL (without the leading "http://"). They can type their new URL into the edit box, or simply copy it from their Web browser's Location box and paste it into the edit box. When they press ENTER, the CGI program receives their URL as a parameter and checks to see if it already exists in the database. If it finds the URL, the CGI program displays the name of the company to which it belongs. If it doesn't find the URL, it displays a message saying so.

Here's the Bourne shell script version of our document-based CGI program:

```
#!/bin/sh
echo Content-type: text/html
echo
echo "<HTML><HEAD><TITLE>URL Search</TITLE>"

if [ $1 ]; then
   COMPANY=`grep $1 cgi-data/list.txt \
            | head -n 1 \
            | cut -f 2 -d ,`

   if [ "$COMPANY" ]; then
      echo "</HEAD><BODY><H2>Found!</H2>"
      echo "The URL <I><B>"$1"</B></I><P>"
      echo "belongs to: <I><B>"$COMPANY"</B></I>"
   else
      echo "</HEAD><BODY><H2>Not found!</H2>"
      echo "The URL <I><B>"$1"</B></I><BR>"
      echo "was not found.<P>"
   fi
else
   echo "<ISINDEX prompt=\"URL:\"></HEAD><BODY>"
   echo "Enter the URL to check (\"http://\" is assumed):"
fi

echo "<p><a href="/cgi-bin/urld.sh">Next search</a>"
echo "</BODY></HTML>"
```

Follow along as we explain what these commands do (we won't go into all the nuances of programming here). The first few lines of this script output the required MIME content type for the HTTP header and start sending the HTML tags and text to define a Web page. Notice, though, that the third ECHO statement begins the definition of the HTML head section and defines a title for the page, but then does not terminate the head section with a </HEAD> tag. This is because we don't yet know if we need to include the <ISINDEX> tag (which is a head section tag). To determine that, we first have to see whether or not the program was called with any arguments.

The first *if* statement performs this test. The Bourne shell assigns arguments to variables by number; a variable named *1* is the first argument, the second argument is named *2*, and so on. Anytime you use a variable in the Bourne shell, you precede the variable name with a dollar sign. Thus, *$1* refers to the first argument. This first *if* statement tests for the existence of a single argument (if argument $1 doesn't exist, then you know that there are no arguments).

Let's assume this is the first time the program has been called, so the *if* test causes command execution to jump down to the lines following the outside *else* statement (the one that is not indented).

```
echo "<ISINDEX prompt=\"URL:\"></HEAD><BODY>"
echo "Enter the URL to check (\"http://\" is assumed):"
```

Since we've recognized that this is the first time the program is being called (because there were no arguments), we know that we should include the <ISINDEX> tag, finish the head section, and display a message in the body section that will prompt the user for a URL.

Finally, command execution falls off the end of the *if* statement, and the shell executes the final two lines (which simply display an anchor to do another search) and completes the HTML output by terminating the body section and the document. At this point, the reader sees the Web page shown in Figure 13-5.

Now let's assume the reader types the URL **www.amd.com** into the edit box. This URL is already in the database, so we'll follow this line of logic first. When the reader presses ENTER, the browser runs the script again from the very beginning. This time, however, the test of $1 reveals that a parameter was passed to the script. In fact, the variable $1 holds the text string "www.amd.com". So, instead of running the commands in the *else* portion of the *if* statement, the

FIGURE 13-5. *The urlsearch program interface*

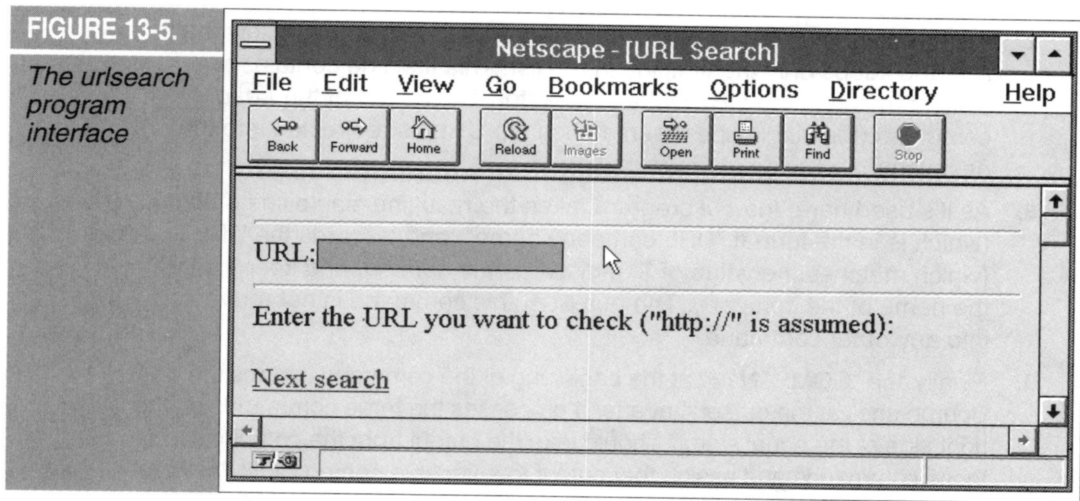

shell runs the commands in the *then* portion (the commands above the outside *else*). Here's the first of those lines:

```
COMPANY='grep $1 cgi-data/list.txt \
             | head -n 1 \
             | cut -f 2 -d ,'
```

This is really one statement split across three lines for easier reading. The "\" character at the end of the first two lines tells the shell to continue reading the current command on the next line. If you prefer, you can think of this command as being all on one line:

```
COMPANY='grep $1 cgi-data/list.txt | head -n 1 | cut -f 2 -d ,'
```

Four things are happening in this command (here is where we get some help from external Unix programs; the C version of this program uses no external programs, so you'll be able to see each part of the process separately):

1. The *grep* command searches the text version of the database (a file named *list.txt* in a directory named *cgi-data* below the *cgi-bin* directory) for all lines that include the URL the reader entered. It's possible that this command will return multiple lines because two or more businesses might have their Web pages on the same computer (as is the case with some Web business directories). The output of the *grep* command is directed into the next command—the *head* program.

2. As it's used here, the *head* program strips off any lines that follow the first line and keeps only the first line in the list. This first line contains the closest match to the URL we're looking for. The output of the *head* command (the single line that matches the URL) is redirected into the next command, the *cut* program.
3. As it's used here, the *cut* program takes the resulting single line of text (which is in the format "URL,company name") and discards the URL (which matches the value of $1), discards the comma, and keeps only the name of the company. The output of this command is not redirected into any other command.
4. Finally, the "COMPANY=" at the beginning of the command informs the Bourne shell at the outset that after it processes the three commands on the right side of the equal sign, it should take the output from the combination of those commands and assign that output to a variable named COMPANY. In our example, the variable COMPANY gets the value "Advanced Micro Devices (AMD)". Note that if the *grep* command (in step 1) had failed to find a matching line, the subsequent commands would still be executed, but they would essentially be passing an empty string among themselves and assigning that empty (or null) string to the variable COMPANY.

The next and final part of this shell script is an *if* statement that determines if the variable $COMPANY contains a value, then either reports that the URL was found and prints the name of the company or reports that it wasn't found.

The following listing shows the equivalent of this shell script written in the C language. This version is somewhat longer than the shell script version because it uses no external programs or utilities. In effect, the program was written to include the functionality of the *grep*, *head*, and *cut* commands used in the shell script.

```
/*  urlsearch-d.c
 *  Document-based version of the urlsearch program.
 *  CGI program to find a URL in a database.
 *  On the first call, this program provides an <ISINDEX> edit box for a
 *  user to enter a URL to search for. On the second call, the program
 *  searches the database for the URL and displays the results.
 */

#include <stdio.h>                          /* standard include files */
#include <string.h>

main(int argc, char *argv[])
{
```

```
    FILE *ifile;                                  /* variable declarations */
    char buf[256], instr[64], *p;

    printf("Content-type: text/html\n\n");        /* output HTML header */
    printf("<HEAD><TITLE>URL Search</TITLE>\n");  /* and HEAD section */

    if (!(ifile = fopen("cgi-data/list.txt", "rt"))) {
       printf("Can't open input file!\n");    /* open database file */
       exit(0);
    }

    if (argc > 1) {                              /* if an arg was passed in */
       strncpy(instr, argv[1], 63);
       instr[63]=NULL;

       while (p = strstr(instr, "\\~"))           /* prepare the search string */
         strcpy(p, p+1);

       while ((p = fgets(buf, 256, ifile))   /* search the database */
         && strncmp(instr, buf, strlen(instr)));

       if (p) {                                  /* display results */
         p = strchr(buf, ',');
         printf("</HEAD><BODY><H2>Found!</H2>\n");
         printf("The URL: <I><B>%s</B></I><P>\n", instr);
         printf("belongs to: <I><B>%s</B></I>\n", &p[1]);
       } else {
         printf("</HEAD><BODY><H2>Not found!</H2>");
         printf("The URL: <I><B>%s</B></I><BR>", instr);
         printf("was not found.");
       }
    } else {
       printf("<ISINDEX prompt=\"URL:\"></HEAD><BODY>");
       printf("Enter the URL you want to check (\"http://\" is assumed)");
    }

    printf("<P><A HREF=\"/cgi-bin/urlsearch-d\">Next search</a></BODY>\n");

    fflush(stdout);                              /* flush output stream */
    fclose(ifile);                               /* close input file */
    exit(0);                                     /* end program */
}
```

In C you have a few more details to take care of—such as opening and closing the database file and flushing the standard output stream—but you should recognize the similarities between the body of the program and the shell script version. The same two nested *if* statements remain; again, the first tests for the existence of arguments passed into the program when it is executed, and the second checks to see if a matching line was found in the database.

Form-Based Interfaces

Now that you know everything there is to know about document-based CGI programs, let's increase the pressure a little and get into form-based CGI programs.

We mentioned earlier that form-based queries are in some respects more straightforward than document-based queries. One reason for this is that with form-based queries, you don't have to worry about making the CGI program handle all the input and output that may be necessary under various circumstances. The HTML tags in an actual HTML document file create a form on a Web page; the CGI program doesn't even enter into the picture until the form is filled in and the reader clicks the submit button. In contrast to a document-based CGI program, all a form-based CGI program does is accept some input, process it, and display some output.

We'll look at the HTML tags for creating forms in the next section and discuss some of the tools at your disposal for defining field types. You'll see a more complex form with several fields, and you'll learn how to point a form at a particular CGI program. Before we get into these topics, however, let's look at what goes on behind the scenes.

Refer back to Figure 13-1, a screenshot of a fairly elaborate form. (We'll actually go through the process of creating this form in the next section.) To begin our discussion of CGI programs, you need one piece of information about the form itself: Each field has an assigned name, and you assign the field a name inside the HTML tag that creates the field. For example, the name field in the form in Figure 13-1 is called *name*, the address field is called *address*, and so on.

Unfortunately, form-based CGI programs don't accept the same type of input as document-based ones. Recall that document-based CGI programs are passed the contents of a single edit field as a parameter. Since forms may have far more than one field, this method of getting information into the CGI program isn't practical. Instead, form-based CGI programs get their input from the standard input stream.

So what does that mean to you? Well, it means that you handle the input slightly differently from inside the program. Also, if you test your script from the Unix command line you can't pass sample input into the program in the same way as with a document-based CGI script. You can test a document-based CGI script as you write it by typing its name followed by the parameters you want to pass in.

Take another look at an example given earlier in the chapter for running a document-based CGI program from the command line:

```
wordsearch congress amendments
```

In this example, the words *congress* and *amendments* are parameters (or arguments) being passed into the program. Inside the program, you can access them simply by using the variables $1 and $2 (assuming *wordsearch* is a shell script).

In a form-based CGI program, though, the Web server that runs the program will never pass any parameters to it. Instead, it makes the field contents available to the program as a long string of characters on the standard input stream. To test a form-based CGI program from the command line, therefore, you have to create a text file that contains the information you want to pass into the program. Then when you run the program, you have to tell it to take its standard input from the file.

For example, to get the same two words (*congress* and *amendments*) into the *wordsearch* program via the standard input, you would create a text file that contains the two words and save it. Let's assume the file is named *words.txt*. You would run the script with the command line

```
wordsearch < words.txt
```

The less-than symbol tells the operating system to take the contents of the file named *words.txt* and make it available to the *wordsearch* program on the standard input stream.

In addition to using the standard input stream instead of parameters, there is a fairly significant difference in the form of the information your browser sends to the Web server. Since form-based queries can work with more than a single field, there has to be a way to distinguish between the fields. Hence, Web browsers send field data to the server as a name/value pair. For example, say the *name* field contains the text "Scott Rogers". When the reader clicks on the form's submit button, the browser sends the data to the server in the form

```
name=Scott+Rogers
```

Notice that in addition to the field name and an equal sign, the browser also replaced the space between the first and the last names with a "+" symbol.

With forms that have more than a single field, the browser separates each field with the "&" symbol. The standard input stream for a name and address might arrive at the CGI program looking like this:

```
name=Scott+Rogers&address=6209+Boulder+Street&city=Los+Angeles&
state=CA&zip=92167
```

The main reason some people say form-based queries are much more complicated than document-based queries is that you have to parse this kind of string into individual variables. But if you want your form to have more than a single field, you have to use form-based queries. And they're not really all that difficult. Besides, the Unix *cut* command (or the C *strtok()* function) can make quick work of parsing this kind of string.

If you're not up to parsing input streams in the language you want to use, some tools that can help you are available on the Net, including some that come with the most popular Web servers for Unix systems—CERN and NCSA. See Appendix B for their addresses.

Now let's use the same examples we used to demonstrate document-based queries to study form-based ones. We'll write both a Bourne shell and a C version of our database search engine, but this program will be form-based rather than document-based.

You won't learn how to create the form that serves as the front end to this CGI program until we get into the next section of this chapter, but that won't hinder you here. All you have to know at this point is that the form looks very similar to the ones we created in the last section that prompt users to enter a URL (and tell them that "http://" is assumed). The only major difference is that the form-based query has a button that users click when they want to submit the contents of the fields. Let's assume that the edit box field is named *theURL* and that a user has entered the URL www.amd.com into the edit box and clicked the submit button. Here's the shell script:

```
#!/bin/sh
# A Bourne shell script as a form-based CGI program
echo Content-type: text/html
echo
echo "<HTML><HEAD><TITLE>Search Results</TITLE></HEAD><BODY>"
read input

URL=`echo $input \
      | cut -f 2 -d = \
      | sed -e s.%2F.\/.g -e s/%7E/\~/g \
      | tr -d "\r"`
```

```
COMPANY=`grep $URL cgi-data/list.txt \
      | head -n 1 \
      | cut -f 2 -d ,`

if [ "$COMPANY" ]; then
  echo "<H2>Found!</H2>"
  echo "The URL: <I><B>"$URL"</B></I><BR>"
  echo "belongs to: <I><B>"$COMPANY"</B></I>"
else
  echo "<H2>Not found!</H2>"
  echo "The URL: <I><B>"$URL"</B></I><BR>"
  echo "was not found."
fi

echo "<P><A href="/wcr/part2/13/urls_sh.html">Next search</a>"
echo "</BODY></HTML>"
```

Right away you can see a number of similarities to the document-based version of this script. The script starts out by printing the MIME content type followed by a blank line, then prints the HTML code to define the head section. But notice that, in this case, we can go ahead and finish the head section because there is no question whether or not the script was called with parameters.

Immediately after the line that defines the head section is a command you haven't seen before. The *read* command is used to capture the standard input that the Web server feeds to the program when it runs it. The word right after the *read* command (*input*, in this case) is the name of a new variable, which is assigned the value of the standard input string.

After reading the standard input string and assigning it to the variable INPUT, $INPUT will have the value "theURL=www.amd.com".

Since this form has only one field, we don't need to worry about parsing the input string. In fact, we can just use the *cut* command to take only the text to the right of the equal sign. Easy, right?

Unfortunately, it's not quite that easy. When Web browsers send the contents of form fields to a Web server, they translate some characters into other characters, or strings of characters, to represent the original character. You've already seen that spaces between words get translated into plus signs. That's so the spaces don't trick the utility programs used to parse the different fields. But other characters get translated as well; for example, the slash character (/) is translated into the string "%2F" and a tilde character (~) into the string "%7E". As you know, both of these characters are prevalent in URLs, so we'll have to translate them back into slashes and tildes before we can do our search in the database.

In the last section, you saw how useful the Unix *head* and *cut* programs are for processing text. Two more programs for processing text that exist on nearly every Unix computer are *sed* and *tr*. Both are filters—that is, they can accept their input from the standard input stream and put their output onto the standard output stream. Therefore, like *head* and *cut*, *sed* and *tr* can be linked to each other, each program taking its input from the previous program's output.

The *tr* program converts any occurrence of a specified character in a stream into another character (or deletes the character altogether). But our current problem isn't converting one character into another; it's converting a string of characters (such as "%2F") into a single character. The *sed* program will accomplish this nicely.

For a more general-purpose form that people will type text into, you need to write a more robust translation routine or use some of the tools available on the Internet for parsing CGI arguments and input streams. However, for this example, the only valid characters are those that can appear in a valid URL. This means we only have to worry about translating slashes and tildes.

Finally, PCs introduce another problem: If the standard input stream comes from a PC, chances are it will be terminated by two control characters instead of the single one that Unix uses. On Unix computers, lines are terminated by a single new-line character (a linefeed, which is a decimal 10 in ASCII code). PCs, on the other hand, terminate lines with a carriage return (a decimal 12) and a linefeed. This might not be an important factor in many cases, but if you're comparing strings as you do with a search program like this one, it is critically important. A string of characters terminated by a carriage return and a linefeed is not the same as an identical string of characters terminated by only a linefeed. This is a job for the *tr* program. Use *tr* to find any carriage returns and delete them from the string. (Of course, the only one it should find will be at the end of the input stream.)

Here's the heart of the shell script that prepares the variable $URL to be used for the search:

```
URL=`echo $input \
      | cut -f 2 -d = \
      | sed -e s.%2F.\/.g -e s/%7E/\~/g \
      | tr -d "\r"`
```

At first, $input contains the string "theURL=www.amd.com". The command echos this string and pipes it into the *cut* command, which throws away everything except "www.amd.com". Next, the string "www.amd.com" passes through the *sed* filter, which translates any "%2F" characters back into a slash and any "%7E" characters

back into a tilde (in this case, there aren't any in the string). Then *sed* passes the string off to the *tr* program, which deletes any carriage-return characters lurking at the end of the line. Finally, the resulting output from *tr* is assigned to the variable URL, which is now ready to be used with the search.

The rest of the shell script is nearly identical to its document-based equivalent: It uses the *grep*, *head*, and *cut* programs to find a matching line in the database, then tests the value of the $COMPANY variable to see if the search succeeded. If it did, it prints out the company name. If not, it says so.

The following listing shows the C language version of the form-based query. Again, no external programs or utilities were used to parse the input; it's all done right here in C so you can see exactly what needs to take place. One difference in functionality between the C program and the shell script is that, in the C version, we used a *while* loop to convert any character that had been translated into a "%" string.

```
/*  urlsearch-f.c
 *  Form-based version of the urlsearch program.
 *  CGI program to find a URL in a database.
 *  This program takes its input from an HTML form field and
 *  searches the database for a matching URL.
 */

#include <stdio.h>                  /* standard include files */
#include <string.h>

main()
{
  FILE *ifile;                      /* variable declarations */
  char buf[256], instr[64], *p;

  fgets(instr, 64, stdin);          /* read standard input stream */
  instr[63]=NULL;

  p = instr;
  while (*p) {                      /* parse input string to strip */
     if (*p=='%') {                 /* out unnecessary characters */
       strncpy(buf, p+1, 2);
       buf[2]=NULL;
       *p = strtol(buf, NULL, 16);
       strcpy(p+1, p+3);
     }
```

```
      p++;
   }

   if (p = strchr(instr, '='))          /* save only characters to */
     strcpy(instr, &p[1]);              /* right of equal sign */
   if (p = strchr(instr, '\r'))
     *p=NULL;                           /* strip off carriage returns */
   if (p = strchr(instr, '\n'))         /* and new-line characters */
     *p=NULL;

   printf("Content-type: text/html\n\n");        /* output HTML header */

   if (!(ifile = fopen("cgi-data/list.txt", "rt"))) {
      printf("Can't open input file!\n");        /* open input file */
      exit(0);
   }

   while ((p = fgets(buf, 256, ifile))           /* search database */
        && strncmp(instr, buf, strlen(instr)));

   printf("<HEAD><TITLE>Search results</TITLE></BODY>\n");
   if (p) {                                      /* display results */
     p = strchr(buf, ',');
     printf("<BODY><H2>Found!</H2>");
     printf("The URL: ");
     printf("<I><B>%s</B></I><P>", instr);
     printf("belongs to: ");
     printf("<I><B>%s</B></I></BODY>", &p[1]);
   } else {
     printf("<BODY><H2>Not found!</H2>");
     printf("The URL: ");
     printf("<I><B>%s</B></I><P>", instr);
     printf("was not found.</BODY>");
   }

   printf("<p><a href=\"urlsearch.html\">");
   printf("Next search</a>");                    /* prompt for next search */

   fflush(stdout);                               /* flush output stream */
   fclose(ifile);                                /* close input file */
   exit(0);                                      /* end program */
}
```

Forms

Now that you know how to process the data a form sends to a CGI program, we'll get down to the fun part of forms: designing them.

Before we begin, though, you should understand how this section relates to the CGI programs you just learned how to write. Designing forms in HTML has nothing to do with document-based queries—only form-based ones. The single text box provided by a document-based query is rendered by the browser if a document's head section contains an <ISINDEX> tag. As the author of a document-based query, you have virtually no control over the positioning or appearance of the single edit box. With form-based queries, you have complete control over the number and types of fields on your forms, as well as their positioning and sizes.

The Form Element

In the last section, you learned how to write a CGI program for form-based queries; now you'll learn how to design forms and associate them with your CGI programs.

The tag to begin a form definition is <FORM>, and the terminator is </FORM>. As with other complex elements in HTML, such as the Table element, the body of your form definition goes between the opening and terminating tags.

A Web page can contain as many separate forms as you would want to put on a single page—there is no inherent limitation—but each form must point to a CGI program that you provide to process the form's input.

The Form element accepts four attributes:

- ACTION
- METHOD
- ENCTYPE
- SCRIPT

The ACTION attribute associates a form with a CGI program. You can think of this as a required attribute because a form without an association to a CGI program to process the input is pretty much useless. The parameter to the ACTION attribute is simply a URL that references your CGI program. For example:

```
<FORM ACTION="http://www.leafy.com/urlsearch"
```

However, this anchor tag is not finished yet; another parameter to the Form element is also required in most cases. The METHOD parameter tells the browser which of two possible protocols to use to send the form data back to the Web server.

Actually, the METHOD parameter isn't required; it's just that the default value is the one you usually don't want to use. To change it to the other option, you have to include it in the element.

The two possible protocols for sending form data are GET and POST. GET is the default, but POST is the one you'll want to use most of the time. GET is only appropriate in rare cases or when the form itself is small, because this method sends the form data to the server by appending it to the end of the URL that points to the CGI script. It provides far less flexibility than POST, so we won't discuss it further here.

The POST method sends the form data as a string of fields separated by the "&" character and tells the server to make that data available to the CGI program on its standard input stream. Sound familiar? In the previous section (on writing form-based CGI programs), the programs we wrote only handle the POST method.

The ENCTYPE attribute tells the browser what MIME content type to use to send the form data to the server. Similar to how a CGI program has to announce its MIME content type to a browser, browsers have to announce a MIME content type when they send data back to the server. When a CGI program sends data to a browser, the content type is almost always "text/html". When a browser sends field contents back to the server, however, it certainly isn't HTML. The MIME content type the browser uses to send form fields is "application/x-www-form-urlencoded". Since this is the default type, you can safely omit this attribute from the Form element tag.

The final attribute to the Form element isn't really in use yet. In fact, it's not even part of the HTML 3 specification yet (though it may be in the future). The SCRIPT attribute will be used to point to a script on the server that the browser will download and use to validate fields as the user types into them. Of course, several hurdles must be overcome to implement this. For one thing, no standard scripting language is now available on all computers.

Usually, then, you'll use a Form element with two of its attributes—ACTION and METHOD. Because it has become somewhat of a convention to place the METHOD attribute before the ACTION attribute in the tag, the completed tag will look like this:

```
<FORM METHOD=post ACTION="http://www.leafy.com/urlsearch">
...(body of the form description)...
</FORM>
```

Next, we'll look at what you put inside the Form element to describe the body of the form. You can mingle virtually any HTML elements you like inside a form definition for comments, headings, labels, and text, but the elements that relate to

the form itself break down into two basic categories: fields and buttons. Interestingly, the tags you use to define fields and buttons don't break down quite as logically. The tag you use to create a button is the same one you use to define most fields, and two special fields have their own unique tags. Logic isn't always one of HTML's greatest strengths.

Field Types

This section is split into three parts. The first part describes the fields that should work with virtually every browser in use. These were defined in the HTML 2 specification. The second part covers fields that are new with HTML 3. Browser developers are working on supporting these field types now, and some browsers may even support some of them by the time you read this. Finally, the last part gives you a glimpse into the future with some fields being considered for future versions of HTML.

Field and Button Element Attributes

The HTML 3 specification calls for each of the elements in this section (and in the following section on buttons) to accept the new attributes of HTML 3 that all elements accept: ID, LANG, CLASS, ALIGN, and, in a few cases, MD. (See Chapter 10 if you need to refresh your memory on what these attributes do.) Since they don't apply to the function of any particular element, we will omit them from the lists of attributes that each element takes.

One attribute is required for all field elements: the name. Since the name is passed back to the server when the user submits the form, it's needed to identify the field. In the examples that follow, we've made up names for the fields depending on the field type. For example, radio buttons are named *rb*. These names have no special meaning, and you can use whatever names you'd like.

Level 2 Field Types

These are the field types that were defined in the HTML 2 specification. Virtually all the major browsers, with the exception of character-based (nongraphical) browsers, now support them.

TEXT BOXES The text box is your basic edit box. It can accept virtually any type of data, including letter characters, words, spaces, numbers, and punctuation marks. The text box tag is

```
<INPUT type=text name="tb">
```

Street address: 1224 Dutton Drive

Other useful attributes to the text box include *value*, *size*, and *maxlength*. Use *value* to initialize the field (set a default value). You can specify the width of the text box in characters or en units with the *size* attribute. And *maxlength* specifies the maximum number of characters users can enter into the field.

SCROLLABLE TEXT BOXES A scrollable text box is a box that can accept multiple lines of text. It comes with slider bars and thumbnail controls for moving around in the text-box window. This is one of the two fields that don't use the <INPUT> tag. The tag for a scrollable text box is

```
<TEXTAREA name="ta">
```

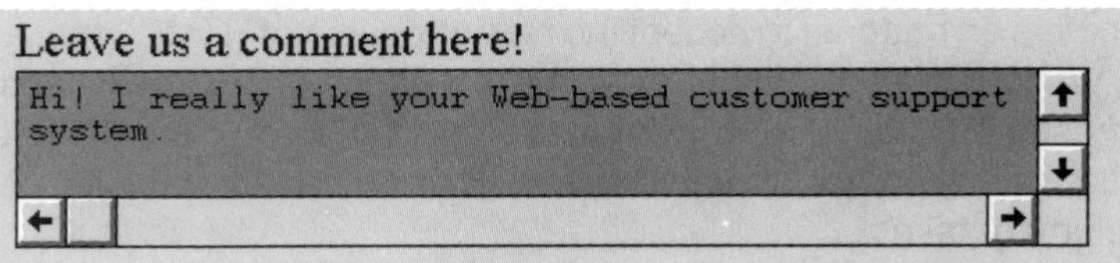

Other useful attributes include *rows* and *cols,* which you can use to set the visible size of the scrollable text box. (These don't limit the amount of text you can put into the box, just the size of the box.) For example:

```
<TEXTAREA name="ta" rows=3 cols=50>
```

CHECKBOXES A checkbox is a small square box that displays an X when you click it. Click it again, and the X will disappear. Checkboxes are useful for fields that are analogous to a yes/no (or on/off) option.

```
<INPUT type=checkbox name="cb">
```

Include:

Summary information: ☒
Detail information: ☐

Another useful attribute is *checked*. Use *checked* to set the initial state of the checkbox (the default is unchecked). When a browser submits form data to the server, a checkbox field will be reported as either on or off (for example, "cb=on"). The *checked* attribute takes no parameters. To use it, just include the word *checked* with the other parameters. (The *checked* parameter is also used with radio buttons; the following section shows an example of it.)

RADIO BUTTONS Radio buttons represent a field that can have one value out of several possibilities. They get their name from the old-style car radios that had buttons for choosing among several radio stations. At any time, one button must be depressed. Press another button, and the first button will pop out.

```
<INPUT type=radio name="rb" value=1 checked>
<INPUT type=radio name="rb" value=2>
```

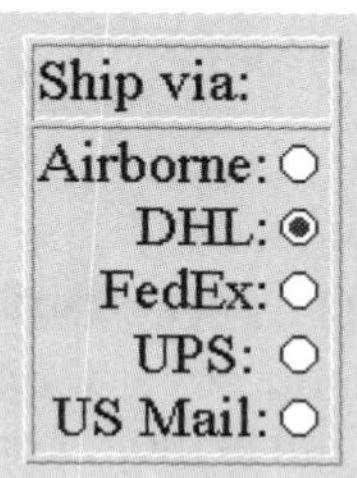

Since radio buttons only make sense in the context of a group, those of the same set must have the same name. This is how you describe a group, or set, of radio buttons to the browser. Radio buttons must also have the *value* attribute, which tells the browser what to send to the server as the field's contents when the form is submitted.

In the above code, the first radio button will be checked by default. If the user checks the second radio button and submits the form, the field content will be sent as "rb=2".

PASSWORD FIELDS A password field is like a text box, but when you type into it you can't see the characters you're typing; they're displayed as asterisks or some other symbol. You can see how many characters were typed, but not the characters themselves.

```
<INPUT type=password name="pw">
```

Enter your password: *****

As with the text field on which it's based, you can control the length of an entry into a password field with the *maxlength* attribute and the display size with the *size* attribute.

HIDDEN FIELDS Hidden fields don't show up on a form at all, and they are used not so much for the reader's benefit as for the Web developer to keep track of information like transaction numbers. On a secure Web site that requires a password for entry, for example, you wouldn't want authorized users to have to enter their password every time they try to load a new page. Instead, you can have them enter and submit their password once, then make the server send back a secret code that will preload into a hidden field with the *value* attribute. Thereafter, when they submit their form, the secret code will be passed back to the server, allowing the CGI script to identify them as authorized users who have already "logged in" and provided a password.

```
<INPUT type=hidden name="hd">
```

SINGLE-CHOICE LISTBOXES (THE SELECT ELEMENT) A listbox allows the user to make a single selection from among several options. Functionally, the listbox is similar to a group of radio buttons but is more compact.

The listbox and the multiple-choice listbox we'll look at next are the other field types that don't use the Input element. The listbox is also called the Select element because that's the tag you use to describe one.

Mark the options in a listbox with the <OPTION> tag. After the last <OPTION> tag, you must terminate the Select element.

```
<SELECT name="sb">
  <OPTION>Red
  <OPTION>Green
  <OPTION>Blue
</SELECT>
```

Choose your primary color: Cadet blue

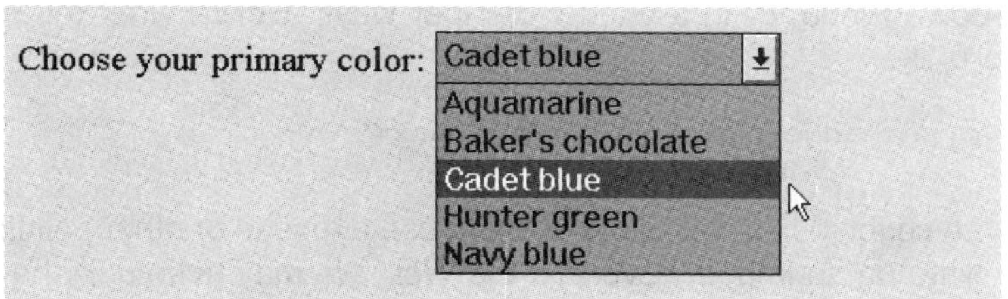

MULTIPLE-CHOICE LISTBOXES (SELECT) A multiple-choice listbox is essentially the same as a listbox, but it allows the user to make multiple selections from among the options. The tags are the same as for the listbox. All you need to do to make it a multiple-choice listbox is to include the *multiple* attribute in the <SELECT> tag.

```
<SELECT multiple name="mcsb">
  <OPTION>Red
  <OPTION>Green
  <OPTION>Blue
</SELECT>
```

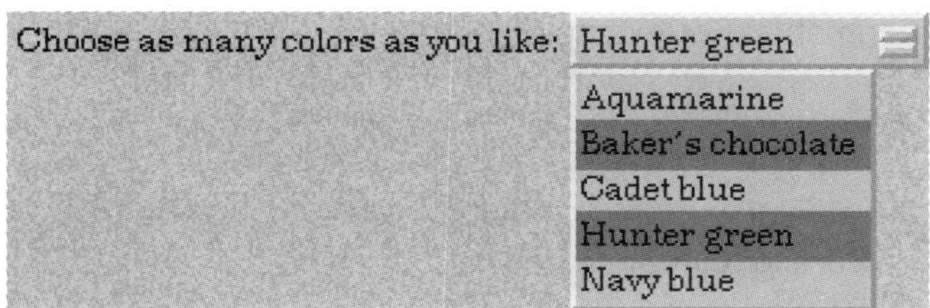

Level 3 Field Types

The three field types described here are new with HTML 3. Some browsers may not yet support them, so be careful in your implementation. As of this writing, no browsers support these field types, so it's difficult to tell what the consensus will be as to how they will be rendered.

RANGES The range field will allow the user to enter a number between a specified minimum and maximum value into a field. How browser developers will choose to render this field type is up for grabs. It may ultimately look just like a text box into which users can only type numbers, or it could be implemented as a spin control, as a drop-down menu, or in a variety of other ways. Here's what the syntax will probably look like:

```
<INPUT type=range name="rf" min=0 max=5>
```

SCRIBBLE A scribble field will allow users to use a mouse or other pointing device to draw or write on an image. (Even on the Web, we may eventually have to sign on the dotted line!) The tag for a scribble field will need to include the SRC attribute to specify the image to send to the browser.

```
<INPUT type=scribble name="sf"
src="http://www.ardvaark.com/imgs/dottedline.gif">
```

FILE The file field will allow users to attach one or more files on their own system to the content of the form. This field will probably be rendered as a list of file names with *Add* and *Delete from list* buttons. Pressing the Add button will probably cause a standard file-selection box to pop up on the system running the browser (like the one that pops up when you choose File¦Open from your browser's main menu).

By using the ACCEPT attribute, you can control, or suggest, the MIME content type for file attachments. For example, the tag

```
<INPUT type=file name="ft" accept="image/*">
```

will cause the file-selection box to default to displaying image files, which includes files with extensions like .GIF and .JPG.

Future Field Types

Although they're not part of the HTML 3 specification, there is some exciting talk about new field types in future versions of HTML. These may include audio fields that you could use to record and play back audio messages. There's also talk of

tables, or grids, that would allow users to view and edit a multirow view of database tables and of enhancing the scrollable text box to include other data types, such as images and sound.

Buttons

Two types of buttons can be put on forms: *Submit* and *Reset*. When you press a Submit button, your browser sends the contents of your form fields to the remote Web server, which passes it along to the CGI program specified by the form.

A Reset button will reinitialize all the fields in a form to their default values. This is essentially a quick way to blank out a form without having to reload the page.

You specify both Submit and Reset buttons with the <INPUT> tag; just use a different attribute to specify the one you want. The syntax for a Submit button is

```
<INPUT type=submit>
```

The syntax for a Reset button is

```
<INPUT type=reset>
```

Please fill in each of the following fields

Name:

Street:

City,State,Zip:

Reset | Submit Query

Return to home page

The default label on a Submit button is "Submit query," and the default label on a Reset button is "Reset." However, you can override these labels with both buttons by using the *value* attribute. For example:

```
<INPUT type=submit value="Send form">
```

will display a Submit button with the text "Send form" on the face of the label.

[illegible]

[illegible] the words shown [illegible]
tools [illegible] and [illegible] next [illegible]
images and sound [illegible]

[illegible]

[illegible] you [illegible]

[illegible]

[illegible]

Part 3

Advanced Web Topics

Chapter 14

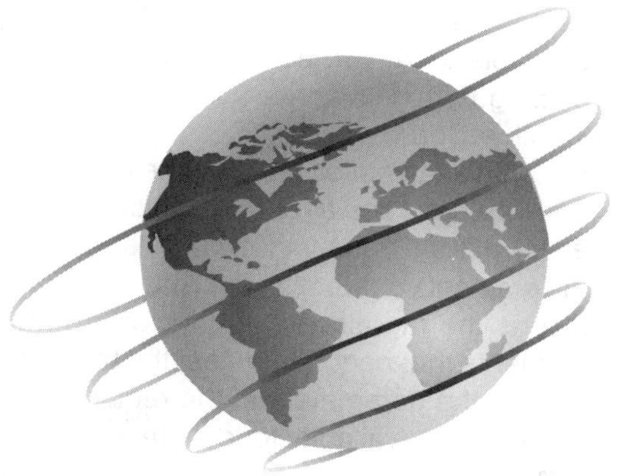

Tools for Authoring HTML Pages

After eight straight chapters of technical information, you're probably thinking you're ready to lighten up a little. In this chapter, we'll slow the pace of the details and look at some of the tools you can use to make the process of creating Web pages easier and more enjoyable. We'll look at two broad categories of tools: editors and HTML converters.

There are two types of editors. "Official" terms for them haven't emerged yet, so we'll call them *graphical editors* and *tag editors*.

A graphical, or WYSIWYG (pronounced "wiz-ee-wig"), editor is used to edit only the content of HTML documents. (The term WYSIWYG is an acronym for "What You See Is What You Get.") By "only the content," we mean that your page looks just as it will look with a Web browser—you don't see any HTML tags at all. Since you can't see or edit any of the HTML tags, your focus is on the content—the words, sentences, pictures, and links in your document. Most of the graphical editors available today are actually document templates for commercial word-processing packages, so in a sense you use them to turn your word processor into a graphical HTML editor.

With a tag editor, you see the HTML tags in your pages along with your content, and you *don't* see a representation of what your page will ultimately look like. A tag editor assists you by inserting the HTML tags where you want them. You just pick the element you want from a menu or by clicking a button on a toolbar, and the editor inserts the tag along with its closing tag (if it's an element that needs one). For elements that need attributes, the tag editor pops up a dialog box and prompts you to fill in the parameters to the required attributes, then insert the tags. Most of the tag editors available today are not add-ons for another type of program (like templates for a word processor), but rather are standalone programs.

The second category of HTML tools, *converters,* are programs or macros that translate files from popular word-processing document formats or other common formats into HTML.

Tools for Authoring Web Pages

There are three primary reasons why you might want to use tools to help you produce your Web pages. First, you might not like dealing with HTML directly, or you might just want some help remembering the attributes to the different HTML tags.

Another reason is that you may prefer working in a word-processing environment to that of a plain text editor. (A word processor's spell checker and thesaurus can be two compelling reasons to do your original work in a word processor.)

Finally, you might like working directly with the HTML tags but find that it's faster or more convenient to write your pages with a program that will insert the tags for you and prompt you for the proper syntax.

Regardless of your reasons for wanting to use an authoring tool, plenty of them are available. In fact, it seems that HTML authoring tools are the hottest new category of software development. New programs are springing up every day, and everyone from developers at the largest software companies to the hobbyist is jumping on the bandwagon by creating programs and making them available on the Internet.

But authoring tools are not a panacea for developing Web pages. They won't necessarily make your development process any faster or smoother, and many Web authors feel that these tools simply are not worth the trouble of learning or using them.

For one thing, most of the Web authoring tools available today aren't HTML 3 compliant. "Big deal," you may think, "most Web browsers aren't either." But although few Web browsers are *fully* HTML 3 compliant, most of them—especially the popular ones—do support some of the most important features of HTML 3. For example, tables are an HTML feature that nearly every browser developer has already adopted. Several of the Web authoring tools fall short when it comes to including a table on a page. Other examples of HTML 3 features that most authoring tools don't support are custom backgrounds, inline figures (as opposed to inline images), and the ID attribute that makes any element a hypertext target. And we won't even mention cascading styles.

If you do choose to use a Web authoring tool, you generally have to figure out how to use other tools to make up for its shortcomings, or ultimately even edit your HTML source file manually anyway.

Finally, since you wouldn't be likely to publish a Web page you created with a graphical editor before trying it out with a real Web browser, why not just edit your HTML in a window and test it with a browser simultaneously? Whenever you make a change to the HTML, you can just click the Save button in your editor and the Reload button in the browser to test it. It doesn't get much easier than that.

But plenty of people do believe that Web authoring tools save them time, or allow them to concentrate on the content of their documents rather than the markup code. If you find yourself in this camp, then that's all the reason you need to find tools that work for you.

In this chapter, we're going to show you the types of tools that are available and give you examples specific to some of the packages. We'll also give you pointers to more complete and up-to-date information on authoring tools.

Although we'll also give you URLs for the software we discuss here, there is a drawback to doing so. Thousands of people trying to download a file from the same machine at the same time can quickly overload a host system, so be responsible when you retrieve these packages. Some of the packages are made available by organizations that graciously provide disk space and network bandwidth at minimal or no cost. Since you don't have to pay for the software or the bandwidth, try to find mirror sites or other sites near you that also provide these files. This will help avoid overloading the host system as well as long expanses of the Internet.

Graphical Editors

Editors aren't for everyone. If you've followed along with the examples in the book and done some experimenting on your own, editors may not get you very excited. However, they can help inexperienced Web authors jump in and start creating pages quickly. Even if you're an experienced Web author, if you hate having to refer constantly to this book because of the many tags with different attributes and parameters, an editor may be just the ticket for you.

In this section, we'll look at graphical editors. With these editors, you work directly with a document that looks just as it will appear in Web browsers. Graphical editors attempt to shield the user completely from the markup code and allow you to design your pages visually rather than textually. We're going to take a detailed look at only one editor—Internet Assistant, which is Microsoft's entry into this arena. We'll briefly mention other editors, highlighting any special features that set them apart from the others, and give you information about where to find them.

Microsoft's Internet Assistant

Microsoft has planted a heavy foot in the field of HTML authoring tools with its Internet Assistant package. Internet Assistant is an add-in package for Microsoft Word for Windows that practically turns Word into a Web browser.

Internet Assistant has two modes: browser and edit. In browser mode, you can load Web pages and follow links just as you do with any browser. In this mode, Internet Assistant provides a Word toolbar with all the usual buttons and commands a Web browser needs for navigation (see Figure 14-1).

In this mode, however, Internet Assistant diverges from Web browsers: It loads each page as a Word document, keeping each successive page that you load in its own window. You wouldn't want to use Internet Assistant to browse the Web for very long because you'd soon run out of memory, but Word's rendering of HTML documents is as good as that of any Web browser.

FIGURE 14-1.

Internet Assistant in browser mode

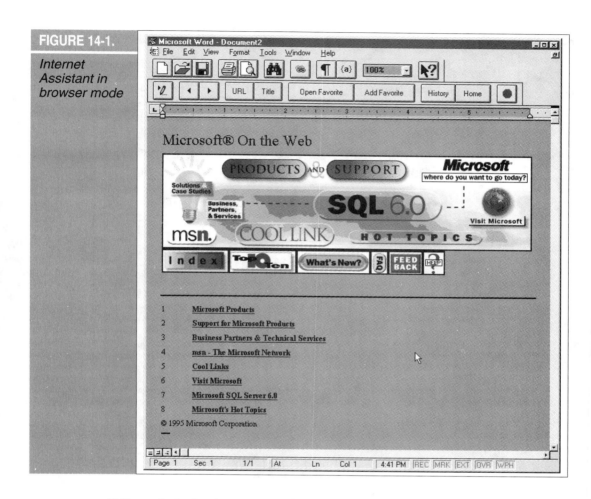

Edit mode looks the same as browser mode except that it provides a Word toolbar with buttons for the elements you'll use most often to create and edit HTML pages (see Figure 14-2). If you know how to use Word, you'll essentially know how to use Internet Assistant. For example, to create a heading, you just pick the heading style you want from the drop-down style list in the toolbar and type your heading, or you can select the heading text first, then pick the heading style.

One of the great advantages of using Internet Assistant is that you have all of Word's capabilities at your fingertips—the spell checker, the thesaurus, AutoText, and so on. Creating links to image files, or other Web pages, is easy: You just click the appropriate button on the toolbar and fill in the URL in the dialog box. For images,

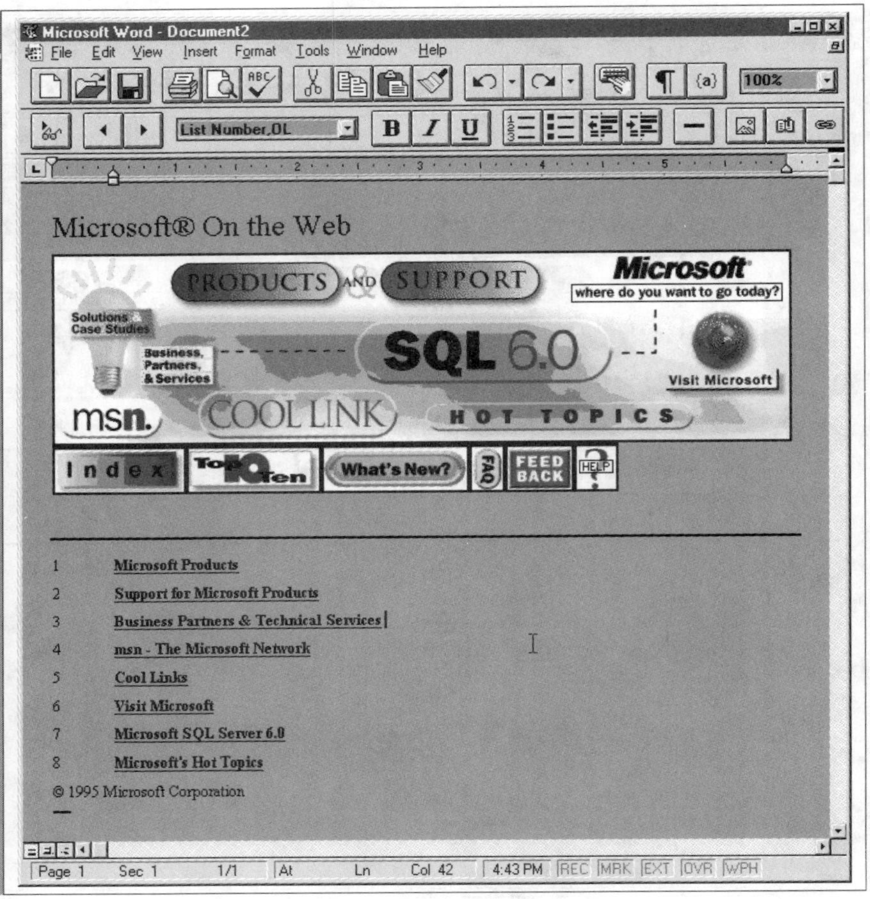

FIGURE 14-2. *Internet Assistant in edit mode*

Internet Assistant instantly displays the image at the appropriate spot in your document, and it applies blue shading and an underline to anchor text, making it look like an anchor should in a browser. One click of a button puts you back into browser mode; another click on your new anchor tests your link to another document.

One drawback to using Internet Assistant is that your original documents aren't stored as HTML files—they're stored as Word document files. To create your final product, you have to go through the extra step of saving it as an HTML file. If you ever have to edit the resulting HTML file outside of Internet Assistant, you get into the classical Catch-22 of any source-code generator: If you go back to Internet

Assistant to make a change to your document and regenerate the HTML file, you'll have to re-edit the newly generated HTML file and reapply your changes.

To alleviate this problem, Microsoft offers another product called *Word Viewer*. Word Viewer allows remote users who don't have Microsoft Word to view your Internet Assistant documents in their native Word file format. Of course, to use Word Viewer, they have to be using a computer that can run Microsoft Windows programs, so this isn't an ideal solution.

Internet Assistant is a free product from Microsoft (*yes—a free product from Microsoft*) and is available from their Web server at http://www.microsoft.com/pages/deskapps/word/ia/default.htm.

ANT_HTML

Another option for users of Microsoft Word is a document template developed by Jill Swift called *ANT_HTML*. ANT_HTML is similar to Internet Assistant, but it doesn't have a browser mode so you can't follow links.

ANT_HTML and its newer cousin, ANT_PLUS, both work with Microsoft Word under Windows and on the Macintosh. (ANT_Plus can import HTML documents into Word as well as writing them to HTML files.) The ANT suite is shareware and is availble at ftp.einet.net/einet/pc/ for the PC and at ftp://ftp.einet.net/einet/mac/html-aids/ for the Mac.

Quarterdeck's WebAuthor

WebAuthor is another add-in for Microsoft Word for Windows users. In several respects, WebAuthor may be superior to Microsoft's own Internet Assistant. For example, with WebAuthor, no conversion is necessary between Word document formats and HTML; WebAuthor automatically converts your documents to pure-text HTML files when you save them, and it automatically imports HTML documents into Word when you load them.

WebAuthor is a cornerstone of Quarterdeck's new suite of Internet tools. Unfortunately, it's a commercial product for which you will have to pay real money, but you can order it online. You can get the latest information on WebAuthor from Quarterdeck's Web site at http://www.qdeck.com/.

Emacs Helper Modes

Help is available for die-hard emacs users, too. These helper-mode add-ins for emacs allow you to create and edit your HTML files in a full WYSIWYG environment. (Are there any tasks for which there isn't a corresponding emacs helper mode?) There are even helper modes that turn emacs into a full-fledged Web browser (see Chapter 5).

There are two helper modes that we are aware of for editing HTML documents. For the latest information and locations, check out http://www.santafe.edu/~nelson/tools/ and ftp://ftp.ncsa.uiuc.edu/Web/html/elisp/html-mode.el.

Live Markup

Live Markup is a little different from the other graphical editors we've discussed. For one thing, it's a standalone program, not an add-in for a word processor. Also, Live Markup isn't truly a WYSIWYG editor. It's sort of a hybrid creature.

Live Markup shields the user from the HTML tags, and it renders the HTML elements similarly to how they will appear in Web browsers (for example, 1-heads are displayed at a larger size than 2-heads). It also includes in the editor window something called an *element selector*, a kind of handle by which you select each element of your page.

Live Markup is neither particularly intuitive nor particularly stable. With time, however, the authors will probably work out the kinks. You can get the evaluation version of Live Markup at http://www.mediatec.com/mediatech/.

Tag Editors

If you enjoy or don't mind working with the HTML markup code, a tag editor may be for you. Essentially, it's a standard text editor that has buttons or commands for inserting HTML tags. This saves you from having to type the tags into your documents manually, but it can also be a real aid when it comes to remembering the proper syntax and attributes of the many elements of HTML.

WebEdit

WebEdit is a fun new tag editor written by Kenn Nesbitt. It embodies many of the best features of tag editors and allows you to work in an organized and uncluttered environment. WebEdit lets you work on a number of documents at the same time, but you need to have a multitasking brain to use this feature.

WebEdit is a standalone program, not an add-in for a word processor. Of all the Web authoring tools we've looked at, WebEdit is the most compliant with the HTML 3 specification. It knows about the ID, CLASS, and LANG attributes, tables, and even inline figures. The program provides a helpful toolbar for inserting the tags you need most often (see Figure 14-3).

WebEdit is available at http://wwwnt.thegroup.net/webedit/webedit.htm.

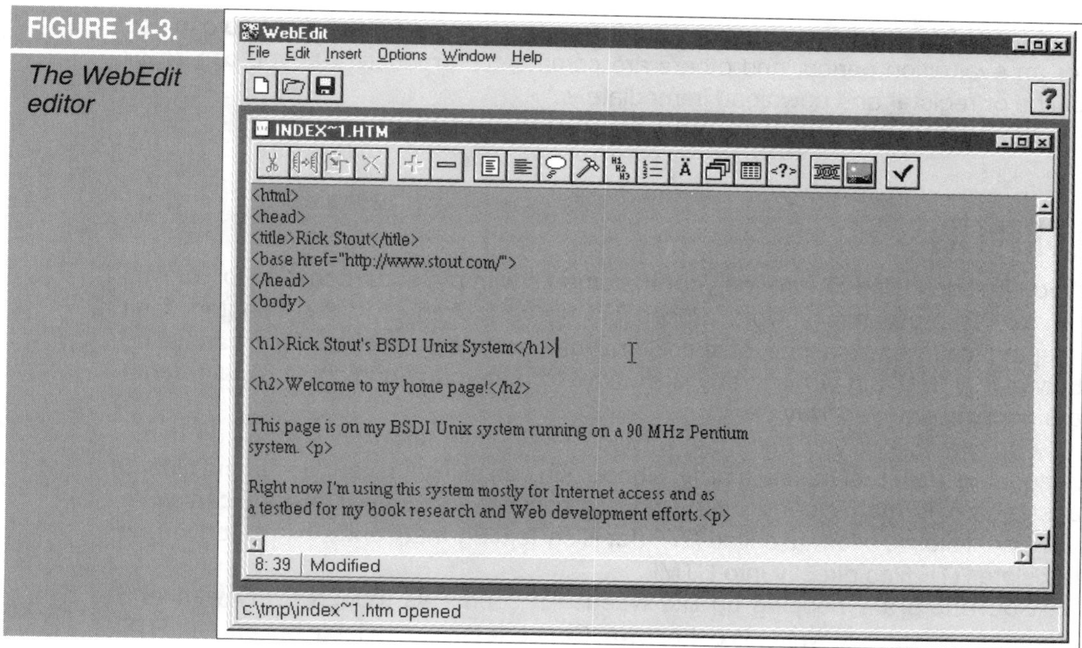

FIGURE 14-3.

The WebEdit editor

SoftQuad's HoTMetaL

HoTMetaL from SoftQuad is a perennial favorite among some Web authors. However, the HoTMetaL environment is lacking in some areas. For example, this editor doesn't yet provide a toolbar for selecting elements, and the entire program is menu-driven—that is, you're constantly working with the menu tree to insert tags and perform actions on your documents.

Among many other sites, you can find HoTMetaL at http://www.sq.com and ftp://ftp.ncsa.uiuc.edu/Web/html/hotmetal/. The NCSA site tends to be busy, so you might want to check the World Wide Web FAQ for a list of mirror sites for HoTMetaL.

Other Tag Editors

So many tag editors are becoming available every day that your choices can seem endless. For the most up-to-date and complete list of editors, check the section of the World Wide Web FAQ on editing tools (http://sunsite.unc.edu/boutell/faq/editinghtml.html). Another source for information on tag editors, and HTML authoring tools in general, is the large directories, such as the Yahoo server at http://www.yahoo.com. Look in the sections for *Internet software* and *World Wide Web software.*

Many of the available packages are free, some are shareware that you can use for an evaluation period, and others are commercial products that you can order online or register and download immediately.

Table 14-1 lists some of the most popular tag editors.

Converters

If you just don't like to work on your documents with a standard text editor, or with *any* of the programs or word processors we've looked at in this chapter, don't despair; you can use one of the filters, or converters, available for translating between HTML and virtually any document format you can imagine. Again, more are popping up every day.

For example, if you don't use a Mac or Windows and you're stuck on some antiquated word processor, in all likelihood you can still save your document files to a standard format. Nearly every word processor in modern history can write document files to a format called *RTF* (for Rich Text Format), and several converters translate RTF files directly into HTML.

Converters are popping up like weeds—it seems as though every weekend programmer wants to write his or her own. Converters are available not only for RTF but for WordPerfect, PostScript, FrameMaker, LaTeX, BibTeX, Texinfo, DECwrite, Interleaf, QuarkXPress, PageMaker, Scribe, PowerPoint, and even nroff and troff, the Unix text-formatting tools.

TABLE 14-1. *Popular HTML Tag Editors*

PACKAGE	PLATFORM	URL
BBEdit extensions	Mac	http://www.uji.es/bbedit-html-extensions.html http://www.york.ac.uk/~ld11/BBEditTools.html
HoTMetaL	Windows	http://www.sq.com
HTML Assistant	Windows	ftp.cs.dal.ca/htmlasst/
HTML Editor	Windows	http://dragon.acadiau.ca/~giles/HTML_Editor
HTML Writer	Windows	http://lal.cs.byu.edu/people/nosack/
Phoenix	X Window	http://www.bsd.uchicago.edu/ftp/pub/phoenix/
TkWWW	X Window	http://www.w3.org/hypertext/WWW/TkWWW/Status.html
WebEdit	Windows	http://wwwnt.thegroup.net/webedit/webedit.htm

For a full list of HTML converters, visit the "official" list of converters and filters at http://www.w3.org/hypertext/WWW/Tools/Filters.html. This page is maintained regularly by the W3 organization.

Finally, if your favorite authoring tools don't do tables and you use Microsoft Excel, a tool is available to convert your Excel worksheets into HTML tables. The introductory page for this Excel macro is at http://rs712b.gsfc.nasa.gov/704/dgd/xl2html.html.

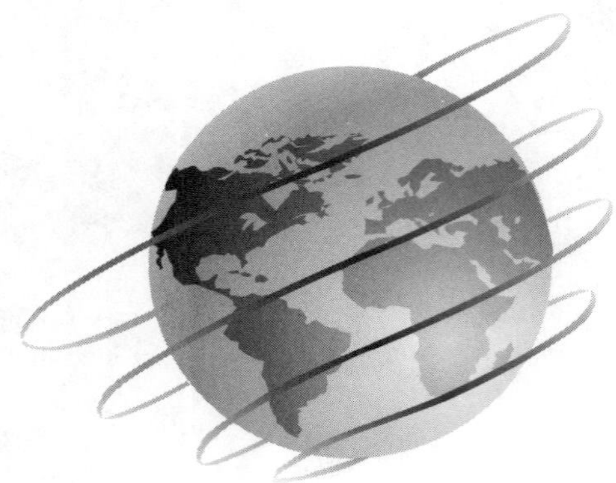

Chapter 15

Finding a Home for Your Pages

By all accounts, the Web is growing by leaps and bounds. Some say the number of HTML pages available on the Web is doubling every few months. When you hear astonishing statistics like this, try to remember that in addition to the huge number of companies and organizations providing pages on the Web, there are even more people reading these pages who haven't yet established their own presence.

Establishing your presence is a process of learning how the Web (and the Internet) works, how to connect to it, how to find a place for your Web pages to reside, and how to produce those pages.

The main hurdle you have to overcome in establishing a presence for yourself or your business is *accessibility*. There's not much point in creating a web of HTML pages for the public to use if your computer isn't connected to the Internet 24 hours a day, seven days a week. At the moment you have only two options—either you purchase a permanent connection to the Internet for your computer or you lease space from some other business or organization that has a permanent connection and will host your pages and make them available at all times.

In the next chapter, we'll look at what's involved in putting your own network onto the Internet. But to jump into the Internet this way, you've got to be pretty serious about putting your business on the Net and ready to spend some bucks on equipment and an Internet connection.

If this sounds like something you would eventually like to do, but you're not quite ready to take the plunge, consider a two-phase approach. Start out by renting or leasing space on another organization's computer. You'll have complete control over the content and administration of your Web pages, but the initial capital, commitment, and risk will be much lower. Once you have a feel for the benefits of being on the Web and have an idea of the administration requirements for maintaining your web, you can consider bringing your web in-house.

In this chapter, we'll give you pointers for finding companies that will be pleased to host your Web pages, tips on getting the best value for your money, and suggestions on how to make your presence known once you're established.

Renting a Home for Your Web

In Chapter 2, you learned about Internet service providers (or ISPs). We discussed connection options as well as some of the other services ISPs provide, such as electronic mail and Usenet news feeds. One service many ISPs provide but that we didn't talk about was hosting Web pages.

Many of the larger ISPs provide a range of services to businesses, including hosting Web pages, providing listings (sometimes even categorized listings) of the businesses they host, creating and maintaining Web pages, and scanning photographs to create GIF and JPEG images.

In addition to ISPs, a fledgling industry of businesses that offer Web services exclusively has arisen in response to the growing demand for companies that create, host, and serve Web pages for organizations that (due to the time or expense involved) don't want to set up their own network on the Internet.

Table 15-1 lists some of the largest companies that host Web space. This list includes both ISPs, whose primary business may be selling Internet access, and companies that specialize in hosting and serving Web pages.

The ways businesses hosting Web pages charge for their services are as numerous as the companies themselves. Each is a slightly different variation on a few familiar techniques. This can make comparing services and prices a troublesome exercise.

For example, some companies charge by the month, while others charge by the year. If that were the extent of the variations, it would be simple to compare pricing on a monthly basis. More often, however, they charge different rates for individuals,

TABLE 15-1. *A Few of the Companies Hosting Web Space on the Internet*

COMPANY	HOST
BizPro OnLine	www.bizpro.com
CTS Network Services	www.cts.com
Engineering International	www.rt66.com
Evergreen	cybermart.com
Global Shopping Network	www.gsn.com
InterConnect West	www.icw.com
Open Markets Commercial Sites Index	www.directory.net
Primenet	www.primenet.com
Teleport	www.teleport.com
Web Communications	www.webcom.com
Xmission	www.xmission.com

businesses, and large businesses. Some even have additional charges for disk space, Internet bandwidth consumed by people reading your pages, or the features you put on your Web pages—interactive forms, email links, and so on.

Let's work a couple of specific examples so you'll know what to expect when you investigate the market for yourself. We won't mention the names of the companies when we look at pricing because their rates and services may change.

Let's assume that you want to create a web with a total of eight pages. One popular company charges $240 per year for the first page and $120 for additional pages. There are no extra charges for disk space, bandwidth, or special services; the annual rate covers all the extras. Thus, the annual and monthly fees for eight pages would be:

First page:	$240
Seven additional pages (at $120 each):	$840
Annual total:	$1,080
Monthly total:	$90

For an additional fee, this company will also help you create your pages and scan photographs. They also collect minimal fees to make changes to your pages or to replace graphic images.

Another company that hosts Web pages for many businesses ties its charges more closely to the Internet traffic your site generates. This company has standard monthly fees, with maximum allowances for disk space and network traffic. The monthly fees and the size of the allowances depend upon the number of employees your business has. This company considers a business with 16 or more employees to be a large business.

The monthly fee for a large business is $95, with a disk space quota of 10 MB and a monthly traffic quota of 400 MB. Eight HTML documents, even if they have a considerable number of graphic images, should easily fit into 10 MB of disk space. And since 400 MB of network traffic is the equivalent of 40,000 page requests (based on an average page size of 10K), if the average reader browsing your web reads four of the eight pages, that works out to about 10,000 readers per month. If you attract more readers than expected and exceed your traffic allowance, the additional bandwidth is billed to your account at a reasonable rate.

For a business of fewer than 16 employees, the monthly fee is $30. The disk quota is 5 MB and the traffic allowance is 200 MB, or about 20,000 page requests at 10K per page. Again, if you exceed your quotas, the excess is billed monthly at minimal additional rates.

Publicizing Your Web

Once you've designed your web and found a home for it, you'll want to announce your arrival to the world. While there is no definitive way to do this, you can do a number of things to make your presence known.

One of the best ways to start attracting readers quickly is to get your web listed in as many of the online directories as you can. Most of these directories provide a "What's New" section (see Figure 15-1) in addition to providing a categorized pointer to your web. If you can get your web listed in several What's New listings, you'll begin attracting some traffic immediately.

Table 15-2 lists a few of the many directories of sites on the World Wide Web. Some of these directories don't focus exclusively on businesses, but the ones that include other types of organizations provide a "Business" or "Commerce" category where you can list your business.

You can add your web to many directories and indexes on the Web yourself. By filling out a form and submitting your information, you can often have your site listed in a few minutes; the longest you might have to wait is overnight. But the best thing about advertising your web on Web directories and indexes is that it's almost always free.

Other places you should be sure to look into are the home pages of Web browser developers and ISPs. When Web users first install browser software, many of them

TABLE 15-2. *Directories on the Web*

COMPANY	URL
ALIWEB	http://web.nexor.co.uk/aliweb/doc/aliweb.html
EINet	http://www.einet.net
Open Markets Commercial Sites Index	http://www.directory.net
Virtual Yellow Pages	http://www.imsworld.com
Whole Internet Catalog	http://www.gnn.com
WWW Virtual Library	http://www.w3.org/hypertext/DataSources/bySubject/
Yahoo	http://www.yahoo.com

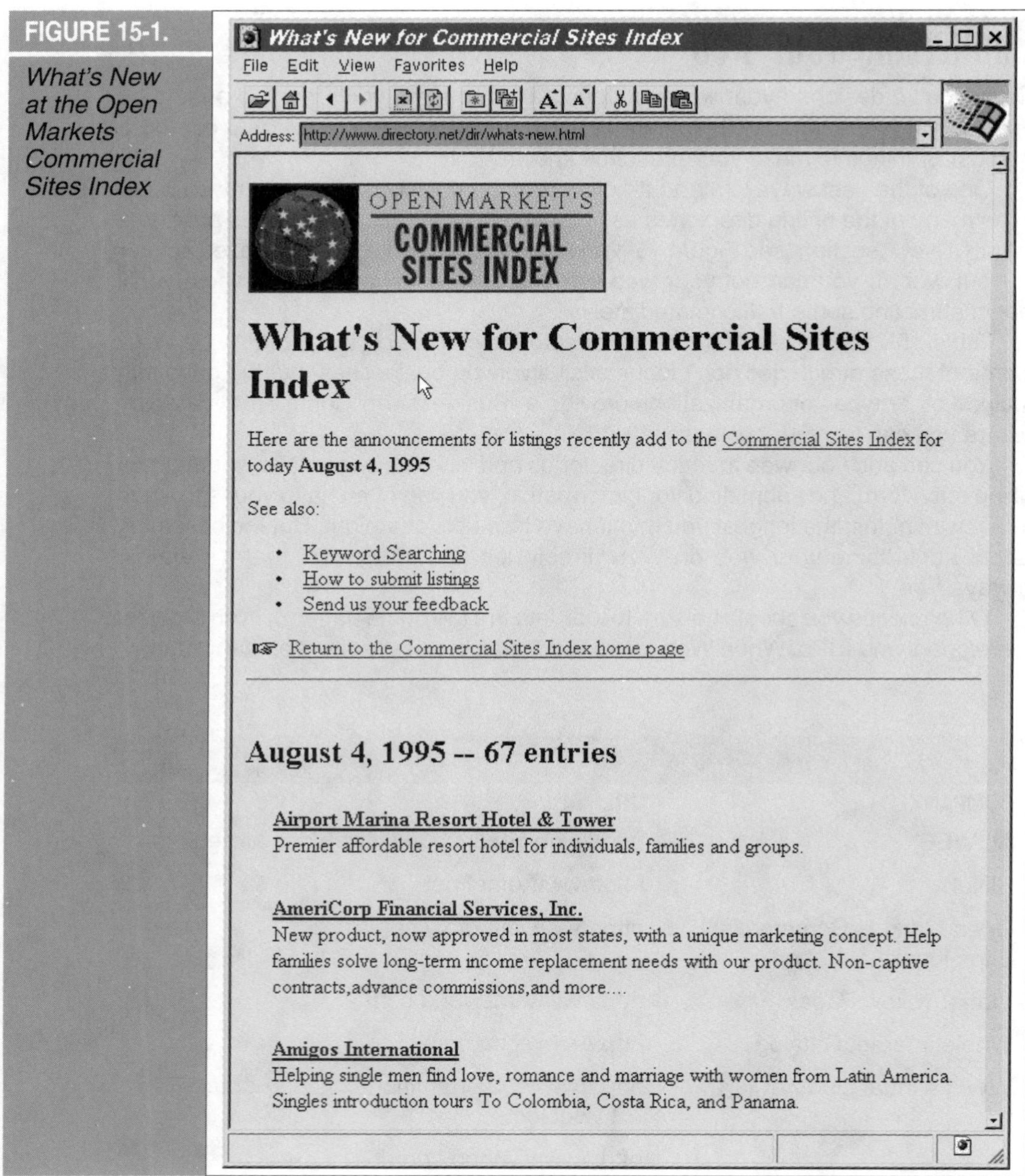

FIGURE 15-1. *What's New at the Open Markets Commercial Sites Index*

point to the home pages of the company that developed the browser. For example, Mosaic points to the NCSA web, and Netscape points to the Netscape web. These pages almost always have a "What's new on the Internet" anchor to follow. Until the users figure out how to change their home page, they will likely see their developer's web with this link on it. The default configuration of Netscape even displays a button in the browser that takes the reader directly to Netscape's What's New page (see Figure 15-2).

When new Web users discover how to change their home pages, they often change them to the home page of their ISP. ISPs often include What's New links. Some of them point to the links to Web service providers or to the Mosaic or Netscape What's New links, but many of them manage their What's New lists themselves. Figure 15-3 shows the What's New page for a major ISP. This page has more than 100 listings of new businesses and organizations on the Web.

Many people who use the Web read Usenet newsgroups to find out about new resources and sites. Take a few days and read the newsgroups comp.infosystems.announce and comp.infosystems.www.announce. Once you have a feel for the type of information that flows through these newsgroups and the protocol people use, go ahead and post a message announcing your new site. The reason we suggest that you read these groups for a few days is that if you don't follow the protocol, you can actually do yourself more harm than good. In fact, it would be a good idea to read the FAQ (Frequently Asked Questions) list for the group before you post.

Finally, many people subscribe to mailing lists to keep current with the latest and greatest on the Internet and the Web. One such mailing list is the www-announce list at the W3 organization. To subscribe, you can send an email message to www-announce@w3.org with the words *subscribe www-announce* as the body of your message. After you've subscribed, read the messages for a few days to get a feel for the protocol of the list, then post your announcement. Actually, you don't have to subscribe to the list to send a message to it, but it's best if you understand the etiquette of any list before sending a message to one.

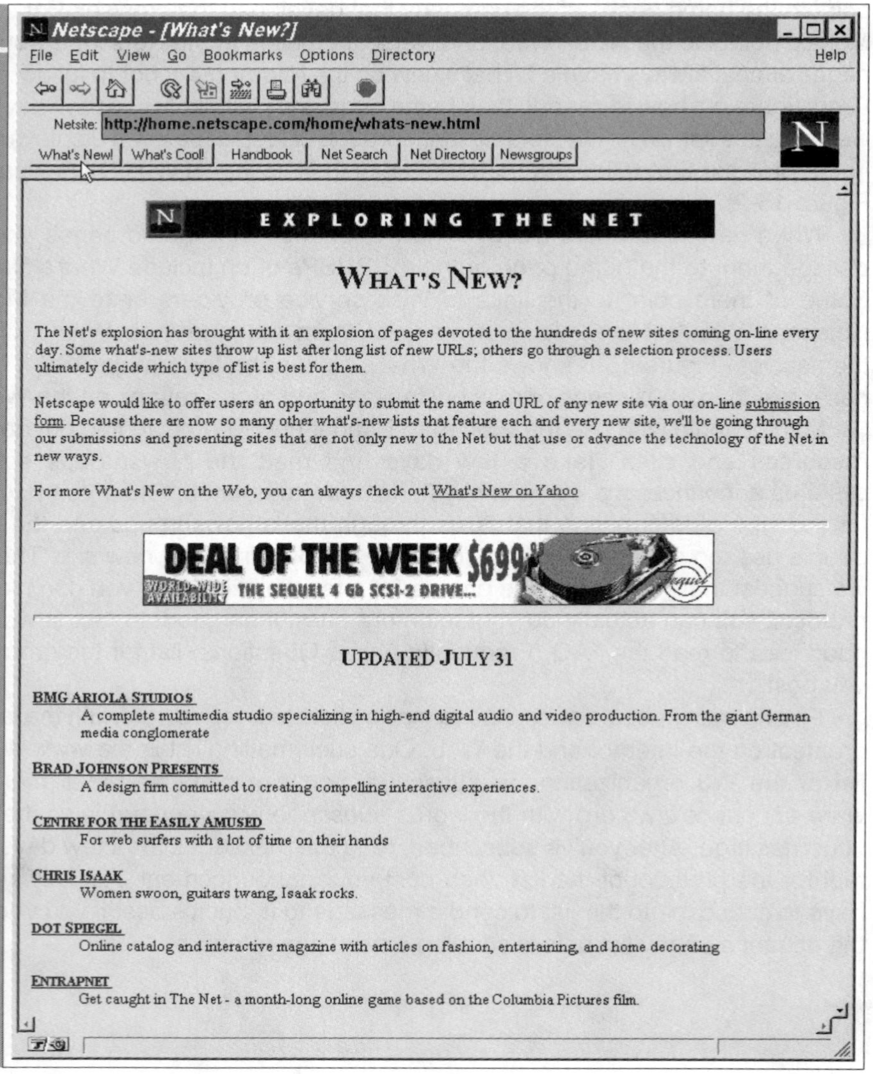

FIGURE 15-2. *Netscape's What's New page. (The cursor is pointing at the button that takes you there.)*

Netscape - [What's New?]

File Edit View Go Bookmarks Options Directory Help

Netsite: http://home.netscape.com/home/whats-new.html

What's New! | What's Cool! | Handbook | Net Search | Net Directory | Newsgroups

EXPLORING THE NET

WHAT'S NEW?

The Net's explosion has brought with it an explosion of pages devoted to the hundreds of new sites coming on-line every day. Some what's-new sites throw up list after long list of new URLs; others go through a selection process. Users ultimately decide which type of list is best for them.

Netscape would like to offer users an opportunity to submit the name and URL of any new site via our on-line submission form. Because there are now so many other what's-new lists that feature each and every new site, we'll be going through our submissions and presenting sites that are not only new to the Net but that use or advance the technology of the Net in new ways.

For more What's New on the Web, you can always check out What's New on Yahoo

DEAL OF THE WEEK $699 WORLD-WIDE AVAILABILITY THE SEQUEL 4 Gb SCSI-2 DRIVE...

UPDATED JULY 31

BMG ARIOLA STUDIOS
A complete multimedia studio specializing in high-end digital audio and video production. From the giant German media conglomerate

BRAD JOHNSON PRESENTS
A design firm committed to creating compelling interactive experiences.

CENTRE FOR THE EASILY AMUSED
For web surfers with a lot of time on their hands

CHRIS ISAAK
Women swoon, guitars twang, Isaak rocks.

DOT SPIEGEL
Online catalog and interactive magazine with articles on fashion, entertaining, and home decorating

ENTRAPNET
Get caught in The Net - a month-long online game based on the Columbia Pictures film.

FIGURE 15-3.

A major ISP's What's New page

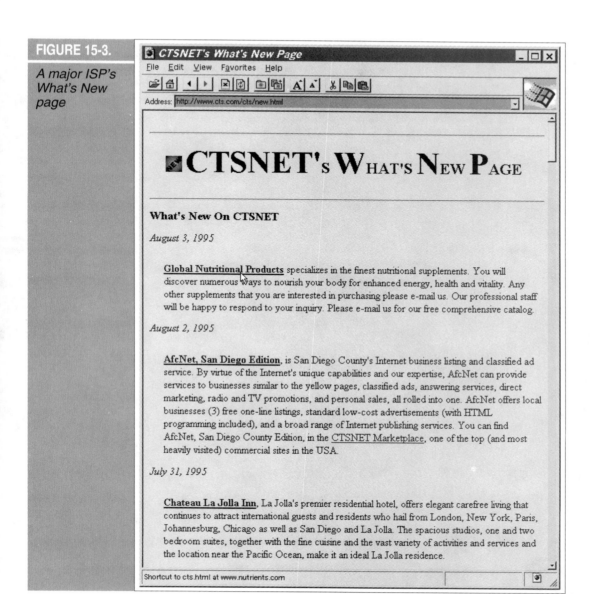

CTSNET's What's New Page

File Edit View Favorites Help

Address: http://www.cts.com/cts/new.html

CTSNET's What's New Page

What's New On CTSNET

August 3, 1995

Global Nutritional Products specializes in the finest nutritional supplements. You will discover numerous ways to nourish your body for enhanced energy, health and vitality. Any other supplements that you are interested in purchasing please e-mail us. Our professional staff will be happy to respond to your inquiry. Please e-mail us for our free comprehensive catalog.

August 2, 1995

AfcNet, San Diego Edition, is San Diego County's Internet business listing and classified ad service. By virtue of the Internet's unique capabilities and our expertise, AfcNet can provide services to businesses similar to the yellow pages, classified ads, answering services, direct marketing, radio and TV promotions, and personal sales, all rolled into one. AfcNet offers local businesses (3) free one-line listings, standard low-cost advertisements (with HTML programming included), and a broad range of Internet publishing services. You can find AfcNet, San Diego County Edition, in the CTSNET Marketplace, one of the top (and most heavily visited) commercial sites in the USA.

July 31, 1995

Chateau La Jolla Inn, La Jolla's premier residential hotel, offers elegant carefree living that continues to attract international guests and residents who hail from London, New York, Paris, Johannesburg, Chicago as well as San Diego and La Jolla. The spacious studios, one and two bedroom suites, together with the fine cuisine and the vast variety of activities and services and the location near the Pacific Ocean, make it an ideal La Jolla residence.

Shortcut to cts.html at www.nutrients.com

Chapter 16

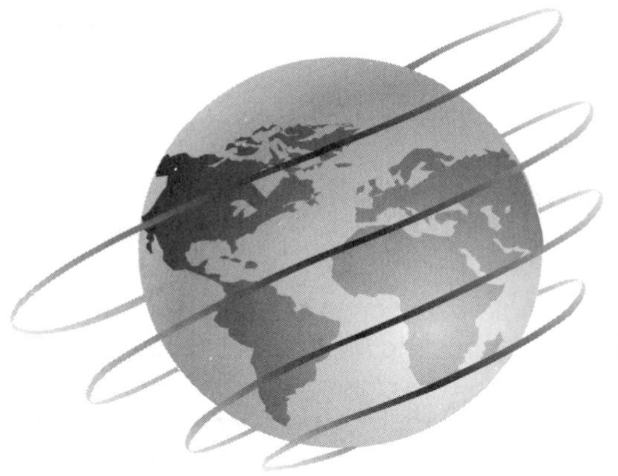

Networking with the Internet

By now, you're probably convinced that putting up your own Web server and offering your products and services online can only benefit your business. But how do you actually go about doing it? Is it complicated? Do you need consultants and contracts, or is it something you can do yourself? And how do you protect your confidential files and information from intruders?

These are a few of the questions addressed in this chapter. It begins with a primer on how to network PCs and the issues you'll face, cutting through the techno-speak to give you the facts you need. You'll learn the meaning of networking terms like *protocol* and *topology*. But rather than loading you up with details and leaving you to choose among the many options, we'll give you a straight-up example of how to build your network and integrate it into the Internet.

The second half of this chapter deals with network security. You'll learn about firewalls and gateways, and you'll be introduced to the two most common types of firewalls. You'll also receive some sound advice for protecting your internal network from new-age outlaws.

Putting It All Online

In Chapter 2 ("Getting Connected"), you learned about the various ways to connect a single-user computer to the Internet and that, with a SLIP or PPP connection, you actually extend the Internet to your own computer. But the focus was on connections for people who simply want to use the Internet and browse the Web. What if you have, or want to set up, a network of computers, and you want them all to be able to access the Internet simultaneously? Or what if you want to put your own permanent Web server online? With these more ambitious goals come some more serious solutions.

In this section, we'll lay the groundwork for you to implement your own network on the Internet, fire up your own servers, and arrive on the Web ready for business.

Networking Considerations

In the business world, there are a handful of good reasons to connect computers together. One of the most compelling is that a network allows many people to work on the same data at the same time. They may be using different programs to work with the data, but the underlying sets of databases and tables are shared by all the users.

For example, let's look at the operations in a small medical laboratory. A clerk sits at a workstation and enters orders for lab tests from doctors. At another workstation, a lab technician performs the tests and enters the results. Still other

people print out the log reports and test results for the doctors. Without a network, these jobs would be much harder and probably much slower.

Businesses both small and large have come to rely heavily on networks for automating the things they do, from operations and accounting to research and development.

For most of the past decade, the premier company in the business of networking PCs has been Novell, Inc. Today, Novell networks still outnumber every other type of PC network in the business world, but this is changing. With the easy networking built into every modern operating system, the need for expensive and complex third-party systems has all but disappeared.

Figure 16-1 shows the classical PC network configuration. A dedicated computer runs a special *network operating system* and basically provides disk space to the other computers on the network that connect to it. Typically, PCs on the network see the network computer as just another disk drive. On the PCs, A: represents the floppy drive, C: represents the local hard disk, and F: (or some other similar label) identifies the additional disk space provided by the special centralized network computer. The other computers on the network can use files on this computer just as they would use files on their own hard drives. A centralized network computer that lends disk space and serves files to the other computers is called a *file server*.

With today's fast Pentium computers and 32-bit operating systems, it's seldom necessary to dedicate a machine to the task of serving files. You still can if so many

FIGURE 16-1.

The classic network with a central file server

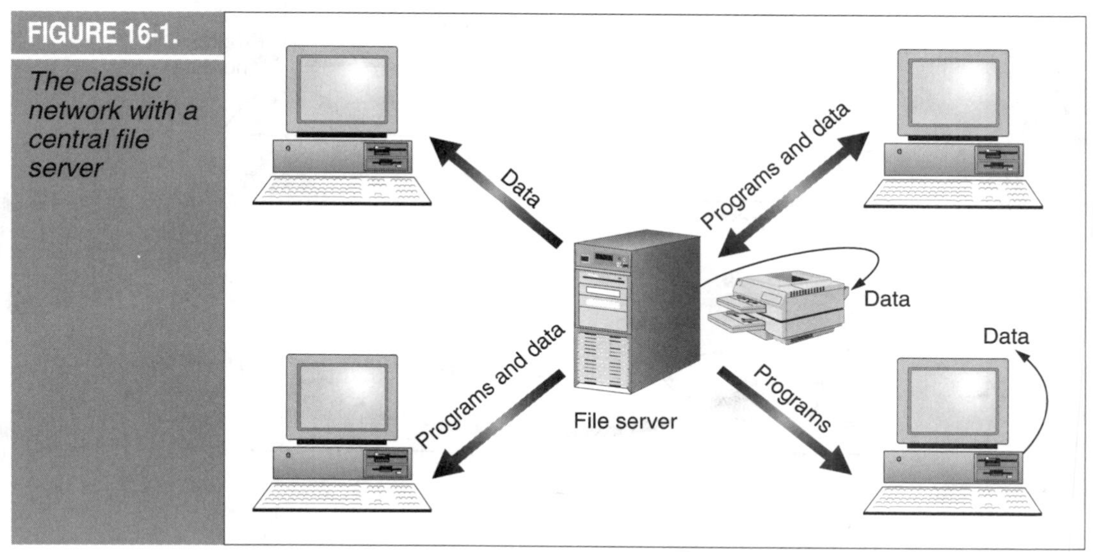

people need to access resources on one machine that the system becomes sluggish, but many businesses can do away with dedicating machines to single purposes.

Figure 16-2 shows the more common way to network PCs today. With this scheme, there is no centralized file server—just a collection of computers. Each may have resources of value to other systems and people on the network. For example, the user of computer A may share that computer's entire disk drive with anyone else on the network (such as computer D), while the user of computer C has a color printer that is shared with anyone who cares to use it. The user of computer C may keep the company's accounting and transaction records in a directory named *\Accounting* and share only that directory, and only with other people in the accounting department. Such a scheme is called *peer-to-peer networking*.

Besides sharing program and data files, there are some other good reasons to network computers. You can use a file server for overflow disk storage space, it's easier to back up centralized data, and you can provide remote access to tape-drive devices for backing up noncentralized data. Networks also make it possible to use electronic mail and to share such information as schedules, calendars, and technical reports.

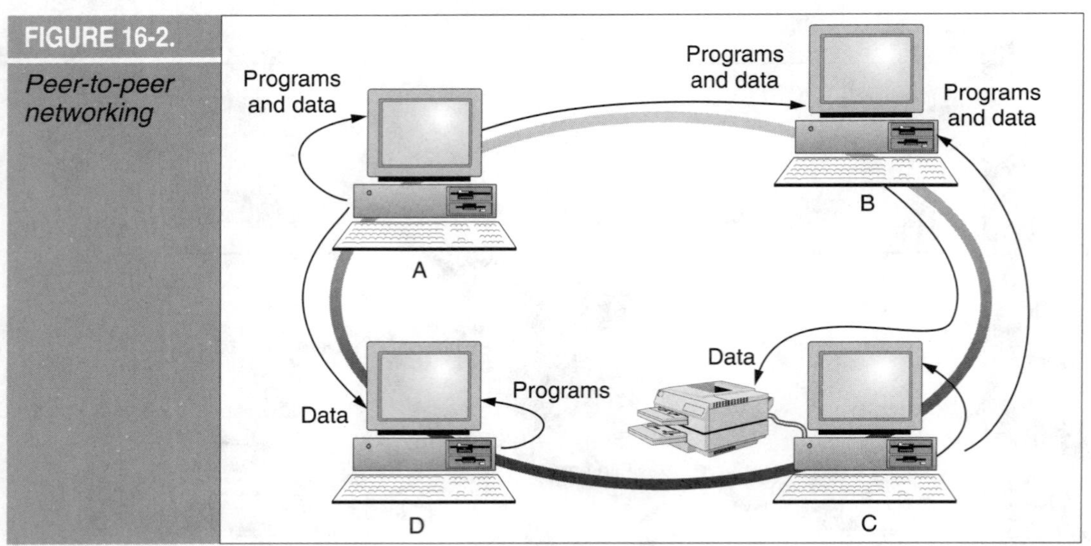

FIGURE 16-2. *Peer-to-peer networking*

Putting together a network of computers used to be a complex and arcane task. It's gotten so much simpler, however, that it now comes down to just a handful of concepts and considerations:

- Protocols
- Topology and cabling
- Network interface cards
- Network software

Network Protocol

The protocol of the Internet is TCP/IP. As explained elsewhere, TCP/IP is really a suite of protocols. The term *TCP/IP* refers to two protocols: *IP* (for Internet Protocol), which defines the routing between computers on the Internet, and *TCP* (for Transmission Control Protocol), which defines how data is wrapped into packets to be delivered by IP.

In addition to these basic components of TCP/IP, most of the applications people use with the Internet also have their own protocols that define how they work with TCP/IP. For example, *NFS* (for Network File System) is a protocol that allows a computer to use disk space and files on another computer over a TCP/IP network connection. *FTP* (for File Transfer Protocol) allows systems to send and retrieve files to and from a special area of another machine. Others include *SMTP* (Simple Mail Transport Protocol), *NNTP* (Network News Transport Protocol), and of course *HTTP*, the HyperText Transport Protocol of the Web.

In the largest sense of the term, TCP/IP includes all of these protocols. To be on the Internet and use its resources and services, your network has to support TCP/IP. This isn't to say that TCP/IP has to be your only protocol, but it is the most important one for connecting to the Internet.

In addition to TCP/IP, you may want (or need) to run additional protocols. For example, if you want to integrate your network with an existing Novell network, you also need to use the IPX protocol that Novell servers and clients use to communicate. For Microsoft networks, you want NetBEUI.

Don't worry about understanding these protocols right now. At this point, you only need to be aware of the protocols you'll use on your network. Later, we'll get into the nuts and bolts of what they do and how to use them together.

Network Topology and Cabling

Technically, the term *topology* refers to the physical layout of a network. A *linear bus* topology is a single cable—terminated at both ends—to which the computers are connected (see Figure 16-3). A *ring* topology is similar, but the ends of the cable are joined. A *star* topology has a central hub from which cables run to each node, or

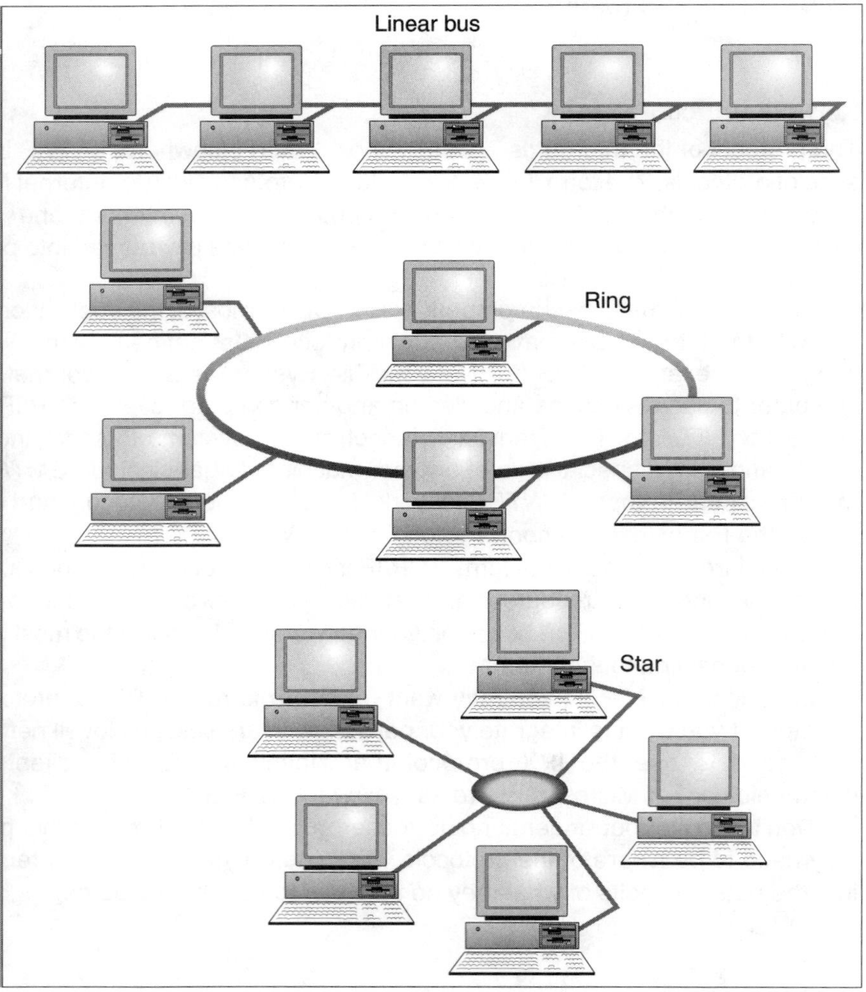

FIGURE 16-3. *Common network topologies*

computer, on the network. There are others as well—even hybrid technologies that combine two or more of these common topologies.

Practically speaking, nobody decides on a network topology by weighing the benefits and drawbacks of each wiring scheme, then looks at the hardware and software protocols available to implement it. Instead, you look at a whole network package and either accept or reject it in its entirety. As a result, the term *topology* has (at least informally) taken on greater meaning; it now includes the protocols computers use to communicate under that topology. The protocols we're talking about here are at an even lower level than TCP/IP or IPX. Here, we're referring to very low-level programming burned into the hardware in the network cards that go into the computers on the network.

Figure 16-4 shows the relationships between these levels of protocols. At the lowest level is the physical wire that connects the computers. Just above the level of the wire is the *firmware*, or programming, on each computer's interface card. Next is a driver that allows the computer's operating system to communicate with the network interface card. Last is the network protocol, which allows each computer's operating system to actually use the network.

The topologies and protocols we're talking about here have names like *Ethernet*, *Arcnet*, and *Token Ring*. These are actually trademarked names, but used broadly they also describe types of networks, including their topologies (in the technical sense of the term). For example, Arcnet is a trademark of Standard Microsystems Corp. (SMC), but it describes a star, or distributed star, network. Token Ring is a trademark of IBM, the only company with significant network products for a ring-topology network.

Ethernet is a little different. Originally it was a trademark of Digital Equipment Corp., but it has become so widely used, and so many companies manufacture Ethernet products and software, that it is now nearly a public standard.

There are two standard Ethernet topologies: the *linear bus* and the *logical linear bus*. The linear bus variant is defined by a standard called *10BASE2*, which was set by the Institute of Electrical and Electronics Engineers. The logical linear bus is defined by another standard, called *10BASE-T*.

A 10BASE2 Ethernet network uses a coaxial cable (similar to a cable television cable, but slightly thinner) to connect computers on the network. With this type of network, the cable really is a single wire terminated at both ends.

A 10BASE-T Ethernet network uses a centralized piece of equipment called a *concentrator* to simulate a linear bus. Therefore, instead of physically *being* a linear bus, the concentrator *simulates* one and provides ports for wires to run directly to each machine on the network. Since 10BASE-T concentrators use telephone wire to run to each computer, many organizations find it convenient to locate their

FIGURE 16-4. *Protocol layers of a network; the shaded boxes represent the components you need for a TCP/IP network*

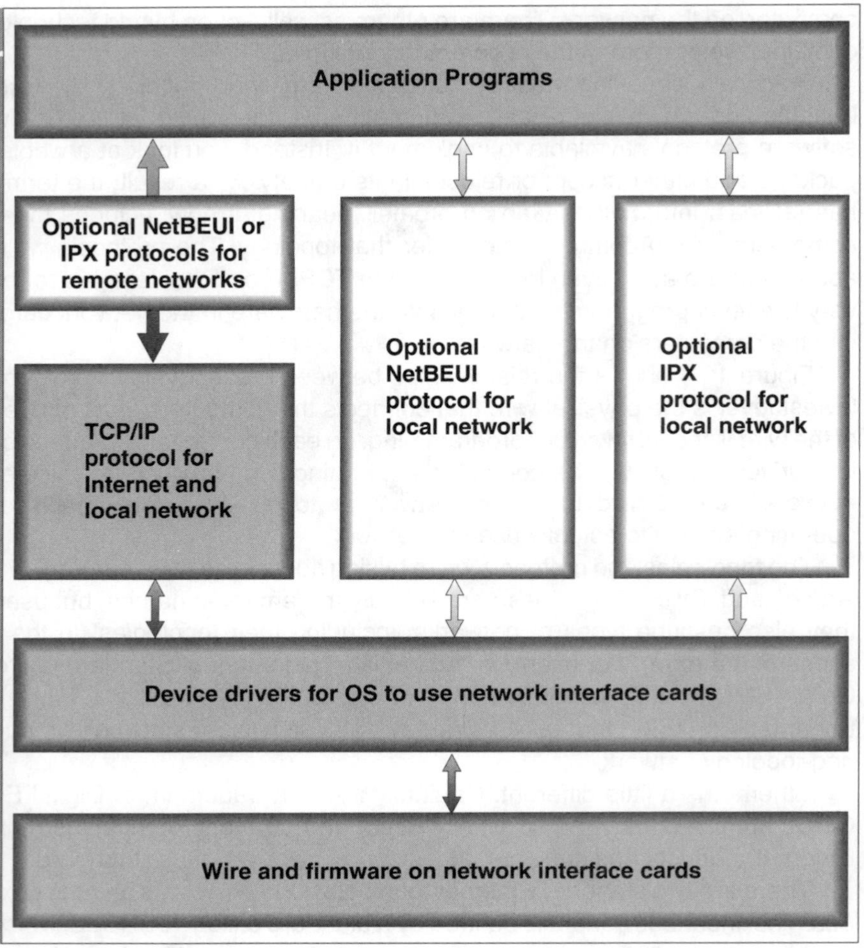

Application Programs

Optional NetBEUI or IPX protocols for remote networks

TCP/IP protocol for Internet and local network

Optional NetBEUI protocol for local network

Optional IPX protocol for local network

Device drivers for OS to use network interface cards

Wire and firmware on network interface cards

concentrators in a telephone wiring room and run patch cables for the network into the building's built-in telephone wiring.

Network Interface Cards

Network interface cards are circuit boards that you plug into a computer to provide the physical connection between the computer and the network cable. Once you know the topology of your network, choosing network interface cards is a relatively easy task: You look for cards to match the network topology you've chosen. For example, if you've decided on an Ethernet network, you should buy Ethernet cards.

In the case of topologies other than Ethernet, you don't have a choice as to the type of connector to use on the outside of the card to attach the network cable. For Ethernet networks, however, you have to make sure the cards you buy match the network you're implementing. If you're planning on a 10BASE-T network, you'll need cards with modular plugs for *unshielded twisted pair* (UTP) wiring. These look similar to a standard modular telephone plug except that they're larger. For 10BASE2 (also called *thin-net*) networks, make sure your cards have a *BNC* connector. These are similar to cable TV coax connectors but are made of heavier metal.

Another alternative with Ethernet is to get combination cards that provide all three of the possible connectors you might need. The combo card provides a port for a UTP connector, a BNC connector for thin-net, and an AUI (or AAUI for Macs) port for the older thick-net networks. Figure 16-5 shows what a combo card and its connector ports look like. Combination cards are a little more expensive, but the flexibility you gain can be worth the extra cost in the long run.

NOTE *When selecting network interface cards, avoid the temptation to buy eight-bit cards. They are substantially cheaper than 16-bit cards, but 16-bit and 32-bit cards are dramatically faster.*

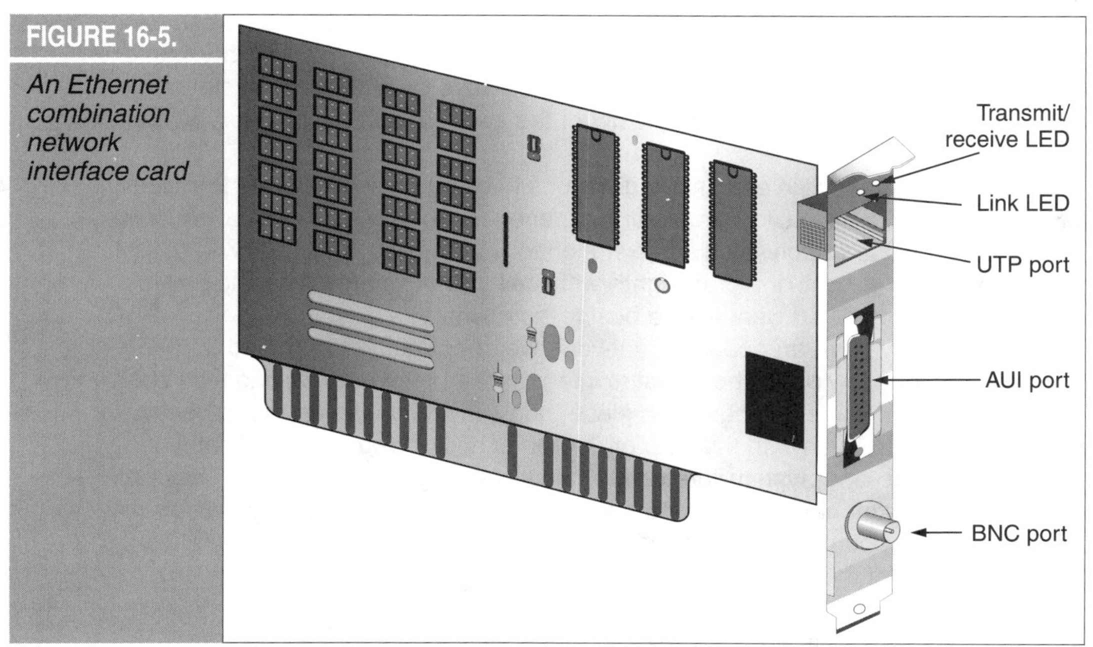

FIGURE 16-5. *An Ethernet combination network interface card*

Finally, when selecting network interface cards, try to stick to name-brand products. You might be able to find some good prices on off-brand cards, but you'll have better luck in the long run if you stay with the leaders. Names to look for include 3COM, Intel, Novell, SMC, and Western Digital.

Network Software

As mentioned earlier, all modern operating systems have built-in support for networking. What this means to you is that beyond buying computers, network interface cards, and cabling, all you really need are operating systems for your computers. Unix, Windows 95, Windows NT, OS/2 Warp, and the Mac have the software built in; all you have to do is configure the operating system of each computer to recognize and use the network.

If you do need to buy any third-party software, most likely it will be a minor part of your system, such as a utility or a specialized program. We'll discuss one such utility in the next section.

Building a Network from the Ground Up

One of the reasons planning a network was a daunting task in the past is that each decision you made had implications for the other choices. For example, if you planned to use OS/2 Warp on your computers, it didn't make a lot of sense to use anything other than OS/2's built-in networking software and IBM's proprietary Token Ring topology and network protocol. You could always build a hybrid system, but doing so greatly increased the complexity of the setup and administration of your network.

Some choices result in even more decisions to be made, while others limit your options, all of which makes for a frustrating experience. So we're going to cut through the maze of options and give you some straightforward advice on a great way to set up a network that will both integrate tightly with the Internet and the Web and provide all the benefits you could want from a business network.

If you already have an operating network, we're not going to pretend that you can learn in these few pages how best to integrate it into the Internet and the Web. With so many networking schemes in place today, it would take an entire book to cover this subject. Even with the help of reference books, you would probably still need consultants and system integrators. However, if you don't already have a substantial investment in network hardware and software, you're in an excellent position to make sound decisions about how to move forward to make your network a seamless part of the Internet.

What we present in the following section is an example of an excellent network system for many people and businesses. There are a huge number of alternative

solutions, however, so keep in mind that you are always the final judge of what is right for your business.

Our Plan

Our hypothetical network will be small, to make it easy to understand. It will consist of only a half-dozen or so computers, each of which will be able to function as a workstation or a server. We want to be able to use Internet services at any workstation, and we want a high level of integration between the computers on the network. In other words, we want the ability to use resources such as disk drives, subdirectories, CD-ROM drives, tape drives, and printers across the network from any workstation we choose.

We have decided on Microsoft's Windows 95 operating system for the workstations. Windows 95 gives us the most flexibility in selecting application programs for users because it can run MS-DOS programs, Windows 3.x programs, full 32-bit applications written specifically for Windows 95, and most of the applications written for Windows NT. Also, the networking tools built into Windows 95 are easy to configure and set up, they offer excellent security, and they integrate easily into the Internet.

We have also decided to use a single Unix computer to run Web and FTP servers for our network and to act as a traditional file server for the other machines on the network (in addition to the peer-to-peer capabilities all the workstations will have). If your business is small, you don't know Unix, and you can't afford or don't want to hire a system administrator, you may forgo the Unix system. Instead, you can opt for a Windows NT or Windows 95 computer to serve Web pages and FTP archives. If you know Unix and want the best of both the Windows and Unix worlds on your network, however, using a single Unix computer is a good way to go.

Protocols

Because we want to use both Internet services and local network services, our network will need to use two network protocols: TCP/IP for Internet services and NetBEUI for networking with Windows 95.

NetBEUI is included with the Windows 95 operating system. Unix doesn't have NetBEUI, but this isn't an issue because all communications with the Unix computer use TCP/IP. Both Unix and Windows 95 have TCP/IP built in.

Network Topology and Hardware

For our network, there is no compelling reason to use anything other than Ethernet for the network topology. Because Ethernet is so prevalent in networks connected to the Internet, there is plenty of support for it in both hardware products and software packages. Also, if there were any one network topology you could consider native to Unix, it would be Ethernet. Many Unix systems even come preconfigured to look for an Ethernet network the first time you fire them up.

Whether you decide to use 10BASE2 or 10BASE-T Ethernet (thin-net or twisted-pair wiring) depends on the geography and layout of your network. If you have a small number of machines located fairly close to each other, thin-net is simple and easy to install: You just run a wire between each machine (as you saw in Figure 16-3) and terminate both ends with a special terminator.

For larger networks, you might want to consider 10BASE-T. The initial cost of a 10BASE-T network is somewhat higher because you need a concentrator, but for larger networks that cost can be offset by simpler and cheaper wiring.

The Internet Connection

If you want to provide Internet access for more than two or three users, a modem connection just won't be fast enough. This is especially true if you anticipate traffic coming in from the Internet in addition to users accessing Internet services. To handle a larger number of users and at speeds greater than a modem connection can provide, we'll get a special digital phone line called *ISDN* (for Integrated Services Digital Network).

An ISDN line does require some additional hardware. To interface an ISDN line with a network, you need an adapter card called a *terminal adapter* or an external box called an *ISDN router*. Terminal adapters work like internal modems. You place the card inside the machine, and the end of the card—exposed at the back of the system—sports a modular plug for the ISDN phone wire.

An ISDN router is typically a box that looks very similar to an external modem. It's about the same size, and it has flashing lights on the front and a modular plug for the ISDN line in the back. But the back of the router also has an Ethernet connector for connecting directly to an Ethernet network. (This is a good example of how Ethernet support is built into a product.)

For a single PC that isn't on a network, using a terminal adapter (the card that goes into the PC) is the easiest way to interface with the ISDN line. For a network, the easy way to interface with an ISDN line is with an external router. However, this isn't a strict rule; a Unix computer on the internal network can house a terminal adapter card and act as a gateway between the Internet and the other computers on the internal network. You can also use an external router with a single PC by putting a network interface card into the PC and creating a network between the router and the PC. Of course, this would be an expensive way to connect a single computer.

For our network, we'll opt for an ISDN router. An external router can take the routing load off the Unix computer and provide an additional level of security to the Unix system and the internal network.

Chapter 17 covers ISDN and other high-speed Internet access schemes in more detail.

Bringing It All Together

One of the first things you need to do to bring up a network on the Internet is to obtain IP addresses for each computer (and router) on the network. You also need to come up with a domain name for your network. The best way to do this is to talk to your Internet service provider. The people there are accustomed to requests for IP numbers and registering domain names and often have processes set up to do it efficiently. Alternatively, you can do it yourself by communicating directly with the Internet Information Center (at http://rs.internic.net/). Even if you do it yourself, however, you still have to communicate with your provider to tell it to do routing for your network. (The provider may charge you an extra fee for this service.)

Figure 16-6 shows a diagram of our hypothetical network. The Internet connection is through the router, which is itself a node on the Ethernet network's linear bus. The router directs traffic between the Internet and the internal network. You can also use the router to create alias names for the machines on your internal network. For example, you can instruct the router to pass along any incoming traffic for a machine named *www.ournet.com* to a machine named *win95-c.ournet.com* or *unix2.ournet.com*.

For example, let's say we register the domain name *abc.com*, and we name the Unix machine *unix* (so its fully qualified domain name is *unix.abc.com*). Let's name the workstations *pc1*, *pc2*, and so on so that their fully qualified names are *pc1.abc.com*, *pc2.abc.com*, and so forth.

When the router is registered on the Internet, any traffic directed to any machine name in the domain *abc.com* will come directly to the router, and the router will decide where to send it from there. When you configure the router, you can program it to route any incoming traffic to any machine based on the machine name.

Say we want the Unix computer to be the main server for FTP, mail, and Web requests. When we set up the router, all we have to do is configure it to send to *unix.abc.com* any packets addressed to *ftp.abc.com*, *mail.abc.com*, or *www.abc.com*.

If you want an added level of security, you can also program the router to refuse to respond to any initial requests coming in from the Internet for any other machines on the network. That way, the only accessible machine from the Internet is the Unix computer—which runs mail, FTP, and Web servers—but the workstations on the

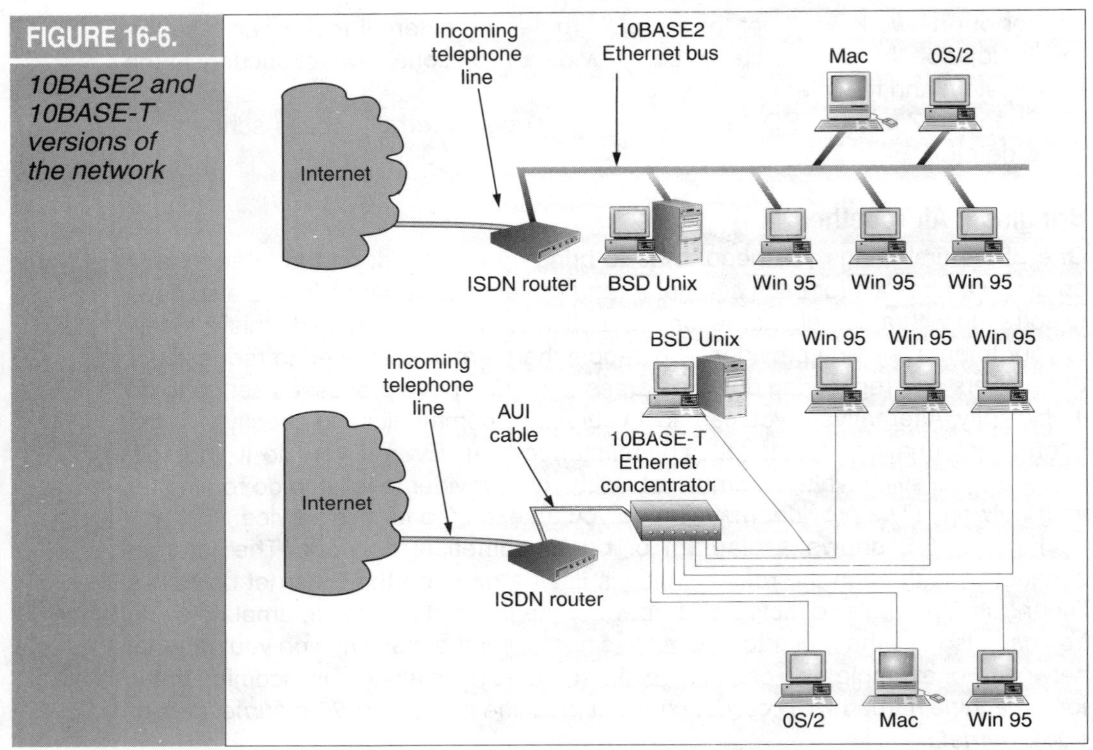

FIGURE 16-6. *10BASE2 and 10BASE-T versions of the network*

internal network still have full access to the Internet. The next section takes a closer look at this and other security measures, and the next chapter discusses routers.

THE UNIX SYSTEM We won't go into the details of setting up a Unix system for use with a network or the Internet. Entire books are devoted to these subjects, and Unix systems come with substantial documentation. Again, if you're not equipped with the skills to set up and administer a Unix system and you're not inclined to hire a system administrator, you can forgo the Unix system altogether. Chapter 18 discusses an excellent Web server for Windows 95 and Windows NT computers. There are also servers for Macintosh computers and even Windows 3.1 machines. Similarly, you can find FTP and mail servers for non-Unix computers. However, Unix computers are excellent platforms for client/server applications, and if you have at least one on your network, you'll gain a great deal of capability and flexibility.

If you do opt to set up a Unix computer, consider a few variants of Unix. Sun Microsystems has been the leading manufacturer of Unix computers for a number of years. Sun makes excellent and powerful systems that are quite at home on the

Internet. In fact, there may be more Sun systems than any other type of Unix system on the Internet. Unfortunately, Sun's computers also come with a hefty price tag.

Another option is a Unix system that runs on an ordinary PC. A Pentium PC running Unix is a robust and cost-effective alternative. With a small network and a fast PC Unix system, chances are you won't even come close to using up the system's capacity.

We're partial to the BSD (for Berkeley Software Distribution) variant of Unix. A number of nearly free versions of BSD Unix operating systems for PCs, including Linux, FreeBSD, and NetBSD, are available. If you want support and regular updates, you may be better off going with a commercial distribution. Berkeley Software Design Inc. develops and distributes BSD/OS, a fully commercial version of BSD Unix; the company's Web page is at http://www.bsdi.com/.

The other major variant of Unix is called *System V* (pronounced "system five"). A couple of years ago, a number of Unix developers got together and formed an organization to promote the idea of a new version of Unix that would merge the worlds of BSD Unix and System V Unix. This new version was called *System V Release 4* (or often SVR4). These vendors did indeed develop and release SVR4, and it did combine BSD and System V. The trouble was, nobody bought it—at least, not enough to make it a viable product. About that time, Novell (the PC networking company) bought the rights to Unix from AT&T and began licensing its own version.

In spite of the push toward SVR4, a company called The Santa Cruz Operation (SCO) remains the major vendor of System V Unix operating systems for PCs. SCO was the lone holdout that never supported the trend toward SVR4. Its Web page is at http://www.sco.com.

Ironically, while all this was going on, BSD developers continued their efforts to make BSD Unix a great PC operating system. Today, BSD-based operating systems—unlike the System V variants—are flourishing.

How you actually go about installing and configuring a PC Unix operating system varies widely from brand to brand, but it's probably not as difficult as you think. For example, BSD/OS comes on a single CD-ROM along with a single boot floppy disk. You insert the CD into your CD-ROM drive, insert the diskette into your computer's A: drive, turn the computer on, and follow the directions, responding to questions or prompts as required. When the installation is complete and the system comes up, you'll have a robust system fully configured for use with a network, with the Internet, and with functioning Web, FTP, and mail servers.

THE WINDOWS 95 SYSTEM When you install Windows 95, it does a reasonable job of detecting all the devices in your system. It also detects most conflicts between hardware settings in your system (if there are any). After Windows 95 boots for the first time, all you need to do is bind the TCP/IP and NetBEUI protocols to the Ethernet card. You do this by opening the Control Panel and going into the network configuration applet (see Figure 16-7).

When you open the applet, you should see a line describing your network card. If you click the Add button on the panel, it will ask you whether you want to add a device or a protocol. Choose Protocol, then choose the NetBEUI protocol. This

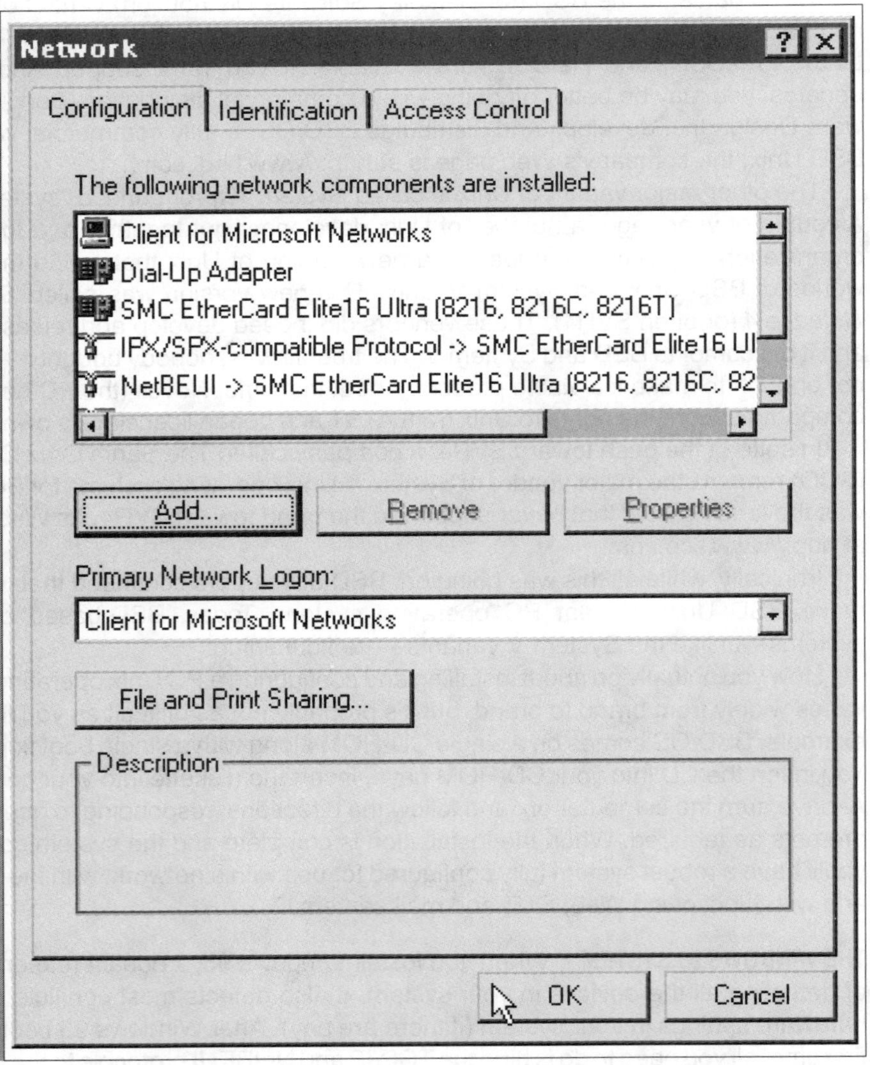

FIGURE 16-7. *Windows 95 network configuration applet*

allows you to do peer-to-peer networking with the other Windows 95 (and any Windows NT or Windows for Workgroups) computers on the network. Choose Add again, and add TCP/IP.

Now double-click on TCP/IP, which should be in the network configuration applet's main window. This brings up the TCP/IP Properties panel (see Figure 16-8). Under the Bindings tab, connect the TCP/IP protocol to your network adapter device. Then click the IP Address tab and enter the IP address for that computer and the subnet mask for your network. (Your Internet service provider or network administrator should be able to give you these numbers.)

Next, click on the DNS Configuration tab. Enter the name of the workstation you're working on and the domain for your network, then click the Enable DNS button.

Finally, click the Gateway tab and enter the IP address of the router. That's all there is to it. Just click OK to exit the network configuration applet. Windows will want to restart itself. After it does, the workstation will be on the local network and on the Internet. (This procedure is covered in more detail in Chapter 3.)

Network Security

In this age of data superhighways and digital cash, we are in essence exploring a new frontier. And like the frontier of the Old West, the information age can be a lawless and ruthless place. But also like the Old West, the vast majority of the people are good-hearted folks who just want to stake their claims and make a living.

But there are always troublemakers. On the Internet, the outlaws are called *hackers* or *crackers*. They won't steal your horse or your boots, but they may do even worse. Trade secrets, personal information, credit-card numbers—it's all up for grabs. And the scary part is that there isn't a lot you can do about it. Most data-robbers are never even detected, let alone prosecuted.

There are, however, some solid measures that you can take to hold hackers at bay. Some steps are just common sense; others amount to digging a moat around your network and posting guards at the drawbridge. How elaborate your security system has to be will depend on how much money you have to spend and how much you don't want your privacy violated.

Unfortunately, security is a matter you can't take too lightly when you're thinking about putting your organization on the Web. It may seem like an odd consideration if your goal is to make information available to the public, but you've got to be sure that the only information you make available is the information you want known.

FIGURE 16-8. *Binding TCP/IP to the network card*

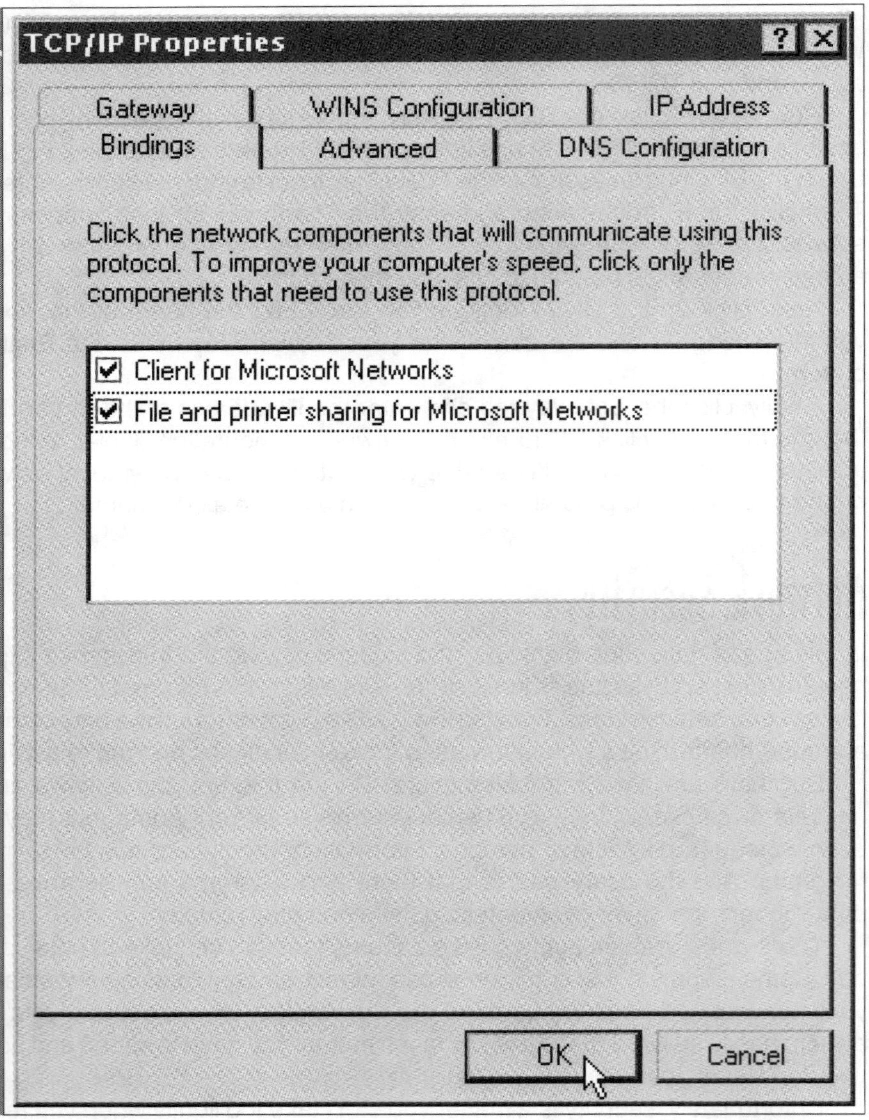

Security for Web servers is just a single aspect of network security. In fact, the issue is much larger than configuring a Web server to be secure. As we've said before, the majority of computers on the Internet are Unix machines. And Unix is a

large and complex operating system, with many nooks and crannies into which potential hackers can pry.

Today, many Unix systems come out of the box configured to begin immediately providing many services to the Internet community, not just Web service. For example, when you first fire up a new Unix computer, it's probably ready to run at least some of the following services and servers:

- A Finger service
- A mail server
- Telnet and rlogin daemons
- Several types of Anonymous FTP servers
- A network file system

In addition, system administrators often implement services that aren't initially on most systems, including:

- A Gopher server
- A Web server
- A Usenet news server
- A talk daemon

All of these network services can be exploited by unwelcome visitors. However, the most common way for a hacker to break into a system is simply to guess a password and gain access to a shell account. Once a hacker has gotten that far, you can consider your system and all the information on it to be compromised.

So who are these hackers and what do they want? Who they are is a great mystery. During the cold war, there were some famous cases of system administrators working with the FBI and CIA to track down hackers who turned out to be spies. (One of these cases was chronicled by Cliff Stoll in a great book entitled *The Cuckoo's Egg*.) Since the cold war ended, however, there has been no dramatic decrease in hacking incidents.

Who hackers are, and what they want to accomplish, has to do mostly with who the intended victims are and what types of information they have on their computers. For example, large corporate research facilities on the cutting edge of technological development probably attract more hackers interested in selling secrets to the competition than would a company that sells widgets on the Web. On the other hand, the company that sells widgets may fall prey to criminals interested in obtaining credit-card numbers and expiration dates. And then there's the run-of-the-mill snoop who just wants to see if he can read your private email, see what projects you're working on, and find out how much money you make.

Whatever their motivation and regardless of their intent, you don't want hackers mucking about on your computers. Unfortunately, you can't do much more to deter them than you can to stop burglars from entering your home and stealing your TV set. In fact, the analogy is pretty complete, and all of the clichés and adages apply: "Good fences make good neighbors," "That'll keep the honest ones honest," and so on. But with computers and networks, as with your home, there is little you can do to keep a really determined intruder out.

So should you give up and just consider your computers attached to the Internet to be fair game for anyone determined enough to figure out how to get in? Absolutely not. If you do that, you're letting them win. There's plenty you can do to make a hacker's work difficult, frustrating, and unrewarding without sacrificing your own productivity and your preferred work style.

This section of the chapter describes security-related terminology and concepts on a systemwide level. In other words, the material here applies not only to Web servers and clients, but to entire networks on the Internet that offer access to computers for user accounts, file transfers, electronic mail, Web access, and other services. Keep in mind that this is only an overview; even books devoted entirely to the topic of Internet security don't go into detail about specific versions of operating systems or the precise lines of code required to implement specific security measures. So don't worry that this section will be too technical—it isn't. But it will give you a solid understanding of the security measures you can take to protect yourself and your network. Besides, when you get to the point of needing to implement some of the more complex security measures discussed here, you're going to have to hire a guy with a pocket protector anyway.

The First Line of Defense

Your first line of defense is to enforce an adequate password-protection mechanism on each and every machine you have that's connected to the Internet. Most break-ins are the result of users choosing poor passwords. Studies have revealed that as many as 25% of the passwords on a system can be guessed easily. (A hacker only needs one to do damage.)

It's exceedingly easy for a hacker to find out some valid usernames on a system, then guess passwords to match. Every Unix system has a user named *root*, and most have at least a few other usernames as well, such as *sys*, *daemon*, *bin*, *operator*, and *admin*. If any of these usernames have guessable passwords, you might as well tell the hacker where to find the keys to your house, too. These accounts carry special meanings and have higher privileges than ordinary user

accounts. If hackers were to get into your system on one of these accounts, they would have free rein. They could look at anything and change or delete anything.

Ordinary user accounts also pose a big problem. Hackers tend to be very computer-savvy, and they often know how to exploit bugs in programs on the system to gain higher levels of access. When such bugs are discovered, they often cause a flurry of activity—at least within the Internet community—as network administrators race to figure out a way to patch the holes as quickly as possible.

NOTE *A few months ago, the news networks reported on a program called Satan that was released to the public. They reported that the program helps criminals and hackers break into computer systems. The truth is that Satan is a very useful tool for helping system administrators find and patch the holes in their own systems.*

Some Unix systems come out of the box with a few bogus user accounts already created on them. For example, some contain the famous *guest* account with the password preset to *guest*. Hackers know about all these accounts, and your best bet is to remove them from your systems completely.

These accounts, however, are the easy ones on which to enforce good password protection (either by the system administrators' changing the passwords themselves or by removing the accounts from the systems). System administrators are usually far less able to induce their ordinary users to choose good passwords, and ordinary users often don't understand the importance of doing so. After all, if a password is secret, how will the administrator know if a user chooses a poor one?

Hackers can easily collect ordinary usernames for a system. It's especially easy if they can ever get onto the system, even if only for a few seconds. Consider the time it takes to type the command

```
mail badguy@foo.org < /etc/passwd
```

Within seconds of typing this command, the bad guy will have a copy of your computer's password file (it doesn't actually contain the passwords, but it will serve as a nice directory of every valid username and sometimes the users' full real names). Armed with this information, the hacker can try to log into any or all of the accounts listed in the password file with all the obvious passwords users often choose—their last names, their names spelled backward, the usernames themselves, and so on.

Even if hackers can't get onto a system initially to mail themselves a copy of the password file, there are other ways to collect usernames. Unaltered, the *Finger* daemon on many Unix systems will dutifully report the usernames (and real names) of everyone who has an account on the system. All the hacker has to do is type

```
finger @foo.com
```

for a nice list of users and other information, such as how long it's been since they've logged into the system. Accounts that appear to be inactive or haven't been used for a long time are especially attractive to hackers.

Another easy way to collect usernames is simply to subscribe to mailing lists and Usenet newsgroups. Each time you send a mail message or post an article to a newsgroup, you announce to the world your username and the name of the computer your account is on. Hackers may even get more information on passwords to try this way—the names of your children, your street address, and so on.

If a hacker is particularly determined, he will run a dictionary program against a user account anyway. A dictionary program takes each word in a dictionary and methodically tries to log into your computer using that word as the password. To defend against this approach, users must choose passwords that aren't regular words—for example, "xe7toMay" or "91xBpd!".

Most of the newer versions of the Unix operating system give system administrators a few tools to manage user passwords. Administrators may be able to require that users choose a password of at least a minimum number of characters, that the password include a mixture of upper- and lowercase letters, that it include numerals, or perhaps that it conform to all of these rules. Enforcing requirements like these will make most passwords virtually impossible to guess.

In spite of the availability of these tools, most system administrators still don't require users to choose good passwords. But you can enforce strong password security, and if you hire someone to administer your systems or network, you can require that person to do the same.

Beyond excellent password management, there is really only one more thing you can do before you get into serious security issues, big bucks, and sophisticated security systems: Simply don't run any servers or daemons you don't need. Or, if you do need them occasionally but not for the general public, don't allow people to use them anonymously. For example, if you don't want people using FTP to log into your system to retrieve files (or if you don't offer any files of value anyway), don't run an *ftpd* daemon, or at least disallow anonymous FTP logins. These measures won't always be practical for the main machines of a full-service provider, but if your intent is only to serve Web pages, then all you need is a Web server.

Building a Fortress

Enforcing passwords and using other common-sense measures to deter hackers sometimes just isn't enough. If you've got a lot at stake, you may need to take more active steps toward protecting your security and privacy.

Companies or organizations with internal networks typically have a special computer called a *gateway*, or *router* (like the ISDN routers we talked about earlier), through which all traffic going to and coming from the Internet flows.

Refer back to Figure 16-6 for an example of how typical networks are connected to the Internet. That figure shows two types of Ethernet networks connected to the Internet by an ISDN line. In both examples, an ISDN router routes traffic between the internal network and the Internet. Networks with other types of connections, such as Frame Relay, might have a different type of router, and networks with a modem connection may connect directly to one of the computers on the network that does routing. But with this type of configuration, no special barriers are in place to discourage intruders.

The terms *gateway* and *router* are used slightly loosely, but generally the term *gateway* refers to a computer on an organization's network. Often a gateway is an organization's main computer, and it's often a Unix machine. In a typical unmodified—and unsecure—network, there is nothing very special about the gateway. The primary difference between a gateway computer and a standard Unix machine is that the gateway's kernel (the core programming of its operating system) is set up to monitor network traffic closely and do routing between the machines on the internal network and the Internet (and vice versa). In every other respect, the gateway functions as a typical Unix computer on the internal network, and it can provide all the Internet services listed earlier to both internal users and users coming in from the Internet.

A router performs the same functions, but generally the term *router* refers to a box that looks more like a modem than like a complete computer. The router has a connector for the Internet connection (a modular phone-type plug, in the case of ISDN) and an Ethernet connector for connecting to the internal network. Like the gateway, the router monitors network traffic and routes that traffic between the internal network and the wild wild Internet.

Without any special programming, neither a gateway computer nor a router does anything to make the internal network more secure; they simply route packets of data from computers on the outside to computers on the inside and vice versa.

However, you can configure most routers and any gateway to provide some additional security. (At least, you can configure any gateway for which you have the source code to the kernel's internals.) With most routers, you can specify computers and networks for which you refuse any incoming traffic at all. This is called *host screening*. You can do the same thing with a gateway if you modify the source code for its kernel to drop packets coming from an offending host.

As you might have guessed, host screening isn't the ultimate security measure. After all, for screening to be effective, you have to know the hosts from which the intruders launch their attacks. And you can only know that after they've been successful at least once. Also, if the intruder hails from a large network or an Internet service provider, you may end up denying welcome traffic as well.

Firewalls

For serious security, you need a *firewall*. A firewall is usually a separate computer that sits between the Internet and an internal network. It is dedicated to sniffing all traffic for troublemakers and enforcing strict security measures. Most often, a firewall computer serves no other purpose than dealing with security issues.

There are many types of firewalls; indeed, there is no formal definition of a firewall nor any organization empowered to come up with one. But most firewalls fall into one of two categories: *dual-homed gateways* and *screened host gateways*.

A dual-homed gateway (sometimes called a *bastion host*) is similar to the regular unsecure gateway we discussed before, but with a couple of very important differences.

The unsecure gateway sits between the Internet and the internal network, but logically speaking it's simply another machine on the internal network—just as all the internal machines are full-fledged nodes of the Internet. That is, the logical connection between the internal machines and the Internet at large is contiguous. Think of it as one unbroken wire that comes in from the Internet and winds around to each machine on the internal network.

The dual-homed gateway breaks that wire cleanly. It is the terminus of the connection from the Internet, but it is also connected to the internal network, although in a completely different way. In the parlance of programmers and Unix system administrators, a dual-homed gateway "talks to two separate network interfaces." Figure 16-9 shows how packets of data from one side of the firewall can't possibly get to the other side without the gateway's knowing about it. Software running on the gateway has to receive packets from one interface and pass them along through the other interface.

The downside of the dual-homed gateway is that the computers on the inside network have no direct contact with computers out on the Internet. Instead, the computers on the inside network make contact with the outside world by communicating their requests to special programs, called *proxies*, that run on the gateway machine. When a proxy receives a request from a machine on the internal

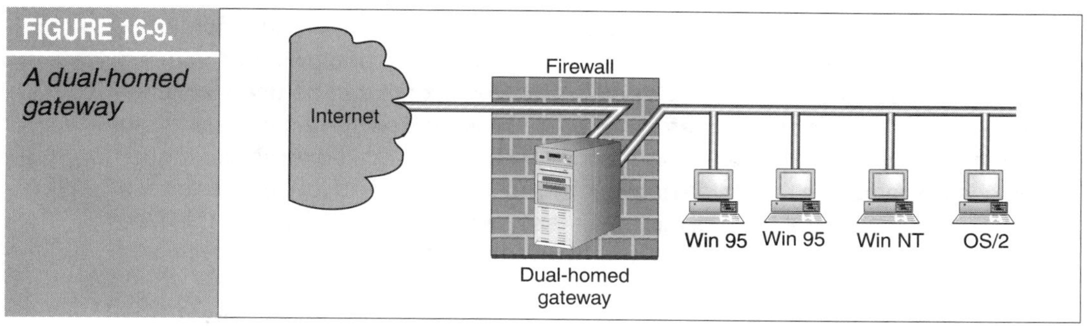

FIGURE 16-9. *A dual-homed gateway*

network, the proxy itself makes the request of the desired host on the Internet, then simply relays any traffic between the two machines.

The other type of firewall is the *screened host gateway.* A single contiguous connection runs between the Internet and all the machines on the internal network, but a router sits between the screened host gateway and the Internet. This router is configured in such a way that it only sends incoming traffic directly to the screened host, which can then validate all incoming requests (see Figure 16-10).

Both dual-homed gateways and screened host gateways examine all network traffic in detail. The gateway machine knows exactly what type of traffic is allowed, and to what machines; for example, if an organization has one machine set up to serve Web pages to the outside world and no other machines are allowed to do that, the firewall will deny any requests from the outside to get at Web documents on a machine on the inside other than the designated Web server.

Similarly, if one machine on the internal network has an FTP server and is allowed to serve files anonymously, the gateway can deny FTP requests to connect to machines other than the allowed FTP server. The screened host will allow the connection to take place directly, while a proxy on the dual-homed host will mediate communication between the outside requester and the FTP server.

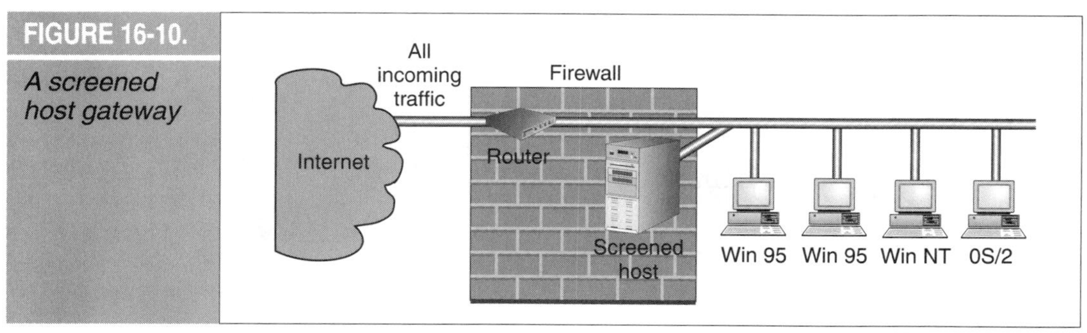

FIGURE 16-10. *A screened host gateway*

Generally speaking, whether a gateway machine is set up as a dual-homed or screened host, it is dedicated to being a security firewall and allowing or denying connections according to a defined set of rules. However, it can be used for other purposes as well. For example, there's no reason why a gateway machine can't also run servers to serve Web pages or file-transfer sessions; in fact, doing so can further protect the machines on the inside network by reducing the need for outside access to the internal network. Of course, this assumes no protection is needed for the Web pages you want to serve, or for files you want to make available anonymously (which may very well be the case).

There are additional benefits to using a firewall machine as a server. For example, the CERN Web server running in proxy mode on a firewall machine will cache external documents requested by clients inside the firewall. This means that if a number of internal users tend to browse the same Web pages, the proxy won't have to go out to the machine on the Internet and retrieve a new copy of the page with every request. Page access for users on the internal network is much faster, and less Internet bandwidth is used.

Restricting Access to Your Web Server

In addition to all the systemwide security measures you can implement with a firewall, with most Web servers you can also restrict access from unwanted networks, hosts, and users. You can also restrict access completely or on a page-by-page basis.

How you do this depends on the particular server you use, but most of them work in similar ways. Implementing security at the server level is easy to understand: To deny access to any networks, hosts, or users, you simply specify in a configuration file that you want to deny them access. To implement the restriction, you specify a command in a configuration file.

The following code fragment shows a section of the *access.conf* file for the NCSA server.

```
# Controls who can get stuff from this server.

<Limit GET>
order allow,deny
allow from all
deny from .abc.com xyz.def.edu
</Limit>
```

Note that the options and configuration language look a lot like HTML. The section that begins with the tag <Limit GET> defines the criteria for accepting and denying access to the server. The first line of the section:

```
order allow,deny
```

specifies that the order of the following commands will apply first to allowing access, then to denying it. As you can see, access is first allowed to anyone, then denied to some specific hosts and users.

Alternatively, if the order is reversed:

```
order deny,allow
```

you could first deny access to everyone, then explicitly allow certain hosts.

You can also control access to specific pages by putting a file named *.htaccess* in each subdirectory that contains Web documents. In each of these files in each directory, you can put code similar to the example we just saw to either allow access to anyone, then deny access to certain individuals, or deny access to all, then explicitly allow certain individuals.

Security with Windows 95 and Windows NT

Most of the discussion of security in this chapter relates to Unix computers, but with the number of Windows 95 and Windows NT computers on the Internet increasing, it's important to discuss the primary security issues for these computers as well.

In the section "Our Plan" earlier in this chapter, we mentioned a Web server for Windows NT and Windows 95. In addition to running Web servers, however, Windows computers can offer other Internet services, including FTP, mail, and news.

Generally, Windows machines leave fewer holes for hackers to get through. There are several reasons for this (it's not simply that the software is better); one is that PCs running Windows are primarily single-user machines, and they never grant any kind of shell access or direct access to the operating system. Nonetheless, you still need to take precautions to protect your data.

Your primary tool to defend these machines is password protection. Use it.

Here's an example of why you should be sure to use passwords with Windows. Windows makes networking very easy; on a local network running Windows 95, all you have to do to make a disk drive (or any other resource) available to others on your network is right-click the object and select the Share command from the shortcut menu that pops up. You can then walk over to another machine on the network and access that disk drive or resource directly.

This is very slick. It's also potentially very dangerous. Here's why: If your Windows 95 machine is on the Internet, unless you do something special, your system won't know the difference between someone on your local network who is allowed to access your disk and someone on another continent accessing it through the Internet.

Of course, intruders of this type would have to know that your machine was running Windows 95, but that wouldn't be too difficult to determine—especially if they should run across your machine because they were browsing your Web pages or doing a file transfer.

With Windows 95, you can set access permissions for disks to read-only or full access. Each type of access carries a different password. As long as you password-protect all of your shared resources, you'll be relatively safe.

Chapter 17

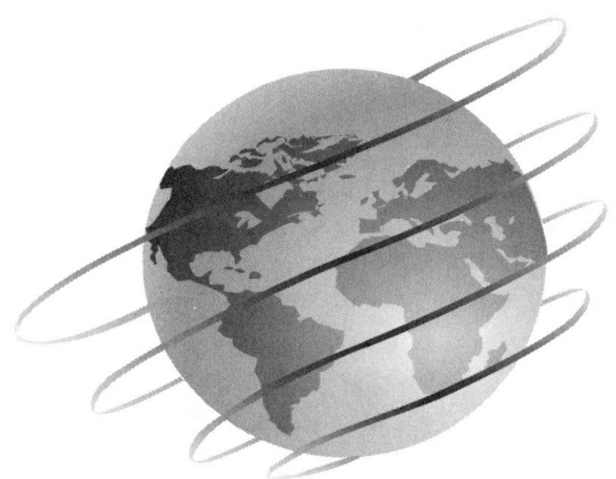

High-Speed Connections to the Internet

A 28.8 Kbps modem may be adequate for a single user browsing the Web; it might even be adequate, though slow, for small networks of two or three computers. However, if you plan to connect a large network of computers to the Internet or want to implement your own Web server, you need a faster connection. In this chapter, you'll find out about the best and most practical options available.

Types of High-Speed Connections

The three major types of high-speed connections are dedicated leased lines, frame relay, and ISDN (see Table 17-1). In this section, we'll discuss the basics of each connection strategy and lay the groundwork for the information presented in the rest of the chapter.

Leased Lines

The oldest and most common type of high-speed connection to the Internet is the *leased line*. With a leased line, you contract with your phone company to provide a direct connection between your network and your Internet service provider (ISP). Your equipment doesn't initiate calls to your service provider because you're not

TABLE 17-1. *High-Speed Connection Types and Throughput*

TYPE	BASE SPEED (KBPS)
V.32bis modem	14.4
V.34 modem	28.8
56K leased line	56
ISDN BRI (1 channel)	56-64
ISDN BRI (2 channels)	128-132
Frame relay	56-1,544
Fractional T1	256-1,280
ISDN PRI	1,544
Full T1 (24 channels)	1,544
T3	44,736

dialing into the telephone company's network. The line is permanently connected from end to end and, once configured, stays up 24 hours a day.

Leased lines come in a handful of capacities. The most common are 56K, T1, and T3. A 56K leased line connects to your network with a standard telephone wire (a pair of copper wires). While this is the least expensive of the leased lines, its total throughput barely surpasses that of a dialup 28.8 modem connection. Most 28.8 modems conform to a standard called *V.34* and can compress data at ratios of up to 4:1, so a V.34 modem that achieves only a 2:1 compression ratio has roughly the same throughput as a 56K leased line. Obviously, a 56K line is only going to support a few more users than would a dialup modem connection; if your objective is to serve Web pages, read on.

The T1 is carried by a *four-conductor wire*, two standard (one-pair) phone lines wrapped around each other in a single sheath. The connector at the end of the wire is a modular RJ-45 jack, which is similar to a standard modular phone plug but slightly larger. The T1 can carry 1.544 megabits per second (1.544 Mbps) of data, roughly 27 times the capacity of a 56K line or a 28.8 modem that's compressing data. A T1 can easily support hundreds of users or dozens of network connections. In fact, many smaller ISPs themselves connect to the Internet with a T1.

A T3 is a very high-capacity (and very expensive) trunk line. It is usually only used by large ISPs and the large communications companies that tie the Internet together, such as AT&T and SprintLink. A T3 can support hundreds of networks and tens of thousands of users. Unless you plan on becoming a very large ISP, you will probably never see a T3.

Of the options we've discussed so far, the most practical are a 56K line and a T1. The difference in capacity and cost between the two is quite large, however; with another option called *fractional* (or *partial*) T1 service, you can start out with a relatively low level of bandwidth over a T1 connection—maybe 128K or 256K—and then increase your bandwidth as your usage expands simply by calling the phone company. Since the wiring is the same for both full T1 and fractional T1 service, all the phone company needs to do is flip some levers or turn some knobs (or whatever it is they do) to increase your bandwidth.

NOTE *If you only need 56K service to start out with but anticipate your needs growing in the future, consider fractional T1 service. You'll avoid paying twice for wiring installation, and the difference in service costs may be less than you'd expect.*

Frame Relay

Frame relay is a newer technology than leased lines. The idea is that rather than paying for a leased line that runs from your own network directly to your ISP's

network, you tie your network into the phone company's frame relay switch, which then routes data traffic between your network and your provider's network.

Frame relay supports speeds of 56K to 1.544 Mbps, and the service costs are scaled accordingly. As with leased lines greater than 56K, you'll have to ask the phone company to do some wiring work.

ISDN

If modem speeds just aren't fast enough for you but you can't justify the expense of a full or fractional T1, ISDN may be just what you need. ISDN stands for *Integrated Services Digital Network*, and it might be the direction of the future for voice communications as well as data transmission. ISDN uses existing telephone wiring, but it uses that wiring digitally rather than in the old analog way. As a result, it permits far greater accuracy and capacity on the same wires. With ISDN, you can get data speeds ranging from 64 Kbps to 1.544 Mbps (T1 speed).

ISDN is a very cost-effective way to get faster Internet access than modems allow. It's also relatively simple to use, and it's available today. For these reasons, we're going to take a closer look at connecting your network to the Internet with ISDN in the section "Getting Up to Speed with ISDN" later in the chapter.

What Should It All Cost?

Understanding how the technologies behind high-speed access work is simple compared to trying to make sense of their costs. One reason for this is that there are so many variables to consider. The one assumption you can make is that a high-speed line is going to cost significantly more than a dialup modem connection.

With a dialup modem connection, you pay a fee to your phone company for your telephone line and another fee to your service provider for access to the Internet. If your modem calls to your provider are local, chances are the total cost of your Internet connection will be very reasonable—probably less than $10 per month for the phone line and around $20 or $30 per month for your Internet account.

With high-speed lines, you also pay both the phone company and your service provider, but the numbers can increase quickly. Furthermore, the decisions you make about your service can dramatically affect your bill. Let's look first at how ISPs typically charge for Internet connections.

The amount you pay your provider for an Internet connection depends largely on the bandwidth capacity of your network connection. Many providers themselves have only a single T1 connection to *their* providers, and it's perfectly reasonable and acceptable for them to oversell their bandwidth. They may even sell their T1 connnection's 1.544 Mbps capacity three, four, or even 10 or more times.

Overselling network bandwidth isn't like overselling airplane seats or hotel rooms. When a hotel books, say, 110 guests for 100 rooms, it's taking a calculated risk that 10 or more of the guests won't show up. This is a risk because when guests do arrive at a hotel and check in, their rooms can't be used by anyone else for the rest of their stay.

This isn't the case with network bandwidth. When you buy network bandwidth, you specify a maximum capacity, but you almost never come close to using it all. And when you do use it, it's usually in short bursts. Even people browsing the Web with 28.8 modems use only a small percentage of their allotted bandwidth (think of the time spent reading Web pages as opposed to pulling them down).

To continue the hotel analogy, think of what booking hotel rooms would be like if the guests only needed rooms for five or 10 minutes. The manager of the same hotel with 100 rooms would know that the hotel could easily accommodate a thousand guests in the same night because none of the guests would need their rooms for very long, and they would come and go all night. There might be an occasional bottleneck here or there when an elevator or hallway filled up, but for the most part 100 rooms could easily accommodate the thousand guests.

Not only is it acceptable for providers to oversell their bandwidth, it's to your advantage if they do. If ISPs were to partition their bandwidth strictly and make your portion available to you and no one else, you would have to pay a much higher rate for your connection, and you would seldom see any difference in performance.

However, when you tell your ISP that you want a certain amount of network bandwidth, the provider has to make it available to you. That means you could do some big downloads or serve a lot of Web pages and use big chunks of your (and the provider's) bandwidth. Therefore, you have to pay more for higher-speed connections.

In addition to deciding on the speed of your connection, you have to decide whether or not the connection needs to be open 24 hours a day, seven days a week. (If you want to put your own Web server online, it won't be too popular if it's not accessible all the time. See Chapter 18 to learn how to set up a Web server.) Plan on paying your ISP an additional $300 to $500 per month for full-time access beyond what you pay the provider for your bandwidth capacity and what you pay the phone company.

It's hard enough to follow the pricing strategies of one provider, but the comparison gets more difficult when you're considering several providers. Before you make a decision, you'll have to do some shopping around to find the best combination of rates and services. You might not have many choices when it comes to your phone company and its service charges, but you do have choices for your ISP.

Here are a few numbers to give you a very rough idea of what the services discussed in this chapter will cost you.

The phone company will charge you roughly the same amount for a leased line whether you're getting a fractional T1 or a full T1. That's because the wiring is the same regardless of what bandwidth you buy to put into the line. The line is capable of a maximum of 1.544 Mbps throughput, and the phone company doesn't care what percentage of that capacity you actually use. In contrast, the *distance* of your leased line from end to end does matter. Figure on paying the phone company between $300 and $500 per month for a leased line, depending on the distance between your network and your ISP.

For the Internet connection at the other end of your leased line, pricing isn't so simple. Again, it depends on the capacity you need. Very roughly, 128K of bandwidth costs around $1,000 per month, and each additional pair of channels (128K) costs between $100 and $300. The rate for additional channels usually drops as you add more bandwidth.

As a rule of thumb, a full T1 connection costs approximately $3,000 per month (for both the phone company and the Internet service).

ISDN can be a much more cost-effective way to connect if you need only a 64K or 128K connection. The phone company will probably charge you less than $30 per month for ISDN service that can handle a capacity of 128 Kbps; however, it might charge for your access time. For example, in California, Pacific Bell charges a penny per minute during normal business hours. If you keep your line open all the time, that's an additional $100 or so per month in usage fees at 64 Kbps. If you use the full capacity of the ISDN line all the time (128 Kbps), that could mean another $100 per month in usage fees.

The amount ISPs charge for ISDN service varies widely, but count on at least $300 a month for dedicated 56/64K access. For the full 128K, you'll probably pay another $150.

Again, the prices quoted here are only rough estimates. You may find bargains with some providers. While there's not much you can do about your phone company's charges, the cost of Internet access is definitely ruled by the free market. If you can find a small ISP with ample unsold bandwidth, chances are you can get a bargain price.

Getting Up to Speed with ISDN

ISDN isn't really a new technology, but until recently it wasn't offered as a service to businesses or residences. In fact, only in the last couple of years have many local and regional telephone companies begun offering ISDN. As with any new

technology or service, some of the pioneers who tried it out in the early days have horror stories to tell about how it was implemented.

The reasons for this aren't surprising—in fact, they make sense. Phone company personnel weren't experienced at implementing ISDN until they had set up a few ISDN connections. Consultants and value-added resellers weren't able to form opinions about what worked and what didn't until they had done some ISDN installations. And system administrators didn't know how to configure their systems and networks to use ISDN until they had done it at least once. In short, when a technology or service is new, it's new to everyone, and there are bound to be some problems.

By now, ISDN is better understood by all parties. Your telephone company shouldn't be surprised if you call and ask about getting ISDN service; the products you need to connect your computer or network to the Internet are plentiful; most ISPs now provide ISDN access points; and consultants and product resellers now know how to install and use ISDN products.

What Is ISDN?

Most of the world's telephone networks have been in place and unchanged for years. In fact, the last significant change in telephone technology from the user's point of view was the switch from rotary-dial telephones to touch-tone dialing in the 1970s. And that upgrade was accomplished without rewiring the network—all that changed is that we started using the newer tone-dialing telephones, and the phone companies upgraded their switching devices to support tone dialing. Even today, the wires that run to and through many older buildings have remained the same for decades.

With the older system, sometimes called *POTS* (for Plain Old Telephone Service), the telephone company's switches and the phones we used were analog creatures. The telephone itself was a rather unintelligent machine; it rang a bell when it received a signal from the phone company's switch, and it carried voice signals by modulating and demodulating them at both ends of the conversation. The basic technology goes clear back to Alexander Graham Bell.

ISDN represents the most dramatic change to the world's telephone system in a long time. With ISDN, our telephone networks are coming into the digital age. ISDN switches, lines, and telephones operate digitally. As with the upgrade to tone dialing two decades ago, the switch to ISDN won't require new wiring in most cases; it's just a new way of using the old wiring.

So what does all this mean to you? It means that if you use ISDN, the same physical telephone wire that runs into your home or office can operate much more efficiently, enabling it to carry much more information. The same single telephone

wire (which is actually a pair of copper wires inside a sheath) that once could carry only one conversation or data transmission can now carry three separate conversations or data transmissions simultaneously!

What's even more important for data communications is that, because the signals carried by the wire are already digital, there's no need to use a modem to convert digital computer data into an analog signal for transmission over the wire. This translates into much higher efficiency, accuracy, and data transmission rates.

As you saw in Table 17-1, the fastest modems today can send data over a standard phone line at a rate of 28 Kbps. When the same phone line is converted to ISDN, it will ultimately be able to transfer data at 128 Kbps. (Until the telephone utility's entire network is converted to digital switches, however, the maximum speed will only be about 112 Kbps.)

Sorting Out Your ISDN Options

You can buy two types of ISDN service from your telephone utility: the *Basic Rate Interface* (or BRI) and the *Primary Rate Interface* (or PRI). The BRI—the service described in the preceding section—converts an existing phone line to a digital line that can support up to three simultaneous calls, with an aggregate transfer rate of 128 Kbps.

The PRI is a much higher-capacity connection that's appropriate for larger businesses and organizations. It has an aggregate transfer rate of 1.544 Mbps (approximately 12 times the rate of the BRI) and is delivered by a T1 trunk line, which is a two-pair phone wire with a modular RJ-45 jack (as described earlier in the chapter).

If you want to use ISDN for a single computer or a small network, you'll most likely want a BRI connection. It takes a standard two-conductor telephone line and breaks it down logically into three separate channels: a single *data channel* (called the *D* channel) and two *bearer channels* (called *B* channels).

The D channel carries data at 16 Kbps. Although it's called the *data channel*, it's used primarily for call setup and administration, not for carrying data. The channels that matter the most to the user are the two B channels, each of which can carry data at 56 or 64 Kbps. To put this into terms we use more often (bytes instead of bits), 56 Kbps is about 7,000 bytes per second. By contrast, a PRI is composed of 23 B channels and a single 64 Kbps D channel.

Equipment You Will Need

Because ISDN is still relatively new, if you ask your local phone company what equipment you need to use ISDN, you'll probably get the following list of devices:

- A network termination device (or NT1)
- A power supply
- A terminal adapter
- An aggregation device

Your next question will be, "Where do I buy these things...Radio Shack?" Unfortunately, you can't buy them in stores. Treating each device as a separate item is somewhat misleading because often all of them are built into a single box. It's likely that all you'll need to do is buy one product—an ISDN router—and you'll be ready to go.

For example, let's say you have an Ethernet network using the TCP/IP protocol, and you want to connect it to the Internet with BRI ISDN. All you need is an ISDN router with a built-in NT1. The router will have ports on the back for:

- A power cable
- An Ethernet network connection
- The ISDN phone line
- A serial port for configuration

Table 17-2 lists a few companies that make ISDN routers and accessories.

Let's look at how an Ethernet network is set up for ISDN Internet access with an Ascend Pipeline 50 ISDN router. The Pipeline 50 is shown in Figure 17-1.

The Pipeline 50 has a built-in NT1, or network termination device, and comes with a power supply (a power cord, similar to a modem's). In addition, it has the necessary terminal adapter built in, and software in the router handles aggregation (we'll explain this in a minute). In short, it's everything you need to put between your Ethernet LAN and your ISDN phone plug.

TABLE 17-2. *A Few Manufacturers of ISDN Routers*

COMPANY	LOCATION / INFORMATION
Ascend Communications, Inc.	http://www.ascend.com/
Combinet Inc.	http://www.combinet.com/
Gandalf Systems Corp.	http://www.gandalf.com/

FIGURE 17-1. *The Ascend Pipeline 50*

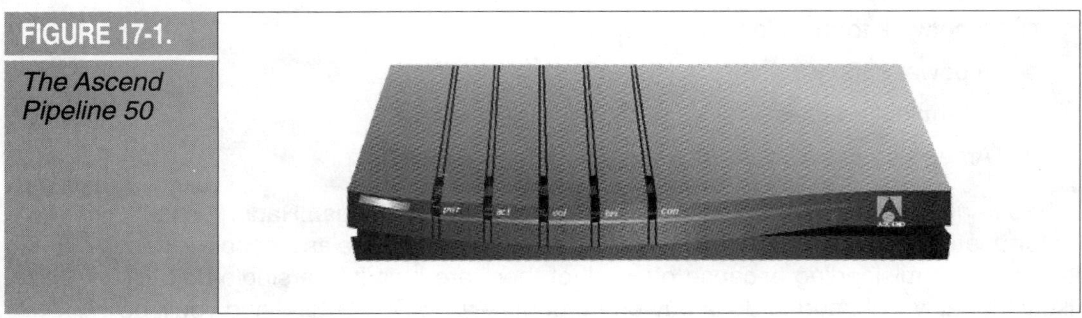

The back of the Pipeline 50 sports plugs for the power cable, the ISDN phone line, a serial port connection for configuring the device, and two types of Ethernet connectors: a 10BASE5 (AUI) connector for thick Ethernet and a modular plug for 10BASE-T (UTP) Ethernet.

If your network is 10BASE-T or thick Ethernet, you're all set. If you have a 10BASE2 (thin-net) network, however, you need a *transceiver*, an adapter that plugs into the AUI port (or the 10BASE-T port) on the back of the Pipeline and provides a 10BASE2 (BNC) connector for your thin-net network. Transceivers run around $40, and you should be able to find them (or at least order them) at most computer stores. You can also order them online at http://www.blackbox.com.

Figure 17-2 shows how you attach the Pipeline 50 to your network. It simply becomes a network node, just like each of the existing computers on your network. In fact, the router is really a small computer in its own right. It even gets its own IP address and machine name.

To configure the router, you can attach one end of a serial cable to the router's serial port and the other end to a terminal or another computer. For example, you can connect the cable to a computer running Windows, then run Windows' HyperTerminal program and set the terminal session for the proper COM port, VT-100 emulation, and 9,600-baud 8N1. Next, press CTRL-L to redraw the screen, and you'll be in the Pipeline's configuration program (see Figure 17-3).

You can set several options in the Pipeline's configuration menus, but the ones you need to be most concerned with are:

FIGURE 17-2. *The ISDN router is a node on the network and acts as the network's gateway to the Internet*

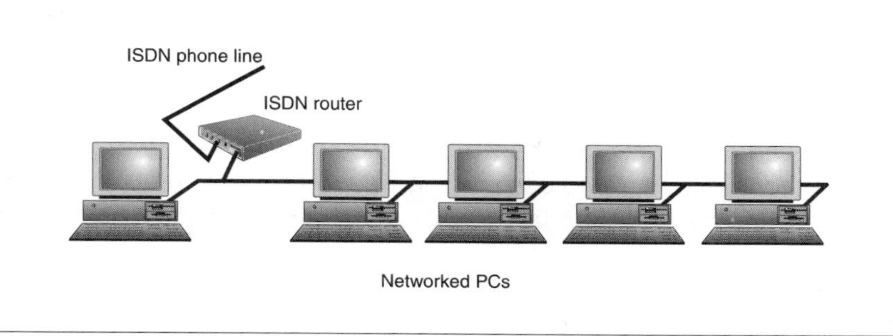

- The IP address for the router
- The name you chose for your router
- The IP address of the gateway to which the router connects
- The name of the gateway computer to which the router connects
- The phone number the router should dial to connect to the gateway
- The login name and password for your router on the gateway computer
- The router's own phone numbers (there may be two)
- The SPID numbers (your phone company will give you these)

FIGURE 17-3. *The Pipeline 50's configuration program*

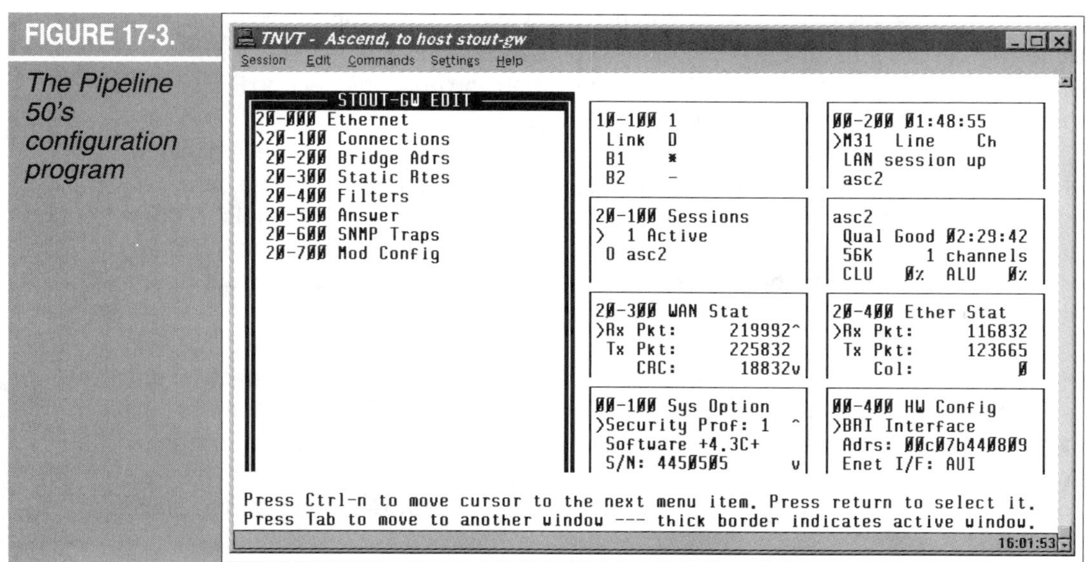

In addition to these, you can set many other options; for example, you can configure the router to drop the ISDN line after a specified interval of no activity. It will automatically reinitiate the connection as soon as it receives traffic to route to the gateway computer.

You can also configure the way the router manages the BRI's two B channels. You can force the router to use only one channel, to use both channels at all times, or to open the second channel only after a certain percentage of the first B channel's capacity has been exceeded for a period of time (which you can also specify).

For example, one person browsing Web pages seldom needs the bandwidth of both B channels. Most Web pages (even those with graphics) are less than 20K; using only one B channel, a 20K Web page will load in about three seconds (at 6.5K per second).

If you're going to be doing some significant file transfers, however, you might want to make sure you're using both B channels to get the highest possible throughput. Using the Pipeline 50's configuration options, you can set the router to open the second B channel after a sustained period (10 seconds, for example) in which more than a specified percentage (such as 80%) of the router's capacity was in use. This way, most Web pages and small file transfers will use only one of the two B channels; shortly after you initiate a large file transfer, however, the second B channel will kick in and your transfer rate will double. This is called *channel aggregation*.

Why not just configure the router to use both B channels all the time? You can, but it will cost you money you don't need to spend. In addition to a (usually very reasonable) monthly rate for ISDN service, most telephone companies also charge a per-minute amount for each B channel you use. The charge is usually small—a penny per minute—but the cost adds up. And when you open the second B channel, that rate doubles to two cents per minute.

In addition, telephone companies usually charge a higher rate for the first minute of a B channel connection. The first minute often costs as much as five cents, so you want to minimize the number of calls you initiate on your B channels. A good practice is to open up the second B channel only when you need it—after 10, 20, or 30 seconds of saturation on the first channel—then hold it open until it hasn't been used for a longer period, such as five or 10 minutes.

Besides the penny-per-minute charge for each B channel, you also have to consider what your ISP will charge you for bandwidth; you can't expect to pay modem rates for ISDN's much higher capacity. Many ISPs use T1 connections for their own Internet connections. A T1 is 24 bearer channels of 64 Kbps each. If you open up both of your B channels and do some large file transfers (or serve many Web pages), you can quickly use up a significant percentage of your provider's bandwidth. Since

bandwidth is what ISPs sell, you have to pay for what you use. Don't be surprised if you have to pay your provider a higher rate for using both B channels.

Another popular router from Ascend is the Pipeline 25. It's similar to the Pipeline 50, but it has a couple of useful features the Pipeline 50 lacks. First, the back of the Pipeline 25 has two analog (POTS) phone ports into which you can plug a regular analog telephone or fax machine. If you happen to be using both B channels when you pick up the phone to make a call (or when a call comes in), the router will automatically deaggregate the B channels and allocate one to your network connection and the other to the phone or fax call.

Another nice feature of the Pipeline 25 is that it does data compression in hardware—rather than in software like the Pipeline 50—for faster compression and decompression.

On the downside, you have to pay extra for the Pipeline 25 to do network routing (routing is standard with the 50). Also, the Pipeline 50 allows you to configure the router by using a telnet program to connect to it. With the 25, you must use the serial port on the back of the unit with a terminal or with a computer that has a terminal emulation program.

Still another popular ISDN router is the Everywhere family of routers from Combinet. The Combinet product that competes with the Pipeline 50 is the 2050D. The 2050D has a built-in NT1, and it sports 10BASE-T and 10BASE2 (BNC) Ethernet ports instead of the Pipeline 50's 10BASE-T and AUI.

So what is ISDN hardware going to cost you? It's not cheap; it will probably cost more than most people would want to spend if they just wanted to surf the Web. But if you're on the Net a lot or you're connecting a small network, it's not too bad, and prices should begin falling sharply as more competitors enter the market.

Today, a basic ISDN router such as the Pipeline 25 or the Combinet 2050D will run at least $600 to $700. This is just a basic router; if you want it to do network routing and compression, you might have to pay an additional $200 to $300 for each service. Thus, a fully equipped ISDN router can cost between $1,200 and $1,500.

To put the price into perspective, keep in mind that these boxes can do routing for an entire network of computers and include security features that let you screen incoming traffic. Today, ISDN cards that slip into an expansion slot in PCs are beginning to hit the mainstream PC catalogs and superstore shelves. Motorola has delivered such a card already; it includes a built-in NT1 and serves as the terminal adapter for a single PC. Motorola's card is going for less than $400—not much more than a top-of-the-line modem.

[illegible]

Chapter 18

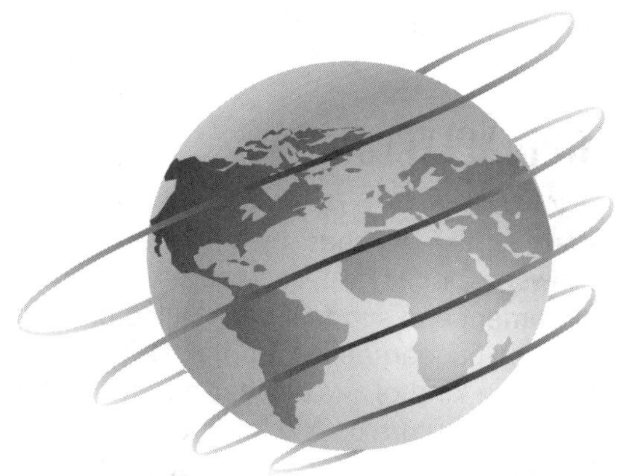

Web Servers

If you're putting your own systems on the Web, you've got to know about Web servers and how to get the most out of them. This chapter begins with a general discussion of Web servers, then takes a closer look at two very good ones—one for Unix, and one for Windows 95 and Windows NT. The discussion also includes some URLs to Web locations where you can find the latest information on Web server products.

Next, you'll learn how to create clickable imagemaps for two popular Web servers. Imagemaps have gained a reputation for being difficult to create, but with the new graphical tools available today they're really not hard at all.

Finally, you'll find out about a package for analyzing Web server log files that will give you flashy and informative reports you can integrate into your web. We'll look at one package in detail and give pointers to several others, along with more information on log analysis tools.

Web Servers

A *Web server* is a program that runs on a computer connected to the Internet. The Web server watches the Internet connection and waits for requests from Web browsers for HTML documents. When it receives a request, it finds the HTML document and sends it back to the browser that requested it.

As you learned in Chapter 11, computers are usually connected to the Internet by some kind of wire, either a network cable or a telephone-type line. Either way, most computers on the Internet have only a single *physical* connection to the Net, but the computer's operating system (or other system software) splits that physical connection up into a number of *logical* connections. Think of these logical connections as separate conduits, or pipelines, through which separate exchanges of data take place simultaneously. These conduits are called *ports*, and the computer's operating system and system software identify each port by a number.

By default, Web servers and Web browsers use port 80. You can use different ports, but doing so defeats the purpose of participating in a homogeneous World Wide Web that functions the way everyone expects.

Do You Need a Web Server?

Not everyone who uses the Web will need or want a Web server; having one means keeping a computer connected to the Internet more or less full-time. After all, a Web server isn't much use on a single, unconnected computer; its primary function is to serve pages to other remote computers.

If you're only interested in using the Web to read the many existing Web pages, you can skip this chapter altogether. If you're thinking about leasing space for your

web of pages on another company's computer, you can also skip this chapter; that company will already have a functioning Web server and the people to operate it. If, however, you're thinking about putting your own computer on the Internet and implementing and maintaining Web pages yourself, this chapter is a must-read.

Do You Have What it Takes?

The fact that you plan to run a Web server implies that you want to make your pages available to people 24 hours a day, seven days a week. If you don't have a permanent connection, potential readers won't be able to connect to your web when they want to, and they may become discouraged and lose interest in the material or resources you offer.

Readers can become equally impatient with your web if your Internet connection doesn't have the bandwidth to support a number of readers simultaneously. When you're starting out, it's hard to estimate the traffic your web will generate. Most of the best Web servers have software for monitoring such statistics as the number of page requests per hour and the number of kilobytes of data transferred during a period. If you watch these statistics carefully, you can pinpoint your peak-volume periods and determine how these transfers compare to the total bandwidth of your network connection.

For example, let's assume an average page size (without graphics) of 2K. At 200 page requests per hour, that's an hourly transfer rate of 400K. A reasonable throughput from a 28.8 Kbps modem is 10MB per hour. It would seem, then, that a 28.8 Kbps modem could easily handle 200 2K page requests per hour. But page requests don't equate to readers. If the average reader checks out five of your pages, 200 page requests equal only 40 readers per hour.

Also keep in mind that many of the page transfers will be happening simultaneously and that any pages with even medium-sized graphics will quickly gobble up a 28.8 modem's throughput.

Most graphic images you will encounter or put in your pages will range from 2K to about 40K in size. If you assume an average graphic size of 20K and one graphic per page, an average page size with graphics would be 22K. This means that 200 page requests per hour will result in an hourly transfer rate of more than 4MB—nearly half of a 28.8 Kbps modem's hourly capacity! Unfortunately, you can't schedule the delivery of your Web pages for when it's convenient or when bandwidth is available; you've got to deliver them when the reader wants them, and do it quickly.

As a rule of thumb, a modem won't provide enough bandwidth to serve Web pages to the world—even if you expect as few as 200 page requests per hour. If your goal is not to attract the masses but rather to serve a very few pages infrequently, maybe you can get away with only a modem connection. But watch those statistics!

The slowest connection we would recommend for serving Web pages is ISDN (Integrated Services Digital Network). With ISDN, you can reasonably expect between three and six times the throughput of the fastest modems. However, even this type of connection might not be enough if you've advertised your arrival to the Web and hope to attract as many readers as possible. It can be an affordable way to get started, though, and if you use up your capacity quickly you can increase the bandwidth of your ISDN connection relatively easily.

If you're serious about arriving on the Web in a big way, you'll probably need a frame relay or full T1 connection. These are terms telephone companies use to describe different types of permanent leased connections. Don't contemplate them unless you have a serious business plan and a budget that can handle thousands of dollars per month in connection fees. (We looked at ISDN, frame relay, and T1 connections in Chapter 17. If you skipped that chapter, you should know that you can't expect to set up a serious Web server without an adequate connection.)

To run a Web server, you also need a fast computer running a multitasking operating system. Today, most Web servers on the Net are running on Unix computers ranging in size from "big iron" (what we used to call minicomputers)—such as HP, Sun, Silicon Graphics, Irix, and Indigo workstations—down to PCs. Other common Web servers are Macs and PCs running Windows NT, Windows 95, and OS/2. You seldom see a Web server that runs DOS or Windows 3.1—and you wouldn't want one if you did. A DOS computer would have to be dedicated to serving Web pages (and even then couldn't do it adequately), and the multitasking capabilities of Windows 3.1 were shaky at best.

Web servers for Unix computers are widespread, and some of the best ones are free (you'll learn about some of these later in the chapter). Servers for Windows 95, Windows NT, the Mac, and OS/2 are quickly coming to market; they tend to be commercial products, but they're typically reasonably priced and very capable.

Implementing a Web Server on Your System

A Web server provides four major functions:

- Serving Web pages
- Running gateway programs and returning their output
- Controlling access to the server
- Monitoring and logging server access statistics

The way these functions are implemented can vary dramatically from server to server. This section introduces one of the most popular Unix servers, along with one for Windows 95.

NCSA httpd

The organization that brought you Mosaic also maintains a robust and versatile Web server for Unix systems. Called simply *httpd* (for HTTP daemon), NCSA's Web server is precompiled for a variety of Unix systems, including:

- HP-UX
- IBM AIX
- Irix
- Linux
- OSF/1
- Solaris
- SunOS
- Ultrix

NCSA keeps httpd on its FTP server at ftp.ncsa.uiuc.edu in the directory */Web/httpd/Unix/ncsa_httpd*. If NCSA doesn't have a binary package for your Unix system, you can also download the source code from that location. The Unix system we used to test NCSA's httpd is a Pentium PC running BSD/OS version 2.0. Since NCSA didn't have a binary package for BSD/OS, we downloaded the source code and built the server from scratch. The whole process, from compiling the program to configuring and using it, took less than an hour.

Unix-based servers typically consist of a single binary executable program that starts automatically when the computer is booted. The Web administrator configures the server by changing its configuration files. For example, the NCSA httpd server expects to be in the directory */usr/local/etc/httpd*. (This is configurable, but that directory is the default.) In this directory are the executable program file and several subdirectories. Table 18-1 lists the directories and their functions.

Of course, all of these directories are configurable. That is, the system administrator can change them to any other location on the system.

The following is a portion of the NCSA server's main configuration file, *httpd.conf*.

```
ServerType standalone
Port 80
StartServers 5
MaxServers 20
User nobody
Group #-1
ServerAdmin rick@rls.com
```

```
ServerRoot /usr/local/etc/httpd
ErrorLog logs/error_log
TransferLog logs/access_log
AgentLog logs/agent_log
RefererLog logs/referer_log
PidFile logs/httpd.pid
ServerName www.rls.com
```

To set or change a server option, you edit this file with a text editor such as vi or emacs and save the file. The version of this file that comes with the NCSA server has ample comments and suggestions for each line, but we've omitted them here to show you the meat of the configuration file. (You shouldn't delete them from an actual configuration file.)

TABLE 18-1. *Default Directory Tree for NCSA's httpd Server*

DIRECTORY	PURPOSE
/usr/local/etc/httpd/	The root web directory. Contains subdirectories for configuration files and documents.
/usr/local/etc/httpd/cgi-bin	Contains executable CGI scripts (gateway programs).
/usr/local/etc/httpd/cgi-src	Contains source code for CGI scripts.
/usr/local/etc/httpd/conf	Contains the server's main configuration option files.
/usr/local/etc/httpd/htdocs	The root document directory (where the server's home page goes).
/usr/local/etc/httpd/icons	Contains graphics files that the server provides automatically, such as folder and document icons for listing the files and subdirectories in an FTP directory or a directory with no default HTML file.
/usr/local/etc/httpd/logs	The server keeps log files in this directory showing the machines from which requests have come, errors, and so on.

The following is a portion of the access log generated by the NCSA server.

```
mac.cino.com - - [06/Jul/1995:19:48:43 -0700] "GET / HTTP/1.0" 304 0
home.adrea.com - - [06/Jul/1995:19:50:11 -0700] "GET /local/sysinfo.html
HTTP/1.0" 200 740
pc8.culea.com - - [06/Jul/1995:19:54:42 -0700] "GET /cgi-bin/bsd-man
HTTP/1.0" 404 -
nc32.netcom.com - - [06/Jul/1995:19:59:38 -0700] "GET / HTTP/1.0" 200 1417
sparc2.crps.com - - [06/Jul/1995:19:59:40 -0700] "GET /bsdi/bsdi.html
HTTP/1.0" 200 1825
plnt.crypto.com - - [06/Jul/1995:19:59:48 -0700] "GET /cgi-bin/bsdi-man
HTTP/1.0" 200 608
nix.hyper.org - - [06/Jul/1995:19:59:58 -0700] "GET /wcr/ HTTP/1.0" 304 0
137.21.166.20 - - [06/Jul/1995:20:00:06 -0700] "GET /html/www_faq.html
HTTP/1.0" 200 117724
cac.psu.edu - - [06/Jul/1995:20:00:10 -0700] "GET /html/html2/html-2.txt
HTTP/1.0" 200 125216
sparc2.crps.com - - [06/Jul/1995:20:00:29 -0700] "GET /html/ns_ext.html
HTTP/1.0" 200 1033
mac2.ax.com - - [06/Jul/1995:20:00:35 -0700] "GET /nsbmarks.html HTTP/1.0"
200 4742
home.servo.com - - [06/Jul/1995:20:02:36 -0700] "GET /icons/text.xbm
HTTP/1.0" 200 527
ra3.slink.com - - [06/Jul/1995:20:02:36 -0700] "GET /icons/blank.xbm
HTTP/1.0" 200 509
gas.alto.com - - [06/Jul/1995:20:02:36 -0700] "GET /icons/menu.xbm
HTTP/1.0" 200 527
sparc2.crps.com - - [06/Jul/1995:20:02:39 -0700] "GET /ni.html HTTP/1.0"
200 180
```

The information logged includes the name of the machine from which the request came, the date and time, the action requested (the name of the document requested), the resulting success or failure code, and the number of bytes of data transferred as a result of the request. This format is more or less common among Web servers and is thus called the *common log file format*.

Don't think that working with a Unix-based Web server is a completely nongraphical experience, though; some X Window-based programs allow you to work with a Web server's configuration files and view or monitor the log files in the X Window graphical environment.

NOTE *A word of caution about Unix programs: A Unix system is still the best platform for heavy Internet traffic and for providing Internet services of all kinds. However, if you don't know Unix, getting such a system up and configured for the Internet would take some effort. In fact, it's probably too daunting to contemplate unless you plan to do it for fun and you're not under any time pressure. If you've got a mission-critical schedule, hire a Unix expert to set up your system and monitor and maintain it thereafter. Alternatively, consider Windows NT or Windows 95.*

NCSA provides an excellent web of pages to help you with installation. If you know Unix, a quick read through the overview and the step-by-step installation instructions should be all you need to get your server up and running. The documentation is at http://hoohoo.ncsa.uiuc.edu/.

WebSite

WebSite, from O'Reilly & Associates, is a powerful new Web server for Windows NT and Windows 95. This commercial product retails for about $500, but its ease of use and superior interface are well worth the price—particularly if you're not a Unix expert and are not planning on becoming one or hiring one.

O'Reilly & Associates offers information on WebSite at its own Web site (http://www.ora.com or http://gnn.com/gnn/bus/ora/item/website.html). Right now, the company sells WebSite from its online bookstore or by direct order. WebSite has already found its way onto the shelves of software stores.

As with any professional Windows program, the included setup program makes installing the software a breeze. We tested WebSite on a Pentium computer running Windows 95 and got the server installed, configured, and serving pages in less than five minutes.

Figure 18-1 shows WebSite running under Windows 95. When you're actually running it in a production environment, though, you'll usually minimize this program window. In fact, when you start the program, it automatically minimizes itself. The minimized icon tells you when the server is idle and when it's being accessed.

In addition to the server, WebSite comes with a handful of administration tools and utilities. Also included is a complimentary copy of Spyglass's Enhanced Mosaic.

Among the administration tools are an imagemap editor (discussed later in this chapter), a program called *WebView* for viewing your Web hierarchy graphically, a program called *WebIndex* that creates a searchable index of words in your entire Web hierarchy (the index can be searched from a Web page), and a server administration program that you use to set all the configuration options for the server.

Figure 18-2 shows the server administration program. By selecting the tabs at the top of this panel, you can set or change the general options for your server. In addition, you can customize more advanced configuration settings relating to map-

FIGURE 18-1.

The WebSite server running under Windows 95

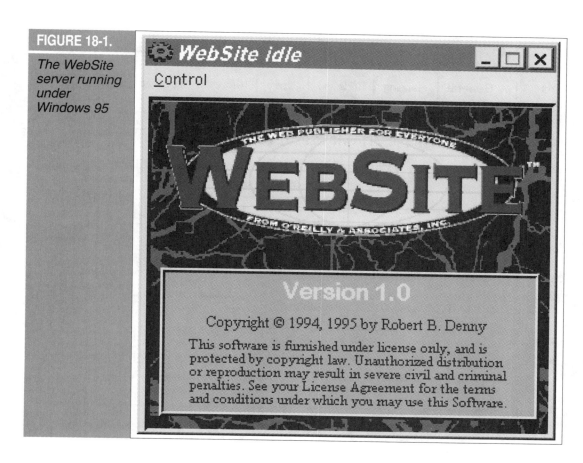

ping directory path names to other directories, indexing, user and group controls, access control, logging, and CGI options. Detailed online help is available on each panel.

WebView is an amazing tool that may help shape the development of tools for managing Web sites. WebView lets you graphically view your entire hierarchy of Web pages, as well as all the graphics and other files to which they're linked. The WebView program window (see Figure 18-3) shows your entire web, beginning with the default page for the server (the home page). Not only can you view your web, you can also change the links from this program window and even edit the HTML source code by double-clicking on a page icon.

WebSite's log files conform to the common log file format. As a result, they look identical to those created by NCSA's server and other Web servers. The only exception is that WebSite's logs provide the IP address of the requesting system

FIGURE 18-2. *WebSite's Server Admin program*

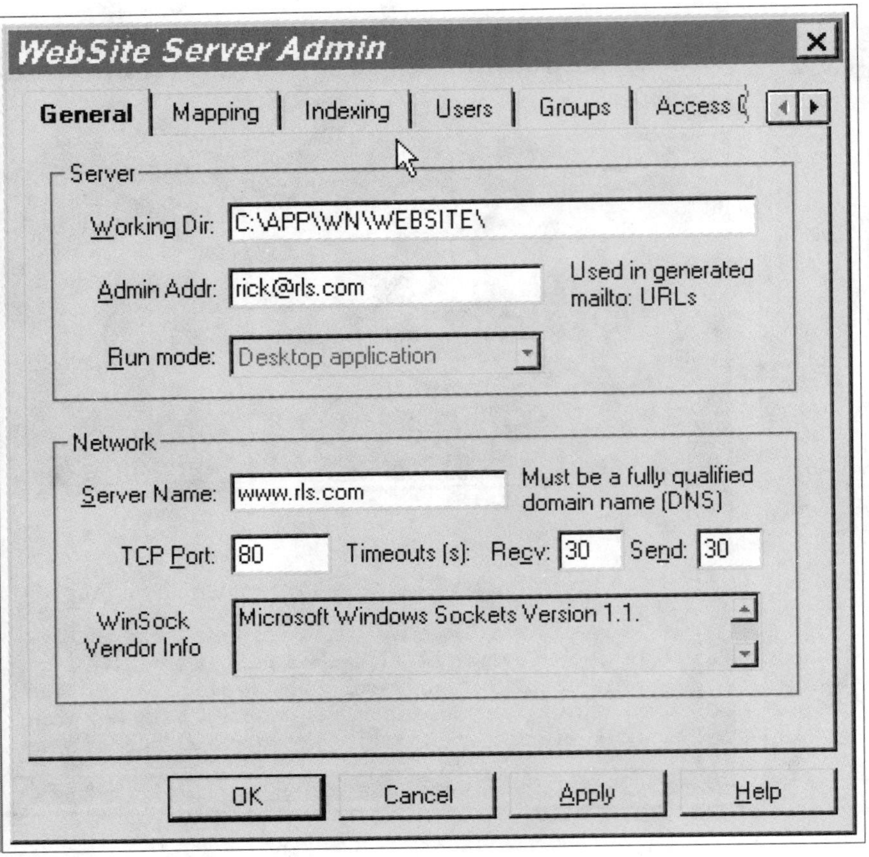

WebSite Server Admin

General | Mapping | Indexing | Users | Groups | Access

Server

Working Dir: C:\APP\WN\WEBSITE\

Admin Addr: rick@rls.com — Used in generated mailto: URLs

Run mode: Desktop application

Network

Server Name: www.rls.com — Must be a fully qualified domain name (DNS)

TCP Port: 80 Timeouts (s): Recv: 30 Send: 30

WinSock Vendor Info: Microsoft Windows Sockets Version 1.1.

OK | Cancel | Apply | Help

rather than the host and domain name. This is only a default setting, however. If you prefer, you can enable DNS (domain name service) reverse lookups simply by clicking a checkbox in the Server Admin dialog box. From then on, WebSite's access log will show the host and domain names of requesting systems rather than the IP addresses. Doing this increases transaction times because the server has the extra step of contacting a name server to translate the IP address into the host and domain names.

More Unix Servers

Since Unix has been on the Internet longer than any of the newer operating systems, it's no surprise that most Web servers are for Unix. NCSA's server is one of the most

FIGURE 18-3.

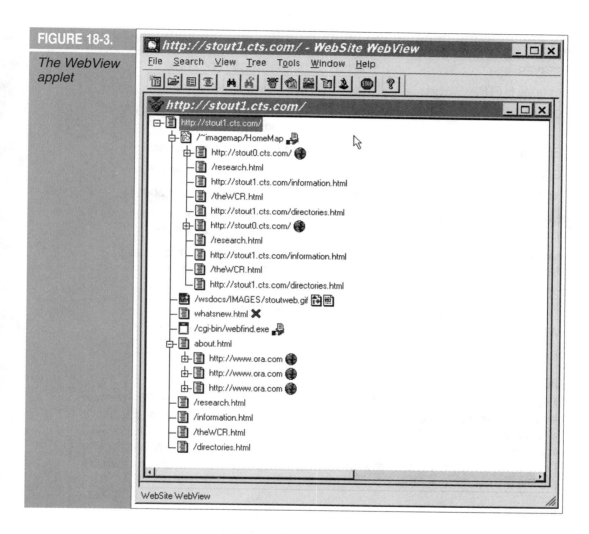

The WebView applet

popular for Unix systems, but it is by no means your only choice. Table 18-2 lists a few more popular Unix servers, and the following sections describe each one.

Apache HTTP

Apache is a replacement daemon for NCSA's httpd. It uses the same command-line options and configuration files, but it fixes some of the bugs in the NCSA server and offers other improvements as well. Apache's developers claim it will eventually be faster than NCSA's daemon.

TABLE 18-2. *Some Unix Web Servers*

SERVER	COST	INFORMATION / LOCATION
Apache HTTP	N/A	http://www.apache.org/
CERN httpd	N/A	http://www.w3.org/hypertext/WWW/Daemon/Status.html
EIT httpd	N/A	http://wsk.eit.com/wsk/doc/
GN Gopher/HTTP Server	N/A	http://hopf.math.nwu.edu:70/
NCSA httpd	N/A	http://hoohoo.ncsa.uiuc.edu/
Netscape Commerce Server	$5,000	http://www.mcom.com/comprod/netscape_commerce.html
Netscape Communications Server	$1,495	http://www.mcom.com/comprod/netscape_commun.html
Plexus	N/A	http://bsdi.com/server/doc/plexus.html
WN	N/A	http://hopf.math.nwu.edu/

CERN httpd

Originally developed at the CERN organization in Switzerland, the CERN httpd server is the main competition for the NCSA httpd. (CERN has since ended its active involvement with the World Wide Web and turned over its projects to the W3 organization at the Massachusetts Institute of Technology.) The CERN Web server is very well-liked by many Unix system administrators and Internet service providers (the Plexus server is another).

EIT httpd

Enterprise Integration Technologies Corp. produces EIT httpd, a low-end (but easy to install and use) HTTP daemon. This server is actually part of the EIT Webmaster's Starter Kit. The server is pretty basic (by EIT's own description), but it's still an attractive alternative because it's simple to implement and a great learning tool for beginners.

GN Gopher/HTTP Server

The GN Gopher/HTTP server is a combination Gopher server and Web server. The GN server even uses the same data hierarchy for serving Gopher clients and Web

clients. If your organization has a Gopher server and you're thinking of upgrading to the Web, this server could offer a reasonable alternative to running and maintaining two separate servers.

NCSA httpd

The NCSA server is the favorite of many Unix system administrators and Internet service providers. It consistently ranks high in benchmark tests and ease-of-use comparisons.

Netscape Server Products

Netscape's servers are professional-quality commercial products that offer a wealth of features and configuration options. Unfortunately, all this capability also comes with a serious price tag. Nevertheless, in some areas Netscape is driving the very technology of the World Wide Web. It's on the forefront of some technologies, such as secure servers and secure HTML. Netscape's servers run on a variety of Unix platforms as well as on Windows NT.

Plexus

Plexus is a Web server written in the Perl scripting language for Unix systems. If you know and like Perl, you'll like the flexibility of Plexus. Perl offers most of the features of other servers and adds ease of use for some functions, such as integrating Perl CGI scripts into the functions of the server.

WN

The WN server focuses on the task of serving hypertext documents, meaning the server has advanced, built-in support for such tasks as searching and indexing HTML documents. Also, the WN server provides an alternative way to run gateway programs without the complexity of CGI scripts.

Web Servers for Other Operating Systems

If you're not into Unix, your options aren't limited to the Netscape servers and WebSite for Windows NT and Windows 95. WebSite is too new to have a track record, but we believe it's destined to become a major player in the server market for Windows computers. Table 18-3 lists a few more Web servers for a variety of platforms and includes both public-domain packages and commercial products (see Appendix B for a more extensive list).

Before you decide on a Web server, check out the server section of the World Wide Web FAQ at http://sunsite.unc.edu/boutell/faq/www_faq.html. This FAQ offers

TABLE 18-3. *Some Non-Unix Web Servers*

SERVER	PLATFORM	COST	INFORMATION / LOCATION
Alibaba	Win NT	$450	http://www.csm.co.at/csm/alibaba.htm
GoServe	OS/2	N/A	http://www2.hursley.ibm.com/goserve
HTTPS	Win NT	N/A	ftp://emwac.ed.ac.uk/pub/https/https.txt
MacHTTP	Mac	$95	http://www.biap.com/
NetAlly	Mac	$995	http://www.delphic.com/
OS2HTTPD	OS/2	N/A	ftp://ftp.netcom.com/pub/kf/kfan/overview.html
WebSTAR	Mac	$795	http://www.starnine.com/webstar/webstar.html
Windows httpd	Windows	N/A	http://www.city.net/win-httpd/

a wealth of information on Web servers, lists of Web servers, and even links to detailed analysis and comparisons that people have put together.

Creating Imagemaps

If you've poked around on the Web, you've probably run across more than a few imagemaps by now. Imagemaps such as the one shown in Figure 18-4 can add an elegant and flashy façade to your web or your home page. By clicking on different areas of the imagemap, you can follow links to pages on your own web or out on the Internet.

The ways you can use imagemaps are endless. For example, if your business sells music CDs on the Web, you might create a display of your most popular CDs by setting them against a backdrop and taking a photograph of them. You could then use a scanner to create an electronic version of the image, create an imagemap, and integrate it into your web. By clicking on various CDs in the image, your readers could get information about each title or add titles to their order.

Or you may be with a large company that has offices in every region or state. You might create an imagemap from a map of the country and design it so that when readers click on their own state or region, they get contact information or the location of your nearest office.

Even simple imagemaps can greatly enhance an otherwise bland Web page. Figure 18-5 shows a simple block graphic, created in a drawing program, depicting a logo and buttons to click for each area of interest.

FIGURE 18-4. *Microsoft's imagemap on its main Web page*

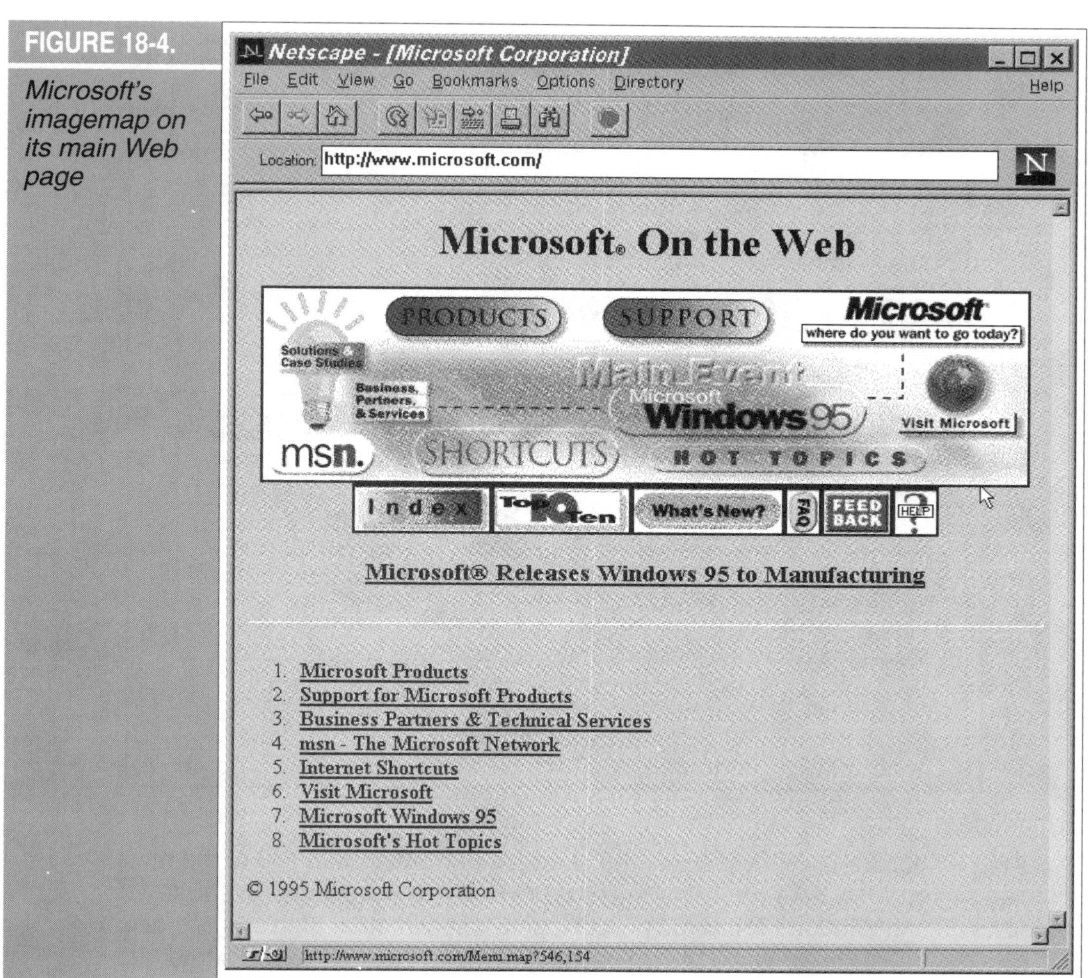

Creating an imagemap used to be complex and cumbersome, but with the tools available today it's a snap. There are three steps:

- Finding or creating an image
- Mapping and assigning the regions of the image
- Integrating the imagemap into your Web server

In this section, you'll learn how to do each of these steps. However, because not all Web servers are alike, we can't show you how to implement imagemaps with

FIGURE 18-5. *A simple imagemap with buttons for hot-spots*

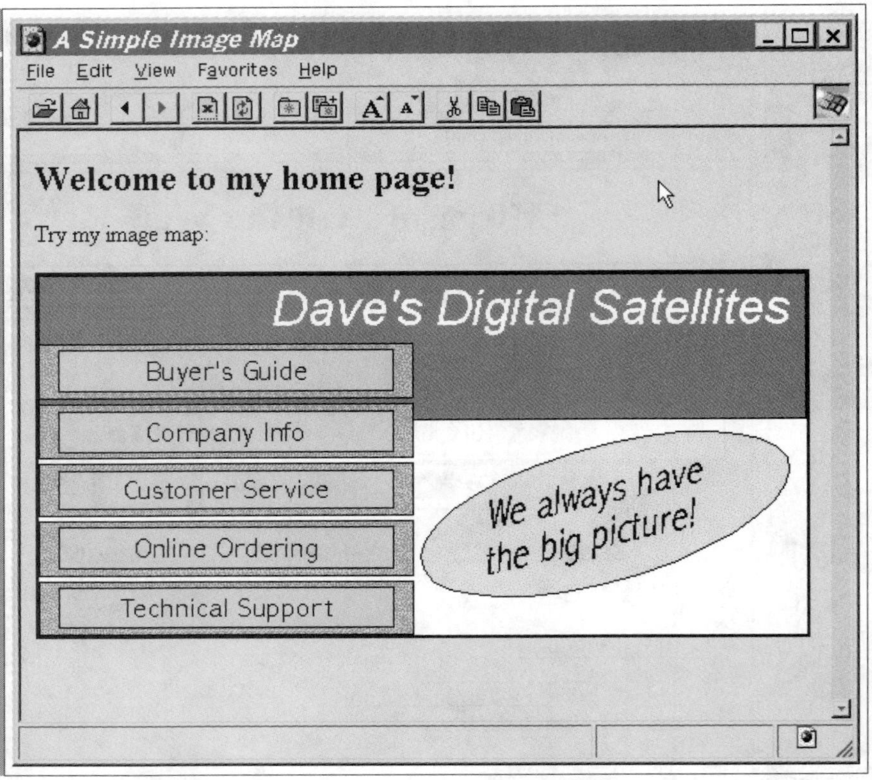

every server. Instead, we'll show you the specifics of working with two of the most popular servers—NCSA's httpd for Unix and O'Reilly & Associates' WebSite for Windows 95 and Windows NT. If you plan on using a server other than one of these, this section will still be of value to you because the procedures are the same; the implementation will just be slightly different. Your server's documentation will fill in the details.

Creating the GIF Image

Even though millions of picture files are available on the Net, you rarely see a public-domain graphic and think to yourself, "Gee, I could use that for a neat imagemap." Somehow, it just doesn't work that way. You may get many good ideas from seeing other imagemaps and looking at graphics, but none may be just right for you.

Besides, you may want to include the name of your company or organization on your imagemap or add some other kind of information. If this is the case, you'll have to create the image yourself. But this isn't hard to do. In fact, it's kind of fun.

The only rule you need to worry about is that your images ultimately need to be in GIF format. Some newer browsers can render JPEG image files inline, and others may in the future. To ensure compatibility with today's Web, however, you should save your images in GIF format. Just keep in mind that the images don't have to start out that way.

For example, we created the image for the imagemap in Figure 18-5 with CorelDRAW! for Windows. CorelDRAW! saves the files you create with it in a proprietary format, but you can easily export your drawings to other formats, including GIF. This image is simple: It's made up of overlapping rectangles with some text on them and an ellipse, which we rotated slightly. But you're not limited to anything so simple. If you like, you can even scan a photograph and then annotate or otherwise adorn it to your heart's content.

The tools for creating and editing images are plentiful; if you don't have one, just take a tour of your local software store. They'll be loaded with graphics software that will do the trick.

If you use X Window under Unix, you probably won't find any graphics packages at the software store, but you don't need to. A great shareware program for X Window called *XV*, written by John Bradley, is available at ftp://ftp.cis.upenn.edu/pub/xv/. With XV, you can create graphics, annotate them, clip and crop them, and manipulate them in a wide variety of other ways. You can also save your images directly in GIF format.

Creating the Imagemap

Once you've got the GIF image for your imagemap, you're ready to proceed to the next step—mapping the image. In the old days, you had to load your GIF image into a graphics program that could display coordinates for the pointer as you moved it over your image. Your task was to painstakingly record the coordinates for each square, rectangle, circle, ellipse, and so on that you wanted to be a hot-spot in the image. You had to write down these coordinates, then load an editor and manually create the map file in your Web server's format.

While map files still have to be in the proper format for your Web server, much better tools exist for both mapping the hot-spot coordinates and creating the map file. With the best of these tools, you can choose between several of the most popular Web server formats when you save the map file. The program then creates the proper map file for your server.

Although you may not ever have to look at the content of your map file, Figure 18-6 shows you what one looks like. The first line (that doesn't begin with a "#$") sets up the default URL for the imagemap. Your server sends the file at this URL to readers when they click on any spot on your imagemap that you haven't otherwise set up as a hot-spot. The subsequent lines define each of the hot-spots in the image. The syntax is

```
shape URL coordinates
```

FIGURE 18-6.

The map file for the imagemap in Figure 18-7

```
#$MTIMFH
#$-:Image Map file created by Map THIS!
#$-:Map THIS! free image map editor by Todd C. Wilson
#$-:Please do not edit lines starting with "#$"
#$VERSION:1.00.5
#$TITLE:Dave's Digital Satellites
#$DESCRIPTION:Introductory Image Map
#$AUTHOR:Rick Stout
#$DATE:Sun Jul 16 18:29:01 1995
#$PATH:C:\ImageMaps\
#$GIF:Daves.GIF
#$FORMAT:NCSA
#$EOH
default http://www.rls.com/Imaps/default.html
# Buyer's Guide
rect http://www.rls.com/Imaps/buyersguide.html 12,51 236,79
# Company Info
rect http://www.rls.com/Imaps/coinfo.html 12,93 236,122
# Customer Service
rect http://www.rls.com/Imaps/custserv.html 14,134 236,163
# Online Ordering
rect http://www.rls.com/Imaps/ordering.html 14,175 236,203
# Technical Support
rect http://www.rls.com/Imaps/techsupp.html 14,216 236,245
# Big Picture
poly http://www.rls.com/Imaps/bigscreen.html  337,130  397,110  468,109
498,126 488,157
```

Map *THIS!*

Map *THIS!* is a free program for Windows written by Todd Wilson. It's an excellent tool for creating imagemaps for either the NCSA or CERN Web server. However, you do need Windows 95, Windows NT, or the Win32s upgrade for Windows 3.1 because Map *THIS!* is a 32-bit program. (Win32s is a free package from Microsoft that allows Windows 3.1 systems to run some 32-bit software.)

To create an imagemap, you open your GIF image in the Map *THIS!* program, draw boxes and circles around your hot-spots, and choose the NCSA or CERN format. When you "save" your file in Map *THIS!*, it creates the map file for your server.

Figure 18-7 shows Map *THIS!* with an image in its program window. From the toolbar, choose the rectangle, circle, oval, or polygon tool you need to define a particular hot-spot, then stretch it around the desired area on the image. While you work, you can keep the area list (also shown in the figure) open. Map *THIS!* uses the area list as a record of each area you've selected on the graphic. After you define an area (or have defined them all), you can edit each entry in the area list to provide a URL for it and an internal comment that Map *THIS!* will build into the map file.

When you're done defining areas and assigning them URLs, choose File¦Save from the menu bar. Map *THIS!* will prompt you for more information, including a title, an author, a default URL for areas not covered in your selections, a description of the image, and your choice of the NCSA or CERN format. After you've filled in this

FIGURE 18-7.

Map THIS!, *an imagemap program for Microsoft Windows (with visible area map)*

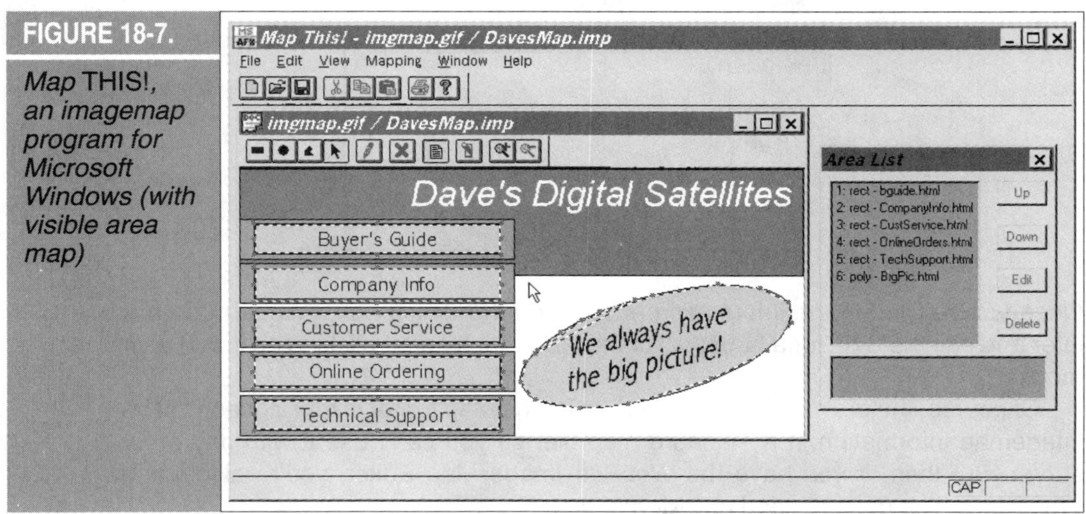

information, Map *THIS!* prompts you for a file name and creates your imagemap map file in the specified format. Map *THIS!* builds the title, author, and commentary information you entered into comment lines at the top of the map file.

You can find Map *THIS!* at http://galadriel.ecaetc.ohio-state.edu/tc/mt.

WebSite Image Map Editor

The WebSite Image Map Editor is part of WebSite, a commercial product from O'Reilly & Associates. WebSite is slightly unusual in that it doesn't use a typical map file. In fact, WebSite doesn't store your imagemap information in any kind of file at all. Instead, it stores the information as *registry keys*. You don't need to understand what that means; just don't go looking for a map file on your file system, because you won't find one.

Like Map *THIS!*, the WebSite Image Map Editor is simple to use. It really only requires that you open your GIF image, mark the hot-spots in it, and assign URLs and descriptive comments. As you can see in Figure 18-8, it even looks similar to the program window of Map *THIS!* (how different can two programs look if they have virtually the same features and functions?).

With the WebSite editor, immediately after you create a new imagemap by selecting a GIF file, the editor prompts you for a default URL and a comment relating to the whole imagemap. After you define each hot-spot, a dialog box pops up prompting you for the target URL and a comment for that hot-spot:

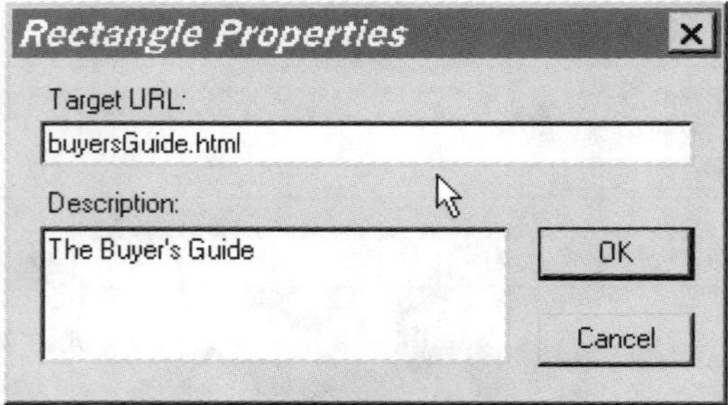

Once you've filled in the information and closed the dialog box, you can go back later and edit the URL for a hot-spot (or background) by right-clicking on it with your mouse.

Of course, the drawback to the WebSite Image Map Editor is that it doesn't save imagemap information in a standard map file, so you can't use it with any other server. But then, if you have the WebSite Image Map Editor, you're also using WebSite, which doesn't need an external map file.

FIGURE 18-8. *WebSite's Image Map Editor*

Other Imagemap Tools

Although we looked only at Map *THIS!* and the WebSite Image Map Editor in detail, you certainly have other options—other Windows programs, Mac programs, and even X Window programs can also be used to create map files. The functions of these programs are all pretty much the same, so the techniques for using them are quite similar.

The important thing to look for is a tool that you enjoy using and that produces map files for your server. Table 18-4 shows a few more options for imagemap tools, and by the time you read this, additional tools will have cropped up. Check the current World Wide Web FAQ and the Yahoo directory for the latest lists of imagemap tools.

Implementing Your Imagemap

At this point, two of the three steps for producing a working imagemap are behind you: You've created your GIF image and mapped it out. Now all that remains is to integrate it into your web.

TABLE 18-4. *A Few of the Available Imagemapping Tools*

NAME	PLATFORM	LOCATION / INFORMATION
glorglox	Unix	http://www.uunet.ca/~tomr/glorglox/
MacMapMaker	Mac	ftp://ftp.uwtc.washington.edu/pub/Mac/Network/WWW/MacMapMaker*
Map THIS!	Win32	http://galadriel.ecaetc.ohio-state.edu/tc/mt
Mapedit	Windows X Window	http://sunsite.unc.edu/boutell/mapedit/mapedit.html
MapMaker	X Window	http://icg.stwing.upenn.edu/~mengwong/mapmaker.html
WebMap	Mac	http://arpp1.carleton.ca/machttp/doc/util/map/webmap.html

Implementing an Imagemap with the NCSA Server

One of the programs that comes with the NCSA httpd package is *imagemap*, in the directory */usr/local/etc/httpd/cgi-bin*. As you might have guessed, it's a CGI script—actually, a binary program written in C (the source code should be in */usr/local/etc/httpd/cgi-src*)—but it's a gateway program like those you saw in Chapter 13.

All you have to do is create a link to the imagemap program in the HTML document that will contain your imagemap. In the HTML code for your document, you have to pass the server three pieces of information:

- A reference to the imagemap program
- The path to the map file
- The path to the GIF image to display

Here's how it works: You create an anchor that references the imagemap program and passes it the location of the map file. The hot-spot for the anchor (what's between the <A> and </A> tags) is an <IMG> tag that references your GIF file. You need to use the ISMAP attribute with the <IMG> tag to let the server know you're referencing an imagemap. For example:

```
<A HREF="http://www.rls.com/cgi-bin/imagemap/imaps/homemap.map">
<IMG SRC="/imaps/homemap.gif" ISMAP>
</A>
```

Before you get too perplexed, let us explain the slightly strange thing about this code. The HREF parameter in the <A> tag looks like it references a file named */cgi-bin/imagemap/imaps/homemap.map*, but it doesn't. Actually, it references the gateway program (*/cgi-bin/imagemap*) and passes it the string "/imaps/ homemap.map" as an argument. It looks odd, but that's the way it works.

Of course, the paths */cgi-bin/imagemap* and */imaps/homemap.map* are relative to the Web server's root directory—not to the root directory of the disk. And the <IMG> tag does need the ISMAP attribute. Also, since the HTML code you write to implement an imagemap on your own system will likely be on the same system, you may be able to get away with relative references rather than absolute ones that include the full system name. You'll have to experiment a little with this yourself.

That's all there is to it!

Implementing an Imagemap with WebSite

If you thought implementing an imagemap couldn't get any simpler than with the NCSA server, hold on. Although the WebSite server doesn't create an imagemap file on your hard disk, you still assign your imagemap a name. Since WebSite stores imagemaps internally, it already knows about all the imagemaps you defined for your server; all you have to do is reference them in your HTML page. For example, let's say you name your imagemap *HomeMap* and the associated GIF file *HomeMap.GIF*. Let's also say you place *HomeMap.GIF* in the server's */wsdocs/ IMAGES* directory.

In the WebView program, you can simply double-click the icon for the page in which you want to place the imagemap. This displays the Notepad editor and places the HTML source code for that page in the editor. At the point where you want your imagemap to appear, you simply type in the following lines:

```
<a href="/~imagemap/HomeMap">
<img src="/wsdocs/IMAGES/HomeMap.GIF" ISMAP>
</a>
```

Finally, save the file and fire up your favorite Web browser to test it out.

Gathering Statistics for Your Web

All the Web servers you're likely to consider using maintain a set of log files that typically includes:

- An access log
- An agent log
- An error log

The server logs every access in the *access log*. You saw the format for the access log earlier in this chapter—it contains the requesting system's name or IP number, the date and time, the path and name of the document requested, the resulting success or failure code, and the number of bytes transferred.

Proposals are in the works for new features that would allow Web browsers and Web servers to identify the number of pages an individual reader hit in a session. Right now, usage statistics are driven by the number of page hits, so there's no way to distinguish between a single reader hitting five different pages and five users hitting the same page.

With better information about which pages users read, Web administrators will be better able to track the effectiveness of their webs. This is important for several reasons. For one, they'll be able to see the paths readers follow through the links on their Web sites. This will make it obvious which pages are accessed often and which are routinely missed. In addition, advertisers paying for Web space want to know how many readers are seeing their ads, not just the number of times each page was hit (by an unknown number of readers).

The *agent log* contains the name and version of the contacting agent (usually a Web browser). Web administrators can use the agent log to see which browsers readers are using to view their pages. Figure 18-9 shows a portion of an agent log from the NCSA server.

The server records any errors that occur in the *error log*. Errors include requests for pages that don't exist, requests for pages for which permissions are inadequate, attempts to run CGI scripts that don't exist, and user authentication errors. The error log includes the date and time, the host and domain name of the requesting system, the nature of the error, and the reason for the error.

Because these Web server log files are in a common format, anybody can write programs to analyze them. If a program works for one server that uses the common

FIGURE 18-9. *NCSA's agent log*

```
Mozilla/1.1N (Windows; I; 16bit)
EIT-WebView-Browser/1.0
Mozilla/1.2b3 (Windows; I; 32bit)
EIT-WebView-Browser/1.0
Mozilla/1.1N (Windows; I; 16bit)
Mozilla/1.2b3 (Windows; I; 32bit)
Mozilla/1.1N (Windows; I; 32bit)
NCSA Mosaic/2.0.0b4 (Windows x86)
Enhanced_Mosaic/2.00 Win32 Spyglass/9
NCSA Mosaic/2.0.0b4 (Windows x86)
EI*Net/0.1  libwww/0.1
Mozilla/1.2b3 (Windows; I; 32bit)
EI*Net/0.1  libwww/0.1
NCSA Mosaic/2.0.0b4 (Windows x86)
NCSA Mosaic/2.0.0b4 (Windows x86)
EI*Net/0.1  libwww/0.1
Mozilla/1.2b3 (Windows; I; 32bit)
NCSA Mosaic/2.0.0b4 (Windows x86)
Mozilla/1.1N (Windows; I; 16bit)
Mozilla/1.1N (X11; I; BSD/386)
```

log file format, it should work for every server that does. As a result, many people are developing programs to analyze log files and provide useful statistical reports and charts.

One of the most exciting of these programs is called *VB Stats*. VB Stats is a Visual Basic program that runs under Windows and operates on any log files in the common log file format. It takes the server's access log and imports it into a Microsoft Access database. Running one of the programs included with VB Stats produces reports of usage statistics in the form of a collection of linked Web pages (HTML documents), complete with inline 3-D graphs and links to other pages containing detailed graphs and stats by week.

Figure 18-10 shows the root Web page produced by VB Stats, depicting total accesses of the server by week. By following the links to the weekly analyses, you can get information on the top 10 sites accessing your web, the top 10 objects of interest on your web, and the top 10 sites by total bytes transferred (Figure 18-11).

FIGURE 18-10. *Web page produced by VB Stats*

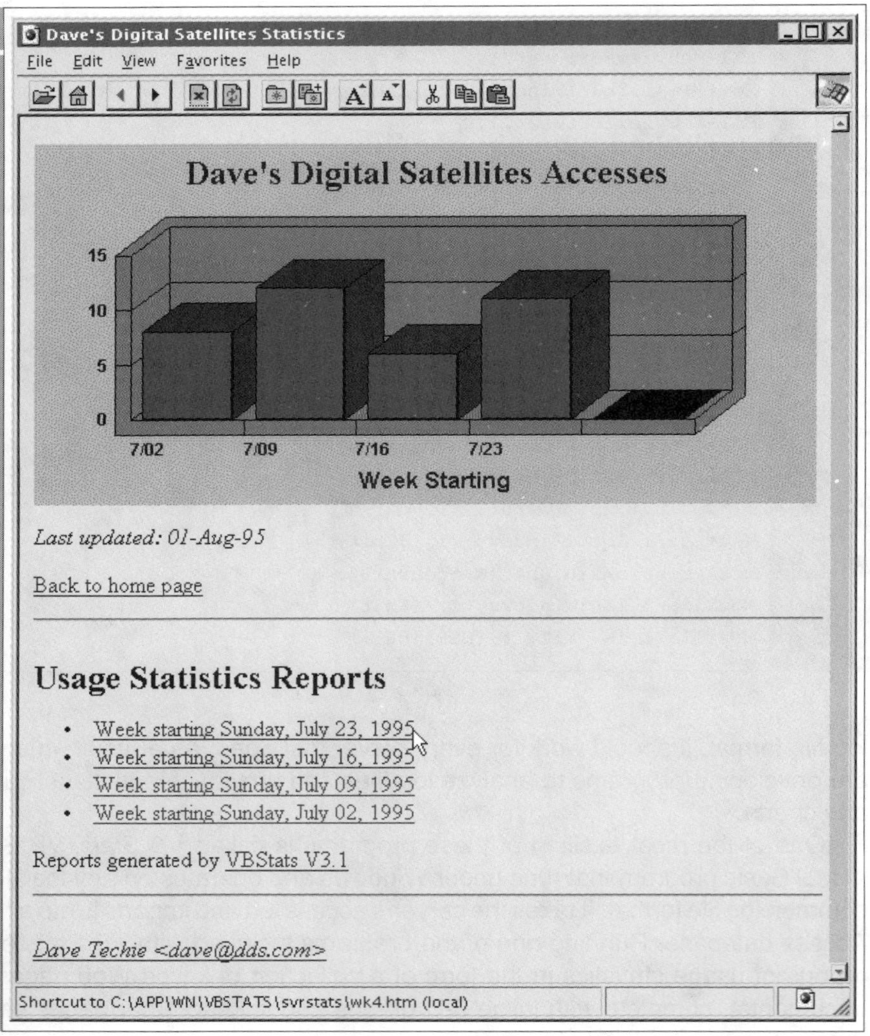

Dave's Digital Satellites Statistics
File Edit View Favorites Help

Dave's Digital Satellites Accesses

15
10
5
0
7/02 7/09 7/16 7/23
Week Starting

Last updated: 01-Aug-95

Back to home page

Usage Statistics Reports

- Week starting Sunday, July 23, 1995
- Week starting Sunday, July 16, 1995
- Week starting Sunday, July 09, 1995
- Week starting Sunday, July 02, 1995

Reports generated by VBStats V3.1

Dave Techie <dave@dds.com>

Shortcut to C:\APP\WN\VBSTATS\svrstats\wk4.htm (local)

You can schedule VB Stats to run automatically with the Windows scheduler, or you can connect it to a Web page and run it as a CGI program so the stats can be updated remotely. You can also just run it by hand periodically when you want to update your statistics pages.

Since VB Stats is a Windows program, it integrates very easily with Windows-based servers. (We tested it with WebSite under Windows 95.) But VB

FIGURE 18-11. *VB Stats' weekly analysis page*

Server Statistics

File Edit View Favorites Help

Dave's Digital Satellites Accesses

15
10
5
0
7/02 7/03 7/04 7/05 7/06 7/07 7/08
Daily Totals

Return to Report Index

Period Totals:

- Accesses: 45
- Data Volume: 57 KB
- Index Queries: 0
- **By method:**
  - GET: 45

Top 10 Objects by Access count:

- /: 13
- /wsdocs/images/wizards.gif: 10
- /wsdocs/images/webview.gif: 10
- /wsdocs/images/website.gif: 10
- /wsdocs/readme.html: 2

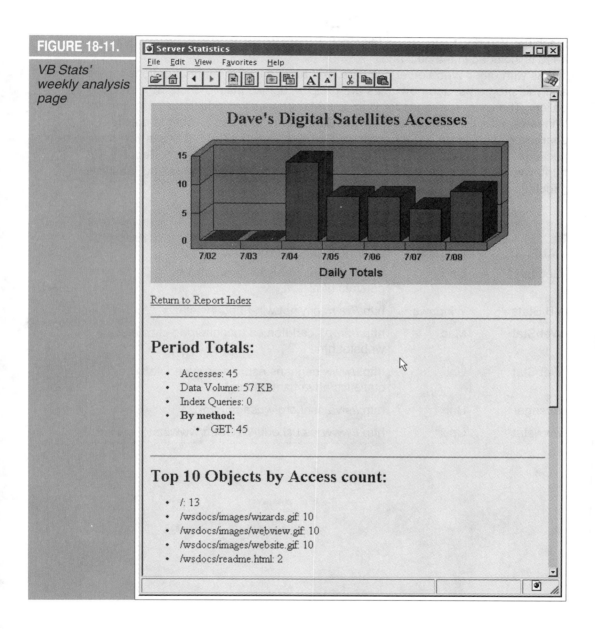

Stats doesn't care what server created the access logs it uses (as long as they're in the common log format). If your main Web server runs on a Unix machine, you can still use VB Stats to create your usage reports; all you need is one Windows machine. You don't even need Microsoft Access or Visual Basic—everything you need is included in the package.

As with other Web server software, you have a broad range of options for log analysis programs, and new ones are popping up like plastic ducks in a shooting gallery. There are packages for Unix and Macs as well as additional programs for Windows. Like every other tool for the Web, many of these packages are free or shareware, and all are easily accessible on the Web. Table 18-5 lists a few more packages, but check the current Web FAQ and the Yahoo directory (at http://www.yahoo.com/Computers/World_Wide_Web/HTTP/Servers/Log_Analysis_Tools/).

TABLE 18-5. *A Few of the Available Log Analysis Tools*

NAME	PLATFORM	LOCATION / INFORMATION
Getstats	Unix	http://www.eit.com/software/getstats/getstats.html
VB Stats	Windows	http://www.city.net/win-httpd/#vbstat
WebStat	Mac	http://arpp1.carleton.ca/machttp/doc/util/stats/webstat.html
WebStat	Unix	http://www.pegasus.esprit.ec.org/people/sijben/statistics/advertisment.html
wusage	Unix	http://siva.cshl.org/wusage.html
wwwstat	Unix	http://www.ics.uci.edu/WebSoft/wwwstat/

Chapter 19

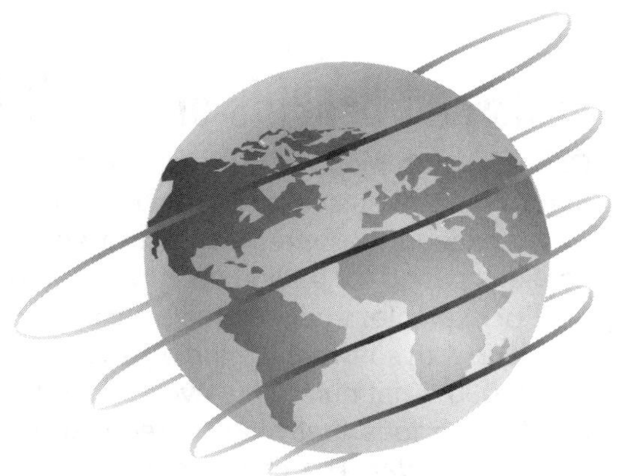

Doing Business on the Web

In Chapter 6, "Weaving a Better Web," you learned some techniques for creating an interesting and readable Web site. Here, in the final chapter, we'll focus more on the business considerations behind creating a Web site and on how to attract prospective customers and keep your current customer base happy and secure.

First, we'll look at the numbers—does it make financial sense to spend the money to create your own Web site and put it online? Then we'll go over some issues that any business owner or manager thinking about starting a company web should consider, regardless of the type of business or industry.

Finally, we'll look at computer- and Internet-related businesses on the Web—specifically Internet service providers, companies that offer Web services, and product fulfillment companies. These types of businesses are unique in that their products or services are tied directly to the Internet or the Web.

Costs and Benefits of Establishing a Web Presence

Consider for a moment the cost of creating and placing a full-page ad in a national magazine. Advertising in even a relatively obscure trade or industry magazine can easily exceed the one-time cost of setting up a permanent Web presence. The payback period for putting up a Web site is usually just a matter of months.

For example, a conservative estimate of what it would cost to set up a computer, load it up with software (including a Web server), and get it connected to the Internet is $10,000. That number is even inflated enough to cover consulting fees and any initial setup fees that may be required by your telephone company and Internet service provider. The cheapest full-page ad in the most obscure national industry publications is $2,000 per run. In more mainstream magazines, it's not uncommon to see ad space as high as $8,000 per issue.

It doesn't take an accountant to figure out that after a few months of an ad campaign, you will have spent as much on the print advertisement as you would have spent to set up a Web server. But the story doesn't end there. Both a print ad and a Web site will generate leads, but the Web site will continue to generate leads, promote awareness of your company and your products, and create goodwill among your customer base every single day.

Another benefit of running your own Web site is that by putting your product catalog online and offering interactive forms for people to order your products, you're actually getting your customers to do their own order entry. This can cut down on clerical errors dramatically, not to mention reducing work loads among your clerical staff.

Integrating a Web form (and the corresponding CGI program) with a database or accounting software isn't something you should take lightly. But neither is it difficult for someone with the right collection of skills. Such a project will require cooperation

between your Web administrator, network administrator or information systems people, and accounting personnel.

Of course, if you wear all those hats, you're probably inclined to do such an integration yourself; it really isn't that difficult on a small scale. For example, one of the premier Web servers for Windows 95—WebSite from O'Reilly & Associates—integrates very easily with one of the premier database management systems for Windows 95, Microsoft Access. (See Chapter 18 for more on WebSite.)

General Business Ideas for the Web

The Web is good for business in so many ways that it's impossible to list them all. In fact, comparing a professional presence on the Web to business necessities such as a telephone system and a fax machine may seem outrageous, but it isn't—and such comparisons will be common in the near future. But perhaps a better comparison today would be to contrast setting up your own Web site to attending trade shows and advertising in industry publications. Most managers and executives agree that advertising and marketing through trade shows and magazines is an absolute necessity if you want to stay abreast of your competitors.

Today, establishing a presence on the Internet—specifically the World Wide Web—is nearly as important as using these traditional marketing techniques. The audience you reach on the Web may be somewhat different from the one you reach through trade shows and magazine ads, but in many cases it might even be a more desirable one.

For example, let's say your company sells home health-care equipment. At trade shows, the majority of your audience consists of administrators from home health-care companies and hospitals. While these people are responsible for making purchasing decisions, they may not fully understand the benefits of your products. On the Web, however, you will likely attract doctors, home health nurses, and other people on the frontlines of the health-care field. These people will understand the benefits of your products and purchase the products directly, or at least make a pitch for them with the management of their organizations.

Most businesses can use the Web to their advantage in three ways:

- Business or institutional promotion
- Product or service promotion
- Technical and customer support services

Business promotion refers to presenting your company in the best possible light and showing how your business stands out from the competitors. *Institutional promotion*, on the other hand, refers to promoting your industry as a whole. For example, we've probably all seen TV commercials that promote milk, but not specifically the product of any one dairy or company.

Of course, *product and service promotion* refers to advertising your products or services. This type of promotion doesn't have to look like an advertisement. In fact, the best product promotion often *doesn't* look like an ad. Possible alternatives to traditional advertisements include endorsements, magazine review reprints, and a good stock of supporting (and easily available) documentation and specifications.

Businesses that provide technical support (such as manufacturers of equipment or computer software) can attract potential customers by making it obvious that they provide online support in addition to the traditional telephone support. If your business involves ongoing relationships with customers, giving them a way to monitor their own account activity or balance or even manage their account online will give them a sense of security and a feeling of control over the relationship.

The World Wide Web is the only medium today where a company can quickly, easily, and inexpensively combine all these promotional strategies into a single, elegant presentation that will be viewed by thousands—if not hundreds of thousands—of people in the course of a year. Moreover, if you combine a professional presentation with interactive forms, readers have a fast, easy way to respond to promotions. It used to be that one of the most effective ways to draw respondents was to place coupons in print ads that the reader could clip out. The Web is vastly more effective.

The following sections discuss techniques for gaining a competitive edge in each of the three areas mentioned earlier. We'll give you specific examples of how you can integrate these services into your Web site and show you examples of how some real companies have done that.

Business and Institutional Promotion

As we alluded earlier, a promotion doesn't have to *look* like a promotion. In fact, the less it looks like one, the more effective it's likely to be. In this section, we'll discuss some ideas for promoting your business, no matter how large or small it is.

The Company Overview

The best way to introduce your business to potential new customers is with a page that provides an overview of your company, your company's products, and your industry. Some people who happen across your web may never have heard of your company nor have any idea what products or services your company sells. When these people stumble onto your page, what they want first is this information.

Don't make the common mistake of putting up page after page of monotonous detail about every notable event that has ever happened in your industry or company. The best overviews are short and sweet. They should mention who you are, what you make or what services you provide, and why you believe your products or services are superior to those of your competitors. If you think more detail is needed, provide a link to them rather than making the overview read like a book. Figure 19-1 shows the "Information" page for a business called *Flower Stop*. This page gets right to the point: It tells the reader who the company is, what products it sells, and where it sells them.

FIGURE 19-1.

Company overview or information pages should be brief and to the point

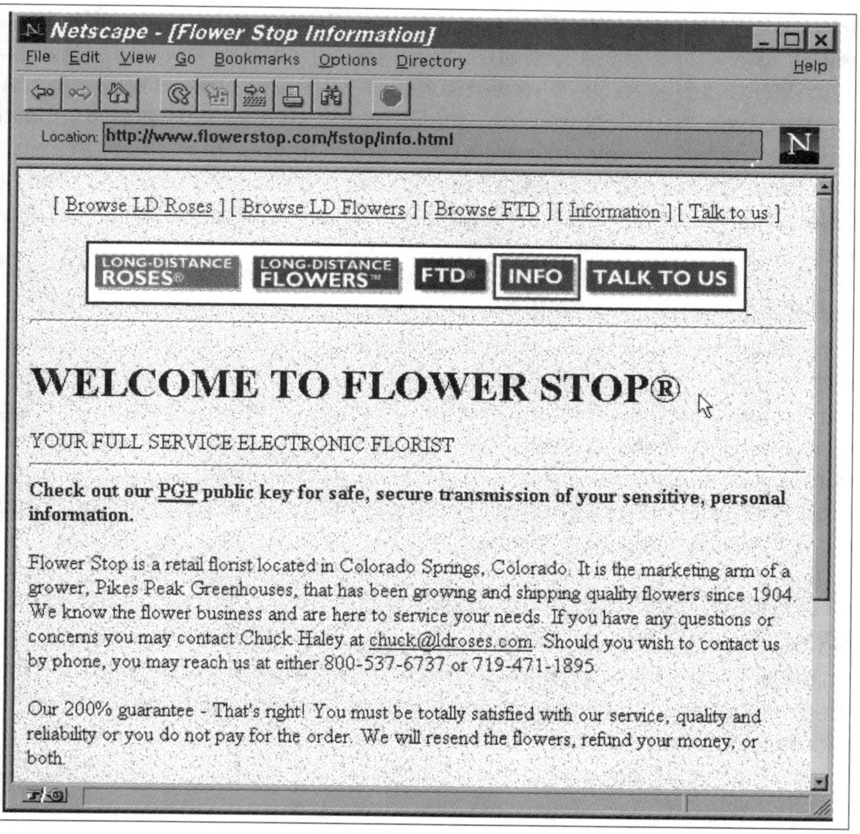

Netscape - [Flower Stop Information]

File Edit View Go Bookmarks Options Directory Help

Location: http://www.flowerstop.com/fstop/info.html

[Browse LD Roses] [Browse LD Flowers] [Browse FTD] [Information] [Talk to us]

LONG-DISTANCE ROSES® LONG-DISTANCE FLOWERS™ FTD® INFO TALK TO US

WELCOME TO FLOWER STOP®

YOUR FULL SERVICE ELECTRONIC FLORIST

Check out our PGP public key for safe, secure transmission of your sensitive, personal information.

Flower Stop is a retail florist located in Colorado Springs, Colorado. It is the marketing arm of a grower, Pikes Peak Greenhouses, that has been growing and shipping quality flowers since 1904. We know the flower business and are here to service your needs. If you have any questions or concerns you may contact Chuck Haley at chuck@ldroses.com. Should you wish to contact us by phone, you may reach us at either 800-537-6737 or 719-471-1895.

Our 200% guarantee - That's right! You must be totally satisfied with our service, quality and reliability or you do not pay for the order. We will resend the flowers, refund your money, or both.

Historical Information

A company background page is another nice touch. The history of your company can give potential customers a sense of the permanence and stability of your business as well as information about where you've come from and where you're headed. How elaborate you get with your history is a matter of preference. Figure 19-2 shows the history page for Boeing Aircraft Co. As you can see, it includes a photo of Boeing's founders taken in front of their first airplane, built in 1918.

Figure 19-3 shows another spin on the history page. Besides including a page on the history of the company and its founder, Hershey Chocolate Co. also provides a page with the history of chocolate.

Staff Information

Providing information about the staff and founders of your company is a great way to make potential customers feel as though they know you. An effective way to do this is to create a page with links to pages for each of your employees and staff. Each page can read like a mini-resume and provide professional information such as education, technical training, qualifications, and awards and competitions. You can also include whatever personal information your staff members are willing to announce to the world. Hobbies and interests make for enjoyable reading and will help readers see your staff as real people. See Chapter 3 for some examples of employee pages.

Other Company Information

If your business has been recognized in trade magazines or journals, create a page with reprints of the relevant articles. A review by a neutral (and sometimes critical) third party adds to your credibility and can go a long way toward establishing a foundation of trust. Also, if your business has entered and shown well in competitions—especially if it has won any awards—don't be too shy to boast a little. Figure 19-4 shows a page from a small graphics and design company listing awards it's won and articles it's published.

Product or Service Promotion

No medium is better suited to putting products before a large audience than an online catalog. Once you get your readers to the catalog, however, you have to give them all the information they need to make a purchase decision. Product and service promotion should include:

- Product information
- Product pricing
- Online ordering information

FIGURE 19-2.

The history page for Boeing Aircraft Co. includes photos of the founders and the original factory and headquarters

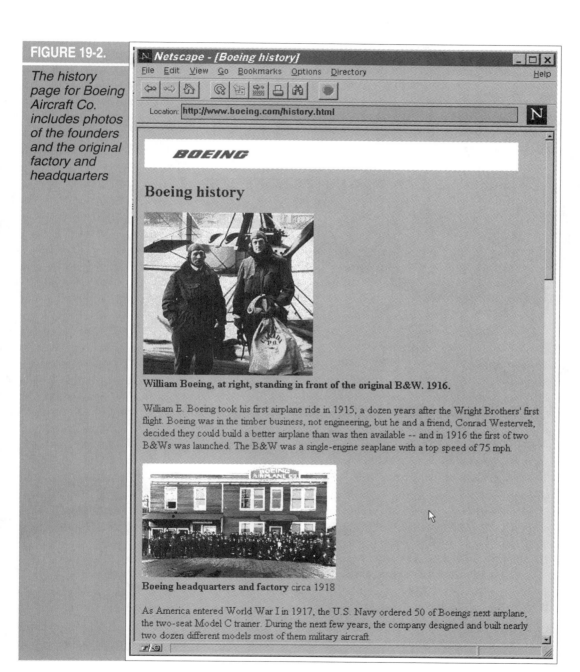

Netscape - [Boeing history]

File Edit View Go Bookmarks Options Directory Help

Location: http://www.boeing.com/history.html

BOEING

Boeing history

William Boeing, at right, standing in front of the original B&W. 1916.

William E. Boeing took his first airplane ride in 1915, a dozen years after the Wright Brothers' first flight. Boeing was in the timber business, not engineering, but he and a friend, Conrad Westervelt, decided they could build a better airplane than was then available -- and in 1916 the first of two B&Ws was launched. The B&W was a single-engine seaplane with a top speed of 75 mph.

Boeing headquarters and factory circa 1918

As America entered World War I in 1917, the U.S. Navy ordered 50 of Boeings next airplane, the two-seat Model C trainer. During the next few years, the company designed and built nearly two dozen different models most of them military aircraft.

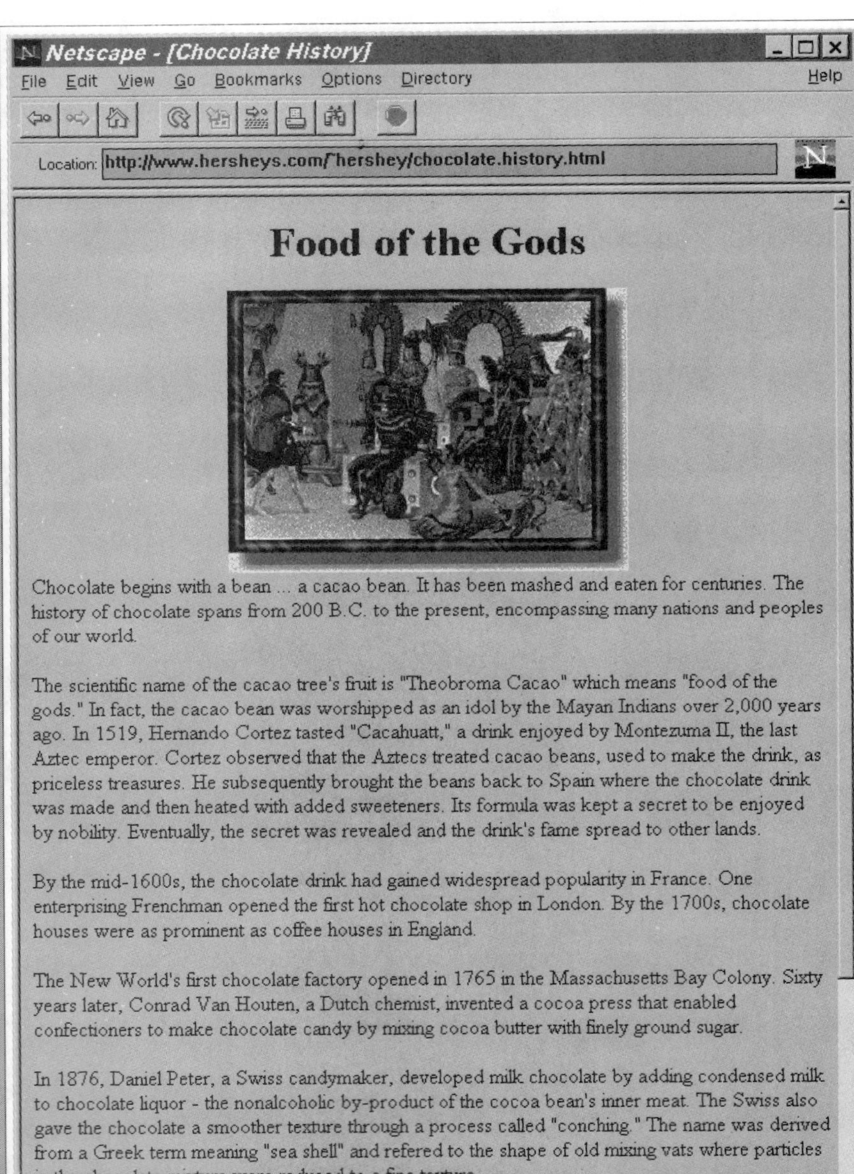

Netscape - [Chocolate History]
File Edit View Go Bookmarks Options Directory Help
Location: http://www.hersheys.com/~hershey/chocolate.history.html
Food of the Gods
Chocolate begins with a bean ... a cacao bean. It has been mashed and eaten for centuries. The history of chocolate spans from 200 B.C. to the present, encompassing many nations and peoples of our world.
The scientific name of the cacao tree's fruit is "Theobroma Cacao" which means "food of the gods." In fact, the cacao bean was worshipped as an idol by the Mayan Indians over 2,000 years ago. In 1519, Hernando Cortez tasted "Cacahuatt," a drink enjoyed by Montezuma II, the last Aztec emperor. Cortez observed that the Aztecs treated cacao beans, used to make the drink, as priceless treasures. He subsequently brought the beans back to Spain where the chocolate drink was made and then heated with added sweeteners. Its formula was kept a secret to be enjoyed by nobility. Eventually, the secret was revealed and the drink's fame spread to other lands.
By the mid-1600s, the chocolate drink had gained widespread popularity in France. One enterprising Frenchman opened the first hot chocolate shop in London. By the 1700s, chocolate houses were as prominent as coffee houses in England.
The New World's first chocolate factory opened in 1765 in the Massachusetts Bay Colony. Sixty years later, Conrad Van Houten, a Dutch chemist, invented a cocoa press that enabled confectioners to make chocolate candy by mixing cocoa butter with finely ground sugar.
In 1876, Daniel Peter, a Swiss candymaker, developed milk chocolate by adding condensed milk to chocolate liquor - the nonalcoholic by-product of the cocoa bean's inner meat. The Swiss also gave the chocolate a smoother texture through a process called "conching." The name was derived from a Greek term meaning "sea shell" and refered to the shape of old mixing vats where particles in the chocolate mixture were reduced to a fine texture.

FIGURE 19-3. *Hershey's history page describes the evolution of chocolate from ancient times*

FIGURE 19-4.

Awards and publications make great decorations for a company Web site

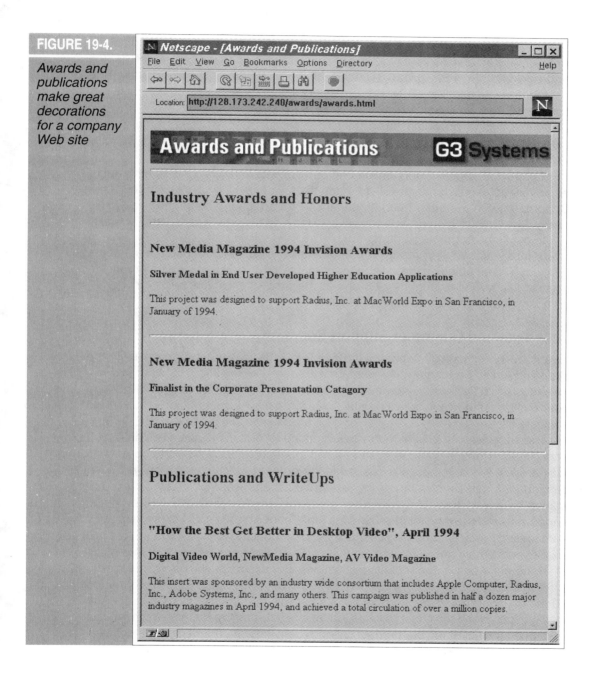

Netscape - [Awards and Publications]

File Edit View Go Bookmarks Options Directory Help

Location: http://128.173.242.240/awards/awards.html

Awards and Publications G3 Systems

Industry Awards and Honors

New Media Magazine 1994 Invision Awards

Silver Medal in End User Developed Higher Education Applications

This project was designed to support Radius, Inc. at MacWorld Expo in San Francisco, in January of 1994.

New Media Magazine 1994 Invision Awards

Finalist in the Corporate Presenatation Catagory

This project was designed to support Radius, Inc. at MacWorld Expo in San Francisco, in January of 1994.

Publications and WriteUps

"How the Best Get Better in Desktop Video", April 1994

Digital Video World, NewMedia Magazine, AV Video Magazine

This insert was sponsored by an industry wide consortium that includes Apple Computer, Radius, Inc., Adobe Systems, Inc., and many others. This campaign was published in half a dozen major industry magazines in April 1994, and achieved a total circulation of over a million copies.

Product information should normally include photographs of your products as well as written details, but you might want to consider placing a link to the photographs on your product information page rather than including the photographs themselves. This way, potential customers with slow connections can choose not to view the pictures.

In addition to providing basic prices for products or services, remember to mention any special pricing deals that may apply. Volume discounts and educational discounts can generate business you wouldn't otherwise get.

If you want to take orders online and don't expect your Web site to generate a large volume of sales, maybe all you need to provide is a link to a *mailto URL* (see Chapter 11). On the other hand, if you anticipate a higher volume than you could easily deal with using email, you can set up a form-based order system and integrate it with gateway programs (Chapter 13).

Before you lead your readers off into detailed product information, it may be a good idea (depending on the number of products you carry) to provide a product or product-line overview. Figure 19-5 shows the product overview page for a small company that manufactures and sells kites.

Technical and Customer Support Services

Nearly every technology company must deliver technical support services via the Web and email. Fortunately, if you integrate these services into your web, you can see substantial savings on phone bills. Furthermore, you'll promote goodwill among your customers because you'll be able to react to their inquiries more quickly and consistently.

The simplest way to offer tech support on the Web is to include a link on a Web page that customers can use to send email to a special tech support account. As mail arrives, it is automatically queued in the order in which it was received. Tech support staff can simply start at the top of the list and work their way down. That makes it easy to track the volume of email messages handled during a certain period, and you can monitor the size of the email queue as a simple way of estimating the time lag between receiving an inquiry and responding to it.

Beyond simply answering email, you can also use your web to alleviate much of the need for answering repetitive questions. For example, you can offer a link to a "Tech Support" page from your home page. That page can offer links to the top 10 tech support questions and other links to take readers directly to areas where they can download the latest patches, drivers, or information. You can even provide links that cross over to your product catalog area, where readers can get technical specifications or find out about prerequisite or alternative products (see Figure 19-6).

FIGURE 19-5.

Sky Vision Kites' product information page begins with a product overview, then offers detailed information on each kite

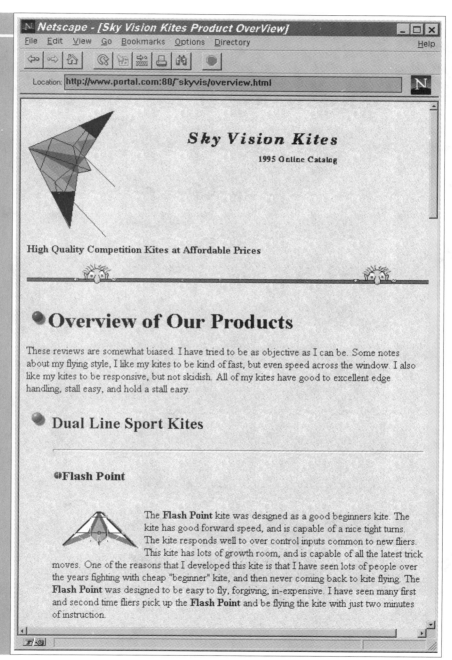

Netscape - [Sky Vision Kites Product OverView]

File Edit View Go Bookmarks Options Directory Help

Location: http://www.portal.com:80/~skyvis/overview.html

Sky Vision Kites

1995 Online Catalog

High Quality Competition Kites at Affordable Prices

Overview of Our Products

These reviews are somewhat biased. I have tried to be as objective as I can be. Some notes about my flying style, I like my kites to be kind of fast, but even speed across the window. I also like my kites to be responsive, but not skidish. All of my kites have good to excellent edge handling, stall easy, and hold a stall easy.

Dual Line Sport Kites

Flash Point

The **Flash Point** kite was designed as a good beginners kite. The kite has good forward speed, and is capable of a nice tight turns. The kite responds well to over control inputs common to new fliers. This kite has lots of growth room, and is capable of all the latest trick moves. One of the reasons that I developed this kite is that I have seen lots of people over the years fighting with cheap "beginner" kite, and then never coming back to kite flying. The **Flash Point** was designed to be easy to fly, forgiving, in-expensive. I have seen many first and second time fliers pick up the **Flash Point** and be flying the kite with just two minutes of instruction.

FIGURE 19-6.

The technical support page for a small software company

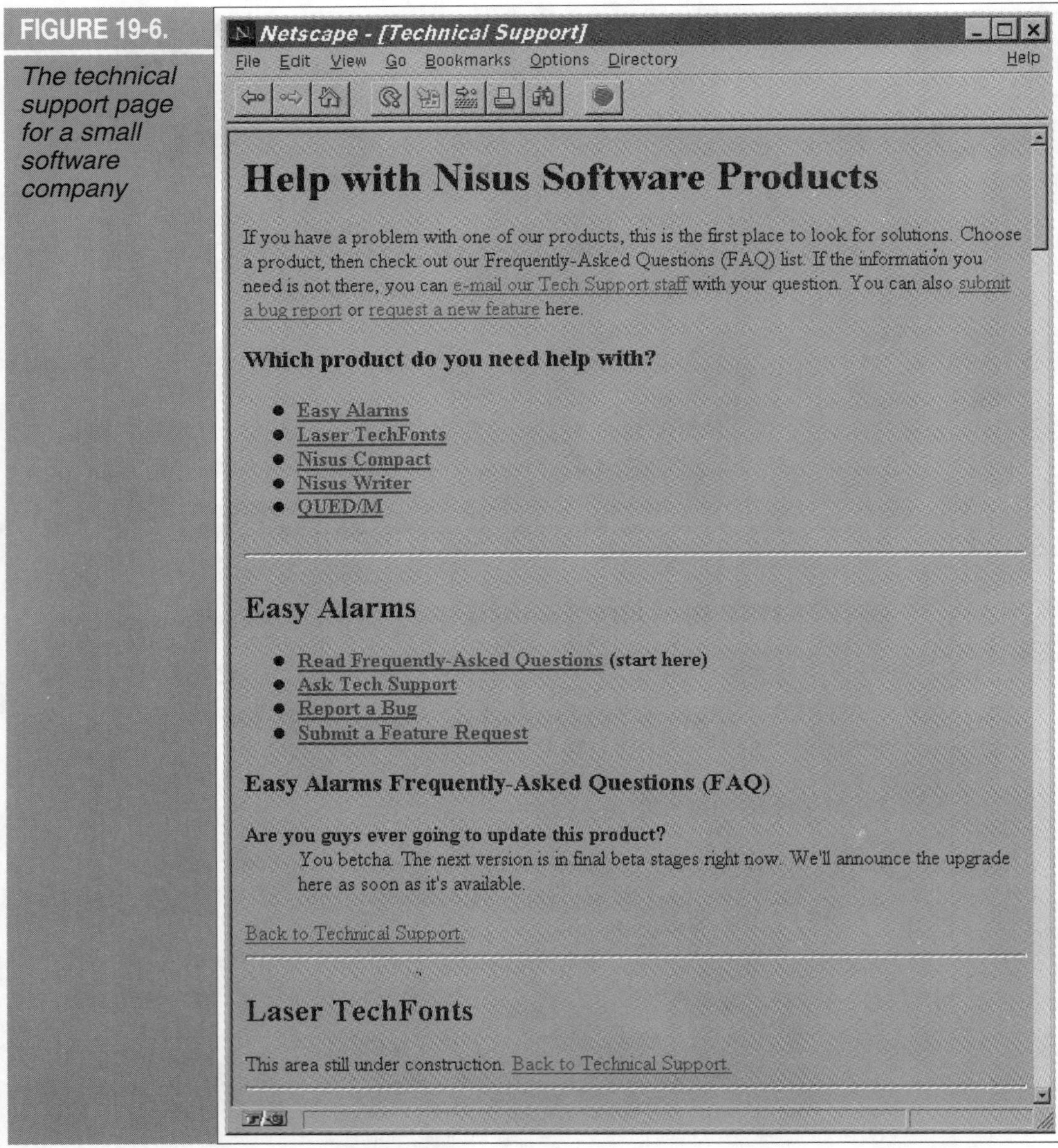

Customer support may be one of the next big areas to go online. Perhaps one reason online customer support isn't yet widespread is that people still have concerns about how to keep customer information secure and confidential. Given the recent strides toward secure HTML and the fact that other security measures will be coming out soon, customer support will likely occupy more Web real estate in the future.

Figure 19-7 shows the customer service page for a diamond company. As you can see, it offers links for forms, gift certificates, and company information and policies.

Services you can offer your customers include tracking their orders, checking the status and activity of their accounts, and checking shipment or availability dates. In the near future, your customers may even be allowed to make payments online. One company that's providing such online services today is Federal Express (see Figure 19-8). At the FedEx Web site, you can schedule pickups, track your shipments, and even check the status of your account.

Help Your Readers Find Their Way

In addition to the usual company and product information, you can add a number of enhancements to your pages to make readers feel welcome and give them the sense that their voices are heard by the company. A few suggestions:

- Provide a help button for people new to the Web. You don't have to provide detailed instructions on using Web browsers, but you might give some general guidance on how to get around on your web. Along with these tips, you might provide direct links to some of your company's most popular resources for people having difficulty finding their way around.
- Provide a link on your home page to a list of the most frequently asked questions about your business or industry (along with the answers, of course).
- Create an index page of your entire web and provide a link to it from your home page. An index can be simply an outline view of your Web pages, as shown in Figure 19-9. This happens to be the index of Microsoft's web, a fairly respectable Web site. It's up to you to decide how much detail you want in your index.
- Offer a "Top 10" page with links to the 10 most popular pages or resources on your web. This can be a real timesaver for people who know what they're looking for but don't know exactly where it is.

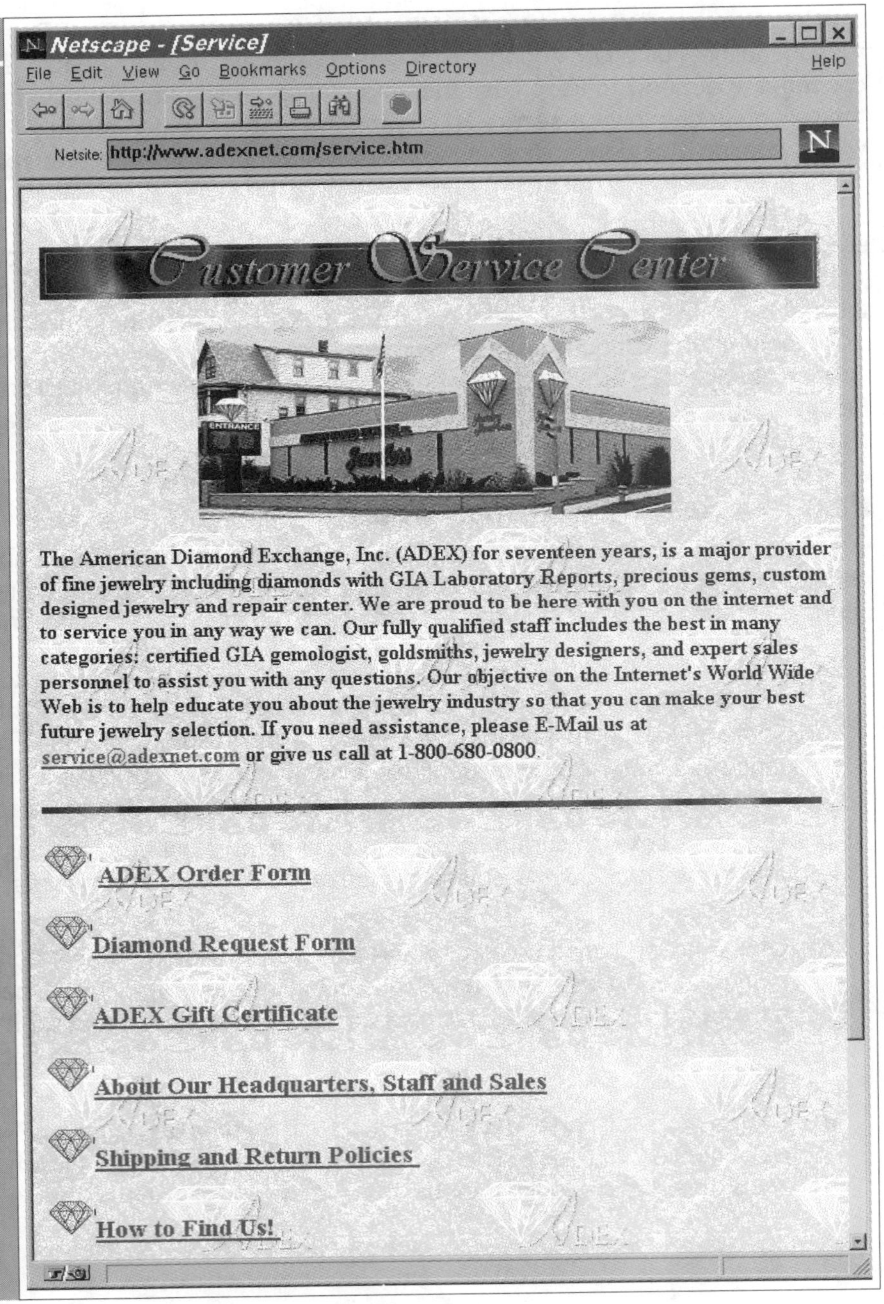

FIGURE 19-7. *The American Diamond Exchange provides an extensive customer service page*

Netscape - [Service]

File Edit View Go Bookmarks Options Directory Help

Netsite: http://www.adexnet.com/service.htm

Customer Service Center

The American Diamond Exchange, Inc. (ADEX) for seventeen years, is a major provider of fine jewelry including diamonds with GIA Laboratory Reports, precious gems, custom designed jewelry and repair center. We are proud to be here with you on the internet and to service you in any way we can. Our fully qualified staff includes the best in many categories: certified GIA gemologist, goldsmiths, jewelry designers, and expert sales personnel to assist you with any questions. Our objective on the Internet's World Wide Web is to help educate you about the jewelry industry so that you can make your best future jewelry selection. If you need assistance, please E-Mail us at service@adexnet.com or give us call at 1-800-680-0800.

ADEX Order Form

Diamond Request Form

ADEX Gift Certificate

About Our Headquarters, Staff and Sales

Shipping and Return Policies

How to Find Us!

FIGURE 19-8.

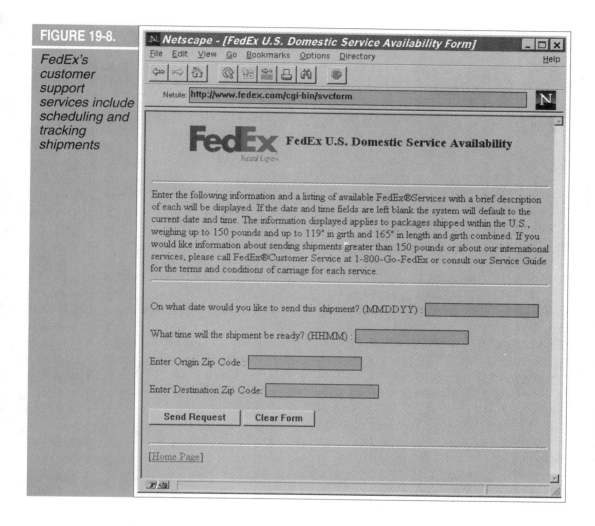

FedEx's customer support services include scheduling and tracking shipments

Netscape - [FedEx U.S. Domestic Service Availability Form]

File Edit View Go Bookmarks Options Directory Help

Netsite: http://www.fedex.com/cgi-bin/svcform

FedEx Federal Express

FedEx U.S. Domestic Service Availability

Enter the following information and a listing of available FedEx®Services with a brief description of each will be displayed. If the date and time fields are left blank the system will default to the current date and time. The information displayed applies to packages shipped within the U.S., weighing up to 150 pounds and up to 119" in girth and 165" in length and girth combined. If you would like information about sending shipments greater than 150 pounds or about our international services, please call FedEx®Customer Service at 1-800-Go-FedEx or consult our Service Guide for the terms and conditions of carriage for each service.

On what date would you like to send this shipment? (MMDDYY) :

What time will the shipment be ready? (HHMM) :

Enter Origin Zip Code :

Enter Destination Zip Code:

Send Request | Clear Form

[Home Page]

- Let readers provide feedback to the web manager on the design, mechanics, and aesthetics of the company's web as well as the products and services it offers.
- Let readers provide feedback to the company's management. An interesting way to set up such a service is to use a metaphor of a bygone era—the suggestion box.

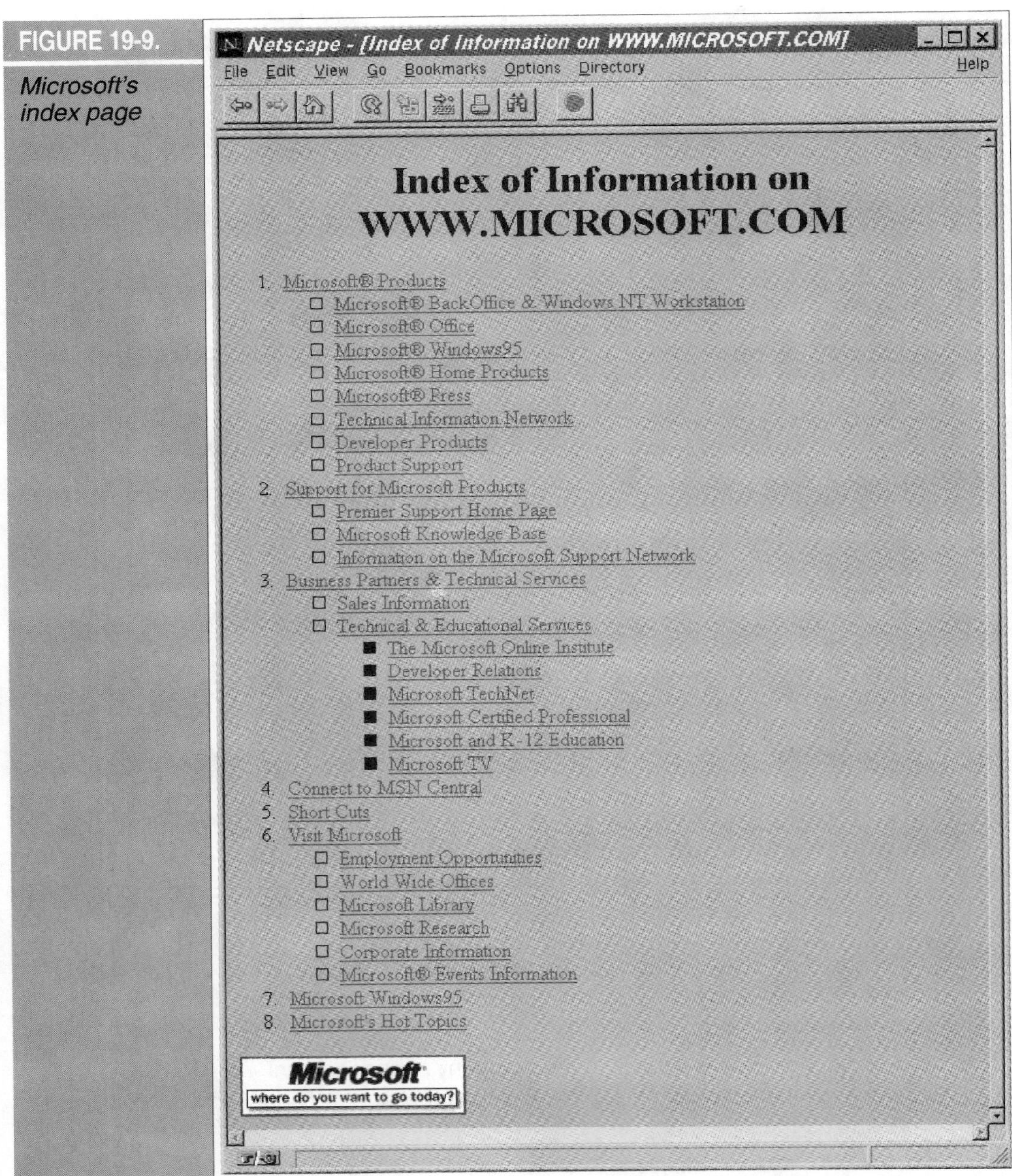

FIGURE 19-9. *Microsoft's index page*

Computer- and Internet-Related Businesses on the Web

A large number of the companies on the Web do business that's related to computers, software, networking, and the Internet—a much higher percentage, in fact, than in the business world in general. There are a number of reasons for this; one of the most obvious is that no self-respecting technology company would want to look as though it didn't have the technical know-how to be on the Internet and have a Web site.

Others are on the Internet because it *is* their business. For example, Internet service providers couldn't very well sell access to the Internet if they weren't themselves connected. Still other technology businesses are on the Internet for the same reasons as every other company—to increase their visibility, attract new customers, and serve existing customers.

In this section, we'll look at these technology companies and investigate some of the special problems they have and the services they offer.

Internet Service Providers

The rapidly rising demand for access to the Internet has unleashed a blizzard of startup businesses selling Internet access. For a while it seemed as though everyone with a computer on the Internet wanted to begin selling access to his or her computer. While this may sound positive because competition is usually desirable, many of the startups had neither the funding nor the technical knowledge to service their accounts, equipment, and software adequately. This resulted in poor service and a lot of frustrated new Internet users.

Thankfully, this rage has quieted down, and many of the smaller providers have pooled their resources and expertise with other providers. Today we have a handful of large, national Internet service providers (with more, such as AT&T, coming online) and a few dozen regional providers that service smaller areas, such as the San Francisco Bay Area or New England. But the vast majority of providers are local; they serve only a single city or perhaps an area the size of a county. Consequently, in most metropolitan areas there is still enough competition to keep rates low and services high.

At the bottom of the Internet provider chain are entrepreneurs with a single computer, some form of high-speed network connection, and a bank of modems connected to telephone lines. A year or two ago, it was feasible to start up a small business selling Internet access and work toward profitability. With a capital investment of less than $10,000, a small provider could expect to cover costs and even become profitable if it could attract enough users.

This really isn't the case anymore. The technical hurdles associated with becoming an Internet service provider aren't trivial. Not only do you need startup capital, but you also need a great deal of technical knowledge and experience. It's not easy to find people who are experienced with TCP/IP networking and Unix systems. In addition to these complications, Internet service providers may be required to pay an annual membership fee to an organization called the *Commercial Internet Exchange*, which routes commercial Internet traffic. Membership in CIX runs $10,000 per year.

World Wide Web Services

The World Wide Web brings a whole new collection of opportunities for the creative and the imaginative. Entrepreneurs have found a ready market in the mad rush to get onto the Web, and companies of all sizes are now providing services that include:

- Web page design and coding
- Photo imaging and digital photography
- Graphic illustrations
- Video sequence conversion
- Web page hosting
- Domain-name registration
- Online order or lead processing and forwarding

Figure 19-10 shows the home page of a small graphics company that does digital photography, imaging, multimedia integration, and Web page design.

Product Fulfillment Companies

An altogether new type of business is beginning to emerge on the Internet: a *product fulfillment company*, a sort of escrow company for information and data. These companies specialize in creating secure Web sites to handle financial transactions and product fulfillment. By specializing in this niche, they can deliver services at a much lower cost than other companies using traditional marketing and distribution methods.

Here's an example of how it might work: Let's say you have a small software development company. Rather than using the traditional distribution channels (which would require expensive packaging and marketing), you opt to market and sell your products directly to users through the Internet—through your Web site, to be specific. And to avoid the cost of putting together a package to compete on software store shelves—producing boxes, books, and diskettes, mastering and duplicating CD-ROMs, and so on—you decide to deliver your product electronically via the Internet.

FIGURE 19-10.

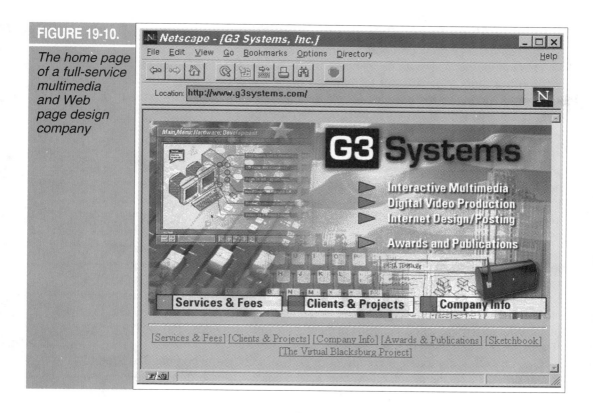

The home page of a full-service multimedia and Web page design company

So how do you accomplish this? You certainly can't make your products available anonymously, or before long you'll have no product to sell. Creating a secure area for each transaction would require direct action on your part for a sale to take place and would become onerous if you did a substantial business.

These are the kinds of problems product fulfillment companies handle for you. A small business like the one in our example would contract with a fulfillment company to accept and process payments—usually credit-card payments, because they can be processed automatically and almost immediately.

Once the fulfillment company has collected payment information and verified or authorized the transaction, it can automatically make a secure download area available to the buyer. Using special software, it can verify (and certify) that the product was delivered, to whom it was delivered, and when it was delivered.

The products you can sell through a fulfillment company aren't limited to software. Any business with a product that can be delivered electronically can use a fulfillment company to handle the complexities of secure financial transactions and secure delivery of the product. These products can include books, reports, any type of data or information, services (such as insurance), and such intangible products as Certificates of Deposit and pork-belly futures.

This industry is still in its fledgling state. As more and more small businesses entering the market decide not to fight the battle for shelf space, and as larger businesses recognize the benefits of delivering products immediately to the user at lower costs, this type of business will become more common.

Computer and Software Companies

Computer manufacturing companies and software developers are more at home on the Web than any other type of business. Since computers and software are what drive the Internet (in fact, the Internet wouldn't exist if it weren't for many of these companies), businesses in these industries must have a formidable presence on the Internet and the Web to be taken seriously.

Establishing a Web presence isn't just a fad; it's becoming a necessity for delivering services to customers and end users. Just a few years ago, many hardware and software companies felt compelled to operate in-house bulletin board systems with dialup phone lines for delivering the latest product news, technical information, drivers and utility software, and customer support. Today they can use the Internet as a more elegant means of delivering these services, and the corporate BBS is becoming a thing of the past.

Like any other company, a computer or software company can use the Web to deliver product specifications, quote prices, and solicit online ordering. Beyond the general benefits of using the Web, however, these companies have the added advantage that at least some of their products (or some parts of their products) can be delivered via the Internet.

For example, one of the biggest support issues for a hardware company is developing and updating software drivers and utilities for its hardware products. While drivers and utility programs aren't the main product of such a company, they are nevertheless very important for keeping the customer base happy and keeping the products working with new operating systems and other new hardware.

Using the Web, a hardware company can organize and document its drivers and utility programs in a much friendlier way than simply putting a README.TXT file in an FTP directory along with a bunch of other cryptic file names. You can see an example of this in Figure 19-11.

As you read in the section on product fulfillment, software companies can even choose to deliver their products directly to the end user. Shareware developers have done this for some time, but the concept is completely new to commercial software developers. Not many of them deliver their products that way now, but they probably will in the near future.

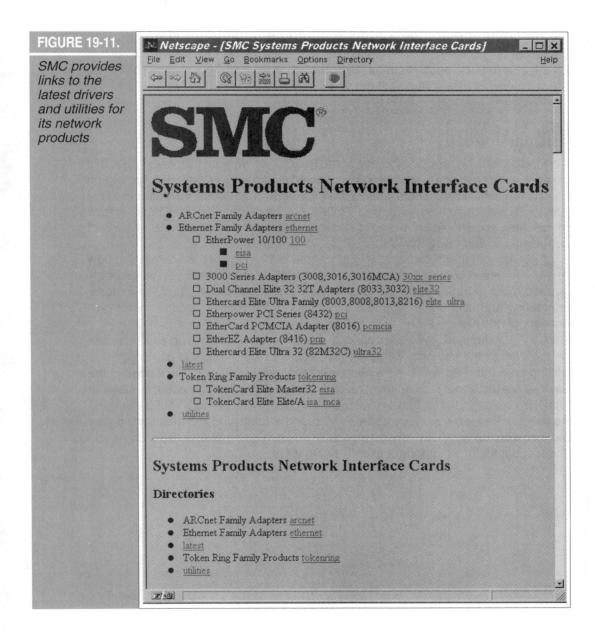

FIGURE 19-11. *SMC provides links to the latest drivers and utilities for its network products*

If you weren't previously aware of how much software is freely available on the Internet, just take a look at Appendix B and the software categories in the catalog at the back of the book. Many companies make their products available on their FTP servers and Web pages; some even provide the source code if you care to have it. By no means do the tables in Appendix B represent *all* the free software available on the Internet—no book could be large enough to list it all—but they will point you toward plenty of new software to get you started.

The Last Word

Congratulations on reaching the end of the book! If you've read all the text up to this point, you can consider yourself to be knowledgeable about both the Internet and the World Wide Web. There should now be light in all those dark corners that previously held the unknown for you. While there are always specific circumstances to consider, you should have a solid understanding of the most important basics of connecting to and using the Web.

If you bought this book because you wanted to learn about the Internet and how to get connected so you can begin surfing the World Wide Web, you've probably learned more than you cared to know initially. We hope you've found the material interesting and useful even if you don't intend to put your business or your own network on the Net.

On the other hand, if you were curious about the benefits of putting your business on the Web or the technical details of doing so, you were probably convinced that getting onto the Web would be a necessity long before you got to this point in the book. A final tip about putting your business on the Web: Don't be afraid to start out small. It's easier (and less expensive) to start modestly and build on your successes. As you now know, the money and time you spend establishing and maintaining your presence on the Web can vary dramatically. You can do as little or as much as you choose, but the most important thing is being there.

Catalog

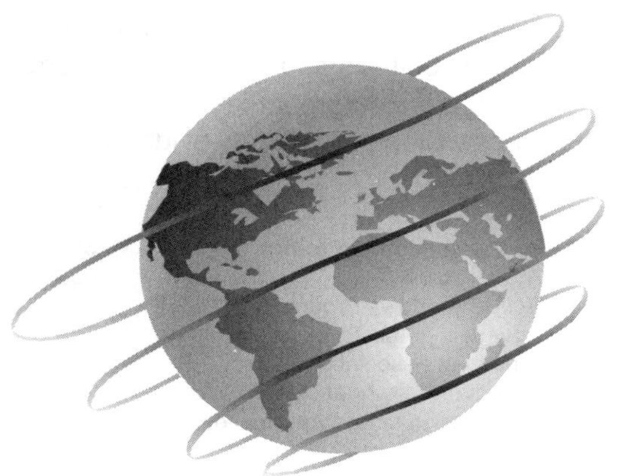

A Guide to Businesses on the Web

In the following pages is a catalog of nearly a thousand businesses that have established a presence on the World Wide Web, organized into 50 categories (the businesses are listed below by category). The businesses here represent dozens of industries and range from home-based businesses on up to some of the largest corporations in the world.

In addition to offering a home page, many of these businesses offer extensive information about themselves, sometimes including a company history and financial information. Most offer an online catalog of products and services, and some offer online ordering through their webs. The icons to the right of each company name indicate what each page offers—company information, product information, and/or online ordering—and a legend for the icons appears at the bottom of each right-hand page.

By no means does this catalog represent all, or even most, of the businesses on the Web; it's just the tip of the iceberg. It should, however, show you the breadth of the types of companies doing business on the Web and how they are doing business, along with plenty of ideas for putting your own business online if you aren't there already.

Advertising and Marketing

A.C. Nielsen

The company that records what you're watching on TV also offers insights into global markets and information about trends in marketing and market research.

Address: http://www.nielsen.com

Active Windows Productions

Active Windows Productions specializes in publishing and marketing. They also provide information about advertising and the media.

Address: http://www.actwin.com

Advertising Age

Advertising Age magazine provides marketing strategies, advertising tips, and daily news updates. They also feature and analyze big players in the fields of marketing and advertising.

Address: http://www.adage.com

American Association of Advertising Agencies

AAAA is an organization of advertising agencies. Membership benefits include access to advertising-related information sources, published management studies, consultation, group insurance, and retirement plans.

Address: http://www.commercepark.com/AAAA/AAAA.html

American Business Information

ABI offers marketing information on businesses in the U.S. and Canada. Their database includes press releases, business magazines, newsletters, annual reports, and newspapers.

Address: http://www.abii.com

Apollo Advertising

This service allows users to advertise free of charge. Apollo Advertising, one of the first advertisement catalogs on the Web, provides a system where you can find information, services, and products worldwide by hooking up.

Address: http://www.apollo.co.uk

Centor Freed 

This marketing agency, which compares itself to a fishbowl, displays advertising techniques used with other clients. Their goal is to provide users with information that will improve their businesses.

Address: http://www.rawfish.com

Data Systems Support  

DSS develops sales and marketing automation systems for enterprisewide sales and marketing operations. Their product addresses sales-force automation, lead generation, telemarketing, and telesales.

Address: http://www.dssny.com

dc Information Services 

This company provides information about Washington, D.C., including its tourist attractions, special events, hotels, and nightlife. Their goal is to promote the city, jumpstarting the tourism industry and stimulating the economy.

Address: http://www.dc202.com

e-Coupons 

Get lots of free stuff just by filling out some electronic forms at e-Coupons. e-Coupons offers free products by mail in return for your time answering several questionnaires. Products and questionnaires are arranged by category—national, local, college, and Internet business.

Address: http://www.e-coupons.com

Electronic Pen 

Electronic Pen provides interactive marketing, advertising, and design for the Internet. They also develop marketing campaigns and corporate identities for dozens of clients in a variety of fields.

Address: http://www.epen.com

EXPOguide   

EXPOguide provides access to trade show and conference information by title, location, and date. It also provides information about conference halls and show services to make your conference more successful.

Address: http://www.expoguide.com

Harpell/Martins

This page offers information about Harpell/Martins' advertising and marketing services, as well as the option to investigate three separate, independent client companies: SpeedSim, Inc., Nashoba Networks, Inc., and Raptor Systems, Inc.

Address: http://www.harpell.com

Hemisphere

Hemisphere Corp. gives readers business advice and allows them to communicate with one another on the Internet. This page is for people who want to talk business, with both fellow users and the experts at Hemisphere.

Address: http://www.hemisphere.com

Insight Marketing Alliance

Insight plans and administrates seminars, corporate meetings, training sessions, trade shows, and industry parties. They specialize in trade shows and pulling all the pieces together so that you don't have to worry about them.

Address: http://www.cykic.com/insight/insight.htm

Interactive Marketing Services

This company uses electronic technologies to help organizations market and sell their products and services. IMS also has its own online shopping network, as well as a mailing list for users.

Address: http://www.imsworld.com

Interactive Media Works

Interactive Media Works is a full-service interactive marketing agency that specializes in telephone, fax, and Internet-based marketing.

Address: http://www.imworks.com

International Marketing

The International Marketing Corp. seeks to assist companies in need of direction and connections. Their page offers a list of organizations worldwide that can lead smaller companies into the global marketplace.

Address: http://www.internationalmarket.com

Internet Business Pages

The Internet Business Pages gives companies the opportunity to advertise their products and services online. Businesses are categorized by city.

Address: http://www.ibp.com

Knowledge Plus Multimedia Publishing

Knowledge Plus offers extensive and innovative marketing services to companies seeking to increase their exposure.

Address: http://www.kpp.com

LMB Marketing

This company's goal is to help other businesses in sales and marketing. They offer a magazine and advice on an inexpensive media campaign that can increase profits.

Address: http://www.lmb.com

Machine

The Machine is an online company providing advertising services for other online businesses. The page offers individual company advertisements and a current list of clients.

Address: http://www.machines.com

Motivators

Motivators is a full-service promotion products/premium agency. For companies, they offer a line of customized products, such as pens, awards, buttons, towels, and T-shirts.

Address: http://www.motivators.com

NetMarket

NetMarket gives its clients increased commercial visibility on the Internet through services like the Digital Dressing Room, SmartClerk, and Virtual MOM. A list of clients, a link to open a NetMarket account, and information on the newest technology in the company are also offered.

Address: http://www.netmarket.com

Pacific Data Resources

Pacific Data Resources is a marketing and design firm specializing in helping companies create a presence on the Internet. Their page offers services and client information as well as Internet demographic data.

Address: http://www.pdrc.com

Parallax Technology Group

This marketing communications company gives products and companies increased visibility and accessibility. This page describes how their services can be applied to the user's company.

Address: http://www.parallaxtech.com

Results Direct

Results Direct tells why it's beneficial for companies to advertise or market their products on the Internet. Also provided is a representative list of the company's clients and an option to read about past projects.

Address: http://www.resultsdirect.com

Ross Roy Communications

Ross Roy is a marketing communications agency that designs and integrates marketing plans. Their page offers a list of clients and a description of the company's varied capabilities and services.

Address: http://www.rossroy.com

Susanna K. Hutcheson Writing

Susanna K. Hutcheson Writing organizes direct-mail marketing and advertising services. Services range from copywriting to organizing radio and TV air time.

Address: http://www.fn.net/~shutches

Traders' Connection

Traders' Connection offers a database of classified ads described as the world's largest. Members have access to the database as well as other Internet services and opportunities.

Address: http://www.trader.com

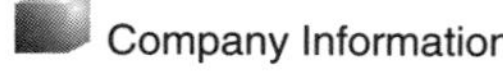 Company Information  Product Information  Online Ordering

Virtual Media Resources

Virtual Media Resources offers consulting services to advertising and marketing companies needing demographic and media research information. The page offers current news, related links, and a sampling of the company's clients.

Address: http://www.vmr.com

Wahlstrom

Wahlstrom is a marketing company specializing in directory marketing services. Their Web site offers information on the Internet and other interactive media, an online version of the company's newsletter, a partial list of clients, and links to related sites on the Web.

Address: http://www.wahlstrom.com

WolfBayne Communications

This marketing and public relations firm specializes in high-tech business-to-business communications. WolfBayne's pages include information about their industry, products, and clients.

Address: http://www.bayne.com/wolfbayne

Xpand

Xpand, Inc., offers both online and CD-ROM advertising services. Their page features a virtual trade show offering products for sale.

Address: http://www.xpand.com

Agriculture

AggieNet

AggieNet is an organization of Texas A&M University students, faculty, and alumni. They offer information about Aggie alumni and Aggie merchandise, sports updates, Aggie jokes, and University and alumni directories.

Address: http://www.aggienet.com

Global Agricultural Biotechnology Association

This nonprofit organization provides information to promote agricultural biotechnology. Their goal is to teach people about the industry.

Address: http://www.lights.com/gaba

Information Services for Agriculture

This company provides information services to the agricultural industry. ISA's pages include crop production data, weather information, market information, and links to other agricultural sites.

Address: http://www.aginfo.com

Pilatus - Luwasa Hydroculture Plant Protection

Luwasa's goal is to protect plants. The company uses many of its own innovative methods, such as hydroculture, to create lush, healthy plants.

Address: http://www.usa.net/pilatus

Plantation Bulb

This company specializes in American-grown bulbs, fruits, flowers, nuts, and plants. Their page provides pictures of some of their products as well as information on how to get a catalog.

Address: http://www.forman.com/tyty

United Breeders

This artificial-insemination service organization for cattle breeding uses the latest embryo-transfer technologies to produce cattle with superior genes.

Address: http://www.ubi.com

Airlines, Aircraft, and Aerospace

Air Charter Guide

The Air Charter Guide offers information about various charter operators and brokers throughout the country. The page offers charter advertising and information about the charter industry's international brokering agencies.

Address: http://www.guides.com/acg

American Airlines

This page tells what American Airlines has to offer, such as membership in their AAdvantage Travel Awards program, ideas for vacations around the world, shipping services, Admirals Clubs, and special programs like duty-free shopping.

Address: http://www.amrcorp.com

 Company Information  Product Information  Online Ordering

Avionics Communications

Avionics Communications publishes books, newsletters, and market reports. They provide an online catalog of avionics products, including books and software.

Address: http://www.avionics.com/avionics

Cathay Pacific Airlines

Cathay Pacific Airlines, which offers nonstop service to Hong Kong, provides pictures of their planes as well as information about frequent-flyer programs and tours of Hong Kong.

Address: http://www.cathay-usa.com

Douglas Aircraft

Douglas Aircraft, a division of the McDonnell Douglas Corp., builds airplanes. This page offers a tour of their main facility as well as news of current and future programs.

Address: http://www.dac.mdc.com

Grumman

Grumman designs and manufactures advanced electronics for aircraft, spacecraft, computerized test equipment, and other products. They also develop, install, and operate computer systems for managing information.

Address: http://axon.scra.org/Organizations/Grumman/Grumman.html

Lauda Air

Lauda Air joined forces with Lufthansa to create one of the world's largest executive travel markets. They offer flights throughout Europe, Asia, and the U.S., and their page offers information on flight times and prices.

Address: http://www.laudaair.com

Lockheed Martin Missiles & Space

This major defense and aerospace company develops space systems, missiles, and other high-technology products.

Address: http://www.lmsc.lockheed.com

Lunar Resources

The Lunar Resources Co.'s goal is to establish a lunar base, making it possible for people to live on the moon.

Address: http://www.access.digex.net/dcarson/Lrc.html

Malin Space Science Systems

This company designs, develops, and operates instruments such as cameras and monitoring equipment to fly on spacecraft. They developed and operated the Mars Observer Camera until its loss, and they provide research to the Jet Propulsion Labaratory for future space missions.

Address: http://www.msss.com

McDonnell Douglas Aerospace

MDA, a member of America's space program, provides a full range of engineering support to NASA and the aerospace community. They specialize in automation and robotics; guidance, navigation, and control; mission analysis and integration; and systems engineering.

Address: http://pat.mdc.com

Mexicana Airlines

Mexicana Airlines offers information about vacation packages, rates, and frequent-flyer programs as well as popular hotels, tour guides, and restaurants.

Address: http://www.mexicana.com

NorthStar's Aircraft for Sale

This page features aircraft for sale. Listings, descriptions, and prices of the planes are provided.

Address: http://www.toronto.com/flyer/northstar

Southwest Airlines

Southwest Airline's home "gate" offers information about its flight schedules, specific aircraft, and cargo. This page also provides convenient forms for inquiring about flights and rates.

Address: http://www.iflyswa.com

Virgin Atlantic

Virgin Atlantic is a British airline that provides transportation worldwide. Virgin's pages provide a list of flights organized by destination and arrival date. Each page also offers information about times and rates.

Address: http://www.fly.virgin.com

Art

Art Online

Art Online is a gallery of artwork for sale. The categories include African American, Native American, wildlife, nautical, and rock art. Choose from rare, limited-edition originals and prints to open-edition posters.

Address: http://www.artonline.com/artonline

Collection

The Collection is an Internet art gallery containing visual images by contemporary artists whose works are available for purchase or simply browsing.

Address: http://www.thecollection.com

Electric Gallery

The Electric Art Gallery lets you view and purchase works of art from virtually any time period.

Address: http://www.egallery.com/egallery

Find Arts

This interactive site lets you view artists' work and even access their home pages through dealers or galleries.

Address: http://www.Find-Arts.com

FunnyFarm

FunnyFarm is a company that markets and distributes Robert Marble's humorous pictures. They offer a two-for-one deal and a satisfaction guarantee on the prints.

Address: http://www.funnyfarm.com

Internet ArtResources

Internet ArtResources offers complete online information on artists, galleries, museums, shows, and other art events. They also provide access to many books and magazines.

Address: http://www.ftgi.com

Internet for the Fine Arts

Internet for the Fine Arts is an online site providing resources for all aspects of the fine arts, including information on artists, galleries, organizations, events, and publications.

Address: http://www.fine-art.com

Lunds Auctioneers and Appraisers

Lunds Auctioneers and Appraisers is an online auction house selling fine art and collectables. Their page lists new items and offers a catalog with descriptions, pictures, and prices.

Address: http://www.lunds.com

Santa Fe Fine Art

This online center provides information on local photographers, painters, sculptors, and printmakers. The page offers a list of artists and a description of their work.

Address: http://www.sffa.com

Wentworth Gallery

The Wentworth Gallery brings all of its paintings, lithographs, and sculptures to this online site. These pages provide information on artists, styles, and individual pieces.

Address: http://www.wentworth-art.com

Automotive

Autolink

Autolink offers catalog design and production for auto dealers. For consumers, they provide used-car listings that include prices, descriptions, and availability.

Address: http://www.autolink.com

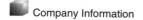

Chrysler

Chrysler Corp. provides information about their cars as well as a special-offers section, a statement of the company's "Customer One" initiative, and an 800 number to call for further information.

Address: http://www.rossroy.com/chrysler.htm

DealerNet

DealerNet presents links to the pages of dealers for nearly every car manufacturer. Find out about all the latest makes and models, used cars, special-interest automobiles, boats, and RVs.

Address: http://www.dealernet.com

Dee Zee

As one of the largest manufacturers of truck accessories, Dee Zee makes equipment for companies such as Chrysler, Honda, Mazda, Mitsubishi, and Nissan. They also provide information about products for sportsmen.

Address: http://www.deezee.com

Eagle

Eagle is a car-manufacturing division of the Chrysler Corp. This page provides pictures of cars and information about their technology.

Address: http://www.eaglecars.com

Ford

Ford's Worldwide Connection lets users preview the latest Ford, Lincoln, and Mercury models and locate the nearest dealers to take a test drive.

Address: http://www.Ford.com

General Motors - Cadillac

Cadillac provides information about its newest contributions on the road and to sports, including golf and the America's Cup. Specific information is provided about Cadillac's products and dealerships.

Address: http://www.cadillac.com

Goodyear Tire & Rubber

This page offers information about tires, including a buyer's guide and answers to frequently asked questions. A calendar of events is also provided for Goodyear's blimp and racing team.

Address: http://www.goodyear.com

Harley-Davidson of Stamford

Harley-Davidson is on the Web. Visit this page to see their current line of bikes, parts, clothing, and memorabilia and for fellowship with other Harley enthusiasts.

Address: http://www.hd-stamford.com

Insurance Express

Insurance Express is the first company to offer auto insurance via the Internet. Users can access quote forms and ordering information by state.

Address: http://www.insrexpress.com

IntelliChoice

AutoExplorer is the online site for IntelliChoice, a company that publishes consumer reports on how to select and purchase cars and trucks. This page offers various books, guides, and software that provide custom vehicle information.

Address: http://www.intellichoice.com

Mercedes Benz Oldtimer Center

The Mercedes Benz Oldtimer Center details their current inventory of classic cars for sale. These pages include classified ads, news reports, and advertising.

Address: http://www.specialcar.com/journal/mbotc/mbotc1.htm

Mobil

Mobil is one of the largest oil and fuel companies. Their manufacturing and marketing techniques are highlighted on this page, along with news about the Mobil 1 racing team and opinion editorials focusing on the company.

Address: http://www.mobil.com

Company Information  Product Information Online Ordering

Saturn

This page offers news and information about this relatively new car company. Answers to frequently asked questions are provided, as well as access to *The Saturn Magazine* and a peek at the new-car lineup.

Address: http://www.saturncars.com

Shell Oil

This oil company lets readers rate the quality of service at Shell stations. They also offer news and information about the Shell Chemical division and the oil industry in general.

Address: http://www.shellus.com

Shen Mitsubishi

This page provides pictures and information about the new cars at Shen Mitsubishi, including features, specs, used-car listings, discount coupons, and order forms for more information.

Address: http://www.systemv.com/autolink/shen/mitsu.html

Tech Auto Sound

Tech Auto Sound is a full-service auto sound store in Endicott, N.Y. Their web includes detailed information about each of their products, which can be ordered online.

Address: http://www.icw.com/techauto/techaut1.html

Texaco

This page offers information not only about Texaco's specialty—gasoline—but about its racing team and the Metropolitan Opera as well. Customer service is also available.

Address: http://www.texaco.com

Volvo Cars of North America

Volvo offers information on current models, dealership locations, and buyer programs and options. They also describe company safety guidelines and post company news.

Address: http://www.volvocars.com

Banks and Banking

Bank of America

Bank of America, part of the BankAmerica Corp., provides various financial services. They offer checking and savings accounts, loans, credit cards, and investment services such as stocks, bonds, annuities, and mutual funds.

Address: http://www.bankamerica.com

Bank of Montreal

This page provides background on the Bank of Montreal, rates, a corporate profile, what's coming in the future, and company news.

Address: http://www.bmo.com

Bank One

Bank One is one of the first full-service banking institutions to offer services on the Web, including automated payments from consumers to billers, transfers, and consumer payments for stores on the Web.

Address: http://www.eft.bankone.com

Banque Paribas

This French bank provides general information about its operations, including branch offices and subsidiaries.

Address: http://www.paribas.com

Barclays Bank

This centuries-old British bank offers banking products, travel insurance, the BarclayCard, computer operations, and one-stop Internet banking services.

Address: http://www.barclays.co.uk

CitiCorp/Citibank

Citibank operates a global, full-service consumer franchise encompassing branch banking, credit and charge cards, and private banking.

Address: http://www.tti.com

Dime Savings Bank of Williamsburgh

The Dime Savings Bank of Williamsburgh offers fixed- and adjustable-rate mortgages for customer properties located within an area including New York City and Long Island. Free mortgage workshops are offered at several of their branch locations.

Address: http://www.the-dime.com

First Federal

First Federal Savings and Loan of Rochester, N.Y., provides information on loans, accounts, branch locations, and other bank services.

Address: http://www.firstfederal.com

First Union

First Union Corp., located in Charlotte, N.C., comprises eight financial institutions that offer banking services on the Web.

Address: http://www.firstunion.com

First Virtual Holdings

First Virtual Holdings is an electronic merchant banker—a financial services company created specifically to enable anyone with Internet access to buy and sell information worldwide.

Address: http://www.fv.com

Mastercard

Apply for Mastercard online or check the nationwide list of ATM machines for one near you.

Address: http://www.mastercard.com

Montgomery Securities

Montgomery Securities is an investment and brokerage firm supporting growth companies in the consumer services, technology, health-care, finance, and real estate industries.

Address: http://www.montgomery.com

Naval Air Federal Credit Union

This credit union is owned and controlled by its members and is open to the military as well as approved civilian businesses. Their page offers information about membership and loans.

Address: http://www.nafcu.com

NetEdge Systems

This company brings ATM services to the Internet. They provide information about upcoming events in the electronic banking industry, news, and employment opportunities.

Address: http://www.netedge.com

Toronto Dominion Bank

TD Bank offers a wealth of interesting and valuable resources, including daily market reports and commentaries, currency exchange data, advice for small businesses, and even PC software.

Address: http://www.tdbank.ca

Wells Fargo

Wells Fargo offers online banking through the Internet, resources relating to personal finance, small business banking, and commercial and corporate banking.

Address: http://www.wellsfargo.com

Books and Publications

Britannica Advanced Publishing

Britannica Online offers a searchable and browsable collection of Britannica's latest article database, hundreds of articles not yet in print, *Merriam-Webster's Collegiate Dictionary*, and the *Britannica Book of the Year*.

Address: http://www.eb.com

Castle Hill Books

Castle Hill specializes in stocking out-of-print and antique books on British archaeology, topography, and countryside.

Address: http://www.kc3ltd.co.uk/business/castlehi.html

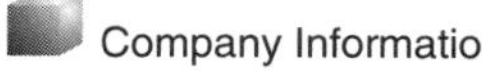

 Product Information

Federal Employees News Digest

The Web site of the weekly *Federal Employees News Digest* offers information about the publication, current features, a reader's forum, and a marketplace for books and other publications offered by the company.

Address: http://www.clubfed.com

Haslam's Book Store

Haslam's Book Store specializes in new, used, and out-of-print books. With a vast archive and search facility, the user can find even the rarest of books. Haslam's page also offers links to many book publishers.

Address: http://www.haslams.com/haslams

InfoCafe

InfoCafe is a complete online bookstore specializing in computer books and business-related books. If you can't find the book you want, you can try the interactive search facility.

Address: http://www.infocafe.com

MultiMania Production

MultiMania Production is the creator of *The Baguette*, an online magazine available in both French and English and offering French-related topics ranging from the Eiffel Tower to snail hunting. Subscription information is available.

Address: http://www.mmania.com

Multimedia Newsstand

Subscribe to your favorite magazine or order your favorite video at this online site, which offers more than 200 videos and 500 magazine subscriptions.

Address: http://mmnewsstand.com

Pan Asian Publications

Pan Asian distributes Asian materials including bilingual books, videotapes, audio cassettes, and computer CD-ROMs. They focus on bringing high-caliber Asian works in a variety of languages to libraries, schools, and other centers of information in the U.S. and Canada.

Address: http://www.panap.com

Virtual Book Shop  

The Virtual Book Shop offers a selection of rare and unique books online. With many topics to choose from, there's something of interest for everyone. This page features an online catalog, a list of member bookstores, and a facility for searching the book database.

Address: http://www.virtual.bookshop.com

WordsWorth Books   

WordsWorth Books is a discount bookstore in Harvard Square. Their web offers information about featured publishers, services they provide, and the Virtual WordsWorth service, which provides online access to databases, catalogs, search systems for hard-to-find books, and a listing of literary awards.

Address: http://www.wordsworth.com

Business Services

Aaron Cohen Associates 

This is a team of architects, interior designers, space planners, and librarians offering architectural and interior design services for information centers. Their page provides information about planning, design, and research.

Address: http://www.acohen.com

aBCD Printing   

aBCD prints documents for legal, corporate, commercial, and financial organizations. Request a quote or place an order online. Those in the printing industry can use "Printer's Link" to talk to other printers.

Address: http://www.abcdprint.com

Accounting.Com 

This company provides accounting, bookkeeping, and payroll services for small businesses. Their page offers budgets and forecasting as well as employment information and a method for consulting with a CPA.

Address: http://www.accounting.com

Active Information Management

AIM creates dynamic document management systems and documentation for mainframe software products.

Address: http://www.activeinfo.com

Aegiss

Aegiss Corp. designs and implements knowledge-based information management systems.

Address: http://www.aegiss.com

Aleph

Aleph translates documents, both business and personal, into other languages. Choose your own translator from Aleph's online database of qualified linquistic experts to translate your documents.

Address: http://www.aleph.com

Ameritech Library Services

This company provides the latest technology and information systems to libraries all over the U.S. and the world. Their page includes information on Ameritech's library management systems and new technology, including Internet access products and information and training services for libraries.

Address: http://www.amlibs.com

Buck Information Systems

Although this company specializes in computer communications, they provide many computer-related services that let companies distribute information effectively over the Internet.

Address: http://bisinc.com

Business Plan Consulting

Business Plan Consulting, Inc., provides business consultation, financial guidance, market research, and sales strategies. This page offers a company overview, descriptions of their financial services, and information about their Presentation Skills Training.

Address: http://www.info1.com/BusinessPlan

Calvert Group

The Calvert Group is the leading sponsor of mutual funds. With an expanding number of tax-free funds, this group is committed to investing funds responsibly and providing investment alternatives.

Address: http://www.calvertgroup.com

Cameron's Publications

Cameron's Publications provides specialized marketing information to managers of tennis, golf, and yacht clubs, nightclubs and lounges, hotels, and restaurants. They also offer strategies to bartenders, waiters, and waitresses to help them increase their profits.

Address: http://www.cameronpub.com

Dataquest

Dataquest is one of the leading developers and providers of market research statistics, analysis, and consulting services.

Address: http://www.dataquest.com

Dimension Specialist

DS develops electronic forms and bar-code technologies. Some of their other products include a pen-based system for using ordinary business forms as source documents, a radio identification system, pogs, and laser check stock.

Address: http://www.dspecialist.com

Docunetworks

Docunetworks is a laser printing company with sites all over the world. They avoid high shipping costs, tariffs, and other international guidelines or regulations. This page provides information on how to use this service.

Address: http://www.docunetworks.com

Edelman Public Relations Worldwide

Edelman Public Relations Worldwide creates and manages public relations programs for products, services, and companies.

Address: http://www.edelman.com

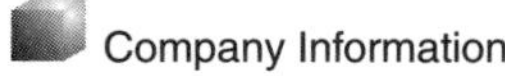 Company Information  Product Information  Online Ordering

Environmental Support Solutions

ESS provides software, products, services, and training to help companies comply with government mandates concerning environmental regulations.

Address: http://www.environ.com

Equifax National Decision Systems

Equifax National Decision Systems provides marketing strategies, consulting, and advanced targeting technologies to aid companies in various industries, including retail, financial services, and commercial real estate.

Address: http://www.cts.com/browse/ends

Express Systems

Express Systems, a software management company, helps companies manage their software assets by ensuring compliance with licensing at minimum expense.

Address: http://www.express-systems.com

Faxon

The Faxon Co. is a serial publication subscription agency that provides libraries, publishers, and businesses with consolidated billing and payment services and publication information.

Address: http://www.faxon.com

Federal Express

FedEx is one of the world's largest express transportation companies, delivering documents, packages, and freight to more than 192 countries each working day. This page describes their domestic and international shipping services and tracking software.

Address: http://www.fedex.com

First American Group Purchasing Association

This organization helps small and medium-sized businesses save money on the products and services they need. This page offers information about their programs, vendor listings, and frequent-purchaser incentives.

Address: http://www.firstgpa.com

Fleishman-Hillard Capabilities

Fleishman-Hillard Capabilities is a multifaceted public relations company whose services range from corporate communications strategy and implementation to marketing and international economic development.

Address: http://www.fleish.com

Focus: Forward

Focus: Forward provides value-added services and products to help clients solve "sales-call reluctance" problems and earn what they're worth. At this site you'll find information about management workshops and exactly what sales-call reluctance is.

Address: http://www.focusforward.com

FranNet

FranNet provides information and advice about franchising and current franchising opportunities. It starts with the basics—"What is franchising?"—and moves on to more advanced information, such as how to select a franchise.

Address: http://www.frannet.com

Global Fax Network

Global Fax Network develops, markets, and provides interactive voice- and fax-based information services for a variety of industries, including media, public relations, marketing, health care, and education. These services include interactive job lines, TV/radio station hotlines, broadcast fax, fax-on-demand, and faxmail.

Address: http://www.cts.com/browse/globefax

Global Job Net

Global Job Net is an employment assistance facility for both jobseekers and employers. GJN strives to protect jobseekers' privacy by informing them of interested employers via email.

Address: http://www.globaljobnet.com

GlobalTech

GlobalTech provides comprehensive client/server services to the information management community, including technical management, Internet resources, information infrastructure, and assistance in a variety of markets, including manufacturing, insurance, banking, and communications.

Address: http://www.globaltech.com

Home Office Mall

Home Office Mall offers a variety of resources that can keep a business running. Services include tracking FedEx packages, the Wallstreet Report, and easy access to airline reservation systems.

Address: http://www.home-office-mall.com

IntelliMatch

IntelliMatch is an online employment service that uses its own "Watson and Holmes" software to make strategic and successful matches between employers and prospective employees. This page includes an Online Job Center, where information is provided on companies using IntelliMatch services, available jobs, and related products and services.

Address: http://www.intellimatch.com

JobCenter

JobCenter brings together employers and potential employees. Companies can describe the types of workers they're looking for and users can post their resumes, and the service will make the matches.

Address: http://www.jobcenter.com

JobLink

This employment service is for companies seeking workers with technical skills. The goal is to match a job description posted by an employer to an employee's resume.

Address: http://www.jobweb.com

JobServe

JobServe sends daily information to those on the mailing list about employment opportunities in computer-related fields in the United Kingdom. Users designate what they're interested in and receive pertinent job information when it's available.

Address: http://www.jobserve.com

JOBTRAK

This employment listing service caters to recent college graduates. JOBTRAK is connected with career centers of universities and also provides a guide to graduate schools to interested students.

Address: http://www.jobtrak.com

LifeLink

LifeLink specializes in disaster preparedness information, services, and supplies to help businesses prepare for, and recover from, disastrous situations.

Address: http://www.lifelink.com

Mail Boxes Etc.

Mail Boxes Etc. is a leading franchiser of neighborhood postal, business, and communications service centers. This page describes MBE's many services and products, including a private mail-receiving service with 24-hour access, packing and shipping services, stamps, printing, photocopying, and office supplies.

Address: http://www.mbe.com

Netback

Netback offers file backup and registration services via the Internet. They offer four main packages and information on other computer topics.

Address: http://www.netback.com

Personal Training Systems

Peter Norton has developed three tutorials on CD-ROM and audio cassette that show how to use a Mac, Windows, and Netscape. This page offers information about the Macintosh tutorial, the Windows tutorial, and the new Netscape Navigator.

Address: http://www.ptst.com

Professionals Online International

Professionals Online is a directory of resources that are arranged geographically and by profession to provide easy access for professionals seeking specific services, jobs, and/or other professionals. Topics include sports, entertainment, business, accounting, law, government, computers and technology, and banking.

Address: http://www.prosonline.com

Schlumberger Ltd.

Schlumberger Ltd. provides products and services to the gas, water, and electricity distribution industries and to the petroleum industry. This page offers news for shareholders, publications, employment opportunities, and resources connected to the petroleum industry.

Address: http://www.slb.com

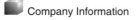

SK Writers

SK Writers provides employment services to professionals in the technical publications industry (writing, editing, and graphic design) by matching prospective employees with positions in high-tech companies in the Silicon Valley. On this site you can place a help-wanted ad or search for a position in the job listings.

Address: http://www.skwriters.com

Talent Network

The Talent Network provides qualified professionals to production companies. There are databases for different professions and services as well as an option to have your own services listed on the network. The page also includes links to related sites.

Address: http://www.talentnet.com

Trade Point USA

Trade Point USA is an organization established in cooperation with the UN Conference on Trade and Development to facilitate international trade. The I-TRADE service page offers extensive company listings, trade information, and important news.

Address: http://www.tpusa.com

United Parcel Service

UPS, one of the largest package distribution companies, transports more than 3 billion parcels and documents annually with 500 aircraft, 130,000 vehicles, and 2,400 facilities providing service in more than 200 countries. This page offers information on using UPS, software and utilities, package tracking, and other resources.

Address: http://www.ups.com

USADATA

USADATA offers consumers information on a variety of U.S. markets, emphasizing trends within those markets through demographic research. The page provides information on a variety of categories, such as travel, finance, and autos, as well as data reports and a map of U.S. markets.

Address: http://www.usadata.com

VTLS  

VTLS, Inc., supplies automation systems and other information services for libraries and similar organizations around the world. The page offers extensive company and services information, as well as data on other Internet services, software, and Web links.

Address: http://www.vtls.com

World Wide Business Center  

World Wide Business Center offers a variety of information services to keep businesspeople up to date on the latest news and developments. Features include news, editorials, company listings, training information, employment opportunities, resources, and travel information.

Address: http://www.wwbc.com

Chemistry and Biology

Ciba Geigy AG 

This Switzerland-based biological and chemical group concentrates on health care, agriculture, and industry. Their page includes Ciba's vision for the future as well as news about the environment.

Address: http://www.ciba.com

Dow Chemical  

Dow manufactures and supplies more than 2,500 product families, including chemicals and performance products, plastics, hydrocarbons and energy, and consumer specialties such as agricultural products and pharmaceuticals.

Address: http://www.dow.com

Electronic Materials Recovery 

This company provides customers with easy, one-stop access to disposal of scrap metal and computer and electronic surplus material.

Address: http://www.computersurplus.com

Interactive Simulations

Interactive Simulations develops scientific solutions for the biotechnology and pharmaceutical industries, primarily through the development of innovative software for molecular modeling, simulation, and drug design.

Address: http://www.cts.com/browse/isigen

Lehle Seeds

Lehle Seeds is the only commercial producer of *Arabidopsis* seeds in the world. The page offers books, bulletins, opportunities, resources, and a list of science journals and miscellaneous resources relating to *Arabidopsis* seeds.

Address: http://www.arabidopsis.com

Midland Certified Reagent

MCRC manufactures synthetic nucleic acids for biological research, including custom DNA and RNA oligonucleotides. They also perform complete gene construction, including sequence verification, isolation, and enzyme purification.

Address: http://www.mcrc.com

Monsanto

This science-based company discovers, manufactures, and markets agricultural products, performance chemicals, prescription pharmaceuticals, and food ingredients.

Address: http://www.monsanto.com

Promega

Promega specializes in applying biological and molecular biological research to the development of new products for all aspects of the life sciences (such as neuroscience and genetic identity). On this page you'll find news updates on related issues as well as information on developments within the company.

Address: http://www.promega.com

Rohm and Haas

Rohm and Haas produces specialty polymers and biologically active compounds, resins, agricultural chemicals, plastics, and additives. This site offers extensive product information as well as an online comment form.

Address: http://www.rohmhaas.com

Scientific Products Information Network

SPIN provides this database of scientific information and products for researchers in the cell sciences. Users can find virtually any desired topic in the database or browse the catalogs for products. Also listed are companies selling SPIN products.

Address: http://www.spindex.com

Sumitomo Chemical

Sumitomo's Web page lists a variety of information about the company in English and Japanese. There is an image processor for analytical pathology (in Japanese) and a link to other chemical Web sites.

Address: http://www.sumitomo-chem.co.jp

Whatman LabSales

From pH instrumentation to safety equipment, Whatman LabSales Inc. provides laboratory science and research products.

Address: http://www.whatman.com

Clothing and Apparel

American Diamond Exchange

This page provides information about diamonds and gives the user a chance to see the company's selection. They also describe ideas for custom jewelry design and repair as well as career and business opportunities.

Address: http://www.adexnet.com

Barnum Shoe

Barnum Shoe is a footwear vendor. Their Web page has information about the company and a catalog of men's and women's footwear and other items.

Address: http://www.tiac.net/users/pwb/barnum.html

Blue Chip Designs

Blue Chip Designs recycles computer chips to create high-tech jewelry.

Address: http://www.cybermalls.com/cymont/bluechip/bcyb003.htm

Burlington Coat Factory

Burlington Coat Factory manufactures garments and textiles, such as pillows, sheets, and comforters. They provide information about their stores and employment opportunities.

Address: http://www.coat.com

Colortech

Colortech is a producer and distributor of printed T-shirts, custom clothing, hats, and mugs. On this page you can view their products, create your own design, find out how to get a free shirt, and order online.

Address: http://www.webcom.com/~color

Historical Interaction

Historical Interaction offers a unique and rare collection of authentic treasure coins handcrafted into beautiful pieces of jewelry. Their products include coins featuring Alexander the Great, Trajan, and Constantine, as well as pieces of eight in silver reales and gold escudos.

Address: http://www.cts.com/browse/khobbs

Merrell Footwear

Merrell Footwear offers shoes for the outdoors, such as hiking boots, sport sandals, and ski boots. This page features company information and a product catalog.

Address: http://www.outdoorlink.com/merrell

Milne Jewelry Title Page

The Milne Jewelry Co. brings you its online catalog of exquisite Southwestern jewelry, handcrafted of genuine stones and sterling silver. Merchandise ranges from bolo ties, pendants, and earrings to Zuni fetishes. Their Web pages also feature a history of Native American jewelry making.

Address: http://www.branch.com/milne/Milne01.html

Net Threads

Net Threads offers a line of apparel and products with an Internet theme, including original T-shirts, mouse pads, custom email, embroidered shirts, coffee mugs, and customized bumper stickers (with email address or Web page address).

Address: http://www.mindspring.com/net-head/home.html

NetDiamonds

This page features a catalog of jewelry from NetDiamonds, ranging from diamond earrings to gold bracelets, all with a quality guarantee.

Address: http://www.netdiamonds.com/netdiamonds

new stuff

This "just for girls" company allows women and girls with an interest in dance, theater, or fashion to create their own elaborate costumes courtesy of B. Famous On Stage, a theatrical costume design team.

Address: http://www.newstuff.com

Planet Reebok

Reebok is at or near the top of the competitive athletic shoe business. This page enables readers to see Reebok's Research and Design Development, communicate with sports stars, and see the many events with which Reebok is involved.

Address: http://www.planetreebok.com

Playware

This online lingerie catalog offers everything from nightgowns to men's and women's underwear. They offer full-color pictures of many different styles, as well as a video of lingerie models.

Address: http://www.playware.com

Product Net

This is the online presence of the upscale "product" boutiques of L.A. and New York. This women's clothing label is marketed in many major department stores and has been featured on the covers of fashion magazines such as *Vogue*. Browse through a catalog of clothing for the upcoming season.

Address: http://www.productnet.com

R.F. Moeller Jeweler

This page provides a Jewelry Information Center that offers specific jewelry information, an online catalog of estate jewelry, a listing of upcoming special events, and an option showcasing "R.F. Moeller's Most Wanted Items."

Address: http://www.rfmoeller.com

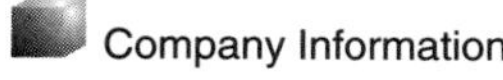

 Product Information 

Registry

This company specializes in the estate and antique jewelry markets. They sell jewelry to retailers and offer an illustrated online catalog on their page.

Address: http://www.registryltd.com

Steamed Heat

This "company on the edge" offers sexy clothing for men and women as well as erotic works of art. Everything Steamed Heat sells is listed in a catalog that you can order through an 800 number.

Address: http://www.steamedheat.com

STUFF.com

STUFF.com sells a variety of logo T-shirts. Their product line includes two Internet-theme shirts.

Address: http://www.stuff.com

T-Shirts.com

T-Shirts.com carries a fun line of preprinted, Internet-related T-shirts, including the increasingly popular "Byte Me." They also do custom orders.

Address: http://www.T-shirts.com

Computers: Hardware

Adaptec

Adaptec is one of the leading manufacturers of SCSI interface cards, network devices, and other I/O products. Their page includes information on hot topics, their complete product line, access to drivers, and technical information about their products.

Address: http://www.adaptec.com

Advanced Logic Research

ALR is a leading PC manufacturer in the U.S. Their Web server provides information on their product lines and awards the products have won as well as employment opportunities.

Address: http://www.alr.com

Advanced Micro Devices

AMD is one of the largest merchant-suppliers of integrated circuits in the U.S. Their pages offer information about their microprocessors, embedded processors, memory products, logic devices, and other products.

Address: http://www.amd.com

APC

APC is a manufacturer of products that protect computers from power surges and brownouts. Through their web, they offer product information, customer service, and technical support.

Address: http://www.apcc.com

Apple Computer

Apple offers information on its line of Macintosh computers and software as well as technical support, information on research and technology, and developer services.

Address: http://www.apple.com

BusLogic

BusLogic manufactures SCSI and RAID products, including SCSI host adapters and controllers for ISA, EISA, Microchannel, VLB, and PCI buses.

Address: http://www.buslogic.com

Compaq

On its pages, this leading PC manufacturer offers information on new products, service and support, upgrading Compaq products to Windows 95, and much more.

Address: http://www.compaq.com

Data Exchange

Data Exchange specializes in repairing computer peripherals, contract manufacturing, and end-of-life product support. They currently repair more than 750 products.

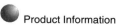

Address: http://www.dex.com

Data General

Data General creates advanced computer systems that employ the newest technologies and offers a complete set of information management services.

Address: http://www.dg.com

Dell

Dell is a major manufacturer of PCs and peripheral equipment. They offer technical support through their web as well as corporate information and employment opportunities.

Address: http://www.dell.com

Design Acceleration

Design Acceleration, Inc., provides hardware design engineers with simulation analysis tools to reduce design time.

Address: http://www.designacc.com

Digital

Digital Equipment Corp. (DEC) offers access to a wealth of information about the company and its products and services.

Address: http://www.digital.com

Digital Products

DP Inc. manufactures a complete line of network print-server products. Product descriptions are available online, as is technical support for their growing customer base.

Address: http://www.digprod.com

Direct Data Storage

DDS sells SCSI controllers and SCSI disk and tape drives online. They say that they will try to beat anybody else's prices on identical products, and they offer a 30-day money-back guarantee.

Address: http://www.harddisk.com

Encore Computer

Encore is a supplier of open, massively parallel, scalable computer and storage systems for mission-critical applications.

Address: http://www.encore.com

Gilltro-Electronics

Gilltro-Electronics developed the Giltronix line of products, including local connectivity products, peripheral sharing devices, low-cost workgroup connectivity, and high-performance local and remote access systems.

Address: http://www.giltronix.com

Heurikon

Heurikon manufactures single-board computers that are typically embedded in larger systems, such as video-on-demand systems, simulation systems, and printer controls.

Address: http://www.heurikon.com

Hewlett Packard

As a major manufacturer of computers and peripheral devices such as printers, HP offers volumes of company and product information on their substantial web of pages. They also offer news and tips for people upgrading to Windows 95.

Address: http://www.hp.com

IBM

This company needs no introduction. IBM's web offers volumes of information about the company and its operations, technology, research, and products.

Address: http://www.ibm.com

IBM Personal Computers

This is the home page for IBM's Personal Computer division. It offers product information, file libraries, support, and news about the PC industry.

Address: http://www.pc.ibm.com

Intel

Check out Intel's web for detailed information about their latest CPUs, PCs, and components. Intel also offers developer support, information on embedded design products, and communications and networking products.

Address: http://www.intel.com

National Instruments

This company develops software and hardware products for PCs and workstations to help scientists and engineers in their research. National's pages offer information about developer programs and a news update option.

Address: http://www.natinst.com

NEC

NEC makes computers and peripherals ranging from monitors to CD-ROM drives. Besides the basics, NEC's pages offer product overviews, support, service, information on events and trade shows, R&D, and even information on buying used equipment directly from NEC.

Address: http://www.nec.com

NECX Direct

This online computer store sells hardware, software, and networking and accessory products. This secure site features more than 20,000 products, daily specials, and good prices.

Address: http://www.necx.com

Network Wizards

Network Wizards makes temperature sensors and system console managers.

Address: http://www.dicon.com

Online Computer Market

OCM is an online center for computer products and information ranging from software, hardware, and research companies to resellers and consultants. OCM offers information on trade shows and upcoming computer events as well as a list of clients and a directory of computer links on the Web.

Address: http://www.ocm.com

Overland Data

Overland Data supplies everything you need for desktop applications—half-inch tape drives, software, connecting cables, and expert service.

Address: http://www.cts.com/browse/odisales

PC Market

PC Market is a computer store doing business on the Web. Their products are categorized into hardware, software, and communications, and they also offer technical support through their web.

Address: http://www.pcmarket.com/~nms

Play, Inc.

Play, Inc., manufactures a video-frame grabber called the Snappy Video Snapshot, which attaches to a PC parallel port and captures still images from a camcorder, VCR, or TV tuner.

Address: http://www.play.com

Power Computing

Power Computing is a manufacturer of Macintosh clones. They claim their systems are 100% Mac-compatible but exceed the Mac in features, expandability, service, and support.

Address: http://www.powercc.com

RICOH California Research Center

RICOH manufactures computers, printers, copy machines, fax machines, and other technology products.

Address: http://www.crc.ricoh.com

Road Warrior International

Road Warrior Outpost offers products, services, and information for portable computers. One option lets customers shop for used computers or advertise their own. The page provides information about new products, monthly specials, and past issues of their newsletter.

Address: http://www.warrior.com

 Company Information  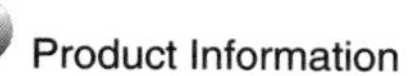 Product Information  Online Ordering

Seagate

Seagate is a leading manufacturer of data storage products (such as hard disk drives). In addition to product and company information, Seagate offers technical support and human resource information through their web.

Address: http://www.seagate.com

Silicon Graphics

Silicon Graphics manufactures high-end Unix workstations. Their pages offer extensive information on their computer services and products, including the Indy, Indigo2, and Onyx systems.

Address: http://www.sgi.com

Sparco Communications

Sparco supplies computer hardware and software products. In addition to product and service information, they provide a list of manufacturers, special offers, and frequently asked questions.

Address: http://www.sparco.com

Standard Microsystems

SMC is a leading manufacturer of networking products for PCs, including Ethernet network interface cards, switches, LSI chips, and Fast Ethernet products. SMC's Web pages offer product overviews, drivers, and technical information.

Address: http://www.smc.com

Sun Microsystems

Sun is the largest manufacturer of turnkey Unix computers. These pages describe Sun's hardware and software products and offer links for sales and service, technology and developers, and back issues of Sun's magazine-style Web pages. You can't order products online, but you can leave your name and address for more information.

Address: http://www.sun.com

Supra

Supra is a leading manufacturer of modems for PCs and Macintosh computers. Supra's pages include product and support information as well as a file library that includes drivers and flash ROM upgrades. You can also enter a contest to receive a free SupraFAXModem 288.

Address: http://www.supra.com

Texas Instruments

Texas Instruments is a high-profile supplier of technological products, including defense electronics, notebook computers, software development tools, calculators, and other technology products.

Address: http://www.ti.com

Toshiba America

Toshiba America is the American branch of the electronics giant. Toshiba's page offers information about the company's divisions and products.

Address: http://www.toshiba.com

TouchWindow

TouchWindow, a product of SCT Inc., is a touch-screen product for the ultimate in user-friendly interfaces. TouchWindow works on any computer that has a graphical user interface and a mouse.

Address: http://www.touchwindow.com

U.S. Robotics

No, USR doesn't make robots—they make digital and analog communications equipment, including modems, remote access servers, fax servers, and communications hubs. Check out RoboWeb and find out more about their products and services.

Address: http://www.usr.com

WebFactory

WebFactory sells top-quality computers and Internet products, both hardware and software. Their products include workstations from Silicon Graphics; routers from Cisco, Livingston, and Ascend; and bridges from Combinet.

Address: http://www.webfac.com

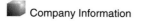

Well Connected Mac

The Well Connected Mac is the online information source for everything regarding Macintosh. The page provides related Mac sites on the Web, current and back issues of *MacWeek*, and extensive information on Mac products and services.

Address: http://www.macfaq.com

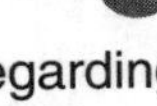

Wiltec

Wiltec manufactures IBM-compatible 9-track and cartridge tape systems. They guarantee their products and provide free expert advice and support to customers.

Address: http://www.wiltec.com/wiltec

Xerox

Xerox's page provides links and information about their divisions, operations, and products.

Address: http://www.xerox.com

Computers: Software

Access Graphics

Access Graphics is a distributor of software and computer systems. Their products focus on document imaging, enterprise networking, computer telephony, and CAD creative graphics, and their pages include a catalog and a description of services.

Address: http://www.access.com

Adobe Systems

Adobe develops software for creating, displaying, and printing electronic documents. Among their notable products are the PostScript and Display PostScript graphics languages.

Address: http://www.adobe.com

Alisa Systems

Alisa develops electronic mail message and directory integration software—specifically AlisaMail, which provides messaging capabilities between numerous PC LAN, WAN, and other host-based mail systems.

Address: http://www.alisa.com

ALVE Software Engineering

ALVE is a software engineering company that develops new software technologies.

Address: http://www.alve.com

Arachnae Management

Arachnae is a software development company that manufactures the Arachnae Information Retrieval System (AIRR II), an object-oriented text search engine.

Address: http://www.arachnae.com

Belmont Research

Belmont Research offers software development and consulting services in several areas, including clinical research, software technology, and federally sponsored research and development. They also offer information on job openings.

Address: http://www.belmont.com

Bentley Systems

Bentley is a leader in professional computer-aided design (CAD) products and services to engineers, architects, drafters, and organizations whose overall success relies on CAD.

Address: http://www.bentley.com

Berkeley Software Design

BSDI develops and sells BSD-based Unix operating systems for Intel-based computers. Their current product, BSDI 2.1, includes the X Window system, networking software, development tools, a Web server, and many other programs and utilities.

Address: http://www.bsdi.com

Beverly Hills Software

Beverly Hills Software sponsors this page, called *The Windows NT Resource Center*. The Center offers a respectable collection of application programs and drivers available for downloading, an area for NT consultants, a job center, a users group, and information about NT-related publications.

Address: http://www.bhs.com

BioData

BioData provides computer services and applications for the life sciences industry.

Address: http://www.biodata.com

Borland International

Borland is a major software development company offering applications and development products, mostly for Microsoft Windows. Also check out Borland's FTP server at ftp://ftp.borland.com.

Address: http://www.borland.com

Cadence Design Systems

CDS develops and markets design automation software and services to accelerate and advance the process of designing electronic systems.

Address: http://www.cadence.com

California Software

CS Inc. develops software for the Internet. Their products include the InterAp suite, a collection of Windows-based Internet applications for the home or office.

Address: http://www.calsoft.com

Computer Conversions

Computer Conversions is a leader in computer data recovery, recovering damaged or lost data from computer backup tapes and cartridges. They provide data conversion for more than 2,000 computer systems and for all formats, including tapes, diskettes, cartridges, and opticals.

Address: http://www.cts.com/browse/cci

Cygnus Support

This innovative company provides support for commercial and free software. Cygnus' Web pages tell about the firm and the products they support.

Address: http://www.cygnus.com

Cykic Software

Cykic Software specializes in connectivity technology. Their products include a Web server called *Hype-It* and a set of database management tools called *MultiBase*.

Address: http://www.cykic.com

Danish International

This software development company develops Bingo Search, which allows users to locate desired products such as camcorders, Mac notebooks and desktops, and printers. The search is based on feature selections and product information.

Address: http://www.danish.com

DataViews

DataViews develops graphical development software ranging from simple GUI builders to complex, dynamic real-time representation software.

Address: http://www.dvcorp.com

Daylight

Daylight develops software for construction and enhancement of in-house chemical information systems and turnkey applications for handling chemical information.

Address: http://www.daylight.com

Dazel

Dazel is a leading supplier of output management software for client/server enterprises.

Address: http://www.dazel.com

DeLorme Mapping

This New England-based mapping company specializes in mapping software and databases for the consumer, education, and government markets.

Address: http://www.delorme.com

Dubl-Click Software

Publishers of software for the Macintosh, Newton, and Windows, Dubl-Click offers information and demo versions of their products.

Address: http://www.dublclick.com

EarthWatch Communications

EarthWatch develops a software package that integrates weather data with a global database to simulate the world's weather patterns. EarthWatch sells directly to the broadcast and educational markets.

Address: http://www.earthwatch.com

Elite Software

Elite Software develops software for architects, engineers, and contractors. They have provided mechanical, electrical, and plumbing design programs since 1979.

Address: http://www.elitesoft.com

Ellery Systems

Ellery Systems develops distributed computing applications and offers system integration, engineering services, and consulting services worldwide.

Address: http://www.esi.com/esi

Empress Software

A marketer of sophisticated data management software, Empress provides a foundation for scientific, engineering, and business organizations using Unix and Windows. Their projects have involved medical diagnostic systems, weather forecasting, space exploration, flight simulation, and other diverse systems.

Address: http://www.empress.com

Ensemble Information Systems

Ensemble Information Systems designs and develops information software that delivers business news and information to desktop PCs. Products include OpenMarket, Relevant Enterprise Edition, and Relevant Personal Edition.

Address: http://www.ensemble.com

Esix Systems

Esix is a publisher of System V Release 4 (SVR4) Unix operating systems for Intel-based PCs. Esix's page offers product information and technical support online.

Address: http://www.esix.com

eSoft

eSoft is the world's oldest manufacturer of BBS software that is still in operation today. The Bread Board System (TBBS) is their primary product, but eSoft also develops enhancement products for TBBS, including an Internet connectivity product.

Address: http://www.esoft.com

ESQ Business Services

ESQ develops, manufactures, and supports software products that increase the service and reliability levels of Tandem computer networks. Their OpenNET software product line provides easy and cost-effective operating solutions.

Address: http://www.esq.com

Expersoft

Expersoft develops and markets XShell, a distributed, object-oriented management system that conforms to the Object Management Group's Object Request Broker architecture.

Address: http://www.expersoft.com

ExperTelligence

ExperTelligence develops products in the areas of object-oriented programming, artificial intelligence, graphical user interfaces, hypertext, and object-oriented databases.

Address: http://www.experTelligence.com

FirstBase Software

FirstBase develops the FirstBase RDBMS application builder toolkit and offers consulting for Unix systems, programming, and Web development.

Address: http://www.firstbase.com

Forman Interactive

This company specializes in Web publishing and catalog-building software. Their premier product, Internet Creator, allows people to create their own linked pages and catalog.

Address: http://www.forman.com

Frame Technology

Frame Technology is a leading developer of software for writing and publishing. Frame software is used by professionals around the world to create, revise, and distribute documents.

Address: http://www.frame.com

Franz

Franz creates dynamic, object-oriented software technology that lets people build applications that can easily adapt to changing needs.

Address: http://www.franz.com

FreeBSD Unix

The FreeBSD organization publishes a BSD-based Unix operating system for PCs that includes networking, development tools, servers, and application programs.

Address: http://www.freebsd.org

FutureSoft

This page provides information about DynaComm's communications packages and products. It includes a list of worldwide DynaComm distributors, software release notes, and technical support.

Address: http://www.fse.com

Galt Technology

Galt Technology, makers of quality software and shareware applications—from screensavers and time displays to hangman games—provides its software online.

Address: http://www.galttech.com

Global Technology Associates

GTA develops software products ranging from real-time data acquisition systems to virtual environments.

Address: http://www.gta.com

Groupe Bull

An international information technology group with a worldwide network of information system skills, Groupe Bull combines technological and business partnerships to develop individualized solutions for clients to work and communicate more effectively.

Address: http://www.bull.com

GroupWorks

GroupWorks is a Windows-based groupware product that offers features of Personal Information Managers, project managers, electronic schedulers, document managers, and bulletin board applications.

Address: http://www.hyperdesk.com

Harlequin

Harlequin products include ScriptWorks, DylanWorks, KnowledgeWorks, and others for the fields of electronic publishing, symbolic processing, and Web applications.

Address: http://www.harlequin.com

Harris Computer Systems

Harris develops products for government and commercial markets. Their products include real-time computing systems and applications for simulations, engineering analysis, ranging, and telemetry.

Address: http://www.hcsc.com

Indotronix International

IIC specializes in software solutions and professional services. Their pages offer extensive information about the company, its services, and employment opportunities.

Address: http://www.iic.com

Instrumental

Instrumental develops performance management, operations, accounting, and billing applications for Unix computers.

Address: http://www.instrumental.com

InterCon Systems

InterCon develops and markets Internet products, such as SLIP and PPP dialers, for Mac computers and Internet client applications.

Address: http://www.intercon.com

Intuit

The makers of the popular Quicken personal finance software package have their computers up, but as we go to press, they aren't accepting Web connections yet. Hopefully they will eventually offer information about Quicken and Intuit's other products.

Address: http://www.intuit.com

JSB

JSB develops, markets, and sells the JSB MultiView software family, a variety of products that enable character-based terminals to perform more than one function at a time and allow PC users to access client/server Unix applications.

Address: http://www.jsb.com

Kitchen Wisdom Publishing

Originally a cookbook publishing company, Kitchen Wisdom is now a software development company offering Internet and network diagnosis services. They also provide free tips for using and converting Adobe's PostScript files to other formats.

Address: http://www.wiskit.com

Lotus Development

The developer of one of the world's most popular spreadsheet programs offers industry news, tips, and other useful information on their Web site.

Address: http://www.lotus.com

MathSoft

MathSoft is the publisher of Mathcad, a popular math calculation application. MathSoft also develops a variety of other software tools for PCs, Macs, and Unix computers.

Address: http://www.mathsoft.com

Microsoft

Microsoft makes a wealth of product and industry information available on its Web server. Areas addressed include Microsoft application programs, customer support, the Internet, and Windows 95.

Address: http://www.microsoft.com

NaviSoft

NaviSoft develops network publishing tools and software. Their pages provide information on new beta programs and product information.

Address: http://www.navisoft.com

Pacific Internet

PacNet is a supplier of Internet-specific products and bundled access products, including everything you need for getting a Mac onto the Internet. Two of PacNet's products are Provider-In-A-Box and Web-In-A-Box.

Address: http://www.pacnet.com

Peachtree Software

Peachtree is the developer of one of the oldest and most popular accounting packages for PCs.

Address: http://www.peach.com

Pencom Systems

Pencom offers software consulting, technical staffing, contract programming, and system administration services.

Address: http://www.pencom.com

Phylon Communications

This software company specializes in communications technology. They created PlayLink, on online interactive game center that allows the user to dial up a friend and play a game through a headset and hookup.

Address: http://www.phylon.com

Plant Software

Plant Software's main product is E-GLUE, a sort of electronic sticky pad for Windows NT and Windows 95. They offer a technical support guide, news updates, and a gallery.

Address: http://www.theplant.com

Pronotes

Pronotes develops voice-activation software, concentrating on medical dictation. They provide information about the field and a link to follow for a free demo.

Address: http://www.pronotes.com

Qualcomm

Qualcomm is a software development company specializing in advanced communications systems and products. Qualcomm is also the developer of the popular Eudora Internet email package, which you can order online.

Address: http://www.qualcomm.com

SanSoft

SanSoft is a software developer specializing in COBOL tools. Their products and services include migration assistance from Wang to Open Systems. They also develop general-purpose utilities for accessing and managing COBOL data.

Address: http://www.sansoft.com

Santa Cruz Operation

SCO is a leading developer of Unix operating systems for PCs. Their system is based on Unix System VR3.2, and extensions for such services as networking and development are available.

Address: http://www.sco.com

SAS Institute

This software research and development company created the SAS System, an information delivery product. Their page offers information about the company's role in the workplace as well as employment opportunities.

Address: http://www.sas.com

SBT Accounting Systems

This company supplies multiuser database accounting software to customers all over the world. They provided the first commercial accounting software used on the Internet.

Address: http://www.sbtcorp.com

Scientific and Engineering Software

SES writes software for modeling and simulation, hardware and software design, client/server performance, object-oriented analysis and design, and business process re-engineering.

Address: http://www.ses.com

Second Nature Software

Second Nature Software produces more than 70 software programs for Windows and the Macintosh, concentrating on screensaver and wallpaper programs. Second Nature's pages provide information about available screensaver images, free software, and sample images.

Address: http://www.secondnature.com

Serif

Serif, Inc., develops low-cost, easy-to-use desktop publishing software for Microsoft Windows. Current products include PagePlus, DrawPlus, and PhotoPlus. In addition to information about their products, Serif offers service and support through their web.

Address: http://www.serif.com

Softdesk

Softdesk is a leading provider of architecture, engineering, and construction software. Softdesk's pages offer extensive resources, including information on upcoming seminars and events, employment opportunities, workshops, press releases, and clients.

Address: http://www.softdesk.com

software.net

This online software store has more than 7,800 products ready to ship and an expanding selection of electronically deliverable products for Windows, OS/2, DOS, Mac, and Unix systems.

Address: http://www.software.net

SpeedSim

SpeedSim, Inc., develops and sells software to reduce the time and cost of verifying digital logic designs. Their page offers specific information on software and company technology as well as current news.

Address: http://www.speedsim.com/speedsim

SPRY

Since CompuServe acquired SPRY Inc. in early 1995, the URL listed below will take you directly to CompuServe's Web page. But you can still get support on SPRY's products, including Internet Office and Internet- and Mosaic-In-A-Box, at http://support.spry.com.

Address: http://www.spry.com

Spyglass

Spyglass develops applications for the Internet and the World Wide Web. Their products include a Web browser and a Web server.

Address: http://www.spyglass.com

Starwave

Starwave Corp. creates interactive programs for entertainment, family, and sports. Their programs include SportsZone, Ticketmaster Online, Mr. Showbiz, and Outside Online. They also offer information on employment opportunities with the company.

Address: http://www.starwave.com

Symantec

Symantec is the publisher of leading software for PCs. Their products include The Norton Utilities and Norton Desktop for Windows as well as a collection of valuable tools for Windows 95. On their web, Symantec offers products and information, a press center, service and support, and an anti-virus reference center.

Address: http://www.symantec.com

systemV

systemV is a supplier of Unix Open Systems for Intel x86 processors. They offer products from SCO and Solaris in addition to general support of the Unix, TCP/IP, and Internet environments. They also provide host capability, HTML page creation, and online support for applications.

Address: http://www.systemv.com

Talyon Software

Talyon Software publishes the Plus&Minus accounting software package, claimed by Talyon to be one of the fastest and most powerful programs on the market. Their site provides a tutorial manual and system requirements.

Address: http://www.talyon.com

Template Graphics Software

Template Graphics Software specializes in cross-platform graphics software tools for professional developers. TGS is Apple Computer's official OpenGL technology and product partner. These pages offer extensive company information and product descriptions.

Address: http://www.cts.com/browse/template

UNIROM

UNIROM supplies CD-ROM disks at discount prices. Their categories of disks range from art and business to entertainment and education.

Address: http://www.unirom.com

Veritas

Veritas produces FirstWatch, a fully redundant, high-integrity and -reliability system for mission-critical applications for Unix client/server environments. FirstWatch is currently available for Sun and HP systems.

Address: http://www.tidalwave.com

Virtus

Virtus is a developer of virtual reality, 3-D modeling, and multimedia products such as Virtus Player, a 3-D model publishing utility. Virtus's pages include information on their products and VRML (Virtual Reality Markup Language) technology as well as employment opportunities at the company.

Address: http://www.virtus.com

Visioneering Research Laboratories

This company specializes in custom computer imaging software on platforms such as Sun, Silicon Graphics, DOS, and Windows. Besides information on their products, VRL's pages offer a free service called the Imaging Machine that may be able to install imaging software automatically on your machine.

Address: http://www.vrl.com

X Inside

X Inside develops and sells accelerated X Window servers for Intel-based PCs running Unix. X Inside's OEM distributors include BSDI, ICL, and Siemens-Nixdorf. Their Web pages include product and ordering information as well as graphics board compatibility.

Address: http://www.xinside.com

Directories and Consortiums

Asia Online

This page offers directions to Web sites related to Asia. Users can find information about travel, conventions, and corporations on the world's biggest continent. This is the complete guide to Asian cyberspace.

Address: http://www.asia-online.com

Asia Trade

Produced by Asia Internet Online Publishing, this is a directory of Asian business and leisure sites on the Internet. It provides information about travel, business, and education on the Asian continent.

Address: http://www.asiatrade.com

CommerceNet

CommerceNet is a membership-based organization that provides online directories, catalogs, databases, and other commerce-related information for member companies and other participants.

Address: http://www.commerce.net

CommercePark

This page is a virtual commercial park. CommercePark solicits business tenants to inhabit the park for a monthly fee. Their page also includes an FAQ, benefits list, rates, and contact information.

Address: http://www.commercepark.com

Desk Shop Galleries

With links to Photo Antiquities and Flags by Claudia, Desk Shop Galleries also serves as a starting point to other directories on the Net.

Address: http://www.deskshop.lm.com

EcoMall

EcoMall bills itself as "a place to help save the earth" and offers a product catalog, a list of ecologically minded companies, a classified section, and investment information.

Address: http://www.ecomall.com

Electronic Commerce Associates

Electronic Commerce Associates offers a collection of online catalogs. Readers interested in using ECA's services for their own catalogs and products can contact the company.

Address: http://www.eca.com

Europages

Europages is the European Business Directory, providing business data on more than 150,000 suppliers in 26 European countries. Companies can be found by name, business type, or location.

Address: http://www.europages.com

European Web

The European Web has a variety of services for all needs: links to European commercial sites, PC anti-virus utilities, commercial pages containing product information, and business advertising opportunities.

Address: http://www.zram.com

FractalNet

FractalNet features several advertising businesses. Among its offerings are a real estate company, a university bookstore, a record shop, and a skin products company.

Address: http://www.fractals.com

Global Network Navigator

GNN is an excellent directory of resources on the Web and a starting point you'll want to put in your bookmark file. GNN offers new and exciting links on the Web and a collection of online publications and directories.

Address: http://www.digital.com/gnn/gnn.html

GTSI Online

GTSI Online is an electronic catalog and ordering system for government customers, with more than 20,000 hardware, software, and networking products as well as customer support, specials, and other features.

Address: http://www.gtsi.com

ImagePlaza

ImagePlaza offers information on and descriptive images of a wealth of companies, products, and services. Information can be gathered using two search categories: Travel and Area Information and The Plaza.

Address: http://www.imageplaza.com

infoPost

infoPost allows companies to advertise their products and services. The pages of this web also offer information about the regions of the world, a diverse classified ads section, and a marketplace called The Shopper.

Address: http://www.infopost.com

Northwest Electronic Web Service

NEWS offers links to businesses, companies, services, and cities in the Northwest. Readers can access information in such areas as education, science, travel and recreation, business, and government. These pages also feature links to newspapers around the world.

Address: http://www.thenews.com

Open Market's Commercial Sites Index

The Commercial Sites Index is a directory of thousands of companies—both small and large—doing business on the Web. The directory is accessible alphabetically by company name and is searchable.

Address: http://www.directory.net

Pacific Information eXchange

PIXINET is a Hawaiian mall offering links to Hawaiian businesses and other directories and resources on the Internet.

Address: http://www.pixi.com

Period.Com

Period.Com is a collection of information resources with such categories as travel, airlines, technology, software, and Internet services. Their pages feature elaborate graphics, news, and other information.

Address: http://www.period.com

Sales and Marketing Exchange

This online site allows sales, marketing and PR professionals, and providers to advertise their services, products, and links for their Web sites. Choose from such categories as MarketingWeb, SalesWeb, PRWeb, and AdWeb.

Address: http://www.sme.com

SilverPlatter World

This company uses databases worldwide to provide a library of electronic information. There is an index of Internet resources and a resource called SilverPlatter World for Physicians, which provides helpful information to the medical profession.

Address: http://www.silverplatter.com

Starting Point

As the name implies, this is a starting point for browsing the Web. Readers can choose a category and then select from a list of sites.

Address: http://www.stpt.com

Tennessee CommerceNet

This company lets Tennessee-area businesses advertise their products and services. Information is provided on local real estate and insurance companies.

Address: http://www.tenn.com

Company Information  Product Information Online Ordering

World Wide Yellow Pages

World Wide Yellow Pages, a product of Home Pages, Inc., offers listings of online businesses. Users can obtain price lists and information on how to get their company a listing on the page.

Address: http://www.yellow.com

World-Wide Web Virtual Library

The Web Virtual Library is an extensive directory of resources, companies, and information on the Web. Subjects range from aboriginal studies to zoos.

Address: http://www.w3.org/hypertext/DataSources/bySubject/Overview.html

Education

InfoVid

InfoVid is a guide to the best educational, instructional, and informative videos from around the world. There are more than 3,500 hard-to-find titles on a wide variety of subjects, including auto repair, aerobics, boating, business, crafts, and computers.

Address: http://www.branch.com/infovid

Institute of Financial Education

The Institute of Financial Education is a nonprofit organization providing training services for the staffs of financial institutions and businesses. Information is offered on course selections and programs.

Address: http://www.theinstitute.com

Internet College Exchange

This site offers college-related information for students, parents, and guidance counselors. University descriptions and financial aid tips are available, as well as an option that lets users purchase merchandise from the school of their choice.

Address: http://www.usmall.com

Kids at Heart Software

Kids at Heart develops educational software for children. Their premier product, called Candy Store Math, focuses on math curriculums for children ages 7 to 12, and the program automatically adjusts itself to your child's skill level.

Address: http://www.cts.com/browse/kidheart

Knowledge Products

Knowledge Products offers audio cassettes featuring biographies of famous people, interesting discussions, and narrations of important events. The cassettes are narrated by well-known personalities, including Walter Cronkite and Ben Kingsley.

Address: http://www.cassettes.com

MathPro Press

MathPro Press offers compendiums and indexes of mathematical problems. The page offers math puzzles and information on the books published by MathPro Press.

Address: http://www.wwa.com/math

Peterson's Education Center

Peterson's Guides offer educational information and materials of all kinds. Peterson's is an amazing source of information on educational issues and public, private, and vocational/technical schools, colleges, and universities.

Address: http://www.petersons.com

Princeton Review

Princeton Review is a test-prep and education center. Their page includes information about their books and software as well as career advice. They also list phone numbers of schools and testing agencies.

Address: http://www.review.com

Sargent-Welch

This company distributes science education materials and supplies to the U.S. and Canada. The page offers information on available products and materials for science fair projects as well as resources for teachers, including a textbook list.

Address: http://www.sargentwelch.com

Scholastic

Scholastic Inc. provides educational material from preschool through high school. New online features include a student-written magazine, online libraries, stores, and descriptions of projects.

Address: http://www.scholastic.com

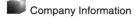

SciTech

This company provides scientific and technical information for children. There is also information on a science summer camp and a selection of T-shirts.

Address: http://scitech.lm.com

Student Services

Student Services, Inc., is an organization dedicated to helping students find financial-aid opportunities. They offer the Money for College Directory, which lists thousands of scholarships, and their own online database lists more than 180,000 scholarships and assorted financial-aid opportunities.

Address: http://www.studentservices.com

Electronics

Alden Electronics

Alden Electronics is a primary provider of weather data collection systems, marine electronics, and specialized imaging products. Alden has pioneered many new systems, from receiving the first satellite pictures from space to mapping the profiles of the world's oceans.

Address: http://www.alden.com

AMP

This company develops and manufactures a wide variety of electronic/electrical interconnection devices. They are also a recognized authority on all aspects of interconnections, such as molding and plating.

Address: http://www.amp.com

Beeper and Stereo Store

As authorized dealers for Kenwood, Sony, PPI, US Amps, Profile, Infinity, OZ, and Kicker, the Beeper and Stereo Store allows online ordering of stereo and component systems, amps, car electronics, alarms, beepers, and other electronics products.

Address: http://www.carstereo.com

Data-Doc Electronics

Data-Doc Electronics provides high-quality products for computer connections, including cabling adaptors, computer interface cables, and printer-sharing products.

Address: http://www.datadoc.com

Electric Power Research Institute

EPRI develops and produces high-value technological advances through their networking partnerships with the electricity industry. EPRI's page features information on their products, projects, and publications.

Address: http://www.epri.com

Electrotex

Electrotex is a distributor of more than 45,000 items of electronics supplies, components, equipment, and tools.

Address: http://www.electrotex.com

Exide Electronics

Exide Electronics manufactures UPS (Uninterruptible Power Supply) hardware and power management and monitoring software. You'll find product information, press releases, news of upcoming events, and job opportunities.

Address: http://www.exide.com/exide

J J Electronic Plaza

J J Electronic Plaza offers information on products and services from electronic stores, vendors, Internet service providers, and others. Also featured are a classified ad section and an information center.

Address: http://www.jjplaza.com

Jerry's World

This electronic superstore provides a wealth of computer-related products and information. Categories on the page include Jvalue, a listing of merchandise on sale, JNews, Jerry's World Multimedia Vendor, and JWorld Computer Industry Directory.

Address: http://www.jworld.com

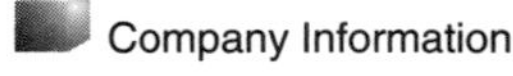  

Company Information Product Information Online Ordering

Panasonic Technologies

Panasonic Technologies provides the locations of its various U.S. research labs. The page also offers suggestions for other interesting Web sites.

Address: http://www.panasonic.com

Philips Electronics North America - Philips Semiconductors On-line

Philips Semiconductors is one of the largest semiconductor suppliers in the world, offering such products as multimedia for PCs, wireless communications, microcontrollers, and audio and video products.

Address: http://www.semiconductors.philips.com/ps

Richardson Electronics

Richardson Electronics, Ltd., is a worldwide electronic components company whose Web pages offer such products and services as security systems, power semiconductors, cathode ray tubes, and electron tubes. Options include information on upcoming seminars and trade shows.

Address: http://www.rell.com

Sabtech Industries

Sabtech Industries produces interface boards and other hardware and software products for military applications.

Address: http://www.sabtech.com

SaRonix

SaRonix supplies quartz crystal and crystal oscillator products to the electronics industry.

Address: http://www.saronix.com

Savantage

Savantage specializes in electronic design automation systems, focusing on electrical and thermal performance, reliability, routability, manufacturability, and cost.

Address: http://www.savantage.com

SeaSpace

SeaSpace develops sophisticated remote-sensing products to acquire, process, and analyze weather satellite data. They develop and sell their TeraScan systems throughout the world and serve academic and commercial users as well as government agencies.

Address: http://www.seaspace.com

Sony Electronics

Sony is one of the largest electronics companies in the world. This page updates consumer and computer products and offers an opportunity for feedback.

Address: http://www.sel.sony.com

Engineering

Da Vinci Design

Da Vinci specializes in engineering custom tools and patent work. Their page offers an FAQ on patent information and has links to other interesting engineering resources.

Address: http://www.sccsi.com/DaVinci/davinci.html

DynAl

DynAl is an engineering firm that strives to provide practical, common-sense applications for a wide variety of engineering and programmatic problems.

Address: http://www.dynal.com

Electrotek Concepts

Electrotek Concepts is an engineering services company that solves utility and industrial power system problems. The company provides new and inexpensive solutions for enhancing efficiency in electrical transport.

Address: http://www.electrotek.com

Felix Heating, Ventilation, and Air Conditioning

Fernando Felix is a licensed HVAC contractor. This page provides the company's phone number and email address.

Address: http://www.catalog.com/rmg/fhac_01.htm

ICEM CFD Engineering

ICEM CFD Engineering produces computational fluid dynamics software and electronic cooling simulation systems. The page includes a list of related links.

Address: http://icemcfd.com

InterCAD

InterCad specializes in converting paper engineering drawings into computerized CAD systems and databases.

Address: http://www.village.com/intercad/welcome.html

Maya

Maya's engineers, human-factors specialists, and graphic designers help clients develop advanced-technology products that are functional but also easy to use and aesthetically appealing.

Address: http://www.maya.com

Silver Engineering

This high-tech firm develops space systems and ground support equipment. They offer design assistance and products ranging from satellite components to simulation equipment.

Address: http://www.isso.org/Industry/Silver/silver.html

Teledyne Brown Engineering

Teledyne Brown Engineering supports the U.S. military and space programs. They have enhanced the U.S. space initiative, ballistic missile defense, and environmental services.

Address: http://www.tbe.com

Viewlogic Systems

Viewlogic Systems develops software for the design automation and computer-aided engineering markets. Their page provides company locations and information about their consulting services.

Address: http://www.viewlogic.com

Entertainment

American Gramaphone Records

American Gramaphone Records is a company started by singer/songwriter Chip Davis. This page includes a list and description of his albums.

Address: http://www.amgram.com

Digital Planet

Digital Planet is an interactive entertainment company. Its activities include enhancing corporate presence on the Internet; developing multimedia marketing, promotion, and consulting; and producing CD-ROM adventure games and educational materials.

Address: http://www.digiplanet.com

Mix 101.5 WRAL-FM

This North Carolina radio station plays a variety of hits from the '70s, '80s, and '90s. You can check out the station's music mix, plus morning show hosts Bill and Sheri, other on-air personalities at the station, photos of MIX events, and concerts sponsored by the station.

Address: http://www.wralfm.com

Movietimes.com

Movietimes.com offers a comprehensive guide to movie theaters in the San Francisco Bay Area and surrounding counties, plus information on movie studios including Paramount and MGM. Additional features include movie reviews, a chat room, and a site-of-the-month pick.

Address: http://www.movietimes.com

Raymond Interactive Theatre

RIT is an online theatre for interactive role-playing. Plays are always underway, and other links lead to information about upcoming plays and about becoming a ticketholder, which enables you to join the play.

Address: http://www.rit.com

Rock Around the World

This excellent music and entertainment site is offered by the 1970s Rock Around the World radio show. Options include news and interviews with major and minor rock stars, new releases on rock and alternative music, profiles of new artists, regional music charts from around the world, and much more.

Address: http://www.ratw.com

Ticketmaster

Ticketmaster Online provides the latest news and information about the entertainment industry, concert schedules, movies, and backstage gossip.

Address: http://www.ticketmaster.com

United Media

United Media owns United Features Syndicate, Inc., which publishes daily comic strips such as Peanuts, Doctor Fun, and Dilbert, plus editorial cartoons, syndicated columns, books, magazines, and other publications.

Address: http://www.unitedmedia.com

Film, Production, and Video Services

Abekas

Abekas Video Systems, Inc., is a leading manufacturer of professional video production, postproduction, graphics, and broadcast equipment. Their page offers press releases, news of trade shows, and an opportunity to contact the company.

Address: http://www.abekas.com

Digital Theater Systems

DTS produces cinema sound delivery systems that provide true sound using digital time codes that faithfully render filmmakers' original recordings.

Address: http://www.dtstech.com

Global Village Stock Footage

The Global Village Stock Footage Library offers online access to a database describing more than one million video clips and images of stock footage from around the world. If Global Village doesn't have the footage you're looking for, they will help you find it by connecting you to an online network of more than 150 stock footage agencies.

Address: http://www.nbn.com/footage

HoloCom

HoloCom offers a wide array information about holography and holograms. They provide information on the latest holographic designs and techniques, the companies that produce holography products and images, and links to other sites relating to holography.

Address: http://www.holo.com

Hype!

Hype! provides information on movies, music, television shows, video games, and comics. There are contests, polls, reviews, and news areas about video and computer systems.

Address: http://www.hype.com

InterStudio Ltd.

InterStudio is a group of international dealers that buy and sell new and used broadcast, video, film, post-production, and pro-audio equipment. They also offer musical instruments and memorabilia and list any current music equipment exhibitions.

Address: http://www.interstudio.co.uk/isl/

Kodak

Visit Kodak's web to find out what the world's premier photographic film manufacturer is up to. Read about their extensive line of products, from aerial film scanners and digital photographic products to X-ray film.

Address: http://www.kodak.com

MCA/Universal Cyberwalk

This Web page provides access to information and updates regarding MCA Records, Universal Pictures, Universal Studios Hollywood, and other MCA/ Universal subsidiaries. Includes product information, music, videos, and guided tours.

Address: http://www.mca.com

Rule Broadcast Systems

RBS provides audio, video, and multimedia rental equipment for industry, broadcasting, and other professionals and organizations.

Address: http://www.rule.com

Total Video

Total Video is an online marketplace for video and digital production products and services.

Address: http://www.totalvideo.com

University Video Communications

University Video offers video materials documenting technological issues and achievements in university classrooms around the nation. You can test-drive Web-cast demonstration videos and view abstracts for more than 125 video lectures.

Address: http://www.uvc.com

Videomedia

Videomedia Inc. is the creator of the V-LAN Machine Control Network, a microcomputer-functioning videotape editing system. The company specializes in producing compatible computer and video equipment for a variety of uses such as processor-intensive animation. There are also links to related sites.

Address: http://www.videomedia.com

Videonics

Videonics provides a variety of products and services in the field of computer video editing and post-production. Videonics' pages include extensive information on video editing, a section on articles and seminars, and a listing of dealer locations.

Address: http://www.videonics.com

Financial Services

1-800-TAX-LAWS

This company consists of tax professionals (CPAs, attorneys, and enrolled agents) from across the nation. Besides a toll-free number to find a tax professional in any user's area, this page offers information on filing taxes online and even a humor section.

Address: http://www.5010geary.com

American Mortgage Listings

This page is a mortgage service listing to help users find loans and to help lenders, private investors, and mortgage brokers nationwide access loan listings. The listings are categorized by location, property type, and loan range.

Address: http://www.loanlist.com

American Stock Exchange

The world's second largest auction-marketplace, AMEX serves more than 800 innovative companies. Their page features a market summary, news, and listed companies.

Address: http://www.amex.com

Berkshire Information Services

BIS provides information about emerging growth companies available to the investing public.

Address: http://www.growth.com

Dun & Bradstreet Information Services

D&B is a widely recognized firm that provides global business information and expertise. They offer online business background reports for a nominal fee, tips on strategic business planning, and strategies on research and tactical marketing.

Address: http://www.dbisna.com

Fidelity Investments

Fidelity Investments offers brokerage services, investor tools, and information on mutual funds and other topics relating to personal investments.

Address: http://www.fid-inv.com

 Company Information  Product Information  Online Ordering

HSH Associates

HSH Associates is a financial publishing firm and one of the largest publishers of mortgage and consumer loan information in the nation. Its database of residential mortgage information provides insight into the mortgage and consumer loan markets.

Address: http://www.hsh.com

J. P. Morgan

Institutional character and a worldwide reach make J.P. Morgan a leader in global finance. Strategic advice, capital raising, market access, operational services, and asset management are the cornerstones of their business.

Address: http://www.jpmorgan.com

Norwest

This financial services company provides financial products and services to clients ranging from consumers to agricultural producers and large corporations. Norwest's page includes financial articles, economic forecasts, a link to search utilities, and an online shopping helper.

Address: http://www.norwest.com

Principal Financial Group

PFG offers a diverse array of financial services. Its many subsidiaries include America's Health Plan, Inc., and the Principal Mutual Life Insurance Company. These pages describe the extensive services for both individual and business financial planning offered by PFG.

Address: http://www.principal.com

Quote.Com

Quote.Com provides quality financial market data, including current quotes on stocks, commodity futures, mutual funds, and bonds. They also offer business news, market analysis and commentary, financial information, and company profiles.

Address: http://www.quote.com

Stock Research Group

SRG provides current stock and investment information to investors. SRG's pages cover breaking news and developments, up-and-coming companies, an online newsletter, and daily market reports for several exchanges.

Address: http://www.stockgroup.com

Stockdeck Communications

Stockdeck Online publishes corporate profiles for hundreds of publicly traded companies. Stockdeck offers links you can follow for up-to-date stock quotes, to register for additional information, and to many business publications ranging from business, commerce, and investing to sports and leisure.

Address: http://www.stockdeck.com

Tax Prophet

The Tax Prophet is an online service that provides information on all aspects of the Internal Revenue Code, business law, and taxation for foreigners. You'll find extensive information on tax services and a variety of helpful publications on related topics.

Address: http://www.taxprophet.com

Wall Street Direct

Wall Street Direct is a one-stop page for stocks, bonds, and financial information. Here you'll find a bookstore, broker listings, market predictions, seminars, product reviews, publications, press releases, and special offers.

Address: http://www.cts.com/browse/wallst

Your Life

Your Life is a service of Canada Trust that provides helpful information and articles on a variety of financial matters, from family financing to retirement planning. Their extensive material explains financial matters for readers of all backgrounds and experience levels.

Address: http://www.yourlife.com

Food and Beverage

20 Tank Brewing Co.

The 20 Tank Brewing Co. is a brewery/pub located in San Francisco. This page offers general information about their menu and operating hours, the brewing process, and available merchandise.

Address: http://www.and.com/20tank

American Homebrewing Association

This company offers information to users wanting to brew their own beer. The AHA is hoping to attract members, who receive five issues of the magazine *Zymurgy* as well as invitations to conferences, competitions, and forums (not to mention advice from expert brewers).

Address: http://www.aob.org/aob/aha.html

Arabica Coffee Co.

This company sells gourmet coffee at commercial-blend prices and provides door-to-door delivery. They also offer an opportunity for people to be tasters and refer others.

Address: http://www.ibos.com/pub/ibos/coffee/coffee.html

Barbra Jean's Famous Candies

Barbra Jean's Famous Candies makes assortments of chocolates, fudge, and other treats available for ordering, either individually or packaged in gift baskets.

Address: http://www.bjcandy.com/~bjcandy/menu.html

BearBoat Pinot Noir

BearBoat is a vintner that produces Pinot Noir wine. They also make apple juice, and you may order cases of both online as well as BearBoat T-shirts. The page features a contest and a wine-related hot-list.

Address: http://www.bearboat.com

Bloomington Brewing Co.

This page offers information on Bloomington Brewing Company's beers, merchandise, specific recipes, history, and brewing techniques. Also offered is a virtual tour of the brewery and, for purchase, a copy of the business plan that made the brewery successful.

Address: http://www.intersource.com/~oneworld

Brew Online

Brew Magazine is for the true beer connoisseur. It's a guide to America's brewpubs and microbreweries, providing information on new beers and breweries around the nation.

Address: http://www.and.com/brew

Buffalo Bill's Brewing Co.

This page offers information on history, the brewing process, types of beer, available merchandise, and the brewers themselves at Buffalo Bill's Brewing Company.

Address: http://www.and.com/bb

Cask Brewing Systems

This supplier and servicer of brewing systems for the cottage brewing industry provides information and assistance, from staff training and recipes to consultation. Cask's pages offer information on products and installation, ingredients, and recipes for the beers.

Address: http://www.tcel.com/~gobrew/cask/programs/comp.html

Celestial Seasonings

Celestial Seasonings Online offers a variety of teas. Here you'll find their selection of teas, gifts, and apparel available for online ordering.

Address: http://www.usa.net/celestial

Coca-Cola

Coca-Cola is the leading soft-drink company in the world. Their page provides important information for stockholders.

Address: http://www.cocacola.com

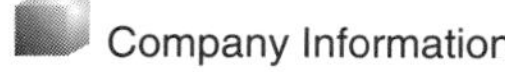 Company Information  Product Information  Online Ordering

Diedrich Coffee

Diedrich Coffee, a family-owned company, imports and roasts arabica coffees from around the world. They participate in all areas of the coffee industry, from owning their own Central American plantations to manufacturing roasting machines.

Address: http://www.diedrich.com

Foodmaker

Foodmaker owns the Jack-in-the-Box fast-food restaurant chain. Foodmaker's page offers words from the "founder" (Jack), press releases, and promotions.

Address: http://www.foodmaker.com

Forest Hill Vineyard

As the first winery to go online on the Internet, Forest Hill was featured in "Shopping the Cyber-Mall" in the April 1995 issue of *Smart Money*. With seven vintages, Forest Hill has proven itself to be one of the most distinguished Chardonnay producers in California.

Address: http://www.branch.com/wine

Goodies from Goodman

Goodies from Goodman ships delectable gifts, such as fruit baskets, Godiva chocolates, gourmet food gifts, and smoked meats, anywhere in the nation.

Address: http://www.branch.com/goodies

Grapevine

This Web page is devoted to the Northern California wine country, wineries, wine products, wine education, travel, and life style through a directory of wine-related services. There are many links to individual wine home pages, and news updates, such as wine auctions, are regularly posted.

Address: http://www.winery.com

Harvard Espresso Co.

As a small cafe, Harvard Espresso Co. now offers the famous coffees that have been enjoyed on Capitol Hill in Seattle via the Web, giving everyone the opportunity to purchase and enjoy the high quality and great taste.

Address: http://www.coffees.com

Hawaii's Best Espresso

Hawaii's Best Espresso Co. offers coffees from paradise. Choose from several varieties of Kona coffee—known for its rich, smooth flavor—in both light and dark roasts. They also offer Italian espresso, a blend of gourmet Central and South American beans roasted to perfection in Italy.

Address: http://planet-hawaii.com/~bec/

Hemispheres Restaurant and Bistro

Hemispheres Restaurant and Bistro is a fine dining restaurant in Toronto, Ontario. It serves lunch, dinner, and Sunday brunch. This page gives the user an opportunity to browse the menu and wine list and "meet" the chefs.

Address: http://www.hemispheres.com

Home Chef

Home Chef is a culinary magazine offering restaurant-quality recipes that are efficient and easy to make. In addition to recipes, their page offers links to other food resources on the Net, cooking techniques, and helpful hints.

Address: http://www.homechef.com

HotHotHot!

If you like fiery foods, check out this list of gourmet hot sauces. We tried "Dave's Insanity Sauce" and still haven't recovered.

Address: http://www.hot.presence.com

Independent Grocers Alliance

This supermarket network's page provides news on upcoming events and projects as well as information on supermarket locations and IGA food labels.

Address: http://www.igainc.com

Lobsternet

Lobsternet ships live Maine lobsters directly from the Atlantic Ocean to your door. They pack your lobster in a foam-insulated cooler with a frozen gel-pac and ship it overnight delivery. Lobsternet also sells lobster claw T-shirts.

Address: http://www.branch.com/lobster/lobster.htm

Company Information   Product Information   Online Ordering

Magic Windows

Use Magic Windows to check out the wine lists of numerous wineries in the U.S. and Canada. This page allows you to choose from a vast selection of wines as well as miscellaneous products such as music, bumper stickers, and bath products.

Address: http://www.magicwindows.com/~mwinfo

Maine Lobster Direct

Maine Lobster Direct offers the luxury of ordering fresh Maine lobster 24 hours a day. This page gives the viewer a variety of ideas for serving lobster and offers personalized gift baskets as well as gift certificates. The 800 number makes ordering easy and free.

Address: http://www.maine.com/lobsters

Mama's Cucina

Read homey advice from "Mama" on pasta and pizza recipes. Sponsored by Ragu, these pages also offer advice on Italian language lessons, tours of Little Italy, information on Italian architecture, stories of food and family, and the chance to win a trip to Italy.

Address: http://www.eat.com

Miller Genuine Draft Tap Room

Provided by MGD, the Tap Room offers frequently updated information about clubs, music, fashion, nightlife, food, and restaurants in a variety of cities. Their mail option lets you post messages and updates about culture in your own city.

Address: http://www.mgdtaproom.com

Orfila Vineyards

Formerly Thomas Jaeger Winery, long known for its award-winning wines, Orfila Vineyards is now offering a wonderful selection of great-tasting and healthy gourmet cooking oils.

Address: http://www.branch.com/orfila

Organic Coffee Co.

This company produces and sells organic coffee. Their page provides details on the coffee varieties, roasting processes, price lists, and available merchandise.

Address: http://www.bid.com/bid/cybercafe/occ.html

Pizza Hut

Pizza Hut has teamed up with The Santa Cruz Operation to offer pizza ordering through this Web server. Type your name and phone number into the online form to see if delivery is available in your area.

Address: http://www.pizzahut.com

Quebec Maple Syrup

Pure maple syrup is a rare treat, and thanks to the wonders of technology, Quebec's finest maple syrup is now available to the world.

Address: http://www.vir.com/~jam/syrup.html

Retail Restaurant Consulting Services

This company offers information, advice, and assistance on virtually every issue of interest to the restaurant industry. Consulting services include restaurant development and design, food-service equipment analysis, and health and sanitation reviews. It also publishes an online newsletter and a helpful FAQ on the restaurant industry.

Address: http://www.jaxnet.com/~lonnien/

Sam's Wine Warehouse

Sam's Wine Warehouse is a distributor of wine and spirits in the U.S. Sam's offers thousands of wine labels from more than a dozen countries, a wide variety of grappas, and a fine selection of rare Scotches and cognacs.

Address: http://www.ravenna.com/sams

scotch.com

scotch.com has devoted this page to information on many kinds of Scotch whiskey, the distilling and production of this beverage, and the history and characteristics of Scotland.

Address: http://www.scotch.com

Sokolin's Online

Sokolin's is an online wine shop offering information on wines, wines as investments, and health issues related to wine consumption.

Address: http://www.dsokolin.com

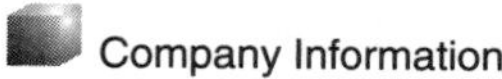 Company Information   Product Information  Online Ordering

Sophisticated Chocolates

Sophisticated Chocolates creates gift-boxed chocolate assortments, chocolate corporate logos, chocolate-filled gift baskets, personalized wedding favors, and many other fine-quality chocolate products.

Address: http://www.branch.com/sophisticated

Southern Comfort

Southern Comfort's Web page offers online guides to a handful of American cities including Austin, Boston, Philadelphia, Buffalo, Chicago, and San Francisco. There is also a "SoCo" drink recipe section.

Address: http://www.southerncomfort.com

Stoli Central

Stolichnaya Vodka, a Russian company, and Carillon Importers, Ltd., have created this page to provide information on drinks from around the world, sites on the Web frequented by "Stoli regulars," and a vodka page in which users can create their own new drinks.

Address: http://www.stoli.com

Taiga Tea Co.

As the only company in the U.S. that offers ginseng products direct from Siberia, Taiga Tea uses the remarkable Far Eastern herb—said to boost physical and mental endurance—in their tea products. Also provided is an FAQ on Siberian ginseng.

Address: http://www.taigatea.com/taigatea

Todd & Holland

Todd & Holland offers a wide selection of choice loose-leaf teas to serious tea drinkers worldwide. These pages allow you to choose from their extensive list of black teas, oolongs and pouchongs, and green teas.

Address: http://www.branch.com/teas

Toucan Chocolates

Toucan Chocolates melds the tastes and textures of tropical nuts with some of the world's best milk and dark chocolates to create a variety of candy assortments.

Address: http://www.branch.com/toucan

Vintage Direct

Vintage Direct is the mail-order branch of a Melbourne-based wine merchant group that provides a variety of Australian wines, culinary products, and cookbooks at direct prices. Note: At present, wine may not be shipped to countries other than Australia.

Address: http://www.sofcom.com.au/Nicks

Virtual Vineyards

Virtual Vineyards allows you to purchase limited-production wines recommended by wine expert Peter Granoff and explore these featured wineries online. Match proper wines with food dishes or pose questions regarding wine to the Cork Dork.

Address: http://www.virtualvin.com

Whole Foods Market

Whole Foods Market is a network of natural-food supermarkets spanning the nation, known in some states as Wellspring Grocery, Bread & Circus, and Mrs. Gooch's. This page offers information on a variety of health issues, available products, recipes, and related Web sites.

Address: http://www.wholefoods.com

Winecountry Virtual Visit

FreeRun Technologies offers a collection of "virtual visits" to California's wine country—the Napa Valley and Sonoma County. Once inside, you'll get information about sightseeing activities, lodging and dining, shopping and current events, and the wineries themselves.

Address: http://www.freerun.com

Wines on the Internet

Wines on the Internet offers information on wines and wineries. You can sample their products in the virtual tasting room or take a tour of the winery. They also offer software and product information, online ordering, and many other resources for wine enthusiasts.

Address: http://www.wines.com

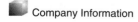

Zima Beverage

This page provides information on the new Zima Gold, upcoming events, merchandise available on "Z Street," and a special room on the Web called the Freezer that is available only to members of "Tribe Z" (a sort of Zima club).

Address: http://www.zima.com

Games

Adventure OnLine Gaming

This online gaming service develops multiplayer role-playing games. Site users can test new games, read articles and stories in its *Adventure Zine* gaming magazine, and participate in various contests.

Address: http://www.gameworld.com

Game Experience

The Game Experience Inc. Web site provides product and ordering information for games available for play on Sony PlayStation, Sega Saturn, 3DO, Super NES, Sega Genesis, and PC CD-ROM.

Address: http://www.gamex.com

Gamer's Den

This site specializes in multiplayer play-by-electronic-mail (PBEM) games and currently offers a commercial space-based game, Phoenix. You can purchase an account online to continue play after the first two free trials. There is also information regarding future game offerings and related publications.

Address: http://www.den.com

Lava Mind

Lava Mind is a company specializing in game development. The page offers product reviews and information about their games, including Gazillionaire and Zapitalism, sneak peeks at the company's latest games, links to other game sites, and movie, book, and article reviews.

Address: http://www.lavamind.com

OKbridge - 'Bridge on the Internet'

OKbridge makes it possible for people around the world to play bridge together live through the Internet. This 24-hour bridge club is inexpensive and easy to use, and it provides rubber, duplicate, and team play.

Address: http://www.cts.com/browse/okbridge

Outland

Outland is an online game center where users can play games with other Internet users from all over the world or get information on other game Web sites. For a small fee, users have unlimited access to such games as chess, Spaceward, and Backstab.

Address: http://www.outland.com

Rocket Science Games

Rocket Science is an entertainment company that creates and produces original video and CD-ROM games. These pages contain information on their current games, online merchandise, and company news.

Address: http://www.rocketsci.com

Virtual World Entertainment

Virtual World Entertainment brought the world's first digital theme park to the Web. VWE's pages offer detailed information on the interactive games they offer as well as a listing of the 1995 Grand Masters and other interesting links.

Address: http://www.virtualworld.com

VR Slingshot

VR Slingshot is a 3-D dogfight simulation game that is available as both a demo and a commercial product. It features three exciting cybersports: Energy Duel, Disc Eliminator, and Cyberball. For other features and requirements, check out this Web page.

Address: http://www.cts.com/browse/vrman

Graphics and Special Effects

Algorithm Inc.

Algorithm Inc. is a research and development company specializing in graphics programming and virtual reality. They also provide links to information about a variety of relevant books and CD-ROMs.

Address: http://www.algorithm.com

Art Store

The Art Store is a virtual art gallery that lets you view sequential thumbnail sketches of art by contemporary artists. A description of the art and an artist's statement accompany each graphic, with options for ordering specific prints.

Address: http://www.gtp.com/art

Beautiful Beautiful Women

This company sells CD-ROMs of—you guessed it—beautiful women. A screensaver and calendar are included at no additional cost.

Address: http://www.cts.com/browse/bbw

Century III

Century III is a commercial and corporate studio production, post-production, and multimedia company. You'll find sample art from their current projects and information on the types of post-production services, equipment, and facilities they offer.

Address: http://www.digital.net/~century3

ERDAS

ERDAS specializes in software for image processing, raster-based GIS, and softcopy photogrammetry. Applications of their software include natural resource management, environmental monitoring, urban/regional planning and site selection, geotechnical exploration, forestry, cartography, agriculture, and defense.

Address: http://www.erdas.com

Picture Network International

PNI offers more than a quarter million stock images from 35 of the world's top picture agencies. Categories include food, business, travel, history, science, and medicine, as well as images of famous personalities and the seasons.

Address: http://pni4news.wwa.com

Precision Digital Images

Precision Digital Images provides a collection of high-performance digital imaging solutions for professional and commercial applications, such as medical imaging, machine vision, virtual reality, and videoconferencing.

Address: http://www.precisionimages.com

SciNetPhotos

This is the online showcase site for the work of Hank Morgan Photography, specializing in photos pertaining to science. More than 30,000 images are available for viewing.

Address: http://www.scinetphotos.com

Sudden Images

Sudden Images takes presentations created with Persuasion or PowerPoint and converts them into full-color slides within 24 hours. Their page includes pointers on making professional slides and methods for translating ideas into high-quality presentations.

Address: http://www.slideimages.com/browse/slides

Health and Medicine

Comfort, Etc.

Comfort, Etc. furnishes products for stress reduction and life-style improvement from more than 75 worldwide suppliers. There is an online catalog of merchandise, and the company accepts QUIK CHEX faxes.

Address: http://www.icw.com/comfort/catalog.html

Cyberspace Telemedical Office

The goal of the Cyberspace Telemedical Office project is to increase worldwide access to health information and services. The project's page is designed to be a one-stop shop for health and wellness information, products, and services, providing at least 15 categories of interest to consumers and health professionals.

Address: http://www.cts.com/browse/drcarr

Dicon

Dicon develops instruments and software for use by eye-care practitioners. Dicon's products include kinetic fixation systems, autoperimeters, and analysis tools.

Address: http://www.dicon.com/dicon

Dr. Art Ulene's Nutrition Strategies

These pages offer information on nutrition, weight loss, and low-fat cooking for a healthy life style with Nutrition and Weight Loss Tips of the Week. Information is available on nutrition expert Dr. Art Ulene, health insurance, and Dr. Ulene's own line of vitamins.

Address: http://www.vitamin.com

E-Zee Vision Eyewear

E-Zee Vision offers eyewear in four frame styles and a variety of colors for men, women, and children at reasonable prices.

Address: http://www.eyeglass.com

Eli Lilly and Co.

Eli Lilly is a pharmaceutical company offering health-care products. Their web offers information about the company, including financial data, press releases, reports, career opportunities, contact information, and answers to frequently asked questions about Eli Lilly.

Address: http://www.lilly.com

Enrich International

As one of the leading distributors of herbal supplements and products, Enrich offers programs and natural, nutritional products for a healthier life style.

Address: http://www.enrich.com

F1RSTMARK

F1RSTMARK has links to thousands of businesses in the medical and health-care fields and information about their products and services. F1RSTMARK also provides a search facility for looking up companies by their services and products.

Address: http://www.firstmark.com

FHP Health Care

Based in Fountain Valley, California, FHP is a diversified Health Maintenance Organization serving people in numerous states. On their Web page, FHP offers a health quiz, information about HMOs, and educational materials in the Fit Kids Club.

Address: http://www.fhp.com

Global Emergency Medical Services

An Atlanta-based company, GEMS provides familiar and reliable medical care for the international traveler. Connections to a nationally recognized trauma center and its affiliated physicians ensure proper care and treatment.

Address: http://www.globalmed.com

Global Nutritional Products

Global Nutritional Products offers supplements designed to enhance energy and health. Their page includes the pricing and description of products.

Address: http://www.kaiwan.com/~health/branch.html

Hsu's Ginseng Enterprises

Hsu's Ginseng Enterprises ships ginseng directly to the user from Wausau, Wisconsin. This Web page offers information about how ginseng affects health, descriptions of its uses, and ginseng recipes. Catalogs are offered in Chinese and English.

Address: http://www.hsuginseng.com

Internet Health Resources

Internet Health Resources provides valuable and accessible information on all aspects of the health-care industry. This site's goal is to educate users about one of America's most important and controversial issues.

Address: http://www.ihr.com

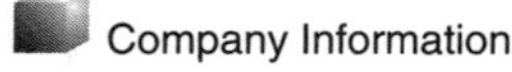  Product Information 

Life Technologies

Life Technologies develops products for use in life sciences research and biomedical manufacturing. Their products are used in the study of diseases, including AIDS, cancer, diabetes, Alzheimer's, cystic fibrosis, and Down's syndrome.

Address: http://www.lifetech.com

Living Large Network

Living Large Network is a self-improvement page offering a supportive atmosphere in which people can learn and grow. Advice and helpful suggestions are provided on issues such as stress and self-esteem.

Address: http://www.lln.com

Plants Publishing

This small business offers information on the use of plants and herbs for treating diseases and ailments. Their page also has pointers to similar resources on the Net.

Address: http://www.plant.com

Proteus Hyperbaric Systems

This company designs and manufactures hyperbaric systems for research and hospital use, including the Proteus III, their most advanced product. The page also provides extensive information about Hyperbaric Oxygen Therapy.

Address: http://www.hyperbaric.com

Relax the Back Store

This company offers products to relieve back pain. They provide extensive information to help ease stress at work, at home, or in the car. There are graphics to illustrate the detailed descriptions of each product.

Address: http://www.relaxtheback.com

Roxane Laboratories

This company developed the Roxane Pain Institute, which works with cancer and AIDS patients in symptom and pain control. The page offers a library of health-care resources and information on specific types of medicine.

Address: http://www.roxane.com

Sachs Group

This online site is for a leading health-care information provider that serves hospitals, physicians, and health-care organizations. The page offers press releases and updated news pertaining to health care.

Address: http://www.sachs.com

Sunrider International

Sunrider International gets customers on the road to healthy life styles. From skin care to weight management, they give advice on how to take care of your body.

Address: http://www.sunrider.com

Ted Edwards

As a radio and TV personality, speaker, and physician with an active interest in preventive medicine, nutrition, and internal medicine, Dr. Edwards offers a weekly health tip, access to previous tips, and general nutrition and health information on his site.

Address: http://www.tededwards.com

U.S. Healthcare

With more than 2 million members across the country, this is one of the largest health-care companies in the country. The page describes the company's services and provides health and medical news. There is even an online art gallery to browse through.

Address: http://www.ushc.com

Walgreens

Walgreens is a nationwide chain of drugstores, filling more than 148 million prescriptions per year. The page provides a list of locations throughout the U.S.

Address: http://www.walgreens.com

Wellspring Media

Wellspring Media offers an assortment of videos promoting healthy life styles. The page has three categories: Health & Fitness, Spirituality, and Personal Development.

Address: http://www.wellmedia.com

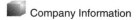

Hobbies and Recreation

Aristo-Craft Trains

With the help of an interactive forum, email contact, product information, catalogs, and great train layouts from across the country, Aristo-Craft makes model trains fun and accessible.

Address: http://www.aristocraft.com/aristo

Atlas Model Railroad

Atlas helps you get started collecting model trains. Listed are railroad resources, a catalog of merchandise, a directory of Atlas retailers, illustrations of railroad sets, and a software modeling program to aid railroaders with any level of experience in improving their sets and layouts.

Address: http://www.atlasrr.com

BoatWorks

BoatWorks is an online marketplace for boats and related products and services, featuring information on boats for sale, manufacturers' products, supplies and accessories, vacations, and a chat section.

Address: http://www.boatworks.com

Gardener's Supply

Gardener's Supply is a company of avid gardeners committed to bringing the pleasures and rewards of gardening to as many people as possible. Their catalog offers practical, earth-friendly solutions to make gardening hours more successful and enjoyable.

Address: http://seidel.ncsa.uiuc.edu/PBM-FAQ/list/gardsupply.

Great Outdoor Recreation Pages

GORP offers information on the great outdoors, including attractions and activities as well as necessary gear, trip ideas, and outdoor safety.

Address: http://www.gorp.com

Houseworks

Houseworks is a world leader in the manufacturing, distribution, and retailing of dollhouse building components and miniature supplies. They feature a hobby builders' supply catalog, a how-to manual for building miniature dollhouses, and a 24-hour information desk.

Address: http://www.miniatures.com

International Treasure Hunters Exchange

The International Treasure Hunters Exchange is for the treasure hunters of the world. The page offers an eclectic assortment of information relating to treasure. News about anything from shipwrecks to metal detecting is available.

Address: http://www.treasure.com

Kingswood Kranium

Kingswood Advertising is an ad agency, but this site is definitely just for fun. They attempt to explore the depths of the human mind, offering some absurd questions and information.

Address: http://www.kingswood.com

Lvalue

Lvalue is an online site offering an Art Gallery, Poster Shop, and Quiz Room. The Art Gallery features works available for purchase from a sampling of international artists, while in the Quiz Room users can participate in contests where they have to guess the authors of literary quotes.

Address: http://www.lvalue.com

Magical Secrets

Learn to be a magician or simply enjoy magic with the help of Magical Secrets. This page lets you order magic props, tricks, effects, illusions, posters, and artwork. It serves as a guide to exploring magic in other venues by offering "Magical Links."

Address: http://www.magical.com

Marine Network

Marine Network offers a database of marine companies throughout the nation. All companies involved provide marine services and products as well as information about available boats and waterfront property.

Address: http://www.marinenetwork.com

 Company Information  Product Information Online Ordering

Sailboats

Sailboats Inc. teaches people to sail, manages marinas, and helps make it possible to purchase a yacht on the Internet.

Address: http://www.sailboats-inc.com

Trading Card World

This page offers lists of dealers, trading show times, dates, and locations, and a card dictionary that holds all the words pertaining to sports and non-sports card trading.

Address: http://www.tradingcard.com

Home Improvement and Household Products

Baskind Co.

M.A. Baskind is an online company offering home improvement and decorating ideas and materials, including wall coverings, window treatments, and architectural millwork. View sample wall coverings, check out tips for measuring and installing wall coverings, and view Baskind's full-color home improvement catalogs.

Address: http://www.ibp.com/pit/baskind

Build.com

This site provides information on where to find merchants, manufacturers, services, and materials for your building and home improvement projects.

Address: http://www.build.com

Calgon

Calgon Corp. supplies specialty chemicals and provides services for industrial applications, such as papermaking and cosmetics.

Address: http://www.calgon.com

Enviro-Care

In an attempt to conserve our most precious resource, "Waterless Technology" was created to provide safe cleaning alternatives to using water. Includes product information, network marketing assistance, and tips for protecting the environment.

Address: http://www.envirocare.com

Home Team

The Home Team is an information service that provides unbiased information about household technology and products for the concerned homeowner. The only products sold by this company are educational tools offering helpful purchasing advice.

Address: http://www.hometeam.com

Lindal Cedar Homes

Lindal Cedar Homes builds homes of cedar wood to the customer's specifications. The page offers local connections for interested users as well as a guided tour of past projects.

Address: http://www.lindal.com

Neff's Safe & Lock Locksmith

This page offers the history of a tiny locksmith company turned big-time. Information about security, staff and services, and electronic access is also available.

Address: http://www.lock.com/lock/lock.html

Quality Custom Cabinetry

Based in the Pennsylvania Dutch Country, QCC builds custom cabinets to the customer's taste or style. Their pages provide a list and gallery of styles as well as dealers across the U.S.

Address: http://www.qcc.com/qcc/home.html

Select Comfort

This marketer of sleep systems offers products, such as mattresses and bedding, guaranteed to reduce back pain and allow comfortable sleeping. The company only sells directly to their customers through their catalog, which provides product information and prices.

Address: http://www.comfort.com

Sure Foot Industries

Sure Foot Industries presents "Sure Tread" at a sale price. This tested and approved anti-slip treatment is used on tiles and enameled tubs.

Address: http://www.worldtel.com/surefoot/surefoot.html

Winter Park Construction

Winter Park Construction (WPC) is a general contracting company serving Central Florida. Their projects range from restaurants and malls to apartments and hotels.

Address: http://www.wpc.com

Importing and Exporting

Actrade International

Actrade helps smaller American companies succeed in export/international trade and domestic, commercial trade finance. Actrade specializes in distributing heating, air conditioning, refrigeration, laundry, and pressing equipment to markets in Europe, South America, the Pacific Rim, and the Middle East.

Address: http://actrade.interse.com

InfoAsia

InfoAsia researches government and trade policies in Asian countries so American and European businesses can enjoy greater access to Asian marketplaces. InfoAsia also provides information about conferences and current events in Asian countries.

Address: http://www.infoasia.com

Muscovy Imports

Muscovy Imports represents fine contemporary artists working in Russia today—established painters and sculptors with international reputations, as well as emerging young artists. This page features oil paintings, bronze sculpture, jewelry, and art objects in the tradition of Fabergé.

Address: http://www.branch.com/muscovy

North Atlantic Resources

This trade management company exports various goods to Russia. The company also seeks business alliances for interested parties on both sides of the Atlantic. Their page is devoted to company history and projects as well as information on investment opportunities.

Address: http://www.nar.com

Trade Compass

Trade Compass offers information on international commerce for both traders and interested consumers. The frequently updated data offered is organized into four categories: Trade News, Marketplace, Trade Library, and Trade Forum.

Address: http://www.tradecompass.com

Trade Reporting and Data Exchange

T.R.A.D.E., Inc., offers vital import and export information for U.S. companies and manufacturers so they can retain a competitive edge and increase their markets. Data is provided on a purchased CD-ROM retrieval system.

Address: http://www.tradeinfo.com

Internet Service Providers

AccuNet

AccuNet is Kansas City's leading supplier of Internet services, which include network consultation as well as Internet access and software. K.C. Commerce Link and Global Network Navigator are prime resources.

Address: http://www.accunet.com

America Online

America Online is one of the most popular online services (as discussed in Chapter 4) and offers access to the Internet and the Web. This Web page offers information about joining AOL and links to FTP sites housing AOL's front-end software packages.

Address: http://www.aol.com

AT&T WorldNet

AT&T has teamed up with BBN Planet to offer one-stop shopping for Internet connectivity. AT&T WorldNet offers high-speed connections to the Internet, hardware, software, training, and ongoing maintenance and service.

Address: http://www.att.com

BBN Planet

BBN (Bolt Berenek and Newman) provides comprehensive Internet service packages for businesses and organizations worldwide. Job opportunities, customer profiles, service offerings, and company contacts are available at this site.

Address: http://www.bbnplanet.com

Best Internet Communications

Best Internet Communications is an Internet service provider in the San Francisco Bay Area. Their page provides information on their services, a price list, a statement of user policies, and an FAQ sheet for quick answers to your questions.

Address: http://www.best.com

Cable Island

Cable Island is an ISP in Toronto offering dedicated and nondedicated dialup ISDN and V.34 connections. They also sell and rent the equipment you need for connecting to the Internet and provide Web services.

Address: http://www.cable.com

Call-Net

Connecticut's ISP for New Haven and the surrounding areas, Call-Net also offers personal Web page services and links to a variety of Web businesses.

Address: http://www.callnet.com

Computing Engineers

With its World Wide Access, Computing Engineers offers Internet access and services to both individuals and businesses.

Address: http://www.adware.com

CTS Network Services

CTSNet is one of the largest ISPs in Southern California, providing shell and SLIP/PPP access to thousands of users. Located in San Diego County, CTSNet is also high on the Commercial Sites Index of companies leasing Web space to other businesses.

Address: http://www.cts.com

Datasync Internet

A full-service Internet provider serving Mississippi communities, Datasync offers three levels of Internet service—telnet-only accounts, regular dialup shell accounts, and SLIP or PPP accounts.

Address: http://www.datasync.com

DeltaNet

Delta Internet Services provides a wide range of Internet access and Web services to individuals and businesses in several California counties. Besides providing Internet access, DeltaNet's services include hosting, training, and consulting.

Address: http://www.deltanet.com

Digital Gateway Systems

DGS is an ISP near Washington, D.C., that serves the Capitol area. DGS also provides on-site training courses on use of the Internet.

Address: http://www.dgsys.com

DirecTell, L.C.

As an ISP for Park City and Heber Valley in Utah, DirecTell offers local weather information in addition to information about the company's services.

Address: http://www.ditell.com

Duck Pond Public Unix

The Duck Pond is a public Unix system in Santa Clara, California. They offer dialup access to shell accounts for a monthly fee.

Address: http://www.kfu.com

ElectriCiti

A full-service ISP specializing in high-speed dialup SLIP and PPP connections, ElectriCiti also offers a Web hosting and archiving service.

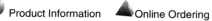

Address: http://www.electriciti.com

eWorld

eWorld is Apple Computer's online service, with more than 40,000 users. eWorld offers links to Apple as well as special-interest sections such as The Mac Zone, The Learning Community, and WebCity. eWorld also offers access to Internet services, such as mailing lists, FTP sites, newsgroups, and the Web.

Address: http://www.eworld.com

Fishnet

Fishnet is a full-service ISP for the Philadelphia area. In addition to Internet access, they offer Web hosting and services such as personal home pages.

Address: http://www.pond.com

Flex Information Network

As Hawaii's first public-access Internet provider, Flex provides full Internet access services, including up-to-date news and weather and surf reports.

Address: http://www.aloha.com

Fleximation Systems

Fleximation Systems is a full-service network integrator and ISP in Mississauga, Ontario. They provide customers with reliable and economical network systems ranging from in-house LAN and WAN installations to worldwide networks using the Internet.

Address: http://www.flexnet.com

FullFeed Communications

FullFeed is Wisconsin's oldest commercial ISP, servicing the entire state of Wisconsin.

Address: http://www.fullfeed.com

Hevanet

Hevanet Communications is an ISP in Portland, Oregon, offering both personal and business accounts. In addition to Internet access, Hevanet also offers Web services and consulting and training.

Address: http://www.hevanet.com

IBM Global Network

Besides their computer lines, IBM is now in the business of selling access to the Internet. IBM offers dialup access and leased lines ranging from 56K and fractional T1s up to full T1 lines. Their pages offer information, pricing, and local phone numbers for many cities and regions worldwide.

Address: http://www.ibm.com/globalnetwork/

Indra's Net

This page includes a list of the businesses and organizations that use Indra's Net. The company also offers a newsletter packed with current news.

Address: http://www.indra.com

Inforamp

Inforamp is a full-scale ISP in Toronto. They offer dialup accounts, SLIP and PPP accounts, and a "no busy signal" policy.

Address: http://www.inforamp.net

MediaCity

MediaCity provides a listing of major features and some information on specific accounts. The page also includes features like The Mall, Net Navigation, Business Resources and Governments, and news.

Address: http://www.mediacity.com

Microsoft Network

The Microsoft Network is Microsoft's online service for users of Windows 95. Although MSN is primarily an online service, it does offer access to parts of the Internet, including the Web.

Address: http://www.msn.com

Naked Pueblo Computing

In addition to providing Internet services, NPC also offers education in computer and software use. The page provides a list of Web sites and relevant articles.

Address: http://www.nakedpc.com/npc

NETAXIS 

This Connecticut access provider offers Internet access to individuals and to businesses of all sizes. Their page offers samples of the company's work, descriptions of new services, and a chance for users to order products directly from the Web site.

Address: http://www.netaxis.com

Netcom   

Netcom is one of the largest ISPs in the U.S., with points of presence in nearly 200 cities and a quarter million subscribers.

Address: http://www.netcom.com

NETInterior  

This ISP maintains a family bulletin board system and provides new communication tools for clients. NETInterior offers information on local events, businesses, and services as well as Internet starting points.

Address: http://www.netinterior.com

Netmar   

This company offers full Internet access and services, including HTML code authoring, full-service desktop publishing, personal Web pages, and Web consulting. The company caters to small businesses.

Address: http://netmar.com

NICOH Net

This Internet provider mainly serves eastern Idaho. Their resources include a users list and a law page, which provides information on past rulings.

Address: http://www.nicoh.com

Northwest Nexus 

This page offers announcements for users, Web page listings, and halcyon.com, which lists specific Internet services and pricing for users in the Puget Sound region and the Pacific Northwest.

Address: http://www.halcyon.com

Performance Systems International

With points of presence in more than 80 metropolitan areas, PSI is one of the largest ISPs in the U.S. Their services include dialup shell accounts, SLIP/PPP services, ISDN, and leased-line connections, including fractional and full T1 service.

Address: http://www.psi.com

Pipeline New York

The Pipeline offers Internet access to New York City customers. Their page includes Pipeline New York Software for Macintosh and Windows, and the first World Wide Web browser for Macintosh that uses a phone connection instead of Internet connections requiring software.

Address: http://www.nyc.pipeline.com

Primenet

Serving Arizona, Primenet is a full-service provider offering dialup shell, SLIP/PPP, UUCP, and Web services. Primenet also offers links to commercial pages and services, user pages, and news.

Address: http://www.primenet.com

RaveNet Systems

As an ISP for the state of Delaware, RaveNet's pages describe their services as well as the many gateways offered, including some to the state's education and business departments.

Address: http://www.ravenet.com

Seanet

Seanet provides individuals and companies with access to Internet services such as email and Usenet newsgroups. This page also offers a classifieds section and a library listing other Internet links.

Address: http://www.seanet.com

SprintLink

SprintLink is an "ISP's ISP." As one of the largest "wholesale" providers, SprintLink offers mostly T1 and faster access services as well as domain-name service and Usenet news feeds.

Address: http://www.sprint.net

SuperNet

SuperNet, Inc., is the largest ISP in Colorado, offering SuperNet Dial and Private-Line services as well as educational and governmental resources.

Address: http://www.hardiman.com

Teleport

Teleport provides Internet email access, mostly in the Pacific Northwest. This page offers the information you need to get their service, access to computer programs you can use, and customer assistance.

Address: http://www.teleport.com

Traveller Information Services

Traveller Information Services is an Internet access and information provider. In addition to detailed information on services and rates, there is a special information section for members of TUG (Traveller User Group), as well as news and current events.

Address: http://www.traveller.com

UltraNet Communications

Serving much of Massachusetts, UltraNet offers low-cost SLIP and PPP Internet access. Their pages feature an overview of SLIP/PPP and UltraNet's local access numbers.

Address: http://www.ultranet.com

Universal Access

UA is an Internet service provider in Santa Barbara, California. Besides access, UA offers Web site development, hosting services, design, and an interesting service that will fax Web pages to your fax machine.

Address: http://www.ua.com

VisiCom Network Services

VisiCom is an ISP for ISPs and businesses. VisiCom offers dedicated T1, fractional T1, and business ISDN connections as well as dialup access in local areas.

Address: http://www.tncnet.com

WELL

The WELL provides Internet access and related services. Their home page features links to community pages, information about WELL services (such as training), and news and weather.

Address: http://www.well.com

XNet Information Systems

This page provides information on XNet Systems' Internet services and prices, including leased line and Web services.

Address: http://www.xnet.com

Law

Bancroft-Whitney

Bancroft-Whitney offers legal information and services to users of its LawDesk software system. This company also uses its Web site to provide information about the legal books and materials it has published.

Address: http://www.bancroft.com

Faegre & Benson

Faegre & Benson is a law firm specializing in Internet legal issues. Their pages offer information relating to Internet legal issues, details about the 275 attorneys in their offices in the U.S., Europe, and Asia, recent court rulings, and where to locate other legal information on the Internet.

Address: http://www.faegre.com

Inter-Law's 'Lectric Law Library

Inter-Law's 'Lectric Law Library is a repository of legal information. The library features an extensive guided tour, which includes images and detailed descriptions of the resources in each room.

Address: http://www.inter-law.com

InterNet Bankruptcy Library

InterNet Bankruptcy Library serves bankrupt companies around the world. This page offers resources pertaining to bankruptcy and insolvency as well as information about how users can get advice and consultation in times of financial distress.

Address: http://bankrupt.com

J & J Ltd.

J & J Ltd. Chicago is an organization that provides patent and technical CAD illustration services to Chicago firms. Services and samples of their work are listed here.

Address: http://www.mcs.com/~jwylde/patents/J_and_J.html

New York Law Publishing

This company offers a service called Law Journal Extra!, which provides access to three online law publications. Their page also includes an online catalog listing hundreds of books, newsletters, and cassettes.

Address: http://public.ljextra.com

Patent Drawing & Design Unlimited

PDDU is located in Santa Cruz, California, and performs patent searches, technical writing, and informal/formal patent drawing. There are links to patent-related items including U.S. Patent Law.

Address: http://www.webcom.com/~scpatent

Saul, Ewing, Remick & Saul

Extensive information is offered about this law practice and its lawyers as well as more general data, including recent developments in related fields and issues of interest in the U.S. government and judiciary system.

Address: http://www.saul.com

Shadow Patent Office

Sponsored by Electronic Data Systems, the Shadow Patent Office offers a wealth of information about U.S. patents, including a searchable index and a listing of millions of patents. Access patent information by date granted or browse recent patents. If you register with the office, you can perform searches of this extensive database.

Address: http://www.spo.eds.com

Silicon Valley Patent Lawyer

Robert Risberg is a California patent attorney. His Web page offers links to other patent, legal, corporate, and research links on the Internet.

Address: http://www.risberg.com

Venable, Baetjer, Howard & Civiletti, LL.P.

Located in the Washington/Baltimore area, this is a leading provider of full business law services. This page features hundreds of law-related articles from a variety of publications, categorized by the three areas of company practice: Business, Labor and Litigation, and Government.

Address: http://www.venable.com

Venture Law Group

This law group specializes in representing public and private technology companies and the venture-capital funds and investment banking firms that finance them. Their page offers company information, a sampling of some of the firm's clients, and information on how to obtain services for your own business.

Address: http://www.venlaw.com

Vorys, Sater, Seymour and Pease

This Ohio and Washington, D.C.-based law firm offers worldwide services in a wide range of legal fields, from antitrust to health care. This page is an online legal information resource, with options covering current top news issues, legal news, and company programs and services.

Address: http://www.vssp.com

Local Interest

BayNet

Operated by BayNet World, Inc., a publisher on the Internet, this site is geared toward providing valuable information about real estate, shopping, entertainment, and other topics in the San Francisco Bay Area.

Address: http://www.baynet.com

Fentonnet

Serving the twin cities of Minneapolis and St. Paul, Fentonnet offers information about area businesses, weather, real estate, government, entertainment, and job offerings.

Address: http://www.fentonnet.com

FOCUS Publications - Orange County

FOCUS Publications specializes in information on Southern California counties. This site has extensive data concerning Orange, San Diego, and Riverside Counties. Find facts on education, real estate, businesses, government, employment, entertainment, and other topics of interest.

Address: http://www.focusoc.com

Forum on the Web

This is a collection of information sources for the Boca Raton, Delray Beach, and Palm Beach County Business Communities in Florida. The directory includes goods and services, business opportunities, databases, and current news.

Address: http://www.apms.com

Mediabridge

Mediabridge bills itself as a "paperless guide to New York," offering information about businesses in New York City, a resource called the Virtual Tourist NYC Project, and a link to TotalNewYork, which offers more resources and information about the Big Apple.

Address: http://www.mediabridge.com

North Carolina's Outer Banks

North Carolina's Outer Banks provides information about the region, including places of interest and entertainment as well as articles, stories, and legends. These pages offer a map of the Outer Banks area, weather updates, and information on becoming a corporate sponsor.

Address: http://www.outer-banks.com

RING! Inc.

This company produces an electronic magazine, *RING! OnLine*, which focuses on the state of Michigan. The magazine covers geography, news, travel information, and many other aspects of Michigan. Classified advertising is also offered.

Address: http://www.ring.com

Santa Cruz County Information Guide

This page offers community information on Santa Cruz County and nearby areas. Topics include Web listings for businesses, public libraries, UC Santa Cruz, and others. Information is also available on other areas in California.

Address: http://www.cruzio.com

Virtual Africa

Virtual Africa provides information on South Africa, including the country's business, travel, and trade. Readers can also use this page to market any services pertaining to South Africa.

Address: http://www.africa.com

WebSource

WebSource provides listings of restaurants, apartments, zoos, and other places of interest in Austin, Texas.

Address: http://www.websrc.com

Magazines

ComStar

ComStar is the leading Web server dealing with multilingual computer information. ComStar provides a bilingual magazine online, *Chinese Computer Digest*, information about multilingual software, and the latest on trading opportunities in China.

Address: http://www.gy.com

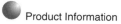

Digital Campus

In addition to being the online site of *Link, The College Magazine*, The Digital Campus offers weekly updated information on news, collegiate sports, campus magazines, video games, and special offers just for college students.

Address: http://www.linkmag.com

Economist

The Economist is a business and news publication that provides perspective through commentary on and analysis of finance, politics, business, science and technology, and the arts. This site offers selections from current issues of the magazine, surveys, and subscription information.

Address: http://www.economist.com

Esquire

The Web page for *Esquire* magazine, Esquire Business to Business online provides a discussion forum, an interactive media kit, news and information about upcoming issues, and an opportunity to get a free gift.

Address: http://www.esquireb2b.com

Maine Antique Digest

Maine Antique Digest is a magazine focusing on art and antiques in North America. Their web offers sample pages from the magazine, including sales, articles, and book reviews. They also provide updates on antique shows and allow users to view all the advertisements from previous issues.

Address: http://www.maine.com

Mother Jones

Mother Jones is a magazine of investigation and ideas from a somewhat left-of-center perspective. Links to current and back issues of the magazine, as well as other interactive information resources, are also located on the site.

Address: http://www.mojones.com

Playboy Enterprises

This page is the online center of the Playboy empire. Options include an announcements section, viewing the latest issue or specific articles, information on Playboy TV, famous interviews, an email directory, and Playboy software information.

Address: http://www.playboy.com

Pollstar

Pollstar - The Concert Hotwire is a provider of accurate, up-to-date information about the music concert industry, with everything from concert tour schedules to box-office results to industry directories, including news and other information about the industry.

Address: http://www.pollstar.com

Popular Mechanics

This online magazine offers information on ways to obtain free software using the Web, daily updated information, clips from the Movie of the Week, an automotive section, a "Time Machine" where 93 years of *PM* issues are available, a Feature of the Month, and a chat forum.

Address: http://popularmechanics.com

Solo Publications

Solo publishes regional magazines, both available online, dealing with two favorite pastimes: *The Southern Aviator* and *Tournament Golfer*. In addition to information about these publications, this Web site offers connections to other aviation-related sites.

Address: http://www.solopub.com

TechWeb

TechWeb is the technology information source, and this page offers more than 16 computer business publications that cover many topics involving your computer. Included publications are *Computer Reseller News* and *Computer Retail Week*.

Address: http://techweb.cmp.com/techweb/WALK/Walk-page1.html

Time, Inc.

Time World Wide provides access to news archives of *Time* and other subsidiary magazines. They also offer links to current and past issues of the magazine.

Address: http://www.timeinc.com

Websight Magazine

Websight Magazine is a comprehensive guide to all aspects of the World Wide Web. The magazine's online site provides all information available in the print edition and offers a discount on a subscription to the magazine.

Address: http://www.websight.com

Ziff-Davis Publishing

Ziff-Davis offers industry news, an ad index, and links to many of Ziff's magazines, including *PC Magazine*, *PC Week*, *Inter@ctive Week*, and *PC Computing*.

Address: http://www.ziff.com

Manufacturing, Machinery, and Tools

Allen-Bradley

This Rockwell International business manufactures industrial automation, offering supplies like software, motion-control devices, and logic processors.

Address: http://www.ab.com

AlliedSignal

AlliedSignal Corp. is an advanced technology and manufacturing company serving customers worldwide with aerospace and automotive products, chemicals, fibers, plastics, and advanced materials. Their businesses include Engineered Material Services, Automotive, and Aerospace.

Address: http://www.os.kcp.com/home/ascorp.html

AMCOL

AMCOL Corp. pioneered many of the first synthetic coolants used in the metalworking industries. They produce environmentally sound and cost-effective lubricants as well as applicators for tube manufacturing, roll forming, and nonferrous extrusion and casting industries.

Address: http://www.pic.net/amcol/homepage.html

KK Tech International

KK Tech produces water purification systems and shrimp feeds for cultured shrimp. This page features information on the company and its products, examples of Ultraviolet systems at work, and ways to get more information.

Address: http://www.hk.linkage.net/~kkt

Marshall Industries

The Marshall Production Supplies Catalog contains such products as test equipment, soldering equipment, hand tools and tool kits, production necessities, lighting and magnification equipment, and workstations and material handling.

Address: http://www.marshall.com

PHD

PHD claims that if it moves, they make it. PHD manufactures industrial automation products such as cylinders, grippers, and built-in sensors. Their page offers extensive information on their products and current company and related news.

Address: http://www.phdinc.com

Plexus

This company is known for designing and testing products, but they also have a manufacturing division and an engineering subsidiary. Plexus offers services that get other companies' products ready for market.

Address: http://www.plexus.com

Qosina

This growing company supplies a variety of products and services to the OEM medical industry. Their page provides a list of upcoming trade shows, a company catalog, and information about Qosmedix, which supplies disposable testers to the cosmetics industry.

Address: http://www.qosina.com

Supply Line

The Supply Line is a source for new and used equipment in industries such as forestry, construction, transportation, and mining. They provide information on upcoming auctions, equipment dealers, manufacturers, and factory outlets. You can also advertise your own equipment here.

Address: http://www.supplyline.com

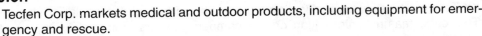

Tecfen

Tecfen Corp. markets medical and outdoor products, including equipment for emergency and rescue.

Address: http://www.tecfen.com

TracNet

TracNet, a division of Corbetco, Inc., offers information about tractors and other heavy equipment. It gives retailers the chance to market their products and buyers a well-stocked site to browse. There is also a manufacturers catalog and an equipment locator to make shopping easier.

Address: http://www.tracnet.com

Merchandise

1-800-FLOWERS

1-800-FLOWERS provides online flower shopping access as well as shipping information. This page also offers information on issues of special interest, such as contests, events, and promotions.

Address: http://www.800flowers.com

Absolutely Fresh Flowers

Absolutely Fresh Flowers specializes in growing miniature carnations in greenhouses. Their shipments, which go to people all over the U.S., contain nearly 150 multicolored carnations and are guaranteed to last at least two weeks.

Address: http://www.cts.com/browse/flowers

Access Market Square

Access Market Square's page offers a catalog organized into several categories: services, art, food, jewelry, electronics, clothes, and videos. They describe each product and how it can be obtained. More than a catalog, this is almost a mall.

Address: http://www.amsquare.com

Adirondack Trading

Adirondack sells a variety of merchandise, including Adirondack chairs, lamps, candles, jams and jellies, and maple syrup.

Address: http://www.amsquare.com/america/adtrade.html

Bargaineers

Bargaineers is a network that provides products for businesses and consumers below wholesale prices. Discontinued and overstocked items from companies like Memorex, Minolta, AT&T, and Leeds are available in sporting goods, toys, electronics, clothing, furnishings, jewelry, and other categories.

Address: http://www.homecom.com/global/index/bargaineers.html

Basket Mania

Basket Mania offers a variety of creatively assembled baskets to meet many gift-giving needs.

Address: http://www.basket.com/basket

Body Shop

The Body Shop is an environmentally conscious skin- and hair-care products company. Their page has a magazinelike appearance and contains articles on social issues and ecological involvement as well as beauty tips and tricks.

Address: http://www.the-body-shop.com

Branch Mall

This company offers a catalog describing a wide range of business opportunities as well as items for sale by predominantly small manufacturers.

Address: http://www.branch.com

CARDS

"Can't Always Remember DateS" has established this site to display and sell its variety of birthday, thank-you, holiday, and everyday greeting cards.

Address: http://www.c-a-r-d-s.com/cards

Comtrad Industries

Comtrad sells wireless phone jacks, speaker systems, and the Koolatron Space-Age cold food storage and warmer.

Address: http://www.icw.com/comtrad

DuPont Performance Lubricants

This Web page furnishes information and updates regarding DuPont's lubrication products for aerospace, automotive, and aeronautical needs.

Address: http://www.lubricants.dupont.com

Flotation Technologies

Flotation Technologies manufactures flotation devices, including buoys and ROV and submersible flotation components. Flotec's Web site offers information and news on their buoyancy products and articles from the Flotec newsletter.

Address: http://www.flotec.com

Flower Stop

Order fresh flowers online through the Flower Stop. The page offers the option to send any kind of flower or FTD arrangement.

Address: http://www.flowerstop.com/fstop

Hot Deals Deadwear

Hot Deals Deadwear features Grateful Dead paraphernalia and merchandise, including T-shirts and attache cases with Grateful Dead artwork. The page provides information on song titles and lyrics and related Deadhead links.

Address: http://www.hotdeal.com/deadwear

JCPenney

JCPenney's online store features a catalog of apparel, home furnishings, and services.

Address: http://www.jcpenney.com

Joke City

This self-proclaimed "funniest store in the world" offers the latest in funny and joke merchandise. If you've ever wondered where to find fake vomit, shrunken heads, fart powder, or double-headed coins, you've found the place.

Address: http://www.jokecity.com

Jostens Ambition Achieved  

Jostens Ambition Achieved is the place to select and purchase college rings. The page also provides information on other graduation products as well as the option to receive the print edition of the company catalog.

Address: http://www.jostens.com

JoyMe by Mail  

JoyMe by Mail offers discounted prices on bestselling books and CD-ROMs. JoyMe offers a comprehensive list of available titles as well as instructions for ordering a print catalog.

Address: http://www.joyme.com

National InterAd 

Sponsored by The Cobalt Group, National InterAd is an online, illustrated classified ad center with categories such as real estate, vehicles, and business opportunities. National InterAd's pages also allow users to place their own ads by contacting the company.

Address: http://www.nia.com

Newbury Comics  

This company sells everything from T-shirts to compact discs to lava lamps. Information about the alternative music scene in New England is also available.

Address: http://www.newbury.com

ONSALE   

ONSALE is an online auction where prices and availability change according to customer demand. Most of the products offered are collectibles or products going out of stock. Customers can shop by category, closing date, or price. All purchasing is done directly with the individual companies.

Address: http://www.onsale.com

Pennsylvania Dutch Marketplace  

This site offers food, flowers, and other products made by Pennsylvania Dutch. Hershey's items, meats and cheeses from Kutztown Bologna Company, and quilts from the Lancaster County Quilt Company are all here, along with other unique products.

Address: http://www.padutch.com

PreVent

PreVent is a disposable breathalyzer that can travel with you anywhere so you can determine if you really are able to drive. This page offers instructions on using PreVent as well as information about the costs of a drunk-driving accident.

Address: http://www.prevent.com

Ring of Fire Enterprises

This company specializes in products such as bumper stickers, plaques, T-shirts, and videos. On online catalog is available for browsing.

Address: http://www.backporch.com

Sharper Image

The Sharper Image offers an online catalog featuring all of its latest products. Included are sections on special items, coupon offers, and specials-of-the-month.

Address: http://www.sharperimage.com/tsi

Shihadeh

Shihadeh has established this Oriental Rug Encyclopedia to provide information on rugs—their history, cost, and cleaning methods. You can also buy and sell rugs at their oriental rug bazaar.

Address: http://www.orientalrugs.com

Upscale Wholesale Shop

Upscale Wholesale provides a wide variety of merchandise at reduced wholesale prices. Recreation products, automotive and pet accessories, and personal and professional security items are available.

Address: http://www.upscale.com

Venger's Orchids

Venger's Orchids is geared toward the hobbyist and is primarily a mail-order firm, but they have a thriving local business as well and always welcome travelers who want to visit. This page also offers orchid listings, announcements, and want ads.

Address: http://www.usa.net/venger

White Rabbit Toys

White Rabbit Toys, located in Ann Arbor, Michigan, offers a wide range of fun, educational, and imaginative children's toys from around the world. You can visit the store online and place orders directly.

Address: http://www.toystore.com

Zeke's General Store

Located in Central Arizona, Zeke's offers a variety of products ranging from chili pepper seeds, pecans, and plants to surplus computer and software products. Zeke's also provides links to other interesting sites on the Web.

Address: http://www.zekes.com

Miscellaneous and Multimarket Corporations

American Material Resources

American Material Resources supplies products such as gas and oil, based on the McMaster-Carr Supply Company yellow page catalog.

Address: http://www.commerce.com/placette

BC Hydro International

Read up on the electric utility company for British Columbia. BC Hydro's pages offer information about their operations, labs, transmission facilities, products, and services.

Address: http://ewu.bchydro.bc.ca/bchydro/bchil.html

Delmarva Power and Light Co.

Delmarva is an investor-owned gas and electric utility operating in parts of Delaware, Maryland, and Virginia. Delmarva's Web pages offer information on the company's operations, marketing contacts, and employment opportunities.

Address: http://www.delmarva.com

Eastern Alloys

Eastern Alloys manufactures and markets zinc alloys. Their pages offer extensive information on the company, its products, and the alloy-creation process as well as a guide to zinc alloys, information on ZA casting alloys (a group of higher-strength alloys), and related information.

Address: http://www.eazall.com

General Electric

GE is a diversified technology, manufacturing, and services company in markets including aircraft engines, broadcasting (NBC), electrical distribution equipment, electric motors and industrial systems, capital services, industrial and power systems, information services, lighting, locomotives, major appliances, medical systems, and plastics.

Address: http://www.ge.com

Motorola

Motorola produces cellular telephones and other electronic and communication devices. Their home page provides information about the company's sponsors, finances, and press releases.

Address: http://www.mot.com

Rockwell International

Rockwell is a diverse technology company specializing in the electronics, automotive, graphics, and aerospace industries. Specific information is offered on these four divisions as well as on current happenings, finance, and employment opportunities at the company.

Address: http://www.rockwell.com

San Diego Gas & Electric

SDG&E offers information on operations, financial information, news, and a useful guide called *100 Ways to Save Energy Around the House and Still Have All the Comforts of Home*.

Address: http://www.sdge.com

Sony Online

Sony's home page offers links to all of the company's major divisions, including their musical production, motion picture and television production, electronics, and publishing divisions and Sony Signatures, the merchandising division.

Address: http://www.sony.com

Warner-Lambert Co.

Warner-Lambert's consumer products range from Dentyne to Actifed. The page offers information under nine categories: Allergy-Cold-Cough-Sinus, Oral Care, Shaving, Women's Care, Antacids, Chewing Gums and Mints, Skin Care, First Aid, and Aquarium Products. This page also includes games and quizzes.

Address: http://www.warner-lambert.com

Westinghouse Science & Technology

The Westinghouse Science & Technology Center seeks to develop and transfer innovative technologies to its customers. These pages feature three product divisions—Systems, Processes, and Technologies; Electronics, Information, and Sciences; and Advanced Energy Conversion.

Address: http://www.westinghouse.com

Multimedia

AcmeWeb

AcmeWeb offers a variety of multimedia services, including network consultation and Web installation. Their page includes a library, a bazaar featuring stores of information, and a description of what's new on the Web.

Address: http://www.acmeweb.com

BETACORP

This multimedia publishing company offers electronic catalogs, interactive marketing, and educational software. BETACORP's page provides information on the company and its products and services.

Address: http://www.betacorp.com

Better Image Productions

This company is a leading provider of digital media communication and information solutions to help its clients change with evolving communication technology. The page offers information on electronic imaging, optical services, creative design, new media, and online design services.

Address: http://www.bip.com

Black Star

Black Star has 60 years experience providing solutions to challenging visual communications projects. The company specializes in the photographic image in both traditional and electronic forms.

Address: http://www.blackstar.com

Eden Matrix

The Eden Matrix system provides access to a vast array of popular and underground media—music, comic books, art, and much more.

Address: http://www.eden.com

ESCAtech Media

As a multimedia communications and technology company, ESCAtech Media examines digital marketing options to ensure clients reach their desired audience. They specialize in resolving the critical issues that surround interactive technology to produce high-tech yet effective presentations for corporations.

Address: http://www.escatech.com

G3 Systems

G3 Systems, Inc., is a multimedia and Internet design consulting firm dedicated to developing interactive CD-ROM and network-based projects for business and industry. The G3 Systems team has won two international design awards for interface design and multimedia development.

Address: http://www.g3systems.com

Web Intertainment

With thousands of titles available, this online site is a place to shop for CDs, laser discs, and CD-ROMs. Accessing the market is simple, and plenty of ordering, payment, and delivery information is provided.

Address: http://www.funstuff.com

Music

Blotch Music

Blotch promotes Seattle-based bands. Download sound clips from a group, and if you enjoy their music, Blotch will provide their CD or tape to you for a nominal price.

Address: http://www.blotch.com/blotch

CD Restore

This company removes scratches from and repairs old compact discs. Their page describes methods and pricing. They also have a satisfaction guarantee.

Address: http://www.eskimo.com/~cdrestor

CDnow!

CDnow! offers more than 140,000 CDs, cassettes, and videos at discount prices, as well as discounted magazine subscriptions, a music video catalog, and hundreds of T-shirts.

Address: http://www.cdnow.com

Haight Ashbury Music Co.

The Haight Ashbury Music Co. offers everything you need to start, sustain, and enjoy a music career. The page provides information on services and sites pertaining to music as well as a store that sells musical instruments and accessories.

Address: http://www.haight-ashbury-music.com

Jim's Ithaca Music Shop

Jim's Ithaca Music Shop is a mail-order business specializing in out-of-the-ordinary music. The page offers favorite artists and groups as well as a list of specially priced titles.

Address: http://www.jims.com

Keola Beamer

Keola Beamer is a Hawaiian songwriter, composer, and singer. The page is dedicated to Beamer's music, tour schedules, and videos.

Address: http://www.kbeamer.com

Le Hit Parade

This unique business is dedicated to promoting French music and lyrics to the English-speaking world. With a current mail-order service and upcoming online ordering, this service makes acquiring the latest hits and classics of French popular music easy.

Address: http://www.lhp.com

Music Scene International

Music Scene International is an online site offering access to music from the newest and most unique artists and labels. Anyone can order a title, but members receive discounts, contest opportunities, giveaways, and more. Bands and musicians can also become members to gain exposure.

Address: http://www.musicscene.com

Music World III

Music World III provides information on the music industry as well as specific artists, albums, equipment, and more. Many fun and interesting options are available, including purchasing albums and music products from the company. Related Web sites are also listed.

Address: http://www.mw3.com

Pepper Music Network

A service of J.W. Pepper & Son, Inc., the Pepper Music Network is an online music catalog that provides sheet music from many publishers as well as music teaching materials and favorite albums.

Address: http://www.jwpepper.com

Racer Records

Racer is an independent record company specializing in alternative music—specifically, what they call "intelligent rock, folk rock, experimental pop, and freeform jazz." Their page provides information on upcoming events, artists, and albums, interviews, and a link to their FTP site.

Address: http://www.racerrecords.com

Schoolkids' Records

Schoolkids' offers an eclectic assortment of music in three main categories: Classical, The Main Store (pop, jazz, and country), and The Annex (the most current and new music of all types, including hip hop and punk).

Address: http://www.schoolkids.com

Sound Wire

Sound Wire offers music by mail, ranging from the newest hits to oldies. A color code makes identifying the music type easy as you browse through the selections. Sound Wire offers clips for listening, as well as reviews of music and related magazines and videos.

Address: http://www.soundwire.com

Sound Works

Sound Works' pages provide audio and video information on wholesale supplies, hardware and software services, commercial music, advertising, and audio restoration.

Address: http://www.soundworks.com

Toby Arnold & Associates

Toby Arnold & Associates offers expertise in the "image music" production industry, creating jingles that influence consumers to shop and purchase items.

Address: http://www.computek.net/inroads/taa

Visual Radio

Current information on 85 independent-label recording musicians is offered on the Visual Radio site. In addition, there is a RealAudio option to hear music clips and a CD-ROM edition.

Address: http://www.visualradio.com

Windham Hill Records

Windham Hill Records is an independent record company based in Northern California. Their page offers information on company projects, products, and concerts, radio news, and a chat line to review and discuss concerts or albums.

Address: http://www.windham.com

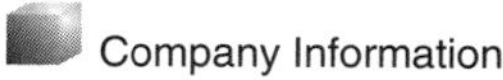

Networking Products

Advanced Computer Communications

ACC is a leading manufacturer of remote area networking products that provide cost-effective interconnection and management of geographically distributed computer networks.

Address: http://www.acc.com

Amber Wave Systems

Amber develops and markets the AmberSwitch, a leading product in workgroup LAN switching. Amber's pages feature news, technical papers, and a directory of interesting places on the Internet.

Address: http://www.amberwave.com

Artisoft

The maker of the popular LANtastic networking products for PCs has put together a web of pages offering information on using LANtastic with Windows 95, their other products and support services, and other items of interest to LANtastic users.

Address: http://www.artisoft.com

Asanté

Asanté manufactures networking hardware and software products to connect PCs, Macs, and peripheral devices to Ethernet networks.

Address: http://www.asante.com

Banyan Systems

Banyan is an old-timer in computer networking products and systems. In addition to company and product information, the page offers white papers and information about their educational and support services.

Address: http://www.banyan.com

Beckman Software Engineering

BSE is a network and communications consulting company. Their web provides information about hardware and software systems for network use. Through BSE, you can also reach VizLab, a visualization facility at the University of Illinois.

Address: http://www.becknet.com

Bellcore  

Bellcore integrates network operations and architectures, effects migrations to new software systems, and develops advanced voice and messaging systems, high-volume databases, and transaction systems.

Address: http://www.bellcore.com

Data Research Associates  

DRA provides client/server automation systems, networking services, and related services for libraries and information providers.

Address: http://www.dra.com

Develcon  

Develcon develops and markets local and remote LAN access products. Their focus is on delivering cost-effective technology with easy installation and administration tools.

Address: http://www.develcon.com

Digiboard  

This long-time manufacturer of high-speed, intelligent serial I/O connectivity products now offers network products as well, including the Digi LANAserver high-speed dialup Ethernet network access system and Fast Ethernet (100 Mbps) products.

Address: http://www.digibd.com

Equinox 

Equinox is a manufacturer of networking products, including SuperSerial I/O boards with speeds up to 920 Kbps, MEGAPORT boards with from four to 96 intelligent serial ports, and ELS terminal servers for Ethernet systems.

Address: http://www.equinox.com

Extended Systems  

Extended Systems offers a number of product lines, including network print servers, printer-sharing products, infrared connections, and client/server software.

Address: http://www.extendsys.com

Farallon

Farallon makes Ethernet networking products, including Fast Ethernet products for the Macintosh market. Their pages feature product listings, tech notes, and demo software.

Address: http://www.farallon.com

FCR Software

FCR develops portable network, routing, and WAN software for the OEM market. FCR's software is designed to run on standard computers such as PCs, Macs, and Sun workstations.

Address: http://www.fcr.com

Nashoba Networks

Nashoba makes network switching products for increased network bandwidth with existing hardware. They strive to make the migration to ATM and other high-speed technologies simple and cost-effective.

Address: http://www.nashoba.com

Network Computing Devices

NCD products include X terminals, PC-X server software, and electronic mail software. Their goal is to make products that "make the network the computer."

Address: http://www.ncd.com

Novell

The giant in PC networking now sells Unix and a variety of other networking and network application products. The Sales button provides links to Novell dealers and VARs on the Web.

Address: http://www.novell.com

ON Technology Corp.

ON Technology offers NetWare optimized workgroup applications and LAN utilities. ON offers extensive information on their products, trial usage, a product catalog, customer service, recent press releases, and a 24-hour hotline for users with questions.

Address: http://www.on.com

Patton Electronics  

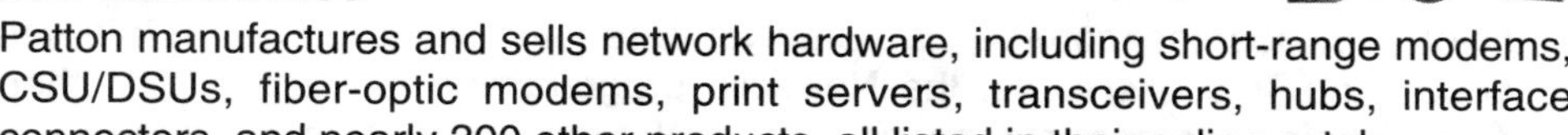

Patton manufactures and sells network hardware, including short-range modems, CSU/DSUs, fiber-optic modems, print servers, transceivers, hubs, interface connectors, and nearly 300 other products, all listed in their online catalog.

Address: http://www.patton.com

Penril Datability Networks 

Penril develops LAN and WAN products for the world market. Their products include access servers, terminal servers, bridges and routers, and ISDN terminal adapters.

Address: http://www.penril.com

Peregrine Systems

Peregrine Systems specializes in networking products, including distributed and administrative management products.

Address: http://www.peregrine.com

Peripheral Technology Group   

PTG distributes PC/Mac and Unix/Internet connectivity products. Their line includes PC-X servers, TCP/IP software and hardware products, HTML tools, disk drives, and print servers.

Address: http://www.ptgs.com

wARE Inc.  

A hardware and software reseller, wARE also offers networking solutions and Internet-related services. The page provides information on related sites and special deals, along with a company directory.

Address: http://www.ware.com

News and Information

Chicago Tribune 

This page offers information from the *Chicago Tribune* about various companies, employers, and job opportunities.

Address: http://www.chicago.tribune.com

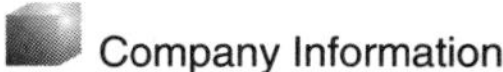 Company Information  Product Information  Online Ordering

ClariNet Communications

ClariNet provides the commercial ClariNet Usenet newsgroups, the Internet Jokebook, the TeleJokeBooks, the Newsclip programming language, and other products. Their page has information on ClariNet staff as well as a listing of job opportunities at ClariNet.

Address: http://www.clarinet.com

EasyNet 2.0

EasyNet 2.0 can lead you to any desired information quickly and effectively with details from well-known sources and publications, providing answers to questions and research for reports.

Address: http://www.telebase.com

Electronic Newsstand

Electronic Newsstand is a source for locating articles from the world's leading magazines, newspapers, newsletters, and catalogs.

Address: http://www.enews.com

Environmental News Network

Environmental News Network offers environmental news and information, mainly from the Northwest and Intermountain regions. The page also provides a monthly bulletin, a calendar of events, a list of environmental services, and a guide to environmental sites on the Internet.

Address: http://www.enn.com

Farcast

Farcast is a news and information service providing its customers with 24-hour access to a collection of news, press releases, reference materials, and stock quotes. Farcast can also arrange to send news articles on a wide range of topics automatically.

Address: http://www.farcast.com

Federal News Service

FNS allows online users to obtain transcripts of the actual words spoken by government leaders on official U.S. government policy matters. This page features information from White House daily briefings, the Executive and Legislative Branches, Congressional hearings, the Supreme Court, and regulatory agencies.

Address: http://www.fednews.com

First Virtual InfoHaus

InfoHaus is a public-access information mall. Readers can browse by categories such as Seller, Topic, Keyword, or Date.

Address: http://www.infohaus.com

Houston Chronicle

This page offers all the news and features included in the newspaper's print edition, plus information on community resources. Breaking news stories that don't appear in the paper are also offered on this page.

Address: http://www.chron.com

InfoPages

InfoPages, a service of Maximized Online, tells readers what's available on the World Wide Web. The page offers a list of events, chat areas, and other interesting sites.

Address: http://www.infopages.com

Information Discovery

This company offers information location services. They use the resources of the Internet and online databases to find information and provide users with tools to locate information themselves.

Address: http://www.I-Discover.Com

Investor's Business Daily

IBD is a newspaper covering the stock market, business, industry, and the economy. Sections include a business news summary, articles on national issues of importance, editorials, and investment information.

Address: http://ibd.ensemble.com

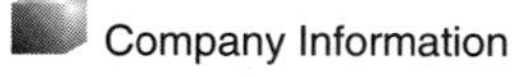

Knight-Ridder Information

Knight-Ridder Information is a leader in electronic information access and delivery, offering the DIALOG and DataStar information search and retrieval services.

Address: http://www.dialog.com

Lexis-Nexis

A division of the Reed Elsevier, Inc., publishing company, Lexis-Nexis offers legal, business, and current news information services to help professionals conduct research expediently. Lexis-Nexis offers extensive company product and service information.

Address: http://www.lexis-nexis.com

Miami Herald and El Nuevo Herald

Order reprints of the *Herald* online, or visit its Superbowl section if you're a sports fan.

Address: http://herald.kri.com

New York Times Syndicate

The New York Times Syndicate, which includes the *New York Times* News Service, provides feature stories, book excerpts, columns, and current news.

Address: http://www.nytsyn.com

Newshare

Newshare sells news through the Internet. Stories of local, national, and international interest are featured. Options include sports, classifieds, and weather. There is also a Current Resources list in which updated information on topics of interest can be found.

Address: http://www.newshare.com

Newspage

Newspage is an online news source from Individual, Inc. They provide stories on a wide variety of categorized topics.

Address: http://www.newspage.com

Providence Business News

This weekly business newspaper covers all fronts of the business world in Southern New England and beyond. It offers current information on business and stock, along with legal and environmental resource guides. Both current and back issues are online.

Address: http://www.pbn.com

RadioSpace

RadioSpace is a radio broadcast agency offering news and programming services to radio stations and other organizations across the country. This company provides sound and text files for broadcasts, interviews, news, and related features.

Address: http://www.radiospace.com/welcome.html

San Diego Daily Transcript

This page offers news and information on every aspect of life in San Diego, including education, technology, current news, finance, and legal matters.

Address: http://www.sddt.com

San Francisco Chronicle and Examiner

These publications have teamed up to offer an online news program, *The Gate*, combining information from both papers. Their pages offer online conversations, sports news, arts and entertainment, and stories and pictures of San Francisco.

Address: http://www.sfgate.com

Sunday Paper

The Sunday Paper is an information and classified ad site. The page provides sections for business news and classifieds.

Address: http://www.sundaypaper.com

USA Today

This online site for the *USA Today* newspaper offers updated news, sports, money, life, and weather information. Subscription information is also available on the page.

Address: http://www.usatoday.com

Verity

Verity Inc. develops products and technologies that make it easier to filter, search, retrieve, analyze, and navigate information sources to get the information you need.

Address: http://www.verity.com

Personal Services

1-800-DEDICATE

Pick a song and record a message for a special person. 1-800-DEDICATE provides an alternative to the greeting card. Songs are categorized by sentiment, such as love, friendship, or apology.

Address: http://www.800dedicate.com

Bay Area Job Finder

Coolware provides this online list of jobs available in the San Francisco Bay Area. Click on various cities on the map to view the listing of jobs offered there. There is a nominal fee for ads more than 16 lines in length.

Address: http://www.coolware.com/jobs/location.html

E-Span

E-Span's Interactive Employment Network provides updated job information that you can search by keyword, region, or industry.

Address: http://www.espan.com

Mass Mutual

Mass Mutual is one of the nation's largest life insurance companies, offering life insurance, health benefits, and investment management. This page gives information about the company, its services, and career opportunities.

Address: http://www.massmutual.com

Molly Maid

Molly Maid offers both a cleaning service and the opportunity to become a franchise owner. The page provides information on the cleaning services, background on the company, and reading material on the requirements of becoming a franchise owner.

Address: http://www.mollymaid.com

ParentsPlace.com

The Parentsplace is a Web information and resource center for parents, offering products, services, and catalogs of merchandise. Chat with other parents about child-related issues on Dialog and Live Chat. These pages include articles, newsletters, and excerpts from books on a variety of interesting topics.

Address: http://www.parentsplace.com

Sun Angel Innovations

Sun Angel Innovations is a unique company dedicated to providing information, products, and services to those seeking spiritual fulfillment and personal growth. Their Web pages offer articles, resources, and a marketplace of available products and services.

Address: http://www.sun-angel.com

Tripod

Tripod is a membership organization designed to provide its members with success in life through their original tools in such areas as finance, health, community, travel, careers, and living.

Address: http://www.tripod.com

UNARIUS Academy of Science

Unarius offers books and video tapes on the sciences of the mind and the universe. They also offer study courses in the psychology and physics of consciousness.

Address: http://www.cts.com/browse/unarius

Pets

AcmePet

This page is about pets. There is a directory of all kinds of animals, including horses, dogs, cats, fish, reptiles, birds, and exotic animals, along with information on where and how to get them and on product supplies.

Address: http://www.acmepet.com

Animal Mania

Animal Mania is a pet store offering a catalog of reptiles, arachnids, amphibians, birds, exotic animals, and supplies.

Address: http://www.paradise.net/animals/

Cohasset Birdhouses Gift Shop

This small company specializes in fine birdhouses and birdfeeders, all handmade of clear pine. Their page describes some of the available products.

Address: http://www.birdhouses.com/birdhouses

Creative Bird Accessories

Creative Bird Accessories offers colorful gifts, clothes, accessories, and books in their international mail-order catalog. They can locate birds and obtain avian veterinarians' answers to your questions.

Address: http://www.webscope.com/cba

Labyrinth Dalmatians

Labyrinth Dalmatians is a kennel aiming to breed champions. For almost half a century, they have been producing top-of-the-line Dalmations in the U.S. This page offers information of all kinds related to Dalmations.

Address: http://www.labyrinth.com/lcs/dals.html

Maggie's Gourmet Goodies

Sheila Magnusson's Web page offers homemade cat-shaped dog biscuits for sale from an original recipe she created for her dog, Maggie.

Address: http://www.vpm.com/mgm

Publishing

Electronic Book Technologies

EBT develops electronic publishing software based on SGML. Their products include the DynaText indexer and stylesheet editor, the DynaBase system for storing and retrieving SGML documents, DynaTag for converting common word processor formats into SGML, and the DynaWeb Web server, which converts DynaText SGML books into HTML for the Web.

Address: http://www.ebt.com

Manual 3

Manual 3, Inc., is an online firm that specializes in writing, publication management, illustration, and graphic design. The page offers not only writing services, but also access to other links associated with documentation.

Address: http://www.manual3.com

MecklerMedia

MecklerMedia specializes in publishing and trade shows and produces a magazine called *Internet World*, which features daily updated news and information on programs, projects, conferences, and seminars to help users understand the computer industry. These pages also list staff and other literary resources.

Address: http://www.mecklerweb.com

Net 101

Net 101 began as an Internet training and consulting firm before adding publishing to their repertoire. This page offers a list of past projects and the companies involved.

Address: http://www.net101.com

O'Reilly & Associates

O'Reilly & Associates is an open systems book publisher dedicated to advancing online publishing technology. Their Web pages feature such subjects as programming, computer security, business and travel, and system and network administration. You'll also find an online bookstore where you can order computer-related books and software.

Address: http://www.ora.com

Peachpit Press

  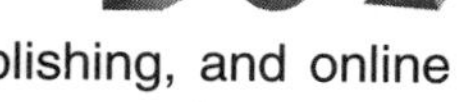

Peachpit Press publishes books about computers, digital publishing, and online communications. Peruse Peachpit's entire catalog by title, author, or category.

Address: http://www.peachpit.com

Precision Proofreading

Precision Proofreading's page features professional services including quality control, copy editing, proofreading, and final output. Also included are links to related editorial information.

Address: http://www.geopages.com/TheTropics/1776/

 Company Information  Product Information  Online Ordering

PrePRESS Solutions

PrePRESS bills itself as the Web site for electronic prepress professionals. The company supplies hardware, software, services, and training to the electronic prepress industry.

Address: http://www.prepress.pps.com

Quixote Digital Typography

Quixote offers digital typesetting and publishing services. They also publish *Serif: The Magazine of Type & Typography*.

Address: http://www.quixote.com

Syllabus Press

Syllabus Press, Inc., publishes *Syllabus* magazine and the *Query* newsletter, which cover technology and related issues for high school and college-level study. This page includes conference information, updated magazine excerpts, and educational tools and software.

Address: http://www.syllabus.com

Thomas Publishing

This company publishes buying guides, magazines, and exchange services. The page offers a peek at the different types of work they have published and keeps users up to date on news.

Address: http://www.nyc.pipeline.com/thomas

Tor Books

Tor Books is a publisher of science fiction and fantasy literature. Their pages provide information on select books and authors, publishing schedules, sample chapters from Tor publications, links to many related Web sites, and an FAQ sheet.

Address: http://www.tor.com

Vannevar New Media

Vannevar New Media is a company offering electronic publishing and applications services, including design and maintenance of Web sites and personal bulletin board systems. The page offers extensive information on the company and its services and includes a portfolio.

Address: http://www.vannevar.com

Williams & Wilkins

Williams & Wilkins is an international publisher of material relating to medicine and the health sciences. This page includes an online catalog of their books, periodicals, and electronic media products.

Address: http://www.wwilkins.com

Real Estate

Accnet

Accnet provides information about real estate and a facility for users to search for property to buy or list property to sell. They constantly update their catalog of houses, condos, and other properties.

Address: http://accnet.com

America's Home Buyer's Page

This magazine has taken all its real estate listings and organized them by state. The page also features a mortgage calculator that enables the user to see how much a new house would cost.

Address: http://www.execpc.com/realty

American Real Estate Exchange

The AMREX Network was created to provide real estate professionals with news about investments, loans and leases, supply-and-demand factors, trends, and industry performance information.

Address: http://www.amrex.com

Antaeus Properties

This company provides property services including investment analysis, site selection, master-site development, preliminary cost estimating, and value engineering.

Address: http://www.hia.com/hia/antaeus

Company Information  Product Information 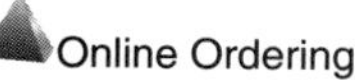 Online Ordering

Apartments on Video

This company offers home videos that show apartments available for rent in the San Diego, Los Angeles, and Orange County areas. The page offers information on the company's services and provides information on where to obtain *Apartments on Video*.

Address: http://www.cts.com/browse/aptonvid

Austin Real Estate Connection

This page provides real estate access information for Austin, Texas. Details include relocation information, loan applications, legal advice, inspector hiring, and building floorplans.

Address: http://www.austinre.com

Coldwell Banker Real Estate

Coldwell Banker was founded in 1906 in San Francisco, California. This site provides World Wide Web referrals to practically any destination you may have in mind. Coldwell Banker locates experienced real estate agents with email capability in your area.

Address: http://www.coldwell.banker.com/cb

General American Credits

General American Credits, Inc., provides lenders with real estate appraisal and title services required for real estate loan decisions.

Address: http://www.gencredits.com

Global Electronic Marketing Service

GEMS offers a page with links to real estate companies throughout the country. Follow a link, and you're presented with links to information on each company's listings.

Address: http://www.gems.com

Global Real Estate Registry

This company covers a small number of nationwide residential and commercial properties. Their site offers assistance in finding an appropriate real estate firm, agent, and home.

Address: http://www.goglobal.com

HIA/Virtual Village

This site directory focuses on real estate and professional services in the NYC metro and San Francisco Bay areas. It provides information in the areas of finance, the arts, speculative physics, innovative software products, and political advocacy.

Address: http://www.hia.com

Home Buyer

Home Buyer provides services pertaining to buying, selling, and leasing houses and apartments worldwide. The page offers color photos of properties and enables customers to get descriptions of homes anywhere on the globe.

Address: http://www.homebuyer.com

Homebuyer's Fair

Purely for residential real estate, Homebuyer's Fair provides relocation and mortgage services, assorted homebuyers' information, classified advertisements, and a section updating developments in Web real estate. You can even view pictures of homes on the market.

Address: http://www.homefair.com

International Real Estate Advisors

This on-line real estate marketing service helps real estate agents, buyers, and sellers. Their page shows you real estate properties, locates properties for your clients, and guides you to related products and services.

Address: http://www.irean.com

Jurock Real Estate Investor

Ozzie Jurock's International Real Estate Net offers a wide range of real estate information, including statistics and advice.

Address: http://www.jurock.com

Long & Foster Realtors

Long & Foster Realtors serves customers in the mid-Atlantic region. Home listings are categorized by area, and the page provides agent profiles as well as lists of area schools.

Address: http://www.home-sales.com

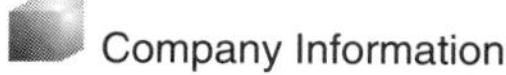

Marcus and Millichap Real Estate Investment Brokerage

This real estate investment company provides financial recommendations and vital data for purchasing a home. The page views property sales throughout the country, keeping customers up on developments in the real estate market.

Address: http://www.mmreibc.com

MoveEasy Professional Real Estate Network

MoveEasy is a free online service providing valuable real estate-related information and services. It connects users with agents across the nation to help buy or sell a home.

Address: http://www.moveeasy.com

Net Properties

Net Properties Corp. provides comprehensive resource information to increase the efficiency of real estate transactions. Real estate companies can display properties through this site.

Address: http://www.intertel.com

New Homes Online

This online magazine shows newly built homes in Florida. Users can contact the magazine or the real estate agents in their area for more information on these listings.

Address: http://newhomes.com

Real Estate On-Line

This online New York real estate resource is sponsored by Bellmarc Realty and offers information on commercial real estate in the New York area and residential offerings in Manhattan and Westchester, Fairfield, and Putnam counties.

Address: http://www.nyrealty.com

Realty Network

Realty Network is a center for information about Atlanta real estate. They provide information about upcoming open houses and available agents around the city. Other options on this page include information about local attractions, restaurants, education, and lodging.

Address: http://www.realty-net.com

RealWorks Real Estate Forum

Created by First Realty Advisors, Inc., this page is designed to help real estate agents around the world by offering information on RealWorks software and popular Internet real estate sites.

Address: http://www.realworks.com

Southern Shores Realty

These North Carolina realtors offer information regarding rentals of oceanfront vacation homes. Also available are maps of the area and descriptions of the property.

Address: http://www.soshores.com/soshores

Stanford Area Real Estate Guide

This guide offers real estate information pertaining to the four communities in the Stanford area—Menlo Park, Palo Alto, Mountain View, and Los Altos.

Address: http://www.paloalto.com

Timeshare Users Group

Timeshare Users Group is dedicated to providing timeshare resort information to timeshare holders and other interested parties. The page offers options ranging from a timeshare database to classified ads to reviews of timeshare resorts.

Address: http://www.timeshare-users-group.com

Security and Ecash

Aladdin Knowledge Systems

Aladdin Knowledge Systems is a leading manufacturer of software security systems, enabling developers to protect their intellectual property and increase their revenues by protecting their products from unauthorized use.

Address: http://www.hasp.com

Cybercash

Cybercash specializes in technology that enables businesses to sell goods and services on the Internet, receiving immediate payment for their products.

Address: http://www.cybercash.com

DigiCash

DigiCash develops and implements methods for secure electronic cash payment using debit cards, credit cards, phone cards, teleshopping and telebanking, and automatic toll-collection strategies.

Address: http://www.digicash.com

McAfee

McAfee is a leading developer of anti-virus and network security software, including VirusScan, RomShield, and NetShield. This page also offers downloadable software from McAfee and other sources.

Address: http://www.mcafee.com

Miros

Miros makes a face-recognition security system called TrueFace. This page provides information on the product and its accuracy, along with a demo showing how TrueFace works.

Address: http://www.miros.com

Raptor Systems

Raptor designs, manufactures, and markets the Eagle product line, providing Internet and LAN security for both corporate enterprises and small businesses.

Address: http://www.raptor.com

RSA Data Security

RSA is a leader in the development of software encryption and authentication systems. Some of their technologies are part of existing and proposed standards for the Internet, CCITT, ISO, and other standards organizations.

Address: http://www.rsa.com

Shopping Malls

America Mall

The America Mall hosts a variety of interesting places to visit. The mall's boarders are neatly categorized and include such titles as Business & Investments, Food & Fashion, and Museums & Art.

Address: http://www.america.com

Downtown Anywhere

Downtown Anywhere is a virtual city offering a Main Street with shopping and services, a 5th Avenue for more shopping, libraries, newsstands, museums, galleries, an education section, and much more.

Address: http://www.awa.com

Emporium One

Emporium One is an online mall sponsored by Internet One, Inc. Options include news updates, ordering information, and a list of clients.

Address: http://www.EmporiumOne.COM

Front Page

The Front Page is a "boulevard of shops and services" offering products and services ranging from art, photography, boat sales, resort information, and a mall to a wide range of business and professional services.

Address: http://www.thefrontpage.com

Global Shopping Network

A collection of industry networks, GSN provides shopping information on the marine industry, sportfishing, the outdoor industry, and more. Online ordering is available to members.

Address: http://www.gsn.com

Global Union Square

Global Union Square is a place to meet and exchange information on the Internet. Services here include an electronic marketplace, global travel information, a gourmet cookbook, real estate and home-planning information, an art gallery, and a section for interactive discussions.

Address: http://www.gus.com

InterMart

This online marketplace provides access to products and services from around the world. There are 15 categories to choose from, ranging from clothing and jewelry to business services.

Address: http://www.shopimart.com

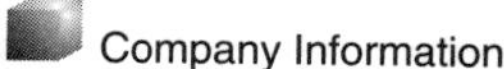

 Product Information 

Internet Commerce Center

This online commerce center brings companies to a marketplace where users can go to shop. The page also provides information on financial news and the current happenings at ICC.

Address: http://www.save.com

Internet Plaza

If you like to shop, make room in your bookmark file for the Internet Plaza. This electronic village offers a business district, a shopping district, a community center, and monthly features.

Address: http://www.xor.com

Net-Mart

Net-Mart features an online shopping directory. Within each store are descriptions of merchandise, along with phone numbers for placing orders and information about employment opportunities.

Address: http://www.netmart.com

Shopping 2000

Shopping 2000 is another online marketplace where companies are listed with their products and services. Online ordering capabilities vary depending on the particular company.

Address: http://www.shopping2000.com

Shopping Expressway

Readers can shop with ease and companies can give their products and services maximum exposure at this online marketplace.

Address: http://shopex.com

Super Mall

The Super Mall offers a wide variety of products, services, and information on promotional events. Also on this site are order forms for information on how to advertise, sponsor, or subscribe to this service.

Address: http://www.supermall.com

Travel & Entertainment Network

TEN offers complete travel and entertainment information as well as shopping opportunities all over the World Wide Web. Options on the page include Travelcom, Showcom, Sportscom, Cruisecom, a reservation system, and a travel agent directory.

Address: http://www.ten-io.com

Village Potpourri Mall

VPM Enterprises of Folsom, California, provides a commercial mall on the Internet as well as a directory of personal Web pages and online business cards. The company offers options to register domain names on its server and to acquire a VPM credit card account for mall purchases.

Address: http://www.vpm.com

VirtuMall

VirtuMall, Inc., allows readers to browse through categories such as food, entertainment, computing, household, and hobbies. They also offer a catalog and a chance to sign up for advertising services.

Address: http://www.virtumall.com

Vista Point Plaza

Vista Point Plaza is an online shopping network that brings products, services, and businesses to the Net. The page offers shopping alternatives and information on how users can market their own products.

Address: http://www.vistapoint.com

World Mall

The World Mall is an online marketplace for worldwide retail, business, and civic-related products and services. There is also information on other Web sites and Web starting points.

Address: http://www.worldmall.com

World Square

A product of World Square Corp., this is an online catalog for shopping. The page presents options related to news, music, art, and automobiles.

Address: http://www.w2.com

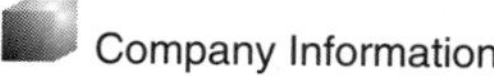

 Product Information

World-Wide Collectors Digest 

World-Wide Collectors Digest provides information on popular collectibles such as baseball cards and comic books. The page covers a wide range of sports, from fencing to hockey. Classified ads are available here, as well as information on manufacturers.

Address: http://www.wwcd.com

Sports

AllSports.Com 

This electronic store features an online catalog of sports clothes. The catalog is divided into categories, and you can order products using AllSport's 800 phone number.

Address: http://www.questtech.com/nfl

American Racing Scene 

This page provides racing news, shop talk, and photographs for auto racing fans worldwide.

Address: http://www.racecar.com

Bentgrass Golf   

Bentgrass Golf sells golf apparel including hats, rainwear, shirts, sweaters, and windbreakers.

Address: http://www.mayavr.com/maya/bentgrass/bentgr.html

C3D Sports   

C3D Sports has created the Portable Line Drive batting trainer for baseball hitters looking to improve their swing. C3D also features the Golf Line Drive portable driving range for golfers.

Address: http://www.c3d.com

Fore Play Golf   

Fore Play is a Web page offering golfing tips, lessons, a quiz, monthly customer appreciation drawings, and product merchandise and information.

Address: http://www.4play.com/sports/4play

fr Progressors

This company develops and manufactures a line of wheels designed for progressive skaters.

Address: http://www.frprogressors.com

H.O. Sports

H.O. Sports manufactures waterskis, kneeboards, wake boards, and accessories. H.O.'s pages offer information on the company's latest designs, products, and clinics and contests pertaining to water sports.

Address: http://www.hosports.com

Linkster's Golf Shop

Linkster's is an online golf store that furnishes information on golf products, books, videos, and other golf-related merchandise.

Address: http://www.golf.com/proshop/linksters/

Los Gatos Tennis Pro Shop

This online California racquet shop features top-of-the-line tennis merchandise, shoes, and apparel.

Address: http://www.sportsmall.com/losgatos.html

Ocean Surfer Home Page

Ocean Surfer has an online surf shop and features news from surf spots, surf market technology, product updates, video reviews, a surfing story-of-the-month, San Diego surfers' perspectives, and news from worldwide surfing clubs.

Address: http://www.cts.com/browse/scwindan

Outdoor Network

The Outdoor Network provides information and news updates on businesses and travel opportunities dealing with outdoor sports (skiing, sailing, windsurfing, kayaking, skating, and more). Hear about a previous sports adventure, order a catalog from your favorite outdoor company, or find out about a sports club or organization in your area.

Address: http://www.outdoornet.com

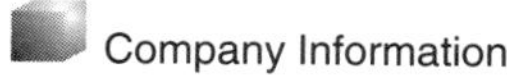 Company Information  Product Information Online Ordering

RaceNews - The MotorSports Network

RaceNews provides information on all upcoming events in auto racing. The page includes editorials and features in addition to daily news and an archive of past information.

Address: http://www.racenews.com

Silver Cloud Sports

Silver Cloud specializes in high-performance golf products, including quality, affordable golf clubs. Its page offers information on leasing programs, clubs and sets, and ordering.

Address: http://www.silvercloud.com

Sports Cards and More

Major-league sports card singles and complete sets are for sale on this Web page. The database is continually updated to reflect cards on hand.

Address: http://www.icw.com/sports/sports.html

Sports Mall

Sports Mall is an online connection to sports merchandise. These pages offer information on how interested parties can market their wares here.

Address: http://www.sportsmall.com

Sportshop

The Sportshop Web site provides collectible sports material. Currently available are 8x10" glossy individual photos of members of the All Star Teams for both the American and National Leagues, provided by Photo File.

Address: http://hkss.com

SportSite

SportSite offers products and information for sports and recreation enthusiasts. Featuring SnowLink, CycleLink, OutdoorLink, and SportLink, SportSite offers information and products ranging from clothing to accessories.

Address: http://www.sportsite.com

SportsLine USA

SportsLine USA features sports news, opportunities, and merchandise. Links include current contests, top stories, league schedules, and updates on current major sporting events, such as Wimbledon and the Tour de France.

Address: http://www.sportsline.com

Thoroughbred Horse Racing Information Link

THRIL provides horse racing information online. Members can get racing statistics, data, and specific articles. For nonmembers, these pages provide a racetrack directory, online shopping opportunities, and news of the industry.

Address: http://www.thril.com

Technical Consulting

American Management Systems

AMS is a technology-based consulting firm offering a range of services, including business re-engineering, change management, and systems integration, development, and implementation.

Address: http://www.amsinc.com

David Solomon Expert Seminars

This company offers seminars and training on Windows programming, covering such topics as Windows 95, Windows NT, and OLE.

Address: http://www.solsem.com

Faludi Computing

Faludi Computing offers comprehensive Macintosh consulting to San Francisco-area businesses. They specialize in implementing Internet and Web services on Macs.

Address: http://www.faludi.com

First Step Research

FSR provides technical consulting services related to computer system architectures and tools, network applications, design, and local access to Internet and Web services.

Address: http://www.fsr.com

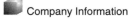

Gateway Communications

Gateway Communications is a consulting firm specializing in connecting to the Internet and providing turnkey packages.

Address: http://www.gateway.com

Global Commerce Link

Global Commerce Link is a technology consulting firm specializing in putting organizations online to do business.

Address: http://www.commerce.com

Honeywell Allied Data Communications

Honeywell's Allied Data Communications Group is a consulting and integration arm of Honeywell. This page offers a wealth of information about the services ADC provides.

Address: http://www.adcg.com

Human Factor

The Human Factor teaches users to find their way through the Internet and the World Wide Web. Users can advertise affordably, and certain nonprofit organizations can get a free page.

Address: http://www.human.com

Ian Freed Consulting

Ian Freed Consulting offers specialized assistance in the analysis, design, and implementation of domestic and international data communications and computer systems. This page provides information on services, projects, and clients as well as other Internet resources.

Address: http://www.ifc.com

Jupiter Communications

Jupiter Communications is a leading research and consulting firm specializing in consumer communications technologies and the Internet. This page provides reports and newsletters, information on upcoming conferences, sponsors, current news, and "interactive data."

Address: http://www.jup.com

NetForce Development

NetForce trains people and companies to use the Internet. They develop new products using the latest technology to assist their clients, and their page includes a section on special Web programs and techniques.

Address: http://www.nforce.com

Nosh Productions

A technology consulting firm owned by women and minorities, Nosh Productions provides computer services such as systems integration, software development, documentation, and custom programming.

Address: http://www.nosh.com

S.M. Stoller

S.M. Stoller Corp. assists both business and government with solutions for technological and information management. This page provides information on their products and services as well as news of upcoming seminars and business training.

Address: http://www.stoller.com

Select HyperMedia

In addition to offering publishing on the Web, this company provides Web page development services and information on current projects, conferences, and company events.

Address: http://www.selectsite.com

Wardell: The Internet Advertising Co.

Wardell IAC provides Internet consulting services and specific services for the World Wide Web. The page offers information on company objectives and services as well as related sites on the Web.

Address: http://www.wardell.com

Woodwind Consulting

Woodwind provides Internet consulting services for business, education, and the arts. This page offers extensive information on Woodwind's recent and current projects, and staffing and contact information is provided.

Address: http://www.woodwind.com/Woodwind/WoodwindConsulting.html

Technology and Research

AT&T Bell Laboratories

Check out the projects underway at AT&T's Bell Labs. This server offers information on Bell Labs' ongoing research and links to other related topics and pages.

Address: http://www.research.att.com

designOnline

designOnline offers information about design technology. It includes data on design companies (including portfolios and resumes), products and services, and the latest news and technology from the design industry.

Address: http://www.dol.com

Enterprise Integration Technologies

EIT is a consulting and research and development firm specializing in information technology, software, and services on the Web.

Address: http://www.eit.com

GammaLink

As one of the earliest developers of computer-based fax tools, GammaLink plays an important role in the PC fax market. In addition, they are a leading provider of core fax platforms for many computer-based fax applications.

Address: http://www.gammalink.com

GIS World

GIS (Geographical Information Systems) is a technology for managing and manipulating geographic spatial data. GIS World, Inc., is the creator of *GIS World* and *Business Geographics* magazines and publishes the annual *GIS World Sourcebook*.

Address: http://www.gisworld.com

Huntsville Microsystems, Inc.

HMI manufactures microprocessor emulators, logic analysis tools, and background-mode debuggers. They also develop an advanced software package called Source-Gate II for analyzing and debugging software.

Address: http://www.hmi.com

IIT Research Institute

This nonprofit research organization develops technical applications for both industry and government to be used in such areas as health and the environment.

Address: http://www.iitri.com

Language Engineering Corp.

Language Engineering Corp. specializes in language processing between people who speak different languages and between people and computers. LEC develops language translation software and natural language processing systems.

Address: http://www.lec.com

Nanothinc

Nanothinc specializes in nanotechnology, the science of making tiny machines. For example, they make machines so small they can be released into your bloodstream to clean out your arteries.

Address: http://www.nanothinc.com

SIGS Publications

SIGS specializes in publishing information on software technology. This page highlights SIGS' program, which offers conferences for education on software and related topics, information on their technology, and titles on CD-ROM and videos. There are also links to related sites and information on upcoming events.

Address: http://www.sigs.com

SRI International

Originally affiliated with Stanford University and called the Stanford Research Institute, SRI is now an independent research organization specializing in engineering research, science and technology, and business and policy matters.

Address: http://www.sri.com

Telecommunications

ACMI

ACMI provides prepaid calling cards, international callback, an international calling card, and other communication innovations. They also have an Advantage Fundraiser program for nonprofit and charitable organizations.

Address: http://www.phonecard.com

ADC Telecommunications

A global telecommunications and networking systems provider, ADC is a leading supplier of transmission and networking systems and products designed for telecommunications, cable television, cellular, broadcast, and enterprise networks.

Address: http://www.adc.com

Adtran

Adtran, Inc., designs, develops, and manufactures electronic transmission products and test equipment for digital communications.

Address: http://www.adtran.com

Alcatel Data Networks

ADN is a joint venture of Alcatel (a supplier of communication systems) and Sprint. ADN's packet, cell, and frame technologies provide high-speed information service to many large companies.

Address: http://www.adn.alcatel.com

American Benefits Group

ALLNET, one of the largest telecommunications companies in America, provides domestic and international long-distance service to residential and business customers. The American Stock Exchange, Time Publishing, UCLA, and many Fortune 500 companies rely on ALLNET's 100% digital network.

Address: http://www.bizpro.com/bizpro/bilmccmr.html

Ameritech

Ameritech started as a telephone service provider, expanding to include cellular, paging, interactive video, and wireless data communications. Ameritech's pages offer company news as well as a list and description of services.

Address: http://www.ameritech.com

And Communications

And Communications does marketing consultation, communications design, and multimedia production. Their page includes information about current projects, and their resume includes the Real Beer Page and 20 Tank Brewery's page.

Address: http://www.and.com

BellSouth Telecommunications

BellSouth, an Atlanta-based company, offers local telephone service in nine Southeastern states. BellSouth also provides mobile communications services and advertising and publishing services, and they market and maintain stand-alone and fully integrated communications systems.

Address: http://www.bst.bls.com

Cable Television Labs

CableLabs plans and funds research and development projects that will help cable companies realize future opportunities and meet future challenges in the television industry. They also transfer relevant technologies and prospective developments to member companies and to the cable industry.

Address: http://www.cablelabs.com

Cablevision

Cablevision operates cable television systems, produces and distributes programming for cable and satellite systems, and sells advertising spots. Their page includes information about their programming, which includes American Movie Classics and an assortment of news and sports stations.

Address: http://moon.cablevision.com

DashOPS

The Dash Open Phone System is a computerized PBX with built-in voice mail, automated attendant, and multiparty conferencing. Their page offers in-depth information on the makeup and technology of the Dash OPS.

Address: http://www.dashops.com

Digital Systems International

DSI provides computer telephony systems, software, and services. Their products include integrated call-center reporting systems, the Campaign Director Workstation, and other call-center stations.

Address: http://www.dgtl.com

Gil Gordon Associates

Gil Gordon Associates is a consulting firm specializing in helping private- and public-sector firms establish successful telecommuting programs and in aiding providers of products and services with effective marketplace strategies.

Address: http://www.gilgordon.com

Hello Direct

Hello Direct offers an online catalog of telephones, accessories, and related productivity tools including headsets, recording devices, and teleconferencing equipment. In addition, they offer information on calling cards and caller ID.

Address: http://www.hello-direct.com

Hill Associates

Hill Associates provides telecommunications training and education services to the telecommunications industry. Their focus is on telephone and data network equipment and service providers.

Address: http://www.hill.com

JABRA

JABRA Corp. offers a variety of software and hardware wireless products to be used as human auditory interfaces (tiny ear phones) for hands-free communication while using a telephone, cellular phone, or computer.

Address: http://www.cts.com/browse/jabra

MCI

This telecommunications company provides information about what's going on within MCI and with their worldwide operations. Their page offers news and information, directories, and even a marketplace for shopping.

Address: http://www.mci.com

Microspace Communications

As a provider of broadcast data and audio satellite services, Microspace serves customers such as paging companies, business music providers, and trading networks. Their point-to-multipoint communication system via four satellites provides inexpensive service and a satellite signal that is conveniently controlled directly by the customer.

Address: http://www.microspace.com

OKI America Inc.

This is the American subsidiary of the Tokyo-based Oki Electric Industry Co. Oki started manufacturing telephones in Japan in 1881 and today builds a wide variety of communications and information processing systems.

Address: http://www.oki.com

Omnet

Omnet develops computer communication systems for scientists doing oceanographic or atmospheric research. Currently, Omnet is working on a project to extend the Internet to research vessels at sea.

Address: http://www.omnet.com

Pacific Bell

Pacific Bell provides data and voice communications to customers throughout California. This page offers information about the company and its products and services.

Address: http://www.pacbell.com

Southwestern Bell Telephone

A division of SBC Communications, Southwestern Bell provides communications services throughout Arkansas, Kansas, Missouri, Oklahoma, and Texas. On SBT's pages, you'll find news updates, extensive product and service information, and fun options for your enjoyment.

Address: http://www.sbc.com

SpaceCom Systems

SpaceCom Systems markets point-to-multipoint satellite distribution systems and provides advanced satellite technology for audio and data.

Address: http://www.spacecom.com

Sprint

Sprint is a telecommunications company that's heavily involved in the Internet. Sprint's pages offer customer service, the company history, and a forum for discussing the future of communications with the experts.

Address: http://www.sprint.com

U-Save Communications

U-Save is an international callback service. Callback services initiate international calls from the U.S. to avoid other countries' exorbitant international calling rates.

Address: http://www.mindspring.com/~cyberdsn/cybermall/u-save/USAVE.HTML

USWEST

USWEST provides communications and marketing services in 14 western and midwestern states. USWEST's pages offer company information, descriptions of products and services, and listings of employment opportunities.

Address: http://www.uswest.com

Wandel & Goltermann

W&G provides telecom and datacom measurement products, including precision laboratory equipment, portable in-service testers, automatic test systems, and a full suite of other test and measurement equipment.

Address: http://www.wg.com/wg

Television Networks and Movie Companies

CBS Television

CBS producers have teamed up to develop this page, which offers an updated, complete schedule with show descriptions, cast photos, scheduling strategy, and news of sales and marketing activities.

Address: http://www.cbs.com

KGTV - San Diego's 10

This online site provides current network, national, and local news. They offer channel programming schedules, editorials, an FAQ sheet, and KGTV departmental information. Companies also have the opportunity to advertise their services using the Marketplace option.

Address: http://www.kgtv.com

MCA/Universal Cyberwalk

MCA/Universal's page offers information on its TV shows and previews of its movies. There is an online music magazine, a bookstore, and other shopping options.

Address: http://www.univstudios.com

MTV Networks

This is the online site for information on four MTV features: MTV News, the MTV Beach House, MTV Animation, and Beach MTV.

Address: http://www.mtv.com

Paramount

This site provides information about released and upcoming movies as well as job opportunities within the company.

Address: http://www.paramount.com

ReZ.n8 Productions

This company specializes in image-branding packages for television programs, stations, networks, syndicators, motion picture companies, and ad agencies. Their credits include the '94 Winter Olympics and the NFL.

Address: http://www.rezn8.com

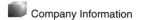

Sci-fi Channel

This online service of the Sci-fi Channel is called The Dominion. These pages offer all sorts of fun for the science fiction fan, including eight directions in which you can head off the main page to find sci-fi shows, products, stories, and related links.

Address: http://www.scifi.com

Walt Disney Co.

Disney's pages offer information on and pictures from various movies from Disney Studios, Touchstone Pictures, and Hollywood Pictures. They include information about Disney films as well as trailers, still shots, and promotional clips.

Address: http://www.disney.com

Transportation and Travel

Above All Travel

Above All Travel offers access to a variety of cruises and expeditions all over the world. The page contains information on each unique adventure, ranging from a cruising expedition in Antarctica to hiking and biking in the Alps.

Address: http://www.aboveall.com

Adventure Shop

The Adventure Shop provides information on all kinds of adventure tours, whether by land, sea, or air. Everything from mountaineering and skiing to river rafting and hang gliding is available. You can also read about adventures that previous travelers have taken.

Address: http://www.ashop.com

AgentNet Worldwide

This source for travel information provides names of local travel agencies, lists of special travel promotions, and sources of other travel information available on the Web. You can also request a flight reservation through this site.

Address: http://www.tiac.net/users/kliger/agentnet/default.html

Alaskan Center

Travel information, community profiles, weather conditions, trip planning, and bookings for flights, hotels, and cars are just a few of the services offered by the Alaskan Center.

Address: http://www.alaskan.com

All-Inclusive Vacations

This page offers a wide variety of travel ideas ranging from Club Med vacations to specialty travel. They allow the user to view an assortment of trips, including the "Destination of the Month" and the "Best Trips for Singles."

Address: http://www.cts.com/browse/vacation

Avid Explorer

Avid Explorer is a center for travel information ranging from cruises to special-value travel packages. Find here Travel Forums offering information for skiers, divers, and snowboarders. These pages include weather reports, travel connections, and a monthly newsletter.

Address: http://www.explore.com

Belize Online

As the official guide for tourism and investment in Belize, Belize Online provides information about this country's history, upcoming events, accommodations, and points of interest.

Address: http://www.belize.com

Conde Nast Traveler Online

This is an online travel magazine that provides information on planning a vacation and all the latest news related to traveling. It provides access to a photo gallery, Beach and Island Finder, forums, a sneak preview of this month's magazine, and much more.

Address: http://www.cntraveler.com

Freeways

Freeways is Alamo Rent A Car's reservation and travel information service. These pages include fun and safety tips for traveling and driving, weather and maps, forums with restaurant tips, and online car reservations.

Address: http://www.freeways.com

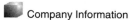

Genie Travel Service

This page makes planning a trip easier. Genie offers airline, airport, and ticket information and will soon even include access to flight schedules and prices so that you can make reservations online.

Address: http://www.genietravel.com

Global Travel Village

Global Travel publishes The Global Travel Village Program and offers bargains on hotel accommodations and rental cars, destinations, extensive advertising services, consultation, and a list of clients.

Address: http://www.neptune.com

Hello America

Hello America provides travel accommodations for every type of vacation imaginable. Clients can choose their ideal vacation or create their own. Possibilities range from educational internships and motorcycle or RV trips to spending a few weeks on a ranch. Hello America makes all reservations and arrangements.

Address: http://www.helloamerica.com

Hotel Discount

Hotel Discount gives users access to hotel rooms throughout the country at up to 65% off regular rates. These pages offer information about hotels in all major cities throughout the U.S., a travel deal of the week, and an 800 number for making reservations.

Address: http://www.hoteldiscount.com

INNroads

This is a guide to country inns and bed and breakfasts throughout the U.S. by region (currently only the West Coast, New England, and the South). Within each region the inns are listed by city or town, with detailed information about location, cost, amenities, and restrictions for each establishment.

Address: http://www.inns.com

Metropolitan Hotel

This Toronto hotel is newly renovated and offers first-class amenities and restaurants. The page provides information about the hotel, its restaurants, rates, and reservations.

Address: http://www.metropolitan.com

Moguls Ski and Sun Tours

Moguls offers ski information as well as custom and prearranged ski trips throughout the U.S. and Canada. This page offers information on group programs and individualized custom tours as well as ski and snowboard trips and family vacations.

Address: http://www.skimoguls.com

Moon Publications

Moon Publications publishes travel handbooks for North America, the Pacific Islands, and Asia. Moon's guides offer tourist information and extensive cultural descriptions and details. They also offer a catalog, links to related sites on the Web, ordering information, and a list of hundreds of bookstores where their guides can be found.

Address: http://www.moon.com

PCTravel

A service of American Travel Corp., PCTravel provides online access to airline reservations and ticket purchase. Find here a demo session to take you through both the ticket reservation system (WEB Reservation System) and ticket purchase system. Included are terms and conditions of the services offered.

Address: http://www.pctravel.com

San Francisco Reservations

SFR is an online site for securing hotel reservations in the San Francisco area. The service is free, and often there are special low hotel rates available. You can choose hotels according to location, price, type, and availability.

Address: http://www.hotelres.com

Tee-Times

Tee-Times creates vacations for golfers. Taking into account budget, skill level, transportation, and lodging, the company organizes trips, often to the scenic courses of North Carolina.

Address: http://www.teetimes.com

Travel Source

Travel Source offers information on unique and exotic travel destinations. Their guide provides extensive options, including cruises, safaris, wine tours, and ski vacations.

Address: http://www.travelsource.com

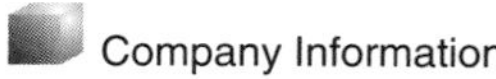 Company Information  Product Information  Online Ordering

Travel Web

Travel Web offers information and brochures on a variety of hotels and motels worldwide. They also provide updated travel news and help users make reservations for trips.

Address: http://www.travelweb.com

TravelASSIST

TravelASSIST provides Internet services to members of the travel and hospitality industries. They provide a directory of small hotels, including bed and breakfasts, and showcase travel-related products and services.

Address: http://www.travelassist.com

Travelogix

Travelogix Online allows businesspeople to make all their travel arrangements on their computer, from hotel to airline reservations.

Address: http://www.travelogix.com

Uniglobe GEM Travel

Uniglobe GEM Travel is an online travel brochure providing information on cruises in Hawaii, Mexico, Jamaica, and Europe.

Address: http://www.uniglobe-gem.com

Vacation Rental Source

The Vacation Rental Source lets users locate vacation accommodations such as condominiums, resorts, and villas. Customers can choose from a variety of regions and learn about the prices, locations, and amenities of the accommodations there.

Address: http://www.vrsource.com

Virtual Destinations: Monterey Bay

This online site offers a wide range of travel and residential information pertaining to Monterey, California, and surrounding areas. Categories include restaurants, lodging, real estate, shopping, and wineries.

Address: http://www.monterey-bay.com

World Span

World Span offers travelers everything they need to know about going abroad. This page includes information about travel agencies, flights, hotels, restaurants, rental cars, cruises, trains, and passports.

Address: http://www.wspan.com

World Wide Web Services

10E Design

10E designs and maintains Web pages, especially for the adventure travel industry and other exotic industries. They offer a magazine called *20th Century Adventures*, a virtual art gallery, and trivia questions.

Address: http://www.10e-design.com

BBS One Online Services

BBS One is a Web service provider that helps businesses and organizations establish their own presence on the Web. They host numerous companies and also provide links to many interesting Internet resources.

Address: http://www.prgone.com

catalogue.com

catalogue.com builds and distributes online catalogs for traditional mail-order and phone-order companies. They take a business's printed catalog and turn it into a graphical, interactive site on the Web.

Address: http://www.arg.com

Databack Services

DBS offers Web presence consulting and page design, including credit-card transactions, product distribution, and market research.

Address: http://www.dbserv.com/dbs/

Digital Creations

Digital Creations develops Web applications and software and offers consulting services.

Address: http://www.digicool.com

 Company Information  Product Information  Online Ordering

Duke-Net

Duke-Net offers personal and business Web pages for a very low one-time fee. They do, however, charge to replace old pages and add new ones.

Address: http://www.duke-net.com

e-Commerce

e-Commerce is a Canadian company specializing in Internet application development and systems integration and in building systems with an eye on reliability and security.

Address: http://www.e-commerce.com

Electric Press

Electric Press is a full-service Web publisher specializing in creating a Web presence for companies. Customers get a dedicated computer on EP's network with a domain name that makes it look as though their clients maintain their own systems. EP also does professional digital graphics and design for their clients.

Address: http://www.elpress.com

Free Range Media

Free Range is a full-scale Web production and Internet services company that creates online environments and interactive promotions for the Web. Their expertise is in creative design, new technology, and account management.

Address: http://www.freerange.com

Home Pages

Home Pages Inc. designs and maintains pages on the World Wide Web. They strive to give their clients the fullest exposure on the Internet.

Address: http://www.homepages.com

Ides Communications Group

Ides Communications Group provides services for the World Wide Web, including development and management of Web sites. The company is experienced with public service and educational organizations, and its page provides detailed information on past projects and clients.

Address: http://www.ides.com

Information Analytics

Information Analytics is an information and software development company that offers online advertising, software information, and various Web pages. They also provide consulting services.

Address: http://www.infoanalytic.com/ia.html

Infovantage

This Internet marketing service helps create custom Web pages, including business home pages and travel and tourism links.

Address: http://www.infovantage.com

Internet Media Group

IMG is an Internet service bureau that provides Web page design, creation, and advertising services. They offer high-speed direct access, the creation of online Internet catalogs, and consulting services.

Address: http://www.mailorder.com

Internet Media Services

Internet Media Services offers communication opportunities on the Internet. The page offers extensive information on the advantages and services they provide.

Address: http://www.netmedia.com

Komuves Consulting

Komuves provides products, services, and consulting for computers, the Internet, and the Web. This business also provides online services, such as site rental and training.

Address: http://www.kom.com

Laran Communications

Laran Communications specializes in online classified advertising, now bringing its services to the World Wide Web. They provide an ad index as well as information on how users can place ads of their own.

Address: http://www.web-ads.com

Mainstream Netservice

Mainstream is a Netherlands-based Web server for business presentation on the Internet. Their page is in both Dutch and English, and there is a form for information on how to advertise plus links to other Dutch servers.

Address: http://www.mainstream.nl

Net Advantage

Net Advantage, Inc., provides professional World Wide Web advertising and publishing services. They offer assistance in setting up and maintaining home pages. For reference, they provide examples of Net Advantage client pages.

Address: http://www.net-advantage.com

NetGrafx

NetGrafx specializes in creating Web pages for businesses and establishing a presence for them on the Web. Included on this page is a list of NetGrafx customers.

Address: http://www.netgrafx.com

Omnibus Direct

Omnibus provides home page construction for business advertisements. It also offers information on flyfishing gear, "futoniture," and mountain bikes, which you can order directly.

Address: http://www.omnibus.com

One World Information Services

One World Information Services offers marketing information to companies who want to maximize their visibility on the Internet. This page includes a client directory, information on developing HTML pages, and a list of interesting Web sites.

Address: http://oneworld.wa.com

Online Solutions

Online Solutions develops Web pages for advertisers on the Net. This page lists previous customers and provides phone numbers and an email address to contact for more information.

Address: http://www.amsquare.com/america/online.html

Open Market

Open Market offers software and other services to coordinate electronic commerce on the Internet and the Web. It also provides company news, options for businesses, and an index of commercial services and products available on the Internet.

Address: http://www.openmarket.com

PoppyWare Web Services

PoppyWare is a Web page design company that also hosts Web pages and takes care of other details. Their server offers links to their customers in the Poppyware Information Plaza.

Address: http://www.poppyware.com

PRoMotion.com

Sponsored by Anne Holmes & Associates, a marketing and public relations firm, PRoMotion.com is an online electronic promotions service specializing in increasing companies' visibility to millions of Internet users. This page provides an extensive list of services offered as well as lists of clients and businesses on the site.

Address: http://www.promotion.com

RS Communications

RS Communications offers Web development services. Their staff has extensive experience with print and broadcast communications as well as data communications, graphics, imaging, and networking technologies.

Address: http://www.rscomm.com

TECH-COMM

TECH-COMM, Inc., creates and provides Web pages for Alabama businesses. There is a local guide to Birmingham and a schedule of Olympic soccer events, which will be hosted by the city in 1996.

Address: http://www.tech-comm.com

Vandelay Industries

Vandelay Industries provides marketing design products and services for the World Wide Web. Their page offers the company philosophy, a portfolio of services, and a price list.

Address: http://www.vandelay.com

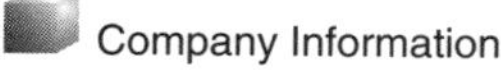 Company Information  Product Information  Online Ordering

Virtual Marketing Corporation

Virtual Marketing Corporation offers marketing services for clients on the World Wide Web. The page offers a Corporate Business Directory listing some of the company's past and present clients.

Address: http://www.vmarketing.com

Virtual Media Communications

Virtual Media Communications, the Internet marketing division of Shandwick/Dorf & Stanton Communications, is a public relations and marketing firm that specializes in creating dynamic Web sites for companies. This page gives extensive information on the company and their services, including examples of home pages created for their clients.

Address: http://www.dorf.stanton.com

VSM Images

VSM is a small Web page design and print-media advertising company located in Tucson, Arizona.

Address: http://www.cris.com/~vaca/vsm.html

Waycool Internet Creations

Waycool Internet Creations, a marketing firm, offers Internet services including page design. The page features a list of clients and related sites on the Web.

Address: http://www.waycool.com

Web Communications

Web Communications provides resources, tools, and services for publication and communication via the World Wide Web, FTP, and electronic mailing lists. Complete lists of available services on the Internet and the Web are offered.

Address: http://www.webcom.com

Web Publishers

Web Publishers offers state-of-the-art advertising and marketing services on the Web.

Address: http://www.webpub.com

Part 4

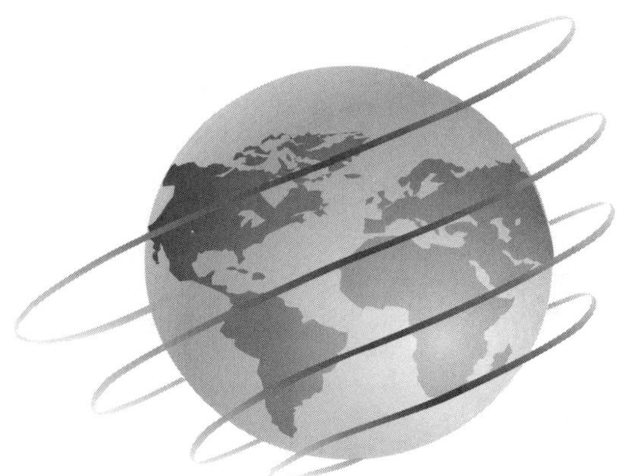

Appendices

Appendix A

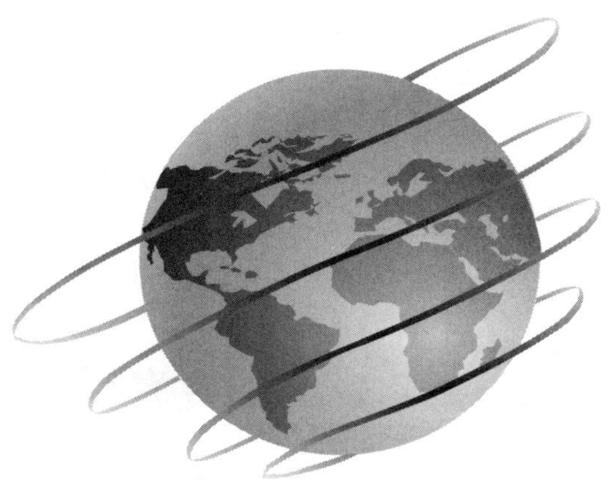

HTML Codes

Use this appendix as a quick reference whenever you're creating Web pages. The HTML codes are categorized by their logical functions into nine tables. For example, the first table contains the head elements and document meta-information elements that apply to an entire Web page. If you want to find a particular element but you're not sure which table it's in, check the index.

This appendix lists the following formatting codes:

- Head-section elements (Table A-1)
- Physical formatting codes (Table A-2)
- Logical formatting codes (Table A-3)
- Miscellaneous codes (Table A-4)
- List and menu elements (Table A-5)
- Anchor attributes (Table A-6)
- Link examples (Table A-7)
- Common entities (Table A-8)
- Tab attributes (Table A-9)

TABLE A-1. *Document Meta-Information Elements and Head Elements*

SYMBOL	DESCRIPTION	LEVEL	TERMINATOR
<BASE>	Records to the URL of the original document itself in cases where the document is read out of context.	0	
<BODY>	Defines the part of your page that is not the head section.	0	</BODY>
<HTML>	Marks the beginning of a Web page.	0	</HTML>
<HEAD>	Marks the beginning of the head section. Define at least the document title in this section.	0	</HEAD>
<ISINDEX>	Informs a browser that the document is an index document that can be searched by keyword. This tag is usually not used in static HTML documents, but rather is sent on the fly by a server generating a searchable document. (See Chapter 13.)	0	

TABLE A-1.	*Document Meta-Information Elements and Head Elements* (continued)		
SYMBOL	**DESCRIPTION**	**LEVEL**	**TERMINATOR**
<LINK>	Defines relationships with other documents and other options, such as fixed banners.	0	
<NEXTID>	A parameter used by some HTML editors to generate unique identifiers for each element.	0	
<TITLE>	Specifies the title the browser will display.	0	</TITLE>

TABLE A-2.	*Physical Formatting Codes*		
SYMBOL	**DESCRIPTION**	**LEVEL**	**TERMINATOR**
<B>	Bold text	1	</B>
<BIG>	Displays the enclosed text in a big font relative to the current font.	3	</BIG>
<I>	Italic text	1	</I>
<PRE>	Preformatted text. Displays exactly as shown.	0	</PRE>
<S>	Strike-through	3	</S>
<SMALL>	Displays the enclosed text in a small font relative to the current font.	3	</SMALL>
_{	Subscript	3	}
^{	Superscript	3	}
<TT>	Displays text in a fixed-width teletype or typewriter-style font.	1	</TT>
<U>	Underlined text	1	</U>

TABLE A-3. *Logical Formatting Codes*			
SYMBOL	**DESCRIPTION**	**LEVEL**	**TERMINATOR**
<ADDRESS>	A special italic font for displaying addresses.	3	</ADDRESS>
<BLOCKQUOTE>	Marks "quoted" text.	0	</BLOCKQUOTE>
<CITE>	Citation	1	</CITE>
<CODE>	Programming language code	1	</CODE>
<EM>	Emphasized text	1	</EM>
<H1>	Marks text for the *Heading 1* style.	0	</H1>
<H2>	Marks text for the *Heading 2* style.	0	</H2>
<H3>	Marks text for the *Heading 3* style.	0	</H3>
<H4>	Marks text for the *Heading 4* style.	0	</H4>
<H5>	Marks text for the *Heading 5* style.	0	</H5>
<H6>	Marks text for the *Heading 6* style.	0	</H6>
<KBD>	Denotes text to be typed on a keyboard.	1	</KBD>
<SAMPLE>	Displays sample text (an example).	1	</SAMPLE>
<STRONG>	Often the same as bold.		</STRONG>
<VAR>	Sets off variable names.	1	</VAR>

TABLE A-4. *Miscellaneous Codes*		
SYMBOL	**DESCRIPTION**	**LEVEL**
<!--.	Starts a comment in the HTML document. Comments are ignored by browsers. Terminate with "-->".	0
<BANNER>	Defines a nonscrolling area of the page for logos, disclaimers, navigational links, and other elements that should always be visible to the reader.	3

TABLE A-4. *Miscellaneous Codes* (continued)

SYMBOL	DESCRIPTION	LEVEL
 	Line break. Use at the end of a line. No end tag.	0
<FIG>	Embeds a reference to a figure (an image file) in a page.	3
<HR>	Horizontal rule. Creates a horizontal line. No end tag.	0
<IMG>	Embeds an inline image.	0
<P>	Marks the end of a paragraph.	0

TABLE A-5. *List and Menu Elements*

SYMBOL	DESCRIPTION	VERSION	TERMINATOR
<DD>	Defines a term in a definition list.	0	
<DIR>	Displays a directory (a list) in columns across the page.	0	</DIR>
<DL>	Definition list	0	</DL>
<DT>	Term defined in a definition list	0	
<LI>	List line item (for any list type)	0	
<MENU>	Defines the beginning of a menu of choices.	0	</MENU>
<OL>	Ordered list	0	</OL>
<UL>	Unordered list	0	</UL>

TABLE A-6. *Anchor Attributes*

SYMBOL	DESCRIPTION
<A>	Marks the beginning of an anchor tag. "</A>" terminates.
HREF	Defines a hypertext reference to another page.
MD	Message digest—an optional checksum for a linked page or image.

TABLE A-6. *Anchor Attributes* (continued)

SYMBOL	DESCRIPTION
NAME	An optional name you can assign to the anchor to make it a destination of an HREF anchor.
REL	Defines relationships with other pages, such as a next and previous page.
REV	Defines a reverse relationship.
SHAPE	Describes shapes within a figure for use as hypertext hot-spots.
TITLE	Describes the reference defined with the HREF attribute (informational only).

TABLE A-7. *Link Examples*

SYMBOL	DESCRIPTION
<A HREF="#JUMP-TO-NAME">Jump Spot</A>	Jumps to another spot on the page.
<A HREF="http://www.xxx.com/foo.html">	Defines a link to another page.
<A HREF="http://www.xxx.com/foo.html#JUMP-TO-NAME">title	Jumps to a specified spot on another page.
<A HREF="xyz.html"><IMG SRC="foo.gif"> </A>title	Makes the image referred to by IMG a hot-spot.

TABLE A-8. *Common Entities*

ENTITY	DESCRIPTION
<	Represents the symbol "<" inside a document.
>	Represents the symbol ">" inside a document.

TABLE A-8. *Common Entities* (continued)	
ENTITY	**DESCRIPTION**
&	Represents an ampersand (&) inside a document.
"	Represents the double quote mark (") inside a document.
	A nonbreaking space
þ	The Icelandic thorn character

TABLE A-9. *Tab Attributes*		
ATTRIBUTE	**DESCRIPTION**	**EXAMPLE**
id	Defines position of a new tab stop.	<tab id=t1>
indent	Defines a new tab in en units.	<tab indent=8>
to	Specifies a tab defined with ID.	<tab to=t1>
align=left	Text resumes just after the tab (default).	<tab align=left>
align=center	Centers following text between margins.	<tab align=center>
to=t1 align=center	Centers following text on tab t1.	<tab to=t1 align=center>
align=right	Aligns following text on the right margin.	<tab align=right>
to=t1 align=right	Aligns following text flush right against tab t1.	<tab to=t1 align=right>
to=t1 align=decimal	Aligns the following number so the decimal point is at tab t1.	<tab to=t1 align=decimal>
dp	Defines the decimal-point character for the "align=decimal" attribute. The default is a period (.).	<tab to=t1 align=decimal dp=",">

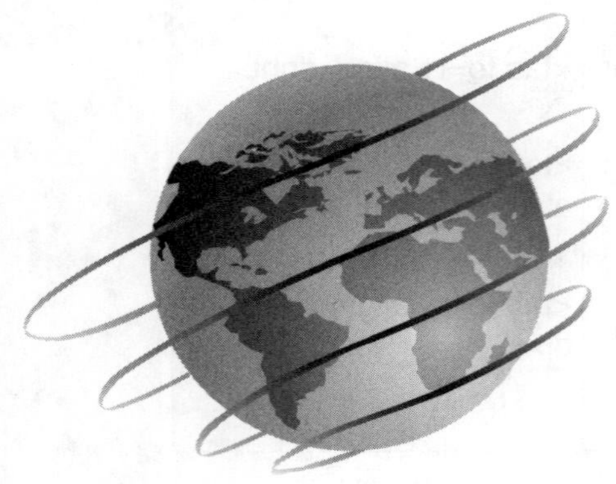

Appendix B

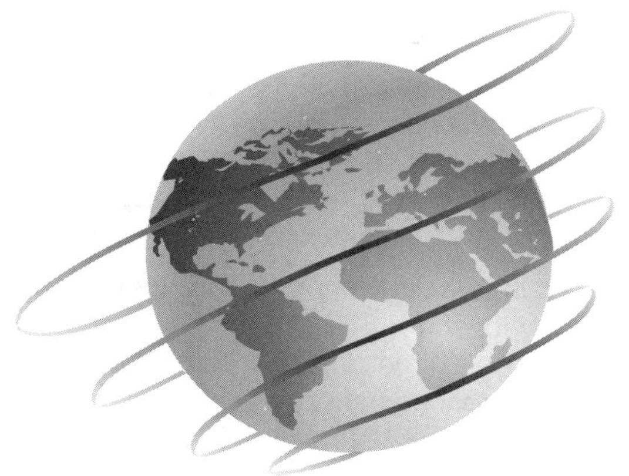

Free Software and Information on the Internet

Throughout this book, you've read about the free software and information available on the Internet. All the information you need to access these resources is collected here for easy reference. Note that some of the file names in these tables contain asterisks, typically in place of a version number for a software package. For example, the file name at the time we go to press might be *winpm201.zip*, but by the time you see the reference and go to the FTP server to download that package it might be *winpm300.zip*. So when you see a file name with an asterisk, be aware that it's there to signify a file whose name may change, and the best course of action is to look at the directory that contains the file instead of trying to retrieve the file directly.

For example, if the reference looks like this:

```
ftp://ftp.risc.ua.edu/pub/network/pegasus/winpm*.zip
```

you should first look at the directory:

```
ftp://ftp.risc.ua.edu/pub/network/pegasus/
```

and, in that directory, look for files that begin with "winpm".

Also, some FTP directory names end with an asterisk. This means you should pull up the directory and look at all the files in it. All of them are probably relevant to the referenced package and might be of interest to you.

This appendix lists the following resources:

- Web browsers (Table B-1)
- TCP/IP utilities (Table B-2)
- Mail programs (Table B-3)
- Viewers and audio players (Table B-4)
- Graphics tools (Table B-5)
- Video utilities (Table B-6)
- HTML editors (Table B-7)
- Web servers (Table B-8)
- Imagemapping tools (Table B-9)
- Web server log analysis tools (Table B-10)
- Web directories (Table B-11)
- FAQ and information files (Table B-12)

TABLE B-1. *Web Browsers*

NAME	PLATFORM	LOCATION / INFORMATION
Cello	Windows	ftp.law.cornell.edu/pub/LII/cello
Chimera	X Window	ftp://ftp.cs.unlv.edu/pub/chimera
DosLynx	DOS	ftp://ftp2.cc.ukans.edu/pub/WWW/DosLynx/
IBM OS/2 WebExplorer	OS/2	ftp://ftp01.ny.us.ibm.net/pub/WebExplorer/
Lynx	Unix	ftp://ftp2.cc.ukans.edu/pub/lynx
MacWeb	Mac	ftp://ftp.einet.net/einet/mac/macweb/
MidasWWW	X Window	http://www.w3.org/hypertext/WWW/MidasWWW/Status.html
Minuet	DOS	ftp://minuet.micro.umn.edu/pub/minuet/latest/minuarc.exe
NCSA Mosaic for Macintosh	Mac	ftp://ftp.ncsa.uiuc.edu/Mac/Mosaic
NCSA Mosaic for Windows	Windows	ftp://ftp.ncsa.uiuc.edu/PC/Windows/Mosaic
NCSA Mosaic for X	X Window	ftp://ftp.ncsa.uiuc.edu/Mosaic/Unix
Netscape for Windows	Windows	ftp://ftp.mcom.com/netscape/windows
Netscape for Mac	Mac	ftp://ftp.mcom.com/netscape/mac
Netscape for X Window	X Window	ftp://ftp.mcom.com/netscape/unix
Quarterdeck Mosaic	Windows	http://www.qdeck.com/
Rashty	VMS	http://www.w3.org/hypertext/WWW/RashtyClient/Status.html
Samba	Mac	http://lake.canberra.edu.au/pub/samba/samba.html

TABLE B-1. *Web Browsers* (continued)

NAME	PLATFORM	LOCATION / INFORMATION
SlipKnot	Windows	http://plaza.interport.net/slipknot/slipknot.html
SPRY Mosaic	Windows	ftp://ftp.spry.com/AirMosaicDemo
The Internet Adapter	Windows	http://marketplace.com/tia/tiahome.html
Viola	X Window	http://xcf.berkeley.edu/ht/projects/viola/
WinWeb	Windows	ftp://ftp.einet.net/einet/pc/winweb/

TABLE B-2. *TCP/IP Utilities*

NAME	PLATFORM	LOCATION / INFORMATION
Chameleon	Windows	http://www.netmanage.com/
FTP Software	Windows	http://www.ftp.com/
MacTCP	Mac	http://www.apple.com/
MS TCP/IP	Windows	http://www.microsoft.com
Net Dial	Windows	ftp://ftp.enterprise.net/pub/netdial/
Trumpet Winsock	Windows	http://www.trumpet.com.au/
Twinsock	Windows	ftp://ftp.coast.net/SimTel/win3/winsock/twnsck*.zip

TABLE B-3. *Mail Programs*

NAME	PLATFORM	LOCATION / INFORMATION
E-Mail Connection	Windows	ftp://ftp.connectsoft.com/pub/emc25/emcsetup.exe
Elm	Unix	ftp://ftp.dsi.com/pub/elm/
Eudora for Mac	Mac	http://www.qualcomm.com/quest/
Eudora for Windows	Windows	http://www.qualcomm.com/quest/
Ladybird	Windows	ftp://papa.indstate.edu/winsock-l/mail/lbird*
NETcetera	Windows	ftp://ftp.airtime.co.uk/pub/windows/netcetera/*

TABLE B-3. *Mail Programs* (continued)

NAME	PLATFORM	LOCATION / INFORMATION
Pegasus	Windows	ftp://risc.ua.edu/pub/network/pegasus/winpm*.zip
Pine	Unix	ftp://ftp.cac.washington.edu/pine/
Post Office	Windows	ftp://papa.indstate.edu/winsock-l/mail/po_*.zip
Pronto IP	Windows	ftp://commtouch.com/pub/commtouch/pip*.exe

TABLE B-4. *Viewers and Audio Players*

NAME	TYPE	PLATFORM	LOCATION / INFORMATION
ACDSee	Image	Windows	ftp://dataflux.bc.ca/pub/acd/acdsee/acdc*.zip
Acrobat	PDF files	Windows	ftp://ftp.adobe.com/pub/adobe/Applications/Acrobat/Windows/acroread.exe
Brian's Sound Tool	Audio	Mac	ftp://src.doc.ic.ac.uk/computing/systems/mac/info-mac/snd/util/brians-sound-tool-*.hqx
LView Pro	Image	Windows	ftp://ftp.ncsa.uiuc.edu/Mosaic/Windows/viewers/lviewp1b.zip
Miscellaneous viewers	Audio	Mac	http://www.qub.ac.uk/sigweb/mac-comms-utils.html
Snd Converter Pro	Audio	Mac	ftp://src.doc.ic.ac.uk/computing/systems/mac/info-mac/snd/util/snd-converter-*
WAVany	Audio	Windows	ftp://ftp.netcom.com/pub/ne/neisius/wvany*.zip
Wham	Audio	Windows	ftp://gatekeeper.dec.com/pub/micro/msdos/win3/sounds/wham*.zip
Wplany	Audio	Windows	ftp://ftp.cica.indiana.edu/pub/pc/win3/sounds/wplny*.zip

TABLE B-5. *Graphics Tools*

NAME	PLATFORM	LOCATION / INFORMATION
GIFTool	DOS	http://www.homepages.com/tools
GIFTrans	DOS	ftp://melmac.corp.harris.com/files/giftrans.exe
Transparency	Mac	ftp://ftp.ned.cornell.edu/pub/aarong/transparency
XV	Unix	ftp://ftp.cis.upenn.edu/pub/xv/

TABLE B-6. *Video Utilities*

NAME	PLATFORM	PLAYS/ CONVERTS	LOCATION
Archive	All	QuickTime	ftp://venice.tcp.com/pub/anime-manga/ software/viewers/
Archive	All	MPEG	http://cuiwww.unige.ch/w3catalog/
Archive	All	MPEG	http://w3.eeb.ele.tue.nl/mpeg/
Archive	All	MPEG	http://www.cs.ucl.ac.uk/movies/
AVI→Quick	Mac	AVI, QT	http://www.lcs.mit.edu/HyperArchive/ Archive/_Graphic_&_Sound_Tool/ _Movie/
FlatMoov	Mac	Flattener	ftp://src.doc.ic.ac.uk/computing/systems/ mac/info-mac/_Graphic_&_Sound_Tool/ mov/flatmoov*.hqx
MPEGPlay	Windows	MPEG	ftp://ftp.ncsa.uiuc.edu/Mosaic/Windows/ viewers/mpegw32h.zip
MS Video	Windows	AVI	http://www.microsoft.com/
Qflat	Windows	Flattener	ftp://venice.tcp.com/pub/anime-manga/ software/viewers/qtflat.zip
Qtime	Windows	QT	http://quicktim.apple.com
QuickTime	Windows	QT	http://www.apple.com/
SmartVid	Windows	AVI ↔ QT	ftp://ftp.intel.com/pub/IAL/multimedia/ smartv.exe

TABLE B-6. *Video Utilities* (continued)

NAME	PLATFORM	PLAYS/ CONVERTS	LOCATION
Sparkle	Mac	MPEG, QT	ftp://src.doc.ic.ac.uk/computing/systems/mac/info-mac/Graphic_&_Sound_Tool/mov/sparkle*.hqx ftp://ftp.cc.utexas.edu/microlib/mac/multimedia/Sparkle*.hqx
VMPEG Lite	Windows	MPEG	ftp://ftp.netcom.com/pub/cf/cfogg/vmpeg/vmpeg*.zip
XingCD	Windows	AVI → MPEG	http://www.xingtech.com

TABLE B-7. *HTML Editors*

NAME	PLATFORM	LOCATION / INFORMATION
ANT	Windows Mac	ftp://ftp.einet.net/einet/pc/ANT* ftp://ftp.einet.net/einet/mac/html-aids/
BBEdit extensions	Mac	http://www.uji.es/bbedit-html-extensions.html
Emacs helper modes	Unix	http://www.santafe.edu/~nelson/tools/ ftp://ftp.ncsa.uiuc.edu/Web/html/elisp/html-mode.el
HoTMetaL	Windows	http://www.sq.com ftp://ftp.ncsa.uiuc.edu/Web/html/hotmetal/
HTML Assistant	Windows	ftp://ftp.cs.dal.ca/htmlasst/
HTML Writer	Windows	http://lal.cs.byu.edu/people/nosack/
Internet Assistant	Windows	http://www.microsoft.com/msoffice/freestuf/msword/download/ia/default.htm
Live Markup	Windows	http://www.mediatec.com/mediatech/
Nick Williams' Editor	X Window	http://web.cs.city.ac.uk/homes/njw/htmltext/htmltext.html

TABLE B-7. *HTML Editors* (continued)

NAME	PLATFORM	LOCATION / INFORMATION
Phoenix	X Window	http://www.bsd.uchicago.edu/ftp/pub/phoenix/
TkWWW	X Window	http://www.w3.org/hypertext/WWW/TkWWW/ Status.html
WebAuthor	Windows	http://www.qdeck.com
WebEdit	Windows	http://wwwnt.thegroup.net/webedit/webedit.htm

TABLE B-8. *Web Servers*

SERVER	PLATFORM	INFORMATION / LOCATION
Alibaba	Win NT	http://www.csm.co.at/csm/alibaba.htm
Apache HTTP Server	Unix	http://www.apache.org/
CERN httpd	Unix	http://www.w3.org/hypertext/WWW/Daemon/ Status.html
EIT httpd	Unix	http://wsk.eit.com/wsk/doc/
GN Gopher/ HTTP Server	Unix	http://hopf.math.nwu.edu:70/
GoServe	OS/2	http://www2.hursley.ibm.com/goserve
HTTPS	Win NT	ftp://emwac.ed.ac.uk/pub/https/https.txt
MacHTTP	Mac	http://www.biap.com/
NCSA documentation	Unix	http://hoohoo.ncsa.uiuc.edu/
NCSA httpd	Unix	http://hoohoo.ncsa.uiuc.edu/
NetAllyl	Mac	http://www.delphic.com/
Netscape Commerce Server	Unix	http://www.mcom.com/comprod/ netscape_commerce.html
Netscape Communications Server	Unix	http://www.mcom.com/comprod/ netscape_commun.html

TABLE B-8. *Web Servers* (continued)

SERVER	PLATFORM	INFORMATION / LOCATION
OS2HTTPD	OS/2	ftp://ftp.netcom.com/pub/kf/kfan/overview.html
Plexus	Unix	http://www.bsdi.com/server/doc/plexus.html
WebSite	Win NT	http://www.ora.com
WebSTAR	Mac	http://www.starnine.com/webstar/webstar.html
Windows httpd	Windows	http://www.city.net/win-httpd/
WN Server	Unix	http://hopf.math.nwu.edu/

TABLE B-9. *Imagemapping Tools*

NAME	PLATFORM	LOCATION / INFORMATION
glorglox	Unix	http://www.uunet.ca/~tomr/glorglox/
MacMapMaker	Mac	ftp://ftp.uwtc.washington.edu/pub/Mac/Network/WWW/MacMapMaker*
Map *THIS!*	Win32	http://galadriel.ecaetc.ohio-state.edu/tc/mt
Mapedit	Windows X Window	http://sunsite.unc.edu/boutell/mapedit/mapedit.html
MapMaker	X Window	http://icg.stwing.upenn.edu/~mengwong/mapmaker.html
WebMap	Mac	http://arpp1.carleton.ca/machttp/doc/util/map/webmap.html

TABLE B-10. *Web Server Log Analysis Tools*

NAME	PLATFORM	LOCATION / INFORMATION
Getstats	Unix	http://www.eit.com/software/getstats/getstats.html
VB Stats	Windows	http://www.city.net/win-httpd/#vbstat
WebStat	Mac	http://arpp1.carleton.ca/machttp/doc/util/stats/webstat.html
WebStat	Unix	http://www.pegasus.esprit.ec.org/people/sijben/statistics/advertisment.html

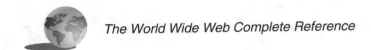

TABLE B-10. *Web Server Log Analysis Tools* (continued)

NAME	PLATFORM	LOCATION / INFORMATION
wusage	Unix	http://siva.cshl.org/wusage.html
wwwstat	Unix	http://www.ics.uci.edu/WebSoft/wwwstat/

TABLE B-11. *Web Directories*

SITE NAME	LOCATION
ALIWEB	http://web.nexor.co.uk/aliweb/doc/aliweb.html
EINet	http://www.einet.net
Open Markets Commercial Sites Index	http://www.directory.net
Virtual Yellow Pages	http://www.imsworld.com
Whole Internet Catalog	http://www.gnn.com
WWW Virtual Library	http://www.w3.org/hypertext/DataSources/bySubject/
Yahoo	http://www.yahoo.com

TABLE B-12. *FAQ and Information Files*

FAQ / INFORMATION FILE	LOCATION
MPEG FAQ	http://www.crs4.it/~luigi/MPEG/mpegfaq.html
HTML Editing	http://sunsite.unc.edu/boutell/faq/editinghtml.html
HTML Converters	http://www.w3.org/hypertext/WWW/Tools/Filters.html
Server Log Analysis	http://www.yahoo.com/Computers/World_Wide_Web/HTTP/Servers/Log_Analysis_Tools/
Winsock FAQ	http://mars.superlink.net/user/mook/winfaq.html
World Wide Web FAQ	http://sunsite.unc.edu/boutell/faq/www_faq.html

Index

G

H

I

L

O

P

Q

R

Y

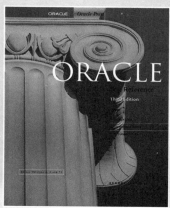

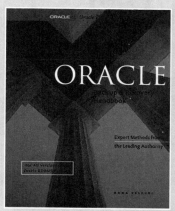

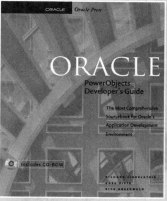

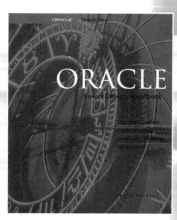

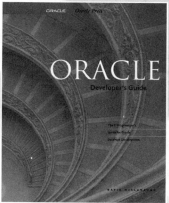

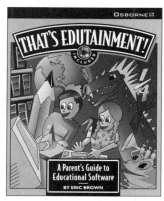

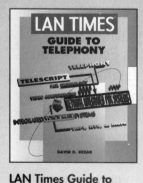

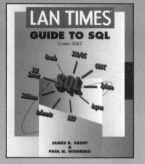

ORDER BOOKS DIRECTLY FROM OSBORNE/McGRAW-HILL

For a complete catalog of Osborne's books, call 510-549-6600 or write to us at 2600 Tenth Street, Berkeley, CA 94710

Call Toll-Free: ***1-800-822-8158***
24 hours a day, 7 days a week in U.S. and Canada

Mail this order form to:
McGraw-Hill, Inc.
Customer Service Dept.
P.O. Box 547
Blacklick, OH 43004

Fax this order form to:
1-614-759-3644

EMAIL
7007.1531@COMPUSERVE.COM
COMPUSERVE GO MH

Ship to:

Name ______________________________

Company ______________________________

Address ______________________________

City / State / Zip ______________________________

Daytime Telephone: ______________________________
(We'll contact you if there's a question about your order.)

ISBN #	BOOK TITLE	Quantity	Price	Total
0-07-88				
0-07-88				
0-07-88				
0-07-88				
0-07-88				
0-07088				
0-07-88				
0-07-88				
0-07-88				
0-07-88				
0-07-88				
0-07-88				
0-07-88				
0-07-88				
	Shipping & Handling Charge from Chart Below			
	Subtotal			
	Please Add Applicable State & Local Sales Tax			
	TOTAL			

Shipping & Handling Charges

Order Amount	U.S.	Outside U.S.
Less than $15	$3.50	$5.50
$15.00 - $24.99	$4.00	$6.00
$25.00 - $49.99	$5.00	$7.00
$50.00 - $74.99	$6.00	$8.00
$75.00 - and up	$7.00	$9.00

Occasionally we allow other selected companies to use our mailing list. If you would prefer that we not include you in these extra mailings, please check here: ❑

METHOD OF PAYMENT

❑ Check or money order enclosed (payable to Osborne/McGraw-Hill)

❑ AMERICAN EXPRESS ❑ DISCOVER ❑ MasterCard ❑ VISA

Account No. ______________________________

Expiration Date ______________________________

Signature ______________________________

In a hurry? Call 1-800-822-8158 anytime, day or night, or visit your local bookstore.

Thank you for your order

Code BC640SL